ANDREW JACKSON

VOLUME TWO

THE COURSE OF AMERICAN FREEDOM, 1822–1832

ANDREW JACKSON

VOLUME TWO

THE COURSE OF AMERICAN FREEDOM, 1822–1832

Robert V. Remini

THE JOHNS HOPKINS UNIVERSITY PRESS
Baltimore and London

For Elizabeth

Copyright © 1981 by Robert V. Remini
All rights reserved
Printed in the United States of America on acid-free paper

Originally published in 1981 as *Andrew Jackson and the Course of American Freedom, 1822–1832,* by Harper & Row, Publishers, Inc.
Johns Hopkins Paperbacks edition, 1998
9 8 7 6 5 4 3 2 1

The Johns Hopkins University Press
2715 North Charles Street
Baltimore, Maryland 21218-4363
The Johns Hopkins Press Ltd., London

Library of Congress Catalog Card Number 97-75802

A catalog record for this book is available from the British Library.

ISBN 0-8018-5912-3 (pbk.)

I had retired from the bustle of public life to my farm, there to repair an enfeebled constitution, worn out in the service of my country. The people of their own mere will brought my name before the nation for the office of President of these U. States. They have sustained me against all the torrents of slander that corruption and wickedness could invent . . . and by a large majority of the virtuous yeomanry of the U. States have elected me to fill the presidential chair. . . . I accept the office given me by the free and unbiased suffrage, of a virtuous people, with the feelings of the highest gratitude.

—Andrew Jackson, Memorandum, 1828

Contents

     A section of pictures follows page 256

Preface

THIS SECOND VOLUME OF THE LIFE of Andrew Jackson presumes to argue a revisionist interpretation both of its subject and the era that bears his name. It offers a thesis that seeks to identify and define Jackson's unique contribution to American political history during the first half of the nineteenth century.

Usually the period in American history from 1816 to 1828 is called the Era of Good Feelings, and the period from 1828 to 1848 the Age of Jackson. My own research has led me to conclude that the Era of Good Feelings ought, more rightly, to be known as America's first Era of Corruption. That designation, admittedly provocative, better explains what occurred during the years immediately following the War of 1812 than the more famous phrase. The Age of Jackson, therefore, if it is to make any sense at all, should be seen as the first conscious effort at political reform in American history. Andrew Jackson was a reformer—the first American President who can be called such. He was committed to an ideology that reflected the beliefs of the Founding Fathers, and he devised a definite program of change and renewal—he himself called it a program of "reform retrenchment and economy"—by which he hoped to end the Era of Corruption and restore the country and its government to virtue and honesty.

Less revisionist in its approach is the book's attempt to demonstrate the influence of the doctrines of "republicanism" on the Jacksonian era. It builds upon the studies of Bernard Bailyn, Gordon Wood, Robert Shalhope, and other historians who have been tracing the ideological strains of the American Revolution from their origins in the eighteenth century into the nineteenth century. It seeks to show Jackson's involvement with and concern for the preservation of this ideology—especially its understanding of the meaning of liberty—and his determination to reassert it as the major imperative of his administration. In sum, then, I see the presidency of Andrew Jackson as a reaction to the corruption of the administrations of James Monroe and John Quincy Adams, and I see Jackson himself as a man of republican principle and purpose who devised a program of reform by which he believed he could best protect and perpetuate the liberty of the American people.

As I investigated the pattern of Jackson's thinking and his goals as President it became evident that the problems of understanding the period from 1816 to 1848 stemmed from a failure among historians to appreciate the role and contribution of the one man most responsible for shaping that age. Jacksonian America has been interpreted from every angle save that of its leading figure. And the standard Jackson biographers have been particularly remiss. Not James Parton, nor John Spencer Bassett, nor Marquis James made any important interpretative statement about Old Hickory or his age. Indeed, Bassett, the most scholarly historian of the group, underestimated his subject to a remarkable degree. In editing six volumes of Jackson's correspondence, Bassett in his preface to volume III quoted a long letter from Jackson to John Coffee in which the General outlined some of the basic tenets of "republicanism"; Bassett concluded that the letter "showed how little intellectual poise he had and how little he grasped the nature of politics at the time" (page xiv). Bassett can be excused for this egregious error since he did not have Bailyn, Wood, and other modern historians to help him understand what Jackson and men like him at the time were talking about when they waxed hot over such questions as corruption, public virtue, and liberty.

In developing certain aspects of my argument I have had the counsel and assistance of a number of friends and colleagues. The notion of republicanism as a motivating force among the Jacksonians first seriously developed in my thinking after several long talks with Wayne Cutler, editor of the correspondence of James K. Polk. He then provided me with chapters from his dissertation on William H. Crawford, which helped me to document the corruption in the Monroe administration. I am very grateful to him. John Niven, presently working on a biography of Martin Van Buren, and Harriet C. Owsley, former editor of the Jackson Papers Project, read several chapters and gave me their criticisms and suggestions. Participants at the 1980 NEH summer seminar for college teachers on Jacksonian America at the Newberry Library offered telling criticism of the chapter on the Era of Corruption and I am deeply indebted to all of them. I must admit, however, that the ideas in this book about Jackson as a conscious political reformer are mostly my own.

I am profoundly grateful to the John Simon Guggenheim Foundation, whose generous support allowed a year of uninterrupted research and writing. Nothing compares to the freedom made possible by such encouragement and assistance. The Research Board of the University of Illinois at Chicago Circle and the American Philosophical Society provided funds for particular research problems. A fellowship from the Huntington Library permitted a month's intensive work among the excellent manuscript resources at that library. Also, the Rockefeller Foundation graciously invited me to spend a month at their Villa Serbelloni in Bellagio, Italy, where the first chapters of this volume were revised and rewritten.

Most particularly, I owe a special debt of gratitude to John W. Delafield and his wife, Anita, who welcomed me to their home and permitted me to see and copy documents from the Livingston Papers. These papers have provided special insights into the Jackson administration and into the thinking that motivated a number of important actions. This book would be the poorer without these documents and I therefore wish to express a special word of thanks to the Delafields for their kindness and generosity.

John McDonough, manuscript historian of the Library of Congress, and John H. Thweatt, senior archivist of the Tennessee State Library and Archives, have always responded enthusiastically to my many requests for information and for copies of documents, portraits, and cartoons. More than once they saved me days of work in searching through voluminous collections to find relevant Jackson material.

The new editor and director of the Andrew Jackson Papers Project at the Hermitage, Harold D. Moser, extended the same courtesies and support that his predecessor provided for the first volume. Whenever new documents or new information came to his attention he immediately relayed them to me. The corrected dates for the birth of Andrew Jackson, Jr., and the death of Lyncoya are only two examples of his interest and assistance in my work.

Originally this second volume was supposed to complete Jackson's life. Unfortunately a great deal of new material and a revised interpretation restricted the book to the story of Jackson's journey to the White House and the four years of his first administration. I therefore am very indebted to my editor, Hugh Van Dusen, who finally consented to a three-volume biography. The third and last volume will cover Jackson's second administration and the final years of his life.

August 1980   ROBERT V. REMINI
Wilmette, Illinois

Chronology of Jackson's Life, 1822-1832

1822, Spring	Convalesces after physical breakdown
1822, July 20	Nominated for President by Tennessee legislature
1823, March 14	Declines mission to Mexico
1823, October 1	Elected U.S. Senator
1823	Builds church on Hermitage property
1823, December 3	Arrives in Washington to begin senatorial duties
1823, December	Reconciles with Thomas Hart Benton
1824, February 14	Receives one vote in congressional nominating caucus
1824, March 4	Nominated for President by Pennsylvania convention
1824, March 16	Receives from President Monroe medal voted by Congress for his victory at New Orleans
1824, May 13	Votes for Tariff of 1824
1824, November	Receives plurality of popular and electoral votes in presidential contest
1825, January	Sustains serious accident
1825, February 9	Defeated for President in House election
1825, February 14	Accuses Clay of "corrupt bargain"
1825, March 4	Swears in Calhoun as Vice President
1825, May 5	Entertains Lafayette at Hermitage

1825, October 12	Resigns Senate seat
1825, October 14	Nominated for President by Tennessee legislature
1826, May 20	Subsidizes founding of *United States Telegraph*
1826, June 4	Supported for President by John C. Calhoun
1826, December	Supported for President by Martin Van Buren
1826–1828	Conducts campaign for presidency
1827, August 22	Supported for President by Amos Kendall
1828, January 8	Visits New Orleans to celebrate anniversary of military victory
1828, June 1	Death of Lyncoya
1828, November	Elected President
1828, November	Encourages John Eaton to marry Margaret Timberlake
1828, December 22	Death of Rachel
1829, January 19	Leaves Tennessee for inaugural
1829, February 11	Arrives in Washington
1829, February	Selects cabinet
1829, March 4	Inaugurated seventh President
1829, March 7	Outlines reform program
1829, March–1831	Involved in Eaton affair
1829, April 6	Meets with foreign ambassadors
1829, August	Vacations at the Rip Raps
1829, September 10	Holds cabinet meeting to evaluate evidence against Mrs. Eaton
1829, December 8	Forwards to Congress his first annual message
1830, January 25	Directs his cabinet to end "conspiracy" against the Eatons
1830, April 13	Attends Jefferson birthday dinner
1830, May	New York and Pennsylvania nominate Jackson for reelection
1830, May 13	Initiates break with Calhoun
1830, May 27	Vetoes Maysville Road bill
1830, May 28	Signs Indian Removal bill

1830, June	Exercises first pocket veto
1830, June 17	Leaves Washington for the Hermitage
1830, August 23	Meets Chickasaw delegation at Franklin
1830, August 27	Informed Chickasaws will remove
1830, September 27	Treaty of Dancing Rabbit Creek signed arranging removal of Choctaws
1830, October	Returns to Washington
1830, October 5	Reopens American ports to British West Indian trade
1830, October	Agrees to establishment of Washington *Globe*
1830, December 7	Forwards to Congress his second annual message
1830, December 10	Submits convention with Denmark to Senate
1830, December	Concludes treaty with Turkey
1830, December	Agrees to reconciliation with Calhoun
1831, February 21	Reads Calhoun out of the party
1831, April	Accepts cabinet resignations and appoints new cabinet
1831, June 25–July 4	Vacations at the Rip Raps
1831, November 24	Andrew Jackson, Jr., marries Sarah Yorke
1831, December 6	Submits French treaty on spoliations to Senate
1831, December 6	Forwards to Congress his third annual message
1831, December	Remodels Hermitage and erects tomb in garden
1832, January	Submits to operation for removal of bullet
1832, January 25	Van Buren's nomination as minister rejected
1832, March 24	Creeks agree to removal
1832, March 27	Accused of maintaining a "Kitchen Cabinet"

1832, April 6– August 2	Black Hawk War
1832, May 9	Seminoles accept provisional treaty for removal
1832, May 22	First Democratic presidential nominating convention concurs in Jackson's nomination for reelection
1832, July 10	Vetoes Bank bill
1832, July 14	Signs Tariff of 1832
1832, July 22	Leaves Washington for the Hermitage
1832, September	Orders preparations in response to nullification threats
1832, September 18	Leaves Hermitage for Washington
1832, October 19	Arrives in Washington
1832, October 30	Treaty of removal signed by Chickasaws
1832, October	Orders further measures against nullifiers
1832, November 1	Becomes a grandfather with the birth of Rachel
1832, November	Reelected President
1832, December 4	Forwards to Congress his fourth annual message
1832, December 10	Issues Proclamation to the people of South Carolina

ANDREW JACKSON

VOLUME TWO

THE COURSE OF AMERICAN FREEDOM, 1822–1832

CHAPTER 1

The Convalescent

HOWEVER BATTERED AND WORN the outer shell of the man appeared to his friends and neighbors upon his return to the Hermitage in 1821, the cold steely blue eyes reassured them that enormous vitality still throbbed within that shrunken hulk. The indomitable will, the force of character, the majestic presence, had not diminished in the slightest. Although a summer in the swamps of Florida had nearly annihilated him, General Andrew Jackson returned to his home outside Nashville, Tennessee, no less active, no less combative, no less involved and concerned about his country's future and destiny.

But he verged on physical collapse. At the age of fifty-five he suffered bodily discomfort that was constant and frequently unbearable. From 1821 until his death in 1845 Jackson's letters speak regularly of his health and indisposition. It became such an obsession that one immediately suspects hypochondria, and no doubt a certain degree of it intruded from time to time. But the truth is that his poor health demanded his attention because of its genuine and frightening precariousness. It is not an exaggeration to say that Jackson suffered physical pain practically every day of his life from 1821 until his death twenty-four years later.

Two bullets lodged in his body. The first resulted from a duel over a horserace, when Charles Dickinson on May 30, 1806, took deadly aim and barely missed killing him.[1] The bullet, as it struck, tore chest muscles, fractured one or two ribs as it entered, and lodged in the chest cavity close to the heart and impinged on his left lung. The bullet remained in his body for the rest of Jackson's life. As it penetrated the thoracic cage it carried with it fragments of cloth, dirt, and other foreign matter. Almost immediately a pulmonary abscess formed. Over the years one respiratory

1

infection followed another and coughing became incessant. During the worst spasms he brought up blood, which convinced him (wrongly) that he had contracted tuberculosis.[2]

The second bullet lodged against the bone in the heavy muscle of the left arm just below the shoulder. During a gunfight on September 4, 1813, with Thomas Hart Benton and his brother Jesse, Jackson was shot twice by Jesse: once in the left shoulder and once in the left arm. Over the next six months bits of bone were expelled from the arm, which Jackson sent to his wife as "souvenirs." It was a long time before he could even slip his arm into the sleeve of his jacket, but the inflammation never totally subsided, and osteomyelitis set in.[3]

Following the gunfight with the Bentons, Jackson campaigned against the Creek Indians. During this campaign he contracted dysentery and malaria, and what with the fever, dysentery, coughing, and sweating he endured it frequently took an act of supreme will to mount his horse and command his troops. Dr. Francis May, his physician, regularly swabbed him with sugar of lead. It was widely believed at the time that sugar of lead, in addition to its astringent powers, could reduce inflammation. So Jackson both drank it and bathed in it. He took it internally to combat his supposed tuberculosis and chronic stomachaches, and externally for its antiphlogistic action. He even squirted it into his eyes when his sight began to falter. For the dysentery, he took massive doses of calomel. Which means that over the years he subjected his system to unbelievable quantities of lead and mercury. Without realizing it, Jackson slowly poisoned himself!

Yet, despite the poison, severe congestion in his chest, a persistent cough, occasional pulmonary hemorrhaging, "intermittent fever," periodic abscesses for which he personally used a lancet to operate on himself, regular and debilitating attacks of dysentery, and a worsening condition of rheumatism, Andrew Jackson would not yield to the infirmities of his pain-wracked body. He kept functioning. He kept going. But the blows and shocks his system sustained through disease, gunfights, malnutrition, and improper medication invite disbelief. How he lived through it all for as long as he did says something important about his will to survive.

Shortly after his return to Tennessee following a brief two-month stint as Territorial Governor of Florida, Jackson suffered a severe physical breakdown. For four months, he wrote, "I have been oppressed with a violent cough, and costiveness." This was followed by an excruciating attack of dysentery that totally immobilized him. In addition he began to complain for the first time of the "great quantities of slime" he brought up with each coughing spell. His lungs, irritated by the perpetual inflammation, had finally produced the characteristic bronchiectasis—which means that Jackson would be tormented by "slime" for the remainder of his life.[4]

His wretched health necessarily affected his general disposition. Always sensitive, frequently petulant, constantly alert to slights, criticisms, or insults, he grew increasingly irascible as the level of pain intensified over the next five years. By 1824 his teeth were decaying very rapidly, no doubt advanced by the calomel and his own indifference to dental hygiene. But before they were extracted in 1828 he suffered severe tooth and jaw aches that murdered sleep and frazzled his nervous system. Thus, he sometimes lashed at his enemies with a savagery that shocked his admirers who were unaware of the degree of his misery. It was as though the sheer fury of his passion, by its intensity, could divert his mind and attention from the torments of his tortured body. What must always be remembered in understanding the next quarter century of Jackson's life is that he suffered constant pain and that by raw will power he forced himself to meet all his obligations and responsibilities.

When his health cracked in the spring of 1822 and he realized he must rest or face the prospect of imminent death, Jackson began to take stock —both of himself and his immediate situation. He pondered the welfare of his children and how much he had neglected them. "I have my little sons including Lyncoya, at school, and their education has been greatly neglected in my absence. Justice to them, require my attention when I have health to give it."[5] The "two Andrews," as Jackson called his children, included his adopted son Andrew Jackson, Jr., and his ward, Andrew Jackson Hutchings. Andrew Jr. turned fourteen on December 4, 1822,[6] and would soon begin elementary classes at Cumberland College, formerly Davidson Academy in Nashville. The boy was not terribly bright and caused his father monumental financial problems. Hardly into his teens, young Andrew soon developed into a spendthrift. The father went to his grave burdened by his son's fiscal recklessness.

The other Andrew, the son of John Hutchings, Jackson's onetime business partner, came to live with the Jacksons in 1817 when his father died after designating the General as the boy's guardian. Just a lad of eleven years, he created a great deal of trouble for his guardian throughout his short, thirty-year life. Always a discipline problem, Hutchings quarreled repeatedly with overseers, abused the slaves, got himself expelled from school later on, and generally behaved in a thoroughly nasty and reprehensible manner. "I have just recd a letter from my overseer Steel," wrote Jackson to John Coffee at a later day, "informing me of a quarrel and fight with Hutchings. It has give me much pain—I have wrote . . . to Hutchings, that he must not attempt to misuse or whip the negroes. . . . I wish . . . him to go to school until he is of age to take charge of his estate."[7] Yet Jackson loved these two boys very deeply and never withdrew his affection or support despite the many problems they both visited upon him.

In a different way, Lyncoya was another problem. The young Indian, now ten years of age, had been raised by Jackson from infancy—ever since he discovered the baby on the battlefield at Tallushatchee during the Creek War.[8] Interestingly, although the child was raised totally in a white man's society, he retained some "Indian habits." At the age of five he fashioned a bow "after the manner of the Indians," which surprised the family because he had had very little contact with "his people" except for the few occasions when tribal chiefs visited the General.[9] He also enjoyed smearing warpaint on his face and then jumping out from behind bushes to frighten other children.

At the age of eight Lyncoya was sent to a "good day school" in the neighborhood and Jackson hoped eventually to enroll him in West Point. In fact the father spoke to James Monroe about an appointment and was assured of the President's "countenance and favour."[10] The following year, 1823, when he was in Washington, Jackson instructed his wife to have Lyncoya write him a letter. "I would like to exhibit [it] to Mr Monroe and the Secretary of War, as I mean to try to have him recd. at the military school, as early as I can."[11] Several weeks later Jackson received the following:

Hermitage December 29, 1823

Dear Father
When the Mad Wolfe & Ogilvie came here from their woods, they said, How do you do, Father? You had not sent them to school as you have me. They could not [speak?] as I can. Their young ears had not known Neither had their war limbs gathered [streng]th from your table, nor rest under [your] roof, yet they called thee Father. [Whe]n as an infant you placed me on your knee [you] Learned me the talk of your Andrews, [and] made me their companion at Home, [their f]ellow in school, and their rival in [their] duty to you. If the Mad Wolfe & Ogilvie [*page torn*] call thee Father & not the bold, may [not] Lincoyer, & be justified? Yes he answers [*page torn*] he can? and since he is not told that [when?] a big man, he must have the white mans [sk]in, but to be just, to [avoid] only evil actions, to do good, is to be the *bigerest* of men, he hopes to have this stature of the ma[n.] Not to feel a blush, when he is told hereafter, *this is the Indian boy I* [once] *raised.*
                                        Your obliged & grateful
                                        Lincoyer[12]
General Jackson

Lyncoya never did get to West Point. By the time he reached the proper age for admission Jackson's "rivals" controlled the government, "which prevented any application for a warrant on the part of Gen Jackson." Instead Lyncoya said he preferred the saddler's trade and in 1827, "his education being sufficient," he was formally bound to a saddler in Nashville.[13]

If the young children in his charge at the moment sometimes added to Jackson's distress, there were other wards who had grown, matured, established careers for themselves, and had increased his joy and happiness. None pleased him more than Andrew Jackson Donelson, the son of Samuel Donelson who had become the General's ward in 1805. Jackson showered the young man with every favor possible. He attended carefully to young Donelson's education, as he did with all his wards. And Jackson had very definite ideas about the education of his children. He believed that West Point was "the best school in the world," far better than Harvard or Yale.[14] He believed that mathematics, rather than languages or classical studies, was essential for mental growth, and West Point was strong in that subject. "It opens and expands the mind," he wrote, "and gives a proper arrangement and system to argument."[15] He was gratified when young Donelson elected to enter the Academy as a cadet in 1817 and supremely pleased when he learned that the young man graduated second in his class. But there had been trouble. About a year and a half after he entered the Academy, Donelson informed his uncle of the mistreatment the cadets suffered on account of the commandant. Physical abuse, customary in those days, was part of this complaint. Donelson told his guardian that he had signed a protest to the authorities and that he might have to resign. Jackson unhesitatingly supported his nephew, warned him to be certain of his grounds and to be prepared to "suffer death before dishonour." If your superior insults or mistreats you, Jackson said, you have my permission to resign. "But if the Superior attempts either to strike or kick you, put him to instant death the moment you receive either. Never, my son, outlive your honour. Never do an act that will tarnish it."[16]

After Donelson graduated from the Academy he served in the army for two years under Jackson as aide-de-camp at Nashville and Florida before resigning his commission early in 1822 and entering Transylvania University in Lexington, Kentucky, as a law student. At this point the ailing Jackson resumed a long and devoted correspondence with his nephew. Some of Jackson's wisest, most loving, and heartfelt letters were written to Donelson during this period. He really cared about this bright, devoted former ward. "I have a great desire that you should turn your attention," the General said, "to writing on various subjects, nothing tends more to expand the mind, and improve the intellect, than writing and investigating various subjects; it gives to thought a wide range, and when your mind is habituated to writing when young, you acquire a facility in managing a subject, that is hard to acquire when of mature age, or the meridian of life. Writing is a good deal mechanical and is only to be acquired by habit at an early age."[17] During the months of his convalescence following his physical collapse, Jackson took his own advice and allowed himself the luxury of ruminating upon many subjects to the young man, from history and politics to morality and the course of nations.

One of my objects in placing you at Lexington was that you might become acquainted with the young gentlemen from various parts of the south and west—that when you enter into professional life, which may be a prelude to political; you may be known—for I will not disguise I look forward, if you live, to the time when you will be selected to preside over the destinies of America. I therefore wish you for the present to steer clear of all political broils. I do not mean that you should be silent on political subjects, but when you speak on them do it with reflection, embracing general remarks unless where it may becom necessary to give an opinion, then, if necessary give it agreable to your opinion of the subject before you, agreable to your ideas of right, and Justice, regardless of consequences, allways keeping in view principles, not men, the public good, seperate from individual views —in short, *measures* that will promote the public good, reguardless, of individual views, or the agrandizement of party purposes.[18]

One of the things that made Donelson so indispensable to the General later on was his immediate recognition of Jackson's needs. He responded to this most recent letter on June 5, 1822, and told his uncle that "as far as my capacity will enable me, and as soon as you can place the confidence in me, it shall be my greatest happiness to relieve you of all business and manifest that sense of gratitude which I have never expressed, and never can, for the many kind and fatherly services which you have tendered me."[19] The General reassured him that he was not needed at the moment despite his grave illness. He wanted Donelson to finish his law education before returning to Nashville. Then he ended with his usual salute: "Your aunt and the little andrews Join me in love to you, and believe me to be your affectionate uncle. *Andrew Jackson.*"[20]

Aunt Jackson, as her many nieces and nephews called her, or Sister Rachel, as her brothers and sisters referred to her, was one of young Donelson's favorites, as she was to practically everyone who knew her. By 1822, after their return from Florida, Rachel had become almost saintlike in her patience, devotion, understanding, and good works. She was known by all as an extremely pious and religious woman whose greatest pleasure was churchgoing and listening to homilies about her Redeemer. In one of her few surviving letters, written to her brother John during a particularly trying period in Florida, she said that she yearned to return home, and only her unshakable religious faith kept her going.

Tell our friends and all I hope to see them againe in our own Country and to know it is the best I Ever seen- What a pitty that some do not know when theay ar well of in this world theay not only hurt themselves but those that is innocent—But stop say to Sister Mary I have Herd but one sermon sinc I herd Mr Hoge he promised me to Come to this place in june but no he never came I have mourned for zion my tears has ran down in the night season—Mr J has been very unwell & no wonder my health is Delicate—The Lord is my help in him will I trust & I will praise him with joyful lips remember me to all my Dear friends The young ones how I want hear them Tell that Jesus the hope of glory is formed in them tell Brother Sanday I have maney things to say to him—farwell my Dear Brother & may you say as pious job I know that my redeemer Liveth[21]

Her return to Tennessee with Jackson in the late fall of 1821 overwhelmed Rachel with joy and happiness. There was a great family reunion of Donelsons. Sisters, brothers, nephews, and nieces crowded around their beloved Rachel and Andrew when they arrived home, although most were shocked at their physical appearance. They were not terribly surprised when the General suffered his breakdown a short time later. For Rachel, "Tennessee is the best Country yet" and the knowledge that she was home at last quickly restored her spirits and health. She nursed Jackson with particular devotion and slowly over the next several months he responded to her attentive care.

Rachel immediately returned to the rhythm of her life on their "farm," as Jackson called their extensive plantation. Her management of the house and the financial accounts always won Jackson's enthusiastic praise. "Recollect the industry of your dear aunt," he reminded the young Hutchings a decade later, "and with what economy she watched over what I made, and how we waded thro the vast expence of the mass of company we had. nothing but her care and industry, with good economy could have saved me from ruin. if she had been extravagant the property would have vanished and poverty and want would have been our doom."[22]

Rachel had grown quite stout over the years. Her health, as she said, was delicate and soon she began to suffer palpitations and occasional chest pains. She may also have suffered from hypertension. She dreaded every occasion that took her husband away from her and sometimes indulged in emotional and hysterical scenes. But she had long since learned that when Jackson identified his duty there was nothing she could do but suffer and accept it. She had hoped that tending his "farm," and seeing the many friends, neighbors, and relatives that constantly visited the Hermitage would fill his life. To a great extent it did. He genuinely hoped to retire from public life after his return from Florida and spend his days in the "bosom of his family," educating his children and enjoying the company of his wife as they sat together each night in the parlor and smoked their pipes and chatted about the family and the concerns of their plantation. Now that his health had failed and he realized how much he needed to rest at home he readily slipped into the routine that Rachel programmed for him to speed his recovery.

What hastened his recovery and buoyed his spirits were the great numbers of friends and relatives who regularly visited the Jacksons. Instead of draining his strength their presence seemed to renew it. Both Rachel and Andrew loved to entertain and, of course, they had the means to do it lavishly. Their home, the Hermitage, provided the necessary setting. Plain, commodious, solid, and built of brick, it stood two stories high. The front faced south, and a guest entered the house through a porch into a spacious hall at the end of which an airy and well-lighted staircase ascended in a spiral to the second floor. There were four rooms leading off the central passageway on the ground floor: the northwest room was the dining room; the southeast and southwest rooms were sitting rooms; and the northeast room was the Jacksons' bedroom, which had a door leading into the garden.

In entertaining friends and neighbors the General especially enjoyed female company, in fact he preferred it to all others. The men could take care of themselves. With a wave of his arm he told his gentlemen guests that the "parlor, the dining-room, the library, the sideboard and its refreshments" were all at their disposal. Also, they could "ring" for the servants if they needed anything more. But the ladies commanded his special attention and gained him a reputation among them as a perfect host. He rarely sat at the head of his table, but preferred a seat between two ladies, "seeking a chair between different ones at various times." He was "very easy and graceful in his attentions," always free, sometimes playful, but never undignified or forward. "He obviously had a hidden vein of humor, loved aphorism, and could politely convey a sense of smart travesty." He had great power of attention and concentration without appearing gossipy. He had developed into a marvelous conversationalist but at times mispronounced words or used them incorrectly; "and it was remarkable, too, that when he did so it was with emphasis on the error of speech, and he would give it a marked prominence in diction."[23]

Rachel matched Jackson's graciousness and warm hospitality, exuding "the very personification of affable kindness." She spoke low but quick, with short and wheezing breaths. She "was once a form of rotund and rubicund beauty, but now was very plethoric and obese, and seemingly suffered from what was called phthisis." (Because of her supposed "phthisis," her doctor prescribed a pipe, so she often rose from her bed at night to smoke for relief.[24]) Another visitor described her in blunter terms: "She is short . . . and quite fat."[25] Still another said she was "an uncommonly ugly woman."[26] One sophisticated and well-traveled New Yorker commented that she was the first woman he had ever seen smoke a cigar but that he thought her manners easy and correct, her conversation "playful," and her sense of humor "keen."[27]

On one occasion the Jacksons entertained a wedding party and included among the guests Judge John Overton, Jackson's longtime friend; the Reverend Dr. O. Jennings, the Jacksons' local Presbyterian pastor, whose daughter was the bride; and Henry Baldwin, the son of the future U.S. Supreme Court justice and one of the groomsmen. After the ceremony the guests streamed into the spacious hall of the Hermitage and scattered through the four large rooms leading from the hall. After several hours of eating and drinking and talking, a small knot of guests sat down with Jackson and his wife in one of the rooms for an evening of conversation. Judge Overton, a "queer-looking little old man" came in first. Small, sharp-featured, with a gourdlike bald head and peaked Roman nose, "he had lost his teeth and swallowed his lips." Since his narrow, prominent jaw curved slightly upward, observers claimed there was always a danger that nose and chin would collide when he talked. As he sat in the Hermitage this day, a bandanna hankerchief thrown over his bald head, he kept "mounching, mounching, mounching" on his toothless gums, looking for all the world like the "Witch of Endor."[28] Next to him sat Jackson, his hair always standing straight up and out. His hair, not then white but "venerably gray," was medium length and evenly cut. Extremely slender and slightly round-shouldered, he stood six feet tall and had strong cheekbones, a lantern jaw, a long, straight nose, and a mouth which "showed rocklike firmness." His teeth were long and loose, as though attempting to escape their sockets, "and gave an ugly ghastly expression to his nasal muscle."[29] As he conversed with his guests, Jackson spoke volubly and with animation, sometimes a bit vehemently and with much declamation but never without "perfect dignity and self-possession." Next to Jackson sat Dr. Jennings, "one of the sweetest men in society," and beside him the overweight Rachel with young Baldwin close by.[30]

In no time at all the conversation turned to religion and Jackson ventured "that some of Swedenborg's conceptions of Deity were the most soo-blime that tapped the drum ecclesiastic." Dr. Jennings challenged this remark and the General launched into an elaborate defense of the "soo-blime" concepts of Swedenborgian doctrine. As he spoke he became more agitated, his eyes flashed, his hair stood at attention, and his clenched right hand gestured for emphasis.

The group was delighted to see the General in such splendid form. Back and forth went the argument and even the Witch of Endor joined in. "Crunch, crunch, crunch," went his chin and nose as they whacked away at each other. "Mumble, mumble, mumble," was all that could be heard. Finally he let out an oath as he tried to win the attention of the group. "By God!" he snapped. Then he realized his mistake. He turned to Rachel, sheepishly. "By Jupiter!" he corrected himself.

Rachel looked at her husband, his face flushed with the excitement of the dispute. She lowered her head a trifle, then reached across and touched Baldwin on the knee.

"Mr. Baldwin, dear," she said in her low soft voice, "you are sleepy!"

The startled Baldwin protested that he was not sleepy at all but wide awake and enjoying the discussion. But his protests were all in vain. Rachel rose, rang for a servant to bring a "candle to light the dear child to bed." When Rachel rose everyone else in the room got to their feet. That ended the discussion and the group then dispersed.[31]

Jackson's "affectionate regard and devotedness to his wife, and his ready submission to her soothing voice," wrote one observer, "even when in his most excited and revengeful moods, were beautiful and commendable traits in his character." Moreover, the observer went on, "it is strong proof of her excellent judgment, self-control, mild temper, and ardent affection for him, that she had such a controlling influence over him."[32]

The influence was indeed enormous. More important, she knew how to exercise it without seeming to dictate his behavior or lecture him on his deportment, even those times when his behavior bordered on lunacy, such as the time he threatened to take potshots with a rifle at a river pilot who was annoying him.[33] Perhaps her greatest influence on Jackson was her deep and abiding commitment to religion. Her own strong faith, her unquestioning acceptance of what she regarded as divine will, and her daily pious and charitable works had a steady and profound effect on her husband. His mother had been intensely religious and had tried to steer him into the ministry. Both mother and wife were strict Presbyterians and both responded with love and appreciation to his acceptance and understanding of their religious needs. From the 1820s to the end of his life there appears in Jackson's correspondence and in his actions a mounting religious conviction that culminated in his officially joining the Presbyterian church. There was, moreover, a steady unfolding of a pious fatalism. In the future he will rebuke his children when they fail to demonstrate the Christian virtue of fortitude in accepting the Lord's will when tragedy strikes and in understanding its meaning in religious terms. Of course, Jackson's religious beliefs were peculiarly his own and not everyone would subscribe to them. Not only was he a fundamentalist in dogma but he encouraged the application of "fire and brimstone." One clergyman, Peter Cartwright, acknowledged that the General "was, no doubt, in his prime of life, a very wicked man, but he always showed a great respect for the Christian religion, and the feelings of religious people, especially ministers of the Gospel." Cartwright then related an incident that he had witnessed. It seems he had preached one Sunday near the Hermitage and Jackson, by special request, invited him to dine along with several gentlemen and ladies. One of these gentlemen, a young lawyer from Nashville, began baiting Cartwright during the dinner about his Christian beliefs. The clergyman tried to evade the argument since he "plainly saw that his head was much softer than his heart." He also "saw General Jackson's eye strike fire, as he sat by and heard the thrusts he made at the Christian religion." Finally, the lawyer asked:

"Mr. Cartwright, do you believe there is any such place as hell, as a place of torment?"

"Yes, I do," replied Cartwright.

Jackson stirred in his seat, his eyes nailed to the lawyer.

"Well," chortled the lawyer, "I thank God I have too much good sense to believe any such thing."

Jackson could keep silent no longer. "Well, sir," he stormed, "I thank

God that there is such a place of torment as hell."

The young man was astonished by the "great earnestness" with which Jackson spoke. Unfortunately he did not have enough sense to leave it at that.

"Why, General Jackson, what do you want with such a place of torment as hell?"

To which Jackson replied, quick as lightning, "To put such d——d rascals as you are in, that oppose and vilify the Christian religion."

The young man gasped and fled the room.[34]

CHAPTER 2

The Era of Corruption

JACKSON'S PHYSICAL BREAKDOWN IN 1822 afforded him considerable time
to do some serious thinking during his recovery. His thoughts almost
automatically turned to conditions within his beloved country and he
could not shake a terrible sense of fear and foreboding. The nation was
still recovering from an economic panic precipitated in large measure by
the Bank of the United States when it reverted to a policy of tight money
and credit. That panic created misery and want across the nation and for
several more years would have a serious economic and political impact,
particularly in the western states. Jackson's agitation over conditions in
the country—and they ranged far beyond the mere financial—reached
such an emotional pitch that he started to prepare what he called "memorandoms" in an effort to sort out his thinking and organize his thoughts.
As he wrote his anger mounted. No doubt his illness and weakened
condition affected his mood. But these articulated thoughts running in
a scattered jumble across several sheets of paper revealed the depth of
his discouragement and disappointment in the affairs of state. He
brooded over what was happening to the nation he had done so much to
defend and protect. He seethed over the caliber of men occupying high
office. The nation was in the hands of incompetents. Worse, criminals.
And systematically they were robbing the people of their precious freedom.[1]

Of course, in these "memorandoms," Jackson principally harped on
the question of Florida and the abuse he had suffered in administering
that territory as governor after its cession by Spain. His only purpose, he
scribbled, had been a desire to insure justice for every citizen no matter
his rank. "I was determined to administer the Govrt. for the happiness

12

of all, and prevent the poor and humble from the Tyranny of wealth and power. this I have accomplished, I trust." And what was his reward? Criticism and vicious obloquy from government officials whose personal corruption blinded them to the enlightened acts of patriots. Even the President, James Monroe, whose administration Jackson steadfastly supported, failed him. The President's appointments, his pusillanimous doubletalk when faced with unpleasant decisions, his lack of recognition of Jackson's accomplishments in Florida—all these and more gnawed at the dispirited General as he sat at his desk citing his complaints. "Strange to tell," he commented, "I have never from the first got a single line of instructions from the President" during my Florida tenure. "All my measures were reported," he fumed, and "none of them . . . were disapproved of."[2] Yet in his annual message to Congress on December 3, 1822, Monroe had the temerity to speak of Jackson's quarrel with Judge Eligius Fromentin as a "misunderstanding of authority."[3] A misunderstanding! What a typical Monroe dodge that was. "The manner in which he speaks of Fromentine and myself, when the facts were before him, that proves that his statement was not true."[4]

The President misrepresented the truth, simple as that. The greatest fraud in the nation sat in the executive mansion in Washington. Only a few years before, Monroe had suggested to Jackson that they alter documentary evidence regarding the seizure of Florida. No wonder the country was riddled with corruption. It started with the administration in Washington, and at the very top. Jackson found it difficult to disagree with a friend who wrote that James Monroe "is a base infamous hypocrite."[5]

Jackson was clearly overwrought, but his fundamental complaint was in fact true. Government officials were indeed engaged in questionable, if not illegal, activities and many of these activities involved enormous sums of money. From the President of the United States down through several cabinet officers into the Washington bureaucracy and reaching beyond to officials in the several states, a degree of malfeasance in the conduct of official business was beginning to come to light in an ever-increasing number of exposures. The country was experiencing such widespread corruption that it worried many men for the safety of American institutions.

Throughout 1822 the newspapers chronicled one swindle after another. By midsummer the New York *Statesman* averred: "That scandalous defalcations in our public pecuniary agents, gross misapplications of public money, and an unprecedented laxity in official responsibilities occurred and been suffered under our government for the past six or eight years are faults not to be concealed."[6] The Washington *National Intelligencer*, seeking to defend the Monroe administration, admitted that "one of the charges brought against the present administration is a gross neglect and waste of public property," but insisted that there "has been less peculation in public affairs . . . than has been supposed." Still that was hardly a defense and the newspaper conceded that "errors of judgment may have been committed by [the President and his advisers] as well as other men."[7]

Like all good politicians Jackson was an avid reader of newspapers and he absorbed the information about the specific scandals as they appeared in the press over the next several years. "Enormous defalcation," trumpeted the Baltimore *Federal Republican* in the spring of 1822, involving naval agents, marine paymasters, pursers, and the like. And these, said the newspaper, constitute only "one of the innumerable instances of corruption in Washington."[8] The situation was rapidly getting out of hand and people were beginning to worry that the entire government was rotten with decay. "There has been no accountability in our public agents," said another newspaper, "from the highest to the lowest."[9] In time it became obvious that the highest meant the President of the United States and the members of his cabinet.

At the Hermitage a gloomy and morose convalescent kept himself abreast of these ever-unfolding public scandals and pondered with a sense of fear and apprehension what was happening throughout the country. Jackson stared at the "memorandoms" spread out before him and then picked up his pen and stabbed the top page again and again as he struggled to find the appropriate words to vent his outrage at the government and its misdeeds. A great many things got mixed up in his tormented mind and what came out was a jumble of incoherence and Jacksonian wrath.

The case, of the opinion of the atto. Genl U.S. on which M. was removed.

The charges as the Sec of the T. swindling the Govrt out of 25500 and giving it to the cherokees in violating the consti. in employing a senator to travel over three states to examine the land offices that he might electioneer for him.

The charges in the papers vs the Post office department etc. etc. etc. etc.

The conduct of other nations towards their officers contrasted with that of our Govt towards me.

The charges for preserving orleans, the necessary urgent, martial law declared, the country and the constitution saved thereby.

The seminole campaign the conduct of congress in that case, the members mutilated and distorted the evidence their Views and object—particularise them

The conduct of the committee of the senate the declaration of Eppes that he consented to the report without hearing the Testimony, Wm. H. Crawford charged with abiding in drafting it.

The Sec of the T. being publickly charged with interfeering with the states election of those favourable to his vews to the Presidency.[10]

And on and on Jackson went, venting the frustration and self-pity pent up inside him, alternating between serious charges of corruption in government and the malice he suffered from Washington officials during his Florida tenure. Much of his venom was directed toward the secretary of the treasury, William H. Crawford, whom he thoroughly detested,[11] and involved his own recent mistreatment by the administration. But what is vitally important is that he thought he now knew the reason for the mistreatment. The administration was corrupt. It had always been corrupt—"corrupt to the core"—and that accounted for its abuse of patriots.[12]

Without untangling and explaining all the specifics of Jackson's charges or cataloguing all the misbehavior of government agents during James Monroe's two terms in office, suffice it to say that sufficient evidence exists, both public and private, to prove that his administration was perhaps one of the most corrupt in the early history of the United States.[13] The years 1816–1828 are generally known as the Era of Good Feelings, because it was a period in which one party ruled the nation and supposedly brought political peace and good will to the country. (Actually there was considerable quarreling and factious bickering within that party.) But instead of an Era of Good Feelings this twelve-year period really deserves to be called the nation's first Era of Corruption.

Public and private misbehavior could be expected. Monroe's presidency followed the War of 1812 and after all wars, as the record amply shows, morality in American life and government plunges. Also, and far more important, the country was entering an era of profound and revolutionary change that would permanently alter every aspect of national life. The industrial revolution had just taken hold and the process of converting a predominantly agrarian and homogenous society into an industrial and heterogenous one had already begun. The economy was expanding —and with it expanded the hopes and aspirations of its citizens. As the economy generated new wealth, men scrambled to grasp everything they could. And none had a longer grasp than government officials.

Although some of the worst offenses were covered up,[14] enough information about government corruption escaped into the courts and public prints to alarm the men like Jackson who concerned themselves about what this corruption might do to their free institutions. Its very pervasiveness was especially disturbing. It spread from Washington—always the fountainhead of corruption—to state and local governments and even into the private sector. The entire nation seemed lost to morality and lofty ethical standards. Newspapers worried over the collapse of public and private virtue, individual correspondence frequently mentioned it, and diaries and journals sometimes provided details. "Mr. West cashr of the U.S. Branch Bank at this place,"[15] recorded one such journal in 1822, ". . . has lately been sent here in place of Mr. Latimer, who became a defaulter to a considerable amount—It is really lamentable & humbling to the pride of integrity—to look at the numerous instances of this kind of fraud which have occurred within the last 3 or 4 years—Scarcely is there a large city, or indeed a small one where there is a Bank—that has not had cause to bewail the aberration from rectitude of some man of (before) unsuspected honesty & one whom the people have delighted to honor—Even now as I passed thro' Richmond a trial was pending against the state Treasr as defaulter for $120,000."[16]

Much of the fraud involved banks in all the states but especially among the branches of the Bank of the United States, an institution chartered and partially owned by the United States government. However, upon investigation, it soon appeared that many men in Washington regularly plundered the treasury as well. Those who disbursed funds or otherwise handled public money skimmed off a little something for themselves as a regular matter.[17] Procedures varied. They ran from outright theft to elaborate systems of converting specie to paper money, with "commissions" going to the officials who arranged the conversions.

Congressmen were probably the worst offenders, at least in terms of the amount of money they pocketed. And "conflict of interest" meant absolutely nothing to them. Granted the term would not come into vogue for another hundred and more years, but surely the ethical sense of some of these congressmen must have given them a momentary pause. The annual fee that Daniel Webster later received for his "services" in safeguarding the interests of the Bank of the United States is fairly well known. But he was not alone. Numerous congressmen took money from corporations to advance the interests of these companies through favorable legislation or other governmental actions. Take Thomas Hart Benton, for example. Recently arrived in Washington as senator from Missouri, Benton served as "legal representative" to John Jacob Astor and received a sizable fee for his services. And Benton earned every penny as far as Astor was concerned. One of the first things Benton did in the Senate was to attack the factory system, run by the War Department, which provided Indians with clothing, tools, and equipment. This operation competed with Astor's American Fur Company and Benton did not rest until he swept the factory system into extinction.[18]

His assault proved relatively simple. Prompted by the economic panic of 1819 into seeking ways of reducing federal spending, the Congress had investigated the Office of Indian Trade operating within the War Department. The investigation revealed a colossal swindle against both the Indians and the federal government.[19] Benton of course provided much of the incriminating evidence.[20] As a consequence Congress abolished the factory system. Thereafter it was simply assumed—nay, understood —that everyone connected in any way with the Indian trade was involved in fraudulent practices and would attempt to conceal their illegal operations.[21] "I believe," said Congressman David Trimble of Kentucky, "there was never a more abominable peculation . . . practiced on the United States."[22]

Trade with the Indians was indeed extremely valuable, particularly the fur trade, and the huge amounts of money involved in its operation encouraged some of the worst examples of bribery. Even the President of the United States fell victim. At a moment of acute financial embarrassment James Monroe borrowed $5,000 from John Jacob Astor. Later, as a favor to his benefactor, Monroe rescinded his previous order about prohibiting foreigners from engaging in the fur trade. He said he had rescinded the order "on further information and reflection." His "further information," provided by Astor of course, revealed that the President's previous order hurt the American Fur Company rather badly.[23] No one ever accused Monroe of having been bribed—who knew about it?—but he could hardly borrow $5,000 and then allow an order of his to inflict an injury on his benefactor.

In addition to accepting money or "loans"—many of which were never repaid[24]—government officers in the Monroe administration used their positions for whatever gain they could squeeze out of them. The charge by Jackson in his "memorandoms" that the secretary of the treasury authorized the inspection of land offices by a United States senator so that he, the senator, might electioneer for the secretary was in fact true. But, again, Crawford was not the sole culprit. The approaching presidential election of 1824, unlike any previous campaign, attracted a large number of candidates, many of whom sat in Monroe's cabinet. Of necessity, therefore, they all used their positions to advance their candidacy. To do otherwise invited defeat. But when they began to operate to undercut each other, that was the moment when the campaign got rough.

The War Department and the Treasury Department were the two most venal departments in the government, which is saying a lot considering the condition of the others. And both departments were headed by fiercely ambitious men who hungered for the presidency in 1824 when James Monroe's eight years in office would end. Both men subsequently decided to knock each other out of contention. Because both were extremely vulnerable to criticism they each landed telling political blows— and these blows staggered the American public.

Within each department a great deal of graft, bribery, and a system of kickbacks flourished.[25] Although neither Crawford nor Calhoun was personally involved—or so it would seem—they knew about these activities but tended to disregard them because by that time these practices constituted the accepted way of doing business with the government and because the political aspirations of the two secretaries required them to "cover up" the malfeasance to avoid unfavorable criticism. Besides, their reputations as administrators were involved.

As a matter of fact, anyone disbursing government funds could find ways of misappropriating the taxpayer's money. One of the most common was defrauding army veterans or those who received a pension or in any way had a financial claim on the federal government. The technique was simple. Hard money (gold or silver) in the form of government funds was used to purchase soft (paper) money and this paper was then passed along to the claimants. The government disbursing officers naturally pocketed the considerable difference between the hard and soft money.[26] Since so many banks were delighted to sell their cheap paper for hard government cash there was never a problem about arranging deals to benefit the government disbursing officials. As an army officer Jackson knew how this system worked.[27] And he hated it with a passion. Paper money and banks were an abomination to him. As he later said to Nicholas Biddle, the president of the Bank of the United States, it was not Biddle's Bank in particular that he loathed. He hated all banks.[28]

In the congressional drive for retrenchment following the Panic of 1819, the War Department attracted a great deal of investigatory attention and, as a consequence, John C. Calhoun, the secretary of war, took a political thrashing. The former superintendent of the Office of Indian Trade, Thomas L. McKenney, tried to defend his old chief by starting a semiweekly newspaper in Washington devoted to advancing Calhoun's political career. The Washington *Republican and Congressional Examiner* embarked on a protracted newspaper war with several other capital newspapers, particularly those supporting the presidential candidacy of William H. Crawford. Whereupon, to no one's surprise, McKenney suddenly found himself in deepening difficulties with Treasury Department officials over his accounts as superintendent of the Indian Trade Office, accounts that took years to settle. A congressional investigation followed. For his loyalty to Calhoun, poor McKenney was subjected to malicious harassment. Still he was lucky. His worse indiscretions as superintendent escaped notice. Had it been discovered in the congressional investigation that his home had been purchased with notes endorsed by a leading supplier to the Office of Indian Trade, the accounts might never have been settled. McKenney was eventually exonerated by the investigation, although certain disturbing "mysteries" remained unsolved. The government had lost a considerable amount of money, but why the sum could not be recovered, read the report, "appears to be inexplicable."[29]

The Indian trade operation was only one source of difficulty for Calhoun. As the depression tightened its grip and reduced government revenues, Crawford's allies in Congress launched a program of retrenchment and aimed their sharpest ax at the appropriations requested by the War Department. The House Committee on Ways and Means, responding to the demands of Crawford's henchmen, slashed the War Department's appropriations from approximately $6 million to $3 million and after 1821 forced the department to stabilize its operations at the lower figure for the remainder of Monroe's administration. In addition—much to Jackson's distress—the authorized strength of the army was reduced from 12,000 to 6,000 men. "The government should be d——d," Old Hickory fumed. In effect, the department lost half its army and appropriations, and Calhoun and his friends regarded the "chopping" as a vicious political move on the part of Crawford's partisans. Jackson agreed. "It is certainly true," he wrote to Calhoun, "that the Military committee of the Senate have and will be wielded by the present Secretary of the Treasury. Their object to effect you, and draw the attention of the nation from his corruption, and intrigue."[30]

But the Crawford cohort in Congress went beyond mere appropriations-slashing. They were out to sink Calhoun's candidacy. So they launched a series of congressional investigations into the affairs of the War Department in an effort to prove corruption and mismanagement. Their inquiries examined a wide range of likely possibilities from the administration of the Pension Act of 1818 to the Yellowstone Expedition to appropriations for fortifications, to West Point, military justice and departmental monetary balances. The issue in each case was "honesty in government."[31] The subsequent investigations turned up all kinds of delicious scandal indicating "curious" if not improper operations, but only the Yellowstone Expedition proved politically damaging for Calhoun. It also brought President Monroe's behavior into grave question. Here is what happened:

In 1818 Calhoun decided to extend the nation's military frontier eighteen hundred miles up the Missouri River to the Yellowstone. He directed that plans for the expedition be drawn up immediately and implemented. Calhoun then gave the transportation contracts for the expedition to his old friend and political ally, Colonel Richard M. Johnson of Kentucky—who just happened to be the chairman of the House Committee on Military Affairs—and to Johnson's brother James. It was a charming arrangement but by no means illegal. It might not be approved procedure in the twentieth century but it was common practice for the early nineteenth. The brothers promptly badgered Calhoun for a hefty advance of money to procure four steamboats for the expedition. The secretary complied. But this request was soon followed by repeated demands for additional advances. The brothers were financially distressed. Bankruptcy was intimated. To save the expedition and rescue the money already expended, more cash was required. At that point Calhoun grew apprehensive. Then President Monroe stepped in and took matters into his own hands. He had been touring Kentucky when Johnson came to him with a hard-luck story about his financial troubles. As chairman of a powerful House committee he was not a man to turn away. Monroe listened sympathetically and then awarded Johnson with a sum of money that dazzled even the congressman with its generosity. For reasons not totally clear, Monroe directed Calhoun to advance $85,000 on the various contracts held by the Johnson brothers together with an additional $57,-500 on receipt of title to the four steamships. But the Johnsons had already received advances on their contracts in excess of $100,000! Calhoun was absolutely stunned. He could not imagine what prompted the President to issue such an order. The amount of money now involved was astronomical. Worse, the government had nothing to show for this fantastic outlay of cash. Calhoun immediately wrote Johnson and begged him not to make any further drafts or in any way draw against the account. But Johnson's notes had already been rejected at the Lexington branch of the Bank of the United States and he was forced to draw once more against the War Department. It was advance after advance, draft after draft, running into the hundreds of thousands of dollars.

Where did all this money go? That is difficult to discover even today. Presumably some of it went to pay for the steamboats—but not much. The four boats that were finally delivered proved worthless. They barely made it to St. Louis, and one of them, appropriately named *Calhoun*, never reached St. Louis at all. The entire expedition only got as far as Council Bluffs, four hundred miles upriver.[32]

It was a colossal boondoggle. Honest men shook their heads in disbelief when they heard about it. "A Government of fraud and deceit," was the judgment of one man.[33] Perhaps outright theft could never be proved in a court of law, but no one doubted that the government had been cheated. When the House of Representatives voted a request for a report on the terms of the contracts for the expedition, Johnson, now United States senator from Kentucky, used the occasion to deliver a speech praising Monroe's frontier policy and insisting that the War Department had exercised "the most rigid economy" ever since John C. Calhoun had become its head.[34]

Another scandal that rocked the War Department—one the newspapers covered in detail and became "the subject of a good deal of discussion in the House of Representatives"—concerned Calhoun's chief clerk, Christopher Van Deventer, who helped his brother-in-law with a $300,000 contract for supplying stone at the Rip Rap Shoal, site of the construction for Fortress Monroe.[35] When Calhoun finally learned of Van Deventer's involvement with departmental contracts he did virtually nothing about it. He simply let the man off with a warning, even though Van Deventer owned a share in his brother-in-law's company! Soon Fortress Monroe got to be known as "Castle Calhoun" and was ridiculed as extravagant and useless. Indeed the *entire* fortification system of the War Department was seen as a national swindle.[36]

In the spring of 1822 a select House Committee on Retrenchment, sponsored by Crawford's friends, reported that private contractors for the army had overpriced their services and produced shoddy work. The committee therefore proposed repealing all laws authorizing the building of forts and other military defenses by contracts with nonarmy personnel. Instead the report urged the employment of regular soldiers for such work under the supervision of the Corps of Engineers. The report, in effect, constituted a censure of Calhoun's administration of the War Department.[37] Although Congress did not adopt the committee's principal recommendations, it did abolish the Office of Department Treasurer and thus prevented the Army and Navy from holding moneys in reserve. It also forbade advances on any contract until the person to whom the contract was given "shall have accounted for and paid into the Treasury all sums for which he may be liable."[38] By instituting the requisition system and requiring Treasury clearance on all contracts, Congress significantly strengthened the Treasury's control of the War Department.

That did it. Calhoun realized he must retaliate if he was to retain control of his department and any semblance of a respectable standing among presidential candidates. And he did—with a vengeance. Long aware of who and what were behind these investigations into his department, he finally set about getting even. He arranged to smear his tormentor with the same accusations that he had suffered. He determined to prove charges of corruption and inefficiency against William H. Crawford in his management of the Treasury Department. In particular he wished to saddle Crawford with the many bank failures that had occurred in the west following the Panic of 1819. If he could link the treasury secretary through mismanagement and favoritism with the currency derangement that devastated western states, Calhoun believed he could cripple, if not destroy, Crawford's chances to replace Monroe in the executive mansion in 1824.

Thus began the "A.B. Controversy." And it shook the entire Crawford governmental apparatus—which was considerable—down to its foundations. It temporarily stopped the Crawford rush for the presidency. The machine that had once seemed unbeatable lost its momentum and initiative.[39] It provided time for other candidates to "gather their forces and enter the race."[40] It completely changed the direction of the presidential election of 1824.

On January 20, 1823, the Washington *Republican* published an article by an anonymous writer who signed himself "A.B.," accusing the public printers, Joseph Gales and William W. Seaton—who were also the publishers of the Washington *National Intelligencer,* a leading Crawford newspaper—of suppressing government documents unflattering to the reputation and public image of the treasury secretary. The documents in question had been requested by the House of Representatives on January 9, 1822, and they concerned the handling of money received by the Treasury Department from the sale of public lands. The accusations of "A.B." clearly impugned the official integrity and personal character of the secretary and brought into question his fitness as a candidate for the presidency. Gales and Seaton promptly demanded an official investigation of what they termed the unfounded and dastardly attack upon their good names and reputation. The select House investigating committee subsequently vindicated the printers and the secretary but failed to discover the culprit or culprits responsible for suppressing the documents in question. And some of this material was in fact very damaging to Crawford. One deleted portion concerned the transfer of deposits by branches of the Bank of the United States to a financially troubled bank in Ohio that was unable to meet demands for redemption in specie of its own paper. Crawford approved the transfer of deposits not only from the Pittsburgh branch of the Bank of the United States but from the Chillicothe branch as well. The action far exceeded what the troubled bank dared hope for.

Another document proved even more damaging. In it—that is in the deleted portion—Crawford confessed that he was willing to permit road construction contracts to be discharged in depreciated western-bank notes. By so doing he would allow the troubled Ohio bank to pay out rather than redeem its depreciated notes and thereby unload its obligation. The investigating House committee chose not to inquire into this remarkable confession by the treasury secretary but rather to pursue exclusively the matter of suppression. It therefore became important to identify the mysterious "A.B." and find out what he knew about the deletions.

Eventually the finger of suspicion pointed at Senator Ninian Edwards of Illinois, whose strong political connections extended from Illinois to Kentucky and included a cousin, John Pope (Henry Clay's chief rival in Kentucky), and Senator Richard M. Johnson and his brother, James, both strong supporters of John C. Calhoun. Edwards's rival in Illinois was Senator Jesse B. Thomas, who backed Crawford. In the contest between the two Illinois factions for federal patronage, Thomas naturally won out, since much of this patronage fell under the control of the Treasury. As a matter of fact, Thomas himself accepted the extremely lucrative post of land-office inspector (which was clearly illegal), the propriety of which was questioned in the House of Representatives during the debate over the "A.B." investigation. He also received more mileage money than any other Congressman from Illinois and this, according to Edwards, constituted a bribe by the secretary of the treasury. As land-office inspector, Thomas toured much of the west and he used these expense-paid excursions to campaign for Crawford. This last disclosure really nettled the Calhoun men.

For Edwards personally it became very important to derail Crawford's developing push for the presidency. But in making his published accusations he chose to hide his identity behind the letters "A.B."

The Washington newspapers friendly to Calhoun, in particular the Washington *Republican* edited by Thomas L. McKenney, began asking embarrassing questions that were later reiterated by the House investigating committee. The questions inferred fraud in the management of public funds. For example, did any of the banks granted public deposits by the federal government accept depreciated notes in lieu of cash? Were public moneys deposited in local banks in cities that had a branch of the Bank of the United States? If so, were these deposits not in reality a loan to the bank and disguised as deposits? And did not the government fail to require security for these deposits?[41]

In Illinois Crawford had earlier permitted the Bank of Illinois to decide which bank notes it would accept from the land-office receivers, all of whom were his supporters. But he allowed no such dispensation to the Bank of Edwardsville, of which Senator Edwards was a director and in which Senator Richard M. Johnson and his brother were heavy investors. Thus the paper notes of the Edwardsville bank could be blacklisted by land-office receivers. Then, after Edwards withdrew from the bank in order to prevent its collapse, Crawford issued a directive to the public-deposit banks instructing them to accept the notes of all specie-paying banks in their state. He also ordered all receivers of land moneys to keep a precise description of the kind of money received. It had come to his attention, he said, that government money had been exchanged for less valuable money "which has been subsequently deposited to the credit of the Treasurer in the banks selected as places of deposit."[42] This, it will be remembered, was the standard technique of government disbursement officers to fill their pockets by exchanging hard money for soft.

Crawford also reportedly bribed the governor of Illinois, Edward Coles, by slipping him sums of money for small favors. In one instance Coles agreed to check the progress of a suit against the Bank of Edwardsville and to handle negotiations with the widow of a land-office receiver. Crawford told Coles that he would pay him however he wished.[43]

As the investigations turned up mounting evidence of possible fraud in both the land-office and banking operations, the friends of Crawford worried over its adverse consequences. So they counterattacked by demanding additional inquiries into Indian and army affairs. The accusations and disclosures of corruption and fraud continued over the next several months. Edwards eventually resigned from the Senate to accept appointment as minister to Mexico. Crawford fired one last blast at the new minister before his departure from Washington, whereupon Edwards turned around and in a long communication to the House of Representatives accused Crawford of six specific charges of misconduct: that he had mismanaged government funds; that he had received depreciated notes from certain privileged banks contrary to an 1816 congressional resolution; that he had deceived the House of Representatives as to the amount of the depreciated notes; that he had misrepresented the obligations of those banks receiving public deposits; that he had failed to report to Congress his decisions to continue deposits of public moneys in certain banks; and that he withheld information and letters called for by the House. In passing Edwards admitted that he wrote the "A.B." letters.[44]

What seemed clear in all the charges and countercharges was that Treasury Department practices and policies toward western banks had been unusual and not in accordance with standard procedures. But it also seemed clear that these departures from the norm were dictated by the dislocation and distress experienced in the west after the Panic of 1819. Westerners, including Edwards, had urged special aid to western banks. It had been given. As a result the government lost money—probably a great deal of money[45]—and some of it mysteriously disappeared. Still, the government in the long run gained by these extraordinary arrangements, for had Crawford not intervened, the sale of public land would have been abruptly halted, worthless paper would have flooded the west, and thousands would have been financially ruined. The final report of the investigating committee issued in the spring of 1824 stated that nothing had been proved to impeach Crawford's integrity or the "general correctness . . . of his administration of the public finances."[46]

Even so, his highly irregular procedures had sent buckets of money sloshing around the west which benefited some institutions and favored individuals largely on the basis of political considerations. Enough evidence surfaced to indicate corruption and favoritism in the government's financial operations. The charges were grave enough to inflict considerable political injury on the secretary of treasury. Worse, they constituted part of a larger picture of general corruption that seemed to touch every department of the government.

Even the secretary of state, John Quincy Adams, was not above suspicion. There was talk that the Florida Treaty had been devised not for territorial gain but simply to win an award of $5 million to reimburse New England insurance companies, which had already paid the claims of American citizens against Spain. In order to obtain this essential clause for the benefit of his business constituents, Adams had sweetened the treaty for other Americans by running the western boundary on a course to the Pacific Ocean. That was the bait he used to win Senate approval for the $5 million.[47]

There was also suspicion about the awarding of consular posts. These appointments had a direct bearing on business operations in the country because the value of goods imported into the United States was based on the assessed costs in the country of origin, not on their market value in the United States, and the consul of the port city decided what value to assign to goods being shipped to America. If the assigned value was placed at a low figure, the importer paid less tariff and thus widened his margin of profit. If his goods were rated on the low side and his competitor's on the high, he could drive his competitor out of business just on the differential in duties, which commonly ran about 20 to 30 percent ad valorem. Manufacturers, particularly, exercised considerable influence in the personnel appointed to represent the nation overseas. They were obliged to—or risk going out of business.[48]

In addition, the assignment of the privilege of publishing the laws raised eyebrows. "Mr Adams . . . gives it to those who support himself" for the presidency, said one man, "thereby making a direct attack upon the freedom and independence of the Press."[49]

Granted some of the talk was nothing but rumor with little hard evidence to support it. Nevertheless enough proof had already emerged during Monroe's second administration to create a climate of suspicion. "I did, before I came to this city [Washington]," recorded one, "entertain a most exalted opinion of the high officers of gov't; but since I have been here it has abated greatly. I find they are not, in reality, quite so good as other men."[50]

In all this ongoing discussion of corruption what must be remembered above all else—indeed it is essential to a full understanding of Jackson's thinking—is that public corruption to the American of the early nineteenth century was not simply a matter of stealing government money. There were far worse forms of corruption, such as subverting the constitutional system, lusting after political power, and placing private interests ahead of the public good. To use one's public office to acquire power or a higher office was far more vicious and destructive and dangerous than mere stealing of government funds. This sort of corruption produced cancerous growths on the body politic that threatened the life of the Republic. Thus the action of John Quincy Adams in providing patronage to his supporters or William H. Crawford in funding electioneering junkets on his behalf were "corrupt" acts, according to Americans of the 1820s, which endangered their free system of government.

A clearer case in point was the determination of certain congressmen —in particular the friends of Crawford—to hold the traditional caucus to nominate the next Republican presidential candidate. Such a nomination was tantamount to election since the Republican party had no rival at the national level. In other words a mere handful of congressmen would elect the President of the United States. While a congressional caucus was not unusual (it had been utilized for decades), at least in the past a political contest between two parties had ensued. Now there was only one party. That fact rendered a congressional caucus totally improper and dangerous. It negated the idea of free elections. For congressmen, rather than the American people, to decide the presidential question was a gross violation of the constitutional system. And for congressmen to insist that a caucus be held to nominate the Republican candidate served as one more indication of the prevailing "corruption in Washington."[51]

Moreover, everyone knew that the decision of the caucus was preordained and that William H. Crawford would receive the nomination because of his popularity among Congressmen and the efficiency of his political apparatus in Washington. Despite all the talk about the mismanagement of government funds, the appointment of land-office inspectors to electioneer for the secretary, and other "corrupt acts," he commanded more Republican votes than anyone else. It appeared to many people, therefore, that Congress was about to "steal" the presidency from control by the American electorate. This suspicion became absolute certainty when Crawford suffered a paralyzing stroke a little later that left him immobile, speechless, and almost blind, and yet congressmen continued to plan their caucus for him anyway. In their "villainy and depravity" they would lift into the executive mansion a man who could not perform his duties. The next President of the United States, if Congress had its way, would be paralyzed, sightless, and dumb. Was any further proof needed that the country was in the hands of desperate and evil men?

Andrew Jackson needed none. His "memorandoms" breathed with agitation and outrage over the affairs of state. They cited "swindling the Govrt," "violating the consti," "perfidious conduct," the "capacity at intrigue . . . and the means mr Crawford employs to reward those who can corrupt to his Views." Parasites attend him, ranted Old Hickory, and they mean to sacrifice me "as a peace offering to the Sec of the T. and therby crush my influence and bring him to the executive chair."[52] Well, "by the Eternal," they would find General Andrew Jackson a tough old bird to sacrifice.

Each day letters came to the Hermitage from Washington from one friend or another citing additional instances of the frightful things going on in the nation's capital. The Vice President, Daniel D. Tompkins, repeatedly disgraced himself. "I dont think he was perfectly sober during his stay" in Washington, wrote Dr. James C. Bronaugh to Jackson. "He was several times so drunk in the chair that he could with difficulty put the question. I understand he will never return here."[53]

Even the newspapers hinted at his condition and mentioned the charge of fraud brought against him in the dispersal of funds during the War of 1812, when he served as governor of New York. His present alcoholism probably stemmed from those unproven charges.[54]

"Out of Congress," Senator John H. Eaton informed Jackson, "nothing grows of moment or interest: they have done nothing and it is difficult to say whether any thing is to be done, or indeed can be done while all is manouver after the Presidential chair."[55]

Maneuvering after the presidential chair, and maneuvering by political pygmies, the likes of William H. Crawford. To think the chair once occupied by Washington, Jefferson, and Madison might soon find the prostrate form of William Crawford sprawled over it.

Even more horrendous to Jackson's mind were the revelations of fraud by the Bank of the United States and the role the Bank had played in triggering the Panic of 1819. The facts presented a dismal picture: the charter of the First Bank of the United States had been allowed to expire in 1811 as a result of the concerted action of state banks and the fear of foreign ownership of the Bank's stock. But the War of 1812 demonstrated the absolute necessity of a national banking system, and therefore on May 10, 1816, President James Madison signed a bill creating the Second Bank of the United States (BUS). The first president of the BUS was Captain William Jones, onetime secretary of the navy and secretary *pro tem* of the treasury. Venal and cunning, he proceeded to speculate in the Bank's stock, to profit from the corrupt practices of the Bank's branch members, and regularly to violate the terms of the charter. It was a typical performance of a businessman-on-the-make in this Era of Corruption. In time Congress launched an investigation, Jones resigned, and Langdon Cheves replaced him as president. Forthwith loans were called in, mortgages foreclosed, and notes of state banks submitted for redemption. Many state banks could not meet their obligations—they had in fact been encouraged to speculate by the BUS—and slid into bankruptcy. Prices collapsed, unemployment rose, and economic havoc spread across the country. A great many people faced misery and want.

Every "community evil" was blamed on the BUS, according to William H. Crawford, so intense was the hatred and anger toward the institution.[56] Soon states enacted legislation to penalize the Bank and prevent it from collecting its debts. In Kentucky—and Kentucky deserves special mention because events in that state would play a significant role in determining Jackson's bank policy after he was elected President—stay laws forbade foreclosures and abolished imprisonment for debt. The state also chartered a Bank of the Commonwealth with authority to issue $3 million worth of paper to combat the economic hardship. These "radical" measures so divided Kentucky that the Republican party split into the Relief and Anti-Relief factions. Small farmers, debtors, and lawyers joined the Relief party; farmers with large landholdings and merchants backed the Anti-Relief party. When the Court of Appeals, Kentucky's highest court, supported the arguments of the Anti-Relief party, the Relief party won control of the legislature, abolished the Court of Appeals, and created a New Court. This rivalry and hostility between the two factions continued for the next ten years.

When Jackson learned what had happened in Kentucky the old judicial magistrate stirred inside him. His natural conservatism and concern over breach of contracts also stirred and he scorched the rascals responsible for creating the New Court in Kentucky.

> The conduct of Kentucky with regard to her Judiciary is to me the most alarming and flagitious, and augurs (if persisted in) the destruction of our republican government—for let me tell you, that all the rights secured to the citizens under the constitution is worth nothing, and a mere buble, except guranteed to them by an independent and virtuous Judiciary, and

should the Demagogues of Kentucky succeed in destroying that indepen-
dance, they place the Judiciary in the hands of these designing demagogues,
and the Judiciary will be become the mere tools of oppression of the people,
and wielded by these men for their wicked purposes. I hope the enlightened
freemen of Kentucky, will assert their rights, and preserve the independence of the Judiciary unimpaired by faction, or the designing demagues
of the day.[57]

The dramatic economic collapse of the nation at the start of a new
decade, coupled with the revelations of fraud by the BUS and its involvement in political elections, provoked a howl of protest from the American
people along with a serious and sustained reaction against increased
government rule in Washington.[58] The American electorate did not require much government from the nation's capital, but what little did
come out of it was expected to be honest and efficient.[59]

This demand for limited government had been preached by conservatives for decades. Almost from the foundation of the nation under the
Constitution they had been arguing the doctrine of minimal government
and urging the necessity of frugality. The central administration can only
be kept honest, they claimed, by restricting it. Unwarranted assumption
of power brings corruption and threatens freedom. When the party system began during the presidency of George Washington the Federalists,
under the direction of Alexander Hamilton, attempted to centralize authority, award the national government increased powers, and allow the
executive full discretion in the administration of the government. The
Republican party, on the other hand, under the leadership of Thomas
Jefferson, opposed centralized government, argued the rights of the
states, and sought to reduce national expenditures. Wherever possible,
Hamilton as secretary of the treasury tried to minimize congressional
interference with the allocation and distribution of the finances. Jefferson, as secretary of state, advanced the doctrine of specific appropriations
in order to guarantee congressional control of the purse strings. By
limiting government spending the Republicans believed they could limit
the opportunities for executive domination.

The passage of the infamous Alien and Sedition Acts during the administration of John Adams proved to many Republicans the necessity of
protecting the states in all their rights and powers. The Alien and Sedition Acts struck at the very heart of individual freedom and provoked
Jefferson and Madison into preparing the Virginia and Kentucky Resolutions passed in 1798. These resolutions proclaimed the need to guarantee states' rights so that when the national government transcended its
constitutional authority there would be some means to redress the wrong
and bring the government to heel. These doctrines of '98, as they were
called, served as gospel for conservatives. Along with the Tenth Amendment to the Constitution they were the libertarian's basic argument for
states' rights.

The defense of individual liberty against increasing demands for governmental authority is one of the great themes of American history prior to the Civil War. It is what Jeffersonian Democracy and Jacksonian Democracy are all about. Fundamental to the thinking of both these historic phenomena is the proposition that the strength of this nation derived from the freedom of its people, not the power of its government. Where Jeffersonians insisted that "government, like dress, is the badge of lost innocence," the Jacksonians proclaimed that "the world is governed too much."

The single most important heritage from the Revolutionary age was freedom. Individual liberty. That was an American's most prized possession. That is what had to be preserved. That is what was at stake in the 1820s and what had been jeopardized by the corruption of the government following the War of 1812, and that was the essence of Jackson's political leadership of this country after he concluded his military career. There really was no other issue. Everything else—banking, internal improvements, tariffs, even slavery in a strange and peculiar way—was secondary. Individual liberty. That was the basic question.[60]

Andrew Jackson was the product of the Revolutionary generation and he absorbed many of its prevailing ideas and beliefs. From colonial days through the Revolution and well into the nineteenth century, Americans believed that those who exercised power were naturally inclined to suppress liberty and that they regularly devised means to limit if not abrogate the rights of the people. They viewed corruption as power's greatest weapon and virtue as freedom's greatest defense. The struggle between liberty and power during the colonial era produced the Revolution and ultimately achieved independence from the British empire for the American people. But the dangers to freedom persisted. They persisted as long as power could be concentrated and the operation of government corrupted. The only defense rested upon the virtue of the American people.

The history of the United States following the adoption of the Constitution was a continuation of this struggle, and the rise of political parties an expression of it. The Federalist and Republican parties quarreled over the limits of power to be exercised by the central administration. They disagreed about the objects of government. They entertained different views about the governed. Whereas Federalists distrusted the people, Republicans maintained that the people would protect and defend their government when its actions were just. Federalists required patronage and large expenditures of money by the central authority to perpetuate their power and position. Republicans claimed that patronage corrupted honest government and that expenditures should be appropriated to carry out the practical and natural services of government; they could not abide artificially contrived projects whose principal aim was to attract votes. Federalists needed a large standing army and navy; Republicans declared that free men had no need for peacetime armies.

After the War of 1812 the Federalist party, which flirted with secession at the Hartford Convention, became moribund and slowly disappeared from the national scene. But its principles did not disappear. They resurfaced in the political thinking of many Republicans who believed that the War of 1812 demonstrated the need for a strong central government capable of advancing the material and intellectual well-being of the American public. As a consequence, demands flooded into Congress following the war urging the passage of a protective tariff, a national bank, and internal improvements such as roads and canals and bridges and many other forms of transportation. The country took off on a nationalistic spending splurge that slowed only with the economic breakdown of 1819.

The events that transpired during the administration of James Monroe —especially after the Panic of 1819—revealed anew that the old tensions between liberty and power had not evaporated. The exercise of increased authority by the central government, the large expenditures of money on internal improvements, the rechartering of the Bank of the United States, the rising demand for greater tariff protection, the revelations of corruption within the government, the abuse of the federal patronage, the demand for a congressional caucus—all these sounded alarm bells in the minds of those familiar with the ideology of "republicanism," the ideology of the Revolutionary generation.

That included Andrew Jackson. His correspondence throughout the 1820s echoed the philosophy of the Founding Fathers. "I weep for the liberty of my country," he wrote, "when I see at this early day of its 'successful experiment' that corruption has been imputed to many members of the House of Representatives, and the rights of the people have been bartered for promises of office."[61] He was growing old, he said, and not likely to live very much longer, "but my fervent prayers are that our republican government may be perpetual, and the people alone by their Virtue, and independent exercise of their free suffrage can make it perpetual."[62] He emphasized the importance of free elections and argued that anyone concerned with the preservation of freedom must therefore condemn the convocation of a congressional caucus to nominate the Republican candidate for President. "I do hope the one last held will put this unconstitutional proceeding to sleep forever, and leave to the people their constitutional right of suffrage. Should this not be the case, it will introduce into our Government, a sistematic system of intrigue and corruption . . . that will ultimately destroy the liberty of our country, a central power will arise here; who under patronage of a corrupt, and venal administration, will deprive the people of their liberties."[63]

Jackson could not emphasize free elections enough as the panacea for all the ills of government. "The great constitutional corrective in the hands of the people against usurpation of power, or corruption by their agents," he said, "is the right of suffrage; and this when used with calmness and deliberation will prove strong enough. It will perpetuate their liberties and rights."[64] So strong was he on this point that Jacksonian Democracy later came to be viewed as the ideology that advocated the widest possible extension of the suffrage.

Realistically, he knew that the most efficient way to check the growing power of the central government was through the instrumentality of the states. But this involved a delicate balance—one must not overtop the other. "To keep the sovereignty of the States and the general govt properly and harmoniously poised," Jackson wrote in 1824, "is the pivot on which must rest the freedom and happiness of this Country."[65] That meant a central government capable of defending the nation from foreign domination, yet one operating within the constitutional limits set by the Founding Fathers. Never may the states regard themselves as superior to the general government. Nor did they possess the right of secession. Jackson is the first statesman to take an absolute stand against secession.

> There is nothing that I shudder at more than the idea of a seperation of the Union. Should such an event ever happen, which I fervently pray god to avert, from that date, I view our liberty gone. It is the durability of the confederation upon which the general government is built, that must prolong our liberty, the moment it seperates, it is gone. The State governments hold in check the federal, and must ever hold it in check, and the virtue of the people supported by the sovereign States, must prevent consolidations, and will put down that corruption engendered by executive patronage, wielded, as it has been lately, by executive organs, to perpetuate their own power; The result of the present struggle between the virtue of the people and executive patronage will test the stability of our government, and I for one do not despair of the republic; I have great confidence in the virtue of a great majority of the people, and I cannot fear the result. The republic is safe, the main pillars virtue, religion and morality will be fostered by a majority of the people, the designing demagogues who have attempted to retain power by the most corrupt means will be driven by the indignant frowns of the people into obscurity.[66]

Because Jackson hammered away at the themes of "virtue, religion and morality" throughout the decade of the 1820s, a great many Americans ultimately turned to him for leadership to help them preserve their freedom and terminate this Era of Corruption.

In many ways, then, Jackson's political thought was a throwback to the Revolution and its most democratic ideals. In his letters and public statements he repeatedly restated the doctrines of the Revolutionary Fathers and he did it in language familiar to many Americans. Thus, in ideology, rhetoric, and commitment Jacksonian Democracy, as it emerged, was strikingly similar in important respects to the democracy of the Revolution.

The initial contours of Jackson's political philosophy changed relatively little as he grew older. Representatives Nathaniel Macon of North Carolina and Henry Tazewell of Virginia, two extremely conservative Republicans, influenced his thought as a young Congressman, as did John Randolph of Roanoke, an ultra-extreme advocate of the states'-rights wing of the Republican party. "My political creed," declared Jackson, ". . . was formed in the old republican school."[67] By the time he concluded his tenure as territorial governor of Florida, Jackson entertained very definite political ideas, which he expressed candidly and forcefully. No ideological novice by any means, he developed pronounced opinions, uniquely his own, that were at once consistent and contradictory, nationalistic and sectionalistic, practical and romantic, conservative and liberal. Yet basic to his thinking, as a bedrock foundation, was the doctrine of individual freedom. "I have risked much for the liberties of my country," he wrote at this time, "and my anxious prayer is, that they may long endure."[68]

As a first principle he affirmed the conservative doctrine of limited government. He opposed a broad definition of constitutional power. He feared the concentration of authority at a central point because such a concentration tended to undermine the rights of the people, inspire corruption, and destroy liberty. Government should not interfere in the legitimate activities of the people. It should stand clear of the normal operations of society. In discussing his reputed "rashness" with an individual who worried about its affecting his performance as President should he ever run for that office, Jackson admitted "I indeed have sometimes been rash, but permit me to assure you, that however in times of toil & trouble, this charecter may have been imputed to me, now in these our times of peace there are some of the politicians of the country who in their construction of constitutional power go greatly a head of where I should dare to venture."[69] As Tennessee's first representative to the lower house of Congress, Jackson came to the capital with fixed ideas about the respective powers of the state and federal governments. In a letter to the governor of his state, John Sevier, he expressed them in tortured syntax and spelling but he expressed them most precisely nonetheless:

> In you [the governor] alone is Constitutionally invested the authority and power of protecting the State in case of Invassion, and to bring to Condign punishment, (through the medium of the Courts of Justice) any person that may Commit acts, that may tend to Endanger the safety and peace of your Government. these are powers, that Consistant, With the Sovereignity retaind. by the States, properly belong to Each Individual State, which never ought on any account to be Surrendered to the General Government, or its officers and when, an attempt is made to arest that perogative out of the hands of the Executive of the State It ought to be opposed. . . . the moment, the Sovereignty of the Individual States, is overwhelmed by the General

Government, we may bid adieu to our freedom, let that be brought about, Either by a Legislative act of the General Government or State quietly, suffering it.[70]

Our freedom. The purpose of protecting state sovereignty was to guarantee individual liberty. Since there always existed the possibility of a diminution of freedom by the central government it was necessary to stand guard and actively oppose every effort to infringe or endanger it. That is why Jackson felt compelled to criticize both Presidents Washington and Adams for their flagrant abuse of authority. The "executive of the Union," he once wrote, referring to Washington, "has . . . been Grasping after power, and in many instances, Exercised powers, that he was not Constitutionally invested with." And the Adams administration compounded the outrage by being guilty of the grossest violations of personal liberty.[71]

As he grew older, Jackson's appreciation for states' rights and individual freedom continued to develop. When he served in the convention that wrote Tennessee's first constitution in 1796 he advocated property qualifications for certain officeholders; but as governor of the Florida Territory he endorsed "residence alone" as a voting requirement. He wanted the suffrage extended to every freeman. Since they were subject to laws and punishments under them, he said, they "of right, ought to be entitled to a voice in making them."[72] At the same time he also recognized the right of a state—far different from a territory—to "adopt such qualifications" as it might consider proper for the "happiness, security & prosperity of the state."[73] He favored liberal suffrage laws but he also recognized the right of the state to enact these laws.

Similarly, Jackson's resentment of strong government also quickened over the years. By definition centralism meant elitism. Centralization excited the interest of the rich because they instantly saw the economic benefits generated by powerful governments. They continually plotted— he invariably thought in terms of "conspiracies"—to gain control of these governments and then subvert them into instruments of their private purpose. They corrupted the republican process of self-government; they connived through fraud to gain the benefits of government exclusively for themselves. Ultimately, he said, a strong central government "is calculated to raise around the administration a moneyed aristocracy dangerous to the liberties of the country."[74] Thus, powerful governments must be opposed not only because they endanger liberty in and of itself but also because they create a "moneyed aristocracy." Again, as governor of Florida, Jackson declared that as long as he functioned as the representative of the United States government and administered its laws, there would be "no distinction between the rich and poor the great and ignoble." His government would treat everyone equally. He worried over the broad powers as governor granted him under his several commissions and he repeatedly expressed the hope that these powers would be reduced and that no one would ever again enjoy such extraordinary authority over the operation of government as he did.[75]

Like Jefferson, who stressed debt reduction as an important article of Republican faith, Jackson also believed that a national debt constituted a danger to free government. Creditors grew rich at the expense of the poor; they fattened on the revenues collected from the masses; and if they were British or French they behaved as though the United States operated solely for their economic benefit. A national debt, he wrote in 1824, is "a national curse, [and] my vow [if I become President] shall be to pay the national debt, to prevent a monied aristocracy from growing up around our administration that must bend it to its views, and ultimately destroy the liberty of our country."[76] As governor, Jackson summed up his administration of Florida as one long effort to protect "the poor and humble from the Tyranny of wealth and power."[77] For Jackson, therefore, total elimination of the national debt became a very real objective. As President it was one of his major achievements. To eliminate the debt, of course, meant reducing government spending. It meant withdrawing the government from such private sectors of the economy as banking. It meant cutting down appropriations for internal improvements.

The ideology of "republicanism," as Jackson comprehended and elucidated upon it in his letters and public statements, also included the notion that society was essentially agrarian in character. Like Jefferson, he emphasized the merits of a settled agrarian order and the need to keep it that way. "I find," he told his nephew, Andrew J. Donelson, ". . . virtue to be found amonghst the farmers of the country alone, not about courts, where courtiers dwell."[78]

Appreciation for the virtue of the farmer did not mean a hostility toward business. Basically, Jackson favored individual enterprise free of government restraint and free of government favoritism. He affirmed the notion widely held at the time that each citizen must be free to enjoy the fruits of his property and labor without interference or regulation. That was what liberty was all about.

Jackson was also an intense nationalist. Although committed to states' rights, jealous of western prerogatives, and extremely sensitive to eastern presumption, he was totally—indeed passionately—devoted to the Union. As a patriot, he had fought in two wars and suffered personal injury and extreme deprivation. As a general, he had scored the greatest military victory in the nation's history. As an ardent expansionist, he had driven the Spanish, British, and Indians from the southwest and called for U.S. acquisition of "all Spanish North America." Both Jackson and the nation came of age at roughly the same time. They had much in common because both extracted recognition of equality through conflict with their erstwhile superiors; both seemed raw, aggressive, untutored, quarrelsome, and a potential threat to the security of others. Any enemy of the

United States instantly encountered his passionate hostility. All his life Jackson believed in an aggressive foreign policy, one absolutely committed to asserting the dignity and honor of the American people. "Peace with all the world, suffering insult & indignity from none," was his guiding principle, he said, "& if this be wrong, my country should be cautious how they ventured to confide her rights & interests into my hands."[79] Nothing set off a Jacksonian explosion faster than a foreign slight or insult. He howled imprecations at any nation that dared defame the reputation of the "Grand Republick." Naturally, then, Crawford's knife-wielding to reduce appropriations by cutting the size of the army met Jackson's total opposition even though it seemed to contradict his concern for economy and reduced government spending. He simply saw it as an attempt to "demolish the army regardless of the injury which must inevitably result to the nation thereby."[80]

The apparent inconsistency in Jackson's political thinking points up an important fact. He was never dogmatic. Despite appearances to the contrary, he could make concessions to seemingly contradictory principles when circumstances dictated. To carry on the practical business of attaining and exercising political power, either at home or abroad, he was perfectly capable of making necessary adjustments. He was a pragmatic politician, not an ideologue. To be sure, he advocated a particular set of conservative principles rooted in a "republican" philosophy of Revolutionary War vintage, but they served as guides to his thinking and actions, not as rigid absolutes that could not be violated.

Like his physical disability—a constant for the remainder of his life—Jackson's political philosophy must be taken into serious account in any evaluation of his later career. A states'-rights advocate of the Jeffersonian school, he regarded the Constitution as a limiting rather than an enabling document. He suspected any concentration of power at a central point and he preached the necessity of preserving the "natural" associations of the people in their respective states. Yet, as President, he contributed his share to widening the scope of the Constitution, enlarging the powers of the central government, and weakening the authority of the states. Like many other Presidents', his thinking and political faith were fundamentally conservative, but his actions frequently pursued the reverse direction.

As Jackson sat in his study in the Hermitage brooding over the state of the nation and the activities of its leaders, he scribbled out his worry over the corruption and intrigue and departure from principle that were eroding American institutions and threatening the freedom of every citizen. "If intrigue, management and corruption can avail," he wrote, ". . . nothing but the virtue of the people can prevent this."[81] Later when he visited Washington his worst fears were all confirmed. "How can a republic last long under such scenes of corruption?" he moaned. Only a moral and virtuous people exercising their constitutional rights of free suffrage could "redeem our nation from woe, & our republican Government from destruction."[82] One thing he had learned over the years was that freedom could be lost by domestic corruption as well as foreign intervention. One could destroy it as quickly as the other.

Leafing through the steadily increasing volume of his mail after his return home from the swamps of Florida, Jackson discovered that his thoughts and concerns were shared by other men. They knew what was happening in Washington and the dangers it posed. One man told him that in Virginia a "powerful party as yet without a head" had begun to emerge, produced by the abberrations from "old republican principles" that had developed over the past five or six years. The writer listed these aberrations: "the excessive accumulation of offices, profuse expenditure of public money and annual increase of the national debt . . . the lust of office and the pride of power about the seat of the General government." These, he said, were "utterly repugnant to the true sinews and spirit of our institutions." Whoever marshals this emerging party, he said very pointedly to Jackson, will call forth an opposition "as powerful as it wou'd be unexpected. It composes the soul and body of this State. If we wou'd preserve the original simplicity of our institutions and perpetuate this grand republic, we wou'd choose our presidents not for the splendour of their manners, but their simplicity and plainness—not for the eloquence of their haranguing, but the soundness of their judgment and their decision of character," not by accommodation of ten thousand competing wills, but by the firm resistance to "every thing not founded in right, and plain solid republican utility."[83]

More and more in 1822 and 1823 there was talk of "simplicity and plainness," and not because of a nostalgic reverence for the past as some golden age of civic purity and patriotism, but because of a conviction that a departure from simplicity and plainness resulted in the aggrandizement of power by bureaucrats who perpetuate themselves in office and fatten themselves on the property of their fellow citizens.[84] In writing to Andrew Jackson, those men most concerned about simplicity believed that he could restore it to government, along with the other principles of Jeffersonian republicanism. Only a man of his stature and accomplishments and eminence could successfully challenge the threat of the Congress to "steal the executive branch" by nominating Crawford in caucus and declaring him the sole Republican candidate. Jackson must, they said, permit his name to be brought forward for the office of President in order "that the great principles of the constitution upon which our republican government rests might be preserved, and our liberties perpetuated."[85]

Although Jackson told himself that he desired nothing except the retirement he had richly earned or that his health was so precarious that he had only a few years left to his life, nonetheless he felt a sense of genuine gratification over the many suggestions that he make the race for president in 1824. After all, he was an intensely ambitious man. And vain.

The presidency had never really been beyond his dreams. With corruption and fraud and retreat from republican principles the order of the day, surely he might make a great contribution to the "Grand Republick" by restoring simplicity and reasserting the doctrines of limited government, frugality, states' rights, elimination of the national debt and—most important of all—honesty in government. "Andrew Jackson and Reform." The temptation tantalized him.

To the increasing suggestions that he run for the presidency, Old Hickory did not say no. Rather he said he would not seek the office. It must come to him. To every application that he enter the race, he told Dr. James C. Bronaugh, "I give the same answer that I have never been a candidate for any office. I never will. But the people have a right to choose whom they will to perform their constitutional duties, and when the people call, the Citizen is bound to render the service required."[86]

Jackson reiterated this general position to Andrew Jackson Donelson, again protesting that he had never been an applicant for any office and that he intended "in the present instance to pursue the same independant, republican course. The people have the right to elect whom they think proper, and every individual . . . when the people require his services, is bound to render it, regardless of his own opinion, of his unfitness for the office he is called to fill."[87] Jackson admitted that he had received many letters "from every quarter of the united states on this subject." His only wish on the matter, he continued, was that in the selection of the President, the people fill it solely with an eye "to the prosperity of the union, the perpetuation of their own happiness, and the durability of their republican form of government, unbiased by the intrigues of designing Demagogues." If left free, he argued, and not "dictated to by a congressional caucus" intent on nominating "as great a scounderal as William H. Crawford," the electorate, he was sure, would make "a happy choice." The elevation of Crawford to the presidency, Jackson flatly declared, was "contrary to the wish of a great majority of the people." It would constitute the final proof that corrupt men had stolen the government.

My everlasting hope, the General concluded, is "that our republican government may be perpetual, and the people alone by their Virtue, and independant exercise of their free suffrage can make it perpetual."[88]

As he wrote these words on August 6, 1822, Jackson had already decided to run for the presidency. The official inquiry to stand as Tennessee's candidate came just a little over a month before in a confidential letter from Felix Grundy. It was quite specific.

> Your friends, wish to know, where there is any cause, unknown to them, which would render it improper to them to exercise their own discretion and Judgment, in bringing forward your name in such way as may be thought best, for the office of Chief Magistrate of the U States at the

approaching Election. The Genr'l Assembly will meet on the 22nd of next month. Then is the time, to take a decisive step.

In an obvious effort to persuade him to say yes, Grundy informed the General of "the Slander which has gone abroad" to the effect that "you are not popular at home." By allowing his name to be brought forward, Grundy said, Jackson would permit Tennessee to put the lie to this libel by voting unanimously in his behalf.

Please deliberate on the matter, said Grundy. "I will call on you."[89]

The business about the "Slander" made an impression on Jackson because he was quite vain and could not bear the thought that such a rumor would go unchallenged. More than that, he wanted to be President. He had earned it by his services to the nation and his performance of duty. Besides, it would thwart that "scounderal," Crawford, and restore honesty to government. But more than anything else he felt it was his "duty" to serve if the people summoned him. So, he decided at length, should the legislature of Tennessee wish to nominate him, he would not reject it. In a strong hand he wrote: "Let the people do as it seemth good unto them."[90]

CHAPTER 3

The Politics of Panic

THE TRANSITION OF AMERICAN SOCIETY from a highly contained, organic whole, with many ties such as the community and the church binding it together, into a highly fluid, unstable society seeking an uncertain direction probably began around the time of the American Revolution with the commencement of a genuine westward movement. Americans, like Andrew Jackson, vaulted over the Allegheny Mountains and within a few years reached the Mississippi River, crossed it, and started populating the other side. By the 1820s the original thirteen states totaled twenty-four with the recent admission of Maine and Missouri. Just a few years earlier, Alabama, Mississippi, Louisiana, Ohio, Indiana, and Illinois joined the Union. A small nation huddled along a thin ribbon of land on the Atlantic coast, struggling to assert its identity and protect its independence, now stretched across a three-thousand-mile continent with seemingly limitless opportunities available to anyone with the courage and fortitude to exploit them.[1]

After the Battle of New Orleans the American people shed their need to demonstrate to the world that the United States had a right to exist or that it could protect its freedom against any and all adversaries. Nationalism quickened with the successful outcome of the war and the nation radiated self-confidence and unbounded optimism. A nationalistic program of internal improvements, protective tariff schedules, and a new national bank (BUS) formed the agenda of the federal government. Naturally, the conflict with Great Britain stimulated the development of American manufacturers. With foreign goods cut off for several years, American capital switched from shipping to manufactures, and this stimulus to home industries signaled the rapid introduction of the industrial

39

revolution, particularly in New England. Technological improvements in such industries as textiles spurred economic change and advancement. Within a few years every step of the operation of manufacturing cloth was done entirely by machine.[2]

Paralleling the revolution in industry came the revolution in transportation. Indeed, they supported each other. The War of 1812 demonstrated the critical need for roads and improved waterways. Because of the coastal blockade by the British during much of the war, American goods were forced to seek inland routes for shipment to their markets. Roads, bridges, highways, turnpikes, and canals were constructed in virtually every state. The Erie Canal, begun in 1817, transformed New York into an "empire state" and opened the entire midwest to a steady flow of immigrants. The great National Road, begun in 1811 from Cumberland, Maryland, steadily inched its way over the mountains and eventually reached Vandalia in Illinois, a distance of nine hundred miles. Steamboating and (a few years later) railroading completed the major components of the transportation revolution at the beginning of the nineteenth century and became the nation's arteries in pumping economic lifeblood to all the areas they served.[3]

In some respects these changes signified the arrival of a new breed of Americans after the war. They were clearly "men on the make," imbued with the spirit of "Go ahead!" and alert to all the possibilities inherent in their newly expanded nation. They were aggressive. They were impatient for change. And they were determined to seize power, leadership, and status from an older political, economic, and social elite. In time they adopted new styles of behavior and invented new techniques to achieve their various goals—styles and techniques that broke with the past and became some of the essential characteristics of modern Americans.[4]

Expanding economic opportunities provided a great impetus for the furtherance of democracy because Americans wanted to get ahead and would suffer no restrictions that might hamper their progress. This attitude opposed political as well as economic restrictions. Political restrictions included the right to vote or hold office based on wealth, religion or social status; economic restrictions took the form of monopolies or exclusive franchises that granted privileges to some but denied them to others. Such privileges generated intense opposition after the War of 1812 because they institutionalized inequality. They reduced opportunity.[5]

Thus the turmoil of change was most visible on the political front. The once-great Federalist party as a viable organization had virtually disappeared from the national scene. The political field became the monopoly of the Republican party so a glib but quite inaccurate phrasemaker on the Boston *Columbian Centinel* dubbed these years at the start of Monroe's presidency the "Era of Good Feelings."[6] At the same time a new generation of politicians emerged and they were determined to grasp the reins of political power. Most of them were gifted politicians. Indeed, the American nation has rarely seen their like before or since. Unfortunately their credentials for governing the nation seemed totally inadequate when compared with those of the Founding Fathers. They had not participated in the Revolution—except for a very few like Jackson—nor signed the great Declaration. They had not framed the Constitution of the United States nor the constitutions of their respective states. They had little to offer the nation except their ambition and their talents. In their struggle to rise to national prominence without the marks of greatness clearly visible to the public, they were forced to rely on their special skills as orators and organizers or on their intellectual prowess in constitutional and legal debate. Henry Clay of Kentucky enjoyed popular favor because of his easy speaking style that combined forceful language with humor and biting sarcasm, while Daniel Webster of Massachusetts overwhelmed his listeners with the power of his eloquence and the drama of his physical presence. On the other hand, John Quincy Adams of Massachusetts and John C. Calhoun of South Carolina attracted support because of their unique and impressive intellectual strengths, particularly as writers.

And then there was Martin Van Buren of New York. The Little Magician! The Red Fox of Kinderhook! These mocking nicknames only underscored his superb political talents. Van Buren perhaps best typified the new breed of American politican after the War of 1812. He instinctively chose political organization as the engine to advance his career. He realized that future political success depended on strong state organizations that could provide a secure base of operations at home and a springboard for national recognition in Washington. Men like Van Buren disagreed with the Founding Fathers, who contended that political parties were little better than factions of designing and dangerous adventurers.[7] These new-styled politicians praised parties as the surest safeguard for a free and representative government. They also recognized them as the speediest instrument by which to change society and achieve their ambitions. A few of them, such as Van Buren, understood the fact that the party system might provide a stable society during a most fluid and unstable era and assist the country in its growth and developing prosperity. This was essentially a conservative position because it demanded balance—balance between interests, classes, and sections.

In the midst of these profound changes that were just beginning to penetrate the fabric of American life, disaster struck in the form of the depression of 1819. That devastating blow to the nation's pride in its accomplishments and optimism about the future shook public confidence. Because it was accompanied by the sensational revelations of scandal in the management of the BUS, followed immediately by disclosures of apparent corruption within the government itself, there resulted a popular distrust of government and a reversal of the postwar trend toward centralization in the operation of the national government. All during the 1820s—and in fact fundamental to the entire thrust of the Jacksonian philosophy as it developed during the General's presidency— came the demand for political and economic conservatism. Less spending was the cry; for less spending meant less government, and less government meant more freedom.

William H. Crawford, the treasury secretary and a particularly astute politician, observed the trend and immediately initiated radical economies, a policy totally in accord with his "anti-power" conservatism.[8] The department that had once served as Alexander Hamilton's instrument for the expansion of federal power became the stronghold of the doctrine of strict government economy. Hamilton had decentralized accounting procedures in order to facilitate spending by the entire government. Crawford restored those functions to the Treasury and tightened the administration of federal monies. Where army and navy accountants had once controlled nearly $40 million, Crawford's new regulations checked this "dangerous" leniency. His fiscal conservatism ultimately restored greater congressional control of the operations of the government, and consequently Crawford gained enormous popularity among Congressmen, particularly among the most conservative Republicans, called "Radicals" or "Old Republicans" because of their rigid opposition to centralized government. To no one's surprise the Radicals converged on Crawford as their presidential candidate and, despite critical reaction around the country, pledged themselves to nominate him in a caucus.

The Panic of 1819 not only altered the operation of the federal government but produced a strong impact upon the several states, and perhaps the development of the Relief and Anti-Relief parties in Kentucky was the most dramatic example of it. In Tennessee all these currents of economic and political change also worked their powerful influences. No longer a frontier society, Tennesseans had gained national attention and respect largely through the exploits of General Jackson. Most Tennesseans, including Old Hickory, thought of themselves primarily as westerners even though they had fashioned their way of life from a southern heritage. In politics the earlier disputes between the Blount and Sevier factions[9] had grown much more complex and sophisticated. Money, patronage, land speculations, the ambitions of strong-minded men—all contributed to the maturing process. The Blount clique still exercised a powerful hold on the electorate, and when Willie Blount completed the three successive terms as governor (the maximum allowed by the constitution), he was succeeded by Joseph McMinn, one of the cohorts within the Blount clique. But the dominating figure of this faction after the war, particularly in middle and western Tennessee, was Jackson's old friend, the "Witch of Endor," John Overton, lawyer, judge, land speculator, banker, and reputedly one of the wealthiest men in Tennessee. A prickly, profane little man, late to marry—he wed Mary (White) May, the widow of Dr.

Francis May—Overton won political leadership by virtue of his keen, pragmatic instincts, his wealth, and his close associations with a number of important and influential men in the state, not the least of whom was Andrew Jackson.[10]

At the eastern end of the state the Blount faction was led by Overton's brother-in-law, Hugh Lawson White, and by Pleasant M. Miller, the son-in-law of William Blount, Jackson's earliest mentor in Tennessee. Related to Overton through his sister, White was also the brother-in-law of John Williams, who had commanded the 39th U.S. Infantry during the Creek War and rendered Jackson invaluable military assistance at the Battle of Horseshoe Bend. Hugh Lawson White served for six years on the state Court of Errors and Appeals as its presiding judge and had been the president of the Bank of the State of Tennessee since its charter in 1811. He also won election to the Tennessee senate in 1817 and recently had been appointed a commissioner to fix claims against Spain under the Florida Treaty. Highly intellectual, but rather rigid in his thinking, something of a Puritan in his manner and behavior, a man of little humor or imagination, White rather resembled Andrew Jackson in appearance except that his long, lean, bony outline radiated none of Jackson's aggressiveness and tension. White was more contemplative, more cerebral. But like Jackson he was a strict constructionist of the old Republican school and he, too, worried over the corruption and centralizing tendencies of the national government in Washington.

This Blount-Overton faction eventually provoked an opposition in Tennessee, which considered itself the successor of the old Sevier party of earlier times. This opposition consisted principally of a powerful alliance among several prominent politicians, including United States Senator John Williams of Knoxville (White's brother-in-law) and Congressmen Newton Cannon and John Cocke. But the leader of the group—in a sense Overton's opposite number—was Andrew Erwin, a land speculator and planter from Middle Tennessee, whom Jackson sued and then refused the judgment when Erwin's wife pleaded for forgiveness. In the matter of ideology and issues, little of substance separated these two opposing Tennessee factions. For the most part, the Overton and Erwin groups were held together by personal friendships and mutual financial interests; but in the case of the Erwin group, practically every one of its members had quarreled with Andrew Jackson—either face to face or in front of a presiding judge. Naturally, then, the Erwin crowd attacked Jackson's Seminole campaign as an unconstitutional and arrogant breach of law and they supported the presidential pretensions of William H. Crawford, whom Jackson detested.[11]

The single event that decisively shaped the future course of Tennessee politics as it entered the decade of the 1820s—just as it did in many other states—was the Panic of 1819. The Overton cronies had largely dominated banking facilities in Tennessee and in Nashville their financial directorate included Overton, John H. Eaton, and William B. Lewis.

John Henry Eaton had risen to fame as Jackson's biographer, and because of his loyalty and ability had been elevated to the United States Senate. A handsome, dignified, and "serene" looking man, he was described by a future Washington editor as "one of the pleasantest fellows I ever met with. He is full of *facetiae*. His jests and humorous stories are always decorous." He and William Berkeley Lewis were brothers-in-law, both having married sisters who were Jackson's wards. Lewis had served as Jackson's quartermaster during the late war and lived close enough to the General to be a regular visitor at the Hermitage right up to the day Old Hickory died. Indeed, the shadowy Lewis's only claim to political influence came from his connection and unswerving loyalty to Andrew Jackson. Tall, solidly built with a strong nose and high cheekbones, Lewis combed his hair diagonally across his forehead in a vain attempt to conceal an increasing baldness. In repose the line of his mouth tended to droop and this gave him a somber, dyspeptic look. Over the years the link between Lewis and Eaton was extended to Overton through mutual financial interests and through Overton to Hugh Lawson White, whose Knoxville bank had a branch in Nashville headed by Overton himself.[12]

Then, in 1817, a third group, largely independent of the Overton and Erwin factions, tried to secure better credit facilities for businessmen in Tennessee by inviting the BUS to open a branch in Nashville. This group was led by Felix Grundy, a onetime War Hawk, and William Carroll, the commanding officer of the Tennessee volunteers at the Battle of New Orleans. The Overton group instantly recognized the full dangers to their interests by this invitation to the BUS, and to prevent this disaster Hugh Lawson White persuaded the legislature to levy an *annual* tax of $50,000 on any bank chartered outside the state. That measure temporarily ended the introduction of the national bank into Tennessee. Jackson himself applauded the result. The efforts to establish a branch in Tennessee, he later wrote, was the action of "the arristocratic few in Nashville."[13]

The Erwin faction also saw the potential danger to the Overton party represented by Grundy and Carroll's proposal, so the Erwin people backed the efforts to bring the BUS to Tennessee. When they failed to block the $50,000 tax they supported the chartering of the Farmers and Mechanics Bank in Nashville, with Carroll as one of the directors.

Then the Panic struck. The Farmers and Mechanics Bank failed, as did several others. White's bank in Knoxville survived in part because of White's enormous reputation for integrity. As the depression deepened and businesses went under, the public cried out for legislative relief. The stocky, beetle-browed, rough-and-tumble Grundy was the fastest man in Tennessee to spot the political possibilities of the discontent and respond to it. He immediately sponsored a series of relief laws which, seemingly democratic and humanitarian, ultimately failed to address the fundamental causes of the distress. One of the more important pieces of legislation passed during the 1819 session was the Endorsement Act or stay law, which provided relief for debtors while maintaining the currency of bank notes by postponing for two years the execution of judgments unless the creditor agreed to accept the depreciated paper money of the Tennessee banks.[14]

The depression hit hardest in middle Tennessee, around the Nashville area, and even the stay law could not mitigate its severity. In desperation Governor McMinn called a special session of the legislature, where Grundy once more introduced a scheme to provide relief. This time he suggested the creation of a new Bank of the State of Tennessee which was authorized to lend at 6 percent interest a maximum of $1 million. These noncommercial loans would be made in limited amounts with funds apportioned among counties according to tax payments and population. And the paper of this bank would be backed by the sale of public lands.

Naturally the Overton faction opposed any measure which effectively took the banking business of the state out of their hands. Besides, Grundy's proposal virtually guaranteed the depreciation of their own banknotes with the issuance of notes backed by the state through the sale of public land. But Grundy tried to win the support of the Overton crowd by placing the directorship of the new bank in the hands of men like John H. Eaton who would see to it that the loans of the state bank were kept as few and as low as possible. Although he was not involved directly, Andrew Jackson himself took a dim view of Grundy's new scheme because of his strong prejudice against paper money and his deep apprehension about the speculative practices of banks generally. The widespread evidence of general corruption among banks totally prejudiced Jackson against them.[15]

With party spirit running higher than it ever had before, with popular resentment against conservative responses to the crisis clearly apparent, the Erwin faction recognized its opportunity to capitalize politically on the situation and trounce the Overton faction in the next election. For its gubernatorial candidate the group wisely passed over their own cohorts —and over the erratic Grundy—and instead chose William Carroll to head the ticket. Carroll was a war hero, probably second only to Jackson himself in popularity, a merchant and part owner of the first steamboat to service Nashville. He suffered financial reverses like so many others in the Panic of 1819 but that only increased his identification with the great mass of the electorate. To oppose him, the Overton faction named Colonel Edward Ward, a conservative and wealthy planter who was Jackson's friend and neighbor. The General favored Ward's election because of his opposition to the new state bank. Carroll said nothing specific about that particular bank, although he blamed the depression on banks generally and said he wished there had never been one in Tennessee.[16]

Interestingly enough, Carroll himself preferred hard money, just like

Jackson, and opposed a paper system to inflate the currency. Indeed, he and Jackson held identical monetary views. At the time of this gubernatorial election Jackson had just accepted the governorship of Florida and had moved to Pensacola, but he did not hesitate to inform his friends of his position on these essential issues. "I am fearfull," he wrote, "that the paper system had and will ruin the state. Its demoralizing effects are already seen and spoken of everywhere. . . . Have nothing to do with the new raggs of the state for be assured it will be a reign of immoral rule, and the interest of speculators will be alone consulted during the existence of the new dynasty. . . . I objected to the new state bank bills, I never had one of them and I never will receive one of them. . . . I therefore protest against receiving any of that trash."[17] Jackson also told William B. Lewis that he did not believe the constitution of the state or the Constitution of the United States permitted "the establishment of Banks in every State."[18] Obviously Jackson's extreme monetary views did not accord with those of his friends in the Overton party, many of whom were closely associated with the banking business. But his long friendships with so many of the Overton people and his personal feuds with the Erwin men kept him from switching sides and supporting the candidacy of William Carroll. Friendship still meant more to Andrew Jackson than banks or hard money or any other financial consideration.

In any event Carroll won a smashing victory in 1821 and for the next fourteen years seemed politically unassailable in Tennessee. He served as governor for the entire period—1821–1827, 1829–1835—except for the two-year break required by the state constitution. "I . . . regret to see it rumoured that Carroll is Gov of Tennessee," wrote the General from Florida, "I hope it is not true for the happiness of my state."[19]

Jackson's gloom worsened in the ensuing years after his return from Florida when the inability of the financial institutions in the state to provide sufficient credit brought renewed efforts to allow the BUS to open a branch in Tennessee by repealing the $50,000 tax. As soon as he heard of the "secret and combined movement of the arristocracy" to abolish the tax, Old Hickory rushed from the Hermitage to the capital, summoned Robert C. Foster, the House Speaker, and "expostulated with him upon the danger of repealing the law." His arguments went unheeded. The tax was repealed and not much later a group of Nashville merchants petitioned the BUS to establish a branch in Tennessee. Because he was such a prominent man in the state Jackson was asked to sign the petition which he vehemently and indignantly refused to do. Before final action was taken on the petition, however, General Thomas Cadwalader, a director of the national Bank, came to Nashville and dined with Old Hickory. In one last effort to win his approval the Bank requested him to write letters of recommendation for the candidates for president and cashier of the proposed Nashville branch. Jackson did so, believing the two men suggested for the posts to be "honest and fit and would direct the institution well and as far as they had control would not wield it to corrupt political principles." So the branch of the BUS came to Nashville in 1827, much to Jackson's disgust. The people, he fumed, would be "cursed with all [the bank's] attendant evils and corruption."[20]

The mounting evidence of corruption within the banking system and within the national government that Jackson learned about in 1822 and 1823 stiffened his conservative economic and political views. And his monetary opinions tended to isolate him more and more from the rest of the Overton faction. Indeed, John H. Eaton and William B. Lewis had been consulted about the directorship of the new branch bank and John Overton himself became a director. Even so, Jackson made no effort to hide or soften his views. In fact he nearly went public. When Patrick H. Darby, editor of the Nashville *Constitutional Advocate,* commenced a slashing attack on speculators and bankers and was nominated for the state legislature in 1823, Jackson supported him. Darby's newspaper hit a very responsive chord in the General. Old Hickory predicted that the public would also respond favorably because there appeared to be "a combination between the secretary, Bank directors, and pension agents to put him [Darby] down. It matters not whether this is true or not," said Jackson, "it is enough that the people think so."[21]

Unfortunately for Jackson the "bankers and speculators" proved too strong and defeated Darby in the election. The strain between the General and the Witch of Endor over this affair did not rupture their friendship,[22] but according to one distinguished historian the defeat forced Jackson to recognize that personal friendships could no longer suffice as the basis for political alliances. In supporting Darby because of the newspaperman's hostility to the speculative system, Jackson was obliged to oppose his oldest and best friends, men who were presently engaged in commencing the management of his candidacy for the presidency.[23] Yet Jackson had come a long way in the past several years. Loyalty was still important to him—fantastically important as a matter of fact—and he could still be persuaded by the Overton faction to overlook his scruples against internal improvements and the tariff and not cause them any trouble over these issues.[24] But more and more his concern about corruption and the need for reform, his commitment to states' rights and the republican ideology of Jefferson and the Founding Fathers, and most particularly his worry over the loss of individual freedom, shaped his future decisions and his subsequent course of action.

After 1823 personal associations no longer locked Jackson into fixed positions. They would still count tremendously in his behavior but he now knew some of their limitations. When as President he decided to kill the BUS, and some of his closest friends objected, Jackson simply ignored them. The friendships remained intact, but he declined to invite these friends to advise him. In relaxing this bond the General even mellowed a little toward Andrew Erwin. In settling the Allison land claim and waiving the $10,000 judgment awarded him by the courts, Jackson eased the bad feeling between himself and the leader of the opposing faction. It suggested that Jackson began to sense that the changes in society required a change from old-style personal politics to politics based on "convictions about public policy."[25] Even now he was committed to and acted upon the conviction that government should not function to provide benefits for a few, that the proper role of government was the elimination of all obstacles to equal opportunity, especially economic opportunity.[26]

Because of Jackson's growing independence of his close personal and political friends in terms of certain public issues that were vital to their economic interests, a rather strange and ironic sequence of events developed in 1822 and 1823 that set Jackson on his course for the presidency. These events also explain in large measure the curious political shifting of his friends over the next twenty years.

Essentially what happened was that Jackson's Tennessee cronies decided to take advantage of his enormous popularity within the state to gain their own advantages by proposing him for the presidency, never calculating that it might produce a tremendous and enthusiastic response throughout the nation. When the unexpected happened and they realized that they had created a potential monster committed to principles and issues inimical to their economic interests, a few of them attempted unsuccessfully to reverse the process they had set in motion. Later a number of them deserted Jackson's party and joined the opposition.[27] It all began understandably enough with the need of the Overton faction to regain lost ground occasioned by the smashing success of the Erwin group through the election of William Carroll as governor. In suggesting the General's candidacy a few of his friends, notably Major William B. Lewis, may have had no other thought than Jackson's advancement. But nearly all the others operated on the basis of their own immediate good.

The movement in Tennessee to nominate Andrew Jackson for the presidency became serious late in 1821 and early 1822 following Carroll's election, when Pleasant M. Miller suggested to John Overton the wisdom of introducing Jackson as a contender in 1824.[28] Since Miller was anxious to win the Senate seat occupied by John Williams of the Erwin faction, he rightly figured that a presidential movement for Jackson in Tennessee would restore the Overton men to favor and in the process win a few political plums for his friends. The fact that the Erwin men supported William H. Crawford for the presidency antagonized Jackson and, as Miller suspected, would encourage the General to agree to a nomination. "As to Wm. H. Crawford," Old Hickory had growled only a few months before, "you know my opinion. I would support the Devil first."[29]

Initially most of the Overton clique preferred John Quincy Adams or, as a second choice, John C. Calhoun. Then when Henry Clay announced his candidacy, a few of them switched to the Kentuckian, including Judge

Overton. Since Jackson had a dim view of Clay on account of his attempt to win a congressional censure of the General for his Seminole campaign, Overton was careful to keep his preference a secret.[30] Then came Miller's suggestion about running Jackson and what it might mean to local politicians. Overton instantly succumbed to Miller's logic, abandoned Clay, and set about with Miller, Lewis, Eaton, and others to plan the campaign. Felix Grundy, who had a sharp eye for the drift of the political wind, deserted Erwin when he learned of the possibility of Jackson's candidacy and joined Overton and Miller. Indeed it was Grundy who ultimately introduced the nominating resolutions at the special session of the Tennessee legislature.

In January, 1822, the Nashville newspapers, at Overton's prodding, hinted at a possible Jackson candidacy. The Erwin faction gasped. But what could they do? They dared not challenge Old Hickory. If they did, they knew they would be swept away in a maelstrom of public protest. So they waited, and when Jackson finally permitted his name to be brought forward and the resolutions of nomination came before the Tennessee legislature during its special session in 1822, they merely dawdled with them for a short time and then supported them.

"Believing that moral worth, political acquirements and decision of character," read part of the opening statement of the resolutions, "should unite in the individual who may be called to preside over the people of the United States," we offer the name of Andrew Jackson. "The welfare of a country may be safely entrusted to the hands of him who has experienced every privation, and encouraged every danger, to promote its safety, its honor, and its glory, Therefore,

"*Resolve,* As the opinion of the members composing the general assembly of the state of Tennessee, that the name of major general ANDREW JACKSON be submitted to the consideration of the people of the United States, at the approaching election for the chief magistracy."[31]

The resolutions passed unanimously on July 20, 1822.

There is some doubt whether the Overton faction really thought that Andrew Jackson—whose sole credential for the presidency was his military record—had much chance for election outside Tennessee. But that, of course, in no way vitiated their purpose. Some of them even assured Henry Clay that he would ultimately get Tennessee's electoral votes.[32] Meanwhile they organized Jackson meetings all over the state and urged the electorate to vote for his supporters in the local elections of 1823. Miller was especially active in this effort, touring western Tennessee in his attempt to defeat John Williams for the U.S. Senate. Unfortunately, other friends of Jackson also entered the senatorial race and thereby divided Miller's strength. John Rhea actually gave up his seat in the House of Representatives in order to stand for the Senate, little comprehending (or simply ignoring the fact) that a split in the Jackson forces benefited no one but the other side.

What came as a complete surprise was the unprecedented outpouring of support that was instantly generated throughout the entire country by the announcement of Jackson's candidacy. Some of the Overton men were flabbergasted, particularly now that the General had begun to express very decided views on economic questions that clashed head-on with their own. That Jackson was popular in the country no one ever doubted. But that he could be wildly popular as a presidential candidate —a supposed frontiersman no less!—vying with such distinguished statesmen as John Q. Adams, John C. Calhoun, William H. Crawford, and Henry Clay seemed incomprehensible to them. It is possible that a few of them wanted to terminate the candidacy immediately and get back to Clay, but whatever actions they took, if indeed they took any at all, were carefully veiled.

The announcement of the Jackson candidacy alarmed the Monroe administration, particularly the three cabinet officers in contention for the presidency themselves. At Adams's behest, and simply to get rid of him as a candidate, Jackson was offered the post of Envoy Extraordinary and Minister Plenipotentiary to Mexico, now that Spanish rule had been thrown off. The idea of General Andrew Jackson as a minister to any Latin American country, let alone Mexico, was absurd. If Monroe thought he had had trouble with his general in Florida it can be imagined what Jackson's presence in Mexico might have provoked. Fortunately it never came about.[33] The Mexican Republic, established after the expulsion of the Spanish, had since been overturned and Agustín de Iturbide had declared himself Emperor. Jackson wisely declined the offer. He explained his reasons to Secretary Adams.

> The present unhappy revolutionary state of Mexico; with an oppressed People struggling for their liberties, against an Emperor whom they have branded with the epithets of Usurper and Tyrant, convinces me that no minister from the U States could at this period effect any beneficial treaty for his country, and of the impolicy of a Republican Representative at a court, which might be constructed as countenancing the Empire in opposition to a Republic. The People of Mexico in their honest efforts for freedom command my warmest sympathies, and their success is intimately connected with the ultimate and general triumph of these liberal principles for which our Revolutionary worthies bled, and which now form the pride and boast of United America. With these feelings and wishes and which I believe to be in unison with my fellow citizens; you may readily conceive that my situation at Mexico would be embarrassing to me independent of the conviction that I was rendering service to my country. To render service could alone constitute any motive for again acting in a public capacity.[34]

Privately, Jackson admitted to another reason. Mrs. Jackson steadfastly refused to go. After Florida, she wanted no more "foreign" adventures. And Jackson had no desire "to treat with ghosts." Besides, "I hate bowing to a Tyrant."[35]

To get lost in Mexico made no sense at all, particularly now that his candidacy had begun so auspiciously. Pennsylvania Republicans quickly declared for Jackson, surprising John C. Calhoun and later crushing his candidacy, since he had depended on Pennsylvania as the centerpiece of his northern support. "If the people of Alabama, Mississippi, and Louisiana follow the example of Pennsylvania," wrote Jackson, "they will place Clay and Crawford where they ultimately will be *Dehors the political combat*, but their intrigues are united, and their friends are industrious."[36]

Despite the early and enthusiastic response to Jackson's candidacy throughout the country, a danger to it developed almost immediately in Tennessee on account of the senatorial race. John Williams had strong backing for reelection in the legislature, possibly enhanced secretly by Overton and William's brother-in-law, Hugh Lawson White.[37] In addition Pleasant M. Miller faced several contenders, all of whom had claims on Jackson's friendship. When it became obvious that Miller could not unite the Jackson men, that he had more enemies than anyone realized, the managers of the General's campaign decided to declare for John Rhea. But that strategy failed, for Rhea could not compel a majority in the Tennessee legislature. Williams's campaign had been extremely efficient in gaining pledges from legislators, and of course he was a great favorite among east Tennesseans. The situation became so alarming that three times Jackson was summoned by his friends to Murfreesborough, the capital of the state at that time, and three times the General refused to respond in the vain hope that he could stay aloof from the tightly entwined threads of national and state politics. He did not seem to realize that if one of his personal and political enemies could win election to the U.S. Senate then it would appear to the nation at large that Tennessee was not really serious about his own candidacy for the presidency. The campaign might collapse then and there. Still, if Williams would pledge himself to support the General a way might be found to escape this predicament. But Williams refused. He had already committed himself to Crawford.[38]

That settled it. In desperation, Major Lewis and John H. Eaton, who were Jackson's chief managers at Murfreesborough, decided on their own "to play a bold and decisive game."[39] They proposed to beat Williams with the General himself! They placed Old Hickory's name in nomination for the United States Senate before the legislature. This produced "great uneasiness and alarm among the more timid members," recalled Lewis, for fear he might be defeated. But Lewis and Eaton concluded that if the General must be politically sacrificed it really mattered little which way the ax fell, whether by personal defeat or by the election of his "bitter enemy."[40] Besides, they confidently believed that they could squeeze Jackson through, however close the final vote. So, much to the chagrin of Williams's friends, the General was formally nominated for the Senate seat by Major Abram Maury, one of the floor leaders of the group and a highly respected member from Williamson County.

As soon as the nomination was made, a messenger, one General Coleman, galloped off to notify Jackson. Again Old Hickory was urged to come to Murfreesborough. But this time the situation was different. This time Jackson's name and reputation had been placed on the line. As soon as he realized this, Jackson saddled, bid adieu to Rachel, and sped toward Murfreesborough. He reached the capital the night preceding the election. He insisted that "I neither vissited or conversed with a member except when vissitted and the conversation introduced by them." When they did seek him out he told them that the Crawford party was massed against him and that their object was his immediate expulsion from the presidential campaign. His words carried great authority, but many of the legislators frankly informed him that they could not vote for him because they had given their pledges to Williams. Much as they wished to bolt in his favor they could not renege on their promise.[41]

The following day, October 1, the "bold and decisive game" was played out. When the votes were finally counted, Jackson was elected senator by the narrow margin of thirty-five to twenty-five, the body of Governor Carroll's party voting against him. The victory was a near-miracle, considering the number of pledges Williams had received. "No person but *Jackson* could have broken down such a combination," commented one man. "Many who voted against him were all alive to his election, but were tied down and obliged to give a vote against him."[42]

Still the victory rankled. It was not what Jackson wanted. "Every intrigue that could exist," scrawled Jackson in a letter to Coffee, sometimes forgetting to complete his sentences as his thoughts tumbled onto the page, "and indeed corruption was restored to. . . . How cruel it was for Colo Williams finding his friends thus situated, and a vote for him contrary to the instructions of their constituents would politically prostrate them, that he did not like Mr Rhea withdraw. how much more magnanimity would have been shewn by him, to have withdrawn than to urge his friends to prostrate their own political standing to elevate his. now his and theirs are all prostrate."[43]

Jackson himself showed little magnanimity toward Williams, however. He expected him to get out of his way once he had been nominated, even though he did not want the office and Williams did. He really behaved very badly. The General's prediction about the future political standing of the men who voted against him came true at the next election. Of the twenty-five legislators who voted for Williams only three were reelected to the next legislature. This further fueled Jackson's belief that the people identified with him and everything he stood for. His will and their will were one.

But now he had to serve in that sewer of corruption, Washington.[44] He no more wanted to be a senator in the capital than he wanted to conduct William Crawford's presidential campaign. "I am a senator against my wishes and feelings," he groaned, "which I regret more than any other of my life . . . but from my political creed . . . I am compelled to accept."[45] His friends swore to him that they had had no choice but to elect him, that his defeat would not have been more "blasting" in its effect than the election of Williams, and Jackson at length "submitted with a good grace," said Major Lewis. "He was a soldier, and knew how to obey as well as command!"[46]

Thomas Ritchie, a leader of the Richmond junto in Virginia, an arch Radical Republican, the editor of the Richmond *Enquirer,* and the most active editorial voice after the Washington *National Intelligencer* for the candidacy of William H. Crawford, noted Jackson's election with a distinct degree of alarm. "General Jackson is elected to the Senate," he wrote in an editorial in November, 1823. "He was the only man in Tennessee who could out turn John Williams. He has done it. The country may yet rue the change."

Without warning, Eaton and Lewis had plucked Old Hickory from retirement and pitched him into Washington. All of which meant leaving the Hermitage just as the cotton was being ginned and prepared for shipment and sale. It meant another separation from Rachel, since he had no time to make the necessary arrangements for her to accompany him to the capital. It meant an absence of four or five months from his home, and it meant facing all the intrigues and corruption and immorality boiling in Washington.

Jackson shuddered. He was too old for this, too worn out, too tired. Still he saw it as his duty, so there was nothing he could do but submit. About the middle of November, together with his colleague in the Senate, John H. Eaton, the General left Tennessee and rode nearly the entire nine hundred miles to Washington on horseback and stagecoach. Another agony. But there were compensations. "I have been greeted by the people wherever I have halted," he informed Rachel, "to avoid much of this was one reason why I took the stage, & even then in many places, on the way side were collections who hailed & stopped the stage to shake me by the hand. This through Virginia I did not calculate on—altho tiresome & troublesome still it is gratifying to find that I have triumphed over the machinations of my enemies & still possess the confidence of the people."[47]

Jackson reached Washington on the morning of December 3, 1823. "We came up in the Steam Boat from Fredericksburgh," he wrote to his wife, "a little after day light, and from the time it was known, I have been waited upon by many. . . . I have been treated with marked attention on the whole rout. . . . But this marked respect altho gratifying—has no charms for me, my heart is with you & fixed on Domestic life, there alone is peace for me."[48]

Together with Eaton and their friend Captain Richard Keith Call, Jackson took lodgings at William O'Neal's boardinghouse on the north side of I Street just east of Twenty-first Street. But he missed his family each day and his letters conveyed his private pain. "This separation has been more sever on me than any other," he repeated several times to Rachel, "it being one that my mind was not prepared for, nor can I see any necessity for—still my country did, and no alternative was left for me but to obey."[49]

CHAPTER 4

Return to the Senate

THE NATION'S CAPITAL TOWARD THE CLOSE of 1823 still retained a calm and bucolic air despite the periodic mayhem that erupted within Congress. A southern city to its core, Washington could be unbearably hot and humid for many months in the spring and summer. Congress usually tried to keep its sessions as short as possible and complete all business by the end of March or early April. Anything running longer guaranteed discomfort. Like Jackson, most Congressmen found lodgings for their enforced stay away from home in boardinghouses or hotels and frequently they "messed" together for companionship and social intercourse as well as to save money.

Wondrous changes had occurred in Washington during the last few years. The burned and charred ruins left by the British after their invasion in 1814 had been rebuilt, removed, or painted over. The President's mansion, so blackened and defaced by fire, had received a fresh coat of paint, and local residents had begun calling it the White House. The new Capitol building, standing on a twenty-two-acre plot about a mile from the White House and enclosed by an iron railing, had a beautiful and extensive view of the city on account of "the sudden declivity of the ground" immediately to the west. One could see the surrounding heights of Georgetown and the windings of the Potomac River as far as Alexandria.[1]

The Capitol building ran a length of 352 feet, in which a "rusticated basement" extended upward to the height of the first story and supported two additional stories. A portico with a long flight of steps projected outward and consisted of a series of Corinthian columns rising 30 feet and extending in length a distance of 160 feet. A pediment with an

55

80-foot span rested gracefully on the columns. In the center of the entire building rose a lofty, flat-topped dome, and each wing of the building supported a smaller flat-topped dome. Most tourists thought the building "of almost dazzling splendor," both inside and outside, and many foreigners agreed that it was "superior to any legislative hall in Europe."[2] The second floor of the south wing housed all the Representatives from the twenty-four states, while the Senators found their chamber in the opposite wing. Both rooms were semicircular in shape and formed like ancient Grecian theatres. The House chamber ran 96 feet at its widest and 60 feet at the highest part of the domical ceiling. The Senate chamber was smaller, 75 feet across and 45 feet high. A series of Ionic columns similar to those of the temple of Minerva supported a gallery on the east side of the Senate room. There was a good deal of imitation Greek and Roman architecture in both chambers, complete with heroic statues and busts, which added a peculiarly grand and awesome splendor to the legislative business of the young Republic. But as most congressional members soon learned, including Jackson, each chamber "was good for every thing but the purpose for which it was intended. It is very hard to speak in it & . . . almost impossible to hear." Sounds skidded around the semicircular walls before ascending into the upper reaches of the domed ceiling. The acoustics of both rooms, including the Supreme Court chamber located in the basement of the building, defied correction—not that any serious attempts were undertaken to improve them.[3]

Even so, acoustical problems did not intimidate congressmen. They just bellowed louder. Given the florid speaking style of the period they seemed to enjoy the need to raise their voices and gesticulate with hands and arms. Several congressmen were master orators whose speeches went on for hours and sometimes days, speeches rich in history and literature and frequently spiced with humor and savage personal attacks. Members of both houses often put on performances to rival those of theatrical troupes. When they did so, large crowds of people packed the galleries.

With the opening of the first session of the Eighteenth Congress in December, 1823, the corridors around both chambers buzzed with talk about the approaching presidential election, the various candidates, and the likelihood of a congressional caucus to choose the Republican candidate. Only the Radicals, the most organizational-minded of the Republicans, trumpeted the need for a caucus and the acquiescence of all candidates to its final selection. Needless to add, they expected Crawford to get the nod, since he was the candidate most acceptable to most Congressmen.

William H. Crawford was "a plain giant of a man," commanding in size and presence. A Virginian by birth, he moved to Georgia where he won a reputation as a compiler of the state's first published digest of its laws. Elected to the United States Senate in 1807, he later served as minister to France and in 1816 became secretary of the treasury in Madison's administration, a post he held throughout Monroe's two terms in office. He might have challenged Monroe for the presidency in 1816 but unwisely stepped aside under the mistaken notion that he would have a clear field when Monroe completed his eight-year tenure. Then disaster struck when he suffered a severe stroke in the summer of 1823. He was only fifty-one years of age but the stroke left him temporarily paralyzed, speechless, and nearly blind. Although his illness became generally known in a matter of months, the seriousness of his condition was hidden from the public. Because he was relatively young, Crawford slowly fought his way back from the worst effects of his illness and by the beginning of 1824 he had resumed some official activities. Still he never fully recovered, although he lived on for several more years. In any event, the Radicals had no intention of deserting him, stroke or no, and they proceeded with their plans to summon a congressional caucus to nominate him as though nothing had happened.[4]

The Radicals' present leader in Congress was the junior Senator from New York, Martin Van Buren. Some Congressmen dismissed him as a crass intriguer, but they underestimated him. A skillful organizer and political broker, as well as a top-flight constitutional lawyer, he created a statewide machine in New York called the Albany Regency, to protect his New York base while he sought the larger sphere of operation in Washington. The Regency was a governing board set up in Albany to oversee and direct the affairs of the Van Buren wing of the state's Republican party, and consisted of many of New York's most impressive political talents, including William L. Marcy, Silas Wright, Jr., Benjamin F. Butler, Azariah C. Flagg, and Edwin Croswell, the editor of the party's newspaper, the Albany *Argus.*[5]

At the age of forty-two, Van Buren exuded confidence, charm, and total self-possession. Short, stocky but not yet overweight, elegantly dressed in the very latest fashion, fair-complexioned with light yellowish-red thinning hair and "small brilliant eyes" under a bulging forehead, he possessed the most exquisitely developed manners of anyone in Congress. He never gave offense if he could help it. Polite to all, even those who ridiculed him, he acquired a variety of techniques over the years to mask his feelings and opinions. Cautious, wary, and shrewd, he understood the value of accommodation and compromise. The "compleat" politician, he expected to win nomination for Crawford in the caucus and then through careful management to place this broken man in the White House.[6]

Van Buren and his allies were hard-pressed to convene a caucus because of the mounting opposition of the other candidates and their friends in Congress. Henry Clay was particularly contemptuous—both of the caucus and its intended candidate. Not only did he dismiss the shattered secretary on account of his health but he regarded Radical principles—strict interpretation of the Constitution, states' rights, strict economy, opposition to federally sponsored internal improvements—as obstacles to the nation's progress. A nationalist to the marrow, he believed that the central government should assist the country's economic growth. In a program termed the "American System" he argued in favor of protective tariffs, internal improvements, and a centralized banking and currency system. He was born in Virginia in 1777, studied law under George Wythe, and later moved to Kentucky, where he won election first to the state house of representatives and then to the United States Senate to fill the remaining months of an unexpired term. Elected to the United States House of Representatives in 1810, he assumed leadership of the War Hawks and became speaker. He was a member of the peace commission in Ghent, Belgium, that wrote the treaty ending the War of 1812, after which he returned home and was reelected to Congress and the speakership. A tall, bony, sharp-featured man with a wide mouth outlined by bloodless lips, he had developed into a most effective public speaker. Combining sarcasm and humor with large chunks of loosely reasoned argumentation, Clay easily dominated the lower house and won its leadership through outstanding political and theatrical skills.[7]

Jackson thoroughly disliked him. In large part, Clay's attack upon the General for his incursion into Florida in 1818 and his attempt to injure the Hero's military reputation destroyed any possibility of friendship. But, let it be remembered, both men were westerners and therefore rivals for the same constituency. Clay saw Jackson as a threat to his main ambition in life. Jackson, on the other hand, pronounced Clay a gambler —a typical western gambler—out to succeed at any cost.[8]

Unquestionably, the best educated and most experienced candidate for the presidency was John Quincy Adams. Born in Braintree, Massachusetts, in 1767 (the same year as Jackson) and educated in the United States, France, and the Netherlands, he was admitted to the bar and began the practice of law in Boston at the age of twenty-three. Because of his experience President Washington appointed him minister to the Netherlands; later he served as minister to Prussia, Russia, and Great Britain. His spectacular rise as a diplomat won him the post of secretary of state in the Monroe administration in 1817. Yet he was cold, forbidding, and sanctimonious; he abhorred partisan politics and managed to alienate both Federalists and Republicans. Still, New England regarded him as its own, despite his lack of a popular following, and genuinely took pride in his singular achievements as secretary of state.[9]

The last candidate—although there had been others who either died or fell away before the canvass swung into full operation—was John Caldwell Calhoun. Born in 1782 in South Carolina of a prosperous family, he was educated at Moses Waddell's academy in Georgia and at Yale College. He then studied law at the famous law school in Litchfield, Connecticut, conducted by Judge Tapping Reeve, after which he returned to South Carolina, started a successful law practice, and entered politics. Elected to the United States House of Representatives in 1810, he quickly emerged as a leading War Hawk and distinguished himself in debate as a brilliant logician and parliamentarian. An ardent nationalist who argued for a strong army and navy, Calhoun was chosen secretary of war by Monroe, from which position he launched his presidential ambitions. Although younger than the other potential candidates he drew considerable support from northern as well as southern states. Pennsylvania backed him until Jackson's candidacy was announced; then it deserted him for the Hero of New Orleans.[10]

The action of the Tennessee legislature in putting forward Jackson's name completely changed the direction and tone of the contest. Its most immediate effect was its devastating blow to Calhoun in Pennsylvania. But it also encouraged other states to imitate Tennessee's action. Small conventions of citizens banded together on an *ad hoc* basis and named him as their presidential choice. Since none but Crawford seemed likely to win nomination by a congressional caucus, all the other candidates accepted their nominations from their own states or from neighboring states. By the time Jackson arrived in Washington to begin his senatorial duties late in 1823 the presidential contest had become a wide-open contest among so many men that shrewd observers feared (or in some instances hoped) that no one could win a majority of the electoral votes as required by the Constitution and that the final selection of the President would fall to the House of Representatives.

Jackson's arrival in Washington brought an immediate change in his appearance, attitude, and behavior. For one thing his health was much improved over the previous year. For another he was the center of attention wherever he went. As hero, senator, and now presidential candidate, he commanded instant recognition and applause. All eyes focused upon him. He felt the stares and realized he was under close scrutiny. One false move and his disgrace would be broadcast around the nation. He was advised to keep his ferocious temper in check but the General had no fears on that score. "When it becomes necessary to philosophise & be meek," he said, "no man can command his temper better than I."[11] But more than anything else, Jackson shrewdly calculated the role he must play in this new environment and situation. As an ambitious young man who learned his political craft from the Blounts back in the 1790s and honed his skills during his many years as major general of the militia, he was no novice at the political game and he looked forward to displaying his talents to the power brokers in Washington. For the last ten years he had enacted the role of hero. That would continue. But now he must assume the manner, style, and deportment of both legislator and contender for the position of chief executive. It was a sizable undertaking but Jackson met it with dash and enthusiasm.

His performance, as it unfolded, was nothing less than brilliant. No sooner did he take his seat in the Senate on December 5, 1823, than he set off a dazzling display of Jacksonian charisma and presence. The figure he cut! The commanding style he revealed! He came like a thunderclap and left observers overwhelmed. "The General is calm, dignified and makes as polished a *bow*," reported Sam Houston, "as any man I have seen at Court. . . . He is much courted by the Great as well as the sovereign folks."[12] Part of the reason for the jolting effect he produced was his physical appearance. Tall and ramrod-straight with a shock of greying hair adding to his height, he possessed strong (but not unusual) features. "Except the eyes," as so many observers repeated again and again, "which are very piercing & when he is excited resemble those of a chafed lion."[13] His eyes had the power to transfix his viewers. But more important than his physical appearance was the total manner of the man. When he walked into a room a charge of electricity seemed to surge through the air. He commanded attention without uttering a word. Some attention undoubtedly resulted from his extraordinary reputation as a hero, but much more was generated by his "hawk-like" look, his graceful manners, his innate dignity, and the ease and naturalness of his commanding presence.

And he worked at making an impression. "He is constantly in motion to some Dinner party or other," wrote John Eaton to Rachel, "and to night stands engaged at a large Dancing party at Genl Browns."[14] Jackson anticipated the effect his appearance and manner would produce in Washington, particularly among the uninitiated, and he thoroughly enjoyed it. "I am told the opinion of those whose minds were prepared to see me with a Tomahawk in one hand, and a scalping knife in the other has greatly changed and I am getting on very smoothly."[15] So smoothly in fact that many of his old enemies went out of their way to approach him and patch up past differences. General Winfield Scott searched for him in the corridors of the Capitol and failing to make contact sent Jackson a brief note intimating a desire to let bygones be bygones. Old Hickory, in his reply, noted that Scott's letter was ambiguous—he could not resist the jab—but since it had been motivated by "friendly views" he was willing to meet Scott anytime "on friendly terms."[16] And so an old unpleasantness was laid to rest.[17]

More important was Jackson's reconciliation with Thomas Hart Benton, now the extremely able and talented senator from Missouri. When Jackson took his senate seat he found Benton occupying the adjoining chair. Several senators who knew about their past differences offered to exchange seats to keep the tension from igniting. But the two old enemies would have none of it. They knew their respective places and they had no intention of budging an inch. They just sat there, eyeing one another with sidelong glances. Each impressed the other. Each had grown tremendously in judgment and wisdom since they shot it out in a barroom brawl in 1813. Before long Benton awed Jackson by a demonstration of his prowess as a parliamentarian. He knew how to maneuver his way through a debate to get what he wanted. Big, powerful-looking, with an ego to match, Benton also sounded powerful when he spoke. He exemplified the new-style western political wheeler-dealer. He had long, black curly hair, side whiskers, and a prominent nose that looked as though it had been broken in several places and indifferently repaired. He measured Jackson with all the thoroughness of a brash, cynical opportunist —and he appreciated the results of his inspection. For his part, as a contender for the presidency, Jackson had even more reason to forget the past. Benton was an army in himself in terms of legislative skill and political astuteness. A fellow westerner and a loyal and devoted lieutenant once he committed himself, he could be an invaluable ally. To regain his friendship made enormous good sense.

It came soon enough. When Jackson was appointed chairman of the Committee on Military Affairs he discovered Benton sitting on the same committee. Constantly thrown together, Jackson finally made the first gesture. "Colonel, we are on the same committee," he said to his old foe. "I will give you notice when it is necessary to attend." Benton responded with equal courtesy. "General, make the time suit yourself; it will be convenient for me to attend at any time." Of course it did not help matters that Benton favored Clay's presidential ambitions, but that could be easily excused since Benton's wife was a niece of Clay's wife.[18] Then, one day, Jackson stepped up to Benton and inquired about the health of his wife. After replying, Benton returned the inquiry. A few days later the General called at Benton's lodgings and not finding him home left his card: "Andrew Jackson for Colonel Benton and lady." Soon thereafter Benton visited Jackson's boarding house and he left his card: "Colonel Benton for General Jackson." They dined together on several occasions at large parties and finally they were both invited to the President's mansion. Benton saw his chance. As soon as Jackson entered the White House Benton walked up to him and bowed. The General immediately shot out his hand, and the two men shook hands and smiled away the enmity of ten years. Next Benton introduced his wife, whereupon Old Hickory opened up with all the charm and "sprightliness" for which he was noted when in the presence of females.[19] Thus began one of the most important political alliances of Jackson's entire life. A little while later Benton deserted to the General's cause and directed his influence in Missouri and in Congress to the service of his old enemy. He was a formidable addition to Old Hickory's party. Never did Jackson show more wisdom and political shrewdness than the moment he decided to court the friendship of Colonel Thomas Hart Benton.

Things got so chummy around Washington that several Tennessee congressmen arranged to invite Henry Clay to dine with Jackson. Every inch a politician, Clay readily agreed.[20] And the General, now running as hard as decency allowed, matched the Kentuckian's political deftness by showing him every courtesy. He simply erased from his mind the House debate over his invasion of Florida and his ugly thoughts about Clay's gambling instincts. He would forgive and forget. Apparently Jackson had decided upon a general amnesty—and might even have included William H. Crawford if necessary.

All of which struck John H. Eaton as wonderful to behold, something he had never seen before in the Old Hero, something he had to convey immediately to Rachel. "It will afford you great pleasure I know," he wrote her, "to be informed that all his old quarrels have been settled. The General is at peace in friendship with genl. Scott, Genl Cocke, Mr Clay and what you would never have expected Col Benton: he is in harmony and good understanding with every body, a thing I know you will be happy to hear." To which Jackson added a postscript in his own hand: "the enclosed information is all true. . . . It is a pleasing subject to me that I am now at peace with all the world."[21]

At the many dinners and dancing parties that Jackson regularly attended, including one given by John Quincy Adams and his wife to celebrate the anniversary of the victory of January 8, 1815, the topic of conversation centered almost solely on the presidential election. But the careful Jackson refused to be drawn into it and sought to remain aloof. There was too much talk about intrigues and schemes and plots, and Jackson not only abhorred such talk but he understood its dangers. "I intermix with none of those who are engaged in the intrigues of caucus, or president makers, nor do I intend," he assured his old friend John Coffee. "I have but one feeling and that is, that the people make a good choice, when I say this, I have to add, that I think it would be a great curse to the nation if the choice fell upon Wm H. C."[22]

When he felt he could spare some leisure time he said he liked to spend it with the O'Neal family, who ran his boardinghouse. "Mrs. Timberlake the maryed daughter whose husband belongs to our Navy, plays on the Piano delightfully, and every Sunday evening entertains her pious mother with sacred music, to which we are invited, and the single daughter who is also pious and sings well unites in the music."[23]

Margaret (Peggy) O'Neal Timberlake was a charming, attractive, and delightful young girl, married to a purser who had trouble keeping his accounts in proper order and whose periodic departures on naval duty encouraged John Eaton, now a widower, to comfort Peggy in her "loneliness." Peggy invited crude and salacious comments because of her behavior and at one point complained to Jackson that she had been "grossly insulted" by his friend, Richard Keith Call.[24] Apparently some of the boarders thought they could sleep with her whenever her husband shipped out.

Otherwise, Jackson spent Sundays at church—and duly reported this fact to his wife. Each week he tried a different denomination: first Presbyterian, then Baptist, next Methodist, all of which he seemed to enjoy if the sermon was interesting and short. He knew how much his church attendance pleased Rachel and his many letters to her went on in a religious vein.

> I trust that the god of Isaac and of Jacob will protect you, and give you health in my absence, in him alone we ought to trust, he alone can preserve, and guide us through this troublesome world, and I am sure he will hear your prayers. We are told that the prayers of the righteous prevaileth much, and I add mine for your health and preservation untill we again meet.[25]

Although Jackson steered clear of all intrigue, his supporters assumed the lead in attempting to block the calling of a congressional caucus. As early as the previous October, Felix Grundy had introduced a series of resolutions into the Tennessee legislature urging Congress to abandon the caucus as undemocratic and in conflict with the spirit of the times. The governor of the state was directed to transmit copies of the resolutions to governors of other states with a request that they be laid before their respective legislatures. Maryland and Alabama endorsed the resolutions but otherwise the states did nothing—except those that favored Crawford (like New York, Georgia, and Virginia), which rejected the resolutions.

The friends of Jackson in Congress tried to link themselves with the supporters of the other candidates to stop the caucus drive but they ran into the stiff determination of Martin Van Buren. Like his fellow Radicals, Van Buren had pledged himself to force a nomination in the traditional manner. "I found many gloomy faces today in the Senate Hall," reported Jackson. "It is said There is to be a *caucus*. This I cannot believe—but it is the last hope of the friends of Mr Crawford, and I have no doubt it will be attempted—with what success time will determine. But it appears to me that such is the feelings of the nation that a recommendation by a congressional caucus would politically Damn any name put forth by it."[26] That politicians would flaunt their arrogance and proceed with their wretched meeting, argued Jackson, only underscored the corruption eating away at the vitals of government. The very idea of it blackened his mood and fired his anger. Intrigue! Corruption! The words were repeated over and over in every letter he wrote. They must be rooted out, he stormed. He must triumph over the "intrigues of this city . . . over my enemies . . . over corruption & [I] will save the nation from the rule of Demagogues, who by intrigue are, & have been attempting to cheat the people out of their constitutional rights, by a caucus of congressional members."[27]

According to Jackson's thinking—and a great many other anticaucus Congressmen—if a small body of men selected the Republican candidate who was automatically elected President because no other party existed to challenge his candidacy, then the people no longer had any say in the selection of the chief executive and the Republic had become a dictator-ship run by an oligarchy.[28] The caucus imperiled liberty. The freedom of all was at stake.

Despite the criticism and protest, despite the cry that "King Caucus" should be knocked in the head, the Radicals issued a formal summons for their meeting. On February 7, 1824, the Washington *National Intelligencer* carried a notice signed by 11 congressmen from as many states calling on their colleagues to join with them on Saturday, February 14, to recom-mend a presidential candidate to the people of the United States. How-ever, the same issue of the newspaper carried another announcement, this one signed by 24 congressmen representing fifteen states and declar-ing it "inexpedient" to hold a caucus since 181 of the 261 members of Congress would probably refuse to attend. The threat of boycott did not surprise nor intimidate Van Buren, since he had already gained this information earlier through a private poll he had conducted. He closed his ears to all protests; he responded to threats with a smile. He was determined to forge ahead, regardless. It was Crawford's only hope, given his broken health.

On the fourteenth of February the gallery doors to the House of Repre-sentatives were thrown open to a waiting throng of caucus friends and enemies. Within minutes all the available seats for spectators were occu-pied and those who could find no room to squeeze into swarmed through the corridors outside. On the floor only 68 congressmen acknowledged the summons, 48 of whom represented four states—New York, Georgia, North Carolina, and Virginia. A total of fourteen states were represented, five of them by a single delegate; and ten states were not represented at all. It was a dismal showing. One congressman moved that the meeting be postponed for six weeks, and this set off a round of applause from the spectators. But Van Buren shook his head, claiming that the meeting had already been postponed twice in the past two months. He prevailed on the rump to proceed, however inconclusive the final results might be. Benjamin Ruggles of Ohio was chosen chairman and E. Calling, secre-tary.

Then the balloting began. When it ended the chair announced to "heavy groans in the Gallery"[29] that Crawford had received 64 votes, 2 of which were proxies—"both sick absent," snapped Jackson, "and one perhaps dead."[30] John Quincy Adams received 2 votes, and 1 each was awarded to Jackson and Nathaniel Macon of North Carolina. The caucus then selected Albert Gallatin for the vice presidency and ended by issuing an address to the people arguing the tradition and regularity of its action and warning of the possiblity and danger of party schism.

Jackson exploded. "Everything is carried by intrigue and manage-ment," he ranted at Coffee. Promises are made, he said, and just as quickly broken. "It is now a contest between a few demagogues and the people; and it is to be seen whether a minority less than one fourth of the whole members of congress, can coerce the people to follow them; or whether the people will assume their constitutional rights and put down these demagogues." The liberties of the people can only be protected by their free exercise of the suffrage, he continued. What the Radicals are saying is simply this: that the "people are incapable of self government; and yet they call themselves Democratic Republicans."[31]

The caucus was actually an exercise in futility. It demonstrated overwhelmingly the weaknesses of the Crawford candidacy. As Jackson had predicted, it "would politically Damn" any name attached to it. Worse, the failure of the caucus destroyed one of the central bonds of the Republican party. As many Crawfordites realized, particularly Van Buren, the Republican party was falling apart, given its many conflicting ideological components, and it would take superhuman effort after the election to pull it back together again. One of Van Buren's principal reasons for insisting on the caucus was his belief that it served the necessary purpose of binding the party together. Without it an important instrument of party discipline was lost. And what could replace it?

Another mistake was the Gallatin nomination. That gesture represented a miserable sop thrown to Pennsylvania since most Radicals actually preferred Clay for the vice presidency. But the Kentuckian made it clear that he had no interest in second place. Then a little later, when it developed that Gallatin hurt the ticket, he was gracelessly asked to resign the nomination. Gallatin happily consented.[32]

The same month that the last congressional nominating caucus plummeted out of existence, John C. Calhoun was eliminated as a presidential contender. His youth and his lack of extensive public service, compared to that of the other candidates, did not inspire confidence; and unless he could match his southern support with real strength in the north he invited resounding defeat. The keystone of his northern strength had been Pennsylvania where his nationalistic ideas and program fired enthusiasm. But once Jackson's candidacy was announced Calhoun's position rapidly deteriorated. George M. Dallas, his most ardent supporter in Pennsylvania, warned him early in 1824 that he might well be discarded by the state convention on account of Jackson's sudden entry into the contest. Sure enough, on February 18, at a meeting of local delegates at Harrisburg, Jackson was unanimously nominated for the presidency, with Dallas himself bowing to the inevitable by offering the resolution in Jackson's favor.[33]

On March 4, the Pennsylvania state convention repeated the action taken by the Harrisburg delegates, but instead of eliminating Calhoun altogether the convention nominated him for the vice presidency, an action later imitated by Maryland, New Jersey, and North and South Carolina. Although his abrupt removal from presidential contention came as a shock, Calhoun was enough of a realist to accept the verdict as final and for the moment set aside his presidential ambitions. With this shift of strategy he suddenly found himself the only national candidate for second place. The friends of Adams also awarded him their support and so, in a sense, the South Carolinian became the running mate of two presidential candidates.

Jackson figured that once Pennsylvania declared for him North and South Carolina would follow—and possibly Virginia, despite the action of a legislative caucus for Crawford in that state.[34] He also calculated that "if I traveled to Boston where I was invited I could insure my election."[35] He worried about losing the election and how it might be stolen from him by the "Demogogues" and "caucus mongers" in Washington.[36] He complained about the call of duty and yearned to return to the Hermitage.

Although Jackson chafed at his life in Washington, claiming the parties and dances were nothing compared to life "amongst the farmers," he managed to direct his affairs at home to a large extent by writing almost daily to Rachel and conveying his wishes. There were two things he wanted constantly attended to: that his overseer, Mr. Parsons, not exceed his authority; and that his slaves be humanely treated. "I do not wish my hands laboured too hard," he told Rachel, "& if you think they are, I know when you name it to him [Parsons] he will moderate—I wish them well fed, & warmly cloothed and they will be then contented & happy This is my wish—I do not want them in any way oppressed, and if they behave well I am sure Mr Parson, knowing my wishes, will treat them well."[37]

He was also very concerned about his son's education—"and also Lyncoya."

> Tell my son how anxious I am that he may read & learn his Book, that he may become the possessor of those things that a grateful country has bestowed upon his papa—Tell him that his happiness thro life, depends upon *his* procuring an education now; & with it, to imbibe proper moral habits that can entitled him to the possession of them. To acquire these proper habits he must beware riligiously on all occasions to adhere to truth, & on no occasion to depart from it—never to make a promise unless on due consideration, and when made, to be sure to comply with it. This rule observed, with a proper attention now to his learning, will make him a great, good, & usefull man, which his papa wishes him, & his little cousin Hutchings, both to become. Having experienced so much inconvenience from the want of a perfect education myself make me so solicitous that his may be perfect, my Dear wife urge this upon him.[38]

Most of all Jackson was extremely solicitous of his wife. She kept him informed of every ache and pain she suffered, and especially how grieved she was over his absence. Their letters to each other invariably contained a medical report, but fortunately Jackson enjoyed relatively good health that first winter in Washington. Not so Rachel. "I . . . sincerely regret that you are indisposed," he lovingly wrote her, "but I trust that kind providence will soon relieve you from the pain that the inflamation of your eye must inflict—with what pleasure would I apply the *cooling wash* was I with you; & how painful it is to me to hear of the least affliction in my absence."[39]

"My health is good," he went on, "altho I am much pressed with business and with Company."[40] Jackson really heeded his senatorial responsibilities throughout this session. Not like the last time. Not like 1798. He attended the Senate session with commendable regularity, despite the fact that Congress did not have a heavy calendar. The session got off to an historic beginning with the President's message in which he warned European powers against extending their system to the western hemisphere or attempting further colonization. Subsequently termed the "Monroe Doctrine," this message delighted Jackson and he termed it "a good one." He had no doubt that the "holy alience" of England, Austria, Prussia, and Russia would attempt to restore South America to Spain. "This must be prevented," he cautioned, "or our government will be Jeopardized—and we will have a bloody contest with the combined despotism of europe." As he wrote these words his intense nationalism peeked through. "For my part," he declared, "I think it best to prevent them gaining a foothold upon the Terra firma of the american continent least when they might be in possession of Mexico, their foreign Bayonets might make an attempt to pierce us in the South & West."[41]

Although attentive to his senatorial responsibilities, Jackson was not active either in debate or in the initiation of legislation. He chose a cautious path. He served on the Foreign Relations Committee and not unexpectedly was assigned as chairman of the Committee on Military Affairs. Whenever the military committee needed to report its business to the Senate, Jackson did so in short, perfunctory remarks that drew little attention. His speeches, four in all, took only a few minutes to deliver, most of them dealing with road construction or fortifications.[42] But his voting record was good. He did not duck away from controversial issues. He recorded his position on virtually every question that came up for a vote.

The two most important and potentially the most troublesome issues before the Senate during this session were internal improvements and the tariff. Neither issue was particularly attractive to the south, although fierce opposition would develop within the next few years; the north tended to favor both, although New England had just started shifting from strong opposition to the tariff to strong support, on account of her developing manufacturing interests. As a conservative, Jackson naturally opposed spending federal money on public works, particularly when they were "local" in nature. But as an ardent nationalist, he supported any measure that contributed to the safety and defense of the nation. Thus, his voting on the question of internal improvements this session was totally consistent. He voted in favor. The bills had to do with road construction, and when questioned about it he justified his position on the ground of military necessity. He was particularly supportive of Secretary

Calhoun's project for a general survey of roads to provide a more systematic program of defense in view of the lessons learned during the late war
with Great Britain.[43] "Congress can constitutionaly apply their funds," he
explained to one inquirer, "to such objects as may be deemed National."
The federal government may build fortresses, roads, and canals "where
they are of a character National, not local," and when they do not "invade
the Sovereignty of the States." The consent of the states through which
these roads or canals will run must be given. The federal government
cannot exercise a superior jurisdiction. To do so would "produce in the
end a consolidation of the States, to the utter destruction of those checks
and balances of power at present existing under our confederation."[44]

    With respect to the tariff, then grinding its halting way through Con-
gress, Jackson was equally consistent. The bill had won passage in the
House after first eliciting an eloquent display of support from Clay and
an equally eloquent display of criticism from Daniel Webster. In the
Senate a flood of amendments to reduce the schedule threatened to
convert the bill to a low tariff, but advocates of protection fought them
to defeat. In nearly thirty separate votes on the amendments Jackson
consistently opposed reducing the rates. In effect he voted with the
strongest protectionists from the largest manufacturing states, like Pennsylvania. On such important items as imported iron, cotton goods, cotton
bagging, wool, and woolens he favored high duties. "On the Tariff," he
commented to Major Lewis, "I am Governed by principle alone.—The
articles of National Defence, & National Independence, I will with my
vote, foster & protect, without counting on cents & dollars; so that our
own Manufactures shall stand on a footing of fair competition with the
labourers of Europe—In doing this, the articles all being of the product
of our own country, tends to promote the agriculturists, whilst it gives
security to our nation & promotes domestic Labour—The balance of the
bill I look to with an eye to Revenue alone, to meet the national debt.
These articles of National defence, are Hemp, iron, lead & coarse Woolens." National defense, paying the debt, promoting "agriculturists," and
protecting "domestic Labour" were the principal determinants of his
vote, and he believed every true American would agree with these principles, "including the south."[45]

    Martin Van Buren reported in his *Autobiography* that he, like Jackson,
had been voting for each provision of the measure but objected to the
duty on cotton bagging because he felt that it disproportionately advanced the interests of Kentucky and would be obnoxious to the cotton-
growing states of Georgia, Alabama, the Carolinas, and Mississippi,
whose electoral votes could be decisive in the approaching presidential
election. Jackson, on the other hand, feared the domino effect one
amendment might have in triggering others, which would ultimately result in killing the entire bill. When the General saw Van Buren switch his
vote on the cotton bagging he turned around—since they were sitting
close to each other—and said to the New Yorker, "You give way, Sir!"

"No sir," replied the Magician, "I have been from the beginning opposed to this clause . . . unless the duty was greatly reduced. Subsequent reflection led me to regard this provision as an exceedingly exceptionable one and I finally determined to oppose it in any shape."[46]

Van Buren further reported that on the following day he spoke to Jackson about the political effect the cotton-bagging provision would have on southern states. He predicted that the motion would be brought up again because the vote had been close, and urged the General to help knock it out.[47] As expected, five days later the clause was reintroduced by Nathaniel Macon of North Carolina and this time was defeated, with Jackson reversing his previous vote.[48]

Because of the proximity of their seats in the Senate, Jackson and Van Buren became well acquainted during those winter months of 1824. Although Van Buren acted as campaign manager for William H. Crawford, Old Hickory pursued a policy of cordiality and amiability with his colleague and tried not to react visibly to the Magician's continuing efforts to vault Crawford into the White House through "corrupt" and undemocratic means. Both Jackson and Van Buren later agreed that their earlier opinion of the other underwent sharp revision. Initially Van Buren regarded Jackson as a military chieftain without presidential stature. Within three years he would salute him as the nation's greatest politician and statesman. For his part Jackson knew about Van Buren's reputation as an intriguer, and "especially about his *non-committalism*" on major issues. With respect to the matter of intrigue there was nothing Jackson could do about that, but as to the non-committalism he decided to judge for himself. One day an important subject came under discussion on the Senate floor and the General noticed Van Buren taking notes. "I judged from this that he intended to reply," said Jackson, "and I determined to be in my seat when he spoke. His turn came, and he rose and made a clear, straightforward argument, which, to my mind, disposed of the whole subject. I turned to my colleague, Major Eaton, who sat next to me: 'Major,' said I, 'is there anything non-committal about that?' 'No, sir,' said the Major."[49]

Van Buren's performance as a Senator impressed Jackson. Whenever he spoke the little man came quickly to the point, presented his evidence logically and clearly, and sat down. No long-winded pieties of limited substance. No playing to the galleries. And Jackson liked that. Van Buren took his senatorial duties seriously and acted responsibly, just like Jackson. Slowly, the two men formed a degree of grudging respect toward one another.

As his votes indicated, the General sided completely with northern protectionists on the tariff measure, and this caused some of his southern friends considerable alarm. Dr. Littleton H. Coleman of Warrenton, North Carolina, a Jackson supporter for the presidency, wrote to the General and expressed his concern over his voting record and warned that he would withdraw his support if Jackson proved, as reported, a friend of protection. The response Coleman's query elicited, which was subsequently published with Old Hickory's permission in the Raleigh, North Carolina, *Star* and the *Niles Weekly Register,* attracted national attention. Some found it an ambiguous muddle; others called it a superb piece of electioneering propaganda. Still others termed it a straightforward, positive statement that was as courageous (since it was written to a southerner) as it was decisive.

> . . . As my name has been brought before the nation for the first office in the gift of the people, it is incumbent on me, when asked, frankly to declare my opinion upon any political or national question pending before and about which the country feels an interest.
>
> You ask my opinion on the Tariff. I answer, that I am in favor of a judicious examination and revision of it; and so far as the Tariff before us embraces the design of fostering, protecting, and preserving within ourselves the means of national defense and independence, particularly in a state of war, I would advocate and support it. The experience of our late war ought to teach us a lesson; and one never to be forgotten. If our liberty and republican form of government, procured for us by our revolutionary fathers, are worth the blood and treasure at which they were obtained, it surely is our duty to protect and defend them. . . .
>
> Heaven smiled upon us and gave us liberty and independence. That same providence has blessed us with the means of national independence and national defense. If we omit or refuse to use the gifts which He has extended to us, we deserve not the continuation of His blessings. . . . I look at the Tariff with an eye to the proper distribution of labor and revenue; and with a view to discharge our national debt. I am one of those who do not believe that a national debt is a national blessing, but rather a curse to a republic; inasmuch as it is calculated to raise around the administration a moneyed aristocracy dangerous to the liberties of the country. . . .
>
> In short, sir, we have been too long subject to the policy of the British merchants. It is time we should become a little more *Americanized,* and instead of feeding the paupers and laborers of Europe, feed our own, or else in a short time, by continuing our present policy, we shall all be paupers ourselves.[50]

Critics who read the letter in print caught the word "judicious" in the opening statement and poked fun at it. Henry Clay supposedly said, "Well by ——, I am in favor of an *in*judicious tariff!"[51] Actually the statement was not as ambiguous nor as politically motivated as his rivals contended nor as some historians later lamented.[52] Granted it remained a strong and useful piece of campaign propaganda; still it was also clear and concise. Jackson called for a revision of the tariff in terms of strengthening the country from foreign danger, protecting labor, and reducing the debt. Again he sounded his keynote theme of liberty. The freedom of the nation. This theme became central to his campaign and figured prominently in major statements distributed by his friends and campaign managers.[53] It undergirded not only his position on such issues as the tariff and internal improvements but his concern over the corruption in Washington and the convocation of the congressional caucus.

Jackson also introduced a variation on the theme. He worried over the rise of a "moneyed aristocracy" because of the national debt and the danger such an aristocracy posed to the liberties of the country. Much of the statement postured defiantly in terms of national well-being, as might be expected, and Jackson could not resist jabbing the British and their mercantile preeminence. The chauvinistic comment about feeding "our own" would certainly not hurt him politically, but Jackson honestly believed this. It was pure Jackson—without subtlety, without pretense, without political fakery.

There were many pressures placed on Jackson because of his tariff stand but he would not back away. "I cannot be intimidated from doing that which my Judgment and conscience tells me is right by any earthly power," he declared. "I therefore will support the Tariff."[54] Obviously neither Jackson nor those who tried to intimidate him thought his statement vague or ambiguous. They regarded it as firm and positive. In any event, the Senate passed this mildly protective tariff in May, 1824, and Monroe added his signature shortly thereafter. Then, as the price of cotton began to slide during the next few years, southerners cited the tariff as the principal cause. If the price of cotton declined following the increase of the protective schedule, they argued, it must be a case of cause and effect. Over the next three years resistance to the tariff redoubled throughout the south, and Jackson himself had second thoughts about the wisdom of his "principles."[55]

The tariff debate concluded the congressional session and Jackson breathed a sigh of relief. Without waiting an extra moment he packed his belongings and headed straight for Tennessee. The past month had him on edge. He wanted desperately to get home. "I am truly wearied of lounging here; doing nothing, but feeding on the public funds," he complained.

Much of his annoyance, naturally, stemmed directly from the presidential campaign and the need for his active participation. A series of attacks on his character and past career forced his involvement. For example, he was reluctantly obliged to permit the publication of a correspondence with James Monroe dating back to 1816 because of the intimation that he had favored the appointment of Federalists when Monroe first came to office. Jackson had indeed recommended Colonel W. H. Drayton, a South Carolina Federalist, as secretary of war. That was all. Nevertheless, this letter was cited as proof of his political apostasy. "Wonder not," Old Hickory pointedly remarked to Major Lewis, "if you see the attempt made to make me a Federalist."[56] Soon the Crawfordites began a campaign to question the Hero's Republicanism, noting that Jackson in his letter to Monroe had commented that appointments should be made without reference to party. Rumor had it that there existed a number of these letters, all written to Monroe, and all similar in content and tone. A copy of one of them got into the hands of Walter Lowrie, senator from Pennsylvania, who threatened to publish it. Jackson felt compelled, therefore, to release the entire correspondence and Senator Eaton was assigned the task of assembling it.

Publication of the letters caused a slight stir among some Republicans because of Jackson's seeming Federalist sympathy. But a larger number of Federalists in New England were horrified to read the General's remark in one letter to the effect that had the Hartford Convention been held within his military jurisdiction he would have hanged the leaders.[57] "Had I commanded the military Department where the Hartford convention met, If it had been the last act of my life, I should have hung up the three principle leaders of the party. . . . These kind of men altho called Federalist, are really monarchrist, and traitors to the constituted Government."[58] Predictably, Jackson did not retract a single word after publication and wisely conducted himself as though nothing further need be said.

But his private letters scalded the Crawfordites. "The Radicals now heap upon me every scurrilous slanderous abuse that falsehood can suggest," he barked in a letter to his nephew Andrew J. Donelson, "I am Glad my name is before the nation, truth is always predominant where reason is left free to combat error, and I have no fear that my character will stand the test of the most exact scrutiny, both my public and private, and I court it from the nation."[59]

Some Radicals drew different and more important information from the publication of the correspondence. What it said about Jackson's character did not disturb them as much as what it revealed about James Monroe. "The correspondence between Monroe & Jackson must satisfy the most sceptical," wrote Martin Van Buren, "that it has been from the beginning the settled purpose of Mr Monroes administration to destroy the Republican Party by amalgamating it with its opponents. With the aid of several of his Cabinet & the effective co-operation of Mr Clays course he has nearly succeeded."[60] Van Buren had been trying to convince all Republicans of Monroe's treachery since he arrived in Washington in 1821. He contended that the President had embarked on a deliberate policy of amalgamation through the impartial distribution of the patronage. Monroe wished to destroy the two-party system and bring about a genuine Era of Good Feelings. The very rock on which the government rested (with all due respect to the Constitution) was about to be sundered. But instead of amalgamating the two parties, said Van Buren, the President would only succeed in reviving the Federalist party and destroying the Republican party.[61] At least, Van Buren went on, the publication of the correspondence with Jackson left no doubt as to the President's intention. Unless Republicans recognized this danger, he warned, the breakup of their party was a virtual certainty. "All hope of the restoration of the party to what it was when Mr Monroe became the chief object of its favor now rests on the fidelity of Virginia & New York," he declared. "Not that there are not sound spots in other parts but without the two pillars I have named the edifice cannot be sustained."[62]

The restoration of the New York–Virginia alliance! Here then was the beginning of the thought processes which would ultimately lead to the creation of the Democratic party, the party that Jackson would head and rededicate to his own brand of "republicanism" rooted in the ideology of the Founding Fathers. Not that Jackson had any sense at present of the concern by some Radicals for the damaging effects of Monroe's amalgamating policy. All he understood as he headed home to Tennessee was that the corruption had reached him in the form of "every scurrilous slanderous abuse that falsehood can suggest." When he first arrived in Washington the Radicals were determined to prod him into "some act of violence," he said, in an effort to destroy his candidacy, but "in this they have much mistaken my charector."[63] They had not realized that he exercised total control over his emotions when it suited his purpose. They assumed he was an untutored frontiersman, deficient in the science of politics and government. They expected him to behave like Sam Houston, who sometimes appeared in Washington dressed in Indian clothes. They thought he would arrive carrying "a scalping knife in one hand and a tomahawk in the other, allways ready to knock down, and scalp any and every person who differed with me in opinion." But he fooled them. He caught them by surprise. Instead of a war-whooping savage as the new Senator from Tennessee they "found a man of even temper, firm in his opinions advanced, and allways allowing others to enjoy theirs, untill reason convinced them that they were in error."[64]

A man of even temper? Unbelievable—and yet exactly so. Firm in the opinions he advanced? That came as a shock, but it was also true. Scrupulous in his conduct, avoiding quarrels of any kind, repairing old ones, and making every effort to impress his colleagues with his statesmanlike deportment and demeanor, Jackson completed his first senatorial session with notable gains to his political reputation. Indeed, on several occasions he positively radiated the charisma of a statesman. That was particularly true when on March 16 he received from Monroe in a simple ceremony the medal voted him by Congress in 1815 for his victory at New Orleans. A few times the Radicals baited him. He never threw the "gantlette" back at them, he said, and his "reply and remarks" so impressed some of his colleagues that "I recd the public congratulations of Governor Barber of the senate as soon as I sat down."[65] If there had been any doubt about whether his presidential candidacy would be taken seriously by the potentates of Washington, those doubts evaporated in the winter of 1824.

General Andrew Jackson proved politically shrewder and wiser than anyone initially suspected.

CHAPTER 5

The Theft of the Presidency

DESPITE THE PRESENCE OF FOUR CANDIDATES in the field and the almost absolute certainty of the presidential election landing in the House of Representatives for a final choice, Andrew Jackson made such spectacular gains during the spring and summer of 1824 that some of his friends entertained vague hopes that he could win a majority of electoral votes and thereby avoid a struggle for the "chief magistracy" in the House.[1] Apart from everything else, Jackson benefited from two special political advantages in 1824 which none of the other candidates enjoyed. One was the presence of the Marquis de Lafayette in the country, and the other was the widespread existence of the militia.

Lafayette had just returned to this country from France. He was in the midst of a triumphant tour, which produced an outpouring of popular affection for him but which also served to remind Americans of their revolutionary heritage, the price and value of liberty, and their eternal debt to a foreigner who assisted in the labor of establishing American independence. Newspapers carried lengthy descriptions of his tour. Everywhere he went, he excited interest. He represented a hallowed history. Giants strode the earth in 1776 and the Marquis de Lafayette was one of them. Just to see him seemed to link the American people with their glorious past. But his presence also underscored the grave deficiencies of the present leadership of the nation and, without uttering a word of reproach, rebuked those responsible for allowing corruption and fraud to seep through the government.

As soon as Jackson learned of Lafayette's arrival in America he immediately wrote him without any thought of its political consequence or possible impact on the presidential question. It was simply an exuberant shout

74

of joy and gratitude—and its composition probably had the benefit of Eaton's more florid pen. "You risked your fortunes with those of *then* hopeless America," Jackson enthused. "But, Thank Heaven, America triumphed; and, now, with the gratitude of Ten Millions of Freemen she salutes you as one of the Fathers of her glorious existence, and as the devoted advocate of independence and national freedom throughout the world. Welcome then—Thrice Welcome to her grateful land!—is echoed from every bosom, and from none with more pure fervor than from the Patriotic citizens of Tennessee."[2]

Lafayette immediately responded—with equal ardor. It gave him great pleasure to hear from one of America's outstanding heroes, he said. He expressed the "relief, joy and pride" he felt "on Receiving the Glorious Account of your Victory" at New Orleans in 1815. "I will not leave the U.S.," he added, "Before I Have Seeked and found the opportunity to Express in person my High Regard and Sincer friendship."[3]

In reminding the country of its revolutionary greatness as he moved among the people, Lafayette also reawakened Americans to the fact that revolutionary heroes still lived and deserved their reverence and gratitude. For example, General Andrew Jackson was one of those heroes. As a boy he participated in that noble enterprise and was scarred on the hand and head for his efforts. The facts of Old Hickory's early life were again reprinted in the newspapers and John Eaton brought out a new and updated edition of his biography.[4] In terms of securing American freedom, Andrew Jackson was the only one of the four presidential candidates who could legitimately claim participation. In terms of presidential advantage, the visit of the Frenchman aided Jackson enormously.[5]

The second advantage the General enjoyed was the existence of militia units in virtually every community in America. If a man belonged to any organization at all he belonged to the militia. Perhaps it was the strongest organization working for Jackson in 1824 because so many men identified with Jackson on account of their mutual military involvement. Edward Patchell, a hat manufacturer in Pittsburgh, wrote to Jackson in the summer of 1824 and told him how he, Patchell, had allowed his friends to put up his name as a candidate for brigadier general in the militia. Eight candidates competed for the rank. A meeting was held in the courthouse where "upwards of one thousand of our citizens" assembled. As each of the candidate's name was called, the men voted by voice, hissing most of the names mentioned. "Untill my name was reached on the list," Patchell reported, "when shouts of Old Hickory resounded from all parts of the house, nine cheers for Old Hickory." Since Patchell had been nominated by Jackson's friends and was identified as a Jackson supporter, he was the clear choice of the cheering mob and subsequently "elected by a much larger majority than any other of my predecessors for any office whatever in this County since the beginning." After the election the crowd rushed forward, lifted Patchell on their shoulders, and carried him to the public square in triumph. Patchell himself admitted he was "very unquallifyed to discharge the duties of any office whatever" and that it was Jackson himself who really carried the election.[6] In company after company the cry "Old Hickory" automatically set off demonstrations of noisy salutes and cheering. How much this meant in terms of organizational strength can only be conjectured. But it is not too far off the mark to say that long before the Democratic party taught voters to "huzza" for Old Hickory a less obvious organization was actively engaged in winning the presidency for their leader and hero.

Clearly the election of 1824 involved colorful personalities who could ignite a mob with the mere mention of their names. But this election also involved issues. The most important political (and ideological) statement produced by the Jackson campaign managers during the canvass was the document known as *The Letters of Wyoming*. First published as a series of eleven letters signed by "Wyoming" appearing in the Philadelphia *Columbian Observer* in June and July, 1823, and authored by John H. Eaton, they were reprinted in pamphlet form in 1824, again under the pseudonym.[7] These letters had such appeal that they were extensively quoted and reprinted in other newspapers around the country.[8] From the tone, style, and content of the letters it is obvious that Jackson himself had a hand in their composition. It is almost as though Eaton had edited and revised sections of Jackson's own "memorandoms," because a constant theme throughout the work is the lamentable fact that the nation had entered an era of intrigue and misrule. Virtue and morality, so characteristic of the revolutionary generation, had disappeared. Corruption—Eaton hammered at this throughout the text—ruled in Washington. "Look to the city of Washington," he wrote, "and let the virtuous patriots of the country weep at the spectacle. There corruption is springing into existence, and fast flourishing." But it also permeated the nation as a whole. Not like the old days "at the close of our revolutionary struggle" when morality and lofty ethical standards directed the hearts and minds of the American people as well as their government. Now the country wallowed in conspiracy and deception as men scrambled "in quest of their own interest and promotion." Only by returning to the principles of the Revolution through the election of Andrew Jackson to the "chief magistracy" could the nation recover its soul. "Remember," Eaton cried, "he was of the Revolution!" He fought, suffered and bled "in the cause of freedom." He lost two brothers and his mother in that struggle. He "is the last of those valiant establishers of the liberty of our Republic, who can succeed to the highest office known to our Constitution."[9]

The Letters of Wyoming forcefully reasserted the ideology of republicanism, the ideology which posited the belief in a perpetual struggle between liberty and power and between their respective instruments of support, virtue and corruption. Republics exist, declared Eaton, just as long as the people "adhere to principles and virtue; the instant these are abandoned, freedom must of necessity . . . be laid prostrate." Our revolutionary fathers have nearly all passed away. "We are not as once we were; the people are slumbering at their posts; virtue is on the wane; and the republican principles with which we set out, are fast declining." What can be done? Who can we turn to? "The answer is plain," declared Eaton. We can "sustain our republican principles . . . by calling to the Presidential Chair . . . ANDREW JACKSON."[10]

In Andrew Jackson, the soldier boy of the Revolution and veteran hero of the War of 1812, Eaton continued, the country had the purest embodiment of the ideals that motivated the Founding Fathers. Who among the current presidential candidates has shown the ability, firmness of purpose, and "devotion to the cause of liberty and his country?" Surely there could be no doubt in anyone's mind. "If one be living it is ANDREW JACKSON."[11]

"He stands aloof from all the contemptible intrigue and management of the day." Like the "Immortal Washington," he was "Revolution-tested." He could reverse the "dangerous trends of the modern age." He could restore "the cherished values of old."[12]

Even Jackson's outrages against liberty were hailed by Eaton as totally in accord with republican doctrine. His suspension of the writ of habeas corpus and jailing of a federal judge during the Battle of New Orleans were noted as further examples of Jackson's virtue and patriotism. The Hero had set aside "constitutional forms," said Eaton, "that the constitution itself might be preserved." Once the crisis passed, the forms had been restored. "WASHINGTON would have done the same," Eaton boldly asserted.[13]

So let the American people remember the record of Andrew Jackson's life when they choose their next President. Let them remember his contribution to their glorious past. "The Constitution and Liberty of the country were in imminent peril, and he has preserved them both!"[14]

The Letters of Wyoming was an important political document not only as a campaign statement but in the continuing discussion of the problem of preserving liberty in a democratic society. It was part of an ongoing process to educate the American people to the idea that the appearance of Andrew Jackson in public life and his elevation to the presidency meant the reestablishment of a republican ideology that had its origins in the Revolution and was the basis for the maintenance and perpetuation of American freedom. Newspapers in practically every state accepted these themes as their campaign slogans in supporting Old Hickory's candidacy.[15] Yet they were not simply quoting routinely from the *Wyoming Letters* but rather writing out of "shared assumptions and values, common beliefs and hopes."[16]

The *Wyoming Letters* enumerated some of the issues of this campaign as the Jacksonians saw them, but it also (and more importantly) provided a blueprint of the ideological intentions of the developing Jacksonian movement. It was a statement of what Jackson's drive for the presidency was all about. It committed an age that would soon bear the General's name to the preservation of liberty as handed down by "our revolutionary fathers." Through Andrew Jackson the course of American freedom would once again surge forward.

In the 1820s these ideals about liberty and virtue were not pious platitudes glibly uttered and devoid of substance and relevance. They had real meaning to the people of this dawning Jacksonian age and were not lightly bantered about by insensitive politicians. These ideals were the very soul of the nation, the principles upon which the political life of the American people depended.

As the campaign progressed during the spring and summer of 1824 little doubt existed in anyone's mind that Andrew Jackson was the leading candidate by virtue of his accomplishments and commitment to the purest form of republicanism. "The rapid march of Genl. Jackson's popularity," reported a New York politican, "has far exceeded the expectations of his warm, decided friends. He may now be called, emphatically, the idol of the people."[17] As though to acknowledge this mounting popular support and the need to reduce it sharply, several publications appeared over the next several months attacking Jackson's character and fitness for high office. One of the bitterest was a pamphlet entitled *An Address on the Presidential Question* published in Nashville and authored by Jesse Benton, the brother of Thomas Hart Benton. Unlike his brother, Jesse could never forget the humiliation he suffered in a duel nor forgive Jackson for his role in it.[18] The *Address* detailed some of the General's less fortunate escapades and less tasteful entertainments. The dueling, the gambling, the cursing, the cockfighting and horseracing, were all recited at length. But what agitated Jackson were the embellishments added to the various accounts. The statements that he fired his pistol during the "Barr Room" brawl with the Bentons in total disregard of the lives of several spectators or that he "exulted" over one fallen adversary "in a strain of *disgusting profanity*" were "positive falshoods," according to the General. He also denied attending a cockfight or similar sports for the last thirteen years. As for the "ballance of the peace," wrote Old Hickory, it "is too contemptible to be noticed."[19] Still it won wide circulation in the newspapers and even appeared in the Nashville *Whig*—which brought down on the head of the editor, said Jackson, "some contempt and harsh ephithets."[20] Jackson dismissed Jesse as the mastermind responsible for this "peace" and singled out the "Crawford Junto" in the persons of Alfred Balch, John P. Erwin, "and Co" as the real movers "behind the scene" in Nashville.[21]

Apart from Jackson's sometimes wild career as duelist, gambler, cockfighter, and all-around ruffian, what troubled a number of thoughtful men in the country was the General's behavior toward the law, individual rights, constitutional guarantees, and the men in authority placed over him. His entire career seemed to contradict the most basic democratic processes for which this country stood. Perhaps no man spelled out his doubts and fears with greater articulation than Albert Gallatin, one of the early leaders and shapers of the Republican party and subsequently secretary of the treasury under Thomas Jefferson and James Madison. Gallatin supported Crawford in this election but recognized that the General was "the most formidable opponent" in his own state of Pennsylvania. Jackson's correspondence with Monore, Gallatin wrote to Walter Lowrie, "the publication of which you have forced," proved beyond doubt that "whatever gratitude we owe him for his eminent military services, he is not fitted for the office of first Magistrate of a free people and to administer a Government of laws." His disregard of party, in particular his opposition to a congressional caucus, "is tantamount to a declaration that political principles and opinions are of no importance in the administration of Government." If talents and virtue are to be the only criteria in the choice of department heads, Gallatin continued, irrespective of party, then we might as well have elected Alexander Hamilton instead of Thomas Jefferson for all it mattered. Disregard the distinctions between parties, he said, "and you immediately loose sight of the principles & substitute men to measures, faction to party, and ultimately & unavoidably favoritism to a selection founded on correct political opinions & merit." The parties such as we have had in the past, Gallatin lectured in words closely resembling those of Martin Van Buren, watch one another and "are one of the best safeguards against illegal or oppressive measures." The party system is our one guarantee protecting our free institutions.

Turning again to the Jackson-Monroe correspondence, Gallatin expressed great dismay over the General's comment about hanging the leaders of the Hartford Convention. "Gen. Jackson has expressed a greater & a bolder disregard of the first principles of liberty than I have ever known to be entertained by any American." And his remark about hanging is typical of the man. He entertains, no doubt very sincerely but very erroneously, "the most dangerous opinions on the subject of military & executive power." Whenever he was entrusted with military authority, Gallatin remarked, he usurped more than legitimately belonged to him. Moreover, "when he thought it useful to the public, he has not hesitated to transcend the law & the legal authority vested in him." His collisions with the judiciary in New Orleans and in Florida and his assumption of the power to make war *repeatedly* against Spain without authorization by the President or Congress were only the most glaring examples.

Finally, Gallatin addressed the one topic that genuinely distressed many men: Jackson, the conqueror, the hero, the "military chieftain." The history of mankind abounds in instances of tyrants raised to power after brilliant victories on the battlefield who then proceed to drench their country in blood and countless years of misery. "Dazzled by military glory," said Gallatin, the people sacrifice their "rights & liberties to the shrine of that glory" and learn too late the awful consequence of their action. "The French indeed have given a late sad example in the oversetting of the Republic & submission to a first rate man." Do we wish to follow their example? Without "any personal disrespect or want of gratitude" to General Jackson for his great services to the nation "it is to me incomprehensible that he can be supported by . . . real friends of liberty."[22]

A powerful and deeply felt indictment of a career that legitimately raised grave problems for the intelligent electorate. Although this statement was never published, its sentiments were repeated in various forms in many newspapers opposed to Jackson's election. Some things in his past career did indeed contradict basic American principles. Some things in his character and personality could jeopardize the normal operation of constitutional government as it was then known and understood. What was not generally appreciated, however, except by a relative few, was his fierce commitment to individual liberty and free suffrage. Without this knowledge it took a profound act of faith for some men to vote for Andrew Jackson in 1824. The fact that so many of them did so says something about the optimism, self-confidence, and courage—if not recklessness—of the American people.

It is obvious that the presidential election of 1824 abounded in discussion over principles. Liberty, public virtue, and centralized power in the federal government were only some of the most important precepts argued over and debated.[23] Many historians have mistakenly insisted that principles had nothing to do with the contest. They regard it simply as a campaign of personality.[24] But they fail to understand the grave concern entertained by many men of the 1820s over corrupt conditions within their society and the danger this corruption constituted to their liberty and republican system. Certainly strong personalities participated. That is beyond dispute. Actually the election of 1824 contained a healthy mix of both personalities and issues.

Because of the principles involved in this campaign, Jackson's candidacy provoked the strongest response—both ways. He was the outstanding candidate in the election, and only John Quincy Adams approached him as a serious rival.[25] Through education, experience, and public service now capped by a distinguished record as secretary of state, Adams drew solid support from New England and the Middle Atlantic states. Crawford, despite his doctor's assurance of his eventual recovery, could not serve as President, and no matter what Van Buren did to shore up his crumbling campaign his physical condition seemed destined to exclude him from the contest. Clay, to his great misfortune, competed with Jackson for votes in the west and south, but he calculated that if the election went to the House of Representatives because no candidate had a majority of electoral votes, then he would be chosen the sixth President of the United States.[26] His mistake in calculation came in thinking that he would be one of the three candidates with the highest number of electoral votes to go into the House election, as stipulated by the Twelfth Amendment to the Constitution.

Although the election of 1824 marked the first presidential election in American history in which popular voting figured in the outcome, that in no way changed the fact that the President was (and still is) selected by electors, all named according to the constitutions of their respective states. In Delaware, Georgia, Louisiana, New York, South Carolina, and Vermont the electors were chosen by the legislatures; everywhere else they were selected by popular vote, either by districts—as in Illinois, Kentucky, Maine, Maryland, and Tennessee—or on a general statewide ticket, as in the remaining thirteen states.

The several states voted at different times during the fall of 1824, some acting quickly like Pennsylvania and Ohio, while others, like Louisiana and South Carolina, proceeding at a more leisurely pace. Not until mid-December did the results of the election look certain, and as many astute observers had long predicted, the final choice belonged to the House of Representatives. Jackson topped all the candidates, both in popular and electoral votes. But he failed to obtain the requisite majority of electoral votes. Out of a needed majority of 131 votes, he fell shy by 32. With so many candidates in the field the odds of his winning in the electoral college were insuperable. Yet he came very close. It was a stunning political performance.

New England, as expected, gave all 51 of her electoral votes to Adams. By comparison the opposition tickets performed very badly. A real contest came in other eastern states. In New York a wild, brawling, bruising fight developed between Van Buren's Bucktails, who dominated the state's Republican party, and the People's party, which supported Adams and Clay. Trickery, intrigue, and probably fraud determined the final outcome. The election in this state alone provided a massive demonstration of the corruption eroding the American political system. By the time the New York electors cast their ballots in the electoral college, more skullduggery had occurred and they awarded 26 votes to Adams, 5 to Crawford, 4 to Clay, and 1 to Jackson.[27] Reportedly there had been an agreement between the Adams and Clay men to supply Clay with four additional votes to ensure the Kentuckian's inclusion in the House election. But Thurlow Weed, a young, astute manager of the Adams campaign in New York, reneged, claiming that the pledge had been given on condition that Louisiana also voted for Clay, and since Louisiana went for Jackson "that left our friends free to vote for Mr. Adams."[28]

Jackson performed better in New Jersey and Pennsylvania, both of which he swept for a total of 36 votes. The friends of Clay and Adams put up a determined fight but the people exercised a direct vote in both these states—unlike New York—and they demanded their Hero. In Pennsylvania Clay had expected his American System to provide strong appeal for his candidacy, but the final popular result came as a rude shock. Jackson polled over 36,000 votes while Clay garnered a mere 4,000. In New Jersey the results were identical, with Jackson's friends conducting a vigorous campaign that ended with Old Hickory capturing all 8 of the state's electoral votes.

In Delaware, where the legislature chose the electors and the old Federalist party still remained an active force, the state finally assigned one vote to Adams and two to Crawford. Over in Maryland, which provided a popular ballot on the districting basis, Adams ran extremely well, outpolling Jackson by a little more than 100 votes. Nevertheless, the General's strength had increased steadily over the past several months and when the electors finally cast their ballots they gave 7 to Jackson, 3 to Adams, and 1 to Crawford. Continuing to the south, Virginia, where the Richmond Junto ruled the political world and remained committed to Crawford and Radical principles, the results were fairly predictable: 24 whopping ballots went to the Georgian. Together with the 9 votes he received from his own state and the 4 he ultimately got from New York, Crawford pushed ahead of Clay in the final tally and assured himself a place among the top three candidates to go into the House of Representatives.[29]

Jackson swept the remainder of the south—almost in toto. He received 15 votes from North Carolina, 11 from South Carolina, 5 from Alabama, and 3 from Mississippi. But in Louisiana a genuine contest developed. Clay amassed an early lead, which Jackson reduced substantially during the final months of the campaign; by the time the legislature met to select the electors the two men enjoyed nearly equal strength. Then the Jackson forces concocted a scheme to wipe out Clay. They arranged a deal with the Adams men to divide the votes between them. Thus, when the legislature finally voted, the Jackson and Adams men defeated the Clay ticket by two votes and then proceeded to award Jackson 3 electoral votes and Adams 4.[30] Obviously the anti-Jackson forces did not hold a monopoly on "intrigue and corruption."

In the west Jackson performed less notably. As anticipated, Kentucky and Tennessee voted for their favorite sons, although Kentucky showed signs of breaking away from Clay. A struggle between the Relief and Anti-Relief parties over policies stemming from the late Panic drove the Relief party to Jackson toward the end of the campaign. Although Clay succeeded in taking all the state's electoral votes, shrewd observers noted that Kentucky had started to slide toward the Hero.[31]

Clay had expected to do well in the other western states where his friends had started campaigning at a very early date. But again Jackson's candidacy advanced rapidly once it started and almost caught up to Clay in the popular vote by the time of the election. Clay just managed to squeeze ahead of the General and snag all of Ohio's 16 votes. In Missouri, where the capable Thomas Hart Benton supervised his campaign, Clay easily won the state's 3 electoral votes. In Indiana the Jackson party ran a well-organized campaign right from the beginning and the Hero had no difficulty in capturing that state's entire vote. Illinois ran a slate of electors for each candidate in each of its three districts. Except for Crawford, all the other candidates did fairly well in the popular vote, although Jackson won the plurality. The General also won two of the three districts; Adams took the third.[32]

The final results of the popular vote around the country showed a clear preference for Andrew Jackson. He polled 152,901 votes against 114,023 for Adams, 47,217 for Clay and 46,979 for Crawford. Jackson's plurality left no doubt about the people's choice, but at the same time Adams demonstrated strong appeal in all the major sections of the country. He did extremely well in New England and the Middle states, but less well in the south and west; and although Jackson ran strong in the east, south, and west, he was totally excluded from New England. In New England alone Adams piled up a vote of over 50,000.

Still it is the electoral vote that counts. Here again Jackson fell short of a majority, receiving a plurality of 99 votes to 84 for Adams, 41 for Crawford, and 37 for Clay. These figures represented eleven states for Jackson with seven for Adams and three each for Crawford and Clay. Once more Jackson was the clear choice. He was the overwhelming favorite in every section of the country but New England. And he was a "gaining candidate." From the beginning of his campaign he had been gathering momentum toward an absolute victory, which in view of the number of candidates in the field would have constituted a stupendous feat if successful. Had the campaign continued for another month the election might have been his. With a little more time Ohio might have capitulated to him. Whether Kentucky could have been enticed away from its favorite son this early, given the political currents operating within the state, remains an interesting speculation. In any event the American people under the operating rules of 1824 had expressed their preference. They wanted Andrew Jackson in the White House. The next move belonged to the House of Representatives.

According to the Twelfth Amendment to the Constitution, when no candidate receives a majority of electoral votes the House selects the President from among the three persons with the highest count, each state having one vote determined by its delegation. A majority of states is necessary for election. Unfortunately for Clay he had the lowest vote of the four candidates and was therefore excluded from House consideration. Since he was a powerful figure in the House and exercised much influence among its members he would have a great deal to say about the final outcome. He could have decided it in his own favor had he been among the top three; now he must decide it for someone else.

In the vice presidential contest John C. Calhoun won over token opposition. He polled 182 votes, while his nearest rival, Nathan Sanford of New York, received only 30. Virginia awarded Nathaniel Macon 24 votes in recognition of his strong Radical stand on the issue of states' rights. In appreciation for his efforts on Crawford's behalf, Georgia gave 9 votes to Van Buren, while Jackson received 13 votes scattered among several states and Clay got 2 from Delaware.

The final results of the election were not known to Jackson when he set out for Washington to return to his senatorial duties with Rachel and his nephew Andrew Jackson Donelson and Donelson's young wife and first cousin, Emily Tennessee Donelson. Although Rachel's return to Washington seemed related to the outcome of the election, Jackson really disliked long separations from his wife and had promised himself the previous spring not to leave Tennessee without her.

The party took off in grand style. They traveled up the Ohio River to Wheeling and there the General placed his family in his own private coach, drawn by four horses, which to some critics showed "aristocratic pretensions."[33] The General himself mounted his saddle horse and rode the rest of the distance to Washington along the Cumberland Road. On the way he learned the final indecisive result of the election. But everyone supposed that the House would respond to the obvious will of the nation and make him President. At one small town in Pennsylvania he was assured by a Presbyterian clergyman of his eventual selection by the House unless, warned the minister, "Congress was corrupted or beguiled by factious intrigues."

"Sir," responded Jackson, his eyes flashing, "no people ever lost their liberties unless they themselves first became corrupt. . . . The people are the safeguards of their own liberties, and I rely wholly on them to guard themselves. They will correct any outrage upon political purity by Congress; and if they do not, now and ever, then they will became the slaves of Congress and its political corruption."[34]

Several people standing by who overheard the remark were forcibly struck by it and its comprehension of the republican ideology, and in that instant knew absolutely that Andrew Jackson "was fit to govern a republic. . . . He was our choice from that moment for the Presidency," they said.[35]

The journey from the Hermitage to the capital took twenty-eight days; on December 7 the party arrived in Washington, where they found lodgings at Gadsby's Tavern. This was O'Neal's old property which Eaton had taken over and sold to Gadsby.

Then the madness began. As the leading presidential contender, as the "people's choice," as some now called him, Jackson was mobbed daily by well-wishers and opportunists of every shape and variety. Not less than fifty to a hundred persons a day clamored to see and talk with him. Graciously but firmly, he tried to keep them at a distance. "Here there is a bustle continually," he informed John Coffee; "the man in office greeted with smiles and apparent friendship, his confidence often sought to be betrayed; surrounded thus, where a man must be always guarded, happiness cannot exist. The best lesson learnt me in my youth, was to pursue principle and never depart from my own judgt when matured. Treat all with complacency, but make confidents of but few. I have profitted much by an adherence to this rule, but still I have been deceived as you know in men, and I have become so well acquainted with human nature, that I am wearied with a public life, and if I could with propriety, would retire, but my lott is cast, and fall as it may, I must be content." And he really did seem content. "All are well and enjoying themselves, the young at parties and Mrs J and myself at home smoking our pipe."[36]

For Rachel, it was pure joy to accompany her husband to the "great city" and not be left alone at home. Staying in the same boardinghouse as the Marquis de Lafayette also pleased her. But what delighted her Presbyterian soul more than anything else was the opportunity to go to church and pray whenever the spirit moved her. "Not a day or night but there is the church opened for prayer," she enthused. "Glory to God for the privilege," was her comment about the prospect of hearing the sermon of one young Methodist minister, for if anything thrilled Rachel Jackson more than a good, rip-roaring, fire-and-brimstone sermon, nobody knew it.[37] Jackson reported that his wife spent her time on Sundays at church, on Thursdays at prayer meetings, and the balance of the week in receiving and paying courtesy calls.[38] Everyone commented on her kindness and hospitality. But she seemed hardly the sort of person one would expect the elegant and commanding-looking Jackson to have married. She "is an ordinary looking old woman," gossiped Louis McLane of Delaware to his wife, "dressed in the height & *flame* of the fashion" whenever she visited the Senate chamber.[39] As for socializing generally, the Jacksons remained properly aloof except to attend a ball at General Brown's home on January 8 to mark the anniversary of the Battle of New Orleans and to attend a reception given by Mrs. Monroe.[40]

From the moment the Jacksons entered Washington the loud and raucous sounds of intense politicking assaulted their ears—and all of it about the presidential contest. Once it became definite that the House of Representatives would make the final presidential selection the Washington scene erupted in rumors of intrigue, plots, deals, arrangements, and plain old vicious gossip, capital-style. "Rumors say that deep intrigue is on foot," Jackson relayed back to his Tennessee henchmen, "that Mr Clay is trying to wield his influence with Ohio, Kentucky, Missouri & Elonois in favour of Adams—others say the plan is to prevent an election all together This last I do not believe."[41] Certainly Clay was the one man who would exercise enormous influence in the final selection, given his prestige and power in the House. And he savored every delicious moment of his king-making role now that he need no longer fret about his own chances. At a dinner party in honor of Lafayette given by Louis McLane, Martin Van Buren, and Stephen Van Rensselaer at their "bachelor quarters," Clay, Jackson, Adams, Calhoun, Rufus King, and General Sam Smith attended and Clay delighted himself in taunting the rivals. "Old Hickory was under par," reported McLane, and the dour Adams looked his usual dyspeptic self. But "Clay was in fine spirits and amused himself a little at the expense of the *rivals,*" chuckled McLane. "J & A sat next to each other on the fire &c &c, a vacant chair intervening." Clay saw his opportunity for a little sport. Sitting on the opposite side of the room, he suddenly rose, strolled over to the two men and plopped himself into the vacant chair. Then, "in his inimitably impudent significant manner," he said to the two men: "Well gentlemen since you are both so near the chair, but neither can occupy it, I will step in between you, & take it myself." Everyone in the room burst out laughing, but neither Jackson nor Adams thought it terribly funny.[42]

Because of his unquestioned influence in the House—although there is some evidence that the extent of his influence was exaggerated—Clay enjoyed the attention and favor of every manager and political broker in Washington. Daily they recited their claims to him. Jackson's friends pointed out the importance of a western president—the first in the nation's history; Crawford's supporters insisted that their candidate was the only true keeper of the Republican faith; and Adams's cohorts reminded Clay that Adams "always had the greatest respect for you, and admiration of your talents. There is no station to which you are not equal."[43] Sighed Clay: "I sometimes wish it was in my power to accommodate each of them."[44]

Most probably Jackson would have rewarded the Kentuckian with high office had Clay come out for him and exerted his influence on the needed delegations.[45] Considering the number of old feuds Old Hickory had laid to rest in the last year and his frequent and relatively pleasant social meetings with Clay it is not impossible that a Jackson-Clay alliance could have been struck. Not that Jackson lifted a finger to initiate such an alliance. That he could never do. That would link him to the other intriguers. As the front-running candidate he had additional reason to avoid any suspicion of appearing to manipulate the outcome. He must remain, he said, on "the high ground the people have placed me on."[46] He told John Coffee that "I will not, have not" interfered in any way with the election. "I would feel myself degraded to be placed into that office but by the free unsolicited voice of the people—Intrigue may stalk around me, but it cannot move me from my purpose. . . . I hope you know, when I mature my course, I am immoveable."[47]

Yet Clay wanted assurances. He wanted the inside track to the presidency. He needed to know that the next President would name him his secretary of state. And if Jackson could not give him those assurances then he would look elsewhere. Besides, the Jackson candidacy made him uncomfortable. Old Hickory was not only a westerner and therefore his natural rival but a "military chieftain" and hardly the proper person to sit in the executive mansion as the successor of Washington, Jefferson, and Madison. Still, there was Jackson's immense popularity to consider, which in time Clay might wield to his own purposes. After eight years at the most he could expect to replace Jackson in the White House.

The danger of rejecting the Hero in the House election should have been obvious. He had won more popular and electoral votes than any of the other candidates and could be designated as the nation's choice. To reject that decision—which the House had the constitutional right to do —risked popular resentment and invited suspicions of wrongdoing. In view of Washington's present reputation for corruption the rejection of Jackson was certain to be seen in that light.

Already suspicions were rife. "Intrigue, corruption, and sale of public office is the rumor of the day," the General declared. "How humiliating to the American character that its high functionaries should conduct themselves as to become liable to the interpretation of bargain & sale of the constitutional rights of the people!"[48] To risk that accusation was madness. Only a desperate man would gamble with this political kiss of death. "I envy not the man who may climb into the presidential chair in any other way, but by the free suffrage of the people," said Jackson. *"The great whore of babylon being prostrated, by the fall of the caucus,* the liberty of our country is safe, & will be perpetuated, and I have the proud consolation to believe, that my name aided in its downfall."[49]

The liberty of the people had been safeguarded by the fall of the caucus; "bargain & sale" in the selection of the president could only jeopardize it once again. And that would set up such a howl of popular protest and outrage as to wreck forever the political ambitions of all who might be involved.

The alternative to Jackson, as everyone realistically knew, was John Quincy Adams. In terms of education, intellectual endowments, and experience in public service, Adams was ideally suited to occupy the presidential chair. More than that, his views on public issues paralleled Clay's as expressed in the American System. Intellectually, though certainly not temperamentally, the two men complemented each other. Thus, to Clay it made considerable sense to advance Adams to the presidency, if he hoped to obtain immediate action on his American System proposals.

More than anything else, Henry Clay loved to gamble. He took risks. He chanced all on a single, wild throw of the dice. Reckless, intoxicated by his sense of personal power, and oblivious to cautious warnings from friends, he presumed he could channel the election in any direction he chose and get away with it.

As the new year commenced and the time for the House election drew closer, the pressures on Clay mounted. Several congressmen sought him out to see what could be arranged. Others offered to play go-between.

Representative James Buchanan of Pennsylvania, a born busybody and a Jackson supporter, had heard that Clay's friends were disturbed over the rumor that the General if elected would "punish" the Kentuckian by excluding him and his cronies from the cabinet. Concerned that these friends of Clay would go over to Adams, Buchanan took his information to Eaton and afterward to Jackson himself. As he stood before the wary General repeating what he had heard, he could not control the nervous affliction that troubled one eye. He kept winking at Old Hickory as he spoke. Clay's friends, said Buchanan after a barrage of winks, gave assurances that they would "end the presidential election within the hour" if the General would first declare his intention of dismissing Adams as secretary of state.[50]

Jackson stared in disbelief at the winking, fidgeting little busybody. Everything he had related to Coffee, Lewis, and his other friends about intrigues and plots now stood twitching before him. Clay obviously wanted to become secretary of state in return for his support and Buchanan had been sent to sound him out with winks and blinks. Actually Clay never authorized anyone to approach Buchanan, nor had he proposed a possible deal. By the time Buchanan spoke to Jackson the Kentuckian had already made up his mind to swing his support to Adams. In fact, Thomas Hart Benton claims that shortly before December 15 Clay informed him of his intention to declare for Adams.[51] Later Jackson found it impossible to believe that Clay had not proposed a deal through Buchanan and only turned to the New Englander when the suggestion was rebuffed. It is not certain exactly what Jackson said to Buchanan during their interview, probably nothing provocative since prudence warned against giving offense. No doubt the Hero quietly repeated his resolution to remain clear of the contest.

If Jackson kept to this resolution—and there is every reason to believe that he did—he was among the very few in Washington who did. Everyone else plunged in with abandon. "It is not at all improbable," Louis McLane told his wife, "that *I shall* ultimately elect J. *if I can.*" The rumor that Clay and his allies would support Adams greatly distressed McLane since he cordially disliked Adams. "To defeat so unhallowed a combination I wd. elect Jackson if possible."[52] Daniel Webster also fancied himself a king-maker. He hankered for the mission to England and at first courted consideration from some Jackson men until he heard that Adams might prove amenable to his desire, after which he worked diligently to line up Federalist support for Adams in Maryland, Delaware, and New York.[53]

The fateful decision came on January 9, 1825. A meeting was arranged between Adams and Clay for an evening's conversation. The two men sat down in Adams's library and eventually reached an agreement about their future roles. "Mr. Clay came at six," Adams confided to his diary, "and spent the evening with me in a long conversation explanatory of the past and prospective of the future." After detailing to Adams all the "disgusting" efforts to win his support by the several managers of the other candidates, Clay asked the New Englander "to satisfy him with regard to some principles of great public importance, but without any personal considerations for himself."[54] Nothing crude or vulgar—like declaring the terms of their political deal—passed their lips. No need. Both men understood one another's purposes. Both men knew what was expected of them when their conversation about the past and future ended. Surely they both realized that in exchange for House support Adams would designate Clay as his secretary of state.

Two days later the Kentucky legislature passed resolutions instructing its delegation in Congress to cast the state's vote for Jackson in the House election. The people of Kentucky preferred Old Hickory over the other two candidates and wanted him as their President. But it was too late. Henry Clay had already decided to support Adams and he had every intention of delivering Kentucky's vote in the House. On January 24 the Kentucky delegation in Congress announced its decision to swing behind Adams, despite the instructions from the legislature and the fact that the New Englander had not received a *single* popular vote in Kentucky in the fall election. On the same day the Ohio delegation also declared for Adams. Obviously Clay had powerful influence with both delegations.

The announcement of Clay's action came like a thunderclap. "We are all in commotion," wrote Robert Y. Hayne of South Carolina, "about the monstrous union between Clay & Adams, for the purpose of depriving Jackson of the votes of the Western States where nine tenths of the people are decidedly in his favor."[55] Other Congressmen also saw the obvious intent of this "monstrous union." It was theft, pure and simple. The west did not want John Quincy Adams. They had voted for Old Hickory. He was their choice. For Clay singlehandedly to overrule this judgment made a mockery of representative government. Was this a free country of elected officials or not? The Jacksonians were beside themselves with rage and indignation. When Martin Van Buren learned from a Kentucky congressman of his delegation's intention to desert to Adams, the Magician was aghast. It defied understanding. It verged on political suicide— particularly for Henry Clay. Van Buren warned of the consequence. If you do this thing, he said to his Kentucky colleague, "you sign Mr. Clay's political death warrant."[56] Could they not see this? It would strike everyone as a "deal"; it would confirm every suspicion of intrigue; it would prove that corrupt politicians in Washington were not above denying the people's right to determine the chief magistrate.[57]

On January 28, 1825, an unsigned letter appeared in the Philadelphia *Columbia Observer* accusing Clay of promising votes in the House to elect Adams in exchange for the office of secretary of state. Thus, within four days after the announcement of the "monstrous union," the public was informed that a private arrangement had been transacted between two venal politicians to deprive the American people of their constitutional rights. True or not, it seemed so obvious that no one needed proof. Almost everybody believed it. The very fact of the "union's" existence was proof enough. Clay, recently elected Speaker of the House over his own feeble protests, hotly denied the newspaper charge by publishing a "Card" denouncing the anonymous slanderer as a "base and infamous calumniator, a dastard and a liar" and calling upon him to reveal his identity and give satisfaction. To Clay's discomfort the "dastard" turned out to be George Kremer, a Pennsylvania representative better known for his eccentricities of dress than anything else. Had Clay actually challenged this ridiculous man he would have seriously damaged his own reputation.[58]

A congressional committee later examined Kremer's charges without uncovering supporting evidence. Jackson's friends did not pursue the matter since Kremer's involvement tended to discredit the entire story. Even so, a great many people believed that some kind of deal had been worked out and that its particulars—the price each paid for the union— would soon be revealed. But no one could resist speculating on the particulars, and most knew that it involved an exchange of office: the presidency for the office of secretary of state. Thus, Kremer's "revelation" elicited little surprise; it only publicly announced what everyone suspected. What made the situation worse and inflicted grave damage on the public attitude toward government was the growing feeling around the country that "skullduggery" was the normal practice in Washington and now even included the selection of the President.[59]

The "monstrous union"—or "coalition" as it was called more commonly—encouraged Jacksonians to consider an alliance with the Radicals. Samuel Swartwout, a New York politician and a relatively longtime supporter of the General, supposedly journeyed to Washington to suggest to the Nashville managers a reconciliation between Old Hickory and Crawford. Rachel reportedly visited Mrs. Crawford to initiate the process; more likely she merely wished to extend a friendly, Christian hand to a woman who suffered a great deal on account of her husband's infirmities. An alliance between Jackson and Crawford would take a lot more than a social visit. It required a total reversal of attitudes between the two men. Besides, after the uproar caused by the "monstrous union," Jackson had too much sense to invite similar criticism; thus it is highly unlikely that anything serious was initiated between the two political factions.

Clay's reputation sank rapidly after his announcement. Louis McLane said that "irretrievable ruin is his inevitable fate." Everybody loved him, but nobody trusted him. Once he seemed destined for the highest office. No more. His coalition "is so unnatural & preposterous that the reports of no committees, nay all the waters of the sweet Heavens cannot remove the iota of corruption." The same held true for Adams, "for so deep and universal is the indignation excited by the coalition, and the affair with Kremer, that from the moment of his election he will encounter an overwhelming opposition in both Houses of Congress [and] throughout the nation. The Jackson men are most violent & implacable."[60]

Thus, even before the House election took place, Washington observers predicted the inevitable consequences of the action taken by Adams and Clay. Their coalition virtually demanded the creation of a party of reform to cast the unclean thing into oblivion where it belonged. And the "violent & implacable" Jacksonians would lead the way. "Thus it is that treachery and duplicity fall in their own snare, and the acts of the villain return the poisonous chalice to his own lips."[61]

The Radicals, long convinced of Crawford's eventual defeat, now regained faith in their broken candidate as the antagonism between the Jackson and Adams men swelled with each passing day. If they bided their time, if they remained steadfast in their loyalty, if they gave no cause for hostility from either of the other two factions they might still capture the presidency. They had nothing to lose by just sitting tight. "Whilst the war rages with barbarous violence between the Jackson & Adams men," wrote Van Buren, "we (Crawfordites) stand aloof *respected for our steadiness, confied in for our sincerity, & admired for our fidelity. . . .* We the subjects of King Caucus, are exempt from injurious imputation of any sort. If in the end we cannot command success we will do more. At all events we will come out of the contest with clean hands." Van Buren could not help laughing out loud at the reversal of events caused by the stupidity and cupidity of Adams and Clay. "Take my word for it, that there is no *honorable profession* extant, in which there are more knaves enjoyed than in this same profession of politics."[62]

Whether Andrew Jackson might have stepped in at this point to respond in a more direct and positive way to the announcement of the coalition between Clay and Adams remains problematic, for he suffered a serious physical collapse at this time that removed him totally from the mounting political turmoil. He had been meeting with congressmen daily because of the intensity of feeling among his partisans over the "treachery and duplicity" of Adams and Clay, and although he attempted to avoid any appearance of plotting and intriguing he listened to the many suggestions offered to him about his immediate course of action. He was closeted late one evening with a particular representative. This congressman tried to convince him about some plan or other. "Long he pleaded (it is said) with the old man, and pleaded in vain." At midnight he left. The General stumbled up the stairs to his rooms, the hall lamp having already been extinguished. On reaching the top landing he mistakenly thought he had one more step to take and as he raised his leg to find the step he lost his balance and nearly fell to the floor. But as he lurched forward he felt something inside his chest tear loose. The indifferently healed shoulder wound from one or both of his duels with the Bentons and Dickinson ripped open. He staggered to his room and collapsed. He lay prostrate on his bed for a week, barely moving. Hemorrhage followed hemorrhage, but by this time he had grown so used to these bloody episodes that they hardly seemed frightening any more except that they quite debilitated him. Weak, listless, sometimes unconscious, he just lay there as the hemorrhages brought him closer and closer to death. Yet he rallied. Somewhere, somehow he found the strength to recover. He willed to survive, or so it seemed to his friends. Hereafter, to the end of his life, the hemorrhages became regular occurrences, not all of which he mentioned in his correspondence unless they were particularly severe or interfered with his duties. Sometimes, when he thought an attack imminent, he tried to forestall it by operating on himself with a lancet or any other sharp instrument at hand. He "would lay bare his arm, bandage it, take his penknife from his pocket, call his servant to hold the bowl, and bleed himself freely. Often, indeed, during his presidency, he performed this operation in the night without any assistance."[63]

The man seemed superhuman. What he did to himself physically defies belief. In any event his fall on the stairway put him out of circulation. The remaining weeks prior to the House election involved some of the heaviest politicking among the members of Congress, but none of it included Old Hickory. Daniel Webster obtained a guarantee from Adams that Federalists would not be purged by his administration, a pledge that aided Webster in winning the Maryland delegation away from Jackson. Webster also told Adams that the Patroon, Stephen Van Rensselaer of New York, would appreciate hearing similar assurances and that he would advise the Patroon to visit the New Englander to obtain confirmation from him in person. Meanwhile Clay worked on the delegations from Louisiana and Missouri, while Adams used his personal friendship with Daniel Pope Cook to woo Illinois away from Old Hickory. While all this was going on Jackson lay on his bed politically bleeding to death.[64]

On election day, February 9, 1825, at the precise hour of noon, the members of the United States Senate, led by the sergeant at arms and their president pro tem, John Gaillard—the Vice President was permanently indisposed and now close to death—filed into the hall of the House of Representatives and took their seats in front of the Speaker. Gaillard was invited to sit at the right side of the Speaker and after everyone had taken his place he called the two houses to order. Spectators crowded the galleries and included foreign ambassadors, governors, judges and other distinguished persons. For over two hours the monotonous business of opening electoral certificates and counting the ballots proceeded with unhurried solemnity, finally revealing to no one's surprise that John C. Calhoun had been overwhelmingly elected vice president but that no candidate for the presidency had received the necessary majority of votes. With that the Senators filed out of the chamber to allow the Representatives their privilege of completing the constitutional business and selecting the next President. The excitement and tension in the room swiftly mounted.

The Speaker, Henry Clay, directed a roll call. As he did so the representatives of each delegation took their seats together in the order in which the states would be polled. The order ran from north to south along the Atlantic coastline and then south to north along the Mississippi Valley. Each state had one vote determined by the entire delegation, with a majority necessary for election. All the delegations received separate ballot boxes from the sergeant at arms into which the secret ballots were deposited. Each state appointed its own tellers, who counted the votes and then prepared the results on two separate slips of paper. These were submitted to a committee of tellers, divided into two groups to serve as a check on one another. Daniel Webster headed the first group, and John Randolph the second.

One moment of high drama occurred during the balloting of the New York delegation. All along Van Buren had hoped that Jackson and Adams would deadlock and eventually force the Representatives to switch to Crawford. The key to his plan, obviously, was to keep as many states deadlocked for as many ballots as possible until exhaustion or some other worthy emotion finally drew them to the Radical position. As it turned out, New York could not reach a decision. Eighteen votes were necessary for a selection. Of the 34-member delegation, 17 preferred Adams, 14 wanted Crawford, 2 leaned toward Jackson, and one man, Stephen Van Rensselaer, seemed to have no strong preference and had encouraged all the candidates at one time or another to think he was sympathetic to their cause. Van Rensselaer was an extremely religious man. He also "messed" with several Radicals, including Louis McLane, who showed him every kindness and courtesy. Van Buren finally obtained a promise from him to support Crawford and under no circumstance to vote for Adams and thereby give him the necessary 18 votes needed for the majority. If Adams won these 18 votes he would add New York to his column and take the presidency.

On the morning of the election as Van Rensselaer headed for the Capitol he was waylaid by Clay and Webster. They pulled him into the Speaker's private office and battered him with arguments about how essential his vote was to the good of the country and the safety of his property. He must vote for Adams, they said. After his release the old man stumbled into the House chamber and slumped into his seat. Try as he might to compose himself, he kept remembering the artful arguments of Clay and Webster. His conscience also reminded him of his previous promise to Van Buren. He visibly trembled. His face registered his indecision. McLane found him "in tears litterally," babbling how "the vote of N. York . . . depended upon him" and "if he gave it to A. he could be elected most probably on the first ballot." What a sorry excuse for a man, sneered McLane. "In the womanish fears, and miserable wavering of *Genl. Vanrennselaer*," he told his wife, I have had a day "full of pain and mortification. Great God, what is human nature!

How few of thy works are worthy [of] thy hands!'"[65]

Tortured by doubts and shaken by the arguments of friends and advisers, Van Rensselaer finally dropped his head to the edge of his desk and prayed for guidance. Then, as his turn came to vote, he slowly lifted his head, and as he did so, lo! there lying on the floor was a ballot marked with a single name: John Quincy Adams. Certain beyond doubt that the Almighty had answered his prayer, he picked up the ballot and placed it into the box. Thus, New York cast its precious vote for Adams and gave him a majority of the states.[66]

Van Buren's *Autobiography,* written a number of years later, is the only source for this incredible story—although McLane's letters to his wife seem to support many of its particulars. Some historians have doubted its authenticity. Whether the story is true or not will probably remain uncertain, but its character certainly conforms to the bizarre pattern of this strange election. Besides, Van Buren had no reason to fabricate such a grotesque incident.

Perhaps more important than Van Rensselaer's single vote, as vital as it may have been, was the concentrated effort of Daniel Webster to convert Maryland, along with the essential work of Clay in winning over Kentucky, Ohio, and perhaps Louisiana. Illinois dumped Jackson, thanks to Daniel Cook and his personal friendship for Adams. For his efforts Cook was subsequently defeated for reelection in 1826, but Adams paid him off with a "diplomatic junket" to Cuba. Even North Carolina deserted Old Hickory, whose delegation abandoned him for Crawford. Missouri's vote was cast by a single delegate, John Scott, who at first seemed undecided. With Clay out of the race, Thomas Hart Benton tried to prod Scott into voting for Jackson since "nine tenths of the people" in the west were believed to be "decidedly in his favor." But Scott's vote was purchased in another, smaller version of a "bargain & sale." Scott's brother was a judge in the Arkansas Territory and had killed a colleague on the bench in a duel. An application to the President for the brother's removal had already been made—since territorial law forbade duelists from holding office—but it had not yet been acted on. Adams personally assured Scott that his brother would keep his office. In fact when the brother's four year-term expired President Adams renominated him, but the Senate rejected it as a gross violation of the law.[67] In any event, to show his gratitude, Scott cast Missouri's vote for the New Englander, to the consternation of most westerners. As a direct consequence, Scott was defeated for reelection in 1826 and never returned to public office.

So the presidential election of 1825 ended on the first ballot. Through hard work, fierce politicking, and several bargains and arrangements, John Quincy Adams was elected the sixth President of the United States with thirteen states as against seven for Jackson and four for Crawford. Jackson, who had won the plurality of votes from eleven states in the general election, was stripped of four of them in the House. The man who had more electoral votes than any of the other candidates, the man who had more popular votes than the others, the man who was judged the choice of the American people, had lost the election through the deliberate conniving of a handful of politicians.

When Webster, the teller, announced the result the vast crowd of a thousand people in the chamber reacted in stunned silence, possibly surprised that the election ended so quickly. Finally, a few Adams partisans realized what had happened and burst into applause. Then the hissing started. But before it could build in volume and possibly create an incident the hypersensitive Clay immediately ordered the galleries cleared. But he overreacted. No demonstration was contemplated. None was planned. Still he could not afford to take any chances and he ordered the people removed.[68]

It was now three o'clock in the afternoon. Messengers quickly streamed to the candidates to relate the news. Nathaniel Macon told Crawford, who reacted as though deeply shocked. Jackson, now back on his feet, listened with controlled anger. Eaton and Donelson both shared his overpowering sense of defeat and loss. That certain representatives would disregard what they all knew was the will of the people staggered the three Tennesseans. That they would brazenly publicize their "depravity" for all to witness said something frightening about the present state of American political institutions. Donelson admitted he was "sickened," and not because of his uncle's defeat—that hardly mattered anymore—but "that every corrupt act was employed to draw the Representatives from their responsibility to their constituents." The "outrages upon the rights of the People, and the character of our Country," he reported, constitute a very long list. More could be anticipated before the denouement. "The closing scenes of this nefarious drama is not yet acted out, nor will it be until the 4th of March when Mr. Adams is to seal with his oath all his corrupt bargains."

Corrupt bargains! Already the term was current, and everyone knew what was involved. "It is rumoured and believed by every body here that Mr Clay will be made Secretary of State." What a scene that will be! The great and powerful Senate of the United States, that bulwark of liberty, said Donelson, will be summoned "to confirm or reject those fitting characters which his Highness may think proper to nominate as his ministers in the arduous work of administering the great concerns of the government whose first principle is *obedience to the Public*. What a farce! That Mr Adams should swear to support the constitution of the U States which he has purchased from Representatives who betrayed the constitution, and which he must distribute among them as rewards for the iniquity."[69]

Indeed. What a farce. If the people submit to this, Jackson wrote, "they may bid farewell to their freedom."[70] His concern was genuine. "I weep for the Liberty of my country," he said. The "rights of the people have been bartered for promises of office."[71]

It was a bitter defeat. Jackson's one consolation was the knowledge that he had received the approving "Judgment of an enlightened patriotic and uncorrupted people" and that he had done nothing to entice a single Representative from his duty to his constituents. "No midnight taper burnt by me; no secret conclaves were held; or cabals entered into, to persuade any to a violation of pledges given, or of instructions received."[72] Thank God he was not in Adams's position. As he repeated many times, how could any man accept election to the presidency knowing the people did not want him and that evil men through "corrupt bargains" engineered his elevation?

Adams did indeed suffer great pangs of doubt. He knew the gossip; he knew the abuse building against him. The day following the House election a committee chaired by Daniel Webster called on the New Englander and officially notified him of his election. The committee found him singularly nervous and uncomfortable. Although his election represented his highest ambition and the culmination of a career spent in public service, Adams experienced none of the overwhelming joy that should have accompanied his accomplishment. At least his Puritan training had prepared him for his ordeal. Following the precedent of Thomas Jefferson, the only previous President elected by the House, Adams simply read a statement of acceptance to the committee, which he then handed to Webster. And that act officially brought the presidential election of 1824–1825 to an end. All that remained undone was the formal offer of the state department to Henry Clay.[73]

"The Election is over," wrote Jackson to his friend John Overton, "and Mr Adams prevailed on the first Ballot." The western states were bartered away by Clay, he said, and together with Maryland they decided the outcome. "Thus you see here, the voice of the people of the west have been disregarded, and demagogues barter them as sheep in the shambles, for their own views, and personal agrandisement." Both he and Rachel were feeling better after a bad siege of illness and he expected to leave Washington in March and reach the Hermitage in April. He looked forward to returning home. It would be good to be among decent men again.[74]

But first there was a reception to attend to honor the President-elect. Monroe gave a levee on February 10 and all Washington turned out for it. The prospect of seeing the defeated Hero come face to face with the triumphant coalitionist was too much to miss. True enough, during the course of the evening, Adams and Jackson chanced upon one another. It happened so suddenly and unexpectedly that people milling around the two men instinctively stepped aside and let them confront each other. Adams was alone but Jackson, the gallant, had a "large, handsome lady on his arm."

For a moment the two men stared at each other. Then Jackson, his face betraying not a sign of anger or disappointment, came forward and reached out his hand in a gesture of hearty congratulations.

"How do you do, Mr. Adams?" he said in a bright and jovial tone of voice. "I give you my left hand, for the right, as you see, is devoted to the fair: I hope you are very well, sir."

Adams accepted the extended hand and in a voice of chilling coldness, replied: "Very well, sir: I hope Gen. Jackson is well!" The crowd felt the chill and began murmuring about how extraordinary it was to see a frontiersman, Indian fighter, and simple soldier so gracious and congenial, while the experienced diplomat, eastern gentleman, and Harvard graduate appeared stiff and rigid and unfeeling.[75]

Louis McLane watched the encounter and told his wife that Jackson congratulated Adams "in quite a manly style. This was carrying the joke too far I think. It shewed the superiority over A. for I assure you he could not have done such a thing to be a King." Jackson's behavior over the next several weeks continued to excite the admiration of everyone who saw him in action. Washington marveled. This supposedly bad-tempered and easily excitable man had locked his temper and emotions under tight control. The presidency had been stolen from him and the people had been "bartered like sheep" to serve the ambitions of demagogues, and yet Andrew Jackson went about his business with an air of serenity and calm. No rude threats. No challenges. No canings or knifings. Instead he hosted a large dinner on February 18 for twenty-two loyal supporters complete with apple toddy, punch, wine, brandy, whiskey, cider, and champagne. It cost him $86.25. They all made a night of it.[76]

The people of Washington were so awed by Jackson's "manly style" that they demonstrated their admiration for him at every opportunity. Wherever he went, either private parties or public assemblies, he was honored. Not so Adams. "He is truly an object of pity."[77] At the theater, one night, the President-elect and his family put in an appearance and immediately the actors on stage cracked several jokes alluding to the House election. Adams received them "with death like silence," according to McLane, who also attended. Then, someone started singing "The Hunters of Kentucky," which referred to Jackson's conduct at New Orleans, and instantly "a universal shout" burst from the audience followed by "repeated cheerings" for several minutes. "I really feared it would have been difficult to quell it," reported McLane. "It was an awful knell for the Prest elect—& he felt it." Then McLane put into words what a great many people were thinking in Washington. "What will he feel, when he hears this shout penetrating every part of the Union? Well may he say, he would not take the office if he could avoid it."[78]

An election so riddled with scandal, one already spoken of as a "corrupt bargain," was hardly worth the winning. Not now. Not with all the jokes and barbs and abuse that went with it. And the last scene of this "nefarious drama"—the offer of the State Department—still had to be acted out. Everyone knew it and waited for it. The suspense was awful.

Five days after the election the suspense ended. Adams fulfilled his part of the bargain and offered the "gamester" from Kentucky the post of secretary of state. Adams had no choice in making the offer, but Clay should have rejected it immediately. By now he knew the risk in accepting. Besides, he was too good a politician not to see the danger. Yet he wanted the post with such a passion that he was willing to chance everything. The position historically led straight to the presidency and he could no longer stifle his craving for the post. He hesitated for a moment when he wrote his good friend, Francis Brooke of Virginia. "I am offered that of the State, but have not yet decided. . . . What shall I do?"[79] For a week he deliberated. He agonized. Then, despite the clear signals of what would happen, despite his own awareness of the risk, he accepted the offer. In that moment he destroyed forever his presidential chances.

No sooner was Clay's decision made public than Colonel Richard M. Johnson rushed to Jackson with the news. Although he did not show it, the information clearly astonished the General. As long as Johnson remained in the room, he stayed calm. Once the colonel left, Jackson started bellowing. "So you see," he raged, "the *Judas* of the West has closed the contract and will receive the thirty pieces of silver. his end will be the same. Was there ever witnessed such a bare faced corruption in any country before?"[80]

Apparently Jackson had actually thought Clay would reject the appointment in view of the earlier reaction to the rumors of a "corrupt bargain." Clay's acceptance of the post, according to Old Hickory, proved beyond question that "a secrete understanding" to thwart the will of the people had been reached. One necessarily proved the existence of the other. When "we see the predictions verified," he wrote—and here he expressed the views of many—"when we behold two men political enemies, and as different in political sentiment as any men can be, so suddenly unite, there must be some unseen cause to produce this political phenomenon." At the very center of the government, at its core, corruption operated to deprive the people of their right of free elections. Will not this corruption now spread like a cancer? Will not outright bribery ensue? "Oh," he moaned, I "shudder for the liberty of my country."[81]

The corruption involved in the presidential election of 1825 was not whether Adams and Clay met in secret and made a deal. (Historians have been arguing over that pointless topic for generations.) The corruption was the decision to hand the presidency to Adams in open defiance of the popular will. Individual interest was placed ahead of the public good. As far as can be determined more Americans wanted Andrew Jackson as their President than anyone else. That fact was contemptuously dismissed. And to make Adams President necessitated delivering Kentucky to him—a state in which he had not obtained a single popular vote. That was corruption with a vengeance. That was corruption to shake the constitutional system to its foundations.

The election of Adams to the presidency and the appointment of Clay as secretary of state set in motion a movement that changed the course of American political history. It confirmed in Jackson's mind the need for reform and the need to restore republican principles and practices in the operation of government. Jackson must lead this reform movement and he must rally the people to his cause. "There is no other corrective of these abuses," declared Old Hickory, "but the suffrages of the people." If the electorate "calmly & judiciously [apply] this corrective, they may preserve and perpetuate the liberty of our happy country. If they do not, in less than 25 years, we will become the slaves, not of a 'military chieftain', but of such ambitious demagoges as Henry Clay."[82]

As for John Quincy Adams, the General had always thought highly of him. He believed him an "honest, virtuous man" committed to the principle that "the people have a right to govern, and that their will should be always obeyed by their constituents." But the lure of the presidency proved that even he could abandon principle and connive with demagogues. Even he would betray the people and barter his soul.

"Would it not be well," Jackson suggested to his campaign manager in Tennessee, "that the papers of Nashville and the whole State should speak out with moderate but firm disapprobation of this corruption, to give a proper tone to the people, and to draw their attention to the subject? When I see you I have much to say."[83] Whether he consciously knew it or not, Andrew Jackson had already begun the campaign for the 1828 election. Whether he knew it or not he had assumed leadership of a movement that historians would later call "Jacksonian Democracy." Whether he knew it or not he had taken command of the first reform movement in American political history.

CHAPTER 6

Organizing an Opposition

THE THEFT OF THE GOVERNMENT was the ultimate corruption. Denying Jackson's right to the presidency was so blatantly scornful of the popular will that some politicians worried for the safety of the constitutional system. If the presidency could be stolen through a corrupt bargain and power seized by a small cabal of ambitious and greedy men, then liberty itself was in jeopardy. It was time to return to the principles and spirit of the Founding Fathers.[1]

But the Jacksonian movement, as it developed, was more than a crusade to restore popular government and root out corruption. It was a recognition that the old divisions between the ideals of Jefferson and the goals of Hamilton had not vanished. It reaffirmed the principles of republicanism, principles which had been overthrown, according to the Jacksonians, by the election of John Quincy Adams. The determination of some men to steal the government in order to reassert Hamiltonian doctrines seemed obvious. The struggle launched in the eighteenth century and continued into the nineteenth still raged. It seemed perpetual: liberty versus power; virtue versus corruption; the people versus an elite.

"An issue has been fairly made, as it seems to me," wrote Vice President John C. Calhoun to Jackson at this time, "between *power* and *liberty*."[2] To preserve and perpetuate that liberty General Andrew Jackson must now lead the people and recover the presidential office.

The Radicals were the Republicans most conscious of the departure of the party from the "doctrines of '98." Many of them, following Van Buren's lead, blamed the fall from grace on President Monroe, and indeed Monroe had much to answer for. The corruption that so disfigured his administration elicited little concern from him. But the Radicals worried less about that than Monroe's amalgamation policy, a policy dedicated to obliterating the divisions between Federalists and Republicans. To undermine that policy and restore the purity of the Republican creed had always been their purpose. Unfortunately they now lacked a titular head. Crawford's physical breakdown necessitated recruiting a replacement. And it took no great political skill to figure that Andrew Jackson qualified on every count. As the principal victim of the theft of the government he made an ideal candidate. Best of all, Jackson's own principles of government—commitment to debt reduction, minimal government, and states' rights—accorded precisely with those of the Radicals. Ironically, then, the man who despised the former leader of the Radicals was soon to replace him as their new party head. By linking Jackson's enormous popularity around the country—a fact not lost on the Radicals—to their commitment to strict republicanism, a party of reform could be organized that would "preserve and perpetuate the liberty of our happy country."[3]

Thus, the Jacksonian movement as it began had nothing to do with the desire of southerners to protect slavery,[4] as sometimes suggested. Despite the Missouri Compromise, that "alarm bell" in the night, it had nothing to do with the "peculiar institution." Slavery was not the coalescing force drawing Republicans together behind Jackson. Nor did slavery represent any great fear among them. The coalescing force was the desire to protect liberty. The great fear was the loss of the government to men who lusted after money and power and would sacrifice liberty to attain them.[5] The "honorable men in this great republic," said Henry Lee to Jackson at the end of the 1828 campaign, "hope by electing you to preserve our liberty."[6]

Immediately upon the announcement of Adams's election, rumors began circulating that a new political alliance had been formed to put down the coalition. Senator Rufus King of New York reported a Jackson-Calhoun combination in train. A "Party is forming itself here to oppose Mr. Adams' administration," he wrote. "South Carolina is headquarters, and I understand that a Dinner takes place today [at] the Quarters of this Delegation, when Gen'l Jackson, Mr. Calhoun . . . and others are to be guests. . . . This first step may serve to combine the malcontents."[7] Although nothing anywhere near a formal alliance developed during this meeting it was, as King suggested, the first step toward that goal.

An alliance between Jackson and Calhoun was natural enough. As secretary of war, Calhoun had always catered to Jackson's needs and temperament—except during the Seminole incident. Now that Clay had a clear shot at the presidency after Adams, Calhoun recognized that his future belonged with Old Hickory. Besides, after what had happened in Pennsylvania he realized that many Americans regarded a Jackson-Calhoun union as appropriate and natural. Finally, there was Jackson's enormous popularity to think about, something not yet tested to its fullest. For the General, a union with the South Carolinian was not unthinkable. Although some of his friends had doubts about Calhoun's loyalty and his true feelings during the Seminole affair, Jackson brushed them aside. "On the subject of Mr Calhoun," he wrote the year before, "I have no doubts myself, but his friends acted agreable to his understanding & instructions; & that he is sincere in his wishes—some have doubted this, but I have not—and I can give you when we meet reasons that will convince you I cannot be mistaken."[8] Besides, this union with the Vice President was a logical step if Jackson intended to coalesce his forces, turn the rascals out of office, and restore the government to the people from whom it had been stolen.

So the work of fashioning opposition to the Adams administration began almost at once. And although Jackson was anxious to escape Washington and return to his farm in Tennessee, he felt a keen obligation to remain at his post until the end of the session. If nothing else, there was the Clay confirmation to witness, and Jackson wished to participate in that small drama.

The inauguration of John Quincy Adams took place on Friday, March 4, 1825, and went off without incident. "After two successive sleepless nights," Adams recorded, "I entered upon this day with a supplication to Heaven, first, for my country; secondly, for myself and for those connected with my good name and fortunes, that the last results of its events may be auspicious and blessed."[9] At 7:30 in the morning he left his house accompanied by a militia and several prominent citizens and made his way to the Capitol, where he was sworn in by Chief Justice John Marshall. Earlier in the morning John C. Calhoun took the oath of office as Vice President in the Senate chamber. In a gracious gesture the members of the Senate voted Jackson, as oldest member—he was less than two weeks shy of his fifty-eighth birthday—to administer the oath to Calhoun. The two men, tall and erect, stood facing each other, their brilliant eyes locked in a magnetic embrace.[10]

After the inauguration there was a general rush to the White House to congratulate the new occupant. Jackson joined the throng and was one of the first to take the President's hand and express his good wishes—or whatever seemed fitting to say to an administration he wished to pull down. Supposedly, Jackson spotted an old friend in one of the rooms of the mansion and said with great emotion, "Colonel, you know how I must feel."[11] Jackson's bitterness—and a touch of "sour grapes"—also peeked out from several letters he wrote at the time. "Yesterday Mr Adams was inaugurated amidst a vast assemblage of citizens," he told Samuel Swartwout of New York, "having been escorted to the Capitol with a pomp and ceremony of guns & drums not very consistent, in my humble opinion, with the character of the occasion.—Twenty four years ago when Mr Jefferson was inducted into office no such machinery was called in to give solemnity to the occasion—he rode his own horse and hitched himself to the enclosure. But it seems that times are changed—I hope it is not so with the principles that are to characterise the administration of Justice and constitutional law. These in my fervent prayers for the prosperity and good of our country will I hope remain unaltered, based upon the sovereignty of the people and adorned with no forms or ceremonies save those which thru happiness and freedom shall command."[12]

The day following the inauguration the nominations for cabinet posts went to the Senate for confirmation, and the voting on them took place on March 7. There was never any question of the outcome. Even on Clay's nomination as secretary of state, the opposition surfaced only in the recorded vote of yeas and nays. Twenty-seven senators voted for approval, including Van Buren and Thomas Hart Benton. Fifteen voted against confirmation, including the two Tennesseans, Eaton and Jackson. The remaining negative votes came mostly from Radicals such as Thomas W. Cobb, Nathaniel Macon, and Henry Tazewell. Another seven senators absented themselves from the vote, such as Richard M. Johnson of Kentucky who left the city the previous week.

For all intents and purposes the vote on confirmation ended the congressional session, a session that had done little more than elect a president. A few days later Jackson and his wife packed their belongings and headed for home, propelled by a fierce desire to escape the "polluted" city and return to family and friends in Tennessee. The Hero left Washington angry and bitter, but he masked his true feelings and acted out the role of defeated candidate with dignity and grace.

Only during the voyage home did he occasionally lose control. For one thing it was a triumphal march; for another the people he met along the way assured him that he, Jackson, was the rightful President and that the will of the people had been bargained away by power-hungry politicians. At Baltimore there was a ball given in his honor. The following day a cavalcade escorted him beyond the town limits to demonstrate the city's appreciation for his visit. Everywhere he reviewed the troops drawn up for his inspection and in most towns the people turned out *en masse* to salute and applaud him. What touched him particularly was the almost universal expression of disappointment over his defeat. It was their defeat, too, they told him. It was the defeat of constitutional and republican government. At West Alexandria, Pennsylvania, the General met an old comrade by the name of Edward McLaughlin who came up to him and offered his sympathy. The voters by the free exercise of their suffrage had done all they could for their hero to elect him President, McLaughlin angrily asserted, "but the rascals at Washington cheated you out of it."

"Cheated." The word clanged inside Jackson's head. "Indeed, my old friend," the Hero blurted out, "there was *cheating*, and *corruption*, and *bribery* too."[13] In each town he visited the people cried out their chagrin and disappointment that their will had been callously and contemptuously set aside by a cabal of politicians. Jackson invariably replied in heated tones about the widespread corruption that now infected the entire government apparatus and how it must be purged if the liberties of the people were to survive. By the time Old Hickory reached the Hermitage he was in high dudgeon about that "poor Devil H Clay" and how through "corruption intrigue and management" he procured the office of secretary of state for himself.[14] He could hardly wait for the next election so that he could have his revenge. For the moment, however, he kept his peace. "My friends say," he told Lewis, "I should not answer whether I'll run in 1828 or resign my seat."[15]

Before leaving Washington Jackson had written a letter to Samuel Swartwout calling into question Clay's reference to him as a "Military Chieftain" as the reason for not supporting him in the House election. This reference had appeared in a letter Clay wrote to Francis Brooke of Virginia and published in the Washington newspapers on February 12. The implication, of course, was that Clay feared for the liberties of the people if a military man sat in the White House. Jackson's response showed deep feeling, and when Swartwout received it he knew he had strong political propaganda which he could use to Old Hickory's advantage. So he published it—without asking Jackson's prior consent. The letter contained several strong passages. For example: "It is very true that early in life, even in the days of boyhood, I contributed my mite to shake off the yoke of tyranny, and to build up the fabrick of free government; and when lately our country was involved in war . . . I made an appeal to the patriotism of the western citizens . . . to support her Eagles. If this can constitute me a 'Military Chieftain' I am one." Then he let fly at Clay. "The cause of freedom and the rights of men," he stormed, would be far safer in the hands of military men than certain demagogues who will do anything for power.

> Mr. Clay never yet has risked himself for his country, sacrificed his repose, or made an effort to repel an invading foe. . . . He who fights, and fights successfully must . . . be held up as a "Military Chieftain": even Washington could he again appear among us might be so considered, because he dared to be a virtuous and successful soldier, an honest states-man, and a correct man. . . .
>
> I have as you very well know, by some of the designing politicians of this country, been charged with taking bold and high-handed measures; but as they were not designed for any benefit to myself I should under similar circumstances not refrain from a course equally bold; that man who in time of difficulty and danger shall halt at any course, necessary to maintain the rights and privileges and independence of the country, is unsuited to au-thority; and if these opinions and sentiments shall entitle me to the name and character of a Military Chieftain I am content so to be considered.[16]

The letter received wide newspaper circulation. This pleased Jackson, and since he had not authorized its publication he escaped criticism for his harsh judgments of Clay. "Mr Clay has used no delicacy toward me," the General wrote Swartwout after being informed of the publication, "and as I have never written any thing whether private or public which my heart and judgement did not sanction, I am not afraid of the publication of those remarks, or any other which I may have made."[17] Clay, of course, could not resist ridiculing Jackson's patriotic self-praise. In an address to his constituents, principally written to answer the bargain charge against him, his delightful sense of humor made light of all the General's comments. Clay even admitted that it had been his "misfortune never to have repelled an invading foe" or led his countrymen to military victory. "If I had," he snickered as he inserted the needle, "I should have left to others to proclaim and appreciate the deed."[18]

Jackson had just arrived at the Hermitage growling his imprecations over his electoral defeat when a copy of Clay's address to his constituents reached him. As he scanned the pages he slowly shook his head. He disregarded Clay's response to his own letter and concentrated instead on the explanations about the bargain.

Jackson muttered his contempt. The address was written, he said, "in a begging cringing tone" to free him of the "corrupt bargain" charge, "but he steers entirely clear of denying this charge. The various papers are commenting on it. . . . how little common sense this man displays. . . . silence would have been to him wisdom."[19]

Within a matter of weeks—nay days—of the House election the major issue of the presidential campaign of 1828 had been cast. The "corrupt bargain" charge entered the newspapers, as Jackson said, and never left. Over and over it was repeated for the next three years. Over and over the Jacksonians reiterated it to demonstrate the need for reform. Over and over it reminded Americans of the moral failures of their age.

In easy doses for the rest of the spring and summer Jackson mixed politics with the running of his farm and the entertainment of his many visitors, the most distinguished of whom was the Marquis de Lafayette, followed later by Frances Wright, the feminist reformer. Lafayette's visit caught Old Hickory at a bad moment. As a result of too much sitting in Washington and too much horseback riding at the Hermitage he suffered "an inflamation in the rectum which communicated to the bladder and affected the prostate glands." Even so he roused himself from his bed to welcome the touring Frenchman and make him feel comfortable.[20] By the end of the summer dozens of visitors had huddled with Jackson and advised him about his future. Apparently there was never any question about running in 1828. The General was told that he owed it to the country, that the people expected him to put down the men who had shown contempt for their will. Tennessee politicians demonstrated what they meant. In October, 1825, before the Adams administration had had a chance to address itself to Congress and propose a program of legislation, the Tennessee legislature passed a resolution that lacked unanimity by three votes but which recommended to the American people that

Andrew Jackson by virtue of his public services and political qualifications merited election to the presidency in 1828.[21] In other words, even before the Adams administration had an opportunity to begin, Tennessee leveled a brickbat at it by declaring that it needed to be replaced at the earliest possible moment. This action officially launched the presidential election of 1828.

At approximately the same time Jackson decided he would no longer continue as United States senator. In the first place his election to the post had come under very unusual circumstances. He never really wanted the office and then found himself in an awkward position when the presidential election landed in the House of Representatives. If he continued as senator, now that he was again a presidential contender, that awkwardness could become acute. Besides, if he intended to give more attention to the campaign—and he did—he was probably better off staying at the Hermitage, where he could meet with politicians relatively free from observation. He might then direct the activities of his friends in their efforts to organize a political party in his behalf.

So Jackson made up his mind to resign (for which he had the consent of his closest advisers) and to submit his resignation personally to the legislature. Upon notification of his nomination for the presidency, Jackson hurried off to the state capital at Murfreesborough to announce his retirement. As soon as they learned of his coming the legislators in both houses invited him to appear before them and address the assembled members. Jackson readily accepted. If nothing else he wanted this relatively large gathering to serve as a public forum to hammer at the theme of "fraud and corruption and intrigue" in Washington which was threatening the liberty of the American people. He also wanted everyone to have his assurance that while everyone else stooped to intrigue and management, he, Old Hickory, had remained pure and unsullied.

The address showed all his political art. To start, Jackson carefully reminded his audience that he had never sought the position to which they had selected him and, of course, he would continue to serve if his "feeble aid" might in some way advance the "security of our Republican system." But he doubted that he was needed in Washington. Moreover, in view of the recent resolution of the legislature in "proposing again my name to the American people for the Office of chief magistrate of the Union," he felt constrained "to ask your indulgence to be excused from any further service in the counsils of the Country." That done, he hurried to his principal concern. Using the likelihood of a proposed amendment to the Constitution being brought before Congress to limit the tenure of the president to a single term of four or six years, Jackson identified his target and drew a bead on it. He not only approved such an amendment so that "some new barier to the encroachments of power or corruption in any of the departments of government" could be provided, but he suggested a provision "rendering any member of Congress ineligible to office under the general government for and during the term for which he was elected." That remark was aimed straight at Clay. The danger to liberty is the breakdown of the system of checks and balances, he said, and the proposed amendment would provide additional protection for that system. "There is no truth more sacred in *politics;* and none more conclusively stamped upon all the state constitutions, as well as the federal constitution, than that, which requires the three great departments of power—the Legislative, Judicial, and Executive to keep seperate and apart." Jackson then drove home his point.

> But if this change in the constitution should not be attained, and important appointments continue to devolve upon the Representatives in Congress, it requires no depth of thought to be convinced, that corruption will become the order of the day, and under the garb of consciencious sacrifices to establish precedents for the public good, evil may arise of serious importance to the freedom and prosperity of the Republic. It is through this channel that the people may expect to be attacked in their constitutional sovereignty, and where tyranny may well be apprehended to spring up in some favourable emergency.[22]

The legislature accepted Jackson's resignation, recognizing the delicate situation that confronted him, and elected Judge Hugh Lawson White of east Tennessee to serve out the General's four last remaining years. White was expected to be a useful member of the Senate, both to the state and to Old Hickory.

Jackson's return to retirement and the care of his farm and children[23] in no way diverted his attention from the presidential contest. He kept up a vast correspondence with his supporters in every section of the country, repeating the charges of corruption against the Adams administration and where appropriate suggesting courses of action to his friends to gain political advantage.[24] He read dozens of newspapers to keep himself informed. Nothing escaped his roving political eye. "I observe the 8th of Janry has this year passed without notice in the City of Washington," he commented to Edward Livingston, "not so elsewhere. It might be dangerous *now* in Washington, to commemorate *military chieftains*—hereafter the defence of our country will be left to the splendour of the government, not to the arms of military chieftains supported by the yeomanry of the nation."[25] Always he took a swing at Clay. He was especially anxious to nail the secretary on the charge that he deliberately and contemptuously disregarded the express wish of the people in Kentucky as transmitted through the legislature. The idea of delivering Kentucky to a candidate who had not received a single vote in the state seemed the height of arrogance and presumption. Surely that "poor Devil H Clay" knows, as everyone else does, said Jackson, "his corruption, and the abandonment of those republican principles which gave him the confidence of the people for the pitiful consideration of the office of

Sect of State. He must have felt his humbled situation to have kissed the hand and bowed the neck to Mr. Adams."[26]

In addition to extending and strengthening his ties with political leaders in many states, Jackson also met the ever-increasing number of committees that appeared at his door to discuss the campaign, request information, and assure him of their support and determination next time to obtain the necessary majority of electoral votes. As a matter of fact toward the close of the campaign he could not step outside the Hermitage without stumbling over some committee or other "who took possession of him bodily, conveyed him to some public banqueting ball, and got him on his legs to speak."[27] However, Jackson carefully avoided the appearance of electioneering. A candidate for the presidency in the 1820s did not actively seek the office. That was considered unseemly. It violated the tenets of true republicanism. So Old Hickory exercised extreme caution in what he did and what he said. He was so attuned to the political implications of his behavior and their effect on the public he even refused a request by Rachel which he knew meant a great deal to her. They were walking one Sunday to the little Hermitage church he had built for her in 1823 when she turned to him and asked him point-blank to join the church and take communion with her. "My dear," he replied in a grave but gentle voice, "if I were to do that now, it would be said, all over the country, that I had done it for the sake of political effect. My enemies would all say so. I can not do it *now*, but I promise you that when once more I am clear of politics I will join the church." Years later, after the death of his wife, Jackson remembered his words and as he did so he broke down in tears.[28]

Jackson's prudence in playing the role of reluctant candidate did not in any way change the fact that he alone headed the elaborate apparatus starting to emerge in 1826 to engineer his election to the presidency. The Jackson party, as it slowly formed over the next several years, took its direction in large measure from the General himself. Not that other leading politicians from other states did not make substantial contributions. They did indeed—vital contributions. But the overall head of the party soon to call itself the "Democratic Republican" party or simply Democratic party was Andrew Jackson.

There was never any serious doubt about that. He served as catalyst drawing several factions together to form a new "combination."[29] He provided the charisma that attracted the popular following.

The evolution of the Democratic party began as a faction of men devoted to Jackson personally. At the center of the Jackson party was a group of Nashville cronies headed by the General himself that included such worthies as John Overton, Hugh Lawson White, William B. Lewis, John H. Eaton, and to some extent Felix Grundy, Sam Houston, and G. W. Campbell. Later they were joined by others in Nashville and elsewhere in Tennessee, particularly when the Calhoun and Crawford factions joined the Jackson party. These men functioned in several capacities. They prepared statements for the newspapers, they corresponded with a wide network of politicians around the country, and they sometimes traveled to other states to visit local central committees set up to provide organizational support for Jackson. In time they formed the Nashville Central Committee. They established communication with state and local committees and with a central committee in Washington. They provided much of the propaganda and campaign material for the election of 1828.[30]

The creation of the Democratic party took several years and the combined efforts of dedicated politicians from every section of the country. Eventually they nailed together an organization structured for the advancement of Jackson and the restoration of republicanism. "What a pleasure it is to see that party almost unbroken rising in almost every part of the Union to put down the men who would have corrupted and betrayed it," said one politician.[31]

The most important work of organization took place in Washington, and that phase of the operation began when Congress reconvened in December, 1825. The Jacksonians began their assault on the administration almost immediately, pressuring fence-sitters to recognize that a two-sided contest was developing and that they must take sides. They had a powerful weapon in their arsenal right from the beginning: the bargain. And they wielded it unmercifully. John Randolph of Roanoke, the eccentric if not addled Senator from Virginia, lambasted the coalition in a speech in the upper chamber by calling it "the coalition of Blifill and Black George . . . the Puritan and the black-leg."[32] Outraged by these remarks, Clay challenged Randolph to a duel and they shot it out on the southern shore of the Potomac River. Both men escaped injury but Clay drilled a hole through Randolph's coat.[33]

President Adams also assisted in the initial stages of the organization of the Democratic party. In rapid succession he committed a series of blunders that reinforced the notion that his administration aimed at seizing power to benefit the few and that it cared nothing for the popular will. His first important blunder came on December 6, 1825, when he submitted his annual message to Congress. In a bold, courageous, statesmanlike, and politically inept assertion of the government's responsibilities to advance the intellectual and economic well-being of the country, Adams laid before Congress a program of public works of breathtaking magnitude, a program immediately denounced by the Radicals and Jacksonians as unconstitutional and visionary. Rooted in Clay's American System, which advocated leadership by the central government to stimulate and influence the economy, the message offered a wide range of proposals that left the Radicals and Jacksonians gasping in disbelief. "The great object of the institution of civil government," the President averred, "is the improvement of the condition of those who are parties to the social compact, and no government, in whatever form constituted, can accomplish the lawful end of its institution but in proportion as it improved the condition of those over whom it is established." In keeping with this principle he proposed the establishment of a national university and an astronomical observatory, the building of an extensive system of roads and canals, the exploration of the western territories and the northeastern coastline, and the creation of a naval academy similar to West Point. It was a stupendous program and one that would take time and money. To accomplish these ends, said Adams in the most appalling statement of the message, the Congress must not give the rest of the world the impression "that we are palsied by the will of our constituents."[34]

An incredible blunder. He invited the Congress to disregard the will of the people—just as he himself had done a few months before. Had he planned it Adams could not have said anything much worse. To provide economic benefit for the few—or so it seemed—the President asked Congress to exercise enormous power (power some denied the Congress possessed) and never mind the people. The Jacksonians guffawed. What further proof did anyone need that Adams and his crew were plundering buccaneers in illegal possession of the government? This message only encouraged the Jacksonians to claim that they represented the democracy against a coalition committed to a moneyed aristocracy. Soon other friendly politicians throughout the country were agreeing that "the approaching contest is, I think, more now than at any former period considered by the sound planters, farmers & mechanics of the country, as a great contest between the *aristocracy* and democracy of America."[35]

Many of these politicians shared their sense of outrage with Jackson by writing him long, impassioned letters. He responded sympathetically, and then took the occasion to state his own position.

> When I view the splendor & magnificence of the government embraced in the recommendation of the late message, with the powers enumerated, which may be rightfully exercised by congress to lead to this magnificence, together with the declaration that it would be criminal for the agents of our government to be palsied by the will of their constituents, I shudder for the consequence—if not checked by the voice of the people, it must end in consolidation, & then in despotism—Yet, I have great confidence in the intelligence, and virtue, of the great body of the american people,—they never will abandon the constitutional ship,—their voice will be roused, & must be heard—Instead of building lighthouses of the skies, establishing national universities, and making explorations round the globe—their language will be, pay the national debt—prepare for national independence, & defense—then apportion the surplus revenue amongst the several states for the education of the poor—leaving the superintendence of education to the states respectively. This will be the safe course to perpetuate our happy government.[36]

Probably as a group the politicians most horrified by what Adams had said in his message were the Radicals. They were utterly dumbfounded —not by the political blunder but by the major proposals. As strict constructionists, as ardent advocates of states' rights, and as fiscal conservatives they were appalled by Adams's program of public works. "The message of the President," sputtered Nathaniel Macon, "seems to claim all the power to the federal Government . . . which the election of Mr. Jefferson was supposed to have settled."[37] As a consequence, the Radicals, led by Martin Van Buren, edged closer to the Jacksonians over the next several months and seriously contemplated inviting the General's friends to help them to extinguish Adams's "lighthouses in the sky," as they derisively termed his program. Those who took the trouble to communicate with Jackson himself were delighted to find his response absolutely in tune with their own thinking.

Adams's message also included a separate item on a proposed conference of delegates from Central and South America to be held in Panama to discuss problems of mutual concern. The United States had been invited to attend the previous spring, and the secretary of state saw it as a marvelous opportunity to cement relations among the nations of the Americas. Such a Congress, Clay figured, would also buttress the cause of independence throughout South America, something wholly in keeping with the spirit of the Monroe Doctrine.

But Jackson hated the idea. "The moment we engage in confederations, or alliances with any nation," he wrote, "we may from that time date the down fall of our republic." The ground taken by the President, he continued, has rightly alarmed "the republicans of the old school of 1798–9." It constitutes an unwarranted invasion of the treaty-making power of the Senate and is nothing less than a barefaced "attempt to destroy the constitutional checks of our government, and to reduce it to a despotism . . . to register the *edicts* of the President." The danger to the nation's freedom was obvious. "It would seem to me," Jackson declared, "that the consent of the people to the expediency of this measure should have been first had, at least by their representatives in congress."[38]

The Radicals agreed totally with Jackson. For them the Panama Congress constituted a serious departure from the established foreign policy of Washington and Jefferson. Like Jackson they worried about it becoming a vehicle to advance the powers of the central government, and in particular the powers of the President. When they learned that Old Hickory had expressed constitutional views basically in accord with their own, many of them were prepared to hail him as their next presidential candidate. What Jackson said could not have been better: "To be represented at a congress of Independant confederated nations, is an event, which I presume, the framers of our constitution never thought of, whilst deliberating upon those enumerated powers, which they conceived necessary & proper, to be given to our confederated government."[39]

Not much later Van Buren decided to visit Vice President Calhoun at his home to talk further about the attitude and position of the Jacksonians on the issue. He simply assumed that Jackson and Calhoun had allied themselves since Clay's appointment. Actually nothing of the kind had yet taken place. No matter. Van Buren was pleased to learn of the Vice President's personal opposition to the conference and the two men ended their brief discussion with an implicit understanding of what they would do.[40]

On December 26, 1825, Adams formally proposed the Panama Mission to Congress by nominating Richard C. Anderson of Kentucky and John Sergeant of Pennsylvania as ministers and William B. Rochester of New York as secretary. The Senate promptly took up the question and the opposition prepared to filibuster it to death. Robert Y. Hayne of South Carolina delivered a notable speech against it as did John Randolph. In his usual acerbic style, and with a sharp poke at Clay, Randolph pronounced the Panama Mission a "Kentucky cuckoo's egg, laid in a Spanish-American nest."[41]

The debate on the issue dragged on interminably, but by the middle of March the administration fought off an opposition resolution declaring the conference inexpedient and won confirmation of the ministers and the secretary. But that did not end the fight. The House tried to hold up the appropriations for the Mission as a means of expressing its opposition but again all it succeeded in doing was to delay approval until early May. Still the delay provided a victory of sorts. One of the envoys died en route to the conference and, because of the delay, the other envoy did not arrive in Panama until after the congress had adjourned.

Thus, by the spring of 1826, a slowly developing opposition to the administration, consisting of Jacksonians, Radicals, and Calhoun men, existed in Congress, which soon burgeoned into a national political party. Adams's repeated stumbling over issues encouraged the opposition to speak out against him and to plan their strategy to defeat his program. This growing hostility finally nudged John C. Calhoun into the Jackson camp. Early in June, 1826, he wrote directly to the General and indicated his willingness to cooperate in the next campaign to rid the government of the present administration. "I believe," he said, ". . . that the liberties of the country are in danger." This was not simply his opinion but that "of the coolest and most considerate of our citizens." The question is whether "power and patronage of the Executive or the voice of the people" will constitute "the real governing principle in our political system." If power can be acquired against the dictates of the majority "our government may indeed retain the forces of freedom, but its sperit will be gone." If the presidency can be transmitted through corruption and management then "we shall soon consider the form of electing by the people a mere farce." I hope for better things, Calhoun said. Your name, General Jackson, "is found, as it always has been, on the side of liberty, and your country." That you may be the "instrument" "of confounding political machinations and of turning the attempts against the liberty of the country, into the means of perpetuating our freedom, is my sincere wish."[42]

To this heartfelt pledge of support, Jackson responded in tones of similar concern and commitment. "I embrace the earliest opportunity to thank you," he said. I have watched the administration and its direction in domestic and foreign affairs "& I am happy to see that the Republicans so well sustained themselves in the just defence of the liberty of the country." Sir, said the Hero, "the people are awake, and are virtuous" and their voice and strength is with us.

> I trust that my name will always be found on the side of the people, and as their confidence in your talents and virtue has placed you in the second office of the government, that we shall march hand in hand in their cause. With an eye single to the preservation of our happy form of government, the missiles of slander will fall harmless at your feet. The approbation of the virtuous yeomanry of the country will constitute a shield which the administration cannot destroy—it will live when the abuse of its [*illegible*] presses shall be forgotten.[43]

The forging of the political link between Calhoun and Jackson was the first important action that eventually produced the Democratic party. It constituted a major step in the structural building of that party by uniting two factions—one essentially southern, the other western—albeit both personal. Less than six months later this initial linking was followed by the decision of Martin Van Buren, the most prominent leader of the Radical faction, to join the Jackson party. This decision—if the Radicals followed his lead—not only meant the strengthening of the southern wing of the Jackson party but gave it powerful northern strength as well.

Sometime late in 1826 Van Buren made his cold and crafty decision. He recognized Old Hickory's popularity. He understood Jackson's central position in all future political developments. Most important of all, he appreciated the need of the Radicals to reassert their doctrines of government in any reordering of political ties. Andrew Jackson was the single answer to all Radical needs and aspirations. "If Jackson was to die," wrote one Radical, "I cannot say how things might turn—rely on it, *he* is the only man that can break down this union. If he can be placed under an honest Cabinet it is the best we can do the Country at present. . . . Any thing to get clear of this cursed union of *'puritan and blackleg.'* "[44] Van Buren also appreciated the mood of the American people. Old Hickory was *their* candidate, cheated of his rights by corrupt and designing politicians. Common sense, if nothing else, dictated a switch to the Hero.

But Van Buren's move to join the Jacksonian party represented a deliberate attempt to revive the two-party system in American politics. Unlike the Founding Fathers, who cursed parties as divisive and destructive, the Magician regarded the party system as an essential ingredient for representative government. Modern, efficient government, he preached, demanded well-functioning political parties openly arrayed against each other. Without parties, a democracy cannot function. A well-defined two-party system provides a balance of power between opposing forces and this in turn safeguards liberty and the institutions of republicanism. The era of a one-party system under James Monroe produced a concentration of power in Washington that necessarily generated corruption and led inexorably to the fraudulent election of John Quincy Adams. Only a revival of the two-party system could restore the healthy interplay between opposing interests and insure order and stability.[45]

Van Buren envisaged a party system consisting of Adams and Clay and their friends on one side, advocating Hamiltonian principles, and Jackson, Calhoun, and the Radicals, on the other side, committed to Jeffersonian principles. Thus, when Van Buren set out to join the Jackson camp he did so not simply to defeat Adams—important as that was—but rather to connect Jackson's enormous popularity around the country with republican principles by which the nation could once more function under a constitutional form of government with the liberties of the people adequately protected. If Jackson were to be elected President in 1828 that election must mean something, something more than personal triumph. Something more than patronage. It must be made to represent the restoration of the two-party system and the rededication of Republicans to the old Jeffersonian doctrines of '98.[46]

Since Jackson had resigned his Senate seat and was not readily available, Van Buren decided to go to the Vice President and see if they could agree to an alliance that would serve all their goals and interests. Later the Magician sent James A. Hamilton, the son of Alexander Hamilton, to visit Jackson at the Hermitage and serve as his emissary. The General responded very favorably to this arrangement and showed particular interest in understanding the character of the public men in New York, especially the differences between Van Buren and De Witt Clinton, one of Jackson's oldest northern supporters.[47]

Van Buren concentrated on Calhoun. The two men met late in December, 1826, at the home of William H. Fitzhugh of Virginia. Coming straight to the point, Van Buren offered Radical support for the election of Jackson in 1828. The Little Magician sat leisurely in an oversized chair, one leg dangling over the other, calmly reviewing the need for a reinvigorated party structured around Jackson and dedicated to pure republicanism. Such a party, he said, would unite the north and the south and forge an alliance between what he later termed "the planters of the South and the plain Republicans of the North." A Jackson victory, Van Buren contended, "as the result of his military services without reference to party . . . would be one thing. His election as the result of a combined and concerted effort of a political party, holding, in the main, to certain tenets and opposed to certain prevailing principles, might be another and far different thing."[48]

To initiate their "combination," Van Buren told Calhoun that he would write to Thomas Ritchie, editor of the Richmond *Enquirer* and a leader of the Richmond Junto, the political machine controlling Virginia, and seek his support for their alliance. A New York–Virginia axis would appeal to all Jeffersonians, no matter their geographical location. Later, Van Buren promised to tour the south personally and talk with other leading Radicals, including Crawford himself. Although it would be very difficult for some Radicals to accept Calhoun on account of his treatment of Crawford in the Monroe cabinet, the Magician thought his southern tour would help bring them around. Besides, they had nowhere else to go.[49]

The irony of Jackson inheriting Crawford's political following was not lost on anybody. Irony aside, Van Buren believed that their party would begin with a sound basis in principles and personnel. The election of Andrew Jackson in 1828 would signal the return of republicanism to government. It would be the beginning of an era of reform.

All the while Van Buren spoke, the Vice President stared at the little man, his magnetic eyes fixed on its object. Finally the Magician finished his presentation and waited for a response. There was a moment's pause, then Calhoun rose from his chair and stretched out his hand. With a smile, Van Buren grasped it eagerly.[50]

CHAPTER 7

"Jackson and Reform"

IT IS NOT SURPRISING that over the next two years Andrew Jackson continued to develop ideas about the causes of his defeat in Congress in 1825 and the agents responsible. That he had been talking incessantly about intrigue and corruption and fraud everyone knew. But now he expressed the conspiracy in terms of an aristocracy seeking power to pursue their own selfish ends. The concentration of power in Washington was the means to achieve these ends and Jackson realized with even greater force than before that his prime objective as President must be the reduction of government participation in the affairs of the American people.

Jackson believed in conspiracies—always did. Simplistic though they were, they provided compelling explanations to account for the bizarre and mysterious in human events. For Old Hickory it made sense to interpret the election of 1824–1825 as a conspiracy of aristocrats seeking power to acquire wealth. Through Clay they arranged Adams's election to the presidency and he repaid them by proposing a program of economic development via the building of roads and bridges and canals that would make the federal government a partner with business in the financial prosperity of the upper class.

Quite naturally, then, Jackson saw his role as the champion of the people. He spoke of them as virtuous and he identified his own will with theirs. The rhetoric of the Democratic party would soon praise the people as good and wise and capable of self-rule, and much of that tone and attitude originated with Jackson—or at least got a powerful assist from him. Also, quite naturally, Old Hickory regarded the movement to place him at the head of the government as one of reform. An era of reform must succeed this era of corruption. His first responsibility, he said, once he became President, would be to "reform the Government" and "purify the Departments" by removing every corrupt agent who had obtained his position through "political considerations or against the will of the people." The exercise of executive patronage through expanded federal power had brought the American experiment in freedom and democracy to the brink of disaster. By reducing government and emptying the departments of all who held their positions to serve special interests he would restore republican rule.[1]

As for specific issues, Jackson's ideas in the late 1820s seemed more reflective, more moderate, and less overweening than they had been. Much of his thinking represented a politician's concern for the broad consensus in order to win election; but some of it indicated Jackson's developing capacity to appreciate another point of view. Only a few issues seemed stuck in a fixed position. On banks and the money question, for example, the Hero hardly budged. He linked them to the general corruption of the times—indeed he regarded them as a major cause—and condemned them as dangerous to the safety of free institutions. On the money question—hard or soft—he entertained very extreme views. Hard money—specie—had his wholehearted endorsement, but paper money he regarded as the instruments of banks to spread their corruption. "Ragg money" weakened the fabric of society and enabled the rich to fatten themselves at the expense of the poor.[2] On the tariff and internal improvements Jackson could be flexible, depending on their relation to the national interest in areas such as defense, but on the Indians he was resolved to remove them west of the Mississippi River. A program of removal had already started and he had participated in it. But this initial effort constituted a very small beginning. Thousands of Indians still resided within the southern and western states and they needed to be removed—for the good of everyone concerned.[3]

Although Jackson's understanding and appreciation of the major issues of the 1820s matured and moderated somewhat, he became extremely cautious and circumspect in giving them voice. There was always the danger of entrapment. The opposition was seen as malevolent and vindictive, necessitating the exercise of every precaution against unwittingly assisting them in their treachery. Yet Jackson's cooperation in providing information and resolving troublesome problems steadily increased as the campaign progressed. Some politicians even demanded personal appearances on some pretext or other, such as celebrating a patriotic day. Although Jackson was really tempted by this innovative campaigning technique, discretion plus Rachel's faltering health convinced him to shy away.[4] Another problem in appearing before the public was the increasing difficulty he experienced with speaking in a declamatory way on account of the loss of many of his teeth. Because of rapid decay, advanced by his overuse of calomel and the general wretched state of his health, Jackson began losing most of his upper teeth between 1826 and 1828.

Finally he consented to wearing dentures. "Genl A. Jackson with comple-
ments to Mr. Earle," he wrote, "requests his attention to getting Doctor
Putnam to finish my teeth. If the Doctor should want my presence the
Genl will thank Mr. Earle to say to the Doctor he must ride up on
tomorrow or Saturday." Jackson thoroughly disliked the ill-fitting dentures and frequently refused to wear them. So it was extremely difficult
and unpleasant for him during this period to appear at a public forum.
Thus, when he was invited to speak at the anniversary meeting of the
Davidson County Bible Society he refused for two reasons: his problem
of articulation and because "I might be charged by my political enemies
with having come forth hypocritically under the sacred garb of religion
thus to electioner."[5]

As the presidential campaign gained momentum in 1827 and as a
swelling army of political managers appeared on the scene to direct a
vigorous demonstration of support for Old Hickory,[6] Jackson was hard-
pressed to meet all the obligations they placed on him: their call for
information; the plea for clarification; the necessity of explaining his
behavior in connection with one event or another. Why had he voted
against George Washington in the House of Representatives in 1796?
What part did he play in the Burr Conspiracy? How did he justify jailing
Judge Hall in New Orleans following the Battle of New Orleans?[7] The
execution of a number of militiamen brought a particularly aggressive
propaganda campaign by the opposition that required Jackson's assistance in answering. The executions of Ambrister and Arbuthnot, the
killing of Charles Dickinson, the tavern brawl with the Bentons—all demanded justifications. But perhaps the most devastating charge leveled
at Jackson, as the campaign swung into full operation, involved the circumstances of his marriage to Rachel. Since General Jackson had taken
a high moral position in this campaign and decried the corruption in
Washington and around the country, the friends of the administration
revived the charge that his was an adulterous and bigamous marriage and
challenged him to explain his own reprehensible behavior in running off
with another man's wife.

As circulated by the anti-Jackson press starting in 1827 and whispered
in private conversations by the friends of the coalition, the circumstances
of Jackson's marriage proved his own moral depravity. And he dared to
accuse Adams and Clay of corruption! According to one popular version
of Jackson's marriage provided by the coalition, Rachel moved in with
Jackson and became his "housekeeper" shortly after he ran off her husband. Later the friends of Andrew and Rachel *"bought* off the claims of
the husband" and when Robards finally obtained a divorce Jackson *"publickly* married" Rachel with whom he had now been living for several
years.[8]

The extraordinary circumstances of the Jackson marriage received
widespread notoriety when Charles Hammond, editor of the Cincinnati

Gazette, made an astounding charge. "In the summer of 1790," he wrote, "Gen. Jackson prevailed upon the wife of Lewis Roberts of Mercer county, Kentucky, to desert her husband, and live with himself, in the character of a wife." Instantly, the Jackson newspapers in Ohio denounced the editor and demanded proof. Starting with the March 23, 1827, issue of the *Gazette* Hammond presented his case, which he later serialized in a pamphlet called *Truth's Advocate and Monthly Anti-Jackson Expositor.* He pointed out that Robards received from the Virginia legislature a statute that authorized a divorce if a jury found against his wife on charges of desertion and adultery. When the legal proceedings were instituted under this law, Hammond wrote, a declaration was filed charging Rachel with "eloping from her husband on July 1, 1790," and living in adultery with another man with whom she continued to live. The jury heard testimony, in particular from one Hugh McGary, and returned this verdict: "We the jury do find that the defendant, Rachel Roberts, hath deserted the plaintiff, Lewis Roberts, and hath, and doth still, live in adultery with another man."[9]

The Jackson press in Ohio screamed a denial. The Cincinnati *Advertiser* called the "assertion a BASE, WANTON AND MALIGNANT FALSEHOOD." Hammond replied that corroboration had recently come to him in a pamphlet published in Knoxville and written by Thomas L. Arnold, a candidate for Congress, who testified that Jackson "tore from a husband the wife of his bosom."[10] T. P. Moore, the Jackson manager in Ohio, issued a quick explanation of the circumstances of the marriage but botched the job sufficiently to make it easy for Hammond to refute the explanation and worsen the case for Jackson.[11]

Finally the Nashville *Republican* offered an explanation, declaring that Robards had deserted Rachel, then threatened to return to Tennessee and carry her back to Kentucky by force, whereupon she fled to Natchez with Colonel Stark and Jackson. Hammond roared with laughter. "A wife whose husband is jealous of her," he wrote, "seeks refuge among strangers, in company with her suspected paramour! And this is evidence of her innocence. What monstrous absurdities the world is expected to swallow where Gen. Jackson is concerned."[12]

There was enough skepticism over certain parts of the marriage story to alarm the Nashville Central Committee. The members quickly arranged to provide a full account of the "true facts" surrounding the breakup of the Robards marriage. John Overton wrote the principal statement, which was supported by documents from various witnesses who knew—or claimed they did—what had happened.[13]

The revelation of the intricate details of this sordid business struck a devastating blow at the Jackson campaign. For the past several years the General had been presented to the public as the child of the Revolution, imbued with its spirit of virtue, committed to high moral standards, and appalled by the corruption pervading the nation's capital. Now he stood revealed as a seducer, adulterer, and home-breaker. What hypocrisy! To think the Jacksonians dared to accuse Clay of misconduct. The utter gall. Jackson's morals were so low that they defied comparison. And this was the man the Democrats wanted to make President. "It would be an indellible dishonor to his nation," wrote one, "to elect Jackson President if the reports which are in circulation as to *the manner* in which he obtained his wife &c *are true.*"[14]

Jackson was visibly shaken by the widespread broadcast in the newspapers of the circumstances of his marriage. But he understood what had brought it about—or thought he did. Henry Clay, charged with corruption in the fraudulent election of a President the people did not want, had responded to the charge by resorting to gutter tactics. Jackson had been informed that Hammond visited Clay in Kentucky and had obtained all the information that later appeared in the *Gazette.* Was this true? the General wanted to know. He immediately contacted Eaton in Washington and asked him to investigate. Eaton confronted Clay and demanded an explanation. The secretary frankly admitted seeing Hammond in Kentucky but denied providing him with any information about Jackson's marriage.[15] Still Jackson suspected him. He persisted in the belief that Clay had engineered this new conspiracy against him. Where else could it originate? Who other than Clay had the opportunity, the access, or the need for this information? In a letter to Sam Houston, Old Hickory released all the fury of his pent-up anger and frustration.

> I am determined to unmask such part of the Executive council, as has entered into the combination to slander and revile me; and I trust, in due time to effect it, and lay the perfidy, meaness, and wickedness, of Clay, naked before the american people. I have lately got an intimation of some of his secrete movements, which, if I can reach with possitive and responsible proof, I will wield to his political, and perhaps, his actual destruction. he is certainly the bases[t], meanest, scoundrel, that ever disgraced the image of his god—nothing too mean or low for him to condescend to, *secretely* to carry his cowardly and base purpose of slander into effect; even the aged and virtuous female, is not free from his secrete combination of base slander—but *anough, you know me,* I will curb my feelings until it becomes proper to act, when retributive *Justice will vissit him and his pander heads.* [16]

The contemptible sewer tactics of the coalition, stormed Jackson, in dredging up the details of his marriage in this campaign was another example of their moral and political bankruptcy. Legitimately charged with corruption for stealing the government, the administration men answered the charge by slinging filth. To Jackson, it confirmed all he had suspected and known about how Adams and Clay had come to power.

It might have been wise to disregard the charges of adultery and bigamy and hope that the American people would dismiss them as something beneath contempt. Of course silence might be interpreted as agreement and do greater harm. In any event Jackson would not permit it so the Nashville Central Committee gathered sworn testimony and issued a long communiqué to the newspapers.[17] During the preparation of the report Jackson stood at Lewis's side, giving advice, making suggestions and hurrying him on to the completion of his task. It was one of the darkest, bleakest moments in Jackson's life.

Other criticisms assailed him. His military career took much abuse, something the General never tolerated—not from anybody. At this time he heard indirectly from his friend Dr. John H. Wallace of Virginia that at a public dinner given to the secretary of the navy, Samuel Southard, the secretary claimed that Jackson had left his army prior to the Battle of New Orleans and was returning home without leave when the then secretary of war, James Monroe, commanded him to return to his post. Said Southard, according to Wallace: *"Mr Monroe and not Genl Jackson was entitled to the credit for the victory at New Orleans."*[18] As soon as Jackson heard the story he wrote to Sam Houston in Washington and asked him to deliver a personal letter to Southard in which he demanded an explanation. "I wish to put down that vile slander," Jackson wrote Southard, "and expose the slanderer . . . and if such order, as aluded to, is on file, the *villain* who has placed it there, shall be unrobed whilst I am living and the nation advised of the *Treachery* and hypocracy of their public functionaries."[19] But Houston, when he read this letter, worried over its severity and showed it to Eaton, Hugh Lawson White, and some other friends in Congress. All agreed that Jackson should "keep out of collisions as to things said and done." In fact Eaton constantly warned the Hero against being "drawn out" and entangled in controversies that might diminish his reputation. "Be still," Eaton told him. "Be at home . . . heedless of whatever may be said or done by any of the 'corrupt crew.' "[20]

Houston suggested that he himself write to Southard and deliver it himself. But Jackson would not hear of it. He wanted the "villain" exposed and he was afraid Southard might put Houston off. So he wrote a second letter which was less combative but still Jacksonian in tone. The letter was duly delivered by Houston and Southard promptly responded. The secretary swore that it had never been his intention to impugn Jackson's contribution to the victory, but he thought Monroe had been particularly energetic in his support and that his many pressing and urgent letters to Jackson in Florida to hasten to New Orleans before the British landed needed to be appreciated. His object, he said, was the vindication of Monroe, not the deprecation of Jackson. Your exploits, he assured the Hero, "form a part of our national glory which I have no inclination to tarnish."[21]

That final statement satisfied Jackson. Not so the Democratic newspapers. They delighted in taunting the hapless Southard with such doggerel as the following:

When Clay and John Adams a bargain first made,
They took Sammy Southard their councils to aid;
But Southard turned out a most consummate ass,
As deficient in brains as abundant in brass. . . .

Ha! Ha! Ha![22]

Jackson exonerated Southard, but he wondered about Monroe. He suspected the ex-President had a hand in this criticism. "I hope he will have prudence to be silent," said the General. If I ever "find Mr Monroe acting hypocritically, or giving out intimations unfounded and untrue to effect my charecter . . . he must not expect me to be silent."[23]

Another attack on Jackson's military escutcheon that did him grave injury was the release of a handbill entitled "Some Account of Some of the Bloody Deeds of GENERAL JACKSON," or "The death of Jacob Webb, David Morrow, John Harris, Henry Lewis, David Hunt, and Edward Lindsey—six militia men, who were condemned to die, the sentence approved by Major General Jackson, and his order the whole six shot." The handbill was bordered in black and at the top showed six black coffins over which were affixed the names of the "murdered" militiamen. This "Coffin Hand Bill" described how the six men wanted to return to their homes during the Creek War at the conclusion of their enlistment, but were charged instead with desertion and executed by command of the pitiless Jackson.

John Binns, editor of the Philadelphia *Democratic Press*, conceived the Coffin Hand Bill and enlivened it with a poem entitled "Mournful Tragedy." He also sprinkled coffins and black borders in every direction and tucked into one corner a picture of Old Hickory running his sword cane through the back of a man stooped over as he picked up a stone. The handbill explained that the man, one Samuel Jackson, had quarreled with the General on the streets of Nashville. As usual Old Hickory responded by brandishing his cane. In an effort to defend himself, Samuel Jackson bent over to pick up a stone and as he did so the General drew the sword from his cane and ran it through Samuel's body, "the sword entering his back and coming out of his breast." General Jackson was subsequently indicted by a grand jury but later acquitted when he persuaded the jury that he committed the act in self-defense. "Gentle reader," said the handbill, "it is for you to say, whether this man, who carries a sword cane, and is willing to run it through the body of any one who may presume to stand in his way, is a fit person to be our President."[24]

Jackson replied to the Coffin Hand Bill through the Nashville Central Committee. These militiamen, he said, mutinied, broke into a commissary storehouse, stole supplies, burned the bakehouse, and then deserted. They were eventually caught, Jackson wrote, "& when I was at New Orleans were tried and condemned to be shot—one was pardoned. But not . . . for crimes committed after their term of service had expired, but for crimes of the deepest dye, perilous to the country, and at a time when every patriots arm was stretched, when every nerve of the Govt was strained to defend our liberties."[25]

Not only the sad demise of the six militiamen but the dreadful killing of John Woods was also reviewed in the press. In fact every "bloody deed" committed by Jackson which ingenious newspapermen could uncover was recounted for the edification of the American public. Charles Hammond in his *Gazette* of June 13, 1828 listed fourteen "juvenile indiscretions" attributed to Jackson between the ages of twenty-three and sixty and which proved, according to Hammond, that his *"intemperate life and character"* render him "unfit for the highest civil appointment within the gift of my country." The list constituted quite an indictment of Jackson's moral character:

1. Quarrels and duels with the late Colonel Waightstill Avery.
2. Engages in a "rencounter with the late Lewis Roberts, who swore his life against him, and Jackson was bound over to keep the peace by Colonel Robert Wheatley."
3. Quarrels "with his old friend and benefactor, Judge Jno. McNairy."
4. Quarrels and challenges William Cocke, "an old man . . . to fight with pistols—compromised."
5. Acts as second for "A. [Alexander] Donaldson, the nephew of Mrs Jackson who fights with young Mr. Winston at the distance of six feet—neither of the boys over 18 years old." Jackson was accused of encouraging the fight and fixing the distance. "The dispute was said to be about some act of gallantry."
6. Carries a challenge from Thomas Overton, the nephew of Judge Overton, to the late John Dickerson. Overton severely wounded.
7. Quarrels and duels with Governor John Sevier. At the time Jackson was a judge of the supreme court of Tennessee.
8. Quarrels with Governor Sevier's secretary, William Macklin, but they did not fight.
9. "Turns *racer*, now about forty years of age. He makes a race with Dr. Purnell, a perfect Virginia Gentleman—Jackson quarrels with and abuses him without measure."
10. Canes Thomas Swann of Virginia in a tavern.
11. Conducts a paper war with N. A. McNairy. McNairy challenges Jackson but they do not fight.
12. Kills Charles Dickinson.
13. Brawls with the Bentons.
14. Runs a sword cane through Samuel Jackson's body.[26]

In addition to these "bloody deeds," Jackson was accused of gambling, drinking, cockfighting, and swearing. Some of the General's friends tried unsuccessfully to argue that Old Hickory never used coarse or blasphemous language.[27] Others converted his vice into a virtue. "His partisans," wrote one critic, "go to every length for him—one of them assured me that he possessed a 'powerful & an omnipotent mind'—while another labored to prove to me that Genl J was great even in his iniquities—that he never used the common vulgar oaths, as 'may I be most essentially d——d etc'—that he never asserted a thing & then swore to it—he was above that—but his oaths were like his actions, great, strong & expressive —his favorite oath being—'by the eternal God'."[28]

As the many accusations leveled against Jackson's private and public life mounted during the campaign, occasioned in large measure by the enormous increase in the number of newspapers at this time and the need to fill their many columns, Jackson spent most of 1827 and 1828 answering them. A barrage of hostile pamphlets raked over every controversial phase of his life. One production by Richard Buckner and Frank Johnson, both former members of Congress from Kentucky, particularly agitated the General because it was derived from Jesse Benton's critical pamphlet published in 1824. As might be expected, Jackson saw the "corrupting influence" of the secretary of state in this production. "I have no doubt but Clay is at the bottom of all this."[29]

Another pamphlet entitled *Gen. Jackson's Negro Speculations, and his Traffic in Human Flesh, Examined and Established by Positive Proof,* authored by Andrew Erwin, another former Tennessee antagonist, claimed that a written agreement existed in Jackson's handwriting which established a partnership with Joseph Coleman and Horace Green for the purchase and sale of slaves, that Jackson later bought them out and regularly trafficked in human flesh in the "lower country."[30]

All these pamphlets and newspaper stories were systematically answered and by 1827 the Nashville Central Committee had a fairly elaborate mechanism for transmitting information to all sections of the country to respond to specific charges when they were leveled. "We want the Cincinnati Jackson committee," wrote William B. Lewis on one occasion, "to call upon our committee, at this place [Nashville], for such information as they may have it in their power to furnish. The documents are all prepared."[31] The members of the committee became so adept at the business of fending off accusations that after a time they began anticipating attacks and where they would come from.[32]

Not that Nashville issued all the major campaign statements. Some excellent pro-Jackson pamphlets were published in New York and Philadelphia and were widely distributed during the closing months of the campaign. They were written with great gusto. Andrew Jackson "has been every where traduced as a blood-thirsty tyrant, a murderer, and a dangerous aspirant," read one. "His adversaries have openly invaded his private sanctuary, and the innocent partner of his bed has been dragged forth with unblushing effrontery, to be made the subject of jest, suspicion, and slander. Their private history has been shamefully and wickedly perverted, and trumpeted through the medium of obscene gazettes, and bandied about in the pestiferous breath of hollow-hearted and treacherous demagogues."[33]

Sometimes more serious controversies boiled out of the wretched mudslinging. One such incident arose on account of Jackson's habit of regaling his guests at the Hermitage with stories about Clay's efforts to corrupt Jackson's own friends in Congress. One of the guests who heard the General's narrative was Carter Beverley, a Virginian, who subsequently published an account of it in the Fayetteville *Observer* in North Carolina. A copy of this story also appeared in the *United States Telegraph*, the new Jackson newspaper established in Washington under the editorship of Duff Green, a close friend of John C. Calhoun.[34] Included in the account was the startling statement that a "member of Congress of high respectability" came to Jackson personally with an offer from Clay's friends. Clay immediately issued a denial and demanded to know the name of this "false" informant.

"James Buchanan of Pennsylvania," retorted Jackson, as soon as he heard the demand. Buchanan not only carried the proposal but claimed that the Adams men had definitely offered Clay the state department in exchange for House votes.

All eyes turned toward Buchanan. On August 8, 1827, he addressed a letter to the editor of the Lancaster *Journal* in which he admitted that he had never been authorized by Clay or anyone else to approach the General. The truth of the matter is that he had simply tried to advance his own position by meddling in presidential politics beyond his proper level. The blinking little busybody did not come out, said Major Lewis, "as he ought to have done, and as was expected of him."[35] Jackson himself spoke of Buchanan's "outrageous statement" but made no effort to prolong the controversy by taking issue with anything in the letter. Nor did the Democrats make any effort to reprimand the Pennsylvanian or expel him from the party. He was playing a significant role in the creation of the Democratic party in his home state and it was deemed necessary to "preserve his friendship and needful influence."[36] For his part, Buchanan wrote Jackson a long, effusively flattering letter saying he was sorry "beyond expression" that the General believed him to be Clay's emissary. He swore anew that he was the Hero's "ardent, decided & . . . efficient friend."[37] So the matter was dropped, although Clay clearly came out of the affair somewhat vindicated.

The intensity of the attacks upon his public career and private history forced Jackson deeper into the campaign. Many of his directions and orders were channeled through the Nashville Central Committee but sometimes he took a direct hand in conducting the canvass. For one thing he opened a correspondence with Duff Green, the new editor of the principal Jackson newspaper in Washington and the person most Democratic editors were looking to for direction and guidance. Green had bought out the old Washington *Gazette* with the financial backing of

Jackson himself (who lent him $3,000) and such other leading Democrats as John H. Eaton, James K. Polk, James Hamilton, Jr., Samuel D. Ingham, and John Branch. Green changed the paper's name to the *United States Telegraph.* He sparked its editorial tone. Indeed his arrival in Washington from St. Louis was one of the first important consequences of the Jackson-Calhoun alliance. Van Buren would have preferred Thomas Ritchie of the Richmond *Enquirer* as the spokesman of the party after Ritchie joined the alliance but the Magician bowed to the accomplished fact. As Calhoun explained: "A paper is already in existence and it does seem to me that two on the same side must distract and excite jealousy."[38] In any event once the newspaper began publication Jackson contacted Green and indicated some of the guidelines he wanted his propagandist to follow. "Should the administration continue their systematic course of slander," he said, "it will be well now and then to throw a fire brand into their camp by the statement of a few facts." However, he wanted one thing clearly understood. "Female character never should be introduced or touched by my friends, unless a continuation of attack should continue to be made against Mrs. J. and then only, by way of *Just retaliation* upon the *known guilty.* My great wish is, that it may be altogether *avoided,* if *possible,* by my friends." Then, as a follow-up, he added: "*I never war against females* and it is only the base and cowardly that do."[39]

When the friends of the administration—now called "National Republicans" to distinguish them from the Democratic Republicans as well as indicate their ideological commitment—accused Jackson of accepting public money for military services not rendered, the General and his friends reckoned it a ploy to lessen the effectiveness of the "corrupt bargain" charge by pretending that Old Hickory himself slipped his hand into the public till. After all, argued the National Republicans, anyone so "morally depraved" as to steal another man's wife must have swindled the government. As soon as he heard this latest accusation Jackson instructed Eaton to go to the War Department and demand the documents relating to his accounts so that he could prove the falsity of the charges. Because he had been so scrupulously honest in all his transactions, because he served his country year after year without furlough and without sick leave, he fiercely resented this trumped-up accusation. "You will have seen what the powers that be, thro their panders have been pouring out all their viols of wrath against me, that falsehood and forgery could invent," he informed Richard K. Call, his former aide, "—that even the War Department has been furnishing false accounts to their panders who has published them to the world to endeavour to induce the ignorant and unwary to believe that I have been using the public money and applying it to my use contrary to law. The vigilance of my friend Eaton in this has entirely discomfitted them." It truly amazed Jackson how far the corruption of the administration had spread. "I have always thought Clay corrupt, that he would do any thing to promote his own views—but I was not prepared to believe . . . that the secretaries of War & Navy were base enough to . . . become his panders, secretely to slander me."[40]

Jackson also told Call how involved he was in conducting the campaign. "I have been constantly employed," he said, "furnishing to various calls on me, the necessary facts and documents, to refute these various attacks on me." But he exercised extreme care in what he said and did. He feared entanglement in controversies that could fix him in the mind of the electorate as a public brawler. "I confess it requires much philosophy to bear things with calmness & equanimity of temper," he admitted to Senator Robert Y. Hayne of South Carolina. "My political enemies have not judged of me rightly. They cannot provoke me to an act of rashness —should the uncircumcised philistines send forth their Goliah to destroy the liberty of the people & compel them to worship Mamon, they may find a David who trusts in the god of Abraham Isaac and of Jacob, for when I fight, it is the battles of my country. I am calm & composed, trusting in the Lord of hosts, I believe him Just, and therefore look forward to a time when retributive Justice will take place, & when Just attonement can be *required and enforced.*"[41]

Journalists, politicians, and sundry local committees (many now called "Hickory Clubs") regularly summoned the Hero's assistance during the campaign or requested direction about how they might advance his cause. The contacts reached a high level by the middle of 1827. Before long Van Buren wrote to him and officially confirmed his arrival into the Jackson camp by informing the General of a tour he would take after the adjournment of Congress to see important Radicals in the south and win their support for the new party. The Magician also tried unsuccessfully to explain the Byzantine nature of New York politics and the rivalry that existed between himself and the governor, De Witt Clinton. The matter concerned Van Buren because Clinton had supported Jackson for many years and had first call on the General's gratitude. The rivalry might have posed a serious problem for the Hero but he was spared the unpleasantness by Clinton's sudden death in February, 1828.[42]

One of the most important men to contact Jackson in 1827 and later assume a major role in the General's administration was Amos Kendall of Kentucky, a newspaperman and former friend of Henry Clay. Kendall had once tutored the Clay children before taking up journalism. He joined the Relief party in Kentucky, wrote scathing attacks upon the Bank of the United States in his newspaper the *Argus of Western America,* and eventually broke with Clay on ideological and personal grounds and joined the ranks of the Jacksonians. Kendall was a spectacularly homely man—nearsighted, stooped, with a chronic illness that produced a sallow complexion accentuated by his prematurely white hair. He seemed perpetually enveloped in a profound silence—until he picked up his editorial pen. Then all manner of thunderbolts shot out of him.

On August 22, 1827, this "quiet man" wrote an introductory letter to

General Jackson. "Although I have never had the pleasure of a personal acquaintance with you," he began, "there are some circumstances of a peculiar nature which induce me now to address you." Kendall went on to say that he was somewhat embarrassed by the course taken by the Democrats regarding the "corrupt bargain" charge, particularly Beverley's "great indiscretion." It allowed Clay an opportunity to pretend he was innocent of the charge. "Mr. Clay never treated me confidentially in relation to his arrangement with Adams," Kendall admitted. "But (I am one of those who were told here by one of his friends, as I think about the 20th day of January 1825, that if Mr. Adams should be elected he would make Mr. Clay his Secretary of State, and I was three times solicited to write to Mr. White, our representative, to vote for Mr. Adams on that account.) Thus urged I did write." However, Kendall told White that Jackson was "unquestionably the choice of Kentucky." Others did as they were urged to do, said Kendall. "Having been one of Mr. Clay's family," he continued, "I should at least have been silent in relation to this transaction, but for the discovery or at least the conviction that Mr. Clay was willing to gratify his ambition at the sacrifice of every tie, regardless of every obligation whether to his friends or to his country. I know not from what source the information relative to the arrangement with Mr. Adams, came; but I now believe that it came from *Mr. Clay himself.* So confident am I that I would risk my honor and my life upon the result of a thorough investigation. It must have come from him before the 10th of January as the letters got up here were written in time to reach Washington before the election."

These final sentences delighted Jackson. They confirmed—not that he needed it—everything he and his friends had been saying since 1825. They proved Henry Clay's "perfidy, meaness, and wickedness."

Kendall told Jackson that what he had written was for *"your own eye only."* He would never disclose to "mortal man" the avenue through which his evidence came to him "unless called on in the name of my country." He then went on to pledge his continued support of Jackson and urged him to come to Kentucky so that they could "finish the war" and ensure victory to their common cause. "The country is eager to see you. . . . We should meet you at our dinner with the most ardent enthusiasm . . . and [it] would redound much to your own advantage and to the success of those principles for which we are all contending."[43]

The arrival of Kendall into the Jackson camp was nearly as significant —although in a completely different way—as the arrival of Calhoun and Van Buren. He and his associate in the running of the *Argus of Western America*, Francis P. Blair—as strange-looking in his way as Kendall—not only brought enormous vitality to the cause by virtue of their journalistic skills but they also added immeasurable strength to the party in a state dominated by Henry Clay. Moreover, as westerners, they soon won Jackson's confidence and ear. Together they provided more energy, ideas, and issues than any two other men in the entire Democratic party.[44]

Other important journalists also joined the Jackson cause. Thomas Ritchie of the Richmond *Enquirer* and Edwin Croswell of the Albany *Argus* followed Van Buren's lead. Isaac Hill's New Hampshire *Patriot,* James Gordon Bennett's New York *Enquirer,* Nathaniel Greene's Boston *Statesman,* Gideon Welles's New Haven *Journal,* Mordecai M. Noah's *National Advocate,* Dabney S. Carr's Baltimore *Republican* and many others contributed valuable support to the Jacksonian movement. Soon the National Republicans complained that the Democrats had established a "chain of newspaper posts, from the New England States to Louisiana, and branching off through Lexington to the Western States."[45] These journalists were joined by a growing corps of imaginative, rough-and-tumble, aggressive politicians: Thomas Hart Benton, T. P. Moore, Littleton W. Tazewell, Henry Lee, Sidney Beese, Levi Woodbury, and many others.

Among these men there was genuine concern for what Kendall had called "the principles for which we are all contending." Theirs was no simple drive to oust a maladroit administration. They contended that misrule and abuse of power existed within the government. Because they believed that corruption abounds where power goes unchecked they demanded an administration that would restrict government power. They also feared that Hamiltonian men of business controlled and directed the Adams administration to advance their economic interests. "Contending as we are against wealth & power," said a future member of Jackson's cabinet, "we look for success in numbers combined by intelligence & impelled by patriotism."[46] Thus, Jackson's election would not only expel a corrupt administration from office but create a new party based on mass support dedicated to the restoration of the constitutional safeguards of liberty.

Jackson himself seemed to understand the larger implications of his candidacy. In his many letters to party leaders around the country he emphasized the notions of republicanism and slowly began to formulate the outline of a reform program. "When the constitution will be so amended as to preserve to the people their rightful sovereignety," he told John Branch of North Carolina, "& restore in practice the proper checks & ballances; when the public debt will be paid, and the executive department of our government freed from the corrupting influence of a monied aristocracy; when Congress will regulate with an eye single to the public weal, and limit by special veto all appropriations, and compel every officer in the government annually to account to congress how the funds entrusted to his care have been applied. Then, and not until then, will our national character be freed from the charges of corruption which is now imputed to it—keep our officers free from temptation, & they will be honest."[47]

By 1828 party leaders were thoroughly aware of Jackson's ideological creed and the ultimate purpose of his election. On the very afternoon that he died De Witt Clinton of New York wrote to Caleb Atwater, his political ally in Ohio, and instructed him on the meaning of Old Hickory's election. "If you wish not to see a second reign of terror—support Gen. Jackson," he wrote, "—if you wish for the restoration of pure, republican principles, support him—if you are a patriot and love your country, support him." In sum, declared the Democratic press, "the parties are Jackson and Adams, democracy and aristocracy."[48]

Corresponding committees set up in the wards and towns of many states focused a great deal of attention on the theme of republicanism. They issued circulars which expounded on the continuing struggle between liberty and power, virtue and corruption, democracy and aristocracy. "When the Pres^t of the United States has been elected in open defiance of the known will of the people," wrote one committee member, "when this same Prest. has in an official message advised & stimulated the representative bodies, not to be palsied by the will of their constituents; when he recommends a system of expenditures glittering & splendid profuse & wildly extravagant the better to increase the power & patronage of the Government to seduce & corrupt the people with their money . . . it is time for every lover of free government . . . to unite upon Genl. Jackson as the next Prest."[49]

Because of the emphasis on republicanism with all its talk about virtue, the campaign managers of both sides went out of their way to smear their opponents with accusations of personal impropriety. Because the Democrats had a powerful issue in the "corrupt bargain" charge, because they could present Jackson as the candidate of morality, the National Republicans were forced to dig into the General's past and expose to the public every shoddy event of his life. Many (if not all) of Jackson's moral delinquencies had previously been known but hardly exploited—until the election of 1828. Now they were exploited with a vengeance, and exploited because the coalition had to counter the "corrupt bargain" charge. Which explains why this election was one of the foulest in American campaigning history.

It also explains the furor over the billiard table that Adams had installed in the White House. This brought anguished cries of moral outrage from the Jacksonians. It not only demonstrated government extravagance, they said, but individual vice. Was it ever intended by Congress, asked Representative Samuel Carson of North Carolina on the House floor, "that the public money should be applied to the purchase of gaming tables and gambling furniture?" Such conduct, he predicted, would "shock and alarm the religious, the moral, and reflecting part of the community."[50]

More than anything else republicanism warned against concentrated power by the central government, which threatened individual freedom. In the perpetual struggle between liberty and power the Democrats had no trouble identifying their position. "Let the cry be Jackson, Van

Buren & Liberty," shouted the Albany *Argus,* mouthpiece of the Magician's party in New York. (Van Buren needed the publicity because he was running for governor of the state.) But elsewhere the Democrats stuck to the national ticket. "JACKSON, CALHOUN and LIBERTY," they cried.[51]

Because of the excitement of the contest and the major issues involved, an unprecedented number and variety of demonstrations for the candidates occurred during the election of 1828. Much of this ballyhoo was conceived and organized by the new breed of politicians who appeared following the War of 1812. They encouraged the public to feats (hitherto unknown) of organized mayhem. Parades, barbecues, dinners, street rallies, tree plantings (hickory trees for the Democrats) and patriotic displays of every variety occurred throughout the Union—most of them for Jackson. Indeed the Hero was the perfect candidate for such nonsense. The grass-root politicians loved him. Said one: "the *Hurra Boys* were for Jackson and . . . all the noisey *Turbulent Boisterous* Politicians are with him and to my regret they constitute a powerful host."[52] The Hurra Boys distributed hickory brooms, hickory canes, and hickory sticks. They stuck them on steeples, on steamboats, on signposts. Poles made of hickory were erected "in every village, as well as upon the corners of many city streets. . . . Many of these poles were standing as late as 1845, rotten momentoes [*sic*] of the delirium of 1828."[53]

"Planting hickory trees!" snorted the National Republicans. "Odds nuts and drumsticks! What have hickory trees to do with republicanism and the great contest?"[54]

Many Democratic politicians tried to enlist Jackson himself in their shenanigans. The Hero appreciated the value of personal contact with the electorate[55] but he worried about its effect on the religious, moral, and "reflecting" part of the community, since it could appear that he was pursuing office for personal gain. Several state central committees issued formal invitations for personal appearances, all of which he politely declined. Then the Louisiana legislature asked him to come to New Orleans on January 8, 1828, to participate in a commemorative celebration of the great victory of 1815. This he could not refuse. Besides, the legislature had issued the invitation, not a Democratic committee. He could argue that he attended a patriotic event, not a political rally. Moreover, the occasion would subtly remind the American people of his contribution to their freedom.[56]

He accepted and arrangements for the journey were turned over to Major Lewis. Although his health was poor and he did not feel up to an extended trip, the General was determined to go. He decided to depart the Hermitage after Christmas and stay in Nashville a few days, leaving on a Saturday or Sunday morning. In proceeding downriver from Nashville to New Orleans he gave Lewis explicit instructions that he did not "wish to stop at any point, except the Natchez, & that only to receive the committee, as I wish to avoid every thing that could draw over me the imputation of electioneering."[57]

Jackson and his party—consisting of Rachel, Overton, Coffee, Lewis, William Carroll, Robert Armstrong, James A. Hamilton (the recently arrived emissary from Van Buren) and a number of politicians and veterans of the great battle, plus the General's cotton crop—boarded the steamer *Pocahontas* at Nashville on December 29 and slowly proceeded downriver to Natchez. Unfortunately, along the way, a steamer of faster speed zigzagged across the bow of the *Pocahontas* several times in a kind of cat-and-mouse game. Infuriated by the constant back-and-forth course of the other ship Jackson finally ordered a rifle brought to him. He hailed the pilot of the other steamer and swore that one more zigzag and he would shoot him. Hamilton, fearing an incident that would have devastating political effects, went below and reported what had happened to Rachel. "Colonel," she replied, "do me the favor to say to the General I wish to speak to him." Jackson immediately responded to his wife's summons, and that ended a near brush with disaster.[58]

The *Pocahontas* arrived in Natchez on Friday, January 4 and the spectators lining the heights above the river shouted themselves hoarse as they welcomed Old Hickory and his party. Cannons boomed; a procession formed to escort Jackson into town; a dinner and a ball were given in his honor; and throughout the day and night the multitude shouted their joy at seeing this "Saviour of His Country."

At midnight the General and his party reembarked. The New Orleans arrangements committee boarded the *Courtland,* which had taken them to Natchez the previous week, and "then both boats, united together, descended the stream" at a speed calculated to get them to New Orleans on January 8.[59]

They arrived precisely on time, just as the arrangements committee had planned. A fleet of steamboats, led by "two stupendous boats, lashed together," advanced toward the *Pocahontas* and kept up a constant fire of artillery that was answered rhythmically from other ships in the harbor and guns planted on the shore. The *Pocahontas,* decked festively with twenty-four flags (one for each state), took its position at the head of the flotilla. Jackson, standing on the fantail of the ship, his head uncovered, was completely visible to the vast multitude packed within the steamboats and standing along the shores. He waved. The people responded with even greater explosions of sound. The screaming and shouting from the thousands of spectators echoed from the river to the woods and then back to the river.

The reception committee formally invited Jackson to disembark and meet his brother soldiers and fellow citizens. A line formed of the "old New Orleans Battalion," headed by Generals Plauché and Labaltat. The emotions generated at the moment Jackson came ashore staggered some observers. "I have no words to describe the scene which ensued," said one. Rachel moved forward accompanied by several ladies from Tennessee and she was immediately greeted by Mme. Bernard de Marigny de Mandeville and other "respectable ladies" who congratulated her on her safe arrival and escorted her to the Marigny house for a reception.[60]

In the evening a sumptuous dinner to honor the General and his lady was tendered. Speeches in both French and English recounted his heroic deeds. The glorious battle of January 8 was relived in word and song. Everyone surrendered to the high emotion that surged throughout the city during this great reunion. All agreed that the world had "never witnessed so glorious, so wonderful a Celebration." Indeed in the forty-odd years of the Republic's existence never had there been such a display of *"Gratitude & Patriotism,"* never had the American people so spontaneously expressed their undying devotion to a national hero.[61]

For four days the celebration continued, a celebration noted in newspapers in every state of the Union. It was a fitting tribute to the heroism of Jackson and his veterans, they said. When it ended, Old Hickory and his party returned to the *Pocahontas* and sailed home. "We had a harmonious & happy meeting with all our friends & compatriots in arms at New Orleans," Jackson wrote the absent Edward Livingston, "the concourse was unusually great." For the remainder of the campaign, lasting little more than nine months, the nation vibrated to the huzzas sounded at New Orleans in remembering that General Andrew Jackson "saved" the nation in its hour of greatest peril.[62]

Except for traveling to Florence, Alabama, on business for his ward Andrew J. Hutchings, whose cotton and cotton gin had been destroyed in a fire, Jackson stayed close to home, conferring regularly with his advisers and attending to his voluminous correspondence. Through it all he tried to stand above the rancor and turbulence of the campaign. "Amongst all the scenes of intrigue, management & slander, with which I have been, and am still surrounded," he informed Amos Kendall, "my great consolation is, that I receive the protection, & maintain the confidence of the virtuous & intelligent citizens of my country."[63]

Although Jackson suffered the worst of the personal abuse that so disfigured this vicious campaign, John Quincy Adams did not escape unscathed. Democrats frequently responded to verbal filth in kind. In a campaign biography of Old Hickory published by Isaac Hill of New Hampshire and entitled *Brief Sketch of the Life, Character and Services of Major General Andrew Jackson,* President Adams was accused of pimping while minister to Russia. Supposedly he procured an American girl for Tsar Alexander I. That Hill would publish this extraordinary story or anyone believe it is a frightful commentary on American politics in 1828. But the canard was widely believed and circulated. In the west the Democrats mocked the President as "The Pimp of the Coalition" whose fabulous success as a diplomat had at last been explained.[64]

Some National Republicans countered by circulating the report that

"General Jackson's mother was a COMMON PROSTITUTE, brought to this country by the British soldiers! She afterward married a MULATTO MAN, with whom she had several children, of which number General JACKSON IS ONE!!!" When Old Hickory read this notice it is reported that he burst into tears.[65]

Adams was also pilloried for conducting himself like a king and implementing the doctrine that "the few should govern the many." "We disapprove," clucked the Democrats, "the kingly pomp and splendour that is displayed by the present incumbent." Other reports accused him of religious bigotry, alcoholism, sabbath-breaking, and a string of other moral and ethical delinquencies. Adams responded in the quiet of his study, pouring out his bitterness and hurt in the secret pages of his diary. He called his tormentors "skunks of party slander."[66]

This "vulgarization" of American politics also included the widespread use of jokes, puns, cartoons, and songs. Indeed the singing of campaign songs became an integral part of the electoral process in 1828 because of the phenomenal success of a song written several years before that recounted the victory at New Orleans. Entitled "The Hunters of Kentucky," its verses had been written by Samuel Woodworth, better known for his "Old Oaken Bucket," and adapted by Noah M. Ludlow to a melody taken from the comic opera *Love Laughs at Locksmiths.*[67] The song became wildly popular during the 1828 campaign, thanks to the Jackson managers who printed and distributed thousands of copies of it. Certain stanzas of the song so moved Americans that they screamed their delight whenever they heard them. They sounded like Indians, whooping and howling their pleasure, said one. The two most rousing stanzas went as follows:

> You've heard, I s'pose, of New Orleans,
> 'Tis famed for youth and beauty,
> They're girls of every hue, it seems,
> From snowy white to sooty,
> Now Packenham had made his brags,
> If he that day was lucky,
> He'd have those girls and cotton-bags
> In spite of Old Kentucky. . . .
>
> But Jackson, he was wide awake,
> And was not scared at trifles,
> For well he knew Kentucky's boys,
> With their death-dealing rifles,
> He led them down to cypress swamp,
> The ground was low and mucky,
> There stood John Bull in martial pomp,
> And here stood old Kentucky.
>
> Oh! Kentucky, the hunters of Kentucky!
> Oh! Kentucky, the hunters of Kentucky![68]

Important as the noise and tumult of the campaign and the participation of the masses in the electoral process appeared to be, the election of 1828 was fought to a large extent in the halls of Congress. Here the leading politicians met regularly during the session, and once the Jackson–Calhoun–Van Buren alliance took shape their friends caucused frequently to discuss and plan strategy. "It cannot but be complimentary to you," Eaton said in a letter to Jackson, "to know that a majority of both Houses of Congress are your friends and advocates. They will take care of your cause and interest without any interference on your part; they only ask of you under any and all circumstances to be *still* and let them manage whatever is to be done."[69] The Radicals were particularly concerned that he avoid any constitutional statement that might reveal him as a latitudinarian. They worried needlessly. "If my name can save the republic with my silence & sufferings, it shall be done," he said.[70]

One reason for exercising caution was the stunning success the Democrats achieved in the off-year elections of 1827. They now controlled both houses of Congress and would be held responsible for the conduct of the government, at least in matters of legislation. That explained their worry that Jackson might say something not in accord with their legislative intentions, and they planned to tailor their business almost exclusively to ensure the General's election to the presidency in 1828.

As the Congress prepared to begin its session, Martin Van Buren called a caucus of Democrats on December 2, 1827.[71] No one questioned his right to assume party leadership. His credentials and political talents gave him full authority. Not that Jackson's close friends were disregarded. Eaton, White, Benton, T. P. Moore, Richard M. Johnson, and others contributed to most decisions relating to the campaign.

The first thing the group decided upon was the important selection of a Speaker of the House of Representatives to replace the administration's incumbent, John W. Taylor of New York. They agreed on Andrew Stevenson of Virginia, largely to accommodate southern interests.[72] The entire House confirmed this decision by a vote of 104 votes for Stevenson and 94 for Taylor. "It is a great triumph," enthused James K. Polk of Tennessee, "a triumph of principle over power and Governmental patronage."[73] Unfortunately, some of the gutter tactics of the campaign intruded into this election. Taylor was splattered with charges of philandering. Even Jackson pelted the hapless Taylor. "I rejoice to hear that Mr. S is appointed Speaker," the General informed Lewis. "It is evidence at least that congress has some respect for itself, by placing a man of good morals over it."[74]

One problem confronting the new alliance of Democrats was the wish of some men to replace Calhoun on the ticket. Crawford's friends wanted to dispose of him, and even some of Jackson's closest advisers doubted Calhoun's past loyalty and were prepared to sacrifice him. Westerners, especially those in Ohio and Kentucky, preferred De Witt Clinton (before he died) but that suggestion made Van Buren wince. Other Democrats argued in favor of leaving the matter to individual state conventions to select whomever they felt would strengthen the ticket in their state. Said one Kentucky politician: "Do we go for *men,* or that *reform* in the Federal Government which is to secure our rights and republican institutions from external and internal enemies, violence fraud and corruption? . . . How will the *cause* of *Jackson and reform,* suffer if Calhoun, Clinton and Crawford should *all* be candidates on that side for the vice presidency? Would it not rather *strengthen* than *weaken* our cause?" In Kentucky, he continued, the Clay party was beaten last summer and that victory "greatly added to our numbers and strength. . . . Mr Clay and his friends are *beaten* but not *conquered;* and we shall have a Hell of a fight next summer. Mr Clays partizans have talents, presses and money; and they will make great sacrafices to save him from destruction. Fraud, violence and corruption will be resorted to in order to regain Kentucky. We shall be greatly clogged with the vice-presidency if we run Mr Calhoun. Great pains have been taken by the Clay party to render Mr Calhoun unpopular in Kentucky."[75]

The same was true in other states. Calhoun drove off Radical votes, said some, and served as an easy mark for the Clay men to shoot at. But Van Buren and other congressional leaders recognized the disastrous effect such an obvious insult to Calhoun would have on the party if they replaced him. They therefore quashed every effort to tinker with the ticket. Indeed, for a time, Van Buren considered calling a national convention to settle the matter for the entire nation but decided against it because it would provide a forum for all the resentments against Calhoun, especially in the north and west.[76]

The Democratic congressional leadership concentrated its efforts instead on enacting legislation that would attract votes from doubtful states. Unquestionably, their monumental tribute to political brokerage was their passage of the Tariff of 1828, more frequently known as the "Tariff of Abominations." The difficulty in adjusting the tariff rates was the danger of triggering a major explosion within the ranks of southern Jacksonians, indeed within the ranks of all southerners. The sliding price of cotton was a disturbing fact of southern economic life during the 1820s, and the blame for this slide centered on the higher protective rates achieved by northern industrialists in 1824. However simplistic this argument, southerners believed it. They felt caught in a system in which they sold their cotton on an open market and were forced (because of the tariff) to buy manufactured goods on a closed one. The government thus favored one section at the expense of another and this, to southerners, was unconstitutional.

The tariff question was further complicated by disagreement within the ranks of northerners over which products deserved protection; also, western farmers required protection for their raw materials, which manufacturers could ill afford. Despite these problems the Jacksonian leaders prepared a new tariff bill. They discounted the opposition in the south because southerners detested Adams, whom they regarded as the "father of all manufacturers." They would support Jackson no matter what the leadership proposed. Also, New England could be expected to vote for Adams, probably in toto. So in shaping a tariff bill the Jacksonians did not trouble themselves to favor that section of the country. Their bill was aimed at the states that could be induced by a favorable schedule of tariff rates to vote for Jackson.

Silas Wright, Jr., of New York, one of Van Buren's brightest lieutenants, prepared the principal provisions of the new bill. Heavy duties were placed on imported raw materials, particularly hemp, flax, molasses, iron, and sail duck, which would hurt New England interests at the same time they would help western farmers. The duty on iron, said Wright, was "the Sine qua non with Pennsylvania."[77] The most important schedule, however, dealt with raw wool and manufactured woolens. The rates, as finally determined, favored Democratic agrarian wool raisers but offered only token protection to the manufacturers of woolen products. Thus the tariff of 1828 deliberately sought favor from states such as New York, Pennsylvania, Missouri, Ohio, and Kentucky—which were regarded as swing states—and discriminated against New England. The south, so totally committed to Jackson, did not enter into their calculations at all.[78]

Despite heavy opposition from New England and the south and after some fine-tuning of the schedule in the Senate, the tariff passed. The bill, according to one commentator, became a "machine for manufacturing Presidents, instead of broadcloths, and bed blankets."[79] Most of the Jacksonian leadership in the Senate—Van Buren, Benton, Eaton—voted with the majority and the Democratic press hailed their achievement as one that provided "a national tariff, which protects, with a just and natural equality, all the great interests of the nation."[80]

Southerners were outraged, however. A few of them even threatened secession if the nation pursued its course in utter disregard of the rights of the south. When the session ended, Calhoun returned to his home and anonymously wrote the *Exposition and Protest,* which formulated his doctrine of nullification. The South Carolina legislature subsequently adopted it. In the *Exposition,* the Vice President asserted the constitutional right of the state to void the tariff within its borders, a doctrine that would receive fuller amplification during Jackson's administration and lead to a controversy that threatened the existence of the Union.

Despite southern pain and threats, the Tariff of Abominations probably helped Jackson in such states as Ohio, Indiana, Illinois, Pennsylvania, and New York, all of them essential to the formation of a Democratic victory in the fall. The hemp provision unquestionably gained votes in Kentucky, although the Jacksonians relied more on Clay's "disobedience of Legislative Instruction" in supporting Adams in 1825 to win that state. They were also bludgeoning Clay for his "latitudinarian construction of the Federal Constitution, which would destroy the state sovereignties."[81]

Some Democrats wondered, however, whether they had unwittingly played the coalition's game. "Our friends I am frank to say have fought their opponents with their own weapons," John Branch told Jackson, "and are therefore not exempt from their full share of those undue influences." Had he the choice, he went on, of either perpetuating "this corrupt dynasty" or using his vote in Congress to influence the pending presidential election "I certainly could not hesitate which of the two to choose. Of two evils I could choose the least; for I verily believe that if by any means Adams and Clay succeed, that the subversion of the liberties of this people would inevitably ensue. Every thing therefore dear to freemen is at stake."[82]

Just as Jackson's contest with Adams was a question of freedom, southerners saw the tariff problem in the same light. It was freedom, not tariff protection *per se*, nor slavery, that lay at the heart of southern fears. Some of them threatened secession, and eventually in 1860–1861 they departed the Union because they believed absolutely that liberty had succumbed to power.

Because Jackson understood this problem and its relation to the preservation of a republican government, he enjoyed almost universal southern support. The fact that he owned slaves had little to do with it. Less than six months before the election the General summed up his thoughts on the matter in a letter to his closest friend, John Coffee. He also defined what he believed was the meaning of the election. Like many others at this time he used the words "power" and "patronage" almost interchangeably.

> The patronage of the government for the last three years has been wielded to corrupt every thing that comes within its influence, and was capable of being corrupted, and it would seem, that virtue and truth, has fled from its embrace. The administrators of the Govt has stained our national character, and it rests with the people to work it out, by a full expression of their disapprobation. The present is a contest between the virtue of the people, and the influence of patronage, should patronage prevail, over virtue, then indeed "the safe precedent," will be established, that the President, appoints his successor in the person of the sec of state. Then the people may prepare themselves to become "hewers of wood and drawers of water," to those in power, who with the Treasury at command, will wield by its corrupting influence a majority to support it. The present is an important struggle, for the perpetuity of our republican government, and I hope the virtue of the people may prevail, and all may be well. From the signs of the times, it appears, that the influence of the administration is on the wane, and the cause of the people will prevail.[83]

The question of freedom and the preservation of a republican government also triggered a sudden release of unanticipated violence during the campaign. Blind hatred of Masons exploded across the western counties of New York in the late 1820s, ultimately affecting the politics of the entire nation. And it all began with the disappearance and presumed death of a man named William Morgan.[84]

Morgan was a stonemason who settled in Batavia, New York, and joined the Order of Freemasonry. A disagreeable and unpleasant sort, he quarreled repeatedly with other Masons and finally decided to get even by publishing a book revealing the secrets of the first three degrees of Freemasonry. The thought of this betrayal outraged other Masons and they appealed to Morgan to cease his madness. But Morgan persisted. He found a publisher in David C. Miller, editor of the Batavia *Advocate.* Consequently, a number of other Masons decided to take matters into their own hands and they seized the page proofs of Morgan's book and set fire to Miller's printing establishment. Then they had Morgan arrested on September 11, 1826, for allegedly stealing a shirt and tie. But the feisty stonemason could not be intimidated even though it was clear that the Masons were serious about silencing him. When the charge of theft against Morgan failed for lack of evidence, the Masons had him immediately rearrested—this time for a debt owed to another Mason. Then events moved swiftly. Someone paid Morgan's bail. As the wretched man stepped from jail he was seized, hustled into a waiting carriage, and presumably taken to Fort Niagara, where he was held captive for a few days and then (according to most sources) drowned in the Niagara River.[85]

The Masons started with harassment, moved to property destruction, and then resorted to abduction and murder. It was a frightening escalation, and when, after an interval of time, no real action was taken against the perpetrators—indeed there was evidence of a cover-up—the people in the western counties of New York suddenly and violently expressed their anger and resentment. The tragedy of one man—an ordinary citizen —became a major political issue and sparked a drive aimed at eradicating the entire Masonic order. Public meetings were called where local citizens denounced the Masons as a conspiracy of aristocrats formed to deprive ordinary citizens of their rights. Freemasons, they declared, dared to place their secret organization ahead of human life. Masons presumed to control everything—government, business, even courts—and bound themselves through fearful oaths to advance the cause of Masonry at all costs.

To some this anti-Masonic outbreak reflected a democratic surge to terminate the alleged privileges of an elite class. To others it was the result of the "disturbed and unsettled state of the public mind" during a period of intense economic and political change. It was a burst of violence in which profound psychological and even religious forces were operating.[86] More likely was the nagging fear among many that the rich and powerful were ordering society for their personal profit. The theft of the presidency to restore Hamiltonian men of business to government provided ample proof that conspiracies existed. If the government itself could be stolen, nothing was safe.

Simply stated, therefore, the antimasonic movement was another expression of mounting concern in the country over the apparent efforts of a self-declared elite to subvert fundamental rights in order to obtain their selfish objectives. Freedom of the individual—in this case poor Morgan —meant nothing to Masons and could be extinguished if it jeopardized their secret organization. As long as Masons controlled the levers of governmental power, liberty for all could be endangered. Thus, antimasonry quickly developed into a political movement, committed to the expulsion of Masons from positions of public trust, and it slowly spread from New York into New England and parts of the midwest.

In no time at all someone pointed out that Andrew Jackson was a high-ranking Mason while Adams was free "from all imputed criminality of that sort." The irony of Adams "the corrupter" becoming the darling of this anti-elitist movement, while Jackson "the democrat" stood revealed as an official of this "aristocratic conspiracy" confounded politicians in both camps.[87]

James A. Hamilton of New York immediately wrote to Jackson for confirmation of his membership in the Masonic fraternity. The General admitted it. "I have to observe that I presided several years as Royal Arch Mason in the great Lodge of Tennessee," he said, "but have not attended the sessions for two years or thereabouts." Moreover, "I have not attended the Chapter for many years, say fifteen or twenty." He quickly added that if Morgan had in fact been murdered to sustain the "power" of the society it would be "a stain on our history. . . . Such an unhallowed use of power can scarcely be credited here."[88]

Jackson's membership in the Masonic brotherhood was a distinct political setback for him, and he knew it. When Van Buren returned to New York from Washington in 1827 he made a hurried tour of the western counties to learn for himself the extent of the political damage. He was staggered by what he discovered. Still he pretended it was less than devastating. The "politics of this State," he assured Old Hickory, "are yet governed by Old Party feelings." Although antimasonry was a real blow, "I am sure I cannot be mistaken in believing, that we shall be able to give you a very decided majority of the votes."[89] What distressed the Magician particularly was the identification of Jackson with a fraternity of men who favored centralized power to achieve their personal ends. The situation improved a trifle when someone "discovered" that Henry Clay was a "Mason of rank." Van Buren's henchmen in New York quickly passed the word. "He has been in Lodges, Chapters &c," said one. "Cannot this be so used with Clay's friends in our Western Districts, or with the people, as to divert that question from mingling with the Presidential one?"[90] After a while the charge of Masonry became a smear. Even Jackson himself indulged in the practice. When several letters unfriendly to his candidacy were circulated by two of his acquaintances the General denounced them. Their "base falsehoods . . . must be stated in bold relief"; besides, both were "Master Masons—and this two, ought to be stated."[91]

The potential danger of the anti-Masonic movement to Jackson's candidacy was at least localized in 1828. Its political strength had only begun to mount. By the late summer of 1828 its threat seemed minuscule, and a great many Democrats declared their confidence that Jackson would win, and maybe win big.[92] "The indications of public sentiment, throughout the union, have anticipated the decision of the ballot-boxes," wrote William C. Rives of Virginia, "& Gen Jackson, as surely as he lives, will be the President of the United States, for four years from the 4th day of March next." Those four years, Rives ventured, "are to form the most important epoch, in my opinion, that has yet occurred in the history of the Republic. On the complexion of those four years, it will perhaps, finally depend, whether we are to remain an united & happy people." Jackson must undo all the harm inflicted by the Adams administration both as to specific policies and general attitude. He must "retrace all the steps" taken by the "corrupt coalition," correct abuses, and restore "the rights of the States." On the matter of the tariff, internal improvements, and the general conduct of the government the American people expect reform. "To insure success in all these reforms, the executive must be seconded . . . by the Legislative Department." By the close of the campaign most Democrats understood that "Jackson and Reform" were their only hope in preserving "an united & happy people."[93]

The managers of the Democratic party in the several states succeeded brilliantly in fixing the campaign slogan "Jackson and Reform" in the public conscience. As early as the congressional elections of 1827 they had discovered the potency of those magic words, and they used them to take the measure of all who would participate in their new party. "Scarce a doubt remains of Ohio's vote being for Jackson & reform at the next election," announced Caleb Atwater in 1827. "We are making it a test at this election, for members of our Legislature. We shall succeed too, without a doubt."[94]

And they succeeded beyond all expectation. The nation seemed ready for General Andrew Jackson and with him his program of reform. By the fall of 1828 even Old Hickory himself sensed victory. The "signs of the times," as he put it, looked very favorable and that in itself helped ease the pain of this long and harrowing campaign. Not that the pace of the canvass slackened at the end. If anything it seemed more intense. He still provided information for committees and met visiting politicians right up to the moment of the election itself. Sometimes the effort almost overwhelmed him. He got so confused with "the hurry & bustle of my company leaving me" that he inadvertently sent a letter intended for Samuel

Ingham, one of his strongest supporters in Pennsylvania, to William Lewis. It was not the company so much that triggered the momentary lapse, he protested, but rather the fact that he was engaged in "watching over an unfortunate individual whose spirit is about to take its flight from its earthly tabernacle—from one in the last stages of consumption." This unfortunate individual was sent to Jackson by Colonel Weakly, who had put him in a carriage and had him delivered to the Hermitage. "I suppose the poor fellow in a state of delirium, requested to be brought here," Jackson continued, "but it is strange to me why the Col should suppose I was more able to watch over a dying man than he. For this I cannot account." Be that as it may, Jackson concluded, "humanity compelled me to take him in, & tender to the distressed, all that a good Samaritan could do, in a few hours the unfortunate being will be at rest, & I will discharge faithfully the last act that humanity can bestow. I barely name this to account to you for the mistake I have committed, as the attention to the sick, & my company occasioned it."[95]

This very characteristic gesture of compassion by Jackson was something few outsiders ever saw. They only knew what newspapers recounted, and a hostile press always presented him as a cruel and merciless man, ruthless and unbending, stern and unforgiving. Yet this "cruel" man could take into his house a complete stranger who was dying of tuberculosis and care for him during his final hours, reckoning it of no great moment. It was simply his Christian duty.

Because of his great sense of humanity those who knew Jackson well declared him a decent man, a just man, a man worthy to sit in the White House and preside over the destiny of the American people.

CHAPTER 8

Triumph and Tragedy

THE SCURRILOUS GUTTER TACTICS of unprincipled politicians and journalists scored deep wounds in the mind and heart of a gentle Christian woman whose sole purpose in life was to serve her God and her husband. "I am denyd maney pleasurs & Comforts in this Life," Rachel wrote. Only her boundless faith in her Redeemer sustained her. The Gospel says that all things are possible in Christ, and "I Can say my soule Can be a testimony to the truth of that Gospel for who has been so cruelly tryed as I have my mind my trials hav been severe." More times than anyone ever realized Rachel broke down and cried hysterically over what was said about her. "The persecution she has suffered," admitted Jackson, "has endeared *her more if possible than ever to me.*" Although he tried to shield her from the calumnies propagated by the press, she knew the extent of the slander and how she had been used to injure her husband. The "Enemyes of the Genls," she told her friend, Elizabeth Watson, "have Dipt their arrows in wormwood & gall & sped them at me almighty God was ther Ever aney thing to Equal it my old acquantances wer as much hurt as if it was them selves or Daughters." Her charity, her decency, her many years of service to all who needed her meant nothing to her husband's opponents.

to think that thirty years had past in happy social friendship with society, knowing or thinking no ill to no one. as my judg will know—how maney prayers have I oferd up for thir repentence—but wo unto them if offencces come theay have Disquietd one that theay had no rite to do theay have offended God and man. in as much as you offend one of the Least of my little ones you offend me. now I leave them to them selves I feare them not I feare Him that can Kill the Body & Cast the Soule into Hell fire. o Eternity awful is the name. this has been a subject my Dear friend that I fear has pained your Sympathezing friendly Disposition toward your friends. let not your Heart be troubled. I am on the rock of ages. in the world I have tribulation. jesus says in me you shall have peace, my peace I gave unto you not as the world &c &c. . . .

I had a hope when I last saw you of haveing the happyness of having you beside me a neighbour but in that I am disapointed. well I remember you allways & should I not see you here I hope to see you with Jesus in the new jerusalem, we shall hav no more sorrow no malevolent Enemies ther to harm us. farwell my much Loved friend & sister.[1]

No more sorrow. No malevolent enemies. Rachel's one abiding hope was surcease from her anguish and torment. She no longer had the strength to face the perpetual disdain and criticism of her husband's political enemies. She needed rest. She needed repose and quiet. Sometimes she seemed so weary that she could barely function around the house. She complained of heart palpitations. She suffered bronchial distress. Often she could scarcely talk above a wheeze.

Then, on June 1, 1828, Rachel suffered a frightful blow when her son Lyncoya died suddenly of a "pulmonary complaint." He was only sixteen years of age. When the hope of educating him at West Point ended with the election of John Q. Adams to the presidency, Lyncoya was apprenticed to a saddler in Nashville in 1827. The following winter he caught a bad cold which so weakened him that he got a leave of absence "and returned, as he said, 'home,' to the Hermitage." Rachel nursed him diligently, tending to his diet and a regimen of exercise. In vain. After "very severe sufferings" Lyncoya "expired under the roof of the hero who had conquered his nation but who followed his remains to a decent grave, and shed a tear as the earth closed over him forever."[2]

Rachel was grief-stricken, and she never totally recovered from the shock. Still she managed a brave front for her husband's sake. Little did he know that his ambition was slowly turning her into a tired, sick, and weary old lady. Even when the tone and mood at the Hermitage took a bright turn toward the closing months of the campaign, Rachel still looked wistful and sad. The idea of going to Washington and living in the White House and confronting some of the people who had vilified her was not something she anticipated with pleasure. But if that is what the General wished her to do, then she would find the strength somehow and yield to his wishes.

And the campaign did end triumphantly. Indeed Jackson's victory at the polls stunned politicians in both parties, so vast did it appear to them at the time. Local Jackson organizations had given much attention to turning out the vote. Not a few central committees brought the electorate to the polls in companies of fifty or sixty marching behind a banner blazoned with the motto "JACKSON AND REFORM." Elsewhere Hickory Clubs distributed flags and bunting to encourage the party faithful to troop to the polls and register their demand for the restoration of virtue and republicanism.

"To the Polls!" commanded Duff Green in his *United States Telegraph.* "To the Polls! The faithful sentinel must not sleep—Let no one stay home—Let every man go to the Polls—Let not a vote be lost—Let each Freeman do his duty; and all will triumph in the success of

JACKSON, CALHOUN and LIBERTY"[3]

Let the Freeman speak and all will triumph in the restoration of liberty! Jackson's election would inaugurate an era of reform to revitalize the nation's commitment to its revolutionary past.

Voting procedures in 1828 varied widely throughout the twenty-four states. State legislatures chose the electors in both South Carolina and Delaware; everywhere else the electors were selected from a general or district ticket by an electorate that was roughly equivalent—except in Virginia, Louisiana, and Rhode Island[4]—to the adult white male population. New York, Tennessee, Illinois, Maine, and Maryland utilized the districting system (which meant that the state's electoral vote could be split), while the others used the general ticket, which awarded all the state's electoral votes to the candidate with the highest popular total. Between 1824 and 1828, four states—New York, Vermont, Georgia, and Louisiana—changed their electoral laws to permit, for the first time, popular selection of presidential electors. This single reform, as the harbinger of many other reforms to come over the next two decades, increased the total number of voters participating directly in American presidential elections by several hundred thousand.

Balloting began in September and ended in November. In each state the balloting occurred over several days and the polls opened at various times even within a single state. By the middle of October partial returns from states with early election dates began to circulate around the country, and they caused some to wonder if a "revolution" was in the making. These first returns indicated a gigantic sweep for Old Hickory. In Pennsylvania alone Jackson ran ahead of Adams by 2 to 1, and the final tally gave the westerner 101,652 popular votes to 50,848 for the New Englander. More important, all 28 electoral votes went to Jackson.

"All Hail Pennsylvania," crowed Duff Green. "Good old Pennsylvania. Victory! Victory! Victory!"[5] By "her virtue and love of liberty," wrote Jackson when he received the tally, Pennsylvania showed herself worthy of her preeminence in the Union. "That state is as firm in the cause of Republicanism and liberal principles as are her native mountains," he added.[6]

Ohio followed into the Jackson column, although not with such a resounding triumph. Again Duff Green claimed it as a stupendous victory. In a letter to Jackson he assured the General that these incredible results were the beginnings of an unprecedented popular declaration of support for him and the principles undergirding his campaign. "It will be a Triumph," he predicted, "such as never was before achieved in the country and permit me to unite with the millions of free men who cheer the 'Hickory Tree.'" [7]

Other politicians had the same reaction as Green. The initial returns looked like the onset of a landslide, and the only way they could account for it was the popularity of Jackson and the "millions of free men" who registered their will at the polls. They called it a triumph of democracy over aristocracy, a victory for the common man, the inauguration of popular government. These quick and glib generalizations characterized the initial impression of the outcome, but they remained the basic interpretation of this election for months and years afterward.

"How triumphant," enthused Andrew J. Donelson, "how flattering to the cause of the people."[8] Even Jackson himself was impressed by what he called his "overwhelming majorities" in the early returns. Because he was such a consummate politician—and getting better with each contest—he summoned Major Lewis to pass the information along to other western states that had not yet voted, so that these results might be used to his advantage. "This is a change that my friends did not calculate upon," he said.[9]

Then Kentucky—Henry Clay's own state!—swung behind Jackson with a handsome majority. "The people of Kentucky," wrote Amos Kendall in announcing the result to the General, "cannot be induced by management, by art, by falsehood nor even by her attachments, to be unjust to our country's defenders, or give her sanction to a corrupt administration of the general government." If nothing else, "the line of Secretary succession is broken. . . . I look forward to a new era under your administration, distinguished not only by reform in the administration of the government, but by such changes in its form as will cut off all inducements to men high in Office to use the patronage of their stations for the purpose of purchasing popularity." In response, Jackson wrote a jubilant letter. Kentucky, he said, had demonstrated its "devotedness to the principles of liberty." He promised with the aid of "Providence" to fortify and strengthen "those points in our Government thro' which our enemies have attempted to invade our liberties."[10]

Perhaps nowhere else had liberty been challenged so directly as in Kentucky when Clay handed over its electoral vote in 1825 to Adams in defiance of the popular will. The victory, therefore, seemed all the more delicious and Jackson could not resist describing it as a triumph for freedom.

"We are beaten," conceded the dejected Clay.[11] "The Hunters of Kentucky" had deserted him.

Although New England went almost totally for Adams,[12] the entire south, most of the middle Atlantic states, and the western states joined

Pennsylvania, Ohio, and Kentucky to give Jackson a total of 647,276 popular votes and 178 electoral votes in the final tally. Adams received 508,064 popular votes and 83 electoral votes.[13] In the electoral college Adams suffered a crushing defeat. In addition to New England he won New Jersey, Delaware, a majority of electoral votes in Maryland, 16 of New York's 36 votes, and a single vote from Illinois. Jackson took all the rest.

Old Hickory glowed. The "virtuous portion of the people have well sustained me," he recorded. His "overwhelming majorities" were "very gratifying to me, and under the weight of executive patronage wielded as it was to corrupt the people, and by propagating its slanders by its panders and corrupt minions, expected to destroy me. in this it has failed, and the suffrages of a virtuous people have pronounced a verdict of condemnation against them and their slanders whilst it has justified my character and course. I am filled with gratitude."[14]

Not unexpectedly Jackson saw his election as a victory for the preservation of American freedom. Not simply in Kentucky, as he had expressed in his letter to Kendall, but around the country. The verdict of the people, he said, condemned and cast out the corruption of the past and "has pronounced to an admiring world that the people are virtuous, and capable of self government, and that the liberty of our beloved country will be perpetual." The presidential election of 1828, he declared, was a "triumph of the great principle of self government over the intrigues of aristocracy."[15]

Everyone agreed—the opposition included—that something extraordinary had happened. Not all would accept Jackson's interpretation of his election but they did acknowledge that something unique in the annals of American politics had occurred. A "great revolution has taken place," was the opinion of one National Republican. "It was the howl of raving Democracy," sneered another disappointed friend of the coalition. Jackson's "triumphant majority," wrote Hezekiah Niles, a journalist of the opposition, resulted from the "ardor of thousands." The coalition of Adams and Clay, said Edward Everett to his brother, was defeated "by a majority of more than *two* to *one,* an event astounding to the friends of the Administration and unexpected by the General himself and his friends. . . . [They] are embarrassed with the vastness of their triumph and the numbers of their party."[16]

Small wonder Americans spoke of the election as a victory of democracy, small wonder historians saw it as inaugurating the age of the common man. Contemporaries believed this, and Jackson and his party propagated it. Their words rang with slogans proclaiming the majesty of the people and their right to self-government. Not only were the people virtuous, according to the Democrats, they were wise.[17]

Jackson's victory did not actually register a "vast" outpouring of voters.[18] It just looked that way. In a country of nearly 13,000,000, some

1,155,340 white males participated in the election, which is statistically rather small. Even so, that small number represented an increase of more than 800,000 over the previous presidential election, so it appeared at the time to signal a far-ranging awakening of public interest in the election of the chief executive.

It was, in fact, an outstanding showing and several factors shaped it. First and foremost was the Hero's enormous popularity among all classes of Americans in all the sections of the country. Second was the conviction that Adams had obtained his office by a flagrant and cynical disregard of the will of the people. And third was the superior organization of the Democratic party. Through the work of local and state committees and newspapers a "concentrated effort," as Van Buren termed it, scored large majorities for Jackson in certain key states in the west and middle Atlantic area. Organization was crucial in Ohio, Kentucky, New York, and Pennsylvania. "Organization is the secret of victory," pronounced one newspaper friendly to Adams. "By the want of it we have been overthrown."[19]

Jackson's personal popularity, so vital in this election, eased the burden of constructing a party organization. The "hurra boys" flocked to his standard.[20] And Jackson's popularity consisted of more than mere gratitude for his military accomplishments. The American people loved Jackson and trusted him. "They believed him honest and patriotic; that he was the friend of the *people,* battling for them against corruption and extravagance, and opposed only by dishonest politicians."[21] They voted to place him at the head of their government with the expectation that he would, in Jackson's own words, "purify the Departments" and "reform the Government."[22] In this "triumph of the great principle of self government," wrote Edmund P. Gaines, who better to lead the people and "cleans the Augean stables" than the foremost Democrat of them all, Andrew Jackson?[23]

The presidential election of 1828, therefore, represented a victory not only for a much beloved and trusted public figure but a demand for the restoration of morality and virtue to civic life, and a reform of those practices that had corrupted officials, expanded government, and endangered freedom. It represented a reaffirmation of the republican doctrines of the Revolution.

When the news of Old Hickory's victory finally arrived at the Hermitage it created "no great sensation." It was almost anticlimactic, since so many people in the household, both friends and relatives, expected it, especially after the first returns came in. They immediately brought the good news to Rachel, who looked a little wistful when she heard it for she realized what it meant in terms of public exposure and comment. "Well, for Mr. Jackson's sake, I am glad," she said; "for my own part, I never wished it."[24]

Jackson himself caught the trace of sadness that flickered momentarily across her face. Although he was filled with gratitude to the American people for their great gift, "still my mind is depressed," he wrote.[25] Naturally the people of Nashville planned a great celebration to salute their Hero and acknowledge the honor he had brought to their state. A "banquet unparalleled" was immediately planned for December 23, the anniversary of the night battle of New Orleans, and Jackson gratefully accepted the invitation to attend. For Rachel, the ladies of Nashville secretly prepared a magnificent wardrobe for her tenure as First Lady and mistress of the White House. They planned to provide something special to impress easterners with the fashions of western dress.

Rachel herself seemed to wilt with all the fuss and commotion. She had no taste for public life, and after what had been said about her in the campaign she shivered at the thought of what lay ahead. She shared some of her misery with her friend Elizabeth Watson, and the sound of her cry brought tears to Elizabeth's eyes.[26]

Rachel's poor health and sagging spirits raised the question of whether she should remain in Tennessee until after the inauguration. If she could quietly slip into the capital at a later time, the transition from Tennessee matron to First Lady might be more easily accomplished. When Senator Eaton heard of the possibility of her delayed arrival he wrote to her from Washington and urged her to reconsider. "The storm has now abated," he insisted, "the angry tempest has ceased to howl. A verdict by the American people has been pronounced . . . that for the honor of your husband you cannot . . . look back on the past. . . . No man has ever met such a triumph before. . . . If you shall be absent how great will be the dissapointment. Your persecutors then may chuckle, and say that they have driven you from the field of your husbands honors."[27]

There was no escaping the truth of Eaton's words. Much as she might wish to wait until the excitement of the inauguration had passed before leaving the Cumberland, Rachel knew her duty.

The thought depressed her. Worse, it sapped her strength. One day she took a long walk and found herself much exhausted by the exercise. She returned home, wheezing and panting. The strain was beginning to tell.

Inside the Hermitage the pitch of activity had already begun to mount in preparation for the departure for Washington and the subsequent inaugural. Jackson was deluged with "addresses of congratulations from committees from various parts," he wrote, "accompanied with invitations to visit them etc. etc. which I am obliged to answer. I receive at least one hundred letters a week, none of which unless from committees, do I answer, indeed it would take ten clerks, and was it not for the aid of Capt A. J. Donelson I could not reply to half of what are necessary to be answered."[28]

For her part Rachel kept as far away from these preparations as possible. "I assure you," she once said, "I had rather be a doorkeeper in the house of God than to live in that palace at Washington."[29]

Early in December, after the final results of the election were known, Rachel forced herself to go to Nashville to buy the clothes she would need for her new position. As she shopped from store to store she soon grew weary. Her strength faltered and she felt uncomfortable. She retreated to the private office of a newspaper editor in town—one of her many relatives—to wait until her carriage could be readied for her return to the Hermitage. While waiting she picked up a campaign pamphlet prepared by the General's friends. It happened to be a defense of her behavior prior to her marriage to Jackson, but what she read staggered her. Never before had she known the full range of the slander leveled against her. The language, the implications, the outright accusation of adultery and bigamy. Now she had it all. Overwhelmed, she crouched in a corner and wept hysterically. When her companions returned to inform her that her carriage was ready they found a completely distraught and terror-stricken woman. Fortunately, the twelve-mile journey home gave her time to compose herself. She was determined not to distress her husband. She even went out of her way to appear lighthearted. But her forced gaiety only attracted his attention and he demanded to know what had happened. With choked-back sobs she informed him of her experience. Jackson now saw in her pitiful condition the human price of his bid for the presidency.[30]

From that moment on Rachel Jackson began a slow mental and physical decline.[31] Perhaps she gave up. Her eyes drifted and fixed themselves on a distant place. The beginning of the end came on Wednesday, December 18, when she contracted a cold and "pleuritic symptoms" set in.[32] Otherwise everything was normal at the Hermitage. The General was busy at his desk writing[33] and Rachel occupied herself with her household duties. Old Hannah, one of her servants, asked her to come into the kitchen to give advice about the preparation of the evening meal. Rachel explained what she wanted and then returned to the sitting room, followed by Hannah. Suddenly, she felt a stabbing pain in her chest and left arm. She screamed as she clutched her heart. Sinking into a chair, she struggled for breath and fell forward into Hannah's arms. Servants came running at the sound of the scream and when they saw the plight of their mistress they themselves began wailing and supplicating the Almighty for mercy. They gently carried Rachel to her bed, while Hannah applied the only remedy she knew. She vigorously rubbed her mistress's side "till it was black and blue."[34]

Still no relief. The pain intensified. The stricken woman writhed in agony. She gasped for breath. She twisted and turned, clutching at the bedsheets for release from the torment.

As soon as he heard her cry, Jackson dropped his pen and raced to his wife. He knelt at her bedside and offered words of comfort. A rider sped into town to summon medical aid. Neighbors were notified. Emily Donelson, the bride of Andrew Jackson Donelson, hurried over from her house nearby. Soon the Hermitage overflowed with relatives, friends, and servants, all trying to give assistance but none capable of rendering any real help.

Dr. Henry Lee Heiskell, visiting from Virginia, and Dr. Samuel Hogg, the Jacksons' regular physician, responded to the General's call. Heiskell arrived first and found Rachel contorted in pain on account of muscle spasms of the chest and left shoulder, accompanied by an irregular heartbeat. He bled her. To no avail. Again. Still no respite. After Hogg arrived they bled her a third time. Only then, very gradually, did the pain subside, and Rachel fell asleep.[35]

Over the next sixty hours General Jackson watched her closely, rarely leaving her side. She rallied somewhat, although she was still weak and listless. She worried about her husband, knowing a great banquet was being planned in Nashville and that he must attend. She begged him to get some rest. Finally he relented and consented to lie on the sofa in an adjoining room and try and get a few hours' sleep. The doctor remained in the house, and Hannah and George agreed to sit up with their mistress. It seemed at last that the General could safely leave her.

It was then nine o'clock, Sunday the twenty-second of December. The General bid his wife goodnight and retired to the next room, removing his coat. He was gone only five minutes. At her bidding the servants lifted Rachel from her bed for the first time so that the sheets might be arranged for the night. While sitting in the chair, supported by Hannah, Rachel suffered another severe attack. She let out a long, loud cry. There was a "rattling sound in her throat." Her head fell forward onto Hannah's shoulder. Rachel died at that moment.[36]

Jackson bolted through the door when he heard the cry. Servants and relatives also rushed in and immediately set up a prolonged and mournful wail. The doctor and Jackson lifted her from the chair and gently placed her back on her bed. The two men stared at each other, half-reading each other's thoughts. The General glanced down at his wife, his face registering his alarm and dread.

"Bleed her," he cried.

The doctor operated but no blood flowed from her arm.

Jackson froze.

"Try the temple, Doctor," he begged.

The doctor obeyed. Two drops oozed from the incision and stained her cap. Nothing more.

Piercing cries from the servants flooded the room. The husband searched her face for any sign of life, refusing to believe that she was dead. He stood by her side for hours, hoping to see some indication of returning life. Only when her hands and feet grew cold did Andrew Jackson accept the fact that his beloved was gone.

The servants prepared a table on which to lay the corpse. In a choking voice, the husband directed their actions. "Spread four blankets upon it," he said. "If she does come to, she won't lie so hard upon the table."

The body was arranged and Jackson spent the night by his wife's side, his face in his hands, grieving. Every once in a while he would look pleadingly into her face and feel for a pulse or heartbeat.

In the morning Major Lewis arrived and found Jackson still sitting in the same position. The General was wholly inconsolable and had quite lost his voice. He remained in the room nearly all the next day, "the picture of despair."[37]

"And this was the way that old mistus died," reported Hannah. "And we always say, that when we lost her, we lost a mistus and a mother, too: and more a mother than a mistus. And we say the same of old master; for he was more a father to us than a master, and many's the time we've wished him back again, to help us out of our troubles."[38]

Thirty-eight years earlier Rachel and Andrew had run off to Natchez and later married. They had been legally married just a few weeks short of thirty-five years when she died. She had been a true and beloved companion, his loyal supporter in all things. She had enough grit and spirit to complain about the things that troubled her—such as his frequent departures to serve his country—but she always went along with whatever he wanted. She had been a blessing to Jackson's life, and now that the most important period of his career was about to begin her calming and devoted presence would be gone. It proved a terrible loss to him and to the nation.

Everyone appreciated what a dreadful consequence Rachel's death might have upon the country. Here was a woman "fondly and excessively loved," a wife who could control the violence of her husband's temper, who healed the wounds he inflicted, and by her charity to all compensated for his notorious failures. "I fear not only the domestic circle," wrote Margaret Bayard Smith, the wife of the Maryland senator, "but the public will suffer from this restraining and benign influence being withdrawn."[39]

Years later, Uncle Alfred, one of Jackson's last servants, gave tours of the Hermitage. In the General's bedroom he would point to a picture of Rachel—one that still hangs there. "This is de picture of Miss Rachel," he would say. "Every morning de general would kneel before it and tell his God that he thank him to spare his life one more night to look on de face of his love."[40]

Andrew Jackson mourned deeply and ceaselessly the loss of his gentle wife. The many hours he sat by Rachel's still form, taking no food or drink, rarely leaving her side, showed how far he would physically push himself for her sake. It was only with great difficulty that his neighbors convinced him to husband his strength by taking a little coffee. Heartsick, grief-stricken, plagued himself by ill health, this sixty-one-year-old man responded once again to the call of duty. He must soon take on the burdens of government.[41]

The news of Rachel's death immediately canceled the reception and banquet scheduled in Nashville in the General's honor. The tables were practically set, "all was expected to be hilarity and joy," reported one newspaper. Now there was gloom. Congratulations dissolved into condolences, smiles into tears, gladness into sorrow. The entire Nashville community went into mourning, so beloved was this kind and charitable woman. The mayor and the board of aldermen voted a resolution urging the people of Nashville to abstain from their ordinary business on December 24 and that churchbells be tolled from one to two o'clock during the hour of her funeral.[42]

As husband and wife had agreed earlier, Rachel was to be buried in her lovely garden, just a few hundred steps from the entrance of the Hermitage. Arrangements for the funeral were quickly concluded. On the morning of December 24, Christmas eve, every road leading to the Jackson home was choked with people. Vehicles of every description, jammed with mourners, trudged across fields and pastures to reach the site of the funeral. Men on horseback, women and children on foot, came to pay their respects. Some ten thousand souls crowded around the mansion and overflowed into the surrounding pastureland. "Such a scene," wrote one eyewitness, "I never wish to witness again."[43] All Davidson County seemed to have converged at this spot to mourn a woman who in her own right had won their gratitude and affection.

At one o'clock, as churchbells began their mournful dirge, the casket[44] was slowly carried from the Hermitage along the curved garden walk to the spot that had been dug to receive it. Sam Houston led the pallbearers. Then Old Hickory himself stumbled out of the house, supported by the ever-faithful Coffee and Major Henry M. Rutledge, one of Jackson's aides in Florida. Jackson looked ghastly as he followed the casket, his face mirroring his sorrow. "I never pitied any person more in my life," said one. Behind the General came a horde of Donelsons, themselves grief-stricken at the loss of Sister Jackson. Brothers, sisters, nephews, nieces, once, twice, three times removed, walked in solemn procession. The servants followed, moaning and wailing. They demonstrated uncommon devotion and love for their mistress. "I never before saw so much affliction among servants on the death of a mistress," reported one observer. "Some seemed completely stupified by the event; others wrung their hands and shrieked aloud."[45] Old Hannah collapsed at the gravesite and had to be carried off the ground. "My mistress, my best friend, my love, my life, is gone," she cried. "I will go with her."[46]

Apparently Jackson spoke first during the ritual, saying something about Rachel's suffering and how deserving she was of "our tears."[47] Then the Reverend William Hume delivered the graveside eulogy. For his text he used the passage, "The righteous shall be in everlasting remembrance." He praised Rachel's religious steadfastness, her tender and loving heart. "The tears of genuine penitence were often shed by her in the temple of the Lord," he said. Her meekness and quiet spirit, her kindness and affability evoked a mood to make her husband "more happy in his own family than in the midst of his triumphs." During the last presidential campaign, he continued, she underwent untold agonies. "Her compassionate heart was wrung with sorrow. Her tears flowed, but there was no malevolence in her bosom." We sympathize with our new President, he said, "in the irreparable loss he has sustained in the death of his amiable lady, whom he deemed so worthy, as he said, of our tears; we cannot doubt but that she now dwells in the mansions of glory in company with the ransomed of the Lord."[48]

Jackson broke down. For the first time since her death tears ran freely down his cheeks. But he quickly regained control. He did not wish to release the catch on his emotions.

The rites concluded, several mourners reached out their hands to Jackson to express their individual sorrow. The old man could barely talk. One gentleman stepped forward and several men standing near Jackson mentioned his name. The Hero caught the gentleman's hand and squeezed it three times. He started to speak but all he could utter was, "Philadelphia." The gentleman was overcome with sadness. "I never shall forget the look of grief," he said.[49]

Slowly the family, along with a small crowd of people, returned to the Hermitage. When he reached the northeast room Jackson seemed to recover his composure, for he began to speak almost immediately and his words were uttered "calmly, firmly . . . and in such deep silence of the crowd" that they were heard distinctly by everyone in the room.

"Friends and neighbors," he began, "I thank you for the honor you have done to the sainted one whose remains now repose in yonder grave. She is now in the bliss of heaven, and I know that she can suffer here no more on earth. That is enough for my consolation; my loss is her gain. But I am left without her to encounter the trials of life alone." Jackson paused at that point as though meditating on what he had just said. "I am now President of the United States," he continued after the pause, "and in a short time must take my way to the metropolis of my country; and, if it had been God's will, I would have been grateful for the privilege of taking her to my post of honor and seating her by my side; but Providence knew what was best for her. For myself, I bow to God's will, and go alone to the place of new and arduous duties, and I shall not go without friends to reward, and I pray God that I may not be allowed to have enemies to punish." His eyes kindled a little as he spoke these words. "I can forgive all who have wronged me, but will have fervently to pray that I may have grace to enable me to forget or forgive any enemy who has ever maligned that blessed one who is now safe from all suffering and sorrow, whom they tried to put to shame for my sake!" With that Jackson ended his short eulogy, but everyone in the room was deeply moved by what he had said. "We can never forget it," said one.[50]

Newspapers around the country announced the death of the wife of the

President-elect. They focused on two points: Rachel's basic goodness, and the slander that had torn her life apart. They remain even now the principal ingredients of her sixty-one-year life.

Jackson shielded the grave with a wooden cover until he could arrange a suitable monument. What he ordered before leaving for Washington was a small, round, white domed roof supported by pillars of white marble resembling in form a Greek temple. Later a tablet was placed directly over the grave. It reads as follows:

> Here lie the remains of Mrs. Rachel Jackson, wife of President Jackson, who died the 22d of December, 1828, aged 61. Her face was fair; her person pleasing, her temper amiable, her heart kind; she delighted in relieving the wants of her fellow-creatures, and cultivated that divine pleasure by the most liberal and unpretending methods; to the poor she was a benefactor; to the rich an example; to the wretched a comforter; to the prosperous an ornament: her piety went hand in hand with her benevolence, and she thanked her Creator for being permitted to do good. A being so gentle and so virtuous, slander might wound but could not dishonor. Even death, when he tore her from the arms of her husband, could but transport her to the bosom of her God.[51]

Even at her death he mentioned the slander. He could not blot it from his mind. Andrew Jackson never forgot.

CHAPTER 9

The First People's Inaugural

"MY HEART IS NEARLY BROKE," the old soldier wept.[1] The "partner of my life," my "dearest heart,"—assassinated by vile slanderers. Although President-elect Jackson could not take pen in hand and write his own letters just yet—his nephew, Andrew Jackson Donelson, had become his most capable amanuensis—he did begin answering his mail within three days after he buried Rachel. Writing to General Jean Plauché and excusing himself for not responding sooner because of the tragedy, Jackson bemoaned his staggering loss, a "loss so great, so sudden and unexpected, I need not say to you, can be compensated by no earthly gift. Could it be, it might be found in the reflection that she lived long enough to see the countless assaults of our enemies disarmed by the voice of our beloved country."[2]

This was his only solace, that Rachel had lived long enough to know that the American people had repudiated "the countless assaults" against them and had awarded him a triumphant vote of confidence. Thank God she lived to see it, he said; without that comfort his victory would have been in vain.[3] The special meaning that Jackson gave to his popular vote intensified his feelings toward the people. He was profoundly grateful to them. Additional bonds of affection and gratitude between this crusty old soldier and the electorate formed and strengthened as a result of the presidential election. They never slackened thereafter.

Democrats around the country offered Jackson their version of the outcome in their many letters to him. But most seemed to agree with Senator Robert Y. Hayne of South Carolina, who told Old Hickory that it was "a triumph of principle over intrigue, of truth over falsehood; in one word, of *the people* over corruption."[4] Democrats anticipated "a new Epoch in the history of our country," added Thomas Ritchie of Virginia, the start of an era of reform based on "wise and constitutional principles."[5]

Although Jackson welcomed these heady versions of the meaning of the popular vote and even bestirred himself sufficiently to write a brief acknowledgement of his election in case a congressional committee should wish to inform him of it officially, he had little desire to attend to any functions connected with the government or the start of his administration.[6] His main concern was the completion of the arrangements for building the tomb for his wife. It was almost impossible for him to concentrate on anything else. "My mind is so disturbed," he wrote, "and I am even now perplexed with company that I can scarcely write. . . . I try to summon up my usual fortitude but it is vain, the time, the sudden and afflictive shock, was as severe as unexpected."[7]

Slowly, over the next several weeks, Jackson forced his mind to attend to his new duties. On Sunday, January 18, 1829 the steamboat that would begin his journey to Washington arrived on the Cumberland. He was not certain whether he would leave that very day or wait until Monday, in view of public disapproval of government officials traveling on the sabbath, something that earned John Quincy Adams considerable criticism during the campaign and about which Jackson would receive a letter of admonition from the Reverend Ezra Stiles Ely of Philadelphia.[8] At length he decided to wait. In his present mood he had no desire to provoke lectures about the sanctity of Sundays.

When at last Jackson appeared in public he was of course dressed in deep mourning—and he remained in deep mourning for an unusually long period of time. In some respects he never stopped mourning his wife. He dressed in a black suit, white shirt, and black tie. Usually he wore a black band on his arm and another black band around his tall beaver hat, a portion of which hung down the back of his neck and was called a weeper. He appeared terribly grave on his first appearance, but observers noted that he still looked every inch the gentleman and soldier.[9] Indeed, he was the most presidential-looking figure to head the nation since George Washington.

Through the Democratic press the Hero let it be known that he wanted no "public shows and receptions" during his journey.[10] Although they tried to respect his wishes on account of his great loss, the public could not resist assembling to catch a view of him when they heard of his presence in the neighborhood. Apart from anything else they needed to reassure themselves that he was well and ready to assume command of the government.

The journey from the Hermitage to Washington began on January 19 and took a little more than three weeks. The steamboat *Pennsylvania* carried the Jackson party along the Cumberland and up the Ohio River as far as Pittsburgh. Two hickory brooms—to sweep the Augean stables obviously—proudly graced the bow of the boat.

Along the riverside crowds of people waved and cheered as the boat paddled by. When the cheering swelled Jackson invariably came out on deck "to salute the good people as he passed with his hat off."[11] Wherever the steamboat stopped a large mass of people thronged the dock to greet him. The "brutal familiarity," as Mrs. Frances Trollope described it, with which common people approached him or spoke to him offended those of finer sensibility. He shook hands with all who reached out to him but he always maintained a dignity and bearing that impressed everyone who saw him.[12]

When the steamboat landed at Pittsburgh and the party prepared to disembark a huge horde of spectators crowded the dock. Their number swelled to such a size that the reception committee feared they would inadvertently tumble the President-elect and his companions into the muddy river.[13] It took Jackson over an hour to get through the mass of people and walk to his hotel a quarter of a mile away.

At Pittsburgh the Jackson party switched to the overland route to Washington, following the Cumberland Road most of the way. It became impossible to restrain the mobs that formed along this route or prevent demonstrations to mark his passage. Everyone had to see him. They cheered and applauded. They begged him to stop and say a few words.

In Washington spectacular preparations were underway for the inaugural. Not since George Washington had a President-elect been absent from the seat of government at the time of his election. So the mayor of the city submitted to the Board of Alderman and the Board of Common Council for their consideration "the expedience of some public assurance to the President-elect of welcome." There were precedents for this, he said, in particular the arrival of George Washington in New York in 1789 to inaugurate the government. Although everyone respected Jackson's state of mourning, still they wanted to assure him that all Washington wished him well.[14]

In addition to the mayor's elaborate plans, the Democrats in the city planned to meet Jackson upon his arrival in Georgetown and then escort him to his hotel preceded by a marching band and the appropriate firing of cannons at given intervals. The Democratic Central Committee in Washington, chaired by John P. Van Ness, neglected to coordinate its schemes with the City Council and went ahead with plans to stage a "great commotion" when their Hero arrived in Washington on February 11.[15]

All these plans were scuttled somewhat by the action of John Eaton, who knew Jackson's real desire to avoid excessive displays of public attention. He dispatched a carriage to Rockville, Maryland, to intercept

Jackson. This enabled the President-elect to dart into the capital in relative obscurity ahead of his party.[16]

So General Andrew Jackson arrived in Washington very quietly on February 11 about midmorning, riding in a plain carriage drawn by two horses and accompanied by a single black servant. He was "preceded by perhaps 10 horsemen."[17] Sly Old Hickory, commented Davy Crockett. He had "stolen a march upon his friends, as he always had done upon his enemies."[18]

The remainder of the Jackson party—William B. Lewis, Andrew Jackson, Jr., Henry Lee, Andrew J. Donelson and his wife, Emily, and their young son, and Mary Eastin—caught up with the General several hours later. They all took up residence in the National Hotel, run by John Gadsby, with whom Jackson had previously and pleasantly resided. This newest and most fashionable hotel was located at the northeast corner of Pennsylvania Avenue and Sixth Street. Jackson's own suite consisted of a bedroom, parlor, and two adjoining drawing rooms that were capable of being opened into an enormous salon. During his brief stay at the hotel Jackson gave several large and expensive dinners. On one occasion the menu consisted of canvasback duck, venison, and turtle soup.[19]

At first Jackson was pleased to greet anyone who cared to visit him at the hotel, and the United States Telegraph so informed the public. The hours from noon until 3:00 P.M. were set aside for these receptions. But so many people took advantage of the invitation and crowded into his rooms—dubbed the "Wigwam"—that Jackson suspended further interviews despite the best efforts of his private secretary, Major Donelson, to keep them running smoothly. These "audiences" took too much out of him and deprived him of valuable time needed for his "public duties."[20]

Of course the suspension of these interviews did not apply to friends and important politicians who hoped to help him inaugurate his administration. They arrived every day. Jackson listened to them attentively and then thanked them for their interest and concern. The Tennessee Congressional delegation visited him immediately. Senators Eaton and White conferred with him daily, as did Lewis and Donelson. The Vice President, John C. Calhoun, let no time pass before making an appearance. Martin Van Buren could not be present because he had been elected governor of New York and had just begun his duties. In his place, James A. Hamilton represented the New Yorker's interests at the Wigwam and found Jackson a willing listener.

The first concern for the new administration was the formation of a cabinet. Almost immediately Van Buren's name came up and no one seriously questioned his preeminent position within the Jackson organization and the need to recognize and make use of it. The fact that he had just been elected governor of New York hardly mattered. When, after extensive consultation, Jackson found that the New Yorker's appointment elicited no strong opposition, he wrote to Van Buren on February

14 and invited him to take the post of secretary of state. No other offer was possible. Van Buren's stature and rank in the party demanded this premier post. Since the position was considered next in line to the presidency the appointment troubled Calhoun and his friends, but there was nothing they could do about it, given Calhoun's situation as Vice President.[21]

Although some of his friends thought the Treasury Department might be a better slot for him in view of the patronage involved, Van Buren himself appreciated the worth of the position at State and he jumped at it.[22] His only problem was his situation in New York. It was bad enough to resign after a short term as governor; worse if he did it weeks after taking the oath of office. Finally, it was agreed to allow him to postpone coming to Washington until the New York legislature adjourned, probably late March or early April. This would also avoid the appearance of anticipating Senate confirmation of his nomination. In the meantime, his "friend and aid," James A. Hamilton, who enjoyed the confidence of both Van Buren and Jackson, might serve as secretary pro tem. The General agreed to this arrangement and on March 4 officially asked Hamilton to take care of the State Department until Van Buren's arrival later in the spring.[23]

In assigning cabinet positions it was necessary to consider all the major sections of the country, and that usually meant giving top priority to New York, Pennsylvania, and Virginia. With Van Buren's selection, New York had received ample reward; but that produced a problem with Virginia, which had a tradition of holding the highest offices of the country. The leading candidate from Virginia for consideration by Jackson was Senator Littleton W. Tazewell, and Calhoun urged his appointment. While Tazewell had expected the State Department, he was offered the War Department instead. Offended, he summarily refused it, whereupon he was invited to take the mission to Great Britain. This, too, he ultimately rejected on the ground of business interests, although he initially accepted it.[24]

Pennsylvania's important role in the election, the size of Jackson's majority in the state, and her "keystone" position in the Union and in the party, all necessitated a major appointment by Jackson. That meant the Treasury. But Pennsylvania's strong protectionist views offended South Carolina, which had passed Calhoun's *Exposition and Protest* during the summer. To prevent such an appointment, South Carolina offered Langdon Cheves for the Treasury. Jackson refused him. He decreed that the state's "movement last summer" in claiming the right to nullify federal law terminated any consideration the state might have enjoyed. He had been fully prepared to appoint someone from South Carolina but not after the nullification pronouncement. "They are fine fellows," he said, "but their zeal got the better of their discretion." Besides, they already had Calhoun as a representative in his administration and he was spokesman enough. Interestingly, although "the Calhoun influence" with Jackson was much spoken of in Washington, James A. Hamilton reported that "it is not however very great."[25]

When Cheves got knocked out of consideration some South Carolinians switched to Louis McLane of Delaware. But that created an even greater problem. McLane was a longtime Radical and a close friend of Van Buren. To place him in the cabinet would strengthen Van Buren's position and further jeopardize Calhoun's. The idea delighted Van Buren, but Calhoun would have none of it.

Pennsylvania offered Samuel D. Ingham and Henry Baldwin. Although Jackson preferred Baldwin for personal reasons there was no getting around Ingham's importance in the Pennsylvania party and his contribution to the presidential campaign. He also enjoyed the support of Calhoun. More than anything else the Hero was determined "not to put into this office either an ultra tariff or an ultra antitariff man," and Ingham had proven his evasiveness by voting against the Woolens Bill in 1827 and absenting himself on the final vote for the Tariff of 1828. He seemed ideal. Ultimately, what made the difference, however, was the Pennsylvania delegation in Congress. A "considerable majority" of that delegation came to Jackson immediately upon his arrival in Washington and "presented Ingham as the candidate of the Democracy of that state. The General immediately assured them that he should have the Treasury."[26] That settled that.

Then Jackson did something exceedingly foolish. He decided he must have a close personal friend in the cabinet with whom he could talk freely and openly. Someone he could trust, someone loyal. Which is a dubious way to fashion a cabinet where needs other than loyalty must be served. Jackson had two possibilities in mind: John Henry Eaton and Hugh Lawson White. White had the edge in terms of intellectual ability and dedication, Eaton in terms of friendship and service. White was the soul of rectitude and a man of uncommon good judgment. His selection would have been preferable. But Eaton had a special claim on Jackson, not only as biographer but as longtime aide and associate. Indeed, Jackson once told Rachel that Eaton "is more like a son to me than anything else; I shall as long as I live estimate his worth and friendship with a grateful heart."[27] What complicated the matter was Eaton's recent marriage to Margaret (Peggy) O'Neal Timberlake on January 1, 1829.

Eaton was a middle-aged widower—whom Van Buren said was "a friend to the friendless"[28]—and Peggy a twenty-nine-year-old beauty when they married. The lady was winsome, witty, somewhat saucy, and distinctly forward, overstepping the bounds of society's limits on young matrons whenever it suited her. She liked to exercise influence. She needed to feel important. After the death of her first husband, Peggy turned over her affairs to Eaton, "and scandal says they slept together," reported Amos Kendall. "I believe the tale is a lie," Kendall went on, "but it is rife among the ladies here, many of whom, I suspect, are no better than they should be. I think her foible is, that she is too forward in her manners."[29] Washington politicians have razorlike tongues, and they promptly sliced poor Peggy's reputation into fragments. "Eaton has just married his mistress," reported one of them, "and the mistress of eleven doz. others!"[30] The talk was grossly unfair but according to the moral standards of the time and the way women were judged, Peggy, by her behavior and attitude, had invited all of it.

Before marrying Peggy, Eaton consulted Jackson about his course of action. He understood the "impossibility of escaping detraction & slander" in this Era of Corruption but had hoped that his past behavior might have shielded him "from the foul aspersions of a condemning and censuring world." He knew Jackson believed in him and considered him an honorable man, "otherwise," he told the General, "your confidence & friendship toward me must have been withdrawn." When visiting the Hermitage earlier in the fall, Eaton explained his present circumstances. "She who had an association with me, been censured by a gossipping world," had been placed in a situation "by the hand of Providence where it was in my power by interposing myself to snatch her from that injustice which had been done her." He could no longer hesitate to do what was "right & proper," he told Jackson. All considerations of "honor, & of justice" required "that at a *proper time* I would tender to her the offer to share my life & prospects with her." Jackson agreed. He had no problem with Eaton's logic or commitment to honor and justice. Thus, it was not Jackson who told Eaton to marry Peggy, as is often stated. Eaton reached that conclusion himself. He simply asked Jackson if he agreed and, he said, "it was a matter of infinite satisfaction to me, to find, that your advice & opinions accorded with my own."

When Eaton returned from the Hermitage to Washington he proposed to Peggy, she accepted, and they planned to marry after the adjournment of Congress the following spring. But then Jackson wrote to him in late November, 1828, a month before Rachel's death, "suggesting the propriety of acting forthwith," whereupon Eaton "again brought this business before *her* and showed what were your [Jackson's] opinions. There was some difficulty, arising from that distrust & deep rooted prejudice which ever attaches to females, in reference to marriages *sooner* than 12 months from their widowhood."[31] Nonetheless, the lady relented and the marriage took place on January 1. Just why Jackson wanted to hurry the wedding is not entirely clear—except that he sometimes acted the romantic busybody[32]—but it probably was something he wanted out of the way before he took over as President. The last thing he needed was more scandal at the start of his administration. Eaton said he was sorry under the circumstances that Jackson would not be present for the wedding, but "the considerations you suggest are of a character so important as to induce us to forego this pleasure, & to close the business earlier than you can be here."[33]

After Rachel's death, Jackson may have had second thoughts about the advice he gave Eaton. But why he would consider him for a cabinet position, knowing the sort of gossip and abuse it would engender, defies understanding. Perhaps Jackson felt he owed Eaton something. Perhaps he thought it would be a kind gesture but that Eaton would refuse it rather than subject himself and his wife to certain vicious slander. If that is what Jackson thought he thought wrong. Eaton desperately wanted the post. So he maneuvered to eliminate White. He wrote to White and told him that Jackson "desired to have me with him." He assumed that Jackson had also talked with White and that White "had declined accepting any situation, as you before had told me would be your feelings." If this is not true, he went on, and White desired the post, "say so to me *in confidence*," otherwise "I should consent to any such appointment."[34] Naturally White stepped aside, and with it Jackson lost his one opportunity to have not only a friend in his cabinet but a man of wisdom and rectitude. That Jackson let the appointment slip from his control demonstrated wretched leadership. It should have taught him a lesson.

Certain "malcontents," as Kendall called them, tried to drive Eaton from the cabinet even before he had been appointed. They made the mistake of going to Jackson and repeating the gossip about how Eaton and Peggy had slept together before their marriage. Jackson showed them the door. It was not the scandal so much that bothered him as it was the "disposition to drive him," to tell him what he could or could not do.[35] He would not be driven. He *could* not be driven. As he said many times, "when I mature my course I am immoveable."[36] But it was more like stubborness, pure Scotch-Irish pigheadedness. He had made a bad decision. Some people tried to get him to see that, but they repeated gossip to make their case and that ruined it. He felt he was being pressured and he would not permit that. So he notified Duff Green of his decision and the Eaton appointment was duly announced in the *United States Telegraph.*

Washington society gasped. If this was any indication of what the new democratic President would bring to the capital then they feared the Republic was in serious trouble.

From start to finish Jackson's handling of the Eaton appointment was a disgrace. The disaster that ensued on account of it he precipitated himself.

Jackson fumbled again when he appointed John Branch, senator from North Carolina and former governor of the state, to head the Navy Department. "By what interest that miserable old woman, Branch, was ever dreamed of no one can tell," said Louis McLane.[37] According to Kendall, "Branch was selected, because North Carolina is a plain, unambitious state, which has thrust forward no claims to high offices although in merit she is not inferior to her more showy neighbors."[38] Which if true is even more idiotic than the reason for appointing Eaton. Branch was an old friend of the President, owned land in Tennessee, and had visited Jackson frequently. In addition, he was a strong states' rights man and a vocal critic of banks—two strong points in his favor as far as Jackson was concerned. Someone mentioned that Branch was noted for his splendid dinners and impeccable manners and therefore might "promote the social prestige of the new party."[39] The way Jackson was headed he needed all the social prestige he could get, but placing one man of impeccable manners into the cabinet with another whose wife was suspected of sleeping with dozens of men guaranteed a free-for-all among Washington gossips and troublemakers.

At the time Eaton supported Branch's appointment, as did White and Lewis[40]—a formidable contingent to say the least. Also, if Virginia and South Carolina went unrepresented in the cabinet, then North Carolina had to have a place to keep southerners happy. But it was a dreadful way of making a selection. Jackson practically backed into it. Again he got what he deserved. Branch did nothing for the navy, but then there was hardly a navy to do anything to.

Still another mistake was the appointment of John McPherson Berrien of Georgia as attorney general. Once more Jackson's friends scratched their heads to figure the reasons for his appointment. "Berrien is a Georgia Crawford man of fine talents," acknowledged Kendall, "but was a federalist until since the last war. I know not what would have induced the General to take him unless it was to satisfy the friends of Crawford."[41] Naturally the Radicals wanted a "strong constitutional Attorney General," and Philip P. Barbour had been put forward along with Berrien.[42] But Eaton and the Tennessee managers preferred Berrien because he strongly supported Indian removal. That was an important consideration. Since his appointment would also please the Radicals (and presumably Van Buren), Jackson went for it.[43] All four of these worthies—Berrien, Branch, Ingham, and Eaton—barely survived two years in office.

Questionable reasons also dictated Jackson's decision to keep John McLean on as the postmaster general. McLean had served John Quincy Adams—not well, indeed disloyally. Which was reason enough to continue him in office, Jackson figured, as a reward for services rendered. But a more compelling consideration motivated the President-elect. Like Van Buren and Calhoun, McLean was widely regarded as a potential presidential contender. He came from Ohio and was popular in the west, so his candidacy seemed to have real merit. As a matter of fact, in explaining Jackson's appointments in a letter to Francis P. Blair, Amos Kendall did not feel it necessary to account for McLean's appointment. Kendall simply said: "It is unnecessary to give the reason why he wished to retain McLean."[44]

During the negotiations McLean let it be known that he found the Post Office Department unequal to his lackluster talents and wanted the War

Department instead. Eaton said he was willing to exchange, as was Branch in case McLean preferred the Navy Department. Since it hardly seemed to matter who occupied what office, they thought nothing of shuffling themselves around at will—like musical chairs. Idiocy begot confusion. Nobody really wanted the Post Office job, as it turned out, and when McLean heard this he consented to stay where he was. But some Jacksonians began to fear that since McLean had been in the Post Office for quite a while and since many of his personal friends were postmasters, he "might not be willing to make those wholesome reforms which the times require." Several cases were put to him for replacements and he seemed disinclined to initiate removals, even though "the General and himself had agreed on the principles which were to guide him."[45] At this point McLean decided to retire from the cabinet altogether. He felt he was in an uncomfortable situation that would most assuredly erode his popularity, particularly if he removed men whom he had appointed himself.[46] In the meantime a vacancy occurred on the Supreme Court and McLean decided to take that post instead. Unfortunately it had already been designated for William T. Barry, the recently defeated Democratic candidate for governor of Kentucky. A solution was worked out when it was suggested that Barry and McLean switch places. Jackson "cheerfully" agreed.[47] Since Barry belonged to the Relief party there were some in Kentucky who disapproved the appointment, but Kendall and his cronies were pleased. "Our friends here are delighted at the change," he wrote.[48]

Barry's appointment was another mistake. He proved to be totally incompetent, indolent, and obtuse, and completely unequal to the assignment. Otherwise he was a grand fellow to have around. In such an important post in terms of the execution of Jackson's reform policy, however, a man of outstanding executive ability was needed. Instead Jackson got another social butterfly, amiable and irresponsible, inexperienced and inept. Since Jackson had already decided on the principles to guide the operation of the Post Office, it was also necessary that the person in charge of the department work closely and intimately with the President and have a sense of what the reform was all about. Barry hardly measured up to the requirements and his tenure became a near disaster.

Indeed, as was quickly pointed out once the appointments were announced by Duff Green in his newspaper, the cabinet was uniformly second-rate with the single exception of Martin Van Buren. "The Millennium of the Minnows!" was the judgment of one man;[49] and surely it ranks among the worst cabinets in the nineteenth century. For an administration intent on restoring the liberty of the American people through a vigorous program of reform, this list of its executive officers hardly inspired confidence. That it collapsed within two years is not surprising.

Even so, the old man liked it. He pronounced his cabinet "one of the strongest . . . that ever have been in the United States."[50] A predictable judgment, and totally distorted. But despite his mistakes and clumsiness in selecting his official family, Jackson did something remarkable: he managed to avoid tipping the scales of his cabinet toward either Van Buren or Calhoun. Both wings of the party were represented—but they did not predominate. Jackson had achieved balance—at least politically. Other than Van Buren and Ingham, none of the members was closely identified with either of the two major rivals for the succession.[51] Consciously or not, the President-elect had ensured that he could hold complete control of his cabinet in his own hands.

Jackson could be expected to dominate his cabinet. That was the character of the man. Quite possibly, then, he deliberately chose weak men in order to direct the affairs of the nation more immediately. Of course, he could have and should have chosen better—Thomas Hart Benton for one—but Jackson had decided against taking any men out of the Senate, where they could serve to greater advantage. Under the restraints of this guideline, therefore, the pickings were necessarily poor. "There are indeed but few men of strict honesty and fewer still of exalted talents among those by which the world is governed," reported Amos Kendall. "Our motto, you know, has been 'Jackson and Reform.' I am disposed to think, that but few of those who have shouted Reform really desire any thing else than the privilege of availing themselves of the very abuses with which we charge our adversaries."[52]

By hobbling the cabinet with inferior appointments, Jackson only increased his own burden. Since he intended to initiate reforms and restore the government to sound principles and practices, he needed skilled administrators to implement his policies once he indicated their general direction. He needed men of integrity who appreciated the motto "Jackson and Reform" and would apply it to the daily operation of their departments. Jackson's failure to find the best men to join him in supervising government operations meant a serious lessening of the reform effort.

Several newspapermen would have been better choices, since they reflected Jackson's own thinking, particularly in their commitment to his program and principles of government. Like the many politicians who visited him at his hotel, a large company of journalists descended on the Wigwam early in February and offered Jackson their talents and advice. Duff Green, Isaac Hill, and Amos Kendall were among the first to talk with Old Hickory. A little later came Thomas Ritchie (who was deeply distressed by the lack of any Virginians in the cabinet), Dabney Carr, Gideon Welles, and Nathaniel Greene. They all met the President-elect in a body on February 12 to receive his commendation for their efforts on his behalf in the late election.

One of Jackson's better conversations with a journalist occurred when Amos Kendall came to visit him and offer his services. Kendall, thin and ghostly-looking, was an obvious candidate for an important position in Jackson's council. Talented, indefatigable, western, a smashing writer, and devoted to "Jackson and Reform," he had already been singled out for special attention by the future contenders for the presidential chair once the General stepped down. Even before the President-elect arrived in Washington, Kendall had been told by McLean that if he went into the cabinet Kendall would be given a chief clerkship; Van Buren promised the same if he took the State Department; and Calhoun guaranteed an auditorship. Kendall himself rather fancied the auditorship but he knew where his best interests lay. "I shall depend on Old Hickory only," he said, and avoid "entangling alliances" with the others.[53]

The interview between Jackson and Kendall went swimmingly. The General rather liked Kendall's soft-spoken, self-effacing manner, perhaps because it was so different from his own. More particularly, his visitor's wide knowledge, keen perceptions, and quiet humor impressed him deeply. Kendall was rabid about the BUS and the need for government reform. Jackson liked that. He therefore decided almost immediately to find a place for him in his administration. For his part Kendall acknowledged that Jackson in person made a profound impression on him. "I only hope," said Kendall, "that his opinion of me improved as much during the interview as mine did of him. He is indeed a noble, honest old man, who intends nothing but to benefit his country."[54] Kendall's reaction was typical. Gideon Welles, fresh from Hartford, Connecticut, was virtually hypnotized by the Hero's "penetrating" eyes and impressed by his "easy and affable" conversation.[55] Jackson's "presence" profoundly affected him.

Kendall had actually come to Washington with the distinct purpose of assisting in the reform of the government. "That there are horrible abuses in the government," he quickly learned, "admits of no doubt." Even in the Congress—especially in Congress!—fraud abounded. In the use of stationery and the frank, and in the charges for traveling, "the most honest of them [congressmen] shame decency." Every member of the Kentucky delegation was paid at the "same rate Clay charges," namely 725 miles. Yet the distance to Washington was only 538 miles. "I do not know how long this abuse has been continued. Yet, if you mention *reform* on any of these points, they are amazingly sensitive!" At the moment when Kendall first arrived in Washington there was nothing he could do about it, "but if I get established here in an independent situation," he wrote, "the country shall know a few secrets, should not Old Hickory contrive to bring them out sooner."[56]

Old Hickory did indeed plan to bring them out, which is why they immediately hit it off at their first interview. They both committed themselves to reform; they both agreed that "a republican government can only be sustained by 'perpetual vigilance,' and that scarcely any man is to be trusted when his interests conflict with his public duties."[57] As they talked Kendall was "happy to find that his opinions agreed so well with my own; that it would give me great pleasure to aid him in any measures of reform." What struck Kendall particularly was the directness and frankness with which Jackson explained the principles that would guide his administration. The President-elect knew precisely what he planned to do. These principles, as the General outlined them, included the following:

1. "All men in office who are known to have interfered in the late election as committee men, electioneerers or otherwise, except by the independent and *decent* exercise of their right of suffrage," he said, "will be unceremoniously removed. So also will all men who have been appointed from political considerations or against the will of the people, and all who are incompetent. He is determined to curtail contingencies, abolish offices and do every thing which the public service will permit, to reduce the patronage of the general government." This retrenchment and reduction of government operation was the first object of Jackson's reform program. It addressed the most immediate problem facing the nation, namely centralized power in Washington. By reducing government he would lessen its ability to corrupt the people and endanger their liberty. In addition he would remove all officers appointed for reasons other than the public good. This would flush out the corrupters and incompetents.

2. "He will suffer no member of his cabinet to be a candidate for the Presidency, and if they intend to take the field they must resign." Jackson's anger and spite toward Clay prompted this decision, but he genuinely believed that Clay's passion for the presidency in 1825 brought the entire constitutional system to near ruin.

3. "Upon the Tariff he is in favor of a middle and just course." There was no change in his previous statement about this issue, but he hoped that it would quiet the hotheads in South Carolina.

4. "In relation to internal improvements, he is wholly opposed to all toll gate projects and every thing which can touch the jurisdiction of the states, and is rather favorably inclined to a distribution of the surplus revenue, if any there should be among the states for the purpose of Internal Improvements." As someone committed to states' rights, Jackson tended to regard internal improvements as a danger. Still he understood their value and importance—especially militarily—and hoped a surplus revenue shared with the states might be the answer to get around the constitutional problem. If he could pay the national debt (something he soon announced as a primary object of his administration), a large surplus might be forthcoming to satisfy the rising need for additional public works.

5. "He said all his cabinet must concur in measures of reform, and if they did not they must leave it." In implementing his reforms he had chosen "plain, business men," he said, in the hope that they might best assist him in achieving his object. Never had there been any question in

his mind that he was seriously and resolutely engaged in a reform of the operations of the federal government, and therefore he must have willing cooperation from his official family.[58]

Apparently nothing was said about the Bank of the United States, although both men detested it and soon found that as westerners their reasons for their antibank views were nearly identical. Earlier, in a letter of Francis Blair, Kendall assured his friend that the branches of the BUS in Kentucky would be under better control. "We have taken steps here which I think will be efficient to take the branches of the U.S. Bank at Lexington and Louisville out of the hands of the Clay men and give them a majority of Jackson Directors."[59] Little did he realize at the time that he and Blair and Jackson would go a great deal further than that.

Nor was anything said about Indian removal, even though it would have a high priority when Jackson came to deliver his first State of the Union address to Congress in December, 1829. At the moment he was apparently thinking solely of the basic principles of his governmental reforms. Later that reform would be expanded to included such specific issues as banking and Indian removal. He mentioned the tariff and internal improvements to Kendall in their conversation because these were contentious issues at the time; banking and Indian removal only became contentious after Jackson had assumed the presidency.

On the face of it Jackson's principles hardly constituted a major reform effort. Certainly when compared with later efforts they appear awfully tepid, if not inconsequential. Yet it must be remembered that this was the first conscious political reform program on a national scale following the first major period of corruption in American history. Moreover, the core of his program contained something major: the reduction of government to end corruption and restore republicanism. His stance was antipower and he was prepared to make whatever changes necessary to limit government and thereby strengthen the nation's bulwark of freedom.

The conversation between Jackson and Kendall lasted approximately an hour but the President-elect made it quite clear that he wanted the journalist close to him. "If the storm waxed violent against his measures," Jackson said, he would need Kendall's editorial talents. "I told a friend the other day," said the Hero, "that you are qualified for the Head of a Department and I shall put you as near it as I can." By this remark Kendall was sure that he would be appointed fourth auditor since that position was presently filled by a Clay man, Toby Watkins. Bringing Kendall into the government was one of Jackson's better and most significant appointments.[60]

Kendall carried the good news of Jackson's reform program to a group of fellow journalists who regularly met together at the home of the Reverend Obadiah Brown. Brown served as a clerk in the Post Office Department during the week and as pastor of the First Baptist Church in Washington on Sunday. In the parlor of Parson Brown's home congregated such Jacksonian literary lights as the acerbic Isaac Hill, the bluff Nathaniel Greene and the calculating Gideon Welles. Sometimes the tall, spare Duff Green joined them; later Mordecai M. Noah popped in, representing the New York interests. All of them were immediately concerned about patronage, and Welles asked Kendall pointedly what Jackson's policy would be. Kendall assured them all that "rewards will invariably take place" but warned that they must serve Jackson's reform intentions. Only those will be removed who "have been violent in their opposition, or made the best use of their status to injure the cause of Jackson." This point is essential, Kendall continued, and in any recommendation it must be "distinctly made out and submitted to the President."[61] The publicists soon forgot about the reform intentions and simply dwelt upon the idea of expelling any and all who belonged to the opposition. Patronage quickly devolved into spoils, and the spoils went solely to the victors.

Once the main business of naming his cabinet had been accomplished, Jackson turned to completing a final draft of his inaugural address. In his collection of papers Jackson left a document entitled "Rough Draft of the Inaugural Address." It is in his handwriting and appears to have been composed by him, probably before he left the Hermitage. The paper is remarkable for its language and ideas. Considering Jackson's limited education the address is quite outstanding. He had been called to office by the "voluntary suffrages of my country," he wrote. A "government whose vital principle is the right of the people to controul its measures, and whose only object and glory are the equal happiness and freedom of all the members of the confederacy, cannot but penetrate me with the most powerful and mingled emotions of thanks, on the one hand, for the honor conferred on me, and on the other, of solemn apprehensions for the safety of the great and important interests committed to my charge." Not bad for an indifferently educated frontiersman, despite some shaky syntax in spots. Few other presidents, before or after, did as well. He said he trusted in the smiles of an "overruling providence . . . for that animation . . . which shall enable us to steer, the Bark of liberty, through every difficulty."

> To the administration of my illustrious predecessors, I will be permitted to refer as mirors, not so much for the measures which m[a]y be demanded by the present state of the country, but as applications of the same principles to the various exigencies which have occurred in our history, and as shedding light upon those which may hereafter arise. It is thus the great moral race we are running, connects us with the past, and is tributary to the events which are to come: thus, that every period of our Government is useful to that which follows, not as the source of principles, but as guides on that sacred fountain to which we must often go for the refreshment of our laws, and the invigoration of the public morals. It is from this source that we derive the means of congratulating ourselves upon the present free

condition of our country, and build our hopes for its future safety. In fine, Fellow Citizens, this is the bulwark of our liberties.

Jackson's long experience in composing addresses to his troops during the years of his military career had amply prepared him for this special task. Some of the phrases in the addresses are stilted but they reflect the style of the age more than any limitation on Jackson's part. By and large he had something vital and appropriate to say, and he said it exceedingly well.

He went on to refer to the duties of the chief executive in terms of foreign and domestic affairs. National defense and the general safety of the Republic were singled out for particular mention. Then he outlined his reform program, extending only slightly what he had said to Kendall. He wished to observe the strictest economy in governmental disbursements, liquidate the national debt, provide a "judicious" tariff, and distribute the surplus on the basis of representation for the purpose of promoting education and internal improvements. He would adhere to "a Just respect for state rights and the maintainance of state sovereignity as the best check of the tendencies to consolidation." With the accomplishment of these goals, he wrote, "I trust the memorials of our national blessings may be multiplied, and the scenes of domestic labour be made more animating and happy."[62]

Jackson discussed this draft with his friends at the Hermitage and later with selected politicians in Washington. He also allowed it to be shown to James A. Hamilton who, in his *Reminiscences*, pronounced it "absolutely disgraceful."[63] Disgraceful it most assuredly was not. Hamilton's comment says something about his own judgment and reliability.[64] Hamilton claimed that he suggested certain alterations in the text and that he even prepared an entirely new address. In any event a second address was put together after much consultation with Donelson, Lewis, Eaton, and others. Then a third. Finally everyone was satisfied and this third draft was the text from which Jackson read at his inauguration and which was later published as the official version. The three drafts are different in many particulars. What is most notable about the final version—other than the lack of the original's vitality and strength—is that Jackson mentions the Indians and his desire to observe a "just and liberal policy" toward them. Also, the need for *"reform."* The word "reform" is underscored. In this regard he said he wished to correct those "abuses that have brought the patronage of the Federal Government into conflict with the freedom of elections." In addition, he would correct the "causes which have disturbed the rightful course of appointment" and placed power in "unfaithful or incompetent hands."[65]

These were significant additions to the address, but on the whole the third version came nowhere near the sweep and animation of Jackson's own version. The revisions were aimed at winning approval from all classes in all sections of the country. Its timid language guaranteed little or no displeasure from Jackson's many friends.

The Radicals were especially concerned that Jackson's address not advance any "ultra latitudinarian" interpretation of the Constitution. They knew him to be fundamentally conservative, but Van Buren felt obliged to remind him (indirectly through Hamilton) that he hoped the address would not express any constitutional opinion at odds with the doctrines of Thomas Jefferson.[66] He worried needlessly. Jackson's political philosophy paralleled Radical doctrine. He only veered from it under the dictates of practical politics. He was a pragmatic politician, fully prepared to compromise whenever it served his need.

Once the address had everyone's approval the Tennesseans prepared for the inauguration on March 4. The town already bulged with tourists, all anxious to witness the beginning of the "people's government" when their Hero would stand before them and take the oath of office. "I never saw such a crowd here before," commented Daniel Webster. "Persons have come five hundred miles to see General Jackson, *and they really seem to think that the country is rescued from some dreadful danger!*"[67] Indeed they did. The danger had been very real to them. It involved something as basic as their right to govern themselves and choose their own President. Maybe some men like Webster could not appreciate that fear, but it was real. Fortunately the nation had been rescued, as Jackson said, by the "voluntary suffrage of the people." Now they must make certain that the danger never arose again.

Soon every hotel room and lodging house was packed with the hordes of people who came from every "point on the compass." It reminded some of the "inundation of the northern barbarians into Rome."[68] Newspapers predicted that the inauguration would draw more people to the capital than Washington had ever seen before. The crowds walking arm in arm gazed "on all around them with the vacant stare of undisguised curiosity and wonder." After Washington filled up, the ever-mounting torrent of people spilled over into Alexandria and Georgetown, taking any accommodation they could find. They slept on the floors of taverns and in open fields "curtained by the unbroken sky."[69] Some boarding houses charged twenty dollars per week—triple the normal cost of most hotels. Only the White House on inauguration eve had available sleeping quarters. John Quincy Adams and his family departed the "President's palace" at around 9:00 P.M. the night before the inaugural and moved into Commodore David Porter's house on Meridian Hill, which Adams rented. Because Jackson had shamefully snubbed him by not calling on him after his arrival in Washington, Adams decided to boycott his successor's inaugural. It was bad form on the part of both men. Jackson certainly should have shown the President the courtesy of a brief, formal call. But he blamed Adams in part for the slanderous articles about himself and his wife that appeared in the Washington newspapers and for failing to put a stop to them. Jackson owed Adams a great deal for his strong support in the past; and it was expecting too much to think that the President could control his partisan press. Jackson should have suppressed his anger and performed what courtesy dictated. But he felt it would be a betrayal of his beloved, and he therefore refused. In any event Adams regarded the snub as inexcusable and so, like his father before him, fled the inaugural ceremonies.

March 4, 1829, the day of the inauguration, dawned bright and sunny, a day made to order for an outdoor celebration. After a long season of cold and rainy weather it was "as if nature was willing to lend her aid towards contributing to the happiness of the thousands that crowded to behold the great ceremony."[70]

The capital awoke to the firing of a thirteen-gun cannon salute. Immediately the streets began to fill with people. The center of the city lay between the President's mansion and the Capitol along both sides of the unpaved but tree-lined street called Pennsylvania Avenue. Here the business and residential sections of Washington could be found. They consisted of narrow buildings of two and three stories usually with shops on the ground floor. The President's house stood out in bold relief at one end. Its stark angularity was emphasized by the white paint hastily applied to it after the War of 1812. The trees planted by President Adams would one day soften the outlines of the building but at present they only accentuated its severe appearance. Clustered nearby were the executive office buildings—Treasury, War, Navy—of Greek revival style done in brick. A mile away and rising from an upward slope sat the Capitol, whose dome looked to some like an "inverted wash bowl." This was the first election in which the inaugural ceremony was planned for the East Portico of the building, and it became the traditional setting for these rituals. An open-air ceremony was scheduled because of the vast numbers of people jammed into the city and the necessity of giving them an opportunity to witness their Hero's final triumph as he took the oath of office. Also, "that they may not hear him," laughed one wag. By 10:00 A.M. the open area in front of the East Portico was thronged with people, as well as the main streets leading to it. Like a mighty, agitated sea, the masses pushed and shoved to get closer to the place where Jackson would appear. They even swarmed up the steps leading to the Portico, so that a ship's cable had to be stretched about two-thirds of the way up the flight of stairs to hold them back. Francis Scott Key stared in wonder at the incredible spectacle of this surging, pulsating mass of humanity. "It is beautiful," he gasped, "it is sublime!"[71]

At half past ten o'clock a group of officers and soldiers of the Revolutionary Army formed a procession at Brown's Hotel and marched to Gadsby's to escort the President-elect to the Capitol. At 11:00 A.M. Jackson emerged from his quarters and was met by "an immense concourse of people" gathered in front of his hotel. When he appeared at the entrance they set up a great shout. They saluted him with cries of "huzza."[72]

The escort positioned itself. Behind them a line formed of officers (Hinds, Call, Patterson, Jones, Spotts, Ross, Robb, Nicholson, and Harper) who had served at New Orleans on January 8, 1815. Then came the Washington Central Committee with Colonel Nathan Towson and the Marshal of the District, followed by Major Lewis and Major Donelson and finally the President-elect himself. Jackson was dressed in a plain black suit, black tie, and long black coat, and because of his height he was plainly visible along the route to the crowds lining both sides of Pennsylvania Avenue.

As the procession moved along Jackson was soon flanked by "hacks, gigs, sulkies, wood-carts and a Dutch wagon." The wagon bore "a freight of females who enjoyed the enviable distinction of keeping by the side of the General all the way to the capitol." Jackson walked eastward along the avenue and with each burst of cheering he waved to the crowd and nodded his head in appreciation. People could single him out from the procession because he was the only person not wearing a hat. How extraordinarily appropriate, thought Margaret Bayard Smith, wife of the Maryland senator, who watched the procession from an upper floor of her house, "the Servant in the presence of his Sovereign, the People."[73]

When he reached the Capitol Jackson headed first for the Senate chamber to witness the swearing-in of the Vice President, John C. Calhoun. Again the crowds were insufferably large and there was genuine fear that there would be injuries from people being knocked down or trodden underfoot. At 11:30 A.M. Jackson arrived in the chamber and was immediately conducted to a chair in front of the secretary's desk. To his left sat the diplomatic corps resplendent in their ribbons and stars and gold trimmings—quite a contrast to the somber, black-suited Jackson. To the General's left sat the justices of the Supreme Court, looking appropriately grave—if not downright worried. A seat had also been provided for the retiring President Adams but it remained vacant during the proceedings and shouted his obvious discourtesy. Members of the Senate sat in their usual places and Representatives from the lower House along with special guests and invited ladies occupied the galleries. It was a scene of republican plainness and austerity and quite appropriate, in view of Jackson's recent bereavement.

At high noon, after Calhoun's swearing-in by the president pro tem of the Senate, a procession formed in the chamber and slowly made its way to the East Portico for the principal ceremony. Fifteen to twenty thousand people (the *Telegraph* claimed thirty) massed together around the Capitol and along the avenues leading to it. As the massive rotunda doors swung open, marshals marched out, followed by the justices. A Marine band took up a position to the right of the steps and other uniformed soldiers stood at attention around the grounds. Two artillery companies prepared to fire their cannons to provide the necessary salutes.

The screaming and shouting of the crowd reached its pitch when General Jackson strode into view.

"There! there! that is he!"

"Which?"

"He with the white head!"

"Ah, there is the old man . . . there is the old veteran; there is Jackson!"[74]

Cries of "huzza" split the air—again and again. The noise "still resounds in my ears," recorded Mrs. Smith a full week later. "Never can I forget the spectacle," said another, "nor the electrifying moment when the eager, expectant eyes of that vast and motley multitude caught sight . . . of their adored leader." In an instant, as if by "magic," the color of the whole mass changed—"all hats were off at once, and the dark tint which usually pervades a mixed map of men was turned . . . into the bright hue of ten thousand upturned and exultant human faces, radiant with sudden joy."[75]

At that moment the Marine band started playing "The President's March" while the artillery companies outside the enclosed yard fired a twenty-four-gun salute. This was answered by cannon posted at the Navy Yard and Arsenal. Ladies seated on sofas and chairs on the Portico waved their handkerchiefs at the Hero. For a moment Jackson "with his tall form, his sunken and deeply grooved cheeks, his locks of silver grey, his high nose, and wide stern mouth" just stared at the spectacle before him. Then in a gesture that thrilled the crowd, he bowed low before them. He bowed to the "majesty of the people."[76]

A table covered with scarlet velvet had been positioned between the two central columns of the Portico with chairs for Jackson, Calhoun, and the chief justice. After bowing, Jackson took his seat—Calhoun on his left, Marshall on his right—and then adjusted two pairs of eyeglasses, one "thrown up on the top of his head, and the other before his eyes."[77] Once the applause and cheers abated, once the cannons ceased (except in the distance) and the band finished its tune, Jackson rose to read his inaugural address. Unlike modern inaugural addresses, this one preceded the taking of the oath of office.

"Fellow-Citizens," he began, and as he spoke the crowd grew very quiet in order to hear him. There was "an almost breathless silence," but not a word reached their eager ears.[78]

"About to undertake the arduous duties that I have been appointed to perform by the choice of a free people," Jackson continued, "I avail myself of this . . . solemn occasion to express [my] gratitude. . . ." It was almost an exact duplicate of the opening sentence of Jefferson's first inaugural address, and everyone thought that wonderfully appropriate. He outlined his program and then closed with a proper invocation. "And

a firm reliance on the goodness of that Power whose providence mercifully protected our national infancy, and has since upheld our liberties in
various vicissitudes, encourages me to offer up my ardent supplications
that He will continue to make our beloved country the object of His
divine care and gracious benediction."[79]

Those who were close enough to hear his words liked them very much.
Those further away were grateful that the address lasted no longer than
ten minutes. It was one of the shortest inaugural addresses in the history
of the presidency and almost set a record.[80] Later, when it was published
it met with general approval. "The address itself is excellent chaste patriotic sententious and dignified," James Hamilton, Jr., senator from South
Carolina, told Van Buren. "As far as I have heard . . . it has given universal
satisfaction."[81] The Democratic press reported that the "address
breathes throughout the pure spirit of republicanism of the Jefferson
school."[82]

When Jackson finished his address the crowd again roared its approval.
He "stood for some minutes amid the shouts of thousands," gestured his
thanks, and sat down, but his manner throughout was so elegant that it
captivated everyone. The "principal personage," wrote James Hamilton,
Jr., "acquited himself with a grace and 'composed dignity' which I never
saw surpassed." Said another: "There was a stateliness and elegance in
the General's manner that charmed everybody."[83]

Chief Justice John Marshall then rose to administer the oath of office.
A Bible was held by one of the attendants. Jackson approached the chief
justice, placed one hand on the Bible, and raised the other. Repeating
after Marshall the words that he would faithfully execute the office of
President, Jackson spoke the final words forcefully, hitting each word with
a smack—"preserve, protect and defend the Constitution of the United
States." The President then raised the Bible to his lips and kissed it
reverently. He shook hands with Marshall. As the crowd erupted Jackson
turned to them and bowed. "Yes," said Mrs. Smith ecstatically, "to the
people in all their majesty."[84]

The crowd was now beside itself and could no longer hold back. In one
great surge the people charged forward, broke the chain barring their
way, and swarmed around their Hero as he received the congratulations
of the guests on the Portico. It took no little effort by the marshals and
friends of the President to free him from this unruly mob. He found
temporary refuge inside the Capitol, but since a public reception was
scheduled in the White House following the swearing-in, Jackson was
obliged to retrace his steps up Pennsylvania Avenue.

He exited from the west entrance of the Capitol, walked down the hill
to the gate, and found a handsome white horse waiting to take him to his
new home. As the Hero mounted, a waiting crowd let out a shout. Everything he did seemed to please them. To accompany him to the White
House, Tench Ringgold, the United States Marshal, and Colonel Nathan

Towson, the inaugural committee chairman, rode beside him. By this time the avenue was again jammed. "As far as the eye could reach," reported Amos Kendall, "the side-walks of the Avenue were covered with people on foot and the centre with innumerable carriages and persons on horseback moving in the same direction. For a full half hour, I stood waiting for the stream to run by; but like a never failing fountain the Capitol continued pouring forth its torrents."[85] Slowly, gesturing his appreciation to the people who cheered and waved to him, Jackson headed for the White House, and oh, said the disapproving Mrs. Smith, "such a cortege as followed him! Country men, farmers, gentlemen, mounted and dismounted, boys, women and children, black and white. Carriages, wagons and carts all pursuing him to the President's house."[86]

Never had there been such an inauguration of a President—not even Thomas Jefferson's. Never before had the ordinary citizen expressed his enthusiasm for a new administration so spontaneously, with such obvious affection and good will. Few inaugurations since have matched it in ardor and excitement. The people had massed in front of the Capitol to witness the "triumph of the great principle of self government over the intrigues of the aristocracy" and now they trailed their adored leader back through the streets toward the executive mansion, reluctant to let him out of their sight.[87] Then it suddenly occurred to a number of ladies and gentlemen who were watching the procession from the safety of their homes that this shouting, "raving Democracy" intended to enter the "President's palace," as they grandly termed the White House. The "palace" was about to be invaded by the rabble—the people. What had the country come to! The masses seemed to think that with Jackson as their President they had a right to attend the inaugural reception, something normally restricted to polite society.

By the time the General arrived at the mansion all the rooms on the lower floor were filled to capacity by a mixture of every conceivable race, color, and social standing. People from the "highest and most polished," said Joseph Story, an associate justice of the Supreme Court, "down to the most vulgar and gross in the nation" poured into the White House. "I never saw such a mixture," he moaned. "The reign of KING MOB seemed triumphant," he added. "I was glad to escape from the scene as soon as possible."[88]

A modest White House reception had been planned. Nothing elaborate, nothing like previous presidential "levees," which had had a regal and elitist tone to them. But what took place verged on public disorder. It became a wild, near-riotous scene. Barrels of orange punch had been prepared, but as the waiters opened the doors to carry them out, the mob spotted them and rushed forward to seize them. The "most painful confusion prevailed" as waiters and guests collided. Pails of liquor splashed to the floor, glasses fell and were smashed or stepped on, and such mayhem ensued "that wine and ice-creams could not be brought out to the ladies." Several thousand dollars in smashed china and glassware were lost during the pandemonium. To add to the general melee, men with "boots heavy with mud" stood on the "damask satin-covered chairs" in order to get a better look at their President. It was a "regular Saturnalia," laughed Senator James Hamilton, Jr. "The mob broke in, in thousands—Spirits black yellow and grey, poured in in one uninterrupted stream of mud and filth, among the throngs many fit subjects for the penitentiary." One "stout black wench" sat quietly by herself "eating in this free country a jelley with a gold spoon at the President's House."[89]

When Mrs. Smith and her family arrived at the mansion they were aghast at the spectacle in progress. "What a scene did we witness!" she gasped. *"The Majesty of the People* had disappeared, and a rabble, a mob, of boys, negros, women, children, scrambling, fighting, romping. What a pity what a pity."[90]

Poor Jackson. They nearly suffocated him with their display of love and happiness. Everyone wanted to shake his hand, or touch him or congratulate him. Amos Kendall caught sight of him standing a few steps from the south entrance shaking hands with "people of all sorts and descriptions." The journalist tried to get to the President but the flow of people surged toward him and bucking it invited physical injury. "Like hundreds of others," Kendall said, "I leapt in at the window of an adjoining room."[91] Still it was impossible to get near Jackson. Finally the pressure got so bad and the danger of actually injuring the President so real that a number of men formed a ring around him as "a kind of barrier of their own bodies." The President, reported Mrs. Smith, was *"literally* nearly pressed to death and almost suffocated and torn to pieces in their eagerness to shake hands with Old Hickory." Happily, he made his escape from his well-wishers and returned to his temporary quarters at Gadsby's. It was 4:00 P.M.[92]

The flight of the President did not dampen the spirit of the mob, however. The mayhem, if anything, got worse. Indeed, it now looked as though the mansion itself was in danger and might collapse around them. To relieve the pressure inside the building, tubs of punch and pails of liquor were transferred to the lawn outside and all the windows were thrown open to provide additional exits for those anxious to keep up with the refreshments. The strategy worked. The "rabble" bolted after the liquor, using the fastest means of exit.

It was wild. For ladies and gentlemen of refinement it was an awful commentary on American life and customs.[93] What would the rest of the world think? What would they say? And, they asked, what had happened to American political institutions to bring this about?

Not everyone thought the reception a scandal. Senator James Hamilton, Jr., declared it a great success. "Notwithstanding the row Demos kicked up," he told Van Buren, "the whole matter went off very well."[94]

The "old man," totally exhausted, rested in his rooms at Gadsby's. He was pleased with the inaugural ceremonies and the favorable reaction to his address. He dined with Calhoun and some of his entourage on sirloin steak cut from a prize ox roasted for the occasion.[95] He planned to retire early since he had no intention of attending the inaugural ball. He was still in mourning for his wife. A six-month period of *deep* mourning was the least he could do for Rachel. The organizing committee for the inaugural knew his decision and did not attempt to talk him out of it. Since admission to the ball involved a subscription there was no danger that the riffraff would crash the scene and make the occasion another free-for-all.

The ball was held in the "spacious and elegant Saloon" at the Washington Assembly Rooms run by Mr. Carusi, the proprietor, and located at C and Eleventh Streets. The "Saloon" was tastefully and appropriately decorated with evergreens and flowers, and a large American flag "waved its broad folds over the heads of the numerous guests." Some 1200 persons attended, so many in fact that pumps had risen in price in the course of the day from $2 to $5 per pair. It was a glittering affair. Ladies gorgeously gowned in tight-waisted, wide-skirted dresses and men dressed in formal black evening clothes provided a sharp contrast to what had taken place a few hours earlier at the "President's palace." The Vice President and his wife, several members of the prospective cabinet and their wives, Major and Mrs. Andrew Jackson Donelson, members of foreign legations, and "numerous distinguished strangers" attended. The newly-wed Eatons put in an appearance, but the other ladies of the official family tried not to notice as Peggy Eaton swept into the room and startled everyone with her presence and beauty.[96]

After dancing for several hours, the company adjourned to the lower room where supper was served "composed of all the delicacies of the season." Dancing was renewed when dinner ended and continued until the guests departed at 2:00 A.M. Everything went beautifully. Only the presence of Peggy Eaton dampened the spirits of certain ladies, particularly since protocol dictated that the cabinet members and their wives sit in fairly close proximity during the supper. Still that was a small price for a wonderful evening. It was "splendid," proclaimed Mrs. Smith. "In perfect order."[97]

Indeed, the ball climaxed a memorable day. The inauguration proved so lusty in its display of the American spirit at its most boisterous, exuberant, and vulgar that the essential ingredients of this inaugural became traditional. It was the first people's inaugural. The people—not politicians or Washington society or the Central Committee—made it uniquely their own. "It was a proud day for the people," reported the *Argus of Western America* on March 18, 1829. "General Jackson is *their own* President. Plain in his dress, venerable in his appearance, unaffected and familiar in his manners, he was greeted by them with an enthusiasm which bespoke him the Hero of a popular triumph."

Speaking from a different point of view, Mrs. Smith had to agree nonetheless, although she tempered her comments with a small warning. "It was the People's day, and the People's President and the People would rule. God grant that one day or other, the People do not pull down all rule and rulers."[98]

The inauguration of General Andrew Jackson, despite the vulgarity and animal spirits unleashed by the occasion, was one of the great moments in American history. And the reason for this, as everyone agreed, was that it represented in a symbolic way a significant advance in representative government for the American people.[99] Andrew Jackson was the people's own President—the first such—and that was something wonderful and exciting. Seeing the crowds and hearing them cheer a government that they themselves had called into existence augured well for the future of a democratic society.

CHAPTER 10

The Reform Begins

ONCE THE "RAVAGES OF THE MOB" had been "repaired and the building prepared . . . for his residence," President Andrew Jackson moved into the White House. And like almost everything else he touched, Old Hickory radically altered the structure and appearance of the executive mansion almost immediately. For it was Andrew Jackson who had the wit and imagination (along with the political skill) to muster from Congress the means to complete the building of the White House and finish its interior decoration. At his direction, the north portico was constructed in 1829, having been designed twenty-two years before by Benjamin Latrobe. In addition, single-story wings were extended east and west from the main building as offices and housing for horses and carriages. And in 1833 iron pipes were laid to bring running water from Franklin Park to the White House. Previously two pumps had provided water via wooden troughs. The first formal garden around the White House was also laid out, and the President himself planted several magnolia trees in memory of his beloved Rachel.

To improve the interior decoration of the house, the Congress allotted Jackson $50,000. A full fifth of this amount went to refurbish the East Room. The furnishings ruined in the inaugural "riot" were replaced. Decorative wooden beams and wood paneling were installed. The upholstery for the twenty-four armchairs and four sofas needed replacement, and three cut-glass chandeliers, several marble-top tables, and a Brussels carpet were also added to the room. Washington society commented unfavorably about the twenty spittoons scattered about the East Room. Not the objects themselves—they were fixtures in most fashionable homes at the time—but the number. Twenty did seem excessive, except there was no telling how Jackson and his western friends might behave and perhaps the White House needed added protection. Because he entertained sumptuously the President also bought a splendid silver service, a new French dinner service, and a set of crystal that included nine sizes of wine glasses. The purchase price came to $4,308.[1]

When Jackson moved into the White House he gathered as much family around him as possible. The Donelsons—Andrew and Emily (who served as official hostess) and their nearly three-year-old son, Andrew Jackson Donelson, Jr.—formed a solid core. Jackson's own twenty-year-old son joined his father in the executive mansion but soon returned to Tennessee to supervise the "farm" and the Hermitage, and only periodically returned to Washington to visit the General and the other members of his family. Mary Eastin, the daughter of William and Rachel (Donelson) Eastin, who was one of Jackson's many wards and the friend and confidante of Emily Donelson, also moved into the White House. Mary's mother and Emily were sisters, although Emily and Mary were only three years apart in age. The winsome nineteen-year-old Mary enlivened the White House with her youthful sparkle and provided Emily with companionship and familial devotion.

Later in the spring, Ralph Earl, the painter, joined the White House entourage. Married to Rachel Jackson's niece, Jane Caffery (who died shortly after their marriage), Earl had often been Jackson's traveling companion. After Rachel's death the new President found his presence very comforting, so he installed the painter in the White House and gave him a private studio where he could work undisturbed.

William B. Lewis, who accompanied the Jackson party from Tennessee to Washington, followed the General into the executive mansion, but a few days after the inaugural he felt a little uncomfortable with this arrangement, since nothing had been said about his status within the new administration. He told the President he planned to return to Tennessee. It was the planting season and his plantation required his presence.

"Why, Major," replied Jackson, "you are not going to leave me here *alone*, after doing more than any other man to bring me here?"

The General looked so forlorn and desperate—at least Lewis liked to think he did—that the Major agreed to stay and it was arranged for him to take an auditorship with the Treasury Department and live at the White House. Lewis provided many services for Jackson, not the least of which was writing to political friends to explain the President's thinking on the major issues before the administration.

In the arrangement of living quarters, Jackson chose the two rooms at the end of the corridor on the southwest side of the building, with his office at the other end of the hall. The Donelsons occupied the northwest corner room facing Pennsylvania Avenue and used the room next to it as a nursery. In these quarters three of Emily's children were born.

All considered, the group comprised a comfortably sized family unit and represented all ages: children, teen-agers, young marrieds, the middle-aged, and the old man himself. Jackson seemed very pleased with this arrangement, at least in the beginning, and the presence of his family so close to him made life much easier all around.[2]

The first and most pressing matter facing President Jackson upon the inauguration of his administration was the necessity of expelling from office those men whose corrupting practices had scarred the operation of the American government for the past ten years. Unfortunately, many historians, including Jackson's most sympathetic biographers, have cynically misinterpreted this reform in the belief that it was a simple matter of patronage and the reward of the party faithful. The "task of *reform*," wrote one biographer quoting from Jackson's inaugural address, "being a brief way of saying, 'Turn the rascals out.'" No doubt to some Democrats, particularly journalists involved in party organization, that was precisely its meaning. Not so Jackson's. Removal from office in his mind was linked initially to the problem of corruption and the concentration of power, and the need to eliminate that corruption and lessen that power in order to protect American freedom. Later, he elevated removal from office into the principle of rotation: namely, that regular change in personnel in office is healthy in a democratic society. "Rotation in office," Jackson wrote within three months of his inauguration, "will perpetuate our liberty."[3]

It was the perpetuation of American liberty that Jackson wished to safeguard and which explains his decision to make his appointments an essential component of his reform program. Not only was he concerned about the corruption to which entrenched officials inevitably succumb, but also he feared the emergence of an "official aristocracy" that would presume to act (as Adams and Clay did) without any regard for the popular will. After a few years in office they tended to view their positions as a matter of right, and even to anticipate bequeathing their tenure to their offspring. As a result of this attitude, the President contended, the worst forms of public misbehavior seeped into the system and corroded the machinery of government. Jackson regarded the Washington bureaucracy as an "Augean stable"—the figure of speech he invariably employed when referring to it, as did his close associates—and he believed he was just the man to cleanse it, having obtained the people's mandate to do so.[4]

But there was nothing particularly extraordinary in the position Jackson took at the outset of his administration. By the time he had been elected President virtually all the leading politicians in both parties recognized the need, if not the wisdom, of regularly cleaning house in all the major departments of the government in order to insure efficiency and integrity. Besides, the success of an administration depended in large measure on the cooperation and support it received from the bureaucracy. For an administration to presume a friendly attitude from appointees of its defeated predecessor, said Edward Everett to the postmaster general, "is to court its own destruction." John Quincy Adams learned that lesson the hard way, Everett went on. He retained and appointed men with "exclusive regard to merit; and what has been his reward? A most furious opposition, rallied on the charge of the corrupt distribution of office, and the open or secret hostility of three-fourths of the office-holders in the Union."[5]

Andrew Jackson was too good a politician to make Adams's mistake. He understood the political necessity of creating a friendly bureaucracy as a preliminary to the successful running of his administration. Moreover, he recognized that there were many men in the Democratic party who felt they deserved a fitting reward for their essential services in defeating the National Republicans. But more than anything else Jackson believed that the people expected him to restore the government to virtue and decency. "I know the General is resolved on making a pretty general sweep of the departments," said Major Lewis. "It is expected he will cleanse the Augean stables, and I feel pretty confident he will not disappoint the popular expectation in this particular. He is determined on making a radical change in the offices—on giving them a complete overhauling and to do this effectually an almost entire new set must be put in."

Prior to his inauguration Jackson prepared an "Outline of principles" respecting his intended reform which he submitted to the heads of the various departments. The document was dated February 23, 1829. In it he directed his cabinet to undertake immediately "a strict examination" into the operation of their respective departments and to report to him directly on "what retrenchments can be made without injury to the public service, what offices can be dispensed with, and what improvement made in the economy and dispatch of business." As much as possible they must limit the operation of government. Because of the "widespread corruption," he continued, he expected removals. But, he added, these removals must emanate from principle. He therefore directed that *only* those who had been "appointed against the manifest will of the people" or whose official station "was made to operate against the freedom of state elections" would be replaced. The appointment power must serve the cause of freedom. In addition, he expected all new appointees to help restore virtue and morality to government. They must conform to a strict moral code. "Connected with the character of the administration are the moral habits of those who may be entrusted with its various subordinate duties. Officers in their private and public relations should be examples of fidelity & honesty; otherwise . . . they will have to be removed." A rigid adherence to this principle, he said, will both "elevate the character of the government, and purify the morals of the country. This principle will be regarded as a fundamental one by the President."[6]

Thus, even before Jackson moved into the White House, he made it clear to his cabinet officers that he planned, as part of his reform, to exercise his appointive power to restore virtue to government and a strict moral code on its bureaucracy. He expected their cooperation. As a consequence some politicians anticipated a general sweep of the departments. Many journalists publicized the happy event with the observation that the people demanded this housecleaning.

The prospect of wholesale removals may have delighted some hungry politicians but it sent a shock of terror through the bureaucracy. Thousands expected dismissal minutes after Jackson entered the White House. Newspapers drummed out the announcement that the "Augean stables" would be cleansed within a fortnight. Over the next several months the propaganda about removals continued unabated. But now the opposition newspapers added their voices to the din. Only instead of describing it in terms of reform they spoke of it as a "Reign of Terror." Intelligent, able, and dedicated servants, they said, had been ousted to make room for political hacks. And many apprehensive citizens believed this distortion. So pervasive was this perception that not many years later a commentator swore that the situation approached the worst excesses of the French Revolution. "Terror . . . reigned in Washington," he said. "The great body of officials awaited their fate in silent horror, glad when the office hours expired at having escaped another day." There were reports that one man "cut his throat from ear to ear, from the mere terror of being dismissed."[7]

This wild exaggeration of what happened during the early weeks of Jackson's administration soon assumed the status of accepted fact. Because an untutored Democracy had expressed its stupid will and elected an ignorant frontiersman to the presidency, the government verged on ruin. "The government," asserted one man, "formerly served by the *elite* of the nation, is now served, to a very considerable extent, by its refuse."[8]

That supposedly was what Jackson had wrought by his rotation principle. Instead of reform he had introduced one of the worst political practices conceivable: the spoils system. An early and generally admiring biographer of Jackson never forgave him for this single lapse. Rotation in office, said James Parton, "I consider an evil so great and so difficult to remedy, that if all his other public acts had been perfectly wise and right, this single feature of his administration would suffice to render it deplorable rather than admirable."[9] Democrats at the time seemed to enjoy their reputation as spoilsmen, as though it confirmed their nonelitism and further identified them with the people. William L. Marcy, himself a man of integrity and one of Van Buren's principal lieutenants in the Congress, told his colleagues on the floor of the Senate that removals were part of the political process. "To the victor belong the spoils of the enemy," he brazenly announced. That baldfaced and arrogant statement proved every critical judgment of Jackson's enemies about the removals. Worse, it diminished the whole concept of reform and the need for rotation to protect the system from corruption and inefficiency.

Needless to say, Andrew Jackson did not inaugurate the spoils system. That system had long been part of the American political scene. Nor did he institute a reign of terror and dismiss thousands from office and replace them with political misfits. In point of fact he dismissed relatively few employees and to a very large extent his appointments were men of similar education and background to those who had been replaced.[10] Jackson's object had always been reform, not the awarding of spoils, and therefore what he did or did not do must be evaluated in terms of this intent.

Within minutes of his arrival in the White House President Jackson was besieged by office seekers. In 1829 they had no difficulty in seeing the President. They just walked into the White House uninvited. If the President was engaged they could wait or request an appointment. Otherwise they expected to be ushered into his presence without further delay. Since Jackson was the "People's President" and his the "People's government," a great many individuals had no hesitation in coming to him directly and requesting employment. He was so inundated by office seekers that at one point he declared he had five hundred applicants for every office available. Despite this time-consuming process he said he was "determined to hear with caution, examine well, and grant offices to none but such as was honest and capable."[11]

Jackson proceeded very carefully with his removals because he insisted on evidence of impropriety before authorizing dismissals. He was sure the evidence existed.[12] But he would not act until he had that evidence in hand. Of course he could not obtain it himself; he relied on department heads to provide it. He also trusted certain individuals whom he assigned to sensitive areas with instructions to report to him directly. One such individual was Amos Kendall, whom Jackson appointed fourth auditor.[13] Kendall had already learned about some "horrible abuses in the government" and once appointed to office he immediately set to work to obtain evidence.[14] He found it in no time. He discovered a "rat"—to use Jackson's word—"marauding on the Treasury." The name of the "rat" was Tobias Watkins, the previous fourth auditor, who fled the city when his misconduct was discovered. Short in his accounts by $7000, Watkins tried to cover up his default. Jackson tracked him. "I am ingaged preparing legal process to pursue and arrest him," he wrote just a few weeks after taking office. "It may be that the Late Secry. of the Navy is concerned in the frauds." That secretary was Samuel Southard and Jackson longed to indict him, considering all the trouble Southard had caused in the late campaign. The President directed that Southard be asked for a written explanation and "should he hesitate he will be called on by a Judicial inquiry, and be put upon his defence. Should a Jury find him guilty, the punishment a Penitentiary offence. As to the Guilt of *Tobias Watkins* in this fraud upon the Treasury, there can be no doubt, but he has disappeared."[15]

Watkins played the role of corrupt government official to perfection. He fled the city, was subsequently apprehended, tried, convicted, and sentenced. He became Jackson's first reform victim. The case made a lovely item for the Democratic press to show existing corruption within the federal government. It also documented the determination and success of the present administration in rooting out and prosecuting the wrongdoers. "Indeed, the affair caused a great sensation."[16] It staggered the public because it came so quickly after the inauguration. Just a matter of weeks. And it seemed to prove everything Old Hickory had said about the condition of the federal bureaucracy.

Jackson beamed. "Assure my friends," he wrote John C. McLemore, "we are getting on here *well,* we labour night and day, and will continue to do so, until we destroy all the rats, who have been plundering the Treasury."[17]

Although Watkins was the most notorious defaulter to be exposed in the opening days of the Jackson administration, he was not alone. Further digging into the records produced additional "rats." Eleven treasury agents were caught short in their accounts. And that was only the beginning. "Among the custom-houses and other receivers of public moneys," reported Kendall, "numerous peculators were discovered and hurled from office."[18] Within twelve months of Jackson's presidency something like $280,000 was discovered stolen from the Treasury Department alone. Frauds in the payment of fishing bounties were stopped. Two collectors engaged in this criminal operation were removed, resulting in a saving the very first year of Jackson's administration of $51,271.41. Miles King, the agent of the Navy Department at Norfolk, was removed because he was discovered "using for his own purposes" about $40,000 of public money for several years, concealing his theft by false returns. Senator Tazewell of Virginia took up King's cause and appealed to Jackson, "distinctly threatening him with consequences in the Senate if he did not revise the decision. You may well suppose that Old Hickory was not to be moved by such means."

The Hero withered the senator with a glance.

Another defaulter of near $12,000, for which he had not accounted, threatened to go to the two Virginia senators, Tazewell and Tyler, if Amos Kendall did not accede to a settlement which he, the defaulter, proposed. Most of these thieves, said Kendall, were as bold as brass.

Within a single year, by flushing out the rats, the administration reduced the expenditures of the Navy Department alone by $1 million. "It is the opinion of the Secretary of the Navy," wrote Kendall, "that if he and myself are left to practice upon our own principles, there will be a permanent saving of a million per annum."

Because of the widespread embezzlements uncovered by his administration, Jackson requested in his first annual message that Congress make the laws dealing with public defaulters more stringent. He also asked that

the two-year statute of limitations be calculated from the date of departure from office (rather than the date of the offense) because so many
"rats" used this statute to escape conviction. In addition Jackson urged
the Congress to revise the revenue laws in order to block the evasion of
customs duties as well as to set the cost of public printing and thereby
close off one source of kickbacks.[19]

Additional investigations by the heads of departments revealed that
many of the exposed defaulters had taken an oath of bankruptcy. Indeed
they had taken it many times. By invoking the Insolvent Debtor's Act
defaulters could escape payment of their debts. This drove Jackson wild
when he heard about it and he subsequently ordered all department
heads to discharge any employee found guilty of invoking this statute.
The President also demanded the dismissal of drunkards, of which the
government had far more than its fair share. To his disgust Jackson
discovered that many employees proved morally delinquent, in one form
or another, and literally scores had spent time in jail. Government service
had become the repository of criminals and moral "degenerates."

These revelations vindicated Jackson's position during the presidential
campaign, and he did not hesitate to point it out. "You will recollect that
in the recent political contest it was said and truly said to be a struggle
between the virtue of the american people and the corrupting influence
of executive patronage," he wrote. Well, that claim has proved totally
correct. But we are presently doing something about it and as quickly as
possible. "You will see from the public journals we have begun reform,
and that we are trying to cleans the augean stables, and expose to view
the corruption of some of the agents of the late administration." Since
"office and preferment" in my administration, said Jackson, will be acces-
sible to both the rich and the poor, "honesty, probity and capability
constituting the sole and execlusive test, will I am persuaded, have the
happiest tendency to preserve, unimpaired, freedom of political action."[20]

One of the hungriest rats to be driven from his nest was the "Register
of the Treasury," a man named Nourse. He defaulted to the amount of
$10,000. When Jackson confronted him he admitted his guilt. Yet he
pleaded to be retained on account of his age! Old Hickory demanded his
resignation. Nourse refused. The infuriated Jackson dismissed him on the
spot. "I would turn out my own father under the same circumstances,"
he fumed.[21]

The moral delinquency within the federal government exceeded even
Jackson's pessimistic prediction. Old Nourse's bland request for reten-
tion on account of his age—as though stealing $10,000 from the govern-
ment in no way reflected upon his ability or efficiency—showed the level
of ethical standards. "The want of moral honesty," declared Jackson, was
pervasive. The improper use of the franking privilege was rampant in
every department, even to allowing wives of officials to frank their letters.

Newspaper subscriptions for certain "privileged" officials were paid for with public funds; supplies running into thousands of dollars had disappeared or never existed in the first place. Everywhere they looked, especially within the Treasury Department, the department heads found traces of the "rats." These were the men, growled Jackson, who talked so grandly about an elite corps of government officials "but who are on the scent of Treasury pap. And if I had a *tit* for every one of these pigs to suck at they would still be my friends."[22]

Because Jackson himself was so scrupulously honest in financial matters and because he found embezzlers in virtually every department, he regularly scrutinized all transactions involving federal funds. No amount was too small to engage his attention. Everything from "incidental expenses" in bridge construction to the costs of building customhouses and running the Florida Territory caught his ever-watchful eye. He even passed on the merits of individual claims and frequently fixed the precise amount to be awarded the claimant.

Jackson's nearly obsessive concern with honesty in government prompted him to badger the secretary of treasury with directives and memoranda to initiate reforms in the department's various financial operations. These memoranda started flying at Ingham almost from the moment he took office. "The Secretary of the Treasury will give the following directions, by circular, to all the Collectors," read one of Jackson's handwritten directives. "That they *use great vigilence & care,* that in every case, the payment of the import duties be *well secured by solvent endorsers,* —that no individual be taken as endorser for a greater sum than *two thirds* of his clear estate. Hereafter no collector to be allowed any percentage on any dues that may be lost to the government."[23] As he wrote these words Jackson's pen tore into the paper again and again, so fired were his emotions. He underscored several words in an effort to convey the intensity of his feelings in the matter. He must restore honesty in government, he contended. That above all else.

The many revelations of dishonesty at the outset of his administration coupled with his own manic concern over corruption convinced him of the need for further action. He realized that a program of reform must do more than simply replace the dishonest, the inefficient, the drunk, and the incompetent. He needed to provide a principle or system, approved by Congress, to attack the main problem. Quite early in his administration Jackson started to keep a private journal, something he called a "memorandum book," and in it he began to articulate some of his ideas about the problem of replacement. This entry comes late in May:

> There has been a great noise made about removals—This is to be brought before Congress with the causes—with the propriety of passing a law vacating all offices periodically—then the good can be sustained. & the bad,—left out without murmers—How ever many who has been in office a

few years, believes he has a life estate in it, a vested right, & if it has been held 20 years or upwards, not only a vested right, but that it ought to descend to his children, & if no children then the next of kin—This is not the principles of our government. It is rotation in office that will perpetuate our liberty.[24]

Rotation in office! That was the solution to the problem. And it was conceived by Jackson in order to "perpetuate our liberty." From this point onwards Jackson was at pains to formulate and advance this principle as one essential to his program of reform. It no longer mattered how *many* men were removed. He had little interest in a quantitative approach to solving the problem. What was needed was the acceptance of rotation as democratic doctrine, as something essential to perpetuating the freedom of the American people.

Consequently Jackson went to Congress with his solution. In his first message to Congress, delivered on December 8, 1829, he explained his doctrine and the reasons for advancing it.

Office is considered as a species of property, and government rather as a means of promoting individual interests than as an instrument created solely for the service of the people. Corruption in some and in others a perversion of correct feelings and principles divert government from its legitimate ends and make it an engine for the support of the few at the expense of the many. The duties of all public officers are, or at least admit of being made, so plain and simple that men of intelligence may readily qualify themselves for their performance; and I can not but believe that more is lost by the long continuance of men in office than is generally to be gained by their experience. I submit, therefore, to your consideration when the efficiency of the Government would not be promoted and official industry and integrity better secured by a general extension of the law which limits appointments to four years.

In a country where offices are created solely for the benefit of the people no one man has any more intrinsic right to official station than another. Offices were not established to give support to particular men at the public expense. No individual wrong is, therefore, done by removal, since neither appointment to nor continuance in office is matter of right. . . . It is the people, and they alone, who have a right to complain when a bad officer is substituted for a good one. He who is removed has the same means of obtaining a living that are enjoyed by the millions who never held office. The proposed limitation would destroy the idea of property now so generally connected with official station, and although individual distress may be sometimes produced, it would, by promoting that rotation which constitutes a leading principle in the republican creed, give healthful action to the system.[25]

The argument Jackson advanced for rotation was the argument of democracy. Offices exist for the benefit of the people. No one has an intrinsic right to them; they are open to all. Removal, therefore, does not in itself constitute a wrong. The only wrong that may result is when good men are replaced by bad. What Jackson advanced was the contention that a popular government had been established with his election and any notion of elitism in the operation of government was inimical to the doctrines of republicanism.[26]

Acceptance of rotation came simply and naturally. It found favor with the American people because it did indeed seem appropriate to democratic government. Instead of Congress legislating acceptance of the doctrine—although within a few years many newly created offices involved some statement about tenure—it simply recognized the fact that each new administration would claim the right to find the personnel congenial to its approach to government. There are disadvantages to Jackson's method—which immediately became apparent in his own administration when to his horror he found that he himself had appointed venal and corrupt men to office—but when properly controlled the system of rotation provides fast response to the changing demands of the American people as expressed through the ballot box. And that, after all, is what democracy is all about.

Skeptics then and later questioned the extent of the corruption that Jackson claimed existed prior to his inauguration. It was fashionable to regard rotation as nothing more or less than a spoils system. The truth seems to be that Jackson was correct in his contention, that corruption was fairly widespread and had been rampant for over ten years. By 1829 it was commonplace in certain departments of the government. Bribes were taken, kickbacks demanded, conflict of interest had become standard procedure. Within a year and a half of Jackson's inauguration nearly half a million dollars was discovered stolen from the Treasury alone—a not inconsiderable sum for the time. When combined with the thefts involving Indians, army and navy contracts, and the operations of the BUS they gave substance to Jackson's insistence that the Era of Good Feelings had really been an Era of Corruption. Any theft is potentially dangerous but in government it is particularly threatening. Since government can be subverted by its servants, the process of subversion frequently begins with the misappropriation of funds. Jackson hoped that over the long haul rotation could provide enough protection to prevent any systematic raid on the Treasury. Of course it was not possible for him to identify all the criminals or obtain sufficient evidence to win convictions in court. But at least he had devised a principle to combat the problem. And it would, Jackson believed, advance the cause of democracy.

With all the "great noise made about removals," both during Jackson's lifetime and afterward, it is extraordinary how few dismissals actually took place. There was no purge. In fact by no definition can Jackson be tagged a spoilsman. Whether he ever had any intention of massive removals is doubtful. His major concern was reform, not spoils. As soon as he felt he had obtained that objective he turned his attention to other matters. It has been demonstrated rather conclusively that during the entire eight years of his presidency only a little better than 10 percent of all office-holders were replaced. In the first eighteen months of his presidency only 919 out of 10,093 government employees were removed. When all these figures and percentages are evaluated in light of normal replacements due to death and resignation or those whose contracts or periods of tenure had expired, plus those dismissed for dishonesty and incompetence, they constitute a very modest record of rotation. Jackson would have removed more had there been a need. Certainly anyone deserving of dismissal for moral or ethical reasons would have been sacked. But once the idea of rotation as a democratic principle caught on, Jackson could afford to keep things operating pretty much as before. He was not attempting a vast overhaul of government personnel. Fundamentally conservative in his thinking, he left things operating as before, only excising what he deemed corrupt. Many officers appointed by Henry Clay, for example, stayed in the State Department because their work was judged satisfactory. Of 612 officers immediately under executive control, only 252 were removed. A great majority of postmasters remained in office—and postmasters were probably the most susceptible to political manipulation. The story is well known about the Albany postmaster who had been proscribed by the Regency because he had supported John Quincy Adams, but when Jackson learned that he had fought in the Revolution he forbade his dismissal. "By the Eternal!" the President stormed. "I will not remove the old man. Do you know that he carries a pound of British lead in his body?"[27]

The speed with which Jackson won acceptance of his principle and the wild furor over the so-called "Reign of Terror" explain to a large extent the trifling numbers of officeholders actually replaced in the eight years of Jackson's administration. Sensitive to the "great noise" generated by his reform efforts, the President slowed his head-chopping almost immediately. He proceeded very carefully in the future when dismissing appointees of his predecessors. He became even more circumspect when the "voice of caution" himself, Martin Van Buren, arrived in Washington to take up his duties as secretary of state.

Van Buren's coach clattered into Washington on March 22. It had been a long and tiring journey from New York. The little man felt quite ill as he arrived at his hotel, totally exhausted and mentally distressed. Even before resigning his position as governor he had been warned repeatedly against accepting a cabinet position. James Hamilton, Jr. told him that if he took the state department he would be cutting his throat. Van Buren himself had doubts. The cabinet was abysmally weak and there was a grave risk that he might sink with it after a few months in office. Then, to top it off, Jackson had made important assignments to foreign posts without informing or consulting him. A bad beginning. Certainly not one that augured well for the future. But he had long since examined the pros and cons of joining Jackson's official family, and as the "head of the new Cabinet" he had decided that the advantages far outweighed the disadvantages. Still his relationship with the President needed immediate attention—his exclusion from recent decisions involving foreign appointments proved that—and to this problem Van Buren concentrated his considerable diplomatic powers.[28]

As Van Buren stepped out of his carriage and entered the hotel, a crowd of office seekers surrounded him. They pursued him to his room and swarmed around him as he dropped to the sofa "on which my health compelled me to lie."[29] He told them he expected to pay his respects to the President within an hour and would therefore listen to them until he had to go. His weakened condition affected them not one jot. They proceeded to fill his ears with their pleas and need for appointive office.

An hour later Van Buren entered the White House to meet with President Jackson. It was their first meeting since they had become political allies.[30] They had never been close before. Their meetings in the Senate as colleagues several years earlier had never advanced to the stage of friendship or intimacy. As a matter of fact they hardly knew one another.

A single lamp lighted the vestibule of the White House and a solitary candle flickered in the President's office as the Magician entered the room. Major Lewis stood by Jackson's side. Van Buren worried about this meeting but the President immediately dispelled his fears with a warm greeting and signs of his obvious pleasure at having his first secretary in Washington at last. Although the General was "quite unwell"[31] and his spirits were depressed by his bereavement and the criticism of his cabinet selections and "Reign of Terror," he nonetheless startled Van Buren by the "affectionate eagerness" with which he greeted the New Yorker. More than that, once their conversation began, Van Buren was struck by the sharpness of his mind, despite his physical and mental fatigue. Like Kendall, Benton, Webster, and dozens of others, Van Buren immediately caught Jackson's intellectual strength. Frequently a visitor sensed it after the briefest conversation. And there was no explaining how it had come about. It simply happened. "The character of his mind was that of judgment," commented Thomas Hart Benton, "with a rapid and almost intuitive perception, followed by an instant and decisive action."[32] Other commentators repeated these observations, all agreeing that his knowledge was more intuitive than anything else. "To him knowledge seemed entirely unnecessary," wrote James Kirke Paulding. "He saw intuitively into everything, and reached a conclusion by a short cut while others were beating the bush for the game."[33]

Like his writing style, Jackson's conversation had "a vigorous flowing current . . . and [was] always impressive."[34] On this occasion it really dazzled Van Buren—perhaps because it was so unexpected. And Van Buren needed to get a sharp fix on Jackson's ability right from the start lest he presume an attitude that could have wrecked their relationship.

The President soon noticed Van Buren's exhaustion from his long journey and in a most solicitous manner—indeed the courtliness of it resembled Van Buren's own best efforts—recommended that his guest retire for the evening and said that they could commence a discussion of business the next day. As he left the White House Van Buren kept remembering the cordiality and kindness Jackson had shown him. What a splendid beginning, he thought. What presence! Years later the little man recorded in his *Autobiography* what his association with Jackson had been like. It started, he said, at the moment he entered the White House. "From that night to the day of his death the relations, sometimes official, always political and personal, were inviolably maintained between that noble man and myself, the cordial and confidential character of which can never have been surpassed among public men."[35]

The next day, rested and ready to begin work, Van Buren returned to the President's office. Jackson was waiting. The conversation began on a trivial note and only slowly turned to the important business at hand. Both continued measuring the other. Both still retained suspicions and doubts about the other. After all, Van Buren was a reputed "magician," the mastermind of the caucus of 1824, and the manager of William H. Crawford's ill-fated campaign.

Temperamentally, physically, every way, the two men seemed quite dissimilar. The long, cadaverous, sharp-featured, excitable Jackson stood in strong contrast to the short, stoutish, ever-cautious Van Buren. But these obvious differences masked many similarities. Both men were widowers, a kind of mutual loss that put them in a special category. Although Jackson's grief was recent, Van Buren, with four young sons to raise since his wife's death ten years before, still appreciated what the President suffered. More important, both men were practical politicians. Different perhaps, but both effective, successful, and attuned to a modern (popular) approach to politics. Also, both were committed to a states' rights philosophy and both tended to a laissez-faire notion of economic theory. Both were Jeffersonian in their approach to government and rather regarded themselves as heirs of Jefferson's political philosophy, although neither was a theoretician. Both believed in limited government. Both understood the need for reform.[36]

The two men talked for hours in Jackson's study. At length the President tendered his secretary an apology. He told Van Buren that he had definite ideas about what changes he planned to initiate in foreign policy and in American representation abroad, but in implementing his ideas he "committed a great mistake" in that he had not consulted Van Buren before selecting several ministers or in introducing some of his reforms. The two most important foreign missions had already been assigned: Littleton W. Tazewell of Virginia to England and Edward Livingston of Louisiana to France. Jackson said he "thought it his duty to apologize" and he hoped Van Buren had not been offended by his action.[37]

Livingston had met Van Buren in Philadelphia just a few days before and had informed the secretary of Jackson's offer, so that Van Buren went into his meeting with the President expecting the matter to be broached and well prepared to state his views. One reason why Jackson came to rely on Van Buren so heavily in the future was his preparedness whenever he was asked for an opinion. He always attended meetings with carefully thought-out arguments to support his position. On this occasion he shrewdly waited until the President brought up the subject of the two missions. Then Van Buren let fire. He "cheerfully" admitted that no two gentlemen were better entitled to the posts offered to them nor with whom his own personal feelings could be more cordial. Van Buren always purred before baring his claws. Nevertheless, he told the General, he was duty bound to state that both choices were unfortunate.[38]

Jackson paled. Van Buren hurried to explain his reasons. He cited both missions as extremely sensitive and important—England on account of the West Indian trade controversy and France because of the spoliation claims—and neither Tazewell nor Livingston, he said, was appropriate for such an assignment. Success would have been much more likely "if those Missions had been entrusted to active young men whose reputation as Statesmen, unlike those of Livingston and Tazewell, were yet to be established," men "who would seize upon those questions . . . with the spirit and vigour of youth and who would be sufficiently ambitious to encounter and resist the rebuffs to which, on such oft debated points, they must expect to be exposed and to submit to the drudgery thro' which final success could alone be hoped for."[39]

Jackson just listened. But the argument impressed him. He especially liked the zeal, the near-fervor with which his secretary spoke. If indeed Van Buren could run his department with this same enthusiasm and determination for success then he need never have worried about naming him to head the cabinet. Although Van Buren spoke in paragraphs he made sense. When he finally finished his brief the President just sat staring at him and puffing away on his old Powhatan pipe with its long stem.

Jackson cleared his throat. With "great feeling" he said that he had had some misgivings about the appointments but having heard Van Buren out he was sure "his course, tho' well meant, had been an unwise one." He wished that it were possible to undo his mistake, consistent of course with his own honor and the decency he owed to the two men involved, but declared that it was too late.

Not necessarily, responded Van Buren in his most diplomatic manner. Neither man had accepted his post, despite the passage of a considerable length of time. Perhaps if Van Buren wrote to them and asked for their immediate decisions, a way out of the difficulty might be found. Of course if they responded favorably and accepted their appointments then the secretary would request that they prepare immediately to start upon their respective missions, and certainly no later than August 1. That would give them four months to settle their affairs and pack. Jackson rather liked Van Buren's take-charge attitude toward his department and immediately agreed to the scheme. Van Buren said he would prepare the letters promptly for the President's approval.[40]

That done, the President asked his secretary to name a possible minister to Spain. "Levi Woodbury of New Hampshire," was the quick reply. Since no member of the cabinet came from New England and since Jackson knew and liked Woodbury from their Senate days together, he approved the choice. Besides, along with Isaac Hill, Woodbury had been most effective in organizing the Democratic party in New Hampshire. A letter went out immediately offering him the post.

As it turned out, Woodbury declined the offer. A trifle miffed by his failure to win a cabinet position, he said that his family opposed accompanying him to Spain and he was disinclined to leave the United States for an extended period of time. Had the mission involved a single and specific object taking no more than a year or two he would have accepted; under the circumstances he must decline. He was ready to serve the administration, he insisted, but not if it required a prolonged absence from his family.[41]

Tazewell and Livingston also declined. Tazewell said he was unwilling to go abroad unless he felt he could render his country a "signal service" and he frankly felt that unlikely at this time.[42] Livingston, on the other hand, declined because of his private affairs which required more time than the August 1 deadline allowed. Once his affairs were in order he would be willing to accept whatever post the administration felt he could handle.[43] Eventually Louis McLane of Delaware went to England and William C. Rives of Virginia to France. The Spanish mission was awarded to Cornelius Peter Van Ness of Vermont.

When Van Buren and Jackson finished their talk an initial bond had been established that grew stronger with each subsequent meeting. From their first conversation Van Buren proved he could tackle his job with enthusiasm and sagacity, and could be relied upon for sound, honest advice. Later he provided repeated evidence of his good judgment, wide knowledge, and unswerving loyalty. In time Jackson found him a good sounding board for ideas, and he appreciated his constant presence—the Magician had no wife to attend to—the ease with which he could converse with him, and the small courtesies the little man frequently bestowed on the members of his family.

As much as he relied on Van Buren over the next several years, the President never surrendered control of his administration on any issue —not to him or to any other person. "I have found the President affectionate, confidential and kind to the last degree," wrote Van Buren shortly after his arrival in Washington. "He has, however, his own wishes and favorite views upon points which it is not my province to attempt to controul."[44] Because the New Yorker learned from the outset that Jackson was the master in his own house, he survived several brushes with catastrophe. Because he never forgot this fact he eventually won the right to succeed the Hero into the White House.

Upon his return to his office Van Buren turned to a pile of correspondence that had been awaiting his arrival. The letters came from every section of the country. Many of them warned him that the administration was off to a bad start and that his own future might be in jeopardy. From among the batch he selected a letter written by his friend Thomas Ritchie, the conservative Radical leader of the Virginia Jackson party and editor of the Richmond *Enquirer*. In it Ritchie authorized Van Buren to show it to Jackson if he thought proper. The letter, he said, was dictated by the "most friendly feelings," but he had to admit that he was greatly disturbed by what had happened since the new administration came to office. He skimmed quickly over the cabinet, only remarking that it disappointed many of the President's sincerest friends. What he viewed "with profound regret" was the way the patronage had been distributed. "We are sorry to see the personal friends of the President appointed; we lament to see so many of the Editorial Corps favored with the patronage of the Administration." True, many of them were well qualified, he allowed, and they "fought manfully to put out a corrupt coalition," but what about the effects these appointments have had? "I go for reform," he said, "but what is reform? Is it to turn out of office all those who . . . decently preferred Mr. Adams? Or is it not rather those who are incapable of discharging their duties, the drunken, the ignorant, the embezzler, the man who has abused his official facilities to keep Gen. Jackson out, or who are so wedded to the corruptions of office as to set their faces against all reform?" Ritchie feared that the administration was headed for disaster. "Under the profession of Reform changes will be made to the public injury. . . . The contest will be for office and not for principle."[45]

Van Buren forwarded Ritchie's letter to Jackson with a covering note in which he said he felt it his duty to show it to him. He signed the note after writing "Yrs affectionately." It was dated March 31, 1829, just a few days since his arrival in Washington.

The letter stung Jackson. He responded testily. "There has been as yet no important case of removal except that of General Harrison," he wrote to Van Buren. William Henry Harrison, old "Tippecanoe," had been named by Adams to the post in Colombia and had hardly reached Bogotá when Jackson summoned him home. You must tell Ritchie, Jackson instructed Van Buren, "that the President has not nor will he ever make an appointment but with a view to the public good and the security of the fiscal concerns of the nation." No personal friend will be appointed unless it will serve the public cause. And if friends are qualified and patriotic "why should I not be permitted to bestow a *few* offices on them?" Of course everyone, he said, mentions Eaton. But Washington and Jefferson also selected "bosom friends" from their state and placed them in the cabinet. In fact Washington appointed two such friends. Tell Ritchie, Jackson concluded, that "before he condemns the Tree he ought to wait and see its fruit. The people expect reform, they shall not be disappointed; but it must be *judiciously* done and upon *principle.*"[46]

Although many observers friendly to the administration continued to misinterpret the rotation policy, Jackson always insisted that he aimed only at restoring the government to virtue and honesty. Sometimes he succeeded brilliantly; other times he failed abysmally.

The worst, as it turned out, was the appointment of the collector of the Port of New York. This was a very sensitive and important position. Some $15 million annually passed through the collector's hands. If any post needed a man of the highest integrity this was it. And when Van Buren heard that Jackson intended to appoint Samuel Swartwout to the post he almost collapsed. Not only did Swartwout have criminal tendencies but the Regency detested him. His appointment, Churchill C. Cambreleng told Van Buren, "would signal general rejoicing among our adversaries."[47] The prospect of millions running through this man's fingers sent shivers down Van Buren's spine. He wrote to Jackson immediately and warned him that Swartwout's appointment would "not be in accordance with public sentiment, the interest of the Country or the credit of the administration." Van Buren should have spoken more harshly, but that was not his style. Instead he said Swartwout was "generous, warm hearted, and high spirited."[48] High spirited!

Jackson refused to listen to this mild-mannered complaint. He appreciated Swartwout because he had been an early supporter in New York —unlike Van Buren. Also, Swartwout was a clever politician and he knew how to advance his candidacy by obtaining many favorable letters of recommendation. Van Buren saw what was happening with these recommendations and alerted his friends. "I don't find a single remonstration agt. the appointment of Mr Swartwout whilst there are hundreds or less on the other side." If the appointment is lost, he said, the blame rests squarely on "our friends" in New York.[49] And the appointment was lost. Jackson disregarded the advice of Van Buren and made Swartwout the collector.

Van Buren considered resigning—what with one thing and another— but this depression lasted only a few hours. When Jackson, as a courtesy, offered to allow him to make an appointment in Nashville, Van Buren appreciated the gesture but declined the offer. "Fair reciprocity," said the President, "is always right, and as I have given you, in your State, a Collector, I leave you, in mine, to give us an Attorney."[50] This was one of Jackson's more inane attempts to compensate for a particularly maladroit political action. Not only was the Swartwout appointment a disaster but he had undermined Van Buren's political standing among his friends in New York. In refusing the offer, the Magician muttered something about being embarrassed by the trust Jackson had shown him, but it was not so much embarrassment as chagrin that Van Buren felt. The trouble with Jackson, wrote Van Buren, is that he truly wants to run the government "honestly faithfully & impartially; but he lacks correct information in respect to the characters of the men of our State and it is at once a delicate and difficult task to be imposed upon me to give it to him in all cases."[51]

As it turned out, Swartwout initially proved to be a very popular collector and Jackson kiddingly told Van Buren that his opposition to the appointment was "the greatest of the few mistakes he had known me to make." So Jackson returned Van Buren's protesting letter, saying that it was a document "which would not read well hereafter" since it contained such egregious error. He implied that the secretary might want to get rid of it. Van Buren accepted the letter but predicted that the "affair was not ended." Jackson just laughed at his obstinacy.[52]

In time, of course, Swartwout absconded with $1,222,705.09. It was a monumental theft. Within months after taking over the collectorship Swartwout had his hand deep in the till. And when his peculations were discovered a few years later the criminal fled to Europe. Jackson was mortified. "Can he live after this?" the President cried, "or will he cut his throat?" Between Jackson and Van Buren the subject was never mentioned again. "I was too sensible of the extent of his disappointment and mortification to do so myself," Van Buren later wrote.[53]

Jackson's opponents doubled over with laughter. All the talk about rooting out corruption in government and here the greatest theft in the history of the Republic occurred in the General's own administration. All the talk about restoring virtue to government, and this single miscreant stole possibly more money than all the defaulters in Adams's administration put together. Here, then, was the bitter fruit of rotation. Here the dreadful consequence of denying the government the service of an elite bureaucracy in order to serve some idealistic democratic principle.

Perhaps this appalling incident taught Jackson a valuable lesson. Perhaps he learned that it takes more than the personal integrity of the President himself to insure an administration free of corruption. Whatever the lesson he clearly suffered from the derision he so richly deserved.

Despite this paralyzing scandal Jackson's reform through rotation improved many bureaus and departments. It rid government service of a number of incompetent and corrupt employees and established the principle that in a republican system government service is open to all. Moreover, no longer would such service become a sinecure for the old, tired, and worn-out. The concept of permanent tenure came to an end, that is until civil service arrived on the scene.[54]

But rotation was not Jackson's sole reform. It was only part—albeit the most publicized part—of a larger program, which applied to both foreign and domestic affairs, and he articulated much of it shortly after his inauguration. He eventually called it a program of "reform retrenchment and economy." Sometimes he spoke very specifically of the changes he planned, at others in sweeping, highly general terms. Sometimes he confided his thoughts to his private memorandum book, at others to selected advisers. What he eventually worked out in some detail was a program mainly consisting of the following: the reduction of the size and operation of the government in order to strengthen the bulwark of freedom; the limitation of government expenditures in order to pay off the national debt; the alteration of the structure of the Bank of the United States, the greatest corrupter in the country; the "judicious" adjustment of the tariff schedule so that harmony between the sections might be restored; the extension of the western boundary to protect the southwestern frontier; the rearrangement of "our affairs" with England and France to win commercial access to the West Indies from the former and to settle spoliation claims with the latter; the introduction of a constitutional amendment governing the election of the President and Vice President, to prevent voiding the popular will as had happened in 1825; and the removal of Indian tribes beyond the Mississippi River so as to "protect and preserve them as nations."[55]

Obviously, some of these intentions are not reform proposals as such, but rather part of a presidential program for change and national improvement. Nevertheless, in Jackson's mind, each one constituted a genuine reform effort because it focused on a problem the solution of which would "protect liberty," or "restore virtue," or "guarantee popular suffrage," or insure "obedience to the popular will," or "eliminate corruption," or reestablish "pure republican principles."[56] In any event he called them "reforms." Take the BUS, for example. From the moment he set foot in the White House Jackson was determined to alter the charter of the national bank. "This being the only way," he told John Overton, a long-time ally of the BUS, "that a charter to the present U.S. Bank, can be prevented, & which I believe is the only thing that can prevent our liberties to be crushed by the Bank & its influence,—for I find from the numerous applications for removals, many are requested on the ground of the injurious effect the interference of the directors of the Bank had on our late election which if not *curbed*, must destroy the purity of the right of suffrage."[57] The Bank's past corrupting influence extended back as far as the administration of James Monroe and had been compounded by its "interference" in the electoral process in 1828. Jackson therefore regarded the alteration of the Bank's charter as just as essential to his reform program as his policy to root out corrupt government officials.

Indian removal was another example of Jackson's reform intentions. The subject had engaged his attention for nearly a dozen years. Almost from the beginning of his negotiations with particular tribes as commissioner in 1818 he had spoken of the necessity of expelling them from within the limits of existing state boundaries.[58] The concept of Indian removal was not original with Jackson. It went back at least as far as Thomas Jefferson. But by the time Jackson became President the resolution of the Indian problem could no longer by delayed or avoided. The state of Georgia had decided that the Cherokee Indians might not remain within her borders as a sovereign, independent nation. The tribe was informed that unless the Indians left the state, Georgia would drive them out. As was their custom, the Indians appealed directly to their Father, the President. A delegation arrived in Washington early in April, 1829, to state their case. Only this time they were not dealing with a President disinclined to face the problem; they were dealing with a man who had set ideas about what should be done. He therefore instructed Eaton, his secretary of war, to prepare a "talk" in reply to the appeal of the Cherokees.[59]

Eaton composed a statement that outlined Jackson's precise position: first, the Indians did not have rights as a sovereign nation as they claimed; second, the United States government did not have the constitutional authority to take action against Georgia in support of Cherokee rights. The government had no more authority in this than it would have to free the slaves within the state. Also, as long as the Indians insisted on the status of a separate, independent, and sovereign state residing within the United States their demands were unacceptable. No country, said Jackson, can long survive such an arrangement—a sovereign nation within a sovereign nation. It would prevent the United States from developing into a strong, independent country. The presence of the Indians jeopardized the ability of the nation to defend itself. Since the Indians wished to preserve their culture, language, and tribal identity Jackson saw only one solution to the problem: removal. Otherwise, they faced certain annihilation.[60]

Thus, Jackson regarded removal as a reform effort because it fundamentally involved the liberty and security of the American people. But, as he readily admitted, many of his plans required the cooperation and concurrence of Congress. Jackson not only understood this but approved it. He did not intend to accomplish his reforms by executive action alone, even in the matter of rotation. He hoped the Congress would pass legislation that would automatically vacate "all offices periodically"—perhaps every four years—to establish the principle on a permanent basis.[61] He also wanted legislation to remove the Indians. All of which meant that he must wait until Congress reconvened in December before he could initiate needed action. Thus his first message to the Congress would constitute a schedule of what he intended to accomplish as President.

Meanwhile he did what he could to inaugurate his basic program. First, he wielded his appointing power. The "rats" scurried from their nests. Then he turned to foreign affairs. He decreed the "reform"—his word again—of the dress to be worn by American ministers serving abroad. He informed Van Buren that although their dress should be such as to distinguish them from "unofficial personages" he wanted it to "conform to the simplicity of our government founded upon, and guided as it is, by pure republican principles." As finally decided and ordered, the ministers were to wear a dress black coat with a gold star on each side of the collar and "under clothes" of black and white at the option of the wearer. A three-cornered "Chapeau de Bras, a black cockade and eagle, and a steel mounted sword with a white scabbard" completed Jackson's recommendations.[62] Van Buren agreed completely with the intent of the President's "reform" and issued a "circular" establishing the new dress code.[63]

More specifically related to his purposes in the field of foreign affairs, Jackson addressed the problem of the southwestern boundary of the country. It was the one area vulnerable to outside attack. He was especially bothered about Texas. "I have long since been aware of the importance of Texas to the United States," he wrote, "and of the real necessity of extending our boundary west of the Sabine. . . . I shall keep my eye on this object & the first propitious moment make the attempt to regain the Territory as far south & west as the great Desert."[64] Some Tennesseans thought that the "propitious moment" had already arrived. Sam Houston, the popular governor of Tennessee, had resigned his office because of marital problems and fled toward the Arkansas Territory to reside with the Indians. Shortly thereafter Jackson was informed that Houston "would conquer Mexico or Texas, & be worth two millions in two years." Commenting that these were the "efusions of a distempered brain," the President notified the Territorial Governor of Arkansas to stand prepared to "put down" any "illegal prospect." But the possible seizure of Mexico had always inflamed Jackson's expansionist fervor. And Texas he regarded as part of the Louisiana Purchase. "Early attention to be paid to the boundary between the U. States and Mexico," he jotted into his private memorandum book. "The line must be altered as by it part of our citizens are thrown into the province of Texas."[65]

As he prepared to initiate his reform programs on both the domestic and foreign fronts as well as write his first message to Congress to ask for their implementation into law, Jackson suddenly lost control of his household and his administration. Through his own folly he created a major public scandal. As a result, all his reforms were temporarily shelved.

CHAPTER 11

The Eaton Imbroglio

IN A CHARMINGLY NAÏVE, if quaintly expressed, comment on the course of American affairs in the nineteenth century, one of Jackson's earliest biographers wrote in 1860 that "the political history of the United States, for the last thirty years, dates from the moment when the soft hand of Mr. Van Buren touched Mrs. Eaton's knocker."[1] Supposedly it was the Magician's manipulation of an unsavory social scandal that produced the political shocks that rocked the nation and ultimately hurled John C. Calhoun into political oblivion and elevated Van Buren to the highest office in the land. This version of the Eaton imbroglio won immediate acceptance if for no other reason than that it added the suspicion of sordidness to an already tawdry affair.

The Eaton marriage was a messy business from the very beginning. It then triggered events which immediately flew out of control. The situation worsened because of Jackson's own single-minded determination, Peggy's overbearing presumption of her rights, the meddling by sanctimonious hypocrites, and the self-serving ploys of ambitious politicians. The marriage itself started everything off by giving Washington gossips enough juicy material to keep them occupied for months. Not only did Peggy's "tainted" past arouse a rush of outrage, but the strange and mysterious death (presumably suicide) of her first husband, John Timberlake, excited delicious speculation. Also, there was a question of Timberlake's accounts as navy purser and the possibility that he defrauded the government in order to pay for his wife's "wanton excesses."[2]

The mismanaged appointment by Jackson of Eaton as war secretary only exacerbated an already unpleasant situation. Not only did it plunge the loose-tongued into conversational exhaustion but it stunned a conventional middle class society of "respectable" and conservative church-goers into anguished concern for the conduct of national affairs. The appointment only confirmed the worst fears of those who worried about having a "military chieftain" at the head of the government.

Naturally, politics immediately intruded and shaped the development of this unfortunate business. And the basic ingredient was the presidency itself: From the earliest stirrings of the new Democratic party two men emerged as its principal architects: Martin Van Buren and John C. Calhoun. A natural rivalry between them and their cohorts seemed inevitable but it was generally understood that Calhoun would succeed Jackson at the end of his presidential term—probably after four years, given the condition of the General's health. But Van Buren had several things going for him. First, he had friends like Alfred Balch in the Nashville Central Committee to advance his interests. Second, several Tennessee cronies of the General actively disliked Calhoun. They heard rumors that the South Carolinian had criticized the Hero's supposedly "unauthorized" invasion of Florida in 1818 and had urged his censure in Monroe's cabinet. None of this sat well with men like Sam Houston and Major Lewis, both of whom tried unsuccessfully to obtain hard evidence of Calhoun's malice. Lewis himself preferred Van Buren for personal reasons. He had more to gain by the New Yorker's advance toward the throne, particularly if he served as kingmaker. Since Lewis was Eaton's brother-in-law, a powerful alliance soon developed between the three men once they gathered in Washington to launch the Jackson administration.

A counterbalance to this influence was the presence in the White House of Andrew Jackson Donelson. He resented Lewis's position of trust and especially his determination to play a key role as presidential adviser and confidant. As a consequence Donelson took an immediate dislike to Van Buren. He later told him, or so the Magician reported, that his feelings were so strong "that 'he could have drowned me' with a drop of water."[3] Donelson's wife, Emily, now serving as Jackson's hostess in the White House, naturally sided with her husband and contributed to the unpleasantness by refusing to socialize with Peggy Eaton.

Because of the mounting nastiness several family members and friends urged Jackson to find another war secretary. But the more they urged him to rid himself of the Eatons, the more obstinate he became. He would not be told what to do. He would not be driven. Then—as usual—he became suspicious that a "conspiracy" might be in progress, one initiated by "Clay and his minions." That only intensified his obstinacy. "I could not, nay I would not," he wrote, "abandon an old and tried friend." It "would have been destruction to him."[4] The very idea that some people thought they could dictate cabinet personnel positively infuriated him. "I did not come here to make a cabinet for the Ladies of this place," he fumed, "but for the nation, and that I believed, and so I do, that Mrs.

Eaton is as chaste as those who attempt to slander her."[5]

Slander. Only two weeks in office and Washington slander engulfed him once again. He wondered whether it would ever end.

In the midst of this developing tragedy Jackson heard of another domestic crisis that left him shocked and puzzled. Sam Houston, an old and loyal comrade-in-arms, had separated from his bride of a few months, resigned as governor of Tennessee, and withdrawn to the Arkansas Territory to reside among Indians. A hundred reports circulated about the cause of the separation but Houston refused to acknowledge any of them. He simply provided his father-in-law with a certificate that his wife was "virtuous."

"My God," gasped Jackson when he heard the report, "is the man mad?"[6]

Houston's friends in Tennessee were saddened and angered by his actions and the people of the state so infuriated that they burned him in effigy in many towns. In fact when he returned for a visit the following year they rudely informed him that he was not welcome to stay.[7]

However disappointed he might be with his old comrade, Jackson defended him. Houston was his friend, a tried and proven friend, and nothing could induce the General to turn his back on him. He sent Houston a token of his regard which the former governor acknowledged with effusive thanks. The rest of society might desert him, he said, but Old Hickory remained steadfast. "You have acted upon the great scale which prescribes benevolence and universal philanthropy," wrote Houston. Had a scepter been placed at his feet it would not have afforded the same pleasure as the simple knowledge that "I *possessed your confidence!* . . . You disregarded the standard calculations of mankind, and acted from an impulse, peculiar to yourself!"[8]

You disregarded the standards of mankind. Precisely so, and he could do no less for the Eatons. Jackson could no more abandon Eaton than he could Houston. And if that meant disregarding the standards of mankind, so be it. Unfortunately he nearly wrecked his administration in the process.

The "Eaton Malaria," as Van Buren called it, grew worse through the meddling action of two clergymen who sought to prevent the administration's certain descent into perdition by its association with a woman of "easy virtue." The Reverend J. M. Campbell, pastor of the Presbyterian Church in Washington, where both the General and Mrs. Jackson had worshipped, felt compelled to communicate the gossip he had heard about one of Mrs. Eaton's pregnancies. Since he was a young man and not on intimate terms with the President, he relayed his information to the Reverend Ezra Stiles Ely of Philadelphia, who had known Jackson ever since the young Tennessean first began to travel east on business in the 1790s. Ely had hoped to transmit Campbell's alarms at some point during the inauguration in March but no opportunity arose and therefore on his return to Philadelphia he wrote Jackson a long letter and recited all the vicious charges reported against Mrs. Eaton: that she had been known practically from girlhood to be a dissolute woman; that she had had a miscarriage even though her husband had been absent for a year; that Rachel Jackson herself had a bad opinion of her because of her disgraceful conduct; and that Peggy and Eaton often traveled together before their marriage and registered at hotels as husband and wife.[9]

The letter nearly gave Jackson apoplexy. He responded in a long outburst of indignation and denial. What especially bothered him was that anyone would invoke the name of his sainted wife to besmirch the reputation of another woman. "You are badly advised, my dear sir," Jackson rasped, "when informed 'that Mrs. Jackson, while in Washington, did not fear to put the seal of reprobation on such a character as Mrs. Eaton.' Mrs. Jackson, to the last moment of her life, believed Mrs. Eaton to be an innocent and much injured woman, so far as relates to the tales about her and Mr. Eaton, and none other ever reached her or me." Besides, was Ely unaware that both Eaton and Timberlake were Masons—as was Peggy's father? "Every person who is acquainted with the obligations of masons, must know that Mr. Eaton, as a mason, could not have criminal intercourse with another mason's wife, without being one of the most abandoned of men." Most of all, did not the meddling Reverend Mr. Ely know that "every secret rumor is circulated by the minions of Mr. Clay, for the purpose of injuring Mrs. Eaton, and through her, Mr. Eaton." Later, Jackson added, "and through the Eatons to injure me."

It was a vigorous defense. Eaton never had a better advocate. The letter ended with an appropriate reminder for the clergyman:

> Permit me now, my dear and highly esteemed friend, to conclude this hasty, and I fear unintelligible scrawl. Whilst on the one hand we should shun base women as a pestilence of the worst and most dangerous kind to society, we ought, on the other, to guard virtuous female character with vestal vigilance. Female virtue is like a tender and delicate flower; let but the breath of suspicion rest upon it, and it withers and perhaps perishes forever. When it shall be assailed by envy and malice, the good and the pious will maintain its purity and innocence, until guilt is made manifest— not by *rumors* and *suspicions*, but by facts and proofs brought forth and sustained by respectable and fearless witnesses in the face of day. Truth shuns not the light; but falsehood deals in sly and dark insinuations, and prefers *darkness*, because its deeds are evil. The Psalmist says, 'The liar's tongue we ever hate, and banish from our sight.'[10]

Several more letters were exchanged between Jackson and Ely, most of them relating to Mrs. Eaton's virtue and purity. By late spring, 1829, the President totally engaged himself in proving "by facts . . . and respectable and fearless witnesses" that a conspiracy had been formed to destroy Eaton and his wife. The more he contemplated it and searched for evidence to expose this "wickedness," the more engrossed he became in tracking down the culprits. Indeed, by midsummer he was obsessed with the affair. He wrote so many letters and statements answering questions, debating points of contention, and collecting evidence of Mrs. Eaton's good character that he exhausted Major Lewis, his principal amanuensis in the dispute. He sent investigators to different cities to check out the hotel-registry report. He interviewed character witnesses. Before he was done with this madness Jackson had brought all the passion and emotion to it that he had once reserved for the defense of his wife.

Whether Jackson consciously or unconsciously equated Peggy's plight with Rachel's hardly matters. His natural sympathy for women in distress, buttressed by his long friendship with Eaton, further strengthened by his growing conviction about a conspiracy, and finally solidified by the pressure exerted on him to coerce him into an action he opposed—all these drove him to heroic lengths to rescue the Eatons. He risked his presidency to defend the lady. He defied social custom—not the first time—to protect her. But as many said at the time, he would no longer be Andrew Jackson had he acted otherwise. And on major issues "when he was under strong convictions" he was immovable. He became stubborn and obstinate, the kind of obstinacy that digs in its heels and snarls defiance.[11]

Whether Peggy deserved Jackson's devoted solicitude is another matter. She could be hard and cold, demanding and ungrateful. She expected the President's full protection and support. Nothing less would satisfy her. And she had every intention of forcing society's acceptance of her whether they liked it or not. Her own servant boy later described her as "the most compleat Peaice of deception that ever god made, and as a mistres: it would be Cruelty to put a dumb brute, under her Command."[12]

In the course of his "research" into the "conspiracy," Jackson decided to assemble the names of every person who had spoken ill of the lady. When he heard about this, Ely advised Campbell to call upon the President and give him what information he possessed. On Tuesday evening, September 1, 1829, Jackson was informed by his doorkeeper that a Reverend Mr. Campbell wished to speak with him. The President went immediately to his office, where he found both Campbell and Major Donelson, although Donelson withdrew almost immediately. After introducing himself, Campbell tried to explain why he had acted through Ely. He then went on to tell about a deceased doctor by the name of Craven who attended Peggy at the time of an alleged miscarriage and claimed that Timberlake could not be the father since he had been absent from home for nearly a year.

Jackson seethed as he listened to this *"vile tale."* When Campbell finished his narrative the President pounced on him. His body shook; his voice cracked. As he paced before the frightened young man he raged, and gestured, and pointed, and threatened, and spoke with such conviction and emotional intensity that he overwhelmed the poor clergyman. Did Campbell not know that doctors were forbidden to reveal the secrets of their patients? Was this doctor, therefore, not a base and contemptible man, unworthy of credibility or respect? And, continued Jackson, now nearly beside himself, would not Campbell himself be held responsible for the *"vile tale"* by the "honorable, moral, and religious party of the community . . . inasmuch as he had avowed himself the author of its circulation?"

Campbell stammered a reply which Jackson cut off by saying that "as a Christian and preacher of the Gospel" it was Campbell's duty to check his facts and if mistaken in them "to repair the injury he had done female character by saying to Mrs. Eaton, and to the world, that on inquiry he found there was no truth in the tale of his dead Doctor." His passion spent, Jackson ended his diatribe on a quieter note. "Justice and Christianity," he lectured, demanded that Campbell repudiate the deceased doctor.[13]

For the next several days the President spent all his time trying to convince Campbell that he was mistaken about his facts. He even invited him back to the White House on September 3 for another go-around. But his efforts collapsed when he ended up quarreling with Campbell about the date of the alleged miscarriage.

This ghastly business reached an absurd height when Jackson decided to call a cabinet meeting at 7:00 P.M. on September 10, before which all the evidence would be placed relative to Eaton's alleged "criminal intercourse with Mrs. Timberlake," as though the cabinet constituted some sort of judicial body. Until this evaluation took place, Jackson decreed, justice to the lady, to the President himself, and to the country could not be done. Of course, it was also a signal to the cabinet that the President expected their cooperation in welcoming the Eatons to Washington society.

In addition to Van Buren, Ingham, Branch, Barry, and Berrien, the President asked Lewis and Donelson to attend this meeting along with the Reverends Ely and Campbell. Eaton was conspicuous by his absence.

After everyone had assembled Jackson began the meeting by stating that once the evidence had been evaluated by the group "I should hold no future conversation with . . . any one . . . in relation to this subject." If only he had kept his word! Then he laid out the evidence provided by Campbell and pointedly stated that the minister had given the date of the alleged miscarriage as 1821, a year in which Timberlake was supposedly away from home. The trap set and the victim neatly tucked inside, Jackson then sprang it shut. Memoranda collected by him, he said, proved that Timberlake was indeed at home in that year.

Campbell interrupted. He did not say 1821. As a matter of fact that very morning he had spoken with Dr. Craven's widow and daughter and both agreed that the date was 1826.[14] Jackson bristled. He would not allow the date change. Campbell had told him 1821 and "by the Eternal!" he must stick with 1821.

The President moved to other evidence, in particular the contention that Mrs. Jackson had had an unfavorable opinion of Mrs. Timberlake. "I declare," pronounced Old Hickory, "of my own knowledge that it is false." So much for evidence on that score.

Next he referred to the story that Eaton and Peggy had passed the night together in a hotel, in particular a New York hotel. On investigation, announced the General, this vicious tale involved nothing more than that they were seen *sitting* on a bed together. He found nothing improper in that. Nor would any other decent-minded person, he added.

His case presented, Jackson then called on Ely to present the results of his own inquiries in New York.

Ely, who had slowly tried to extricate himself from this unholy mess and regain his good standing with the President, reported on his investigations and concluded by stating that there was no evidence to convict Eaton of misconduct.

"Nor Mrs. Eaton either," prompted Jackson.

"On that point," replied Ely, "I would rather not give an opinion."

"She is as chaste as a virgin!" barked the President.[15]

The cabinet sat stony-faced as they heard these incredible words. They dared not say a word. Finally Campbell asked to speak on his own behalf. Jackson nodded consent. The clergyman said he had simply tried to spare the administration grief and the country from embarrassment. He hastened to assure everyone that he had communicated nothing to the opponents of the administration and that he felt his evidence sufficiently grave to justify the course he had taken.

Again Jackson interrupted. The minister had been summoned to give evidence, not pass upon it.

"I perceive that I have mistaken the object of the invitation to come," Campbell replied; "that it was not to give me an opportunity of saying any thing in my justification. I have therefore only to say, that I stand ready to prove, in a court of justice, all I have said, and more than I have said, or would have dared to say three days ago." He bowed to the cabinet and left the room. Shortly thereafter the meeting broke up.[16]

It was a farce. The cabinet of the American government sitting in solemn council to hear evidence about miscarriages and assignations. Sheer madness. The President was engaged in a lunatic campaign in which he had absolutely no business.

When the cabinet adjourned Jackson thought that Peggy had been completely vindicated. He should have known better. In his own household he could not make a convincing case. His official hostess and niece, Emily Donelson, agreed to receive Mrs. Eaton as her uncle's guest in the White House but she absolutely refused to pay the lady the courtesy of calling on her at her own home. Wives of several cabinet officers felt the same way. Emily disliked Peggy because of her "bad temper," she said, and "meddlesome disposition." Eaton's "elevation" to cabinet rank gave Peggy airs that made her "society too disagreeable to be endured."[17] "The ladies here with one voice have determined not to visit her," Emily announced.[18] Other critics began referring to Mrs. Eaton as "Bellona," the Roman goddess of war, and the Eaton affair as the "petticoat war." For some it was all terribly amusing.

The matter of the Eatons' place in society was certain to cause problems as the Washington social season neared. Van Buren gave an "entertainment" for the diplomatic corps early in the administration's life, but fortunately it was a stag affair and passed off without incident. However, cabinet dinners would soon begin and that promised trouble. Jackson told Van Buren during one of their horseback rides together—both men enjoyed horseback riding and soon discovered that this mutual interest gave them an opportunity for uninterrupted conversation—that he planned to postpone his cabinet dinner in order to avoid an outbreak of "violent feelings" among his friends. Still, it could not be postponed indefinitely. Once Congress reconvened in December the matter would have to be squarely faced. Then, with a sigh, Jackson added, "the sooner it was entered upon the better."[19]

Normally the President gives the first formal dinner for his official family, followed by all the other cabinet members beginning with the secretary of state. Jackson's party brought a complete turnout, but so much bad feeling showed on the faces of several cabinet wives that the evening was a dismal failure. The President escorted Mrs. Ingham to the table—an excitable woman particularly offended by Mrs. Eaton—while Van Buren gave his arm to Emily Donelson. Everyone hurried through the meal. Conversation sagged. Even after the meal concluded, the attempt at drawing-room pleasantries went so badly that the company dispersed sooner than usual. The evening was a disaster. Old Hickory retired to his bedroom mortified and humiliated.

He desperately needed Rachel.

Van Buren realized what he was up against as the next in line and therefore attempted to add glamour to his guest list by inviting the widow of Governor Thomas Mann Randolph of Virginia, the sole surviving child of Thomas Jefferson. She cheerfully accepted. In issuing this invitation to Jefferson's daughter Van Buren knew, of course, that his dinner would receive particular attention throughout Washington society. It was assumed that the party was given in her honor.

Yet Van Buren received a note from John Branch almost immediately accepting the invitation for himself but declining for Mrs. Branch and his daughter and offering the transparent excuse of "circumstances unnecessary to detail." John McPherson Berrien, a widower, followed suit. He had a "conditional engagement" out of town as his excuse, and for his daughter, "her state of health." Although Samuel Ingham attended, his wife did not. Nor did the wives of Eaton and William Barry. Mrs. Eaton and Mrs. Barry were "faithful allies" who "resolved to remain behind their batteries." So practically all the ladies of the cabinet officers stayed away, but this, in a perverse way, only added to the gaiety of the occasion. Mrs. Randolph had a smashing good time, "to the satisfaction of all my guests," Van Buren recorded, so the evening ended on a bright and happy note.[20]

A few weeks later, after Congress had assembled, Van Buren gave another party. He almost seemed to court disaster. This time he needed no daughter of Thomas Jefferson to advertise the occasion. The *Washington Journal* did it for him. An article appeared over the signature "Tarquin," accusing Van Buren and his ally in crime, Sir Charles Vaughan, the British minister and a bachelor, of attempting to force an "unworthy person" upon Washington society. It urged everyone who had received an invitation to demonstrate their outrage by not showing up. Naturally this ensured a record turnout. Savage beasts could not hold back the matrons of Washington—except, of course, the Mesdames Ingham and Branch and Miss Berrien. They were all unfortunately indisposed. But the party was a sensation. During the course of the evening's festivities Van Buren was informed that Mrs. Eaton and the wife of Major General Alexander Macomb had collided on the dance floor and that he had better intervene if he wished to prevent a battle royal. Assuming the report was a jest, at least in part, Van Buren begged off interfering between the two heavyweights.[21]

Another of Van Buren's diplomatic friends, who was also a bachelor, gave a ball soon afterward, on December 23, 1829. The host was the Russian minister, Baron Krudener. Since Mrs. Ingham was again indisposed, the host conducted Peggy to the dinner table, as next in rank. Eaton was assigned to Madame Huygens, the wife of the Dutch envoy. The Madame was not amused by this arrangement. At one point she supposedly announced that she would give a party to which Mrs. Eaton would not be invited and that her example would be followed by the Mesdames Ingham, Branch, and Berrien. That would put John and Peggy Eaton out of society with a vengeance.

While Van Buren stirred and seasoned this cauldron of female venom, busy reporters transmitted the details of Madame Huygens's outrage and remarks to President Jackson. Not long afterward Van Buren received a summons to come to the White House at once. The Magician arrived before breakfast and found the General clearly distraught. His eyes were bloodshot and his entire appearance showed that he had spent a sleepless night. He had learned, he said, about Madame Huygens's threats; if they were true and the other ladies planned to ostracize the Eatons, then he had no alternative but to dismiss his cabinet and hand the Huygenses their passports. He regarded the entire matter as a "conspiracy" ultimately aimed at himself, which he must smash before it could proceed any further. Before acting, however, he would permit the Huygenses to defend themselves. He asked Van Buren to interrogate them and report back. The secretary went immediately to the home of the Dutch envoy and explained his mission. Not only did Madame Huygens deny that she said anything resembling what had been attributed to her but she protested that "she had been too long connected with diplomatic life, and understood too well what belonged to her position, to meddle in such matters." So strong was the disavowal that the President received it with "unaffected pleasure."[22] The Huygenses were absolved.

Not the cabinet officers, however. They had to learn that this embarrassment must cease. Although his opponents were women—against whom he never warred—he would stop their meddling interference by threatening their husbands. He had heard that they gave dinner parties and excluded the Eatons. That must end. Sometime before January 27, 1830, Jackson again summoned Van Buren to the White House and told him that he had prepared a paper on the Eaton matter and planned to present it to the cabinet. Van Buren read the paper carefully. He offered one small comment. He suggested that it did not make clear Jackson's determination not to interfere with the domestic affairs or social intercourse of his officers and their families. Furthermore, he felt that the paper should be read to the cabinet, not presented to them. The New Yorker then offered to provide these changes so that Jackson could copy them into a readable script.[23]

The three cabinet officers were duly summoned and the President read them his memorandum. He explained that several members of Congress had informed him that a "combination" had been formed to drive Eaton and his family out of society and thereby "coerce me" into dismissing him from the cabinet. This course, he continued, was "not only unjust in itself, but highly disrespectful to me and well calculated to destroy the Harmony of my Cabinet." Although he abjured any right to interfere in their domestic relations or personal intercourse he felt they had attempted to induce others to exclude the Eatons from society and thereby degrade them.

> It is impossible for me upon the fullest and most mature and dispassionate consideration of the subject to regard this course in any other light than a wanton disregard of my feelings and reproof of my official conduct. It is I, that without any solicitation or desire on his part called major Eaton into my cabinet, and it is I, that with the fullest conviction of the injustice of the imputations which as I firmly believe malice and envy have cast upon his wife continue him there. If her character is such as to justify active measures on the part of my cabinet to exclude her from virtuous society, it is I who am responsible to the community for this alledged indignity to public morales. I will not part with major Eaton from my cabinet, and those of my cabinet who cannot harmonise with him had better withdraw for harmony I must and will have.[24]

The three gentlemen practically fell over one another to assure the President that they would be the last persons on earth to do anything to injure the feelings or character of Eaton and his family. True, they had given dinner parties and excluded the Eatons from the invitation list but that was no indication of a desire to expel them from society. How could anyone get such an idea? Of course "they could not undertake to controle their families" in such things as dinner parties but in all that had happened they had no wish or "intention to wound the feelings of major Eaton." Of that the President could be certain.

"I was bound to believe them," recorded Jackson in a private memorandum. Still he wanted them to understand that a general impression had gotten abroad which he could not tolerate and he instructed them to conduct themselves in the future so as to counteract this impression. They assured him of their cooperation and the interview ended with their insistence "that nothing on their part should be done to destroy the harmony of the cabinet."[25]

If in fact the cabinet officers, by their actions, thought they could force Jackson to abandon Eaton they were badly mistaken. "Heaven and earth may come together," the President told Amos Kendall, "but no base conspiracy shall separate me from Eaton. I have confidence in other men," he continued, "but I have more in Eaton; for my confidence in him has been tried. When he turns out to be dishonest, I will not confide in man."

The one thing to be regretted in the whole affair, Kendall later told his friend Francis P. Blair, "is that the villians here should have operated on any of our own friends, through their wives and daughters." And make no mistake, he told Blair, "the villians of this City are . . . more than a match for their co-villians in Kentucky. There is more intrigue and grovelling corruption with them; but not so much brutal violence." Fortunately, "Old Hickory is the boy for them."[26]

Nowhere does Kendall mention the names of the "villians." Although he speaks of intrigue the perpetrators seemed to have been simply "our enemies." At first Jackson placed the blame on "Clay and his minions," but over the summer and fall months his accusations became less specific. At best he complained of "females with clergymen at their head" who think they can determine "who shall & who shall not, come into society —and who shall be sacraficed by their secrete slanders."[27] At no time did he consider a larger plot having to do with the presidential succession. That came soon enough.

Although the "conspiracy" seemed to have no specific enemy by the close of 1829, the Eaton affair did reveal a loyal friend: Martin Van Buren. Very assiduously over the past several months the Little Magician had taken great pains to prove to Jackson not only his loyalty and dependability but his readiness to provide thoughtful and sage advice on the conduct of public affairs. It was unnecessary for Van Buren to manipulate the situation or the leading characters in this "petticoat war." All he needed to do was let events develop on their own and then act in accordance with his own good judgment and keen political sense. Everything else simply fell into place.

Jackson watched with particular pleasure at the emergence of this staunch ally and friend. By December, 1829, he was speaking openly of Van Buren's sterling qualities. To John Overton, he could not say enough about the support and strength the New Yorker had provided. "I have found him every thing that I could desire him to be, and believe him not only deserving *my* confidence, but the *confidence* of the *Nation.*" And that included the presidency. "Instead of his being selfish and intriguing," continued Jackson, "as has been represented by some of his opponents, I have ever found him frank, open, candid, and manly. As a Counsellor he is *able* and *prudent,* Republican in his principles and one of the most pleasant men to do business with I ever saw. He, my dear friend, is not only well qualified, but desires to fill the highest office in the gift of the people who, in him, will find a true friend and safe depository of their rights and liberty."

That last remark indicated the distance Van Buren had come in Jackson's estimation in a little over nine months. Already it had crossed the General's mind that the New Yorker would be his successor.

But what of Calhoun? "I wish," Jackson confided to Overton, "I could say as much for Mr. Calhoun and some of his friends" as I have for Van Buren. "You know the confidence I once had in that gentleman. However, of *him* I desire not now to speak; but I have a right to believe that most of the troubles, vexations and difficulties I have had to encounter, since my arrival in this City, have been occasioned by his friends. But for the present let this suffice."

Calhoun's "friends" were the problem—not the Vice President himself. Not yet. Although among those "friends" Jackson could have included the South Carolinian's wife, Floride. She too had refused to return a social call by the Eatons. Later Floride Calhoun would be seen by some as the leader of the "female contingent" to ostracize and humiliate poor Peggy.

In any event Jackson did not finger Calhoun as the man immediately and directly responsible for the attack on the Eatons or the cause of most of the administration's "troubles, vexations and difficulties." Probably, at the moment, Jackson simply felt that his Vice President was not doing enough to control his "friends"—such friends as Ingham, for example.

Still, if pressed, the President did have a few complaints. Calhoun objected to the apportionment of the surplus revenue among the states after the national debt was paid, said Jackson in his letter to Overton. Worse, he was silent on the BUS question and was believed to have "encouraged" the South Carolina legislature to adopt the nullification "Resolutions." In fact it was rumored that Calhoun had had a hand in their composition. Also, grumbled Jackson, the Vice President's friends in Congress would probably take a decided stand against distribution of the surplus, both the policy and its constitutionality.[28]

According to William B. Lewis this letter to Overton was written at Lewis's urging. Because of his concern for Jackson's health—indeed, during the summer and fall of 1829 the General's health suffered a distinct setback and manifested itself by severe swelling of the feet and legs—he spoke to Jackson about the presidential succession in case his condition should worsen. The General himself was quite concerned about his "dropsy" and had no qualms about discussing it with Lewis and wondering out loud about his course of action should it become critical. One thing led to another and Lewis broached the question of the succession and whether Van Buren might not be the best man to carry out the principles and reforms by which the General intended to administer the government. After all, if he died there was danger that everything he had wanted to accomplish might die with him. It occurred to Lewis—and he said this flat-out to the President—that Jackson's name (even though he was dead) might prove a "powerful lever, if judiciously used" to lift Van Buren to the presidency. Thus if the Hero would write a letter to a friend expressing his confidence in Van Buren's abilities and patriotism and qualifications for office it could be used at the next presidential election if Jackson died. The General agreed to Lewis's suggestion and wrote the letter to Overton, giving Lewis a copy. "If I die," said Jackson to Lewis, as he handed over the copy, "you have my permission to make such use of it as you may think most advisable."[29]

Obviously, there was a strong feeling among some of the President's close advisers that Van Buren, rather than Calhoun, should succeed the old man. And the General himself said he was very pleased "that the most cordial good feeling exists between Mr. Van Buren, Major Barry, and Major Eaton." The bond between them and its connection to Lewis linked them to Jackson on a very intimate and personal level. The President needed this close tie of friendship and loyalty and he acknowledged his debt to them. "These gentlemen," he wrote, "I have always fancied true, harmonious, and faithful, they not only most cheerfully cooperated with me in promoting the public weal, but do every thing in their power to render my situation, *personally*, as pleasant and comfortable as the nature of my public duties will admit."[30]

Thus within a few months in the life of the administration a situation had developed in which the President lost confidence in the Vice President and certain members of the cabinet and found unexpected comfort from his secretary of state. Moreover, in Lewis, Van Buren had won a powerful ally in the White House who used every opportunity to advance the New Yorker's political interest. At the moment a major blowup within the administration had been sidestepped, but with the political fortunes of several powerful and ambitious men riding on the outcome of this dispute further mischief and intrigue was certain to develop.

By the spring of 1830 the situation eased a little, and Major Donelson hoped that the worst of the danger had passed. The "big battle has ended, no lives are lost," he wrote to John McLemore, "and those who expected to profit by it are disappointed." The President "thinks in the goodness of his heart Mrs. E has obtained a triumph."[31] But Donelson knew better. The "big battle" was yet to come.

CHAPTER 12

"Mine Is a Situation of Dignified Slavery"

"THE PEOPLE EXPECT REFORM," said Jackson at the outset of his administration, "—they shall not be disappointed." It greatly troubled the President that he could not move the reform of the government along as fast as he initially intended, but he consoled himself with the knowledge that reform must be done "*judiciously*" and upon "*principle*" to be effective and long-lasting.[1] His first intention had been to cut the size of the government. Indeed, his cabinet had barely been assembled when he directed them to begin a program of "retrenchment and economy," as he called it, and to report directly to him on their progress.[2] He demanded a reduction in personnel "without injury to the public service," even though that meant reducing the number of offices available for distribution among friends and party leaders. He wanted to do something for General William Carroll, for example, and thought of making him a "charge de affairs" in South America if he would accept. The position might not match Carroll's expectations but, said Jackson, "it is all that can be done for him, as we are trying to curtail our Diplomatic Corps, at least of Ministers of the first Grade."[3]

In initiating his program of "retrenchment and economy"—ultimately he called his entire program one of "reform retrenchment and economy" —Jackson proved to be an outstanding administrator. He not only devoted long hours to the preparation of "principles" for the guidance of his department heads but he met regularly with them and discussed their overall needs and problems. He delegated authority. He provided support. He kept careful watch over many operations of the executive office and paid particular attention to expenditures. He inspected the details of every appropriation authorized by Congress.

Jackson's greatest disappointment during the opening months of his administration was the failure of his department heads to provide the leadership and reforming zeal that he expected of them. But that disappointment grew directly out of his own failure to appoint an adequate cabinet. He kept grumbling that the only reform that seemed to excite the interest of his department heads was Mrs. Eaton's morals. Still the President kept prodding them to "cleanse the augean stables" and restore virtue and purity to the government. "I have given a spurr to industry in every department," he told John Coffee, "and I hope the nation will soon feel the benefit of the change."[4]

And he did achieve a number of significant changes—not all of them as beneficial or successful as he wished, however. Because of his close association with Eaton and a growing regard for Van Buren, the President accomplished more with the State and War departments than with the others. Of course these departments handled affairs that were closest to his interest. Even so, a keen sense of cooperation and mutual concern developed among the three men.

In foreign affairs Jackson's interests were highly nationalistic—if not downright aggressive. He was an expansionist. He wished to secure the American frontiers against possible attack or invasion, and he had long expressed his desire to possess all of Spanish North America. Unfortunately, in agreeing to a treaty with Spain over the western boundary of the Louisiana Purchase, the United States had accepted a line that excluded Texas from U.S. possession. Jackson declared this a great mistake and a possible danger to the future security of the nation. As President he felt an obligation to undo the mistake. He was determined to acquire Texas.[5]

The most obvious and simplest manner of acquisition was through purchase and Jackson told Van Buren that he was willing to go as high as $5 million to acquire the territory. It was dangerous "to leave a foreign power in possession of heads of our leading branches of the great mississippi," he declared; acquiring it was "necessary for the security of the great emporium of the west, Neworleans." Besides, "the god of the universe had intended this great valley to belong to one nation."[6] And that nation—let no one doubt—was the United States.

During discussions of how they should approach the Mexicans about the purchase Van Buren brought Colonel Anthony Butler with him to the White House. This free-wheeling, fast-talking land speculator from South Carolina had formerly served as a member of the Mississippi legislature and supposedly knew a great deal about the area. He more than matched Jackson's expansionist ardor. When the three men met on August 13, 1829, they worked out a position paper that outlined the main American objectives in attempting to buy Texas. First, there was national security. Jackson constantly worried about the nation's exposed southern flank where "enemies" might locate a soft spot (Indian country most especially) to launch an invasion. Second was the need to acquire additional land on which to relocate the Indians presently living east of the Mississippi River. Additional territory would also allow for "a more effective system" for Indian government. Third was the need for the United States to have a "natural boundary—one that cannot become the subject of dispute hereafter, and near to which a dense population on either side can never be settled." These three objects embraced Jackson's basic thinking about expansion and emerged from his concern for national security as a means of protecting the liberty of the American people.[7]

The President hoped that the Mexicans would immediately see how a "natural boundary" would work to their own benefit as well. It would eliminate "collisions" which two peoples of "conflicting laws, habits and interests" were bound to have. The money from the sale could also be used for defense to protect Mexico against Spanish aggression. Finally, and most significantly, the failure of a sale would probably encourage the Texans to establish an independent republic, and this would seriously weaken the "bonds of amity and good understanding" between the United States and Mexico.[8]

The American minister to Mexico at the time was Joel Poinsett of South Carolina, appointed early in the Adams administration. On orders from the then secretary of state, Henry Clay, Poinsett tried to talk the Mexicans into recognizing the Rio Grande River as their northern boundary. His efforts only aroused suspicion and enmity. He eventually did succeed, however, in obtaining a commercial treaty in 1828 in which the Sabine River (which today forms the border between Texas and Louisiana) was declared the boundary separating the two countries.

Following the August 13 meeting Poinsett was formally instructed to approach the Mexican government about the purchase. Jackson thought the timing perfect in view of the "threatened invasion of Spain, connected with the deranged condition of the finances of Mexico." It was suggested to Poinsett that his queries to the Mexicans take on the character of "individual solicitude" for Mexican welfare rather than a grab for territory by the United States.[9] Jackson must have thought the Mexicans were half-witted to be taken in by such "solicitude." The reopening of the question only reawakened the old suspicions and antagonisms.

Ultimately these suspicions plus Poinsett's meddling in Mexican internal affairs brought an unfortunate turn in United States–Mexican relations. In the fall of 1829 Mexico demanded Poinsett's recall. Jackson replaced him with Colonel Anthony Butler, who proceeded to execute every cheap trick his febrile mind could devise to offend the Mexicans and hoodwink the Jackson administration. As requested by Mexico, Butler was named "charge de affairs" and given full powers to conclude a treaty according to the previous instructions given to Poinsett. The duplicity that Butler subsequently practiced as the American representative—a position he held until 1836—may have been encouraged by Jackson himself. For, in stating his desire for an honest transaction with the Mexicans, the President remembered back to the negotiations with Spain over Florida and how Florida became the "theatre for fraud and corrupt speculations." This prompted a most unfortunate comment. "I scarcely ever knew a Spaniard," Jackson advised Butler, "who was not the slave of averice, and it *is not improbable* that this *weakness* may be *worth a great deal to us, in this case.*" It would seem that the President was inviting his minister to gain the cession of Texas by encouraging Mexican greed. In endorsing this letter Butler wrote, *"Gen* Jackson. *Remarkable communication."* Later, Jackson would endorse one of Butler's letters with the words, "A. Butler: What a scamp."[10]

Jackson's other primary and immediate concern with which he had the cooperation and support of the department head and in which he achieved an important and significant change in policy involved the question of Indians and their removal west of the Mississippi River. And this, of course, was related directly to the nation's expansion in the southwest. Expansion and Indian removal compelled Jackson's total commitment because they were linked in his mind to national security and the protection of American freedom.

In appointing Eaton his secretary of war the President not only obtained a personal friend in the cabinet but one committed like himself to Indian removal. Both wished to proceed immediately with the removal but they foresaw certain complications and problems. One complication was the conflict between state law and tribal governance. The states, particularly the southern states, had nothing but contempt for federal weakness and indecision in handling the Indian question. Of particular concern at the time of Jackson's assumption of the presidency was the situation of the Cherokee Nation. This tribe had once held extensive property in Georgia and Alabama. Although their landholdings had been vastly diminished over time, Georgia wanted *all* Indian titles extinguished within its borders. To achieve this goal the state formed an agreement with the federal government as early as 1802 in return for which Georgia ceded its western land claims to the United States. But nothing happened. Meanwhile the Cherokee Nation adopted a constitution in 1827 modeled after the U.S. Constitution and proclaimed itself an independent nation with complete sovereignty over its people and their land. Infuriated by Indian presumption and the failure of the government to keep its 1802 pledge, Georgia decided to settle the matter itself. The legislature decreed that on December 20, 1828, all Indian residents within Georgia would fall under its jurisdiction after six months.[11]

A more direct and dangerous threat to Jackson's policy, however, was the attitude of certain church groups in the country. They disapproved removal, and in light of the revivalistic fervor of the time they might create a storm of protest over any implementation of the policy. A shrewd politician, Jackson worried over public opinion. He therefore did two things. First, he assigned Thomas L. McKenney to undertake the task of molding public opinion in favor of removal.[12] The choice was inspired. McKenney had served as superintendent of Indian trade and had become the head of the Bureau of Indian Affairs in 1824. He was generally recognized as a humanitarian and a man who knew more (and cared more) about Indian affairs than anyone else in the country. Most important of all he favored removal. And it certainly helped his credibility that he had supported Adams's re-election. He was no henchman of the new President. McKenney proved to be highly effective among church groups in presenting the most favorable arguments in support of removal, and he probably accomplished a great deal toward diminishing the possibility of a public outcry against the policy.[13]

The second thing Jackson did was to send Generals John Coffee and William Carroll to visit the Creeks and Cherokees and try to convince them to remove voluntarily. The two men were advised that since Georgia and Alabama were about to extend their laws over the Indians, other states would probably follow suit. Moreover, they were told that the President concurred in the right of jurisdiction expressed by Georgia and that the Cherokees had already been officially informed of his position. "The President is of opinion that the only mode left for the Indians to escape the effects of such enactments, and consequences more destructive . . . is, *for them to emigrate*. . . . He is sincerely anxious . . . to save these people, and relieve the States."[14]

There is no doubt that Jackson believed absolutely that he was pursuing a "just and humane policy towards the Indians." Given the greed of the white man and the certitude that the two races could not intermingle or live side by side, Jackson contended that only through removal could the Indians escape inevitable annihilation. Once relocated beyond the Mississippi the federal government might then exercise "parental control" over their interests and in that way "perpetuate their race." Most Americans probably agreed with this policy. As "hard and cruel" as it was then thought," wrote one contemporary a short time afterward, it "is now universally felt to have been as kind as it was necessary."[15]

To implement this "hard and cruel" yet "kind" and "necessary" action, Carroll and Coffee were instructed by Jackson to learn first who controlled the will of the Creeks and Cherokees. "Go to them," he directed, explain the dangers facing their people, enlarge on their "comparative degradation as a people" and the utter impossibility of their ever attaining high privileges if they stay, and that their own laws were soon to be superseded by the laws of at least four states. Then describe to them, Jackson continued, "the fine and fertile and abundant country" west of the Mississippi where the federal government "could and *would* protect them fully in the possession of the soil, and their right of self government." There, in succeeding generations, they would grow "to be our equals in privileges, civil and religious"; if they refused to go, however, then "they must necessarily entail destruction upon their race."[16]

Carroll and Coffee executed Jackson's instructions to the letter. But the chiefs and headmen who listened to them resisted their blandishments to remove. This was their land. They were the original proprietors of the American soil. They would never abandon their native country, nor would they counsel any other Indian to emigrate west. The refusal was curt, and it was final.[17]

After this rebuff, Jackson proceeded very cautiously. With rising opposition among northern religious groups and with renewed resistance by the Indians themselves, coupled with the continued determination of Georgia and Alabama to force a confrontation, the President recognized that he had a major political problem on his hands that could fly out of control at any moment. Voluntary removal now seemed out of the question. So Jackson ordered the army to remove all white intruders from Indian lands and if necessary to destroy their cabins and fields. He wanted relations with the Indians to remain peaceful until he could go before Congress and get the necessary legislation to begin formal and legal removal.[18]

It was becoming more and more obvious to Jackson that in order to inaugurate his program of "reform retrenchment and economy"—that is, Indian removal, rotation, debt reduction, alteration of the BUS, and the rest—he must go to Congress and explain his program and invite their cooperation and participation. His first opportunity to do this came in December, 1829, when he was obliged by the Constitution to report to Congress on the state of the Union. He started thinking about this first message almost from the moment he entered office. He worked on it for months. Whenever he got an idea he would jot it down on any stray scrap of paper and put it in his large white hat for safekeeping. Most of his ideas or recommendations to Congress found their way to these miniature keepers of the presidential intention. By the time he needed to shape the general outline of his message he had a large collection of these scraps and he simply turned them over to Major Donelson, his secretary, to sort and write out in some semblance of order and clarity.[19] At the same time he asked his cabinet officers for statements relating to their departments. These were subsequently edited and incorporated into the message. Then he called on a variety of advisers to help him shape the final draft. In the beginning he relied principally on Donelson and Lewis. He also came to favor Kendall because of his sound thinking on important issues and his vigorous writing style. But there were many other ghostwriters over the next eight years. For this first message he enlisted James A. Hamilton to provide a final draft. The two men met after breakfast on November 29 and Jackson turned over all the scraps and earlier drafts he had for the message. Hamilton discovered that the most recent draft was the work of several hands, including Jackson's. The section on the Indians extended over many pages. The Bank of the United States came in for heavy attack and was written "at great length in a loose, newspaper, slashing style," which meant that Kendall authored it.

Indeed Jackson had asked Kendall for a statement on the Bank problem and received in reply on November 20 a thoughtful five-page presentation arguing the merits of a totally different kind of banking system, one that would be "regulated and checked." To which Jackson added the words in his own handwriting: "checked the more effectually to guard the rights of the states and the liberties of the people, it shall have my most hearty approbation & support." But Kendall had doubts about his scheme. He protested that it needed more "investigation" before being "thrown before the public."

Nevertheless, Jackson turned the statement over to Hamilton to see what he could do with it. The young man polished the final draft until four o'clock in the morning. During the night, Jackson, who slept in an adjoining room, heard Hamilton moving about and stoking the fire. The President came in to investigate, dressed in his nightgown. He seemed surprised to find the young man still dressed.

"My dear Colonel," said the President, "Why are you up so late?"

"I am at my work," Hamilton replied, "which I mean to finish before I sleep."

Concerned for the young man, Jackson summoned the mulatto servant who slept on a rug in his room and directed him to stay with the Colonel and keep the fire going. At five o'clock, Hamilton finally retired for the night.

At eight the next morning Hamilton went to the President's study to inform him that the work was done.

"What have you said about the Bank?" was the first question asked.

"Very little," came the quick reply.

Jackson's face signaled displeasure. Seeing it, Hamilton read what he had written about the Bank. There were three sentences in all, but the last ended by saying that the Bank had failed to establish a uniform and sound currency.

Jackson looked at Hamilton. "Do you think that is all I ought to say?"

"I think you ought to say nothing at present about the bank," he retorted sharply.

Jackson laughed. "Oh! My friend, I am pledged against the bank, but if you think that is enough, so let it be."[20]

The version of the message prepared by Hamilton proved unacceptable and went through further revisions. Jackson himself worked on the Bank section and wrote out a dozen pages in a private memorandum. He began by giving the reasons for his concern:

"The objections to the present Bank are

1. It is unconstitutional;

2. It is dangerous to Liberty."

Then he tried his hand at revising the scheme suggested by Kendall but he got bogged down in the details. Ultimately he allowed his swipe at the Bank to remain brief. Probably he believed that any elaborate criticism would require the presentation of a substitute banking system, and he was not yet prepared to provide it.

The constant reworking of the message plus his physical debility and concern over the Eaton imbroglio seemed to wear Jackson down. At one point he complained of the burdens of the presidency. "As the meeting of Congress Approaches," he wrote to Robert J. Chester, "my labours increase. I am engaged preparing for them, and this with my other labours, employs me day and night. I can with truth say mine is a situation of dignified slavery."[21]

Still, considering all his difficulties in getting a final version prepared, Jackson produced a remarkable state paper for the Congress when it convened on December 7, 1829. The paper revealed both his determination to get on with his reforms and the extent to which he planned to make changes in the operation and affairs of the government.

The strength of the new administration became immediately apparent with its success in gaining the reelection of Andrew Stevenson of Virginia as Speaker of the House. Together with men like James Knox Polk of Tennessee, Churchill C. Cambreleng of New York, and Richard M. Johnson of Kentucky in the House, and Thomas Hart Benton, Edward Livingston, and Levi Woodbury in the Senate, the administration did not lack for strong, articulate, organized leadership in both houses of Congress.

The President's message was eagerly awaited. Delivered and read aloud by a clerk the day after the new Congress convened, it was a detailed paper, running in excess of 10,000 words, and written in a flat, somber, and prosaic style. It began on a friendly and hopeful note:

> It affords me pleasure to tender my friendly greetings to you on the occasion of your assembling at the seat of Government to enter upon the important duties to which you have been called by the voice of our Countrymen. The task devolves on me, under a provision of the Constitution, to present to you, as the Federal Legislature of twenty-four sovereign States and 12,000,000 happy people, a view of our affairs, and to propose such measures as in the discharge of my official functions have suggested themselves as necessary to promote the objects of our Union.
>
> In communicating with you for the first time it is to me a source of unfeigned satisfaction, calling for mutual gratulation and devout thanks to a benign Providence, that we are at peace with all mankind, and that our country exhibits the most cheering evidence of general welfare and progressive improvement. Turning our eyes to other nations, our great desire is to see our brethren of the human race secured in the blessings enjoyed by ourselves, and advancing in knowledge, in freedom, and in social happiness.[22]

Jackson's own original version of this opening paragraph had a more religious turn and a more personal touch. It was written in his own hand

and is reproduced here with all his original punctuation, grammatical liberties, and personal style.

> It afford me pleasure to congratulate you on your safe arrival at this city, to enter upon a discharge of these important duties which have been assigned by your country and I offer up to the almighty ruler of the universe my fervent thanks for the peace and prosperity he has been pleased to bestow upon our favored country, and implore him at a throne of grace for a continuation of these blessings, and that he may endow by his spirit the councils of the nation with wisdom to discern, and united harmony to enact all laws that may tend to promote the prosperity of his Kingdom, and the best interests of the union.[23]

After the introduction the President proceeded to a consideration of foreign affairs. He started with a typical Jacksonian swing. He said he would ask nothing that "is not clearly right" and "submit to nothing that is wrong." Under the protection of Providence and with the support of Congress and the people he would "cause all our just rights to be respected."[24] After that declaration Van Buren's cooing voice could be heard between the lines. The unsettled differences between the United States and Great Britain, France, and Spain were reviewed one by one. What was needed from Great Britain was a show of amity and good will; from France a resolution of the just claims of American citizens for depredations upon their property committed during the Napoleonic Wars; and from Spain an indemnity for spoliations upon American commerce committed under Spanish authority. Denmark, too, owed American citizens for spoliations but here negotiations had proceeded rapidly over the past year and there was hope that the matter could be settled in the immediate future.

Moving on, Jackson called for an amendment to the Constitution to prevent the election of a minority President as occurred in 1825. "To the people belongs the right of electing their Chief Magistrate," intoned the still-nettled Old Hero. Their choice must not be defeated either by the electoral college or the House of Representatives. *The majority is to govern,*" he declared. "Let us, then . . . amend our system" so that the "fair expression of the will of the majority" will decide who serves as President. As the first expression of the new democracy Jackson asked for the removal of *all* "intermediate" agencies in the election of the chief executive. He also asked that his service be limited to a single term of four or six years.[25]

In the spirit of this new democracy Jackson next analyzed the whole question of rotation and explained what he hoped to do and how it would reform and purify all departments within the government. It was one of the most significant sections of the message.

Turning to the tariff, the next vital if not potentially dangerous topic, Jackson said a number of important things: the existing tariff needed modification in some of its provisions; tariff adjustment should never be attempted except with the utmost caution; and frequent legislation with respect to any branch of industry "must always be productive of hazardous speculation and loss." All sections of the country, he said, should unite in diminishing any inequity or burden over which any one of them might justly complain, and if they do so then an active patriotism not bounded by sectionalism will provide renewed life to the political compact.[26]

Commenting on the prosperity of the government, arising in large measure from the sale of public lands, the President noted that the national debt would be reduced to $48.5 million by the first of January. He could foresee "in a very short time" with the proper exercise of frugality the total extinguishment of the public debt. Relief from this burden would not only increase "patriotic affection" but spur "individual enterprise." He therefore urged the Congress to hold down appropriations. Once he liquidated the debt, the resulting surplus could be distributed among the states for public works and education.

Those who opposed the tariff naturally opposed the distribution of the surplus because by reducing the surplus it also reduced the need to lower the tariff. Tariff rates could be kept high by keeping the surplus low. John C. Calhoun and his southern antitariff friends understood this and they therefore promised all kinds of difficulties over surplus distribution, including the problem of its constitutionality. But Jackson had an answer for them: amend the Constitution. "That this was intended to be a government of limited and specific, and not general, powers must be admitted by all," the conservative President averred, "and it is our duty to preserve for it the character intended by its framers." Therefore, he told the Congress, make an appeal to the states, "the source of power in cases of real doubt," and obtain through an amendment the necessary authority for the distribution scheme. Then Jackson's strong commitment to states' rights came thundering off the pages. To protect the liberty of the people, to preserve the "glorious cause of self-government," it was essential to safeguard the rights of the states.

> The great mass of legislation relating to our internal affairs was intended to be left where the Federal Convention found it—in the State governments. Nothing is clearer, in my view, than that we are chiefly indebted for the success of the Constitution under which we are now acting to the watchful and auxiliary operation of the State authorities. This is not the reflection of a day, but belongs to the most deeply rooted convictions of my mind. I can not, therefore, too strongly or too earnestly, for my own sense of its importance, warn you against all encroachments upon the legitimate sphere of State sovereignty. Sustained by its healthful and invigorating influence the federal system can never fail.[27]

Clearly in the tradition of Thomas Jefferson in the need to preserve the integrity and value of the states as a counterbalance to the national government, Jackson contended that such a balance permitted the majority to rule without jeopardizing the rights of individuals.

With respect to the rights of individuals, the President thought it important that the government lead the way in eliminating imprisonment for debt. A "more liberal policy" than imprisonment for debts owed to the federal government should be adopted, he said, unless fraud is involved. It should be the duty of the republic, he declared, "not to exert a grinding power over misfortune and poverty." To do so reduces the individual to a "useless drone in society or a vicious member of it."[28]

Jackson discussed the question of dishonesty in government. He spoke of the "numerous frauds on the Treasury" that had been discovered and what he was doing to eliminate the problem. In part the trouble was compounded by the size of the government and the extent of its operations. Therefore the President invited the Congress to assist him through a "minute inquiry . . . with a view to ascertain what offices can be dispensed with, what expenses retrenched, and what improvements may be made in the organization of the various parts to secure . . . efficiency and justice in all its operations." By doing this the Congress would achieve a government free from the taint of corruption and vastly strengthened in protecting the liberty of all.[29]

The old soldier then called for a review of the pension law for the soldiers of the Revolution, those "relics of the War of Independence." They have strong claims upon the country's gratitude and bounty. Not only would a revision cost little but it would respond appropriately to the sympathies of the American people.[30]

Next Jackson moved to the Indian question. His original version of this portion of the message, written in his own hand, contained more character and feeling. Where the final version (probably Van Buren's) speaks of the condition of Indians as becoming "objects of much interest and importance," Jackson put it more humanely. "The condition of the Indians within the limits of the U. States is of a character to awaken our sympathies, and induce the enquiry if something cannot be done to better their situation." The policy of the government, Jackson continued, seeks to open to them the ways of civilization and wean them from their "wandering habits" and into a course of life calculated "to present fairer prospects of comfort and happiness." It is wrong, he asserted, to encourage them to the idea of "exclusive self government. It is impracticable." The idea of a free, independent, sovereign Indian state is incompatible with a free, strong American nation. The country cannot be divided. Such a division will only encourage Europe to meddle and play one off against the other, as has occurred repeatedly in the past. Also, the Indians are not ready for such an exercise in self-government. No people were ever free or capable of forming and carrying into execution a social compact for themselves, said Jackson, "until education and intelligence was first introduced." This racist notion—that the Indians lacked sufficient intelligence to govern themselves—was a current belief. Jackson admitted that there were a "few" educated and well-informed men of mind and judgment among Indians but most of the southern tribes he had observed "are erratic in their habits, and wanting in [intellectual] . . . endowments" which are necessary for a people to be "happy and prosperous." The Indians east of the Mississippi River have been told, Jackson went on, that while the government is solicitous of their prosperity they may not continue at their "efforts at independence within the limits of any of the states." And that, said Jackson, was final.[31]

None of the above language was explicitly used in the message, except a few phrases like "wandering life." But the message did speak more specifically to the question immediately at hand, namely the situation in Georgia and Alabama. "I informed the Indians inhabiting parts of Georgia and Alabama that their attempt to establish an independent government would not be countenanced by the Executive of the United States, and advised them to emigrate beyond the Mississippi or submit to the laws of those States."[32]

The fate of the Mohegan, Narragansett, Delaware and other "dead tribes," the message continued, is fast overtaking the Cherokee, Creek, and Choctaw. Surely that fate awaits them if they do not relocate. "Humanity and national honor demand that every effort should be made to avert so great a calamity." But what about protecting the Indians with federal power in the lands they still occupied? "It is too late" for that, Jackson declared. "It is too late to inquire whether it was just in the United States to include them and their territory within the bounds of new States, whose limits they could control. That step can not be retraced. A State can not be dismembered by Congress or restricted in the exercise of her constitutional power."[33]

Yet something can be done, the President announced. "I suggest for your consideration the propriety of setting apart an ample district west of the Mississippi, and without the limits of any State or Territory now formed, to be guaranteed to the Indian tribes as long as they shall occupy it, each tribe having a distinct control over the portion designated for its use." There they may form their own government. They will be subject to no other control from the United States except what is required to maintain peace on the frontier and between the tribes. This emigration should be voluntary, he continued, "for it would be as cruel as unjust to compel the aborigines to abandon the graves of their fathers and seek a home in a distant land." If they remain where they are they are subject to the jurisdiction and laws of the states.

Given the past atrocities and the present continued greed of white men the only sane policy for a just government, Jackson declared, was to get the Indian to a place of safety, which he fervently believed existed west of the Mississippi River.

Turning to other matters Jackson discussed the savings to be effected in the navy and marine corps. He mentioned the correction of abuses in the post office and the need to reform the judiciary so that the circuit court could be extended to those states not presently covered.

Then he dropped a bombshell. At the very tail end of his message, in two short paragraphs, he announced his displeasure with the United States Bank. The charter of the Bank would expire in 1836, he reminded the Congress. To avoid the evils of precipitous action he felt that justice dictated that he raise the subject at this early time. Both the constitutionality and the expediency of the law creating the Bank have been questioned by the people, he said, and "it must be admitted by all that it has failed in the great end of establishing a uniform and sound currency."

That last remark was a stunner. The Bank a failure? On the contrary it had developed into a powerful central banking institution in full control of the credit and currency facilities of the nation and adding to their strength and soundness. But Jackson thought otherwise. Indeed he felt the Bank the most corrupting influence in American life. Therefore he went on to say that if such a financial institution is deemed essential to the operation of the government perhaps a national one could be devised by the Congress that would avoid all constitutional difficulties and provide essential governmental services.[34]

And with that Jackson closed his message. The benediction was short, appropriate and customary.

> I now commend you, fellow-citizens, to the guidance of Almighty God, with a full reliance on His merciful providence for the maintenance of our free institutions, and with an earnest supplication that whatever errors it may be my lot to commit in discharging the arduous duties which have devolved on me will find a remedy in the harmony and wisdom of your counsels.[35]

The message was no great ringing call for reform, nor a passionate pronouncement of republican principle. In language and style it conformed to early nineteenth century conventions. It was ponderous, the sort of thing a committee of writers would concoct. But embedded within the turgid prose lay the broad outline of a program of change and improvement that Jackson made the guide and purpose of his entire administration. That he ultimately achieved most of the objectives of this program not only distinguishes him from most other presidents but measures the degree of his leadership with the Congress and the Democratic party.

In implementing these proposals Andrew Jackson was about to demonstrate to the nation a new kind of presidency, one that would reconstruct the American government and provide a revitalized system worthy of contending with the different problems and issues of the modern world. The American presidency came of age with the arrival of General Jackson in the White House. For good or ill, he altered it permanently.

CHAPTER 13

The Rivalry

FOR JACKSON TO ACHIEVE ANY SUCCESS with his program he needed the cooperation of Congress. That he understood long before he sent down his first message. But it was not Jackson's style to wait and see if Congress would respond positively to his recommendations. He summoned men; he did not wait upon them. He had always played the leader's role. So, almost immediately, he began to intrude in the operation of Congress—slowly at first but gaining momentum with experience and the continued demonstration of popular support in his administration. In the beginning he worked stealthily. Nothing overt. The reelection of Andrew Stevenson as Speaker was a case in point. But with each new session of Congress the President became more skillful at political jockeying and finally succeeded in dictating membership of some congressional committees and winning the right to have a major voice in the writing of important legislation.

Straight off, Congress balked. In fact the members gave the new President a rather difficult time of it. Their first scuffle with him came over his nominations to office, some of which were so bad that they deserved to be rejected. Henry Lee, for example, was provided a small consular post as a reward for his valuable campaign efforts as well as for his friendship with Jackson and Lewis. But his private life gave Senators pause. Ultimately and quite properly they rejected him. Lee blamed the administration for mismanaging his appointment and repaid the failure by turning against Jackson.[1] Then a second appointment got shot down. Isaac Hill of New Hampshire was rejected for a post in the controller's office. Supposedly his blistering attacks on Adams during the 1828 campaign caused the rejection. No doubt his past editorial comments offended many New England congressmen, but his latest foray against the Portsmouth branch of the BUS also annoyed certain Senators who had financial connections with the Bank. (In fact some people later believed that the attack on the Portsmouth branch initiated the general war against the BUS.) In any event Hill returned to New Hampshire, where he won election to the Senate upon the retirement of Levi Woodbury in 1831; it gave him immense pleasure to assume a seat in the very chamber in which he had been rejected. Amos Kendall almost suffered a similar defeat but he just squeezed through the Senate by the casting vote of the Vice President. Lemuel Williams failed confirmation as a customs collector but then won reconsideration; the same thing happened to Samuel Herrick, appointed district attorney for Ohio; and John P. Decatur was rejected as the Portsmouth collector the same day Samuel Swartwout won confirmation for the New York customs.

Then the Senate really went to work on the President. The district attorney for New Hampshire, the surveyor and inspector of New York, Indian agents for the Shawnee and Delaware tribes, a land-office nominee for Ohio, and a receiver for Cincinnati were all rejected.[2] For one reason or another most of them quite properly deserved their fate. But Jackson threw a tantrum over this offense, particularly when the rejects were men he knew and liked. "Let Congress go home, and the people will teach them the consequence of neglecting my measures and opposing my nominations," he supposedly said at one point.[3] Indeed there was real congressional concern over popular reaction to their rejections. "Were it not for the fear of the outdoor popularity of General Jackson," said Daniel Webster, "the Senate would have negatived more than half his nominations."[4]

Actually the number of rejections hardly compared to the total (more than 300 appointees) submitted. Still Jackson resented this "discourtesy." He saw in Congress's intransigence a desire to "lessen my popularity," slow his reforms, and bring his administration into disrepute. The trouble with Congress, he complained to Coffee, was their failure to abide by "the real principles of the constitution as understood when it was first adopted, and practiced upon in 1798 and 1800." If he could drive Congress back to these principles then "I shall not complain of the sacrifice I have made."[5]

Jackson was heartened by the continued strong support he received from the people and the knowledge that Congress appreciated that support and reacted accordingly. He especially appreciated popular response to his first message. He felt it a good omen that so many flattering comments about his recommendations came from all parts of the country. There was some opposition, of course. But these he dismissed as the expected reaction of "all the sordid and interested who prise self-interest more than the perpetuity of our liberty, and the blessings of a free republican government."[6]

Congressional intransigence was not limited to confirmation proceedings, however. The House delivered a sharp rebuff to his bank proposal. The Ways and Means Committee, chaired by George McDuffie of South Carolina—one of Calhoun's closest allies in Congress—addressed itself to the BUS part of the message and eventually brought back a report to the full House expressing its complete satisfaction with the existing Bank. Later, Jackson's friends introduced into the House a series of resolutions declaring the BUS dangerous and a threat to liberty, but the resolutions were promptly tabled. Clearly, the Congress was not intimidated by the White House nor did it expect to take its direction from the President.

All of which ultimately served Jackson. He was put on notice that it would take more than presidential pleasure to activate the Congress. He was forced to summon his best political skills to move his program through the legislative mill. He was also forced to look to his popularity with the electorate and not simply take it for granted. Hereafter Jackson went to considerable trouble to convince the public that he acted on their behalf. Frequently he spoke over the heads of Congress and aimed his remarks directly at the people. As he did so he became an active, involved, and forceful politician. And once he assumed this role he converted political failure into success.

The opportunity to rally the people and win their renewed approval came sooner than anticipated. It developed in consequence of a stormy debate that occurred early in the new session between Senators Robert Y. Hayne and Daniel Webster.

This debate broke out over a resolution restricting the further sale of public lands. But almost immediately the controversy shifted to a discussion of the nature of the Union, the rights of the states, and the status of slavery. In a high-powered, emotional, yet closely argued speech Hayne articulated the doctrines of his friend, John C. Calhoun. Nullification, the theory that a state may declare federal law inoperative within its boundaries, received a formidable presentation by Hayne. The rights of the south, he protested, particularly its right to maintain slavery, must be respected, and any effort to jeopardize those rights would provoke extreme action on the part of the southern states: nullification first, then secession if nullification failed to provide redress.[7]

Webster replied in a two-day speech. It reached a peak of high drama when he shook his finger at the Vice President, the author of nullification, and proclaimed that the Union was composed of people, not states. Webster began his speech slowly, as he usually did, his right hand resting on his desk, the left one hanging limp at his side. The magnificent head would sometimes roll from side to side as though he were attempting to catch the attention of his listeners. His bushy eyebrows and deep-set eyes produced a hypnotic gaze that held his audience enthralled. Once launched into his speech his voice would swell for dramatic effect or hush to a whisper to underscore his meaning. As he became more animated his left hand would work itself behind his back and reach under his coattail, while his right hand swung through the air in great looping gestures. At one point he said in reply to Hayne: "I go for the Constitution as it is, and for the Union as it is. It is, Sir, the people's Constitution, the people's government, made for the people, made by the people, and answerable to the people."[8]

President Jackson had a high opinion of Senator Hayne, whose brother had been his military aide. He also appreciated Hayne's concern for the rights of the states and the right of the individual to protect his slave property. But nullification—that was something foreign. That was subversive. Who ever heard of nullification as a basic right of the states? And secession, the breakup of the Union—that was out-and-out treason. A state secede from the Union? Not while General Jackson sat in the White House.

Major Lewis attended the debate between Hayne and Webster and reported his findings to the President.

"Been to the Capitol, Major?" asked the General as Lewis walked into Jackson's study.

"Yes, General."

"Well, and how is Webster getting on?"

"He is delivering a most powerful speech," came the reply. "I am afraid he's demolishing our friend Hayne."

"I expected it," said the President.[9]

Everyone presumed that Jackson would side with Hayne in defense of states' rights. After all, Hayne cited the consolidation of the government as the greatest evil to their republican system, and no one doubted Jackson's position on that point. Some of Duff Green's editorials of the *United States Telegraph* seemed to confirm this presumption.[10] Most probably if the debate had addressed itself exclusively to states' rights the President would have agreed with the South Carolinian. But the argument drifted and finally centered on nullification and secession and conceivably the breakup of the Union. That Jackson could never espouse. He would rather "die in the last Ditch," as he once said, than "see the Union disunited."[11]

Because of the false presumptions propagated by Duff Green and his own abhorrence of disunion Jackson could not remain silent. He could not give the impression that he sided with the theoretical views of Hayne and Calhoun. But how to disavow the doctrine? What would be the appropriate format?

Fortunately, the problem resolved itself. For the past twenty years it had been the custom in Washington for Republicans in Congress to celebrate the birthday of Thomas Jefferson on April 13. Since Jackson was regarded as the "great restorer and exemplifier of Jeffersonian principles"[12] he was expected to attend and participate in the approaching celebration. And if he attended, then the Vice President, cabinet, and all the congressional panjandrums would also participate. Suddenly it occurred to Van Buren—since his mind naturally inclined to "morbid speculations" concerning Calhoun—that the celebration might become the occasion for "some irregular and unauthorized proceedings" by the nullifiers and their friends, "which might menace the stability of the Union." The occasion might become a "stalking horse" to enlist additional congressional support for the pernicious doctrine of nullification.[13]

Obviously the situation "required the utmost prudence and circumspection on the part of the President."[14] Jackson therefore cautiously reviewed the options available to him. Then, as the day of the celebration approached, the *United States Telegraph* published a program for the proceedings and a "friend" brought it to his attention and suggested "that he had better read it." When he saw the names of the principal participants he immediately concluded that "the celebration was to be a *nullification affair altogether."*[15] That settled it. The moment had arrived for the President himself to put a stop to these nullifiers and make his own position absolutely clear not only to congressmen but to the American people.

He still needed to exercise prudence, however. He must not worsen the situation with threats and fiery words. He therefore worked out very carefully in his mind what he planned to do and say. On the morning of the celebration he prepared three statements. Since he would surely be invited to offer a toast at the affair, Jackson decided that that would be the moment to take his stand.

When he arrived at his office the President found Donelson and Lewis reading the newspapers. He handed each of them in turn the three slips of paper and asked which toast they preferred. Both agreed on the shortest one. It was the most "expressive," they said. Jackson then placed the approved statement in his pocket and threw the other two into the fire.

Van Buren arrived as prearranged and together the four men discussed what might happen that night and how the President should react. The Magician read Jackson's toast and expressed his pleasure in it. Since Van Buren would also be expected to say something in his proper turn, his toast was constructed to conform to the "spirit and tenor" of Jackson's. "Thus armed," recorded Van Buren a number of years later, "we repaired to the dinner with feelings on the part of the old Chief akin to those which would have animated his breast if the scene of this preliminary skirmish in defence of the Union had been the field of battle instead of the festive board."[16]

The dinner was held at the Indian Queen Hotel. A full portrait of George Washington and two busts of Thomas Jefferson adorned the hall. Numerous evergreens added a festive touch. The celebrants sat at two parallel tables, with a cross table at the head "which promoted festivity and sociality." The size and form of the room were such as to accommodate a large crowd. In addition to the President and his cabinet more than a hundred congressmen attended along with high-ranking officers of the army and navy, civil officers of the government, visitors in the city, and distinguished citizens from the District and surrounding cities.

The President arrived at five o'clock and stayed until ten. The affair was organized with John Roane of Virginia officiating as "President of the Day," assisted by George M. Bibb of Kentucky, Levi Woodbury of New Hampshire, Felix Grundy of Tennessee, Churchill C. Cambreleng of New York, William F. Bordon of Virginia, and Walter H. Overton of Louisiana, the vice presidents.

Once the festivities began the guests eagerly anticipated the toasts to be drunk. Twenty-four of them were proposed, and all but six or seven mentioned Virginia and Jefferson and the great principles of states' rights for which both stood. Robert Y. Hayne, chairman of the Committee on Arrangements, spoke long and eloquently of "the glorious stand taken by Virginia in regard to the alien and sedition laws."[17] He referred very pointedly to the recent course adopted by Georgia in relation to the Indians and how, under the standard of states' rights, she had "achieved a great and glorious victory." He paused and then proposed his toast:

"The *Union* of the States, and the *Sovereignty* of the States."

Jackson fidgeted. The toasts were bordering on sedition, he later remarked. Some of them contained sentiments which he knew Jefferson abhorred. He could not bear to "hear the dissolution of the Union spoken of lightly."[18]

Both Jackson and Calhoun were seated near the chair. Van Buren had been placed at the foot of the second table next to a presumed nullifier for safekeeping. It was getting close to the time when the President would be asked to offer a toast. Jackson picked up the list of regular toasts and wrote his own on the back of it. But as he wrote he inadvertently left out a single word.

The regular toasts concluded. The President was then asked to provide a volunteer. He rose.

"Our Union: *It must be preserved.*"

The words ricocheted around the room. The effect was explosive. "The veil was rent," recorded Van Buren, "—the incantations of the night were exposed to the light of day."[19]

Hayne jumped from his place and ran over to the President. He begged him to insert the word "federal" so that the toast could be reported as "Our federal Union." Since that was precisely the word Jackson had inadvertently omitted he "cheerfully assented."[20] If Hayne thought that the insertion would make the rebuke less "pungent," he thought wrong. In fact it "electrified the country."[21]

When the guests had settled down after recovering from the shock of Jackson's forceful declamation, the Vice President rose to offer the next toast.

"The Union," he said in a loud, strong voice. "Next to our liberty, the most dear."

Had he stopped with these words Calhoun would have shared some of Jackson's merit in terms of brevity and pungency. But he could not resist lecturing his audience for a few extra moments and in so doing dulled the edge of his thrusting words.

Next came the political master. Van Buren offered blessings on everyone's house. "Mutual forbearance and reciprocal concession," he preached. "Through their agency the Union was established. The patriotic spirit from which they emanated will forever sustain it."[22]

In all three toasts the keynote was "Union." Calhoun said it came next to liberty. But Webster, in his second reply to Hayne on the Senate floor, insisted that liberty and Union were inseparable—one not possible without the other. That was Jackson's opinion also. Liberty had always been uppermost in his thinking about government and its relationship to the people. But only through a strong Union—not a hyperactive government—could liberty be preserved and perpetuated.[23]

As he left the banquet hall Jackson grumbled over the fact that the Jefferson dinner had been "turned into a piece of political management." And all this because the south hated protective tariffs and demanded substantial reductions. All this because of the Tariff of Abominations and the decision of South Carolina to proclaim its right to nullify federal legislation. Well, the "nullies" would not get away with it. The President later told Kendall that he meant his toast as "a rebuke upon the seditious sentiments which were uttered in his presence." He blamed Duff Green as the person most responsible for "wilfully perverting" the dinner into a political engine. "Green has wholly lost the confidence of the President," reported Kendall, "and . . . there will shortly be a *real* administration paper here." All of this maneuvering, said Jackson, was a simple ploy to force him to adopt a low-tariff stance.[24] Why, they would even calculate the value of the Union. Well, "by the Eternal God," the President ranted, the Union would be preserved, *"Tariff or no Tariff"*; and, said Kendall, all the Hotspurs who attended the dinner "know that Old Hickory *means what he says.*"[25]

Not many days later a Congressman from South Carolina came to the White House to pay his respects and take leave of the President. He was returning to his home state. Jackson received him with great courtesy, as was his wont, offering his hand and begging him to take a seat. After a brief conversation the Congressman asked if the President had anything he wanted him to convey to his friends in South Carolina.

"No, I believe not," came the immediate reply. But then the President remembered his toast and quickly amended his remark. "Yes, I have; please give my compliments to my friends in your State, and say to them, that if a single drop of blood shall be shed there in opposition to the laws of the United States, I will hang the first man I can lay my hand on engaged in such treasonable conduct, upon the first tree I can reach."[26]

The Congressman's eyes almost popped out of his head. He got out of the room as fast as possible.

This brush with the extremist southern position totally alienated Jackson from his Vice President and also severely damaged the relationship of the administration with its so-called mouthpiece, the *United States Telegraph*. At the same time Van Buren continued to gain ground. His relationship with the President grew closer and stronger. Their almost daily horseback rides provided Van Buren with a unique opportunity to display his talents and loyalty. Then, quietly but persistently, he began urging Jackson to stand for reelection in 1832, something the General at first opposed.[27] It accorded with the Magician's ambition to keep Old Hickory in place and stall Calhoun's ambitions for another four years. What Van Buren needed was time both to strengthen his association with Jackson and allow Calhoun (with the help of his friends) to further damage his own. By early spring 1830 even the opposition knew that Jackson was being urged to seek a second term, and some figured that the President had meant all along to run again. "Seeing this" obvious desire by the General, wrote Webster, "VB has been endeavoring to make a merit of persuading him to do so, on the ground of its being necessary to keep the party together."[28]

Van Buren had considerable help with his scheme from William B. Lewis, who wanted to stretch out Jackson's term in order to delay (and eventually block) Calhoun's succession. In addition the Magician signaled his friends in New York to pass a resolution at their next party caucus favoring a second term. The New York cronies immediately translated their leader's request into an appropriate resolution at Albany by placing Jackson in formal nomination for reelection. Pennsylvania Democrats also obliged. Both Henry Clay and John Quincy Adams saw the obvious intent in all this. "The Jefferson dinner was a trick of Calhoun's against Van Buren," wrote Adams, "as the Harrisburg and Albany nominations of Jackson for re-election were a trick of Van Buren's against Calhoun."[29]

The ever-observant Amos Kendall watched the skillful New York operator work his magic. He had to express his admiration. "Van Buren glides along as smoothly as oil and as silently as a cat," he wrote to Francis Blair. "If he is managing at all, it is so adroitly that nobody perceives it. He is evidently gaining from the indiscretions of Calhoun's friends. He has the entire confidence of the President and all his personal friends, while Calhoun is fast losing it."[30]

Almost without lifting a finger to merit his isolation Calhoun was being cut loose from the administration. Everything moved slowly, but it moved nonetheless. Several Washington commentators began to note that a new division had broken out within the party. Kendall informed Blair of the speculation. On one side, he said, was the democracy of the northern, midwestern and part of the southern states, "who will go for reform in all the branches of the government, a gradual reduction of duties, so as to bring down the revenue to the proper wants of the government . . . the abandonment of all pretensions to powers which necessarily create collisions with the states and an honest and efficient administration." On the other, he continued, will be found "the previous anti-tariff men of the South and furious tariff men of the North with the corrupt portion of the late coalition party." It will be headed by Calhoun and John McLean, with Ingham, Berrien, McDuffie, and Green as "its main pillars." Kendall said he would not be surprised if some of the southern leaders within the next twelve months became "hotly opposed to Gen. Jackson."[31]

The belief that the party was slowly dividing into two wings attested to the fact that a major rivalry between Van Buren and Calhoun had developed and was certain to affect the course of party history as well as the presidential succession. And everyone saw that the Magician had the major advantages. Poor Calhoun. He was being murdered by his friends. Without doing a thing—or much of anything—he was losing his hold on Jackson. First there was the Eaton business, including Mrs. Floride Calhoun's refusal to return a social call from the Eatons, and although Calhoun was not yet accused of instigating that imbroglio, Van Buren was the clear gainer. Then there was nullification, a doctrine Jackson rejected outright. Another major setback for the Vice President. Next Duff Green had lost favor with Jackson—an additional defeat. George McDuffie's House report about the BUS also aggravated the General. And now Van Buren steadily worked on the President to stand for another term and had gathered support for his efforts from some of the General's closest associates.[32] "Mr. Van Buren has got the start of Calhoun," confided John Quincy Adams to his diary, "in the merit of convincing General Jackson that the salvation of the country depends upon his re-election. This establishes the ascendency of Van Buren in the Cabinet, and reduces Calhoun to the alternative of joining in the shout of hurrah for Jackson's re-election or of being counted in opposition."[33] Everywhere the push for a second term was seen as an action by Van Buren to "strengthen himself against Calhoun," even among National Republicans.[34] Of course the Magician swore he was doing no such thing.[35]

Actually Calhoun was not without friends and supporters within the Jackson circle. Donelson was one. Isaac Hill was another. "I greatly fear," Hill admitted, "that the day of his usefulness to the democratic party is on the wane. Still, if he has a friend in the world, it is I who wish him well."[36] Francis P. Blair, the Kentucky publicist, was another Calhoun ally and he felt the party owed the Vice President a great deal for past services.[37]

It was difficult for Calhoun to know what to do. He watched with apprehension and alarm. He seemed powerless to ingratiate himself with the President at the same time that Van Buren marched further ahead every month. "V.B.—thro' the petticoat influence," commented Edward Everett of Massachusetts, "—is quietly possessing himself of the President—of his personal influence, if he has any—and of the great Jackson party. Calhoun sees this; but dare not yet break out; because he cannot unite with Clay, & without his strength, he would be an impotent fragment of a party, when severed from his present associates."[38] Although Calhoun was not yet "breaking out," Webster believed he was "forming a party against Van Buren, and as the President is supposed to be Van Buren's man, the Vice President has great difficulty to separate his opposition to Van Buren from opposition to the President."[39] The obvious danger was that Calhoun would become the rallying point of all the opposition to the administration.

While this major rivalry took shape the atmosphere in Washington became supercharged over the continuing social warfare generated by the Eaton affair. One dinner party after another was held during the winter without the presence of Mr. or Mrs. Eaton. Ingham, Branch, Berrien, and Colonel Nathan Towson, the paymaster general of the army, gave large dinner parties, according to Adams, "to which Mrs. Eaton is not invited. On the other hand, the President makes her doubly conspicuous by an over-display of notice. At the last drawing-room, the night before last, she had a crowd gathered around her, and was made the public gaze."[40] Although Jackson expected the "petticoat war" to end following his instruction to the cabinet in January, 1830, the slights and embarrassments continued unabated all winter long. The wives of these officers rejected Jackson's presumption in instructing them in their social obligations. Early in March Levi Woodbury reported on a large party and ball. "The ladies," he told his wife, "being apprised in one of the public papers, Mrs Eaton was to be there and *patronized*—played a little shy—tho' a large number were still there—But more gentlemen than ladies."[41] Mrs. Margaret Bayard Smith, with tongue in cheek, saw the scandal as a sign of advancing democracy. "Our government is becoming every day more and more democratic, the rulers of the people are truly their servants and among those rulers women are gaining more than their share of power." The test of presidential favor, she said, was to be Peggy's friend. Thus does democracy forge ahead![42]

But the slights and bad publicity were starting to affect poor Peggy. It was noticed that she had begun to withdraw from every occasion of possible embarrassment. At one ball, reported Mrs. Smith, Peggy was "treated with such marked and universal neglect and indignity, that she will not expose herself again to such treatment."[43] To make matters worse she was being patronized. Patronized by Van Buren and by the President. Within a few months she even declined a presidential invitation for dinner. "Circumstances my dear Genl are such as that under your kind and hospitable roof I cannot be happy." She was referring to the Donelsons of course, and she complained of the "unkind treatment" she had received at their hands. Jackson showed the letter to his nephew. Donelson reacted in white heat. He swore that the only unkind treatment she received from his family was "their refusal to acknowledge her right to interfere with their social relations. All else is imaginary or worse." Donelson took great exception to Peggy's behavior. Instead of coming to him with her complaints she went to the President "with childish importunities, first aiming to excite his sympathies, and then to pour upon them the poison which they had concocted for all who did not bow to her commands."[44]

So, by the spring of 1830 if not earlier, the Eaton affair and the rivalry between Calhoun and Van Buren became intertwined. "Calhoun heads the moral party," wrote John Quincy Adams with what almost passed with him for humor, "Van Buren that of the frail sisterhood; and he is notoriously engaged in canvassing for the Presidency by paying his court to Mrs. Eaton. He uses personal influence with the wives of his partisans to prevail upon them to countenance this woman by visiting her." He even tried to get Emily Donelson to accept Peggy, but she indignantly refused.[45]

Still Calhoun was not yet blamed for instigating the Eaton scandal. But he was seen more and more as the focal point around which gathered all those who provoked trouble for the administration. Slowly over a period of five or six months a noose began winding itself around Calhoun's neck and it was slowly but inexorably squeezing the political life out of him. Then, without warning, the noose got a sudden and devastating tug. Three days after Jackson gave his memorable toast, John Forsyth, the governor of Georgia, wrote a letter to William H. Crawford. And that was the beginning of the end of John C. Calhoun as successor to President Andrew Jackson.

A conspiracy against Calhoun had been brewing for years. The cause of it went back to the time of Jackson's invasion of Florida and the efforts of some members of Monroe's cabinet, including Calhoun, to censure the General for his supposedly unauthorized seizure of the Spanish colony.[46] Calhoun's opinions had never become public but some men close to Old Hickory suspected him of "treachery." One of them was Sam Houston, who obtained a copy of a letter from Monroe to Calhoun, written September 9, 1818, which indicated that both men disapproved Jackson's action. "When the letter reached me," Old Hickory confessed, "it smelled so much of deception that my hair stood on end for an hour."[47] At the time, however, Jackson was furious with Monroe over the allegation that he, Monroe, was the true rescuer of New Orleans in 1815 and mistakenly thought that Calhoun had made the letter available in order to document Monroe's duplicity.[48]

A cloud of suspicion hung over Calhoun, nonetheless. Major Lewis distrusted him, but because he added strength to Jackson's presidential campaign made no overt move against him. Only William H. Crawford, the South Carolinian's implacable foe, tried to create trouble. He wrote to Van Buren just before the 1828 election and sought to enlist his aid in backing Nathaniel Macon for the vice presidency. Van Buren understood what this would do for the entire Democratic ticket and refused to participate.[49]

At the height of the presidential campaign Van Buren sent James A. Hamilton to Nashville to make himself generally useful and to help improve Van Buren's standing with the Hero. Hamilton became quite intimate with Lewis and Houston during his visit. He also accompanied the Jackson party to New Orleans for the celebration on January 8. On the voyage downriver Hamilton and Lewis discussed the old quarrel between General Jackson and William Crawford. At one point Hamilton offered to try to work out a reconciliation between the two men by visiting Crawford (now a judge in Georgia) on his return to New York from New Orleans. Lewis then asked Jackson if he had any objections to Hamilton's trip and purpose.

"Mr. Crawford is truly an unfortunate man," said the General after a moment's reflection, "and is more deserving sympathy than the enmity of any one, and especially on account of his physical prostration."

"Am I at liberty, then," asked Lewis, "to say to Colonel Hamilton that you are willing that every thing heretofore of an unpleasant nature shall be buried in oblivion?"

"Perfectly so," came the response.[50]

Unfortunately, Hamilton missed Crawford on his trip through Georgia since the judge was riding circuit and not expected back for a week or two. Instead Hamilton discussed his mission with Governor John Forsyth and got the governor to agree to serve as go-between and convey to Crawford everything Jackson had said about agreeing to a reconciliation. In time Forsyth notified Hamilton in a letter that Crawford acknowledged that one of the sore points between Jackson and himself was the charge that he, Crawford, had proposed Jackson's punishment for the Florida invasion at a meeting of Monroe's cabinet. He denied that he ever made such a proposition. Rather it was Calhoun who proposed the General's arrest and punishment, said Crawford.[51]

In April, 1828, Major Lewis visited New York, but on his way north he stopped off in Washington and met Martin Van Buren for the first time. Once in New York Lewis went immediately to see Hamilton, who showed him Forsyth's letter. The letter was pure dynamite, as Lewis well knew, and he realized that if he ever showed it to Jackson it would "produce an explosion" that could jeopardize the presidential election. So nothing was said. The incriminating letter was allowed to sit quietly in Hamilton's correspondence file. But any number of people knew of its existence.

Nothing was said to Jackson, even after his election in November, 1828. Those privy to the information bided their time. Then, a year later, while the Eaton affair boiled away, James Monroe passed through Washington and called on the President. Jackson, courteous as always, invited the former President to dine, and for this occasion he also invited his cabinet, Lewis, Donelson, and Tench Ringgold, the Marshal of the District and a close personal friend of James Monroe. Shortly after they were seated for dinner Ringgold remarked to Lewis that he was happy to see Monroe and Jackson together and enjoying themselves. Monroe had been Jackson's staunch friend during the Seminole campaign, he added, in opposition to every member of his cabinet. Lewis protested that Calhoun and Adams were *reputedly* favorable to Jackson, but Ringgold denied it. "And he repeated that Mr. Monroe was the *only member* of his Cabinet that was in favor of sustaining the General in every thing he did."[52]

After all the guests departed—except for Eaton and Lewis—Jackson rang for a servant to bring his pipe and the three men retired to the parlor. Then the crafty Lewis, Iago-like, whispered to Eaton that Ringgold's revelation about the Seminole controversy completely surprised him. Jackson overheard just enough to ask what the two men were talking about. Eaton repeated Ringgold's remarks.

Jackson seemed incredulous. Ringgold was mistaken, he said.

"I am not sure of that," commented the faithful Lewis.

"Why are you not?" asked Jackson.

"Because I have seen a letter, written eighteen months ago, in which Mr. Crawford is represented as saying that you charged him with having taken strong ground against you in Mr. Monroe's cabinet, but in that you had done him an injustice, for it was not he, but Mr. Calhoun, who was in favor of your being arrested, or punished in some other way."

"You saw such a letter as *that?*" Jackson gasped.

"Yes . . . and read it too."

"Where is that letter?" Jackson's voice became nearly shrill.

"In New York."

"In whose hands, and by whom written?" Jackson demanded.

"It is in the hands of Colonel Hamilton, and written by Governor Forsyth of Georgia."

"Then I want to see it," said the President, "and you must go to New York tomorrow."[53]

The cat was finally out of the bag. Lewis had neatly and deftly released it.

The Major only too obligingly hurried to New York to complete his mission, but Hamilton objected to surrendering the letter without the approval of Forsyth, who had just been elected to the U.S. Senate and was on his way to Washington. When finally contacted, Forsyth insisted on obtaining Crawford's consent, too, before turning over the letter. It was at approximately this time that Jackson mentioned to John Overton that his confidence in Calhoun had been shaken. It had already crossed his mind that "most of the troubles, vexations and difficulties" he had suffered since the beginning of his administration were connected ultimately with his Vice President.[54]

It took a little while before all the necessary authorizations were given and Crawford's charges could be laid directly before the President. In the meantime the Eaton affair continued to sour social relationships and the nullification controversy started along on its long and frightening course. Three days after Jackson proclaimed his toast at the Jefferson dinner, Forsyth finally wrote to Crawford. In his reply, dated April 30, Crawford brushed aside his own past problems with Jackson and accused Calhoun outright of instigating the effort to have the General punished for his action in seizing Florida without authorization.[55]

The letter was placed in Jackson's hands on May 12. It really contained nothing that the President had not heard before from some of the men around him. But instead of hearsay this was hard evidence, an insider's report of what actually took place in Monroe's cabinet. Jackson bristled. A supposed friend had "betrayed" him.

According to a recent historian, Calhoun himself was not altogether a sweet innocent in the drama starting to unfold. The Vice President's opposition to the tariff, leading to his enunciation of the doctrine of nullification, says this historian, committed him to *radical* reductions in the tariff schedule that Jackson was not prepared to honor. In addition, the Tariff of Abominations had won the support of Van Buren and Eaton in 1828 and with both men now holding high positions in Jackson's administration he worried not only about obtaining relief for southerners but about his ability to exercise any influence over the President.[56] Eaton's close association with the General and his attachment to the Magician plus his support of the 1828 tariff were seen, according to this historian, as a threat to any future hope of rate reduction as well as a danger to Calhoun's political fortunes. Eaton, therefore, needed to be gotten rid of. Calhoun's friends saw that. Berrien and Branch, both southerners, probably understood the full implications of Eaton's presence among them, especially in terms of tariff reduction, and their social behavior, according to this historian, probably resulted from their desire to drive him out of the cabinet.[57] Certainly Ingham, who was totally committed to Calhoun and his succession to the presidency, wanted Eaton's ouster. Thus, as one conspiracy shaped against Eaton another one developed against Calhoun, and both involved access to Jackson, the succession, and control of the direction of the President's reform program.[58]

This is as fine a conspiracy theory as one could want. Jackson would have loved it. Unfortunately, it makes more of the tariff issue than the facts can support. There are too many "probablys" to it. Actually there never was a conspiracy against the Eatons—at least not a political conspiracy to drive the secretary out of the cabinet. The ladies of Washington simply disliked Peggy (with apparent good reason, let it be noted) and refused to socialize with her. This petticoat war soon got mixed up with the nullification furor and the developing rivalry between Van Buren and Calhoun. Since Jackson had a "natural" penchant for finding conspiracies in virtually every disagreeable situation, he quickly assumed that the humiliation of Peggy was part of a deliberate design to force Eaton out of his cabinet.

But to return to the conspiracy against Calhoun. When the General received Crawford's letter he could have ignored it had he wished to protect his relationship with his Vice President. But by this time he had more than sufficient reason to demand an explanation for Calhoun's past behavior. So he forwarded Crawford's letter to the Vice President and in his harshest tones requested a reply. "The statements and facts" in this letter, said Jackson in his covering note, "being so different from what I had heretofore understood to be correct requires that it should be brought to your consideration. . . . My object in making this communication is to announce to you the great surprise which is felt, and to learn of you whether all the circumstances of which you and I are both informed, that any attempt seriously to affect me was moved and sustained by you in the cabinet council, when, as is known to you, I was but executing the *wishes* of the government."[59]

In sending his letter and Crawford's, Jackson deliberately provoked a rupture with his Vice President. And his reason was simple. He did it because Calhoun's nullification ideas alarmed him and he worried about the presidential succession and the preservation of the Union. By this time Jackson felt that Van Buren would be a better and safer choice to succeed him, so he had to jettison Calhoun. That is why his letter was a deliberate act of provocation; for, in demanding a response from Calhoun, what did Jackson think he would receive? Proof that Crawford was a liar? Hardly. Admission that what Crawford said was true? If that was so, what could he do with such an admission except initiate a break? "The truth is," said an early Jackson biographer, "that before this affair began" —indeed at the moment the General demanded an explanation from Calhoun—"the President was, in his heart, totally estranged from Mr. Calhoun, and would have been glad of any pretext for breaking with him."[60] Also, by making Calhoun the scapegoat, Jackson could identify to the American people the "scoundrel" who was disrupting his administration.

Calhoun conveniently provided the pretext for the rupture. In fact he provided several. He had a number of options open to him, and he proceeded to take all the wrong ones. The President was deliberately baiting him, of that there could be no question. Jackson said quite specifically that he was simply executing the government's express wishes in Florida and he expected Calhoun to agree with him. He also said that Crawford contested what Jackson had always believed was Calhoun's true position and he wanted to know if "the information given is correct."

This was no time for Calhoun to lie. Too many people stood ready to contest any dissembling. Nor was this the time to get into a shouting match with Crawford or anyone else. At the very least, if he wished to maintain his relationship with Jackson, he must state unequivocally that the General did indeed have full authority to conduct the war in the manner that he had. To do otherwise would terminate their association instantly. Had he been clever or judicious or circumspect he might have considered refusing to stoop to Crawford's level by revealing cabinet secrets or getting into a dogfight over who said what about whom. Done with grace and humility he might have prevented what he so passionately dreaded might happen. But Calhoun, like Jackson, saw a spectacular conspiracy at work, one aimed at his downfall. He believed there was a political design in progress in which Jackson was the appointed instrument and he the victim. The real manipulators of this plot were carefully concealed by artful dodging. Although he did not name names he obviously had Martin Van Buren in mind as the most artful dodger of them all, the one who had most to gain from Calhoun's fall. So he decided to expose the plot and reveal to the President the true purpose for which this past history had been resurrected.

In a fifty-two-page response dated May 25, Calhoun played right into Jackson's hands. And he did it gracelessly which, of course, made the President's task of casting him out easier. The opening shot struck Jackson square in the face. "I cannot recognize the right on your part," said Calhoun in his first sentence, "to call in question my conduct." Hardly an auspicious way to avoid a quarrel, especially when directed to the President of the United States. As to executing the wishes of the government, Calhoun said the worst thing possible. "If by *wishes*, which you have underscored, it be meant that there was any intimation given by myself, directly or indirectly, of the desire of the Government that you should occupy the Spanish posts, so far from being 'informed' I had not the slightest knowledge of any such intimation, nor did I ever hear a whisper of any such before." But did Jackson not realize what was behind this sudden reappearance of Crawford into the political arena? "I should be blind not to see that this whole affair," wrote Calhoun, "is a political manoeuvre . . . and that a blow was meditated against me." He would not say from which quarter the blow emanated but two years before, a certain individual from New York approached him on this subject, which awakened his suspicions.[61]

Jackson received Calhoun's letter on a Sunday as he was about to enter his carriage to go to church. He took it to Lewis and asked him to look it over and see if any portion of it required his particular notice. When he returned from church he retired to his own room to digest the contents but had read only a portion of the exhaustive statement when he was summoned to lunch. As he entered the dining room he appeared extremely agitated but he said nothing. After the meal he returned to his room and finished the letter. Then he summoned Lewis, who later said that "I never saw him more excited under any circumstances in my life than he was on this occasion." Jackson said he had been deceived by Calhoun, a man for whom he had shown only the "warmest friendship, and in whom he had reposed the most unbounded confidence." He felt betrayed. He felt dishonored.[62]

Jackson asked Lewis to take the letter to Van Buren and ask what he thought of it. But the crafty Little Magician refused to read it on the grounds that it was certain to lead to an "open rupture" between the President and the Vice President and that he would be held responsible. If, in time, he must make a public statement about it he wanted "to have it in my power to say" he knew nothing about it.

"I reckon Van is right," said Jackson when Lewis reported back. "I dare say they will attempt to throw the whole blame upon him."[63]

But the blame belonged to Jackson. He provoked the rupture with Calhoun, not Van Buren, and he did it deliberately. Politically Calhoun had done him the greatest favor. He provided the explanation Jackson needed to justify and account for all the dreadful things that had happened since the start of his administration, an explanation which could be offered the people if need be to safeguard their confidence in their Hero. The party line was quickly formulated and easily sold to all true believers. Lewis put it into a single sentence: "Nearly all those who exerted themselves, *first* to prevent Mr. Eaton's appointment as a member of the Cabinet, and afterward, having failed in that, to drive him out of it, were the friends of Mr. Calhoun."[64] This explained the social ostracism of Peggy Eaton. And the motivation behind it was the need for absolute control of the administration to prevent Van Buren or anyone else from slipping ahead of Calhoun into the presidential chair.

Most important, the working out of this explanation provided Jackson with a needed victim. He loved to personalize quarrels. He knew no other kind. He needed someone to accuse of having deliberately conspired to ruin him and his administration. It helped to say that the conspiracy was motivated by personal ambition. In time Jackson figured all the details of Calhoun's cunning. The whole thing "originated in a political combination to put Major Eaton out of the Cabinet, & disgrace me," he wrote, "and weaken my administration for having appointed him." The participants in this "nefarious" scheme were an "apostate clergy & perjured masons" with the Vice President at their head. "I have this moment" read a copy of a letter written by Crawford, Jackson concluded, which "proves Calhoun *a villain.*"[65] This was Jackson's complete scenario of the Eaton imbroglio.

Jackson acknowledged Calhoun's fifty-two-page letter. He penned a sharp rebuke. He denied questioning the Vice President's conduct or motives. "I repeat, I had a right to believe that you were my sincere friend, and, until now, never expected to have occasion to say to you, in the language of Caesar, *Et tu Brute.*" Again Jackson insisted that he had authority for seizing Florida and always believed that Calhoun understood this and agreed. "Your letter to me . . . is the first intimation to me that *you,* ever entertained any other opinion. . . . Your conduct, word, actions and letters I have ever thought show this. Understanding you now, no further communication with you on this subject, is necessary."[66]

Many hands shaped Calhoun's fall. Houston, Lewis, Hamilton, Crawford, the Eatons, Van Buren, Calhoun himself and his friends, and, of course, Jackson. The President deliberately chose to cast him loose. He tagged the South Carolinian the "most profound hypocrite he had ever known" and a man dangerous to the country's best interests and institutions.[67] He decreed his political eclipse. And Calhoun's demise left Andrew Jackson in undisputed control of the Democratic party.

CHAPTER 14

Return to Reform

As the situation in Washington became more confused and combative, Andrew Jackson assumed the air of calm, deliberative statesmanship. He surprised visitors both in appearance and demeanor. While the political atmosphere in Washington, reported one commentator, "seems to be made up of strife, heartburnings, corruption, and sacrifice of personal honour and character," Jackson appeared totally at ease and in full command. "I saw the president and was very favourably impressed by his whole appearance; his manners are graceful and easy, and at the same time dignified; he has neither the ferocity nor coarseness, nor worn out haggardness which is generally given to him."[1] What this reporter failed to realize was that Jackson always drew strength from adversity. It was a unique aspect of his character.

During the first year of his administration the President faced a large measure of adversity. Politics provided a fair share of it, and his health also contributed, since he suffered a severe reversal in late fall. In addition he sheltered rebellion in his own household in the form of the Donelsons' refusal to treat Peggy Eaton as a social equal. And there were other personal traumas. His twenty-year-old son, Andrew Jackson, Jr., had the annoying habit of falling in and out of love, which might be expected in a young man his age, but the trouble with Andrew Jr. was that he seemed to feel he must get married each time he was smitten. His amours caused Jackson considerable apprehension. First there was a young lady in Philadelphia, and the President was obliged to write to her father and make excuses about his son's lack of courtesy in pursuing the romance. Jackson assured the father that his son's intentions were honorable. "He has made known to me," Jackson wrote Major Francis Smith, "the attachment he has formed for you[r] amiable daughter, which he informs me has been expressed to her and if not reciprocated, has at least won her favorable opinion. He has erred in attempting to address your daughter without first making known to you and your lady his honorable intentions and obtaining your approbation, but he has been admonished of this impropriety and he now awaits upon you to confess it."[2] Nothing came of this budding romance begun without benefit of the social amenities, and two months later young Andrew had his eye on another beauty closer to home. In writing to his son about this latest passion Jackson seemed a trifle annoyed.

July 26, 1829

(Confidential)

My son, Having your happiness at heart more than my own, for since I have been deprived of your dear mother, there is no happiness or contentment for me this side of the grave, none but what your society, and your welfare and prosperity, and that of your family, should you have one, can afford. . . . You can Judge of the anxiety I have that you should marry a lady that will make you happy, which would add to mine, seeing you so. You are very young, but having placed your affections upon Miss Flora, I have no desire to controle your affections or interfere with your choice, early attachments are the most durable, and having been raised together in the same neighbourhood, I have only to remark that no good can flow from long courtship. Therefore I would recommend to you to be frank with her, say to her at once the object of your visit and receive her anser at once. . . . Should Miss Flora not favour your wishes, then my son, I have one request to make of you, that is that you will give out all idea of Marriage for the present, until you see and advise with me.[3]

Miss Flora held young Andrew off and refused to give him an answer. His father urged him to have it out with her.

I would like to hear how you have settled the matter with Miss F. she is a fine girl, but you being young she may try to keep you within her toils, without giving you a definite answer. Permit this not to be the case. have a final and positive answer, and let it be as it may, close the matter finally with her. if favorable, Marry, and bring her on with you, if unfavorable, wish her happy, cherish her as a friend, but have it understood that hereafter you remain her friend without any other views. and I beg you my son, that you enter into no more love affairs, until you see me. You have many years yet for the improvement of your mind, and to make a selection of a companion. Remember my son, that you are now the only solace of my mind, and prospects of my happiness here below, and were you to make an unhappy choice, it would bring me to the grave in sorrow.[4]

Apparently young Andrew heeded his father's advice and pressed for an answer. Miss Flora turned him down. Jackson offered consolation by dismissing her as a coquette.

I expected the result you name with Flora—she is a fine little girl, the daughter of my deceased friend and I esteem her much, but as I told you she has give herself up to coquetry and I warned you of the fact. treat her with kindness, but I assure you I am happy at the result, as I seldom ever saw a coquett, make a good wife, and when you marry, if ever, I wish you to marry a lady who will make a good wife, and I, a good daughter, as my happiness depends much upon the prudence of your choice. . . . I had no wish to interfere with your choice, and particularly when you stated, there had been some little engagement. you know I have councilled you from your childhood, to make no promises, or engagements, but what you punctually perform, therefore before engagements are formed, or promises made, it ought to be on mature reflection, and when made religiously performed. I will only add I am happy you are now free from all engagements and I trust you will keep so until you advise with your father on this interesting subject on which your peace and happiness thro' life so much depends.[5]

Andrew Jr. was not Jackson's only domestic problem. His ward Andrew Jackson Hutchings regularly caused grief. The boy could not learn and refused to study. "His conduct has filled me with sincere regret," Jackson wrote to John Coffee, who supervised the boy's plantation near Florence, Alabama. "I know not what to do with him. I cannot think of letting him be lost, and have concluded to bring him here, and place him at the college at George Town under the controle of the Catholics." Jackson thought it an excellent school, "and perhaps under my own eye, I might be able to controle him and convince him of the impropriety of his ways." Jackson said that he had given up all hope of Hutchings ever receiving a liberal education and had decided to direct the professors at Georgetown to confine his studies to "Arithmetic, Orthography, and Mathematics." Although it would be more expensive to educate him in Washington, Jackson feared that if the boy were left in Tennessee "he must be lost."[6] Young Hutchings did in fact move to Washington but the arrangement did not work out. "Here," Jackson wrote a year later, "is a bad place for a youth, who has not a constant eye over him, and my situation is such that every moment is employed in my public business."[7] Hutchings behaved properly at Georgetown for a change but so disliked his location and suffered so much illness that Jackson finally agreed to allow him to return to Tennessee "under a promise that he will abandon his extravagance." It was a promise only partially fulfilled.

Another matter of even greater personal concern to Jackson was the condition of life at the Hermitage. He worried about his slaves and regularly investigated his overseer, Graves Steele, to make certain that he did not mistreat his workers. When he heard about the death of one slave Jackson suspected the worst and directed his son to look into the matter. "I pray you my son to examine minutely into this matter, and if the death was produced by the cruelty of Mr Steel, have him forthwith discharged.

. . . My negroes shall be treated humanely. When I employed Mr Steel, I charged him upon this subject, and had expressed in our agreement that he was to treat them with great humanity, feed and cloath them well, and work them in moderation. if he has deviated from this rule, he must be discharged." Since leaving the Hermitage, Jackson calculated that "I have lost three of my family." Old Ned he expected to die; but the deaths of Jack and Jim he feared resulted from exposure and bad treatment. John Donelson told Jackson that Steele *"ruled with a rod of iron."* This was intolerable. "I cannot bear the inhumanity that he has exercised towards my poor negroes, contrary to his promise." Unless he changed his habits, Jackson ordered, dismiss him and hire another.[8] Charles J. Love, one of Jackson's longtime friends and business associates, regularly looked in on the Hermitage and he assured the President that Steele was doing a fine job and that Jim's unfortunate death resulted from poison and not from punishment.[9] Young Andrew confirmed this, but Jackson kept a close eye on Steele nonetheless. A violent scene occurred when the General learned later on that the overseer did not regularly summon a physician whenever his slaves became ill.[10]

With all these problems and irritations on his mind Jackson took a brief vacation during the first summer of his presidency. In late August, 1829, he sailed down the Potomac for the Rip Raps to spend a few weeks sea bathing. The Rip Raps was a small government-owned islet in Hampton Roads off Norfolk, Virginia, and provided an ideal location for brief respites from the debilitating climate of Washington. The Rip Raps seemed to reinvigorate the President and it became a favorite vacation spot during his eight years in office.

Even on vacation Jackson did not escape entirely the penalty of his office and popularity. Crowds followed him whenever they learned of his presence; letters and dispatches constantly engaged his attention; and of course such nagging problems as the Eaton business rarely left his mind. Since he was a man oppressed by his sense of duty, he never allowed himself to stray too far from the major concerns of his administration.

With the return of Congress in December, 1829, and the presentation of his first message, the machinery began to crank back to life by which Jackson hoped to resume his program of reform. As the session progressed one of the first legislative actions to provide the President with an opportunity to present a major statement of his reform intentions to the nation was a bill to extend the National Road from Maysville to Lexington, Kentucky.

The National Road was begun in 1811 in Cumberland, Maryland, and over the years steadily inched its way westward. This latest extension ran totally within the state of Kentucky and alarmed strict constructionists for fear that the federal government would be committed to small public works that were totally local in their purpose and usefulness. Also, the fact that the road was located in Henry Clay's state did not sit well with some Jacksonians, and several of them spoke against the bill when it was introduced into the House. Advocates of the bill—principally westerners —were annoyed by the opposition. They considered the road a minor matter that would easily and quietly slip through Congress without comment and without fuss. Actually the debate over the Maysville Road lasted the better part of three days before passing the House in late April, 1830, by a vote of 102 to 86.[11]

By the time the Maysville Road bill passed the House Jackson had already taken steps to further his reform intentions. He instructed Van Buren to keep his eye peeled on all congressional legislation and alert him to any measures that the New Yorker thought mischievous and in conflict with his stated objectives.[12] "The people expected reform retrenchment and economy in the administration of this Government," the President reminded Van Buren. "This was the cry from Maine to Louisiana, and instead of these the great object of Congress, *it would seem*, is to make mine one of the most extravagant administrations since the commencement of the Government. This must not be; The Federal Constitution must be obeyed, State-rights preserved, our national debt *must be paid, direct taxes and loans avoided* and the Federal union preserved. These are the objects I have in view, and regardless of all consequences, will carry into effect."[13]

Van Buren spotted the Maysville bill the moment it was introduced into the House by Representative Robert P. Letcher of Kentucky. He waited until it passed and then during one of their horseback rides together brought it to Jackson's attention. He also offered to provide a brief against the bill and this the President gratefully accepted.

The brief impressed the General. The more he studied the provisions of the bill the more it agitated him. The idea of spending federal money for a local road not only seemed unconstitutional but a needless drain on the treasury which would delay payment of the national debt.

The bill safely navigated its way through the Senate, and indeed won the support of such staunch Democrats as Thomas Hart Benton and Edward Livingston. Meanwhile the White House leaked its opposition. Western friends of the road, fearful of the political consequences of a presidential veto, appealed to Representative Richard M. Johnson to speak to Jackson personally and get him to see the advantages of the bill to westerners. Johnson agreed, and when he arrived at the White House he found the President and Van Buren comparing the figures of congressional appropriations to date with the available funds currently in the Treasury. From the expression on Jackson's face Johnson knew that something was wrong.[14]

Johnson explained the purpose of his visit. He recited the fears of their western friends and their concern that a veto would provide Clay with enough ammunition to injure them all.

Jackson's ears picked up at that last remark. Pleased to have caught the

President's attention, Johnson tried to cap his plea with a dramatic state-ment. "General!" he exclaimed. "If this hand were an anvil on which the sledge hammer of the smith was descending and a fly were to light upon it in time to receive the blow he would not crush it more effectually than you will crush your friends in Kentucky if you veto that Bill!"[15]

Jackson rose from his chair. "Sir," he said very solemnly, "have you looked at the condition of the Treasury—at the amount of money that it contains—at the appropriations already made by Congress—at the amount of other unavoidable claims upon it?"

"No! General, I have not! But there has always been money enough to satisfy appropriations and I do not doubt there will be now!"

"Well, I have," snapped the President, "and this is the result," pointing to the Treasury appropriation figures, "and you see there is no money to be expended as my friends desire. Now, I stand committed before the Country to pay off the National Debt, at the earliest practicable moment; this pledge I am determined to redeem, and I cannot do this if I consent to increase it without necessity. Are you willing—are my friends willing to lay taxes to pay for internal improvements?—for be assured I will not borrow a cent except in cases of absolute necessity!"

The mere mention of borrowing money brought Johnson to his feet. "No!" he exclaimed in alarm, "that would be worse than a *veto!*"[16]

The President's tone of voice had been very aggressive during the exchange. But as Johnson moved to end the interview Jackson reverted to his usual pleasant and courteous manner. He assured Johnson that he would not make up his mind until he had thoroughly examined all sides of the question and he thanked him for coming to him and providing such valuable information.

When Johnson returned to the House his western colleagues immedi-ately surrounded him. He related the details of his interview and the President's final promise to study the subject thoroughly. But his private opinion, he said, "was that nothing less than a voice from Heaven would prevent the old man from vetoing the Bill, and he doubted whether that would!"[17]

As Johnson correctly guessed it would take a miracle to get Jackson to sign the bill. The measure totally contradicted his commitment to "re-form retrenchment and economy" and what he felt the people expected of him as President. He could do no less than kill the bill.

Extensive notes in Jackson's handwriting elaborating his objections to the Maysville measure document his central role in formulating the veto message. But he had help with the actual writing, principally from Van Buren. Representative James Knox Polk from Tennessee, who had at-tacked the bill on the House floor, also contributed to the final version.[18]

On the night before the veto was sent to Congress Jackson asked Van Buren to take an early breakfast with him since both houses would meet at an early hour. When Van Buren arrived the next morning he found

Eaton, Lewis, William T. Barry, and Felix Grundy seated at the table, their faces displaying their apprehension. Each one of them believed that the veto would severely damage Jackson in the west. They felt that Clay would use it to hatchet them all to political death. On his way up the stairs to his office Jackson beckoned Van Buren to join him. As they walked the President leaned on his secretary's arm to steady himself. Van Buren remarked that their friends looked frightened.

"Yes," Jackson replied, "but don't mind that! The thing is here," as he touched the breast pocket of his coat with his finger, "and shall be sent up as soon as Congress convenes."[19]

And up it went, causing extreme consternation among the friends of internal improvements. But to the "true believers" of republicanism it "fell upon the ears like the music of other days," said John Randolph, who was about to leave for Russia as U.S. minister.[20] The framers of the bill and their supporters among the National Republicans denounced the veto as an electioneering document. Indeed it was. Most of Jackson's messages had one eye cocked toward the public. In addition, the friends of the measure claimed "that the 'hand of the magician' was visible in every line of it."[21] True, much of the language is so stilted and circumlocutory that only Van Buren could have written it. Still it was Jackson's message. In terms of doctrine and principle, the Maysville veto said exactly what Jackson wanted.

The veto was dated May 27, 1830, and forwarded to the House of Representatives, where the bill originated. In his message Jackson immediately challenged the constitutionality of the measure. "I have given to its provisions," said the President, "all the reflection demanded by a just regard for the interests of those of our fellow-citizens who have desired its passage, and by the respect which is due to a coordinate branch of the Government, but I am not able to view it in any other light than as a measure of purely local character."

The people have a right to expect, Jackson continued, that a "prudent system of expenditure" will characterize government spending "as will pay the debts of the Union and authorize the reduction of every tax to as low a point as . . . our national safety and independence will allow." When the debt is paid, he said, an accumulating surplus is expected to develop that may be distributed to the states for improvements. This is the soundest view of national policy, he insisted, and one which will provide many advantages to the government in the "elevation" of its character. "How gratifying the effect of presenting to the world the sublime spectacle of a Republic of more than 12,000,000 happy people, in the fifty-fourth year of her existence, after having passed through two protracted wars—the one for the acquisition and the other for the maintenance of liberty—free from debt and with all the immense resources unfettered!"

Another concern, the President revealed, is the question of whether a system of internal improvements ought to be commenced without a prior amendment to the Constitution explaining and defining the precise powers of the federal government over it. "This subject has been one of much, and, I may add, painful, reflection to me." The "friends of liberty" have a right to expect that "expedience" will not be made the "rule of construction in interpreting the Constitution."[22]

The veto stopped short of denying federal power over internal improvements. It affirmed the right of Congress to appropriate money for purposes of defense and of national benefit, but that was all. "Sound principle" as well as political "prudence," said Van Buren, imposed this compromise on the President.[23]

Thus did President Jackson kill the Maysville Road. To many it marked the end of all internal improvements by the federal government. A constitutional amendment was not only difficult but impractical, and therefore if his veto was to stand as principle then the program for government-sponsored public works was doomed. "We shall attack the veto," announced Henry Clay; to allow it to stand would be ruinous to the national interest. The veto, he also remarked, "has produced uncommon excitement in Kentucky."[24]

Jackson, on the other hand, pronounced himself perfectly satisfied with the message and the reaction of the people. "The *veto works well,*" he assured Van Buren in late June. "We have nothing to fear from it—it will lead to stability in our government & a system of national improvement that will be desireable & beneficial to our country, keeping the agency & powers of the Federal Gov^t within its proper sphere & the States to manage their own concerns in their own way." As might be expected he viewed his veto as a blow for liberty since it allowed people, through their states, to conduct their own affairs. It was an integral part of his reform program.[25]

Other Democrats agreed with Jackson. "I have only time to express my great delight & satisfaction at the noble & heroic stand our gallant old chief has made against the overwhelming tide of corruption through the gross abuses of the powers the Govt has practically usurped over internal improvements," wrote James Hamilton, Jr., to Van Buren. "His message . . . has had both a soothing & exhilerating effect throughout the South . . . [which] will strengthen his popularity."[26]

But what about the west? His friends feared he had done himself irreparable harm. Not Jackson. "Where it has lost me one, it has gained me five friends," he said, "and in Kentucky has done no harm." He had faith in the electorate. "The great body of the people hail the act, as a preservative of the constitution & the union."[27]

Jackson took pride in the veto because it addressed the principal concerns of his administration. In the "Notes" he wrote for the veto message he played variations on several of these concerns. Nothing in the Constitution, he said in the "Notes," authorized the United States to become a member of a corporation created by the states—this referring to the Maysville, Washington, Paris, and Lexington Turnpike Road Company, incorporated by the Kentucky legislature and whose stock Congress contemplated buying. To permit the United States to become a member of this corporation "is corrupting and must destroy the purity of our govt.," he wrote. "it must lead to consolidation and the destruction of state rights. . . . This will be more injurious and destructive to the morales and Liberty of the people than the U. States Bank so much and so justly complained of."28

Again the concern for "Liberty," again the concern for the "morales" of the people. The Maysville Road bill, like the BUS, jeopardized the "purity" of the government and threatened freedom. By becoming stockholders, Jackson wrote, whether stockholders of a road campany or the Bank, the United States government might "wield its power in your elections and all the interior concerns of the state, this would lead to consolidation and that would destroy the liberty of your country."29

Ultimately, Jackson decided that internal improvements exposed Congress to the temptation of making hasty appropriations, This, in turn, promoted a "corrupting influence upon the elections" by holding out to the people the hope that the success of a particular candidate will "make navigable their neighboring creek or river, bring commerce to their doors, and increase the value of their property." Such a process, he argued, was "fatal to just legislation" and the "purity of public men."30

Such a process had already begun.

When the Congress finally adjourned on May 31, 1830, the members left behind them a last-minute flurry of legislation that drove Jackson into a fit of anger. They met on Saturday and Sunday morning to pass one appropriation bill after another, even though "they knew the Treasury was exhausted by former appropriations."31 The amount reached nearly one million dollars. Think of it, he cried, a million dollars! "Their objects plainly are to make this a more extravagant administration than the last." Well, he would show them. He vetoed again and again. He had struck down the Maysville Road; then he scored a second veto on the Washington Turnpike bill. Next, for the first time in American history, he exercised the pocket veto.* He annulled the appropriations for building lighthouses and beacons, dredging harbors, and other such improvements. He also killed a bill to purchase stock in the Louisville and Portland Canal Company.

It was quite a massacre. But Jackson glowed. By these vetoes, he contended, he had provided "reform retrenchment and economy," just as he had promised he would.32

---

*This is a special veto by which the President may kill legislation by withholding his signature from a bill after Congress has adjourned.

Something of Jackson's commanding presence is conveyed in this portrait by Ralph E. W. Earl. The cape, hanging loosely from his shoulders, adds a touch of majesty. *Ladies Hermitage Association.*

This pencil sketch of Jackson was drawn from life by Edward W. Clay in 1831. Around the eyes and mouth the artist caught some of the physical pain Jackson constantly endured. *National Portrait Gallery.*

This striking portrait by Ralph Earl shows Jackson wearing the large beaver hat in which he kept notes and memoranda. The Hermitage, as originally built, can be seen dimly in the background. *Ladies Hermitage Association.*

"The President's Levee, or all Creation is going to the White House" by Robert Cruikshank satirized Jackson's inauguration in 1829 when a mob invaded the executive mansion. The caricature shows the recently completed south portico with staircases. *Library of Congress.*

"The People's First Inaugural" included an outdoor swearing-in ceremony. This idealized but historically inaccurate depiction of the event decorates the rotunda of the Washington Capitol. *Architect of the Capitol.*

This engraving by J. Sartain after a painting by W. J. Hubard was executed early in Jackson's first administration. The engraver's caption: "The Federal Union—It Shall Be Preserved." *Library of Congress.*

Nephew, ward, private secretary, and liaison with Congress, Andrew Jackson Donelson disappointed his uncle during the Eaton affair. At the height of their disagreement they communicated by letter (four in a single day) even though they resided under the same roof and ate at the same table. *Ladies Hermitage Association.*

Political manager, neighbor, confidant, liaison with Congress, and White House resident, Major William Berkeley Lewis exercised considerable influence during Jackson's first administration. *Tennessee State Library and Archives.*

The mutual friendship and loyalty between John Henry Eaton and Jackson ultimately caused them both personal suffering and humiliation. *Library of Congress.*

This engraving by T. B. Welch from a J. B. Longacre drawing captures some of John C. Calhoun's intensity and drive. *Library of Congress.*

This rare, if not unusual picture of Martin Van Buren is an engraving after a portrait by Ezra Adams. It was executed at approximately the time Van Buren accepted the office of Secretary of State. *Library of Congress.*

Margaret (Peggy) O'Neale Timberlake Eaton was long past her salad days when she sat for this picture, but it is one of a very few portraits extant. *Library of Congress.*

No one encouraged Jackson more in his program of reform than Amos Kendall, newspaper editor, fourth auditor, master propagandist, political organizer, and confidant-extraordinary. *Library of Congress.*

Francis Preston Blair, distinguished editor of the Washington *Globe,* was called "Preston" by his friends, but Jackson called him "Bla-ar." *Library of Congress.*

One of the most damaging propaganda broadsides to appear in the presidential campaign of 1828, the "Coffin Hand Bill" vividly recounted Jackson's execution of six militia men during the Creek War. *Library of Congress.*

The Rats leaving a Falling House.

Two thousand copies of this popular cartoon were sold in a single day in Philadelphia. It ridiculed both Jackson's handling of the administration and his efforts at reform. *Tennessee State Library and Archives.*

No cartoon said as much about what had happened to the presidency during Jackson's administration than "King Andrew the First" which appeared during the election of 1832. *Library of Congress.*

CHAPTER 15

"Brothers, Listen . . . You Must Submit"

IT IS AN AWESOME CONTRADICTION that at the moment the United States was entering a new age of economic and social betterment for its citizens —the industrial revolution underway, democracy expanding, social and political reforms in progress—the Indians were driven from their homes and forced to seek refuge in remote areas west of the Mississippi River. Jackson, the supreme exponent of liberty in terms of preventing government intervention and intrusion, took it upon himself to expel the Indians from their ancient haunts and decree that they must reside outside the company of civilized white men. It was a depressing and terrible commentary on American life and institutions in the 1830s.

The policy of white Americans toward Indians was a shambles, right from the beginning. Sometimes the policy was benign—such as sharing educational advantages—but more often than not it was malevolent. Colonists drove the Indians from their midst, stole their lands and, when necessary, murdered them. To the colonists, Indians were inferior and their culture a throwback to a darker age.

When independence was declared and a new government established committed to liberty and justice for all, the situation of the Indians within the continental limits of the United States contradicted the ennobling ideas of both the Declaration and the Constitution. Nevertheless, the Founding Fathers convinced themselves that men of reason, intelligence and good will could resolve the Indian problem. In their view the Indians were "noble savages," arrested in cultural development, but they would one day take their rightful place beside white society. Once they were "civilized" they would be absorbed.

President George Washington formulated a policy to encourage the "civilizing" process, and Jefferson continued it. They presumed that once the Indians adopted the practice of private property, built homes, farmed, educated their children, and embraced Christianity these Native Americans would win acceptance from white Americans. Both Presidents wished the Indians to become cultural white men. If they did not, said Jefferson, then they must be driven to the Rocky Mountains.[1]

The policy of removal was first suggested by Jefferson as the alternative to the "civilizing" process, and as far as many Americans were concerned removal made more sense than any other proposal.[2] Henry Clay, for example, insisted that it was impossible to civilize these "savages." They were, he argued, inferior to white men and "their disappearance from the human family would be no great loss to the world."[3]

Despite Clay's racist notions—shared by many Americans—the government's efforts to convert the Indians into cultural white men made considerable progress in the 1820s. The Cherokees, in particular, showed notable technological and material advances as a result of increased contact with traders, government agents, and missionaries, along with the growth of a considerable population of mixed-bloods.[4]

As the Indians continued to resist the efforts to get rid of them—the thought of abandoning the land on which their ancestors lived and died was especially painful for them—the states insisted on exercising jurisdiction over Indian lands within their boundaries. It soon became apparent that unless the federal government instituted a policy of removal it would have to do something about protecting the Indians against the incursions of the states. But the federal government was feckless. It did neither. Men like President John Quincy Adams felt that removal was probably the only policy to follow but he could not bring himself to implement it. Nor could he face down a state like Georgia. So he did nothing. Many men of good will simply turned their faces away. They, too, did nothing.

Not Jackson. He had no hesitation about taking action. And he believed that removal was indeed the only policy available if the Indians were to be protected from certain annihilation. His ideas about the Indians developed from his life on the frontier, his expansionist dreams, his commitment to states' rights, and his intense nationalism. He saw the nation as an indivisible unit whose strength and future were dependent on its ability to repel outside foes. He wanted all Americans from every state and territory to participate in his dream of empire, but they must acknowledge allegiance to a permanent and indissoluble bond under a federal system.[5] Although devoted to states' rights and limited government in Washington, Jackson rejected any notion that jeopardized the safety of the United States. That included nullification and secession. That also included the Indians.

Jackson's nationalism, a partial product of his expansionist ideals, and his states' rights philosophy, a product of his concern for individual liberty, merged to produce his Indian policy.

He formally proposed removal to the Congress in his first message. The reaction startled him. It generated a storm of protest whose intensity and power caught him completely off guard. Directed by the American Board of Commissions for Foreign Affairs under the prodding of Jeremiah Evarts, this storm descended on both the Congress and the administration. It sent cries of outrage reverberating in the House and Senate. It gained strength by its religious fervor. How could supposedly decent and civilized men send helpless Indians to certain death in the wastelands beyond the Mississippi? How could they face themselves and their families knowing they had condemned innocents to torment and destruction?

The power and suddenness of this protesting storm delighted the National Republicans. At last they could identify with popular feeling. They immediately accused the administration of betraying the Indians and the many promises given them in the past.[6] Their accusations produced instantaneous results. Petitions opposing removal flooded into Congress.

Under the direction of the President the Democratic leaders in both houses maneuvered to ram a removal bill through Congress. The matter was appropriately sent to the respective committees on Indian affairs in the House and Senate, both of which favored the measure. Jackson had personally arranged the membership of the House committee. In addition, two Tennesseans, John Bell and Hugh Lawson White, headed the committees. As added protection the administration looked to Speaker Andrew Stevenson to break any tie votes and, as it turned out, he was required to do so on three separate occasions to save the removal bill from defeat.[7]

On February 22, 1830, the Senate committee reported the first bill, and two days later the House committee reported the second. As might be expected, given Jackson's interest, the two bills were remarkably alike. Fundamentally they recommended establishing an area west of the Mississippi to be divided into enough districts to accommodate as many tribes as might choose to go west, and removing them there. The scheme also involved an exchange of land for all the tribes residing in the east. Both bills triggered heated debate over the constitutional and moral implications of the exchange and eventually questioned the President's unwarranted extension of executive power.[8]

The Senate bill touched off several wild exchanges when it came up for debate on April 6. Senator Theodore Frelinghuysen of New Jersey led the opposition forces and spoke for three days, for a minimum of two hours each day. A deeply religious man with a proven record of humanitarian concern for the Indians, he attacked what he called the hypocrisy of the Democrats. He insisted that the true purpose of the bill was the ultimate removal of all Indians—not just the southern tribes— or their complete abandonment to the tender mercies of state law and jurisdiction. The Indians had a right to refuse to surrender their lands, he said. To threaten or harass them only invited violence and blood-shed. He pronounced Georgia's dispute with the Cherokees a simple violation of Indian treaty rights. The United States was obligated to protect the civil and political rights of the Indians against all transgressors, including sovereign states.[9]

In the course of his remarks Frelinghuysen noted the intrusion of the President himself in trying to resolve the problem. It was done, he asserted, "without the slightest consultation with either House of Congress, without any opportunity for counsel or concert, discussion or deliberation, on the part of the co-ordinate branches of the Government, to despatch the whole subject in a tone and style of decisive construction of our obligations and of Indian rights." For an administration that spoke so grandly about liberty and the abuse of power by the central government, this action against the Indians was hardly consistent. "We must," he thundered, "firmly protest against this Executive disposition of these high interests." Apart from that, he continued, the Indians themselves have known nothing but our cupidity and greed as we committed one crime after another against them. They listened to "our professions of friendship." We called them brothers and they believed us. They yielded millions of acres to our demands "and yet we crave more. We have crowded the tribes upon a few miserable acres of our Southern frontier: it is all that is left to them of their once boundless forests: and still, like the horse-leech, our insatiated cupidity cries, give! give! give!"[10]

John Forsyth of Georgia responded with savage sectional rage. Frelinghuysen's "speech was plain enough," he said. "The Indians in New York, New England, Virginia etc etc are to be left to the tender mercies of those States, while the arm of the General Government is to be extended to protect the Choctaws, Chickasaws, Creeks and especially the Cherokees from the anticipated oppressions of Mississippi, Alabama and Georgia."[11] What the north and east have already gotten away with is now to be denied the south. Robert Adams of Mississippi seconded Forsyth's argument. He insisted that everyone living within the boundaries of a particular state is subject to the laws of that state. Otherwise chaos reigns. Or has a new set of rights been discovered? In addition to federal and state rights we will now have "Indian rights." What folly! Peleg Sprague of Maine spoke against the bill and charged the Senate with its responsibility to carry out the treaties signed with the Indians. Protection had been "solemnly promised" and we can provide nothing less. Have we not done the Indians enough harm? he wearily asked. Have we not taken enough of their land?[12]

Some Senators asked for an amendment that would guarantee proper negotiations with the Indians in providing for removal, but this was rejected. Frelinghuysen also proposed that removal be delayed until Congress could determine whether the western lands were adequate to the needs of the Indians. Again this was rejected. Finally on April 26, 1830, the bill came up for a final vote and passed by the count of 28 to 19 along fairly strict party lines.[13]

In the House of Representatives both the bill and President Jackson took a worse pounding. Removal came close to defeat. The opposition never really expected to kill the measure in the Senate where the Democrats outnumbered and outmaneuvered them. What they hoped to do in the upper house was arouse public sympathy for the plight of the Indian and the terrible wrong removal involved.[14] But in the House, the National Republicans looked for a triumph. The Democrats in the House were not as well disciplined as those in the Senate, and many of them feared reprisals from certain religious groups like the Quakers if they voted for the bill. Removal might remove *them* from office.[15]

Serious debate on the bill began on May 15, when Henry R. Storrs of New York took dead aim on the White House and fired a powerful salvo. He accused Jackson of attempting to overthrow the constitutional securities of the states and their authority as well as assume the power of Congress to abrogate existing treaties in cases of necessity or war.[16] The friends of states' rights who are such strong supporters of the administration ought to see this, he facetiously remarked. Already the President has given notice that his administration will be one of aggressive action by the central government to address problems and resolve them—with or without the cooperation of Congress. The "military chieftain" is about to demonstrate what his brand of leadership is like. "If these encroachments of the Executive Department," said Storrs, "are not met and repelled in these halls, they will be resisted nowhere. The only power which stands between the Executive and the States is Congress. The States may destroy the Union themselves by open force, but the concentration of power in the hands of the Executive leads to despotism, which is worse. Of the two evils, I should prefer the nullifying power in the States—it is less dangerous."[17]

And so the basic quarrel between Jackson and his opposition was struck over the question of Indian removal. The National Republicans represented legislative government, they said, which was the very essence of republicanism; while Jackson represented executive government, which ultimately led to despotism. For the next eight years the two branches battled over their respective rights and privileges. By the end of Jackson's second term, they had reshaped the process of American government.

Wilson Lumpkin of Georgia dismissed the arguments against the bill as simply an expression of party prejudice. What the Democrats were proposing, he contended, was the means of preserving the Indians against certain annihilation. Removal, he said, was "their only hope of salvation." Their destiny was suspended by a single thread. And thank God there was someone in the White House who understood this fact and wanted to act for the Indian's own good. "No man entertains kinder feelings toward the Indians than Andrew Jackson," he flatly announced.[18]

William Ellsworth of Connecticut pummeled the administration at another sore point. The cost of removal might run into the millions. "We are first to purchase the country they leave, then to remove them, to conquer or purchase the country assigned them, and after this to sustain and defend them for all future time. How many millions will this cost?" This administration with its vaunted claims of retrenchment and economy is starting off by involving the nation in an operation that may well come to five millions—no, five times five millions, he said—before we are done. What kind of economy was that? In conclusion he begged the House "not to stain the page of our history with national shame, cruelty, and perfidy."[19]

By this time the southerners choked with anger each time they rose to speak. Thomas F. Foster of Georgia fairly spluttered as he raged at the bill's opponents. After all, he said, the Indians themselves had come to President Jackson and asked for his assistance. What was he to do? Remain silent? Hardly. "Would this have been like Andrew Jackson? Sir, it would have been at variance with every act of his life." No, he responded to them and he spoke honestly. He told them what would happen unless they removed. If they remained in the east they were subject to state laws just like everyone else. Or, bellowed Foster, "Are we now talking about Indian sovereignty?"[20]

During the debate a number of proposals were put forth that clearly indicated widespread concern over the fact that General Andrew Jackson was the man in charge of Indian removal. Perhaps Wilson Lumpkin believed that the President entertained "kinder feelings toward the Indians" than any other living person but some Congressmen had their doubts. At one point it was suggested that independent commissioners be appointed to implement removal and not leave it to the President alone. One Democratic representative from Pennsylvania, Joseph Hemphill, had many reservations about the bill. Like others he was caught between his position as a loyal follower of the administration and as a representative from a district where many of his constituents opposed removal. Hemphill thought he could escape his dilemna by proposing a substitute bill in which removal would be postponed for a year in order to send out a commission to gather information about the land to which the Indians would be sent. A decent concern for humanity demanded nothing less, he said. In arguing for delay he pointed out that Congress would thereby take the responsibility on themselves and then could intelligently lay out the manner and system of removal and direct the President to execute the law.[21]

When faced with complications or adversity congressmen love nothing better than delay. To many of them, therefore, this substitute bill made much good sense; when the vote was called 98 of them supported it against 98 who did not. The tie was broken by the Speaker, Andrew Stevenson, who voted against the substitute.[22] In this single debate, right at the outset of his administration, Andrew Jackson learned how important it was to have the right man in the right position in Congress. He never forgot it.

Obviously the question of removal had strong opposition, even among Democrats. For the bill to survive the White House had to step in and take charge. Not only did many Democrats oppose removal *per se*, but they feared that the bill was supported by the enemies of internal improvements and that the success of removal would kill the "whole system of internal improvements."[23]

In intruding into the legislative process to get the bill he wanted, Jackson took several actions. First he delayed sending up his Maysville veto. If that veto had been announced it would have killed removal on the spot. Next he pressured Democratic members of the House for their support. They were told quite specifically that the President "staked the success of his administration upon this measure," that he wanted it passed, and that he would not accept a watered-down substitute.[24] At the same time they were advised that Hemphill's bill was unrealistic in that a commission would never complete its mission within a single year.[25] Delay meant death to removal. Did they understand this, and were they prepared to accept the consequences of defeat? Several members of the Pennsylvania and Massachusetts delegations succumbed to the argument; when the bill came up for a final vote it passed 102 to 97.[26]

It was a narrow squeak. Many Democrats voted against the bill. The debate had been "as protracted and excited as any that had ever before taken place" in the House.[27] Considerable pressure on both sides was brought to bear on the Representatives, and many of them feared for their political futures no matter how they voted.

When the slightly modified House bill came back to the Senate for approval there were final attempts by Frelinghuysen, Sprague, and company to encumber it with amendments, such as to restrict removal to Georgia, but they failed. The bill passed handily and Jackson signed it on May 28, 1830. The day following passage of this bill he sent up his Maysville veto.

The Indian Removal Act of 1830 authorized Jackson to carry out the policy outlined in his first message to Congress. He could exchange unorganized public land in the trans-Mississippi west for Indian land in the east. Those Indians who moved would be given perpetual title to their new land as well as compensation for improvements on their old. The cost of their removal would be absorbed by the federal government. They would also be given assistance for their "support and subsistence" for the first year after removal. An appropriation of $500,000 was authorized to carry out these provisions.[28]

This monumental piece of legislation spelled the doom of the American Indian. It was harsh, arrogant, racist—and inevitable. It was too late to acknowledge any rights for the Indians. As Frelinghuysen remarked, all the white man had ever said to the Indian from the moment they first came into contact was "give!" Once stripped of his possessions the Indian was virtually abandoned.

Of the many significant predictions and warnings voiced during the debates in Congress that eventually came true, two deserve particular attention. One of them made a mockery of Jackson's concern for freedom. The President insisted that the Indians would not be forced to remove. If they wished to reside within the state they might do so but only on condition that they understood they would be subject to state law. He would never force them to remove, never compel them to surrender their lands. That high and noble sentiment as interpreted by land-greedy state officials meant absolutely nothing. Fraud and deception also accompanied the exchange of land. Jackson himself tried desperately to discourage corruption among the government agents chosen to arrange the removal, but the events as they actually transpired ran totally opposite to what he expected and promised.

The other prediction that mocked Jackson's commitment to economy was the cost of the operation. In the completed legislation the Congress had appropriated $500,000 but the actual cost of removal is incalculable. For one thing the process extended over many years and involved many tribes. Naturally some Indians resisted Jackson's will and the government was required to apply force. The resulting bloodshed and killing and the cost of these Indian wars cannot be quantified. For a political party that prized economy above almost everything else the policy of Indian removal was a radical departure from principle. Still many Democrats argued that the actual cost was a small price to pay for the enormous expanse of land that was added to the American empire. In Jackson's eight years in office seventy-odd treaties were signed and ratified, which added 100 million acres of Indian land to the public domain at a cost of roughly $68 million and 32 million acres of land west of the Mississippi River.[29] The expense was enormous, but so was the land-grab.

Andrew Jackson has been saddled with a considerable portion of the blame for this monstrous deed. He makes an easy mark. But the criticism is unfair if it distorts the role he actually played. His objective was not the destruction of Indian life and culture. Quite the contrary. He believed that removal was the Indian's only salvation against certain extinction. Nor did he despoil Indians. He struggled to prevent fraud and corruption, and he promised there would be no coercion in winning Indian approval of his plan for removal. Yet he himself practiced a subtle kind of coercion. He told the tribes he would abandon them to the mercy of the states if they did not agree to migrate west.[30]

The Indian problem posed a terrible dilemma and Jackson had little to gain by attempting to resolve it. He could have imitated his predecessors and done nothing. But that was not Andrew Jackson. He felt he had a duty. And when removal was accomplished he felt he had done the

American people a great service. He felt he had followed the "dictates of humanity" and saved the Indians from certain death.

Not that the President was motivated by concern for the Indians—their language or customs, their culture, or anything else. Andrew Jackson was motivated principally by two considerations: first, his concern for the military safety of the United States, which dictated that Indians must not occupy areas that might jeopardize the defense of this nation; and second, his commitment to the principle that all persons residing within states are subject to the jurisdiction and laws of those states. Under no circumstances did Indian tribes constitute sovereign entities when they occupied territory within existing state boundaries. The quickest way to undermine the security of the Union, he argued, was to jeopardize the sovereignty of the states by recognizing Indian tribes as a third sovereignty.

But there was a clear inconsistency—if not a contradiction—in this argument. If the tribes were not sovereign why bother to sign treaties (requiring Senate approval) for their land? Actually Jackson appreciated the inconsistency, and it bothered him. He never really approved of bargaining or negotiating with tribes. He felt that Congress should simply determine what needed to be done and then instruct the Indians to conform to it. Congress can "occupy and possess" any part of Indian territory, he once said, "whenever the safety, interest or defence of the country" dictated. But as President, Jackson could not simply set aside the practice and tradition of generations because of a presumed contradiction. So he negotiated and signed treaties with dozens of tribes, at the same time denying that they enjoyed sovereign rights.[31]

The reaction of the American people to Jackson's removal policy was predictable. Some were outraged, particularly the Quakers and other religious groups. Many seemed uncomfortable about it but agreed that it had to be done. Probably a larger number of Americans favored removal and applauded the President's action in settling the Indian problem once and for all. In short, there was no public outcry against it. In fact it was hardly noticed. The horror of removal with its "Trail of Tears" came much later and after Jackson had left office.[32]

Apart from everything else, the Indian Removal Act served an important political purpose. For one thing it forced Jackson to exercise leadership as the head of the Democratic party within Congress. It prepared him for even bigger battles later on. For another it gave "greater ideological and structural coherence" to the party. It separated loyal and obedient friends of the administration from all others. It became a "distinguishing feature" of Jacksonian Democrats.[33]

As soon as Congress adjourned, Jackson decided to initiate the policy of removal himself by meeting personally with the southern tribes, thereby insuring a proper beginning to his program. The issue had the potential of creating enormous political trouble for the administration and the President was anxious to demonstrate that his policy was humane and economical. He also anticipated Indian opposition, and few men knew how to overcome Indian intransigence as well as Andrew Jackson. The call for the abandonment of the sites of their ancestral graves was sure to provoke resentment and resistance. Indeed, some chiefs swore they would fight. "We will no more beg, pray and implore, but we will *demand* justice," promised the *Cherokee Phoenix* on May 15. "Let us then be *firm* and *united.*"

On May 31, much to Jackson's satisfaction, the Congress closed its session and left the capital. "Congress has this day adjourned," he wrote Coffee, "after a very stormy session." On balance he figured he had scored a thumping success in his first tangle with the legislature. "Altho congress has acted very strangely and contrary in most things to what was expected," he said, "still my administration is going on pretty well." He had obtained removal legislation and vetoed away misguided appropriations. His program was off to a good start. The only irritant still troubling him as he prepared to return to Tennessee was the continued unpleasantness over the Eaton affair. And what made it worse was the resistance to his wishes in his own household. The Donelsons stoutly refused to socialize with the Eatons or acknowledge his demands that they amend their behavior.[34] Jackson tolerated this dissension for as long as he could. Finally he served the Donelsons with an ultimatum: either they treat Mrs. Eaton as he had directed or they could leave the White House and return to Tennessee. He could no longer endure the discord under his own roof, and of course he must have the right to decide social relationships in his own home.

Donelson chose banishment. A man of courage and honor, like his uncle, he could not subject his wife to the humiliation of bowing to Peggy's demands. He regretted that he had no choice.

The decision deeply wounded the old man. Next winter, he told Van Buren, he would live a "bachelor's life, would to god I had commenced it with my administration, it would have prevented me from much humiliation & pain that I have experienced, and have prevented much injury to the innocent."[35]

When the entire family, including Jackson, left for Tennessee on June 17, 1830, the tension ran high. John Eaton planned to meet the party somewhere en route, since he and the President and General Coffee expected to meet the chiefs of the southern tribes once Jackson arrived in Nashville. Donelson even resented the rendezvous. "As matters stand," he explained to Coffee, "the self respect of the Major should have dictated a different course."[36]

Along the way home—estimated at from sixteen to eighteen days if they encountered no difficulty in getting a boat when they reached the Ohio—the President was greatly heartened by the receptions he received and the solid support his Maysville veto evoked from the people. "You may say to our friends in the city," he wrote back to Lewis in Washington, "that the veto is working well, widely different to what our enemies anticipated." Jackson had left the capital with real apprehensions weighing on his mind, and so the reassurances he received from the people lifted his spirits enormously. "There has been, and are things, that have coroded my peace, and my mind, and must cease, or my administration will be a distracted one, which I cannot permit."37

The further west Jackson traveled the larger the receptions grew. The size of the crowds amazed him. At Cincinnati he was met by over six thousand people assembled on the shore. "Surely it was a more numerous crowd, than I ever before witnessed here," he informed Lewis, "some say, eight, but I do suppose that at least six thousand people."38 And to think how many friends warned him that his popularity in the west would plummet if he vetoed the Maysville bill. The people never desert him, he declared.39

Jackson had expected to meet John Eaton in Cincinnati to prepare for the meeting with the chiefs of the southern tribes, but Eaton failed to appear. He assumed that the war secretary had been delayed on account of Peggy's health. Meanwhile the President proceeded to Tennessee, where he received a "remonstrance" from the Choctaw chiefs, which was forwarded to the Senate.

The proposed meeting was scheduled for Franklin, Tennessee, where Eaton himself lived, just a short distance from the Hermitage. The President invited the chiefs of several nations to meet him there, but the Cherokees and Creek chiefs refused him outright. They no longer regarded him as a protecting "Father." Rather they looked to the Supreme Court for redress. Since the President and Congress had betrayed and abandoned them they had no recourse but to sue in the courts. They hired William Wirt, one of the most distinguished constitutional lawyers in the country, to handle their case. Wirt's acceptance of the suit angered and shocked Jackson because the lawyer apparently did not realize that removal was designed for the Indians' own good.40

The refusal of the chiefs to meet Jackson did not unduly distress him. If they chose another path than the one he offered, so be it. Just as long as they understood they were now subject to state law. "Their great father is resolved that if they now refuse," he said, "he will trouble them no more, but leave them to remove or not, as they please, & when they please and at their own expense. If they believe they can live under the laws of Mississippi he is perfectly willing they should do so; but should they find they can not, & become desirous to seek a new home, let them understand, that they must seek it as they can, & in their own way; for no other application will be made to them for a treaty. If they will not listen and be advised, be all consequences which may follow on themselves."41 This was a very subtle form of coercion, whether Jackson realized it or not. Do as I direct, he told the Indians, or suffer the consequences.

Jackson waited for Eaton at the Hermitage, and he summoned General John Coffee to join him there. Not until July 21 did the war secretary and his wife reach Tennessee, and almost immediately the social ostracism of Washington engulfed them. This mortified Jackson. "You know I am immoveable," he wrote Lewis, "I will govern my Household, or I have *none.*" Most probably, he said, he would return in the fall to Washington "with my son alone." In which case he would need a new private secretary. He wanted one "who can write and compose *well,* one who from a brief do justice to any subject." That he was reduced to this necessity only further agitated him. "My feelings have been much coroded here," he said. "Mrs E was met by all the ladies in the place with open arms, *but one.* I will purge the sanctuary in due time, of all its unworthy members."[42]

On July 28 Jackson journeyed to Franklin and was immediately greeted by a "large assemblage of people collected to give Major Eaton a barbecue." A committee invited Jackson to the barbecue but he declined. Instead he agreed to ride out after the dinner and shake hands with all his old acquaintances and former comrades-in-arms. The courtesies shown Peggy at Franklin contrasted sharply with the scorn shown her in Nashville and Washington. Even my family are tools, Jackson complained, "to injure me, disturb my administration, and if possible to destroy my friend Major Eaton. . . . that my Nephew and Nece should permit themselves to be held up as the instruments, and *tools,* of such wickedness, is truly mortifying to me."[43]

Jackson expected to meet with the Indian chiefs of the Chickasaw and Choctaw nations in Franklin around the middle of August. He communicated with various government agents to the tribes and instructed them to use their influence with the Indians to encourage their chiefs to come to Franklin and meet with him and Eaton and Coffee. "I beg of you to say to them," he wrote to one such agent, "that their *interest happiness* peace and prosperity depend upon their removal beyond the jurisdiction of the laws of the State of Mississippi." Congress had provided the "liberal appropriations" whereby they might remove "comfortably" and with a minimum of difficulty. "It was a measure I had much at heart and sought to effect because I was satisfied that the Indians could not possibly live under the laws of the States. . . . I feel conscious of having done my duty to my red children."[44]

The President assumed that the Chickasaws would arrive on the nineteenth and the Choctaws on the twenty-fifth. The Chickasaws did appear on schedule, but the Choctaws chose to remain away. The Choctaw chiefs knew that in a face-to-face confrontation, Jackson would force them to give up their country, and they also knew that their people would kill them if they did so.

On August 23 the President met at the Presbyterian church with the Chickasaw delegation. Twenty-one chiefs and their agent, Colonel Benjamin Reynolds, assembled before their "Father." After a brief and formal welcoming ceremony the President gave the Indians one of his celebrated "talks."

"Friends and brothers," he began, "Your Great father is rejoiced once again to meet and shake you by the hand, and to have it in his power to assure you of his continued friendship and good will. He can cherish none but the best feelings for his red children, many of whom, during our late war, fought with him in defence of our country." He went on to tell them that Congress had given him power to extend justice to the Indians, to grant them lands in the west, to pay the expenses for removal, and to support them for a year. This was the reason he had asked them to come to Franklin and meet him in council, "to point you to a course which cannot fail to make you a happy and prosperous people. Hear and deliberate well," he said, "and under the exercise of your own reason and matured judgment, determine what may appear to you to be done for the benefit of yourselves and your children."

This "talk," which was published in all the newspapers, was intended to reach beyond the Indians to the American people so that they might better understand his purposes. Therefore Jackson chose his words very carefully. He wanted nothing in the text to appear threatening. No coercion or sign of force must be intimated. Yet the coercion was there.

> Brothers:—You have long dwelt upon the soil you occupy. . . . Now your white brothers are around you. States have been created within your ancient limits, which claim a right to govern and control your people as they do their own citizens, and to make them answerable to their civil and criminal codes. Your great father has not the authority to prevent this state of things.

Were they ready to submit to the laws of Mississippi if they chose to stay? for this they must in fact do.

> Brothers, listen:—To these laws, where you are, you must submit;—there is no preventive—no other alternative. Your great father cannot, nor can congress, prevent it. The states only can. What then? Do you believe that you can live under these laws? That you can surrender all your ancient habits, and the forms by which you have been so long controlled? If so, your great father has nothing to say or to advise. . . . His earnest desire is, that you may be perpetuated and preserved as a nation; and this he believes can only be done and secured by your consent to remove to a country beyond the Mississippi. . . . Where you are, it is not possible you can live contented and happy.

The "great father" promised that no force would be used to compel them to consent to removal. The decision was theirs alone. He said he understood fully their feeling about leaving the land of their birth. He knew how painful it would be to bid goodbye forever to the graves of their ancestors. But survival necessitated this move. Annihilation was the alternative.

"Old men!" he called, addressing the ancient chiefs. "Arouse to energy and lead your children to a land of promise and of peace before the Great Spirit shall call you to die." Then turning to the younger warriors, the President renewed his plea. "Young chiefs! Forget the prejudices you feel for the soil of your birth, and go to a land where you can preserve your people as a nation." It was a powerful appeal. It deeply affected the Indians.

The "great father" closed with a warning, thinly disguised: "Reject the opportunity which is now offered to obtain comfortable homes, and the time may soon pass away when such advantages as are now within your reach may again be presented." If you reject this opportunity, "call not upon your great father hereafter to relieve you of your troubles. . . ." If you choose to stay be advised that you are subject to state laws and state regulations. In a few years, he further warned, "by becoming amalgamated with the whites, your national character will be lost . . . you must disappear and be forgotten."

The Indians cried out their dismay when they heard these crushing words. The President paused to let his words sink in. After a moment he began again. This calamity can be avoided, he concluded. If you are willing to remove, say so and state your terms, and my friends Major Eaton and General Coffee, who are authorized to talk to you, will "act candidly, fairly and liberally towards you."[45]

Thus spake the "great father." After hearing him out the Chickasaws withdrew to council among themselves. His words left them shaken and morose. They needed time to talk out their concerns and fears. They needed time for reflection. Four days later they returned with their answer. They met the President, Eaton, and Coffee at the Masonic Hall. The President seated himself in the center of a square formed by the chiefs. One of the chiefs, the secretary of the delegation, approached Eaton with a sheet of paper in his hand. The chief extended his free, right hand which Eaton took and shook. Then the Major was asked to read the paper to the President. He took the sheet, turned to his superior and began:

Franklin, August 27, 1830

To our great father the president. Your red children, the chiefs and head men of the Chickasaws, have had under consideration the talk of our father. . . . On the decision we this day make and declare to you and the world, depends our fate as a nation and as a people.

Father, you say that you have travelled a long way to talk to your red children. We have listened—and your words have sunk deep into our hearts. As you are about to set out for Washington city—before we shake our father's hand, perhaps with many of us for the last time—we have requested this meeting to tell you, that after sleeping upon the talk you sent us, and the talk delivered to us by our brothers, major Eaton and gen. Coffee, we are now ready to enter into any treaty based upon the principles communicated to us by major Eaton and gen. Coffee. Your friends and brothers.

(Signed etc.)[46]

The "great father" smiled with satisfaction. He told the chiefs how much they had gladdened his heart and how good it was to have this "talk" with them. Many of the chiefs, he said, had known him a long time, a friendship that would never be interrupted. He would remember them always. He hoped—and as he spoke the next words his voice choked with emotion—the "Great Spirit above would take care of, bless, and preserve them." Jackson was so moved by the sight of these "gentle children" that he rose from his chair and bade them all an affectionate farewell. The Chickasaws were deeply touched by this unexpected and genuine show of emotion. Suddenly, one of the principal chiefs rushed forward and grasped the President with both hands. "God bless you, my great father," he exclaimed. Then, overcome by the intensity of his feeling, the chief turned away. The President and all the other chiefs stood perfectly still, too affected to say or do anything.

The emotional level of the scene reached an excruciating pitch. The father casting out his children. Each knew his role and what was happening. The Chickasaws loved their father as dutiful children, and yet he was saying goodbye to them forever. He was, said one reporter, "by them so much beloved," still he was telling them they must leave "the land of their youth, where the bones of their fathers reposed." They were all choked dumb by their feelings.[47]

The President could not remain to negotiate the final terms of the treaty with the Chickasaw Nation. He had already stayed eight days with the Indians and it was time for him to return to Washington. Eaton and Coffee had excellent credentials; they enjoyed the President's total trust and the Chickasaws had agreed to negotiate with them. On August 31, 1830, they signed a treaty with the Indians embracing the main principles contained in the President's "talk." The Chickasaws agreed to give up their land, "cross the Mississippi," and find a new home in the west.

Jackson saw this victory as something won against the machinations of dark and hidden forces. The "opposition" had schemed to keep the southern tribes from meeting him in order to create havoc and discord. At least the Chickasaws had responded and yielded to his entreaties. This encouraging beginning, he felt, would draw other treaties after it. "Thus far we have succeeded, against the most corrupt and secrete combination that ever did exist," he snorted, "and we have preserved my Chickasaw friends and red brethren." Unfortunately, for a number of technical reasons, the Senate later refused to ratify this initial treaty and it was renegotiated by Coffee and signed on October 30, 1832.[48]

As for the other southern tribes, Jackson predicted a less happy future. The Cherokees and Creeks had opted to sue in the courts and had placed themselves in the hands of William Wirt, the former United States Attorney General. The Creeks added insult to their other outrages by informing their "great father" that they would not meet him in Franklin. "We have answered," the President growled, "that we leave them to themselves, and to the protection of their friend Mr. Wirt . . . to whom they have given a large fee to protect them in their rights as an independent Nation; and when they find that they cannot live under the laws of Alabama, they must find, at their own expence . . . a country, and a home." As for Wirt, "he had been truly wicked" and will surely bring about "the distruction of the poor ignorant Indians." If only these meddlers would keep out of it and leave Indian removal to him. "I have exonerated the national character," intoned the great father, "and now leave the poor deluded Creeks and Cherokees to their fate, and their anihilation, which their wicked advisers has induced."[49]

The Choctaws also rejected Jackson's invitation at first. They had been expected on August 25 but Greenwood LeFlore, a mixed-blood leader of the tribe, informed Eaton that his warriors were fiercely opposed to attending a convention at Franklin. The "lives of the chiefs and head men of the nation," he wrote, "would be in great danger if they propose of selling the country." Not that they rejected a discussion outright. LeFlore assured the "great father" that the Choctaws would listen most carefully to whatever he chose to tell them. "We wish our father the President would send us a talk by some good men, who will give us time to call a full council, and who will explain to us the views of the government on the subject of the removal of our people west of the Mississippi."[50]

Angered at first by the Choctaw refusal to meet him, Jackson soon recognized that LeFlore's words left open the possibility of future removal. And if both the Choctaws and Chickasaws agreed to migrate, the state of Mississippi would be virtually emptied of Indians, thus tightening the nation's military grip on the lower Mississippi valley and increasing America's security against possible foreign invasion. So the President wrote a cordial acceptance of the offer and appointed Eaton and Coffee to present his "talk."[51]

The commissioners met with the chiefs and headmen at Dancing Rabbit Creek on September 15, 1830. The policy of removal was explained simply as the President wished. Would the Choctaws migrate west and sign a treaty with the United States as evidence of their good faith? If not, they must submit to state law; and if they refused to submit to state jurisdiction, armed force would be used against them. Neither Eaton nor Coffee had Jackson's charisma with the Indians, so they offered bribes to induce agreement. The bribes rarely failed, and on September 27 a treaty was signed. As it turned out this was the first treaty to be signed and ratified by the Senate to implement the removal policy. The earlier Chickasaw treaty had served a valuable purpose, however. It demonstrated the President's willingness to intervene personally to achieve removal of all the southern tribes.

According to the Treaty of Dancing Rabbit Creek, the Choctaws agreed to evacuate all their land in Mississippi and emigrate to an area west of the Arkansas Territory to what is now Oklahoma. In addition the Indians would receive money, household and farm equipment, subsistence for one year, and reimbursement for improvements on their vacated property. In effect the Choctaws ceded to the United States 10.5 million acres of land east of the Mississippi River. They promised to emigrate in stages: the first group in the fall of 1831, the second in 1832, and the last in 1833.[52]

Jackson immediately submitted the treaty to Congress when it reconvened in December, 1830, and Eaton, in his annual report, assured the members that agreement was reached through persuasion only. No secret agreements, no bribes, no promises. Everything had been open and aboveboard! The Senate swallowed the lie whole and ratified the treaty on February 25, 1831, by a vote of 35 to 12. Said one Choctaw chief: "Our doom is sealed."[53]

Since the Treaty of Dancing Rabbit Creek was the first to win Senate approval the President was very anxious to make it a model of removal. He wanted everything to go smoothly so that the American people would understand that removal was humane and beneficial to both the Indians and the American nation at large. Furthermore, he hoped its success would encourage other tribes to capitulate to his policy and thereby send a veritable human tide streaming across the Mississippi into the plains beyond.

The actual removal of the Choctaw Nation violated every principle for which Jackson stood. From start to finish the operation was a fraud. Corruption, theft, mismanagement, inefficiency—all contributed to the destruction of a once-great people. The Choctaws asked to be guided to their new country by General George Gibson, a man they trusted and with whom they had scouted their new home. Even this was denied them. The bureaucracy dictated another choice. So they left the "land of their fathers" filled with fear and anxiety. To make matters worse the winter of 1831–1832 was "living hell." The elements conspired to add to their misery. The suffering was stupefying. Those who watched the horror never forgot it. Many wept. The Indians themselves showed not a single sign of their agony.[54]

Jackson tried to prevent this calamity but he was too far away to exercise any real control, and the temptations and opportunities for graft and corruption were too great for some agents to resist. When he learned of the Choctaw experience and the suffering involved, Jackson was deeply offended. He did what he could to prevent its recurrence. He proposed a new set of guidelines for future removals. He hoped they would reform the system and erase mismanagement and the opportunity for theft.

To begin with, the entire operation of Indian removal was transferred from civilian hands to the military. Then the office of commissioner of Indian affairs was established under the war department to coordinate and direct all matters pertaining to the Indians. In large part these changes reflected Jackson's anguish over what had happened to the Choctaws, but they also resulted from his concern over public opinion. Popular outrage could kill the whole program of removal.[55]

Additionally, Jackson worked out a "project of operations" for removal with the help of his war secretary and several persons in the Office of Indian Affairs. The project was sent to the various superintendents appointed for the "replacement" of each tribe and consisted of three parts:

1. The "initiatory measures," consisting of the enrollment of the Indians to be removed and the evaluation of their property.

2. Payments to be made to the Indians and the articles to be furnished them.

3. Transportation and subsistence.

With respect to enrollment and payments, the superintendents were instructed to ascertain how many Indians were prepared to remove, when they would be ready to go, how many would travel together, what points of departure would be used, what route would be taken, and where to locate depots of provisions and the quantity necessary for each person. As part of the payment, each head of a family upon enrollment was provided with a good rifle, a blanket, a kettle, and five pounds of tobacco as well as one blanket for each member of the family. If these supplies were not immediately available, certificates would be issued to the family head enumerating the articles due him and promising that as soon as they were procured they would be delivered to him personally (and to no other) upon presentation of the certificate.

With respect to transportation and subsistence, an officer of the army was designated as the person responsible to make all purchases and expenditures on the basis of requisitions issued by the superintendents. The location and quantity of these provisions would be decided by the superintendents, who would also select the route of departure and the mode of transportation. Funds for these operations would be remitted to an agent of the subsistence department.[56]

The superintendents were particularly urged to make the President's policy as clear to the Indians as possible. Jackson wanted the Indians to give "their own free consent" to removal but he also wanted them to "understand distinctly the offers which are made to them and all the circumstances attending their removal and settlement." Superintendents were warned to take particular care in their explanations so "that nothing is left of which they can eventually complain." Tell them this, said the secretary of war to the superintendent sent to remove the Cherokees: "Let them know, that the President feels for their situation, that he is satisfied they had better remove and soon, and that where we wish them to go, they will find a mild climate, a fertile country, and the means of preserving their institutions, without the interference of the white people. And then let them know, that we leave the choice to them, trusting that the Great Spirit, who made the white man and the red, will open their eyes to see the path, they ought to travel."[57]

The experience of removal is one of the horror stories of the modern era. Beginning with the Choctaws it decimated whole tribes. An entire race of people suffered. What it did to their lives, their culture, their language, their customs is a tragedy of truly staggering proportions. The irony is that removal was intended to prevent this calamity.

Would it have been worse had the Indians remained in the East? Jackson thought so. He said they would "disappear and be forgotten." One thing does seem certain: the Indians would have been forced to yield to state laws and white society. Indian Nations *per se* would have been obliterated and possibly Indian civilization with them.

In October, 1832, a year and a half after the Choctaw treaty was ratified, General Coffee signed a treaty with the Chickasaws that met Jackson's complete approval. "Surely the religious enthusiasts," wrote the President in conveying his delight to Coffee, "or those who have been weeping over the oppression of the Indians will not find fault with it for want of liberality or justice to the Indians." By this time Jackson had grown callous. His promise to economize got the better of him. "The stipulation that they remove at their own expence and on their own means, is an excellent feature in it. The whole treaty is just. we want them in a state of safety removed from the states and free from colision with the whites; and if the land does this it is well disposed of and freed from being a corrupting source to our Legislature."[58]

Coffee's success with the Chickasaws followed those with the Creeks and Seminoles. On March 24, 1832, the destruction of the Creek Nation begun with the Treaty of Fort Jackson in 1814 was completed when the chiefs signed an agreement to remove rather than fight it out in the courts. The Seminoles accepted a provisional treaty on May 9, 1832, pending approval of the site for relocation. Thus, by the close of Jackson's first administration the Choctaws, Creeks, Chickasaws, and Seminoles had capitulated. Of the so-called Five Civilized Tribes only the Cherokees held out.

Not for long. They found small consolation from the courts. The Cherokees' lawyer, William Wirt, sued in the Supreme Court for an injunction that would permit the Indians to remain in Georgia unmolested by state law. He argued that the Cherokees had a right to self-government as a foreign nation and that this right had long been recognized by the United States in its treaties with the Indians. He hoped to make it appear that Jackson himself was the nullifier of federal law. In effect he challenged the entire removal policy by asking for a restraining order against Georgia.[59]

Chief Justice John Marshall in the case *Cherokee Nation* v. *Georgia* handed down his opinion on March 18, 1831. He rejected Wirt's contention that the Cherokees were a sovereign nation. He also rejected Jackson's insistence that they were subject to state law. The Indians, he said, were "domestic dependent nations," subject to the United States as a ward to a guardian. They were not subject to individual states, he declared. Indian territory was in fact part of the United States.[60]

The Indians chose to regard the opinion as essentially favorable in that it commanded the United States to protect their rights and property. So they refused to submit—either to Georgia or to Jackson. Meanwhile, Georgia passed legislation in late December, 1830, prohibiting white men from entering Indian country after March 1, 1831, without a license from the state. This was clearly aimed at troublesome missionaries who encouraged Indians in their "disobedience." Samuel A. Worcester and Dr. Elizur Butler, two missionaries, defied the law; they were arrested and sentenced to four years imprisonment in a state penitentiary.[61] They sued, and in the case *Worcester* v. *Georgia* the Supreme Court decided on March 3, 1832, that the Georgia law was unconstitutional. Speaking for the majority in a feeble voice, John Marshall croaked out the court's decision. All the laws of Georgia dealing with the Cherokees were unconstitutional, he declared. He issued a formal mandate two days later ordering the Georgia Superior Court to reverse its decision.[62]

Georgia, of course, had refused to acknowledge the court's right to direct its actions and had boycotted the judicial proceedings. The state had no intention of obeying the court's order. Since the court adjourned almost immediately after rendering its decision nothing further could be done. According to the Judiciary Act of 1789 the Supreme Court could issue its order of compliance only when a case had already been remanded without response.[63] Since the court would not reconvene until January, 1833, no further action by the government could take place. Thus, until the court either summoned state officials before it for contempt or issued a writ of habeas corpus for the release of the two missionaries there was nothing further to be done. The President was under no obligation to act. In fact there is some question as to whether the court itself could act since the existing habeas corpus law did not apply in this case because the missionaries were not being detained by federal authorities. And since the Superior Court of Georgia did not acknowledge in writing its refusal to obey, Marshall's decision could not be enforced.[64] Jackson understood this. He knew there was nothing for him to do. "The decision of the supreme court has fell still born," he wrote John Coffee, "and they find that it cannot coerce Georgia to yield to its mandate."[65]

It was later reported by Horace Greeley that Jackson's response to the Marshall decision was total defiance. "Well: John Marshall has made his decision: *now let him enforce it!*"[66] Greeley cited George N. Briggs, a Representative from Massachusetts, as his source for the statement. The quotation certainly sounds like Jackson and many historians have chosen to believe that he said it. The fact is that Jackson did not say it because there was no reason to do so. There was nothing for him to enforce. Why, then, would he refuse an action that no one asked him to take? As he said, the decision was stillborn. The court rendered an opinion which abandoned the Indians to their inevitable fate. "It cannot coerce Georgia to yield to its mandate," said Jackson, "and I believe Ridge* has expressed despair, and that it is better for them [the Cherokees] to treat and move."[67]

Even if Jackson did not use the exact words Greeley put into his mouth, even if no direct action was required at the moment, some historians have argued that the quotation represents in fact Jackson's true attitude. There is evidence that Jackson "sportively said in private conversation" that if summoned "to support the decree of the Court he will call on those who have brought about the decision to enforce it."[68] Actually nobody expected Jackson to enforce the decision, including the two missionaries, and therefore a lot of people simply assumed that the President would defy the court if pressured.[69] In the rush to show Jackson as bombastic and blustery, however, an important point is missed. What should be remembered is that Jackson reacted with extreme caution to this crisis because a precipitous act could have triggered a confrontation with Georgia. Prudence, not defiance, characterized his reaction to both the challenge of Georgia and later the threat of nullification by South Carolina. As one historian has said, Jackson deserves praise for his caution in dealing with potentially explosive issues and should not be condemned for his so-called inaction.[70]

Still the President had encouraged Georgia in its intransigence. He shares responsibility in producing this near-confrontation. He was so desperate to achieve Indian removal that he almost produced a crisis between federal and state authorities. Nor can it be denied, as one North Carolina Congressman observed, that "Gen Jackson could by a nod of the head or a crook of the finger induce Georgia to submit to the law. It is by the promise or belief of his countenance and support that Georgia is stimulated to her disorderly and rebellious conduct."[71]

Jackson chose not to nod his head or crook his finger for several reasons, the most important of which was his determination to remove the Cherokees. But he had other concerns. As the time neared for the Supreme Court to reconvene and deliberate on Georgia's defiance, a controversy with South Carolina over nullification developed. Jackson had to be extremely careful that no action of his induced Georgia to join South Carolina in the dispute. Nullification might lead to secession and civil war. He therefore maneuvered to isolate South Carolina and force Georgia to back away from its position of confrontation. He needed to nudge Georgia into obeying the court order and free the two missionaries. Consequently he moved swiftly to win removal of the Indians. His secretary of war worked quietly to convince the legal counsel for the

*Major John Ridge was the leader of the Cherokee party who held out against removal.

missionaries and the friends of the Cherokees in Congress, such as Theodore Frelinghuysen, that the President would not budge from his position nor interfere in the operation of Georgia laws and that the best solution for everyone was for the Indians to remove. Meanwhile the Creeks capitulated, and a treaty of removal was ratified by the Senate in April, 1832.[72]

Although Senator Frelinghuysen "prayed to God" that Georgia would peacefully acquiesce in the decision of the Supreme Court he soon concluded that the Cherokees must yield. Even Justice John McLean, who wrote a concurring opinion in the *Worcester* case, counseled the Cherokee delegation in Washington to sign a removal treaty.[73] Van Buren's Albany Regency actively intervened because of their concern over a possible southern backlash against their leader. Van Buren himself encouraged his friend Senator John Forsyth to intercede with the newly elected governor of Georgia, Wilson Lumpkin, keeping Jackson carefully informed of his actions.[74] More significant, however, were the letters written by the secretary of war to Lumpkin. These letters pleaded for a pardon for the two missionaries and stated that the President himself gave his unconditional endorsement of the request.[75] Finally Forsyth conferred with William Wirt who in turn conferred with a representative of the two missionaries, and they all agreed to make no further motion before the Supreme Court. That done, Governor Lumpkin ordered the "keeper" of the penitentiary on January 14, 1833 to release Worcester and Butler under an arrangement devised by Forsyth. Thus, while the President held steady to his course and directed the activities of the men in contact with Lumpkin, both the problem of Georgia's defiance and the fate of the two missionaries were quietly resolved without injurious consequences to the rest of the nation. It was one of Jackson's finest actions as a statesman.[76]

Ultimately, the Cherokees also yielded to the President. On December 29, 1835, at New Echota a treaty was signed arranging an exchange of land. A protracted legal argument had gained the Indians a little time but nothing else. Removal now applied to all eastern Indians, not simply the southern tribes. After the Black Hawk War of 1832 Jackson responded to the demands of Americans in the northwest to send all Indians beyond the Mississippi. A hungry band of Sac and Fox Indians under the leadership of Black Hawk had recrossed the Mississippi in the spring of 1832 to find food. People on the frontier panicked and Governor John Reynolds of Illinois called out the militia and appealed to Jackson for assistance. Federal troops were immediately dispatched under Generals Winfield Scott and Henry Atkinson. A short and bloody war resulted, largely instigated by drunken militia troops, and when it ended the northwestern tribes were so demoralized that they offered little resistance to Jackson's steady pressure for their removal west of the Mississippi. The result of the Black Hawk War, said the President in his fourth message to Congress, had been very "creditable to the troops" engaged in the action. "Severe as is the lesson to the Indians," he lectured, "it was rendered necessary by their unprovoked aggressions, and it is to be hoped that its impression will be permanent and salutary."[77]

It was useless for the Indians to resist Jackson's demands. Nearly 46,000 of them went west. Thousands died in transit. Even those under no treaty obligation to emigrate were eventually forced to remove. And the removal experiences were all pretty much like that of the Choctaws —all horrible, all rife with corruption and fraud, all disgraceful to the American nation.

The policy of removal formed an important part of Jackson's overall program of limiting federal authority and supporting states' rights. Despite the accusation of increased executive authority, Jackson successfully buttressed state sovereignty and jurisdiction over all inhabitants within state boundaries. This is a government of the people, Jackson argued, and the President is the agent of the people. The President and the Congress exercise their jurisdiction over *"the people of the union. who are the people of the union?"* he asked. Then, answering his own question, he said: "all those subject to the jurisdiction of the sovereign states, none else." Indians are also subject to the states, he went on. They are subject "to the sovereign power of the state within whose sovereign limits they reside." An "absolute independence of the Indian tribes from state authority can never bear an intelligent investigation, and a quasi independence of state authority when located within its Territorial limits is *absurd.*"[78]

In addition to establishing the removal policy Jackson also restructured the bureaucracy handling Indian problems. Since 1824 a Bureau of Indian Affairs headed by Thomas L. McKenney had supervised the government's relations with the Indians. By the time Jackson assumed the presidency the Bureau had become an "enormous quagmire" from an administrative point of view.[79] McKenney was retained in office to take advantage of his reputation to win passage of the Removal bill. Once Removal passed, McKenney was dismissed. (For one thing he had supported Adams in 1828.) Then the Bureau was reorganized. On June 30, 1834, Congress passed the necessary legislation establishing the Office of Indian Affairs under an Indian commissioner, and this administrative machinery remained in place well into the twentieth century. The Indian service was restructured into a more cohesive operation than had previously been the case. It regularized procedures that had been practiced as a matter of custom rather than law.

Ultimately Jackson's policy of removal and reorganization of the Indian service won acceptance by most Americans. The President was seen as a forceful executive who addressed one of the nation's most bedeviling problems and solved it. Even Americans who fretted over the fate of the Indians eventually went along with removal. The policy seemed enlightened and humane. It seemed rational and logical.[80] It constituted, Americans thought, the only possible solution to the Indian problem.

CHAPTER 16

Jacksonian Diplomacy: Beginnings

UPON HIS RETURN TO WASHINGTON in the early fall of 1830 Jackson had several reasons to feel a certain amount of satisfaction about the course of his administration. After a shaky start as the result of his own mismanagement and inexperience, he began to feel as though the principles for which he had been elected were beginning to take hold. His policy of rotation had succeeded in ridding the government of "countless miscreants" and he believed a healthy atmosphere of honesty had been created within the bureaucracy in Washington. In addition, after a hard battle in Congress, he had gotten approval for an Indian Removal Bill. The resettlement of the Indians had begun with the recent treaties concluded with the Choctaws and Chickasaws. In the process, the rights of the states had been reaffirmed.

Fiscal conservatism was another vital component of his reform program. Although he had a distance to go—particularly with the BUS—he noted real progress in his efforts at "retrenchment and economy." As a result the national debt appeared to be in hand. Upon his return to Washington in late September Jackson ordered the payment of $2 million more toward the debt. That brought the total reduction for 1830 alone to $12 million, a remarkable illustration of the administration's frugality and the strength of the American economy. Jackson exercised scrupulous care in approving expenditures. He hawkeyed the Congress on every major appropriation bill and vetoed with abandon those he dubbed extravagant. Before he was done he had vetoed more legislation than all the previous Presidents combined.

Of the national debt Jackson estimated that about $16 million of the 5 and 4½ percent bonds remained unpaid; $13 million of the 3 percent, and $7 million of the bank stock. If all went well, if the economy kept up its steady growth, if he held the Congress to a strict accounting of their appropriations, and "if I live on the 4th of March 1833 I will, I hope, by the sale of land pay the last dollar."[1]

Pay the last dollar! What a blessing that would be. What a triumph of the principles of republicanism. Not to owe anyone a cent. It would provide the American people with an example of fiscal responsibility and restraint and an example of strict accountability in the use of public funds. Could there then be any doubt of the restoration of the government to morality and virtue?

The Jackson administration also enjoyed several important victories in foreign relations during its early years. Not surprisingly, the President regarded this area as essential to his success in furthering the course of American freedom. He took an immediate interest in the affairs of the state department and even went so far as to decide major appointments at the ministerial level without consulting the secretary. Fortunately this regrettable beginning produced no major shocks. Once Van Buren arrived at his desk a smooth operation was set in motion.

Shortly after his inauguration Jackson summoned the foreign ministers in residence in Washington to meet him in the White House on Monday, April 6, 1829, to enable him "to restate . . . those sentiments expressed in that part of my inaugural address concerning our foreign relations and to add that I am sure the true interest of my country will be best promoted by preserving the relations of peace with all nations." The ministers, no doubt, were pleased to hear these words, especially coming from General Jackson, whom the Spanish had earlier nicknamed "the Napoleon of the woods." At this meeting he emphasized that friendly relations can be preserved only if they are "founded on principles of fair reciprocity." That meant the normal courtesies and respect owed to any sovereign and independent nation. Not like the past when contempt and scorn characterized Europe's attitude toward the United States and had ultimately led to war. Nothing less than global recognition of United States rights and sovereignty was Jackson's object. But he assured the ministers that he entertained no "prejudice to, or undue partiality for any nation, or people, and with personal feelings of the most friendly character towards all." This, too, must have delighted the attentive ministers. "I have no desire to impair the rights or interests of others," the President declared; he said he would "endeavour to effect these objects by the most frank, friendly & sincere negotiations." Where differences existed—and they did exist—"I would desire to settle them on the most fair & honorable terms, in that spirit of frankness so congenial with my nature, and the spirit of our government."[2]

One outstanding difference concerned trade with the British West Indies; it had been closed by Great Britain since the conclusion of the Revolutionary War. Repeated efforts to reopen the trade had failed. But

Jackson was determined to succeed. Somehow he must induce the British to yield and allow American ships to enter the West Indies.

Louis McLane of Delaware served as Jackson's minister to Great Britain. A former Radical Republican, he reluctantly accepted the post after it had been refused by Tazewell.[3] He proved an excellent choice. "He is correct, conciliating and spirited," wrote one man; like Jackson, "he would give no insult, and he would receive none."[4] Early in June, 1829, McLane told Van Buren that if the United States would divorce itself from the errors of the Adams administration, which had bungled the West Indian business, the British might consider negotiating a treaty. In other words, the defeat of Adams by Jackson in 1828 might be viewed as a repudiation of the former President's foreign policy and the British might then respond favorably to a friendly gesture and agree to commercial reciprocity.[5]

Van Buren caught the picture immediately. John Quincy Adams had botched earlier overtures from the British, who were anxious to improve their relations with the United States. Now it was simply a matter of telling the British that Andrew Jackson and his administration wanted to erase all existing difficulties between the two countries and that the lifting of the West Indian commercial restrictions would be a helpful place to start.[6]

Repudiating the foreign policy of one's predecessor is risky business, to say the least. The political dangers can be enormous. But Jackson ached to settle the matter and prove his diplomatic skill, and he felt secure enough to move in a new direction. What soon emerged was an overall Jacksonian foreign policy that sought through practical—rather than formal—means to reconcile the differences that interrupted normal U.S. relations with other countries. Where there had been injury to the United States, Jackson sought redress. He would not offend any nation, as he said, but neither would he tolerate insult either. And basic to it all, indeed the very core of his policy, was Jackson's fierce desire to win global recognition for the independence, sovereignty, and rights of the United States, something not always accorded in the past. The departure by Van Buren (approved by Jackson) from the diplomacy of the past was a willingness to accept any practical means to secure these ends. For example, where the Adams administration preferred treaty negotiations to bring about a reopening of the West Indian trade, Jackson was quite prepared to accept the British desire to do it through a legislative act. Nor was he unwilling to admit Adams's error in failing to respond to Parliament's offer in 1825 to accord American ships the same rights in the West Indies as the United States accorded British ships in American waters. "Practical" diplomacy was what the Jackson administration chose to pursue.[7]

Not that Andrew Jackson would tamely accept any response—or, worse, no response—from foreign powers. If, by their conduct, they chose to see a nationalistic President in full cry, he could oblige them. On the other hand, if he must be conciliatory or accept certain peculiarities or special demands from foreign countries he could also oblige. However, when conciliation and accommodation failed then he was quite prepared to use the threat of force or some other equally intimidating tactic. With regard to Great Britain, for example, he explained to Van Buren in a memorandum dated April 10, 1830, precisely what he meant.

> On the subject of our negotiation with great Britain, we ought to be prepared to act promptly in case of a failure. We have held out terms of reconciling our differences with that nation of the most Frank and fair terms —Terms, if England really had a wish to harmonise, and act justly towards us, ought to have been meet in that spirit of frankness and candor and friendship with which we proposed them. These terms being rejected our national character and honor requires that we should now act with that promptness and energy due to our national character. Therefore let a communication be prepared for congress recommending a non intercourse law between the United States and Canady, and a sufficient number of Cutters commanded by our naval officers and our midshipmen made revenue officers, and a double set on every vessel, etc. etc. This adopted and carried into effect forthwith and in six months both Canady and the Westindia Islands will feel, and sorely feel, the effects of their folly in urging their Government to adhere to our exclusion from the West India trade.[8]

A conciliatory approach with a willingness to accept practical solutions to problems in foreign affairs, but always ready to act with "promptness and energy" to make foreign nations "sorely feel" the consequences of treating the United States contumaciously—that was Jacksonian diplomacy.

In the case of the West Indian trade the British had in fact triggered the President's annoyance by long delays to McLane's gentle prodding. Lord Aberdeen, the British foreign secretary, insisted that his government was more than willing to reconcile differences with the United States—but then nothing happened. The Duke of Wellington, the prime minister, assured McLane early in 1830 that a decision about the trade would be reached before Parliament met. Still nothing. Finally McLane explained to Aberdeen that what he was negotiating was far more important than the West Indian trade. At stake was the future of American-British relations.[9] And that produced the breakthrough.

McLane's aggressiveness and persistence surely revealed his own self-confidence in the success of his mission. He told several friends in Washington that if Congress would only show good will and move immediately to end American restrictions against British ships coming from the Islands on a reciprocal basis, then perhaps the British might quit their stalling. His optimism and plea for Congressional action was shared with administration leaders in the House and Senate.[10] Suddenly, by the spring of 1830, it looked as though an entirely new approach to United States–British relations was emerging.

But Jackson himself contributed the major action to the breakthrough in the negotiations by sending a message to both houses of Congress on May 26, 1830, notifying the members that he expected any day to success-fully conclude the West Indian business on the basis of reciprocity and requesting permission to act independently after Congress adjourned.[11] Since the President had no authority to remove United States restrictions on his own, and to avoid the necessity of calling a special session, he suggested to Congress the "propriety" of authorizing him to do it by proclamation once Britain agreed to permit American ships into the West Indies. Congress complied immediately. The bill passed on May 29 ap-proved presidential action to open American ports to trade with the British West Indies whenever Jackson had assurance that Britain would reciprocate. McLane received notification of the congressional action but was cautioned to use discretion about warning the British of Jackson's intention to recommend a total stoppage of all trade with Canada and other British northern provinces in the event that his negotiations col-lapsed.[12]

Aberdeen and Wellington were duly informed. Unfortunately the death of the king necessitated the dissolution of Parliament and seemed to guarantee another delay. But Aberdeen responded in a little over a month. In view of the congressional action in response to the President's request and the apparent repudiation by the American people of the claims advanced by the Adams administration, Aberdeen said that a pledge could now be given that Britain would remove all restrictions to trade relations between the United States and the British West Indies once Jackson implemented the law by his proclamation.[13]

McLane exulted. "I have the satisfaction to inform you," he wrote Levi Woodbury among dozens of others, "that I have succeeded in my negotiations for the colonial trade! This government consents to restore to us the direct trade with her colonies upon the terms of my proposi-tion." He allowed as how "a good deal of labor & solicitude & persever-ance" went into this "most happy result."[14] Aberdeen had a few condi-tions, principally over interpretation of the American statute, but Jackson agreed to raise no fuss over it. Basically the President got what he wanted. He appreciated that in the "haste and confusion" of the closing moments of the congressional session there could be minor problems in the word-ing of the legislation but he wished to do nothing that would delay or defeat the agreement. He sat quietly and said nothing.

Jackson received notification from McLane shortly after returning from Tennessee in 1830. He positively radiated good will. He had won an important victory in gaining international attention to U.S. demands. A proclamation opening American ports was immediately prepared and Jackson issued it on October 5, 1830. After a series of "Whereases," the proclamation concluded: "Now, therefore, I, Andrew Jackson, President of the United States of America, do hereby declare and proclaim that such evidence has been received by me, and that by the operation of the act of Congress . . . the ports of the United States are from the date of this proclamation open to British vessels coming from the said British possessions, and their cargoes, upon the terms set forth in the said act."[15]

A dispatch informed McLane of Jackson's action. He in turn communicated this to Aberdeen and on November 5, 1830, two days later, the British lifted their restrictions.

It was a diplomatic triumph. A source of annoyance and discord stretching back over several decades had at last been cleared away. It was an important step in a growing sense of friendship between the two nations. Past hostility gave way to mounting cordiality.

The Democratic newspapers trumpeted the victory.[16] The news came in time to influence several congressional elections and it considerably bolstered the administration's sense of achievement. In his second message to Congress in December, 1830, the President expressed his gratitude. More than trade was involved, however. "This event is hailed with great and deserved joy by our citizens," he said privately, "not only on account of the direct benefit which they will derive from it, but as indicating a disposition on the part of Great B to meet us half way in establishing the relations between the two countries upon that fair and reciprocal basis which is the only sure guarantee for their future peace and the steady advancement of their prosperity and fame."[17]

Nor was the West Indian trade the administration's only diplomatic success. Jackson's policy of giving no offense and suffering none included a belief that foreign nations that were responsible for damages to property belonging to American citizens should pay for them. During the fierce Napoleonic wars of the early nineteenth century, Americans had suffered commercial losses at the hands not only of the French but also of smaller nations that had been obliged to enforce Napoleon's maritime decrees. American spoliation claims existed against France, Russia, Denmark, Portugal, the Netherlands, and the Kingdom of the Two Sicilies. Although previous administrations had sought a settlement of these claims, the complaints were rudely brushed aside. Then Andrew Jackson assumed the presidency.

All his life Jackson had been taught that honest men paid their just debts. He believed that this principle also applied to nations. And he was not the man to be lightly dismissed by a wave of the hand. The debts were legitimate obligations and Andrew Jackson wanted them paid. He insisted that foreign nations act honestly and honorably toward the United States, that they accord this nation the respect it deserved. The phrase he had used in his annual message—"to ask nothing that is not clearly right, and to submit to nothing that is wrong"—was something he decidedly meant.

The President's persistence and determination to gain international recognition of United States rights, along with a willingness to engage in endless discussions without tiring or giving up and a disposition to compromise to resolve deadlocks, brought notable successes to several prob-lem areas. A few of these successes were resolved through executive agreements, principally with Russia and Portugal, which accepted and paid the amounts negotiated. These agreements served as unfortunate precedents for the settlement of a widening list of problems in foreign relations, thus weakening the treaty-making power of the Senate. Al-though this constitutional invasion was not deliberate (or conscious) and resulted more from Jackson's own personal presidential style than from calculation, it contributed to the growing authority of the chief executive in assuming the primary role of chief of state. Andrew Jackson had al-ready begun to transform the presidency.[18]

Resolutions of other diplomatic problem areas were more involved. These necessitated considerable diplomatic maneuvering. Probably Jack-son's first success outside the area of executive agreements came through negotiations with Denmark. According to American figures the total claims against that nation stood at $2,662,280.30 as of 1827. Denmark did not dispute the legitimacy of the claims, only the right of the United States to dispute the decisions of its prize courts once they were ren-dered. Henry Wheaton, the *chargé d'affaires* in Copenhagen and an out-standing international lawyer, argued persuasively that prize courts were designed to fix responsibility and when their judgments were unjust an aggrieved nation had a right to protest. Wheaton persisted in his argu-ments and finally the Sieurs Henry Count de Schemmelman, minister of foreign affairs, and Paul Christian de Stemann, president of the chancery, accepted his position. They agreed to allow claims for the "seizure, de-tention, and condemnation or confiscations" of American vessels, cargoes, or property by Denmark in the years 1808–1811 and pay a lump sum of $650,000. This figure represented total victory to Jackson. "We have obtained $150,000 more than our merchants had agreed to accept as full indemnity," he gloated to Overton. "The sum to be paid being *$650,000* $500,000 having been offered by our merchants to have been recd in full." Jackson made no such boast when he reported the settle-ment to Congress: "It is an agreeable circumstance in this adjustment that the terms are in conformity with the previously ascertained views of the claimants themselves, thus removing all pretense for a future agita-tion of the subject in any form." The convention was signed in Copenha-gen on March 27, 1830, and submitted to the Senate for approval on May 27 with a presidential message that said in part: "The convention pro-vides by compromise for the adjustment and payment of indemnities to no inconsiderable amount." In one of its last actions before adjournment the Senate gave its consent.[19]

A far more difficult and serious dispute over spoliations existed with France. Here Jackson's mettle was tested. In one of his private memoran-dums, the President reflected on the instructions to be given the Ameri-can representative to that country. Whoever goes to France, Jackson wrote, should be "friendly, decorous, & peaceful, but firm,—demanding a final answer to our complaints."[20] "Our complaints" centered mainly on damages sustained by Americans because of Napoleon's Berlin and Milan Decrees. Successive administrations badgered the French for payment and got nowhere. "Nothing can exceed the reluctance of a *Frenchman,* or of the *French* government, to pay money," wrote William C. Rives of Virginia, Jackson's appointee to the French post. "This has grown into a proverb here; & when the demand comes in the shape of *indemnities for past wrongs,* the effect upon them is still more revolting. They never will, therefore, pay our claims . . . unless they are made to believe that their interests . . . require it."[21]

The situation was complicated by French counterclaims, some of which related to the Louisiana treaty. No one seemed to know how much money might be involved in all these claims and counterclaims, although in Rives's instructions Van Buren identified five classes of American claims against France, broken down according to time, in which the last class involved claims subsequent to 1805 and came to $6,256,647.69.[22] However, Rives was not given a precise figure to shoot at when negotiating with the French.

It was difficult for the French to give credence to American complaints. Considering all France had done for the United States in the past it refused to believe that the relationship between the two countries could be jeopardized by their refusal to pay these debts. "They have no idea that we would even go to war for them," reported Rives, "& they think our own interests will restrain us from the adoption of any measure directed against her commerce."[23]

Clearly Jackson needed to disabuse them. He expected foreign nations to treat the United States with the courtesy and respect owed to a sovereign and independent nation; and that meant paying legitimate debts. The President rose to the challenge. In his first annual message—in a passage Van Buren did not write—Jackson stated in unequivocal language that he would drive the issue to a conclusion "and in a spirit that will evince the respect which is due to the feelings of those from whom the satisfaction is required."[24] Some in the United States thought his words threatening, and indeed the French foreign minister, Prince Auguste de Polignac, took exception to them. But Rives assured the minister that Jackson had no "intention of holding a menace over the head of a foreign power." Just pay us, he asked, pay what is owed.[25]

Jackson's strong stand in his first message began the process that slowly weakened the French resolve against parting with money. Rives pressed the advantage by warning Polignac that "a *crisis* must soon occur" if the matter was not adjudicated. He also noted the improved United States relations with Russia and Great Britain and speculated on what might happen if France lost the friendship of the United States. "I have come to adopt the vulgar rule of interpreting dreams," Rives told Van Buren,

"& from what is *said* to conclude that the precise contrary will be *done*. This has been always, more or less, the character of French diplomacy, & is . . . a recognized postulate upon which all foreign agents make their calculations in dealing with the government."[26]

Unfortunately these slow-moving negotiations came to a complete halt with the July Revolution in Paris in 1830, and Rives had to begin all over again. "The energetic language of the President's message in December last gave them some uneasiness on this subject," he reported; "but after they got over this *fit of the pouts,* they persuaded themselves that it was meant only to pacify the claimants, at home, & that the government of the U.S. would never make it a serious question between the two nations." He again called for a *"strong* ground taken by the Government of the United States."[27]

Jackson obliged. His second message, in December, 1830, not only pressed the claim but it also cooed cordiality and friendliness. He spoke of the "courage and wisdom" of the French people in initiating a rebellion and the "high character" of their new king, Louis Philippe. These handsome phrases pleased the king and gave the French a convenient excuse to acknowledge the compliments by paying the debt. And it worked. Shortly thereafter the American minister was informed that his Majesty's government was prepared to offer the United States 15 million francs to settle all claims.[28]

The offer shocked Rives. He rejected it out of hand. It was far too little. It was, he said, a "mockery." The French countered by offering 24 million —their last offer—payable in installments over a six-year period. Again Rives rejected it. He demanded 40 million. Eventually the French agreed to raise the figure by 1 million and pay 4 percent interest over the six-year period, and this, they said, was their absolute final offer. It came to a little more than $5 million. Since his instructions never gave him a precise figure to demand and since Van Buren had mentioned approximately $6 million as the estimated claims for the the Napoleonic period, Rives decided to accept. A treaty spelling out the terms and including a reciprocal reduction of duties on French wines and American cotton was signed on July 4, 1831. Jackson received it on September 3 and submitted it to the Senate on December 6, 1831. It received unanimous approval.[29]

The nation broke into wild applause over this diplomatic achievement. The phrase "to ask nothing that is not clearly right, and to submit to nothing that is wrong"—a phrase Jackson himself devised—was hailed in the newspapers as a policy worthy of comparison with Washington's "no entangling alliances." Jackson's administration, declared the Democratic press, had brought a "series of diplomatic triumphs, unequalled with any similar period of government." They noted that through his statesman-like efforts Jackson had obtained $12,500,000 in indemnity from foreign nations while Adams as President got absolutely nothing.[30]

The French ultimately capitulated and agreed to pay the debts because

Jackson convinced them that otherwise they risked the loss of American friendship. Given present political conditions in western Europe France dared not take this risk. On top of that, Jackson's determination to collect the debt could not be turned aside. His persistence matched French delaying tactics. But a great deal of credit belongs to Rives, who encouraged the President to take a strong stand and who himself applied considerable pressure on the foreign ministry. He identified French fear from the beginning of his mission and played on it like a virtuoso.

Still a third, though less significant, diplomatic success was achieved by the fledgling Jackson administration. The injury to American commerce resulting from the exclusion of United States ships from the Black Sea ended when Turkey agreed to a treaty on a most-favored-nation basis. Again Jackson demanded and obtained recognition of American rights. "I felt it my duty," he said, "to leave no proper means unemployed to acquire for our flag the same privileges [on the Black Sea] that are enjoyed by the principal powers of Europe." Consequently he dispatched commissioners to the Sublime Porte and a treaty ultimately resulted in which trade with Turkey was inaugurated for the first time. American vessels were accorded access to the Black Sea without any limitation of time. The treaty also provided for extraterritorial juridical status for American citizens residing in Turkey. "The most friendly feelings appear to be entertained by the Sultan," Jackson informed the Congress, "and an enlightened disposition is evinced by him to foster the intercourse between the two countries by the most liberal arrangements." This treaty began the process of opening the entire Near East to American trade and commerce.[31] It also helped to hurry along a new most-favored-nation treaty with Russia, which was signed on December 18, 1832.

Jackson was not as successful with Mexico, and the fault was largely his own. He had hoped to conclude a commercial treaty with Mexico and an agreement over the boundary separating the two countries. But instead of choosing an honest and able minister as he had for the French and British posts, the President picked a certifiable scamp in Anthony Butler. Several times Jackson came close to discharging his minister but each time Butler outfoxed him with fake hopes for the success of his mission. Old Hickory's expansionist fervor ultimately defeated him. He failed to exercise rational judgment. Even when he realized what dishonest schemes his minister practiced on the Mexicans, Jackson did not recall him. The President lived in hope that one of Butler's frauds might work and deliver Texas into his outstretched arms.

With McLane's outstanding success in Great Britain Jackson informed Butler of his desire to duplicate that victory in Mexico. "How gratifying would it be to me," he wrote, "to include within the list of our good works in the foreign relations of the Union, a Treaty with Mexico adjusting the points in disput in regard to *our boundary,* and establishing a proper commercial intercourse!"[32] As President, Jackson expected to press on with his expansion of the American Empire. Unfortunately for his dreams he compromised his principles and allowed corruption and incompetence to represent him in Mexico.

Despite the fiasco in Mexico Jackson's record in foreign affairs during his first administration was nothing less than outstanding. Only one real embarrassment reached public notice. John Randolph of Roanoke had been appointed minister to Russia and after an interminable delay finally arrived in St. Petersburg in the summer of 1830. He hardly unpacked. He stayed a total of twenty-nine days. Without a by-your-leave he simply abandoned his post. He repacked his bags, headed for London, and then notified Jackson of his action. He wrote, he said, "in pain and sickness." He informed the President that he was going to the continent "to try and renovate my shattered system." He hoped he might return to St. Petersburg in the spring "if it pleases God." Jackson sympathized with his condition, as a fellow sufferer, and offered nothing but understanding and compassion. One year later Randolph tired of his sojourn abroad and returned home.[33]

The importance of choosing competent ministers to implement his purposes was dearly learned by Jackson. He stumbled again and again over the next several years. Many of the mistakes and failures of his administration stemmed immediately from his own inexcusable misjudgments about the people in whom he placed his confidence and trust. He sensed the direction he should pursue but he failed to appoint the proper agents to achieve his objectives. Probably Jackson's principal failure as President centered mainly on his many wretched appointments. A few of them nearly destroyed him.

CHAPTER 17

Founding the Washington *Globe*

ANDREW JACKSON'S SUCCESS IN FOREIGN AFFAIRS was shaped in part by his willingness to compromise—a readiness to find a middle solution to a problem. In similar fashion and in a spirit of conciliation he tried to put his domestic house in order. The Eaton affair was the one persistent problem that seemed to defy solution. It left him angry and bitter. It disrupted his entire life, even necessitating the banishment of the Donelsons from the White House.

Jackson offered his nephew a compromise. As he packed his bags to return to the capital in the late summer of 1830 he said he was willing to have Donelson return with him to Washington and leave Emily home; at the same time Peggy Eaton would also remain in Tennessee. It was not the best arrangement in the world but at least it was a step towards a future reconciliation. Donelson accepted, and this pleased the old man. Once back in the White House, Jackson renewed his efforts to settle the domestic unpleasantness. He offered to take Emily back but only with the understanding that she follow his direction with respect to her social obligations. Emily refused. Both she and her husband were as much committed to principle as their uncle. And he could not command them to give way. The next few months proved extremely difficult for both men. "Altho we have been visited by a vast number of ladies and Gentlemen," Jackson informed Emily, "and inundated as usual, by officer hunters, still we have appeared loansome—several times have I been left to sup alone." The separation from his wife also troubled Donelson. "Pray," Uncle, he wrote, "let me know what are the difficulties which I have to remove before my family can be allowed to occupy the same house that I do."[1]

This disruption of his lifestyle only further soured Jackson's relations with his cabinet. The cabinet! What a mockery of his efforts at reform. Instead of standing united behind him the department heads conspired with Calhoun "to put Major Eaton out of the Cabinet, & disgrace me, and weaken my administration . . . [and] lessen my standing with the people, so that they would not again urge my re:election."[2] Ingham, Branch, Berrien—all of them traitors. The situation, he said, could not go on this way indefinitely. "A cabinet ought to be a unit," Jackson told Donelson; "otherwise like the interests of a divided house it must fall." And fall it will! "Ere long I will have my cabinet as it ought to be, a *unit*," he wrote to John Coffee. "The double dealing of J.C.C. is perfectly unmasked."[3]

By the close of 1830 Jackson knew that he must run for a second term, strike Calhoun from the ticket, and flush away the disloyal and disruptive members of his cabinet. To pull this off without unduly agitating the American people would take all his political skill and wisdom.[4]

He started cautiously. But he soon identified all the major actions he must take. The first important step in the process was Jackson's decision to replace the *United States Telegraph* as the party mouthpiece with another newspaper. Duff Green, the editor of the *Telegraph,* proved highly unsatisfactory as the spokesman of the Democratic party. His editorials lacked fire. Repeatedly, Jackson complained that he did not defend the administration or his policies. Sometimes Green distorted those policies to conform with his own thinking. The nullification issue was a case in point. "The disposition which Gen. Green has exhibited to identify Gen. Jackson and his friends with the nullifiers of South Carolina," said Amos Kendall, "has excited anew their desire for another paper here."[5] Jackson explained his position on nullification to Green several times, not that it did any good.[6] Furthermore, Green was particularly weak on the Bank issue, something very important to Jackson's entire reform program. But everyone knew that Green took his editorial direction from Calhoun, not the President. So when Calhoun's villainy was "unmasked," Green's departure as spokesman was just a matter of time.

But who could replace him? The kind of editor Jackson wanted—aggressive, loyal, committed to his reform policies, and with a "slashing pen"—would be hard to find. As it turned out, however, the selection of an editor proved easier than anyone expected. An obvious choice was Amos Kendall, former editor of the Kentucky *Argus of Western America* whose performance in office since Jackson's inauguration had placed him close the President as adviser and friend. Kendall was highly agreeable to the idea of taking the post himself. Indeed when he first arrived in Washington there had been some thought of forcing Green to take him on as a partner.[7] A little later when Kendall's nomination as fourth auditor appeared to be in jeopardy in the Senate, there was a distinct possibility that he would begin a new paper.[8]

By April, 1830 Green had so "wholly lost the confidence of the President," reported Kendall, that "whether I establish it or not, there will shortly be a *real* administration paper here."[9] When Jackson finally decided to take definite action in the late spring of 1830 he immediately turned to Kendall, who had studied the matter and had definite ideas about what needed to be done to insure success in an otherwise risky venture. But Kendall was also interested in becoming an agent to treat with the Indians on their removal, and Jackson would not tolerate an editor whose head was divided between two interests. Meanwhile William B. Lewis contacted E. W. Gooch, former partner of Thomas Ritchie on the Richmond *Enquirer*, but his demands were excessive so Lewis let the matter drop.[10]

Kendall consulted with William T. Barry, the postmaster general and his former comrade in the Relief war in Kentucky. Both agreed that if Kendall was disqualified, Francis P. Blair was the man for the job. His experience as an editor of the *Argus*, his "slashing" journalistic style, his commitment to Jackson and the principles of reform, and his close association with Kendall and Barry made him ideal. Kendall mentioned the possibility of editing a new paper to Blair and invited him to come to Washington in time for the opening of Congress in December, 1830. "We shall have to war with the giants," he told Blair. "Pluto is with them; we must summon Jupiter and Hercules to our aid. I *know* the President will enter with zeal into my views. Your sentiments in relation to the Bank will make him zealous for you."[11] In the meantime several of Blair's articles on the nullification question were shown to Jackson and the President pronounced them all excellent. Unlike Green, Blair got Jackson's position exactly right. Also, he stated it forcefully and persuasively. Thus when Kendall finally suggested Blair to Jackson the Old Hero responded with enthusiasm.

The decision to oust Green and invite Blair to Washington came the first week in October, 1830, shortly after Jackson's return from Tennessee. In extending the invitation to Blair, Kendall outlined the program an administration paper must follow to satisfy the President. "The course a paper should pursue here is obvious. It must be for a thorough reform in the government." That was the first priority. In addition the paper must be "mildly opposed to the South Carolina nullifiers, in favor of a judicious Tariff and of National Internal Improvements or a distribution of the surplus revenue, for the payment of the national debt . . . against the U.S. Bank and in favor of leaving the states to manage their own affairs without other interference than the safety of the whole imperiously requires."[12] All these things, Kendall believed, had Blair's unwavering support and agreement.

For Blair the offer came at an ideal time. He later revealed that he was a "man of broken fortune, forty thousand dollars in debt."[13] So he jumped at the offer. He resigned as clerk of the court of appeals and president of the Bank of the Commonwealth (his salary was only $1,000), rented out his farm on Benson Creek, and prepared to leave Kentucky. In Washington, meanwhile, Kendall pushed ahead with preparations to inaugurate a genuine "Jackson paper" that would speak authoritatively to Democrats around the country about the major issues and the President's attitudes toward them. Kendall believed that it would take only two thousand "punctual subscribers" (without considering the proceeds from advertising or jobwork) to yield a handsome profit. "So well satisfied am I that a newspaper may be profitable here," he assured Blair, "that I am ready to share an equal responsibility with you, write for it what I can, concede to you $1500 per year of the profits and rely upon an equal division of the rest for my compensation."[14] As for patronage Blair could expect cooperation from Barry and Van Buren as well as the war department, treasurer's office, the second comptroller, and the second and fourth auditors. Other department heads, in time, "would throw their patronage into your hands on its being understood, as it will be, that such a step would be acceptable to the President." In the beginning Blair could expect $4,000 a year in patronage, which would increase to $15,000 later on. "The personal exertions of the President and all his particular friends, may be relied on to give the paper circulation."[15]

Once the question of the editorship was settled Kendall took charge of establishing the newspaper. He negotiated with a printer for publication, started subscription lists, settled postal rates, and arranged other details. "Your time must be wholly devoted to writing and selecting for the paper," he instructed Blair, "and pushing your acquaintance with the affairs of government, members of Congress and gentlemen visitors." With respect to the publication of congressional proceedings "it is the opinion of our friends that if Green behaves well, you ought not to enter into competition with him for any part of it." If the department heads will give you their patronage "I shall prefer your having nothing to do with Congress. We want an establishment here which shall be independent of that body." You ought to see Green, Kendall further counseled, as soon as you arrive in Washington and "assure him of your friendly disposition without yielding to any of his plans or suggestions, or trammelling yourself with promises or pledges." The object was not to supersede the *Telegraph*—as least not yet—"but to furnish an auxiliary paper" devoted "exclusively to the support of the administration."[16]

Be careful of Calhoun's friends, Kendall cautioned. They will ply you with "all sorts of arguments to dissuade you from your purpose; but you must be prepared to turn a deaf ear to them all with the utmost politeness." On the other hand, the "men on whom you may entirely rely are Maj. Lewis, Barry, Eaton and the President." Jackson told me two days ago that you will have proper aid and predicted fifty thousand subscribers within six months. "I could not but smile at the old gentleman's extravagant notions. Van Buren will also treat you kindly."

Kendall promised to have all preparations completed so that the paper could begin publication the first week of the new congressional session. "The sooner it is done," he wrote, "the better; for all intrigue about it will then be at an end." As to lodging, you can board at the printer's, who also takes in a few congressmen during the session. But no final arrangements about this will be made until you get here. Kendall offered his own house for a few days upon Blair's arrival.[17]

Kendall not only arranged for the formation of the new Jackson paper but he immediately solicited subscribers from the most influential men he knew. "Now, I beg of you," he wrote Isaac Hill, "to aid in this enterprise by getting for Mr. Blair all the subscribers you can." He will have no aid from Congress and only a portion of what is available from the executive departments. Kendall then spelled out whose interests would be served. "In lending him your influence and aid, you will do that which will be acceptable to the President and all his real friends here with the exception of Gen. Green and a very few others." Green, of course, is annoyed. He claims, said Kendall, "that I and Mr. Van Buren have brought Blair here." The truth is that Van Buren was never consulted. The paper, he went on, will be "exclusively a Jackson paper and an administration paper." It will not place the interests of Van Buren or Calhoun or anyone else before those of the party and its principles.[18]

Kendall was not alone in drumming up subscribers for the newspaper. Jackson himself lent a hand. "You will receive inclosed the prospectus of a paper to be published here, by Mr. Blair, the former editor of the Ky Argus, and aid of Mr. Kendall," he informed John Coffee. "It is of the true faith, and I hope you and the Winstons will patronise it."[19] A full squad of politicians around the country were pressed into service to provide as many subscribers within their states as they could muster.[20] They were advised to advertise the paper as an administration organ, the sheet responsible for announcing Jackson's policies and will. "Genl. Jackson handed me a letter, this morning, containing a list of subscribers," said Major Lewis, which a southern politician had forwarded to him. He was assured that Judge Hayward would take care of Ohio, Major Campbell would handle Virginia, and Major Smith and Churchill C. Cambreleng, New York. "Without such a paper to sustain the *principles* of this administration," Lewis explained to Overton, "we should be in a bad way." But the paper got off to such a good start by winning a large following, especially in Congress, that its ultimate financial success was assured.[21]

Blair himself finally arrived in Washington to take up his duties on December 1. For weeks the White House had waited for him with keen anticipation. Each time Green failed to produce a satisfactory editorial on a vital issue, someone in the President's entourage would comment, "Never mind. Wait till Blair comes." Finally he arrived. And everyone in the White House was struck speechless by his appearance. A walking cadaver, Blair presented himself looking disheveled and nonplussed. He had a large gash on the side of his head from a recent accident in his carriage as it approached Washington. "Mr. Blair," said the apprehensive Lewis when he first encountered the wispy man, "we want stout hearts and sound heads here."[22]

Blair went immediately to see the President. Jackson studied him. Mousy-looking, hardly weighing more than a hundred pounds, Blair tried to look authoritative but his appearance defeated the intent. The two men sat down and had a long conversation and by the time it ended the President had completely forgotten about Blair's unprepossessing appearance. Within minutes Jackson warmed to the purpose of the interview. He explained that he had been elected "to carry into effect the great principles of reform called for by the people and for which I had been drawn from my chosen retirement." Unfortunately he had been plagued almost immediately by a conspiracy against Eaton, the ambition of Calhoun, a disruption in his own household, the efforts of nullifiers to undermine the principles upon which the Union had been founded, the corrupting atrocities of the BUS, the ineffectiveness of Green's *Telegraph*, and God-only-knows-what machinations of Henry Clay—all these complaints and more poured out of Jackson in this first conversation with Blair.[23]

So immediate was the rapport struck between the two men that Jackson explained to his visitor about the loss of his Rachel and what that had done to his life. He described the unhappiness in his household and how he, Donelson, and Emily all suffered on account of it. He also warned him to be on guard against publishing any articles written by his nephew. "There's my nephew, Donelson," said Old Hickory at one point, "he seems to be leaning toward the nullifiers. But he's my nephew. I raised him. I love him. Let him do what he will, I love him. I can't help it. Treat him kindly, but if he wants to write for your paper, you must look out for him."[24]

And on and on Jackson went, recounting his troubles and his expectations, his wish to restore virtue to public conduct and his frustration in contending with one harassment after another. Jackson was completely open with Blair, telling him frankly what was on his mind without any reserve whatsoever. And this was their very first interview. Obviously the founding of a *"Jackson paper"* in Washington meant a great deal to him and the future success of his administration.

Blair responded with equal candor. He admitted that his antagonism toward the U.S. Bank went back so many years in Kentucky he could scarcely remember its origins. He also affirmed his commitment to hard money. Most particularly he favored reduced government in Washington and said he believed that the world was governed too much. Everything Blair said struck Jackson as right on the mark. Of course Kendall in his many letters over the past two months had coached his friend and even outlined a program of purpose for the editor. Nevertheless Blair spoke his mind freely and his beliefs and opinions were advanced with such conviction and enthusiasm that Jackson had no doubt by the end of the interview that he had found the ideal penman to present him and his policies to the American public.[25]

Jackson practically vibrated with excitement. He insisted that Blair return for dinner. Naturally the little man accepted. But to his horror he discovered on his arrival in the East Room a great company of social dignitaries, all elegantly dressed. Blair had only one presentable coat, and that a frock-coat. He was mortified when he entered the glittering room. He slunk into a corner, dreading the moment of Jackson's appearance. But when the President entered the room he immediately located Blair, walked over to him, and led him to a place of honor at the table at his own right hand. Blair was transfixed. His devotion and loyalty to Jackson from that moment never slackened.[26]

A warm personal relationship between the President and the editor immediately followed. Their families interacted. Mrs. Blair knitted woolen socks for Jackson and regularly entertained him in her home. Her daughter, Elizabeth, whom the General called "Betty," copied letters for him, and he arranged an appointment for one of the sons, Montgomery, to West Point and provided another son, James, with an office in the navy. Unlike Kendall, whose friendship with the President always remained on a business level, Blair practically became a member of Old Hickory's family.[27]

Having satisfied himself about the editor's competence and loyalty and commitment to republicanism, Jackson took extraordinary measures to assist the fledgling journal. Officeholders were "encouraged" to subscribe as an act of good will toward the President. Since congressional patronage was temporarily unavailable, Jackson was anxious that the printing of the executive departments should go to Blair—or a goodly portion of it. He later told the secretary of state of "the pleasure he felt on hearing that he intended giving the job for printing the Diplomatic correspondence to the Editor of the Globe." Jackson assured the secretary that the "work will be done faithfully and *well* and as cheap as it can be by any one." Of course he expected this sort of cooperation from all department heads. "It would be mortifying to see his establishment . . . embarrassed for the want of that support which the work of the Departments afford."[28] When a few cabinet officers failed to respond to the President's obvious wishes an executive order was immediately circulated directing all department heads to prepare a quarterly account of the sums paid, and to whom, for printing in their respective departments. No one missed its intent. The order constituted a command. And the command was obeyed.[29]

Like Jackson and Lewis, other Democrats were startled when they first encountered Blair. Several of them called at the offices of the newspaper after it had been established and expected to find a man of "Kentuckian proportions"—tall, powerfully built, physically imposing, pistols at the ready, knife peeping out of his belt—but were sadly disappointed when led to a shriveled little man sitting in a corner with a writing-pad on his knee, scribbling furiously. They came to appreciate him, however. Those scribblings shook the party and the nation.[30]

The first issue of the new *"Jackson paper"* appeared on Tuesday, December 7, 1830. It was a semiweekly and Blair called it *The Globe*. The name was possibly derived from *Le Globe*, a Parisian newspaper that supported the recent July Revolution in France; or it may have resulted from Blair's delight in claiming that "like the great globe we inhabit [it] was created out of nothing" since he did not invest a single dollar to get it started. It survived in the beginning on partial patronage and subscriptions paid *in advance* for six hundred copies at $10 per annum.[31]

The first issue consisted of four sheets. It announced at the very outset that the editor's purpose was "to dedicate this paper to the discussion and maintenance of the principles which brought General Jackson into office." Blair then proclaimed the *Globe*'s basic philosophy. "The world is governed too much," he declared, and that motto served as the paper's lodestar.[32] It was hoisted to the masthead. "We firmly believe that this Government will come to an end, if end it must, in wicked attempts to govern too much." Fortunately there was nothing to fear as long as Andrew Jackson served as chief executive. "By the firmness of the President, the career of the Government in that path has been arrested."

Subscriptions poured into Blair's office from the moment of the announcement of the *Globe*'s inauguration, and within weeks the paper was a paying success as loyal Democrats signed on and canceled their subscription to the *Telegraph*.[33] Blair set up residence on Pennsylvania Avenue with his family and visited the White House practically every day to speak to the President and take his direction. Everyone knew that Jackson dictated policy, even National Republicans. Unlike the *Telegraph*, said congressman Edward Everett, the *Globe* was *"his* paper."[34]

Blair fulfilled every one of Jackson's expectations. His writing possessed all the vigor and thrust that Green's lacked. His total commitment to the President's program of "reform retrenchment and economy" meant he functioned on the same intellectual wave length as Jackson. There were other similarities. Their temperaments were alike. Both exuded force and energy. Both possessed an aggressive style. In the coming battles it was a great service to the administration to have a newspaper capable of sharing the burden of conflict. Jackson, the thunderer, now had a device to send his roar cascading across the nation.

The founding of the *Globe* provided Jackson with the final instrument he needed to secure absolute control of the Democratic party. It was a vital piece of organizational apparatus necessary for the permanent establishment of the party, and it added structural unity to bind Democrats closer to their leader. The *Globe* aided Jackson not only in proclaiming his principles and policies but in securing discipline and loyalty among the party faithful. It played an essential role in Jackson's continuing efforts to gain control of Congress in order to put through his reform program. As Van Buren once said, a partisan newspaper was the *sine qua non* in the operation of party politics. With it, he declared, we can endure a thousand "convulsions"; without it, we might as well "hang our harps on the willows."[35]

In the coming years few men surrounding Jackson matched Blair's influence in the formulation of policy and the definition of issues.[36] But one reason for Blair's longevity as a presidential adviser was his recognition that only Old Hickory decided policy, ran the Democratic party, and headed the government. Blair might make important contributions to the President's thinking, as did other men, but he knew who ultimately held the reins of power and made the final decisions. Blair never stepped out of line. He served loyally and effectively. As a consequence he gave the President a "blaring" trumpet to sound his call around the nation and summon the American people to follow him as he continued to reform and reshape the structure of American politics.

CHAPTER 18

The Purge

THE IMMEDIATE SUCCESS OF THE *GLOBE* only exacerbated the internecine struggle going on within the Jackson administration and further convinced the President that he must unite his cabinet or get rid of it.[1] The troublemakers, said Lewis, "are what we call here Calhoun Jackson men."[2] Green, however, blamed it all on Van Buren. Indeed, local gossip in Washington insisted that "the President was a mere automaton in the hands of Mr. Van Buren." Supposedly it was done very skillfully, by indirection. Barry and Eaton were judged "entirely subservient" to the Magician, and they "controuled" William B. Lewis who, in turn, controlled the President. Jackson himself was put down as a "weak and unpractised man, of little experience and no business habits—that he scarcely ever read any thing, not even a newspaper. . . . *Gen. Jackson was a plain farmer and not a statesman.*" He simply performed as the Magician directed.[3]

Other rumors fingered Calhoun as the troublemaker. "I became thoroughly convinced, during my stay of nineteen days at Washington," wrote one visiting politician, "that an insidious and unprincipled conspiracy was on foot, among some of the pretended friends of the President, to destroy his usefulness and prostrate his influence in the nation, for the purpose of erecting on the ruins of the true Jackson party, a new *mongrel party,* with John C. Calhoun and John McLean at its head, and Messrs. Ingham, Berrien, McDuffie &c as it main pillars."[4]

None of the rumors flattered Jackson, although rumormongers took pains to place blame for the discord on the contending factions. But in failing to resolve the disunity within his cabinet the President was seen as fumbling and ineffectual, unable to control either his administration or his family. Several concerned politicians visited the President to see for themselves, expecting to find an infirm and despirited old man. They were pleasantly surprised. "The person of Genl Jackson," reported one of them, "is very commanding, altho at first sight you would take him for an old farmer, plain though dignified, free, perfectly affeble in his manner, face wrinkled and war worn—on further view of him he presents the appearance of a man of much tough and determination of purpose, in short his appearance was altogether deferrent from the one which I had fixed in my imagination. I think no unpregidist mind could see him without forming an opinion of him highly favourable."[5]

Despite the seriousness of the internal disorder within his administration Jackson personally suffered no loss of confidence in himself or anxiety about his ability to correct the situation. "The old man is in good health, good *spirits,* and quite *confident,*" reported Lewis.[6] For one thing he was always a man of enormous self-confidence who gained strength from adversity. For another he knew what he had to do and was simply trying to discover the best way to do it at the least political cost. Also he was pleased with the several successes his reform program had already achieved over the past twelve months.

Jackson detailed these successes in his annual message to Congress delivered on December 7, the day following the opening of the new session. He crowed about his triumphs in foreign affairs, the wisdom of the Maysville Road veto and his steady progress toward obliterating the national debt. Rather slyly and cleverly, Jackson argued the right of the executive to use his veto at will to implement his reform program. Many congressmen denied this right, insisting that the veto could be used only to negate legislation deemed to be blatantly unconstitutional. The right of the President to veto any bill at will did not accord with the practice of past Presidents and if sustained added a vast new power to the executive branch.[7]

Naturally Jackson praised his Indian removal policy. "It gives me pleasure to announce to Congress that the benevolent policy of the Government . . . is approaching a happy consummation." Free from the control of the states, the Indians can now pursue their own culture and happiness, he said, "under their own rude institutions"; they will be encouraged to cast off their "savage habits and become an interesting, civilized and Christian community." Toward the "aborigines" of this country, he went on in this racist outburst, "no one can indulge a more friendly feeling than myself" or try to make them a happier and more prosperous people.[8]

After mentioning a need to adjust the tariff schedules, Jackson concluded his second message like his first. He assaulted the National Bank. This worst of all corrupting influences in American life got only a few lines in this long message but what it got spelled trouble.

The importance of the principles involved in the inquiry whether it will be proper to recharter the Bank of the United States requires that I should again call the attention of Congress to the subject. Nothing has occurred to lessen in any degree the dangers which many of our citizens apprehend from that institution as at present organized. In the spirit of improvement and compromise which distinguishes our country and its institutions it becomes us to inquire whether it be not possible to secure the advantages afforded by the present bank through the agency of a Bank of the United States so modified in its principles and structure as to obviate constitutional and other objections.[9]

Raising a constitutional objection to the BUS seemed like a "red herring." Presumably the constitutional question had been settled long ago when Presidents George Washington and James Madison signed separate bills creating the Bank; and if not then, surely when Chief Justice Marshall handed down his favorable opinion about the BUS in *McCulloch* v. *Maryland*.[10]

Not according to Jackson. The Bank, to him, was a malignant and malevolent influence in national life. It was a danger to free elections, a threat to individual liberty. It was also unconstitutional. Jackson cared not a fig for Marshall's arguments.[11]

In the original version of this portion of his annual message Jackson struck harder and more frequently at the question of constitutionality.[12] Jackson permitted the alteration, probably at Van Buren's or Lewis's suggestion, because it in no way lessened the tone or intent of his criticism. His few sentences put everyone on notice that he meant business.

The message went on to suggest the organization of a financial institution as a branch of the Treasury, based on public and individual deposits, but without the power to make loans or purchase property. This bank would handle the funds of the government and might sell bills of exchange at a "moderate premium" in order to pay for the cost of the operation. Since it would not be a corporate body with stockholders, debtors, or property and since it could not manipulate the "hopes, fears, or interests of large masses of the community, it would be shorn of the influence which makes that bank formidable" and a danger to a free society.[13] But Jackson did not offer these suggestions so much as a recommendation as a means of calling Congress's attention to a matter that needed immediate attention.

The message was one of the longest ever submitted to Congress. Much of it dealt with Indian removal and the justification for that policy. But the care and skill that went into the argumentation on all the issues raised in the message indicated Jackson's seriousness and determination to exert forceful leadership of the Congress to resolve the issues in the manner he directed. The success of his reform program depended on it.

The President's persistent sniping at the BUS annoyed many congressmen, however, some of whom believed that the best way to handle his complaints was to ignore them or shunt them aside. When the President's first message scored the BUS for its failures, the House Ways and Means Committee, chaired by George McDuffie of South Carolina, returned a report specifically denying the accusations. That galled Jackson. The fact that Green published this report without comment and that McDuffie was a Calhoun henchman further agitated the President. The Senate Finance Committee, chaired by Samuel Smith of Maryland, turned the responsibility of a report over to the Bank's president, Nicholas Biddle!

Jackson's return to the attack in his second message won the same congressional reaction as his first. The quicker they could bury his complaints the better. Only this time the senator from Missouri, Thomas Hart Benton, entered the contest. His ideas about money, the debt, and the BUS closely paralleled Jackson's. He decided to act on the President's call and fire a blast at the BUS before Congress could quietly quash the matter. Some Democrats, he knew, were willing to accept Jackson's demands for change but preferred to wait until the Bank's charter came up for formal renewal in 1836. "I foresaw that, if this course was followed," Benton wrote, "the Bank would triumph without a contest—that she would wait until a majority was installed in both Houses of Congress—then present her application—hear a few barren speeches in opposition;—and then gallop the renewed charter through."[14]

So Benton rose in the Senate to smite the mighty Bank. With any luck he might arouse the electorate to the dangers posed by this behemoth. As it turned out Benton delivered a most powerful speech, one of his best in a long record of rousing, rip-roaring orations. He pulled out all stops. The chamber reverberated with his blasts. "What a state of things!" he cried. "What a condition for a confederacy of States! What grounds for alarm and terrible apprehension, when in a confederacy of such vast extent, so many independent States, so many rival commercial cities, so much sectional jealousy, such violent political parties, such fierce contests for power, there should be but one moneyed tribunal, before which all the rival and contending elements must appear! but one single dispenser of money, to which every citizen, every trader, every merchant, every manufacturer, every planter, every corporation, every city, every State, and the federal government itself must apply, in every emergency, for the most indispensable loan! and this, in the face of the fact, that, in every contest for human rights, the great moneyed institutions of the world have uniformly been found on the side of kings and nobles, against the lives and liberties of the people."[15]

Benton sizzled with passion. At last Jackson had a real champion in the Senate. At last he had a strong congressional voice. And joined to that voice came the powerful sounds of the *Globe,* which seconded Benton's demand for the Bank's demise. Francis Blair's prejudice against the BUS, like Kendall's, had been nurtured for many years and had risen to passionate heights. His editorials crackled with imprecations against this "moneyed tribunal."[16] And they delighted his chief.

As soon as Benton finished his speech in the Senate, Daniel Webster called for a vote to end the discussion and demonstrate the strength of the pro-Bank forces. Benton's efforts were treated with contempt. His speech went unanswered. By ignoring him the other senators hoped to inform Jackson of their clear intention. But the vote surprised them. It was close—too close—20 to 23. It was a strong vote against the Bank, said Benton, "enough to excite uneasiness but not enough to pass the resolution" for a full-scale debate. "The debate stopped with the single speech; but it was a speech to be read by the people—the masses—the millions; and was conceived and delivered for that purpose."[17]

Blair publicized the speech. Other Democratic journals reprinted it. Soon Benton, whose effort had "emptied the Senate chamber" but "roused the people," heard a chorus of praise from every section of the country. He was later complimented, he wrote, for delivering the opening salvo which "crippled the bank, and given it the wound of which it afterwards died."[18]

As Benton said, these events caused the Bank men considerable uneasiness. A few of them assured Nicholas Biddle that despite the President's huffing and puffing he would sign a recharter bill if it contained a few modifications. But Biddle knew better. The President, he wrote, "aims at the destruction of the Bank."[19]

Jackson savored every word of Benton's speech. It said everything he wished—and with feeling. Moreover, Blair sent it circling the country with just the right opening comments to insure public discussion. By the beginning of 1831 the general opinion that the BUS could win recharter easily or that Congress could simply ignore the President's complaints abruptly changed. What did it, besides Benton's speech, was the *Globe*'s announcement that Jackson would seek reelection to the presidency in 1832; sooner or later, therefore, his complaints must be faced and acknowledged.

Although the decision to seek reelection had come earlier, the formal announcement was delayed until Congress reconvened. Like many other things, it served a political purpose. First it headed off other candidates and signaled the Calhoun faction to get in line. Then it notified the BUS, Nicholas Biddle, and all pro-Bank congressmen that the President demanded serious attention to his complaints, which they had studiously ignored.

Jackson's decision to run for a second term jolted Washington because of its suddenness. Everyone had taken him at his word that he planned to serve only one term. Now they tried to read its larger political meaning and some saw it as a ploy to block any movement in Pennsylvania for John McLean.[20] Calhoun's friends figured that it was aimed at getting rid of the Vice President and that Van Buren had conceived it. They always saw the Magician as their relentless tormentor. Under the circumstances there was only one course of action for them to take and they pursued it with vigor. Somehow a reconciliation between Jackson and Calhoun had to be arranged—somehow a truce negotiated. Since the General was desperate to unite his cabinet, perhaps he might be receptive to the idea. It was worth a try.[21]

Calhoun had not yet arrived in Washington from his home in South Carolina to begin the new congressional session, so it fell to such mutual friends as Senators Felix Grundy of Tennessee and Richard M. Johnson of Kentucky along with Samuel Swartwout (who knew of Van Buren's opposition to his appointment) to make the first move. On behalf of the Vice President, they proposed to patch up the misunderstanding.

Van Buren said that he was sitting with Jackson one day in a room of the White House that had been converted into a studio by Ralph Earl. The painter worked at one of his many portraits of the President. A servant entered to announce that Swartwout was in the President's office and wished to see him. Jackson excused himself. When he returned he told Van Buren that the "whole affair was settled." He recited the terms of the reconciliation but the little man subsequently forgot what they were. "He did not appear entirely satisfied with what he had agreed to," Van Buren reported, "but said the matter was done with and he would think no more about it."[22]

The Magician accepted the decision with his usual outward calm. He even expressed to Jackson "my gratification at the result." As it happened, at precisely this time, the New Yorker gave an enormous party. "It was a great state dinner," recounted one of the guests. A "mixture of all politics" attended the dinner, with Mrs. Randolph and her daughter, Mrs. Trist, Mrs. Johnston, Mrs. Dickinson, and Mrs. Howard of Baltimore the principal ladies in attendance. As usual a number of invited guests failed to appear. Then, all of sudden, who should walk into the room but the Vice President himself. "Among others the Vice President himself" attended, said a startled guest, "in spite of the quarrel supposed to be not so much impending as actually existing between him & Van Buren." The Magician returned the compliment of the Vice President's visit with every show of courtesy. And the dinner itself went gloriously. They sat down at 6:30 P.M. and did not rise until 9:00. "Among the luxuries served were string beans & green peas preserved of course from last spring but imitating very tolerably the fresh article."[23]

The full particulars of the reconciliation were never revealed. There is some evidence to suggest that part of the agreement included the destruction of the correspondence between Jackson and Calhoun concerning the Seminole Controversy, but that is not certain.[24] However, the two men supposedly agreed never to mention the subject again. Another part of the arrangement involved a visit by Calhoun in which he would leave his card for the President; then he would be invited to dine at the White House.

Whatever the arrangements, unfortunately, the reconciliation collapsed almost immediately. For reasons best known to himself Calhoun decided to *publish* the Seminole correspondence, despite the supposed agreement to destroy it, and that single desperate act terminated any possible hope for reconciliation. Perhaps the Vice President thought his action would advance the reconciliation by demonstrating the existence of a conspiracy against him; perhaps he thought he could prove Van Buren's "duplicity" in the conspiracy; somehow he believed that publication would improve his situation, otherwise he never would have committed such an incredible blunder. The stupidity of his action defies belief. It was monumental. Jackson was pathologically sensitive about his actions in Florida[25] and any publication of documents that failed to support all his claims about the adventure was certain to invite a cataclysmic explosion. Calhoun's action was sheer, inexplicable folly.

Senators Grundy and Johnson, who sympathized with Calhoun's motives, went to Francis Blair with a request that he publish the documents in his newspaper. Blair flatly refused. He told them that publication would cause a rupture with the President and surely result in "the ruin of Mr. Calhoun."[26] Perhaps this reaction worried the two men because Grundy went to John Eaton and showed him what the Vice President intended to publish, asking him to point out anything which he felt might cause excitement or be "misconceived."[27] When the reading ended and several of Eaton's suggestions were noted, Grundy asked his friend if it contained anything to which Jackson might feel compelled to reply. Eaton thought not, although he wondered what the newspapers might do with it and where that might lead. As the two men started to leave, Grundy made one last request. "Will you see Gen. Jackson and explain to him what has taken place? I will see Mr. Calhoun, and if the course we have taken be approved you shall be informed."[28]

But Eaton did not speak to the President about it. "Upon reflection," and probably with Lewis's advice, he said, "I thought it improper to do so." The day following the interview Eaton received a note from Grundy "stating that all was right . . . the suggestions offered had been adopted." To this Eaton made no response. Naturally, then, Grundy assumed that the President had also approved.[29] It was a deliberate deception.

A pamphlet containing the Jackson-Calhoun letters, along with a prefatory address, was readied for publication by Duff Green's *Telegraph*.[30] The evening before it was to be issued to the public a copy of the entire pamphlet was sent to Eaton with a request that he show it to Jackson so that he could read it before it came out. Again, Eaton did nothing. Since the Vice President was presumed to be the instigator of the plot to ostracize and humiliate Peggy, Eaton let Calhoun think that Jackson approved the pamphlet and its publication. It was sweet revenge.

Actually the President was not totally innocent of what was going on. He may have been playing cat-and-mouse with Calhoun, pretending to go along with a reconciliation while at the same time keeping up a wary guard. He was very suspicious of the efforts of Swartwout, Johnson, and Grundy, and of course he recognized that they were concerned about Calhoun's political good in attempting this reconciliation. What troubled Jackson was the general Washington gossip to the effect that Calhoun had been gathering correspondence relative to the Seminole affair and that its publication would greatly embarrass the administration. Lewis knew about this as early as January 13, which means that Jackson also knew.[31] "The gossips of Washington," said Van Buren, spread the rumor about the correspondence, and the newspapers "gave loose and contradictory accounts of its contents."[32] In self-defense Jackson also gathered evidence, writing to Overton for assistance in his search. He received two letters from Overton written on January 22 which evidently provided precisely what he wanted. "I am now fully prepared for defence," Jackson responded on February 8, "should it become necessary to make one— The conduct of Mr. Calhoun has been truly astonishing, he has been growling & grumbling, in petto, and his friends intimating that he has written a pamphlet, others of his friends deny this—he has shewn the correspondence between him & myself, & has been cutting his own throat as fast as he can politically—My own opinion is, that the whole has been a political movement, without any intention of comeing out before the public—be this as it may, I am prepared for defence, and will make him understand the old adage, 'O that my enemy would write a Book.' "[33]

So, the old scoundrel knew about the pamphlet all the time. As a matter of fact rumors of Calhoun's plans were so rampant that he could not help but know what was happening. Besides, Blair discussed it with him.[34] It was even bruited about that Calhoun would single out Van Buren as the man responsible for resurrecting the controversy in order to further his political career. "The city all agog about the controversy between Mr Calhoun & Van Buren," wrote Edward Everett to his wife on February 11; "the rupture is supposed to be impending. At the French minister's, Van Buren went up to Calhoun & offered him his hand. Calhoun turned on his heel & went off; and it is said that a very angry pamphlet is to be published by Calhoun in a day or two."[35]

The evidence seems conclusive that Jackson not only knew when the pamphlet would be published but what direction its main thrust would take. Even so, he chose to pretend ignorance. He chose by his silence to let Calhoun cut his own throat. As Francis Granger of New York told Thurlow Weed days before publication, "It will make a devil of a buzzing, but my own opinion is that Calhoun will suffer more by it than anyone else."[36]

The buzzbomb exploded in print on February 17, 1831—nine days after Jackson penned the portentous words, "O that my enemy would write a Book." The fifty-page octavo pamphlet was entitled, "Correspondence between Gen. Andrew Jackson and John C. Calhoun . . . on the subject of the course of the latter, in the cabinet of Mr. Monroe, on the occurrences in the Seminole War." In the introductory address, Calhoun explained to the American people his purpose in publishing the correspondence. "I have come before you, as my constituents, to give an account of my conduct in an important political transaction, which has been called in question, and so erroneously represented, that neither justice to myself nor respect for you will permit me any longer to remain silent; I allude to my course, in the deliberations of the Cabinet of Mr. Monroe, on the Seminole question." There then followed copies of James A. Hamilton's letter to John Forsyth, Forsyth's letter to Crawford, a few letters of Jackson's about Crawford's accusations that Calhoun had called for the General's censure on account of his supposedly unauthorized invasion of Florida, and of course many letters of Calhoun that spoke to his defense. Anyone reading the publication immediately concluded that it had two apparent purposes: to justify everything Calhoun did in Monroe's cabinet; and to prove the existence of a plot to annihilate Calhoun's political career, a plot concocted and supervised by Martin Van Buren. Although Van Buren's name was never specifically mentioned, no one missed the name of the culprit responsible for this monstrous scheme of political assassination. It was so blatant that Van Buren demanded that Green insert a notice in the February 25 issue of the *Telegraph* that he unequivocally denied having anything to do with hatching a plot against the Vice President. Any "assertion or insinuation" that he sought to prejudice Calhoun in the opinion of the President was "unfounded and unjust."

The bomb shook not only Washington but the entire country. "Mr. Calhoun's pamphlet is the all absorbing subject of conversation in this part of the country," wrote John Williams in Tennessee to Van Buren. "The pamphlet & the comments of the Telegraph newspaper have made a strong impression on the public mind." What made it so reprehensible was that it held up the Jackson administration to public ridicule by revealing the scandal of the personal feuding that had been going on in the cabinet for the past two years. He revealed something that the public had not fully realized before. Now they knew, and it shocked and saddened them. Most Democrats agreed that Calhoun had argued his case quite effectively but they also agreed that he had done himself, the President, the party, and the country a great disservice. He washed dirty political linen for all to see, and that was inexcusable. In the northern, middle, and southern states, with the exception of South Carolina, Calhoun's "attack on the President" was uniformly condemned.[37]

It did not take long for the party line to come down from the White House. On February 21 the *Globe* carried an editorial. "Mr. Calhoun's publication . . . was wholly uncalled for. It is a firebrand wantonly thrown into the [Democratic] party. Mr. Calhoun will be held responsible for all the mischief which may follow." The denunciation echoed in hundreds of other pro-administration newspapers. "Calhoun is a dead man." He must be shunned by all loyal Democrats as a disturber of party harmony. "War, open war, is now the cry," trumpeted Amos Kendall. Calhoun and Green must be "put down." The period of tender regard and consideration for the *Telegraph* was over. Having published the infamous pamphlet it deserved to go under. In a matter of weeks, predicted Kendall, Blair will torpedo Green with a "few short hits." To "kill off Duff," Blair later admitted, "was really my interest."[38]

The two newspapers opened fire on one another and a lively controversy ensued. Like Jackson, Blair thrived on controversy. His editorial salvos landed right on target. With the repudiation of the *Telegraph* the administration now needed more than a semiweekly to fight its battles, so the *Globe* was elevated to the status of a daily newspaper. To finance this change "the friends of the President in Washington and elsewhere" were called upon to demonstrate their loyalty.[39]

The decision to read Calhoun and Green out the Democratic party came from Jackson himself. He pronounced the sentence by calling the Vice President's publication an act of self-destruction. "They have cut their own throats, and destroyed themselves in a shorter space of time than any two men I ever knew." Without my consent, he complained, they "published part of my private letters." Surely they deserved the fate that awaited them.[40]

Despite appearances, these events suited Jackson to perfection. Now he could get rid of Calhoun and his friends without appearing to be acting at the behest of Eaton and his wife. Now he could restore harmony to his cabinet by purging it of Calhoun's friends. It took no great political punditry to predict this purge.[41] In fact within five days after the publication it was understood that Samuel D. Ingham, the secretary of the treasury and Calhoun's close ally, would be axed.[42] Ingham and Green were the two most disloyal administration men and once they had been purged a degree of harmony would be restored.

Naturally everyone believed that Van Buren had conjured up these phenomenal events. Only a magician of his skill could produce such wonders. Poor Jackson was a block-headed puppet in his hands. "The President is an ignorant weak superannuated man, scarcely fitter for the office he holds, than a child of ten years old would be," wrote Senator Samuel Bell of New Hampshire, "Van Buren is President *de facto.*"[43] These comments about Van Buren's masterminding the course of events became so widespread that James A. Hamilton felt obliged to write Jackson and assure him of Van Buren's innocence. As one of the important men who set the revelations about the Seminole controversy in train Hamilton knew that Van Buren was guiltless of any manipulation. With respect to Calhoun's publication, Hamilton told the General, "I have the best evidence to prove that Van Buren determined . . . to have no concern in the matter." "It is manifest that he is the object of attack." The poor, maligned Van Buren even believed that Jackson and Calhoun had reconciled.[44]

Actually the publication deeply depressed the secretary of state and he worried about its long-range effect on his career. Letters to his friends invariably inquired about the public reaction to the publication. Their responses disturbed him profoundly.[45] He knew the gossip but he knew not how to contradict it. So he reverted to type. He simply said nothing and tried to appear imperturbable. He avoided all comment. When attending parties he immediately planted himself down at a card table and played whist for the evening. "This prevents his falling in, with company which he does not like."[46]

The division within the party placed Van Buren in an awkward position. He was being made to play the scapegoat, the villain of the piece. He knew there would be a great deal of public sympathy for Jackson—and also for Calhoun, once the initial shock of the Vice President's revelations wore off. Eventually, he knew, Calhoun would be seen as the benighted and innocent victim of a dastardly plot, conceived and executed by a master magician. Only Van Buren would suffer opprobrium. Only he would bear "long-lasting" criticism. "The offence charged against me," he later recorded, "was in every respect a heinous one. . . . It would have been difficult to conceive of a case better calculated to excite the unmeasured condemnation of all good citizens." Van Buren, said one man, "is a gone dog. *he is done.*"[47]

To protect himself and his career, the New Yorker had to turn things around. He had to win public sympathy, and the only thing he could think of was resignation. Nothing else would suffice. But the thought of it depressed him further. During the spring of 1831 he was noticed as "looking pale & spiritless—he has been much secluded of late & has not appeared at the *fetes* as heretofore."[48]

While all this transpired, Jackson seriously contemplated publishing a defense of his actions during the Seminole War in which he would directly accuse Calhoun of deceiving him into thinking he had supported him in Monroe's cabinet.[49] But he wisely decided against it. He shrewdly calculated the enormous political cost such an indulgence would be,[50] and set the project aside. What he really needed to do, as well he understood, was to remake his official family, something he had determined upon months before. But a cabinet purge is a disaster at best, for which the President usually suffers the loss of popular confidence in his ability to lead the nation. Still it had to be done. His cabinet had to be united.

The decision to purge was Jackson's—always had been Jackson's—but the way it finally happened resulted from Van Buren's need to extricate himself from his "uneasy" position.[51] The "unmeasured condemnation" of him by "all good citizens" for his supposed involvement in Calhoun's "downfall" dictated that he retire from his position. To do so might be seen as an act of self-sacrifice to spare Jackson further humiliation. Maybe then he might inherit a measure of public sympathy. Also, Jackson would certainly interpret his immolation as undying loyalty, and his appreciation for such acts frequently verged on the extravagant. Thus it only required a moment's thought for Van Buren to decide what he must do. He later convinced himself that his resignation was submitted to restore the General's "tranquility and comfort." Actually he did it for himself. And he had little choice.[52]

Van Buren explained his reasons for resigning to his son Abraham, who totally agreed with him. The only real hurdle, as they both recognized, was the problem of explaining it to the President. It must be done carefully to avoid giving a wrong impression about his motivation. Several times Van Buren started to tell the President but fell silent at the crucial moment. His son teased him about his timidity. On one such occasion Van Buren and Jackson were out horseback riding when a severe thunderstorm developed and they took shelter in a small tavern near a racetrack. They were confined for several hours. Jackson's spirits were low. Donelson had returned to Tennessee to induce his wife to return to Washington under their uncle's conditions and William B. Lewis was his only companion in the White House.[53] Emotionally, Jackson was drained. He just sat there, saying nothing, looking morose. It was one of the low points in his life. Finally the storm abated. The two men remounted and headed home, riding at a rather brisk canter. Suddenly Jackson's horse slipped on the wet road and almost threw his rider. Van Buren quickly seized the bridle and the horse regained his footing.

"You have possibly saved my life, Sir!" said Jackson. Then he muttered something to the effect that he wondered whether his escape from death had been fortunate or not. He was really low. Van Buren could not bring himself to speak of resigning.[54]

A few days later the secretary tried again. It was a bright, sunny day and as usual the two men went riding. Passing Georgetown, Van Buren noticed he had lost his glove. He told the President to go on while he turned back to look for it. After finding it, Van Buren put his horse to a gallop to catch up. As he rode he felt exhilarated. This is the moment, he thought. He caught up to Jackson and just as they were turning from the Potomac toward Tenally Town the President said something about feeling better once his niece and nephew returned. Their return, he felt, would provide some relief from his domestic troubles.

"No!" cried Van Buren. "General, there is but one thing can give you peace."

"What is that, Sir?"

"My resignation!"

The words jolted the old soldier. Van Buren could never forget the look on Jackson's face as he pronounced the words.

"Never, Sir!" Jackson responded in solemn tones, "even you know little of Andrew Jackson if you suppose him capable of consenting to such a humiliation of his friend by his enemies."[55]

The response was exactly as Van Buren feared. After all, what was the Eaton malaria, as he liked to call it, except a mistaken notion about friendship?

Van Buren fell silent for a moment. After collecting his thoughts he pleaded that Jackson surely knew he would sooner "endure any degree of personal or official injustice and persecution" than appear to desert a friend. But the President had the nation to think about, said Van Buren. If he would just hear him out he thought he "could satisfy him that the course I had pointed out was perhaps the only safe one open to us."[56] For four hours Van Buren talked. Jackson listened, his mind whirring. Then he suddenly interrupted the long monologue with a question. What would Van Buren do if he accepted his resignation? Oh, Van Buren shrugged, probably return to the law.

Out of the question, responded Jackson. That would be an admission of defeat. It would provide a "triumph to our enemies," and that he would never suffer without a fight.[57] They talked of other possibilities. The English mission was mentioned. Not only would it provide a suitable situation for the New Yorker but it would get him out of the country for a spell.

When the interview finally ended Jackson said he would think the matter over. He told Van Buren to return the next day for further discussions.

Jackson knew Van Buren must go. His resignation would simplify things by allowing the President to discharge Ingham, Berrien, and Branch and improve the quality of the entire cabinet. Still it would be hard to lose such a loyal and capable man. Or was the little fellow deserting a sinking ship? He would find out soon enough.

Van Buren arrived at the White House early the next morning. He could tell from Jackson's appearance that he put in a sleepless night. When he spoke the President showed no emotion. He was "unusually formal and passionless."[58]

"Mr. Van Buren," said the General, "I have made it a rule thro' life never to throw obstacles in the way of any man who, for reasons satisfactory to himself, desires to leave me, and I shall not make your case an exception."[59]

The words struck Van Buren like a sledgehammer. The secretary jumped from his chair before the President could say another word. This was precisely what he feared, he cried, and he swore his motives were selfless. If only Jackson could peer into his heart and examine his "inmost thoughts" he would know the truth. "Now, Sir!" he declared, "Come what may, I shall not leave your Cabinet," not until you say "you are satisfied that it is best for us to part. I shall not only stay with you, but . . . stay with pleasure."[60]

Jackson seized Van Buren's hand. The little man had responded with all the melodrama and sentimental gush the old man needed to hear.

"You must forgive me, my friend," Jackson bawled, "I have been too hasty in my conclusions—I know I have—say no more about it now, but come back at one o'clock—we will take another long ride and talk again in a better and calmer state of mind."[61]

Obviously Jackson did not need convincing about the wisdom and necessity of Van Buren's resignation. What he needed were assurances that Van Buren acted out of loyalty. Otherwise he would never have responded so emotionally and quickly to Van Buren's protests of devotion and fidelity.

By the time the two men met again the matter was settled. Jackson asked Van Buren's permission to discuss the matter with Eaton, Lewis, and Barry—his only other trustworthy associates. That night he thrashed the matter out with his friends. Lewis had long championed Van Buren's cause and like everyone else he quickly saw the necessity of letting him go. It would ease the difficulty of demanding the resignation of the others. In the final discussions Van Buren joined the group. When this parley ended, Van Buren invited them all to his house for supper to mark the occasion. As they were walking down the street, Eaton suddenly stopped them.

"Gentlemen," he exclaimed, "this is all wrong! Here we have a Cabinet so remarkable that it has required all of the General's force of character to carry it along—there is but one man in it who is entirely fit for his place, and we are about consenting that he should leave it."[62]

Everyone laughed, but Eaton persisted. Addressing Van Buren, he said: "Why should you resign? I am the man about whom all the trouble has been made and therefore the one who ought to resign." Van Buren remained silent. What could he say? And no one else tried to talk Eaton out of it. Later they asked about Peggy. Would she consent to his resignation? Eaton thought so, but he was asked to consult her first. When he reported back that she supported his decision, Jackson agreed to accept both resignations.

Many historians have assumed that Van Buren executed a "masterpiece"[63] of manipulation in convincing Jackson to accept his resignation and of prompting Eaton to submit his own. Actually there was no manipulation, and Van Buren has been vastly overrated as the precipitator of the cabinet dissolution. What he did came of necessity. He was in a very awkward and dangerous position. Van Buren himself swears he never thought of inducing Eaton's resignation and there is every reason to believe him.[64] Once the New Yorker resigned the obvious thing for Eaton to do was follow suit. Their departure then lightened the burden of dismissing the others.

In the final discussion Eaton said he wished to submit his letter first, to which Van Buren cheerfully acceded. On April 7, 1831 Eaton tendered his resignation and gave as his reason his wish to retire to private life. On

April 11 Van Buren followed as scheduled, but his letter alluded to the suspicions and charges brought against him and his desire to spare Jackson further distress from these unfounded accusations. The President responded graciously to both men, but his reply to Van Buren conveyed a real sense of loss. "In the most difficult and trying moments of my administration," he wrote, "I have always found you sincere, able, and efficient—anxious at all times to afford me every aid."[65]

A short time later Jackson and Van Buren took a walk and suddenly found themselves in front of the home of the Eatons. On the spur of the moment they decided to pay the lady of the house a visit. But their reception was distinctly "formal and cold." Peggy made it very clear that she was deeply disappointed in the President over the resignation of her husband. They stayed long enough to know that her attitude was no "passing freak," but rather a "matured sentiment." A few moments after they left the house, Van Buren turned to Jackson and expressed his surprise at her attitude. "There has been some mistake here," he said.

Jackson shrugged. "It is strange," he muttered, and turned away.[66]

CHAPTER 19

The Kitchen Cabinet

THE *GLOBE* ANNOUNCED THE RESIGNATIONS of Eaton and Van Buren on April 20, 1831. The news astounded the Magician's friends in New York, who had no inkling of the impending purge. At first they imagined a blowup between their leader and the President and they worried over the consequences, particularly *"if the other incumbents were to remain in the cabinet."*[1] But Van Buren reassured his henchmen. There had been no "collision" with Jackson. The President's action had been dictated "by true patriotism" and "is also as wise as it is honest." Notify my friends, he asked his former law partner, Benjamin F. Butler, so that the news will not unduly alarm them. Then he hinted of things to come, alerting his lieutenants to Jackson's larger design. "Of what further changes may take place it does not become me to speak."[2]

The announcement of the cabinet shake-up redeemed Van Buren somewhat from the untenable position he found himself after the publication of the Jackson-Calhoun correspondence. The loss of his high office immediately generated sympathy and many Democrats regarded the resignation "as highly patriotic and as giving evidence of his warm personal attachment" to the President.[3] Calhoun noted the shifting popular mood but still regretted nothing in going public. "I had truth & justice with me," he declared, and "I published the correspondence with great reluctance, and only from a sense of duty to myself & to the people, and not with the least reference to any advantage in a political point of view."[4]

Once he had the Eaton and Van Buren resignations in hand Jackson promptly sent for Ingham and Branch—Berrien was out of town—and told them what had happened. He spoke with them separately on April 18 and left it to them to decide on their own course of action.[5] At first

315

Ingham played coy, demanding more precise information about Jackson's wishes. Jackson invited him back for another interview the next day and informed him flat-out that he wanted his resignation. Ingham returned to his office and executed the request, acknowledging in his letter of resignation the President's "kindness with which you have expressed your satisfaction" with his tenure as secretary. In accepting what he had commanded, Jackson graciously offered to "bear testimony to the integrity and zeal with which you have managed the fiscal concerns of the nation."[6] The exchange of letters with Branch was more formal and curt —but it served the purpose nonetheless. Privately, Branch denounced the President. If it is suggested, he wrote, "that I am responsible for the want of harmony in the Cabinet the charge is unjust. . . . I went as far as a man of honor could go in endeavoring to promote a good understanding. . . . But it seems I was expected to go still farther, and not doing so, it has been held good cause for my dismissal."[7] Berrien was dispatched a short while later in a conversation with the President held on June 13. The formal letters were exchanged two days later.[8]

The dissolution of the cabinet stunned the nation. In the history of the nation nothing like it had ever occurred before. No one ever dreamed it could happen. The American people had only a dim notion of the Eaton scandal and were totally unprepared for the shocking news of the mass resignations. "It produced a sensation." Forty years of orderly government suddenly disrupted by this "catastrophe." To many the government itself seemed on the verge of collapse. It was a constitutional crisis of major proportions, they thought. The resignations were "unexpected," admitted John Tyler of Virginia, and I never thought "that matters would have taken the course they have." Jackson, it appeared, had shaken the government to its foundations. "We live in an age of revolution," chortled Henry Clay as he pondered the political rewards for his party as a result of this debacle. "Who could have imagined such a cleansing of the Augean stable in Washington? a change, almost total, of the Cabinet."[9]

Obviously the public regarded a cabinet purge as virtually the equivalent of the fall of the government. Certainly the government as they knew it. Cabinet officers constituted a vital part of the executive branch and held their posts through the confirmation of the Senate as well as appointment by the President. Their sudden departure without any indication or explanation to Congress raised fears about the future course of republican government in America.

So horrifying did the dissolution appear to the electorate that Jackson's enemies genuinely believed that the resignations would destroy him. The entire incident demonstrated his incompetence as chief magistrate, they said. Surely the people could see that now. Even Andrew Donelson admitted that the resignations cast doubt "upon his *independence, upon his sagacity,* upon his ability to move without the *appliances* of unseen hands."[10] Newspapers of the National Republican party hurried to exploit their advantage. A caricature entitled "The Rats Leaving a Falling House" appeared in the Philadelphia press and was widely circulated. In the picture four sleek rats—Berrien had not yet resigned—with faces resembling the four secretaries scamper around the room as Jackson struggles to maintain his balance on a chair that is breaking under him. His right foot presses upon Van Buren's tail as if to detain him. An "altar of reform" is toppling over along with an "imp," armed with a broom, who has the head of an ass, the body of a monkey, and the wings of a bat. The room is hung with papers on which is inscribed the single word, "Resignation." The President's "spitting-box and broken tobacco-pipe" lie on the floor. Two thousand copies of this print were sold in Philadelphia in a single day.[11] Samuel Ingham thought the caricature terribly amusing. "You have nearly escaped the ludicrous caricatures which the wags are amusing themselves with all over the U.S. at our expense," he told Berrien. "Some of which could not fail to make you laugh especially as your own face is not quite discernible."[12]

Jackson was appalled by the reaction to his purge. It mortified him to think that the public might misunderstand or misinterpret what he had done. His mood blackened. At a wedding party he attended with Van Buren the two of them "resembled funeral guests rather than wedding guests," and at a dinner for the diplomatic corps the President slumped glumly in his seat. Samuel Ingham said he "found it pleasant to see the old chief napping constantly & finally sinking his eyes on his plate for an hour. Mr. V.B. had a sad fit of Dyspepsia, I tried to cheer him up and encourage his appetite, but the viands did not relieve."[13]

Around Washington the purge was seen as Van Buren's supreme achievement. Even Democrats thought so. "I consider the course that has been adopted as a master stroke of policy," wrote Isaac Hill, "worthy of the head and heart of the 'Great Magician.' " Amos Kendall agreed. "The step unquestionably originated with Mr. Van Buren."[14]

Although overrated in arranging the cabinet dissolution, Van Buren did assist in the selection of the new cabinet. He consented to take the London mission—almost everyone (including Clay[15]) acknowledged its suitability either to get him out of the country or to serve as his reward —once Louis McLane agreed to return home. To compensate McLane, he was offered the Treasury post vacated by Ingham. In Van Buren's place, Edward Livingston was invited to head the State Department. At first he hesitated but when he conferred with Jackson their old friendship reasserted itself. "With a slap on the knee," Livingston related to his wife, the President said: "my friend Livingston, you must accept." And so he did. After moving into the State Department office the new secretary could not help thinking that he sat "in the very cell where the great magician . . . brewed his spells."[16]

To replace Eaton, the President wanted Hugh Lawson White, his original choice for the post. In addition to everything else, White's appointment would vacate the Senate seat he held, which presumably would go to Eaton. Jackson wrote to his old friend on April 9 and offered him the position, inviting him at the same time to live temporarily in the White House since the senator's wife had recently died of tuberculosis. "With me you can live (I have a large room for you) who can sympathise with your sufferings . . . and the duties of your office will give employ to your mind." Not only will you "render important services to your country," said Jackson, "but an act of great friendship to me." Unfortunately, White refused. He lacked the necessary qualifications for the office, he said, and abhorred the idea of accepting political favors from a friend.[17]

The rejection saddened Jackson. "I cannot do without you for the next two years," he wailed. So much remained to be done to root out corruption in government and complete the task of reform and these goals were impossible without a united cabinet of strong, active, intelligent, and loyal members.

> The great principles of democracy which we have both at heart to see restored to the Federal Government, cannot be accomplished unless a united Cabinet who will labour to this end. The struggle against the rechartering of the U. States Bank are to be met. The corrupting influence of the Bank upon the morals of the people and upon Congress are to be met and fearlessly met. . . . Between Bank men, nulifyers, and internal improvements men it is hard to get a Cabinet who will unite with me heart and hand in the great task of Democratic reform in the administration of our Government.[18]

But White persisted.[19] Perhaps it was not so much the reasons he gave as a lingering displeasure over the original distribution of cabinet positions and a concern about the Lewis–Van Buren axis that seemed to hold Jackson in its grip. In any event his steadfast refusal nettled the old man. It "has produced unpleasant feelings in me," he confessed, "and from the treachery of *man,* which I have experienced, makes it necessary for me to deliberate well before I fill this place." White's refusal necessarily upset the strategy to replace him in the Senate with Eaton. Eventually the former war secretary ran in 1832 against Tennessee's other senator, Felix Grundy, but was defeated.[20]

Jackson called a meeting with Eaton, Livingston, and Van Buren to discuss a replacement for Eaton, but the best they could offer was Colonel William Drayton of South Carolina. Fortunately he refused the honor. He might have been weak on the Bank question and unenthusiastic about Indian removal. Since removal was central to Jackson's intentions for the war department the conferees finally decided on Lewis Cass. Big, burly, sad-faced, Cass enjoyed a very respectable reputation as territorial governor of Michigan for the past nineteen years. Van Buren liked him and told Jackson that he was "a most able administrator." Born in New Hampshire, Cass trudged across the Alleghenies on foot at age nineteen. He studied law, served in minor political posts in Ohio, fought in the War of 1812, and then received the post of territorial governor in 1813 from President Madison. Most important of all was his soundness on the Indian question.[21]

To provide consideration for New England in the composition of his new cabinet, and possibly gain political capital for the next election from that section of the country, Jackson agreed to offer the Navy Department to Levi Woodbury, former governor and United States senator from New Hampshire and one of Van Buren's supporters. Shrewdly, Jackson first checked out the appointment with Isaac Hill, and although Hill had some reservations he judged him an excellent choice. Jackson said he was "much gratified to learn that the appointment of Mr Woodbury is gratifying to Mr Hill—This will unite all friends in New Hampshire." A bit testy at times and a little temperamental, Woodbury proved an inspired choice. Decidedly above average in ability and intelligence, he brought a strong legal mind to the affairs of the administration and provided Jackson with the loyalty and dedication he so desperately needed.[22]

Even shrewder was the choice of Roger Brooke Taney of Maryland for the office of attorney general. The President knew Taney and admired him both for his legal skills and his talent as a political organizer. An early Jackson supporter, Taney virtually ran the Democratic campaign in Maryland in 1828 as chairman of the Jackson Central Committee. A towering legal intellect, trained in Baltimore, he presently served as attorney general of his state and had earned a commendable reputation as scholar and politician. He was a Catholic, the brother-in-law of Francis Scott Key (who acted as go-between for the President in the negotiations), and belonged to the landed aristocracy of southern Maryland. Scrawny, with bulging forehead, sharp nose, and a slightly protruding lower lip, Taney looked like a clerk on account of his nearsightedness (which caused him to squint) and a perpetual stoop.[23]

The sole departmental officer to survive the purge was William T. Barry against whom only incompetence could be charged. The Senate had already begun to poke around in the operation of the post office and as yet had produced nothing but howls of protest from Barry and assurances of his department's efficient service. But he had proved his loyalty to the Jackson–Lewis–Van Buren team and was therefore retained. Since the post office head was not yet a regular member of the cabinet an exception could be made in his case. The possibility of charges of official misconduct was also given as a reason for retaining him![24]

Despite the genuine worry over the "collapse of the government" and reports that a conniving puppeteer controlled the President's actions, Jackson himself pronounced the cabinet shake-up an important preliminary to his renewed efforts to advance a program of reform. "All things appear to be progressing well *every where*," he said, "—and I have no doubt but the next congress will be more harmonious than the two last

—The electioneering demagogues will *now* have to appear unmasked, & female caucuses to foster & cherish [?] feuds between the families of the heads of Departments will cease, and my whole cabinet will be a unit."[25]

A cabinet united and harmonious. That was Jackson's sole desire, and he hoped he had finally achieved that long-sought goal. His new cabinet was distinctly better than the first in terms of talent, loyalty, and dedication, but it still lacked brilliance or any visible mark of particular distinction. Indeed, with Van Buren gone it almost seemed lusterless.

Unfortunately the transition from the first to the second cabinet produced further unpleasantness, which again embarrassed the administration and endangered the program of reform. Once more it reminded Americans that passionate and violent men controlled national affairs.

It began in May when the *Telegraph* informed the rest of the country (just after the resignations were announced) what had been common gossip in Washington for the last two years. The Eaton scandal in all of its unholy glory tumbled into national view. Among other things, the journal claimed that Ingham, Berrien, and Branch had refused socially to receive the notorious Peggy, implying that their subsequent dismissal from office resulted from their moral rectitude. After the account appeared, Eaton expected the three men to disavow the statement; when they failed to do so he wrote them directly and demanded to know whether they would sanction or repudiate the article.[26] Branch was out of town at the time and Berrien discreetly disclaimed responsibility for the piece, but Ingham blasted Eaton with the full force of his anger and resentment. "You must be a little deranged," he said, "to imagine that any blustering of yours could induce me to disavow what all the inhabitants of this city know, and perhaps half the people of the United States believe to be true."[27]

Eaton promptly demanded satisfaction. Ingham refused. Whereupon Eaton arranged to have him waylaid on the streets. In self-defense, Ingham armed himself and traveled with a small bodyguard, including his son. He appealed to Jackson, naming several others as parties to the assassination plot. Calmly and politely, the President asked those whom Ingham had accused if they were indeed guilty. They naturally denied it.[28] Only Eaton admitted his need to defend his honor. He published a "Card" in the *Globe* admitting he had stalked the frightened Ingham but swore he did not attempt to force his way into Ingham's house. "I passed by, but at no time stopped at or attempted to enter his house, nor to besiege it by day or by night."[29]

The day after Eaton's "Card" appeared in the *Globe*, Ingham fled the city. He took the four o'clock stage and paid the driver a bonus to get him to Baltimore as fast as possible. Jackson called his flight "infamous," "ridiculous & cowardly."[30] Indeed, the entire Eaton affair might be termed infamous. It ruined reputations and terminated friendships. And it was all so needless.

Shortly after Eaton's senatorial defeat, Jackson appointed him governor of the Florida Territory, and still later sent him to Spain as U.S. minister. Unfortunately, the two men quarreled after Eaton's return and they remained estranged to the end of their days. A sad close to a tragic episode.

It was an embarrassing summer for the administration as the *Telegraph* revealed more and more details about the "Eaton malaria." The *Globe* ably defended the President, but many National Republicans confidently predicted Jackson's fall at the next election. "To what new developments are these things to lead?" sighed Governor John Floyd of Virginia. "Step after step our degradation seems hurrying on."[31]

This unnecessary and ridiculous affair left Jackson confused, agitated, and depressed. Almost every letter he wrote during the course of it was a quarrel. He advanced tortuous arguments to prove the rectitude of his cause and actions. When his nephew, Andrew J. Donelson, referred to "Lewis and Co." (revealing his own pent-up jealousy), Jackson tore into him. The petulance and bickering in these letters reached remarkable heights by the late spring of 1831. The President picked over every detail of the Seminole and Eaton controversies as though the fate of the nation rested upon such analyses. He searched his files for documentary proof of his assertions; he asked for written confirmation from participants when his searches proved unproductive; and he dreamed up the most extraordinary excuses to explain away unacceptable variations of his version of the truth. For an intelligent, mature, and responsible individual, Jackson's behavior during this period borders on madness.[32] Small children would be hard-pressed to match the amount, intensity, and utter stupidity of the bickering.

Other than his chronic illness, two factors explain (though hardly justify) Jackson's behavior during the Seminole and Eaton controversies. The first concerned his military career. No one could besmirch that career in any shape or form. The mere whisper of criticism brought nagging (sometimes whining) responses from the old man. He simply could not handle anything less than unstinted praise for his military accomplishments. The second factor concerned friendship and his perception of it. "When have I diserted an old friend, *never,*" he wrote. To him something sacred was involved in the Eaton affair and he would rather die—literally—than abandon his friend.[33]

Of course a constant factor in understanding his bizarre behavior at times was his wretched health and the constant pain he endured. When they started painting his rooms in the White House the smell of the fresh paint almost prostrated him. The "repainting of my dwelling" was "very injurious to my health," he said, "and made me very subject to my excrutiating head ache."[34] These headaches intensified during the worst period of bickering over the Eaton episode. They got so bad that he finally fled to the Rip Raps in late June, where he hoped to find "improved health, and general tranquility."[35] One development that helped his general frame of mind was the restored relationship with his nephew and niece. Jackson had not been above reminding young Donelson over and over how he had brought him up, educated him, and provided him with every advantage only to be repaid with pain and sorrow in his declining years. (Jackson could be a tiresome nag at times.) Finally Donelson relented. Of course the fact that the Eatons no longer belonged to Jackson's official family helped heal the breach. "After what has now passed," Donelson wrote his wife, ". . . I am almost as well satisfied that the view which Uncle takes is correct. If it seperates us from him as members of his family, we can only regret that it deprives us of repaying, by our kind attentions to some extent, his munificent and tender care of us heretofore."[36] Later that fall husband and wife were rejoined under Uncle Jackson's roof.

Ironically the Eaton affair brought Old Hickory an enormous political bonus. It reduced Democratic orthodoxy to a single test: one was either for or against Andrew Jackson. Nothing else mattered. Anyone who dared to contest Jackson's position on men or measures could expect to be condemned, vilified, and read out of the party. The *Globe*, naturally, produced much of that vilification and did not hesitate to single out those who disrupted party harmony by disagreeing with the President. When a meeting of Democrats was organized in Washington to show their support of Jackson and "counteract the false charges" brought against him, Duff Green showed up and tried to move the nomination of Calhoun for Vice President in the coming election. He was virtually shown the door. "Duff Green's course is such that every friend of Genl J. must abandon him," said Felix Grundy.[37]

Calhoun, Green, and their friends were not the only cast-outs. By the end of the congressional session in 1831, after the *Globe* had commenced full daily operations, senators and representatives found themselves in deep political trouble whenever they crossed the President. The Democratic press made their lives miserable. For example, when Jackson undertook to bring about a settlement with Turkey over trade and failed to consult the Senate in dispatching an envoy to conclude a treaty (or even ask its approval for the final agreement), Senators Littleton W. Tazewell and John Tyler of Virginia, both staunch advocates of states' rights, loudly protested. The reaction of the Democratic press was immediate. The senators were denounced "because they had 'opposed Jacksons wishes.'" They were vilified as disturbers of party harmony. They were labeled "dupes" of Calhoun for simply protesting what they considered a "breach of the constitution." And they were accused of aiding the larger "conspiracy" against the President. The "various intrigues" against him, declared Jackson, "gave a key to the attack of Tazwell and Tyler." So effective were these newspaper assaults that congressmen in their private letters chided those who went public when they disagreed with the President.[38]

To differ with Old Hickory or his policies in a public way guaranteed swift retaliation in the form of personal abuse in the newspapers. And because of Jackson's popularity with the electorate and his rejection of public criticism, Democratic congressmen found it politically safer to follow the President's policies and direction. The alternative was obvious: leave the party. In this manner Andrew Jackson slowly assumed tighter control of the entire government by making himself the measure and test by which all Democrats must be judged.

Some Democrats demurred, naturally, particularly southerners and advocates of states' rights. They strongly resented some of his policies and refused to keep silent. They hailed his Maysville veto but they noted with alarm his approval of other internal improvements since writing that veto. They fretted over his pronouncement in his last message that the tariff was constitutional, over his appointments of ministers without the advice and consent of the Senate, over his recommendation for a "worse" bank than the one they already had, and over his proposal to distribute the surplus on the basis of representation. This last proposition, according to Governor John Floyd, was "so monstrous, so dangerous, and so ruinous to our interest, so destructive to liberty . . . that it is not to be tolerated." Jackson had been elected to the presidency to protect freedom by limiting federal power; instead he had been increasing it over the past two years, particularly executive power. "To my chagrine and mortification," fumed Floyd, "every principle and every power claimed by Adams and Clay, as belonging to the Federal Government, has been acted on, or claimed by President Jackson." We exchanged one princely power for another, he said. "To talk about the benefits this administration has brought or will bring to States Rights, is an insult to the plain understanding of all."[39]

What indeed had happened to all the promises about preserving liberty? Quite obviously, Jackson was himself slowly and unconsciously subverting that concept, and he did it by imposing a different definition of the term. Heretofore freedom had meant the right of the individual to be left alone to enjoy the fruits of his labor without interference by government. To a certain extent that notion continued under Jackson. He would revert to it, for example, during the opening phase of the Bank War. But more and more during his presidency the term "freedom" became identified with majority rule. A free society was one that conformed to the will of the masses. Since Jackson represented the people it therefore followed that what he proposed by way of a program of "reform retrenchment and economy" constituted their sovereign command. To reject that program denied majority rule. To contest majority rule jeopardized freedom.

Thus Jackson subverted not only the meaning of freedom but the entire concept of "republicanism" as it had come down from the Founding Fathers. By responding naturally and unconsciously to the new impulses within American society—a dynamic economy, an emerging industrial state, an expanding population, a more involved electorate enjoying greater suffrage rights—he assisted in the conversion of a republic into a democracy.

Jackson was helped in the process by the matchless talents of some extraordinary men. Van Buren, Benton, Blair, Kendall, Taney, and others provided invaluable services both in undergirding Jackson's leadership of a mass electorate and in propagating the notion that a free society functioned best through a party system based on popular support. The *Globe* alone, directed by Blair and Kendall, succeeded in convincing Democrats of the changed ideological meaning of Jeffersonian republicanism. All these men contributed handsomely to the evolving notion of democracy.

Quite early in his presidency Jackson learned to draw upon many talents to assist his administration. In seeking advice he never felt constrained to limit himself to his cabinet or a few close friends. Not that he totally disregarded the cabinet, despite the discord within it. He held meetings with its members and showed them every deference and consideration. That was his style. Even when he fired them he stated publicly that they had performed their tasks with "integrity and zeal" in the management of their departments.

In short, then, Jackson was never *driven* to seek outside assistance. Inviting a wide range of opinion from many men was part of his normal and usual operation. True, once he discovered the "treachery" of Ingham, Branch, and Berrien, Jackson cancelled regular cabinet meetings and tended to look for counsel elsewhere. For that counsel he turned to a large contingent of friends and relatives, some living with him like Lewis and Donelson, who actively sought to direct presidential policies. But other friends also offered their opinions. Some he heeded, like John Coffee and John Overton, his two oldest and best friends, and some he ignored, like his nephew-in-law, John McLemore. Still at any time, depending on the issue, even someone like McLemore might get through to him and have an impact on his thinking.

Closer to home in Washington, Jackson listened more and more to Martin Van Buren. The cautious wisdom, the balance, the integrity, the "loyalty and patriotism" of the Little Magician captured Jackson right at the start of his administration and it never appreciably lessened. Not that Van Buren controlled Jackson, despite the gossips. Van Buren learned soon enough that when Old Hickory made up his mind, the Magician could either acquiesce and shout "huzza" like the rest or suffer exclusion from future consultation. A few times Van Buren came close to losing Jackson's confidence but he hurried back into line in time to avoid banishment. Even when the New Yorker resigned as secretary of state his influence with the President did not wane. Although out of sight he was constantly invited to participate in policy decisions. Jackson wrote him often. "I wish my D'r sir," he wrote shortly after Van Buren's return to New York, "that you would forward me your views on the various subjects I mentioned to you, at as early a period as your convenience will permit. I wish them soon, so as to be able to prepare my message to the next congress with great care." Even after he arrived in England he should feel free to give advice. "Let me hear from you, and any idea that may occur to you, worthy to be presented to Congress, suggest it to me."[40]

After the cabinet blowup probably no one succeeded Van Buren as principal adviser. Amos Kendall probably came closest, for he commanded the President's respect and admiration almost from the moment they met in Washington. Kendall's "radical reform" ideas more nearly matched his own than did those of anyone else, including Van Buren, Lewis, and Blair. Kendall powered those ideas with administrative skill and inexhaustible energy. Moreover, his writing talents and editorial experience proved extremely valuable and he frequently lent them to the administration in the composition of important state papers and messages. Early on, Kendall admitted that Jackson had shown him "marks of his confidence . . . which are quite flattering. In every appeal to him from my decisions, he has supported and applauded me." Even when it looked as though his nomination as fourth auditor would be opposed by the friends of Calhoun, the President reassured him. "Against you!" Jackson barked. "Don't be alarmed—I'll take care of you—if they were to reject you, they might see you where they would like to see you still less."[41]

Both Kendall and Blair added an important new dimension to Jackson's presidency. No previous administration enjoyed the kind of communication with the American people as the General's. It was a whole new concept in running the government, namely having advisers and shapers of policy who could then translate White House decisions into forceful language and announce them with persuasive eloquence to the American electorate. But neither Blair nor Kendall was simply a transmitter of the presidential will. They participated very often in the discussions leading to a major decision. Probably no other two advisers were as important to Jackson in the struggle against the United States Bank as Blair and Kendall. They came to Washington already equipped with fixed prejudices against the institution, ideas which coincided with the President's. As he moved closer and closer to a confrontation with the Bank, Blair and Kendall emerged as his most intimate confidants, replacing earlier aides such as Lewis (who was pro-Bank) and Eaton (who was politically extinct). The fact that he identified with them as westerners also strengthened their position. The two editors sometimes mentioned their western background to explain their identity of purpose with the President.[42]

As a rule Jackson took advice from the men whose thinking most nearly matched his own, and necessarily this shifted with each issue. While he listened to Van Buren on the question of internal improvements, he closed his ears to his advice on the Bank. He practically turned Lewis out of the White House when he began his war on the BUS, and once Indian removal had been legislated into law he no longer needed the assistance of John Eaton in quite the same way as before. Not that he disposed of his advisers after each issue. They just kept changing, sometimes re-emerging, in a kind of kaleidoscopic grouping that rearranged itself in response to Jackson's need and will.

The appearance of Blair and Kendall into the inner circle of Jackson's advisory council marked the beginning of open talk and speculation in Washington about a "Kitchen Cabinet." Because it was a label slapped on the administration by its foes it had little meaning except as a propaganda tool. Supposedly, there existed—according to those who invented and employed the term—a group of aides outside the official cabinet with special talents at political manipulation who advised Jackson on the running of the government, the distribution of the patronage, and the operation of the Democratic party. Since they were not his official advisers, like cabinet officers—the official cabinet was sometimes called the "parlor" cabinet—they were imagined as slipping into Jackson's study by way of the back stairs through the kitchen. And because of Jackson's difficulty with his first cabinet, historians later adopted the term as a convenient means of explaining how Jackson got around the predicament of the Eaton scandal. Since advisers seemed to come and go during Jackson's eight years in office, neither the President's enemies nor future historians put a limit on the number of Kitchen members. They included editors, politicians, official cabinet officers, family, and longtime friends. The list can be interminable and it makes little sense.

It was inevitable that something like the concept of a Kitchen Cabinet would be invented. From the beginning of the dispute between Van Buren and Calhoun, two factions seemed to be operating within the White House, each struggling to control the thoughts and actions of the President. With the arrival of Blair and the establishment of the *Globe,* followed by the resignation of the cabinet, a full-scale "war between the Telegraph and the Globe" signaled the opening of public combat. What had once been discreetly concealed from the public now received a full airing. Green assaulted the "Eaton & Van Buren Jacksonism" rampant in the White House; Blair scored "the Calhoun" wing of "Jacksonism." The dominance of Van Buren in the administration by the opening months of 1831 so infuriated the Calhoun wing that they publicly spoke of "back-stairs influence," "conspiracy," and "plotters and contrivers" as the operative force within the government. Green and Calhoun carefully excluded Jackson from their attacks at the war's beginning, insisting that Van Buren was the sole object of their complaint. They even endorsed Jackson's reelection, hoping of course that Calhoun would be rewarded with second place on the ticket. As the war progressed during the spring of 1831, Green kept referring to the "manipulators" controlling operations in the White House who sent out their "orders" to politicians and newspaper editors all over the country. He named them: "Mr. Van Buren, Major Lewis, and Mr. Kendall." He sometimes referred to the group as "Amos Kendall & Co" and "Amos Kendall, Martin Van Buren, William B. Lewis, & Co." When Donelson used the term in one of his letters to his uncle—"Lewis and Co."—Jackson lashed at him with unbecoming fury.[43]

After the cabinet dissolution John Branch was the first of the former secretaries to accuse Van Buren openly of exercising a strange and "malign" influence over the President.[44] From that moment on there arose a steady, mounting complaint about a group of men skulking around the White House and poisoning Jackson's mind with advice about men and issues that were detrimental to the nation. Critics close to Calhoun spoke mainly in terms of a "Van Buren conspiracy" that had deliberately provoked a quarrel between the President and Vice President, had established the *Globe* to supplant the *Telegraph*, and now schemed to capture the presidency once Jackson stepped down. But it soon became convenient, even for Jackson's friends, to fault his "unseen" advisers whenever they disliked some presidential action or measure. Rather than risk public displeasure by criticizing the President they attacked the "Kitchen Cabinet" instead. Even Blair found occasion to use the term, albeit in a private letter. He assured his sister-in-law that whatever Jackson "conceives the *permanent interest* of the country, his patriotism becomes an all-absorbing feeling, and neither *kitchen* nor *parlor* cabinets can move him."

As far as can be determined at present the first time the concept of the "Kitchen Cabinet" appeared in a document was in December, 1831 when Nicholas Biddle worried in a private communication that "the kitchen ... predominate[s] over the Parlor" in advising the President, particularly on the Bank question. Not until March was the term actually used in print, however; but within a year the concept was well established throughout the nation.[45]

Senator George Poindexter of Mississippi, a sinister-looking profligate who abandoned Jackson for Calhoun and hated Van Buren,[46] published an article in the *Telegraph* on March 27, 1832, which caught everyone's attention because of its use of the unusual term. "The President's press," he wrote, "edited under his own eye, by 'a pair of deserters from the Clay party,' [meaning Kendall and Blair] and a few others, familiarly known by the appellation of the 'Kitchen Cabinet,' is made the common reservoir of all the petty slanders which find a place in the most degraded prints of the Union."[47] With the publication of this piece the expression entered the nation's political vocabulary. Two days later Blair responded in an editorial and denied any influence by a *"Kitchen Cabinet."* Blair credited Poindexter with originating the term (which Poindexter later conceded) and implied that it oozed from his lascivious brain. Thereafter, particularly during the presidential election of 1832, the expression enjoyed widespread use.

Quite obviously, the Kitchen Cabinet never existed—at least not in any of the ways described by the opposition. Granted Jackson received advice from a number of close friends who often helped him to clarify or sharpen his ideas, prepare statements and messages, and carry his decisions to a wide audience of politicians and the electorate. But there was no structure to the operation, no form. Membership in the group shifted from moment to moment and issue to issue. The only stable and permanent element in this unstructured affair was Jackson himself. All others came and went. Only he remained; only he decided who attended council meetings; only he determined the issues for discussion. His was the controlling influence.

Rarely, if ever, did Jackson ask his advisers to decide an issue. Invariably he came to a meeting—either "parlor" or "kitchen"—with a sense of his own direction. He set the problem before the group and heard their reaction, following which he made his decision. Most often he arrived with a decision already formulated. He laid it before his advisers and listened to their criticisms. Then he made his final decision. This latter procedure paralleled what he had often done during his military career. He first examined his own mind, then he heard objections from his senior staff. But the final decision was always his.[48]

If the decision required a public statement in the form of a message, proclamation, order, or whatever, Jackson's private secretary, Andrew J. Donelson, was directed to prepare a draft. Usually Jackson had his ideas scribbled on small notes which he dumped in his nephew's lap and directed him to shape into an intelligible whole. Once the draft was prepared it went to the "parlor" cabinet for final approval before being signed by the President and issued. Frequently, Kendall, Blair, and one or more of the "parlor" cabinet would have a hand in the writing of the draft. All Jackson's messages to Congress bear the marks of half a dozen or more writers. The preparation of these drafts sometimes took months.[49]

A man of strong opinions, a man virtually immovable once he had made up his mind, Jackson still preferred to hear from a wide range of opinion before he acted. His particular style sometimes amazed his friends. "When I find how much oftener you prove to be right than your friends," Van Buren said to him, "it amazes me that you continue so open to advice."[50]

As a matter of fact those who worked closely with him quickly came to recognize his extraordinary talents as an administrator and executive. Indeed, the strength and quickness of his mind immediately won their respect and admiration. "The President has much more sagacity in civil affairs and a much fuller acquaintance with the principles and practice of the government," said the usually hypercritical Levi Woodbury, "than many of his opponents are willing to concede. He is very firm in his opinions—inflexibly upright—devoted to his public duties and marked for his courtesy to all."[51]

Because Jackson was so much the master of his own house the talk of Kitchen Cabinets and the "malign" influence of "Van Buren, Blair, Lewis, Kendall & Co." and all the rest hardly troubled him. To those who had the presumption to mention it to him—John Randolph of Roanoke was harebrained enough to bring it up—Jackson stated a simple truth. "In regard however to these complaints and others of a similar character founded on a pretended distrust of *influences* near or around me," he commented, "I can only say that they spring from the same false view of my character. I should loath myself did any act of mine afford the slightest colour for the insinuation that I follow blindly the judgement of any friend in the discharge of my proper duties as a public or private individual. I am sensible of my liability to err: but rest assured that I have too much confidence in the indulgence of my fellow citizens and in the integrity of my purposes to desire any other shield for my conduct than truth and a fair hearing from those who have a right to judge me."[52]

As a result of his informal, shifting advisory system, Jackson enjoyed personal services that strengthened his political leadership in Congress and around the country. Some of his conferees participated in major decisions, but others like newspaper editors and local politicians advised on matters of removals, appointments, selection of committees, establishment of newspapers, and other party matters. Some regularly gathered information about public reaction to his measures. Jackson frequently asked his political correspondents to report on attitudes in their communities. Still other men performed personal or administrative chores and felt flattered when Jackson called on them for their assistance. Before long, through his informal procedure, Jackson had set up a wide network of advisors and consultants ranging from editors and cabinet officers to government officials, members of Congress, friends, and political leaders in the various sections of the country. Jackson was the center of this network—he was the cause and purpose of its existence. Small wonder, then, he came to dominate the processes of government, including the operation of the Congress.[53]

Once he refashioned his "parlor" cabinet Jackson treated it with marked respect and deference. He regularly met the members each week, first on Saturdays and then on Tuesdays. During crisis periods, such as during the Bank War, they met every day.[54] Not that the cabinet decided anything. It merely advised. The more important an issue, the less likely anyone but Jackson determined the direction of his administration. He expected unanimous support from the cabinet once the decision was made, or if they had doubts they learned to keep them quietly to themselves. Any variation from this invited dismissal.

Jackson preferred his Kitchen over his parlor cabinet. He could consult his Kitchen or not as his mood dictated, dismiss the members or keep them depending on their usefulness and loyalty. He could shop around to find the right men to fit all the tasks necessary to implement his goals. No one person could be expected to fill all the President's needs so he deftly circulated among a number of willing confidants. When a favorite bucked him or tried to prod him into taking the "wrong" direction—as Lewis did on the Bank issue—Jackson quietly closed them down, without fuss. And there were always others waiting to take their place. Appreciating the wealth of talent he could summon at any time, Jackson valued the strengths they brought to his administration. As long as he "had a few Patriots around," he said, he could stand any trial. "When thus situated, I was never long in dificulty."[55] Actually he was his own greatest asset— something he had learned to appreciate a long time ago.

CHAPTER 20

The Bank War Begins

POOR JACKSON SPENT THE SUMMER OF 1831 in Washington—hot, muggy, pestilential Washington. His headaches intensified and his letters frequently complained that he could barely compose his thoughts on account of their severity. "Excruciating" was the word he used to describe them. The absence of his family contributed to his misery. His nephew and niece had not yet returned from Tennessee and he longed to see them. He needed family around him to distract his mind and provide the joy of companionship. Nicholas Trist, recruited from the State Department, served competently as his private secretary but he could not provide the "tender affection and sympathy," the "kindness and love" that only his family could give him. Major Lewis still resided in the White House but whenever Old Hickory began a tirade against the United States Bank for its notorious corruption, the Major coolly—if carefully— disagreed. Clearly Lewis could offer no assistance in his determination to reform that dangerous institution.[1]

Ralph Earl, the artist, also lived in the White House and steadily turned out handsome pictures of the General and his family. During the spring he transported his portrait of Rachel from the Hermitage to Washington in order to make a copy. Under the present circumstances he did not think Old Hickory ought to see it. But the President stopped in "by accident" one day while Earl was copying it. "He stood and gazed at it for a few moments with some fortitude, until as the association rose in his mind he began to weep, and his sobs became so deep that Earl carried the picture away to relieve him."[2]

Thoughts of Rachel. They uncoiled in his aching head quite frequently during the spring and summer of 1831. He had a Bible in which a great many of Rachel's favorite passages had been marked by his wife. "One of these he reads every morning *religiously,*" reported a daily visitor.[3] He sometimes wept when he read them.

The Fourth of July provided the occasion for more misery. A group of "dismissed clerks, and officers" at a celebration in the capital demonstrated their feelings about the administration and toasted the "Hon'rd mrs. Calhoun, mrs. Ingham, and Emily." The inclusion of his niece's name rankled. "No greater indignity can be offered to a lady," he instructed his nephew, "than to toast her for political effect, or for any other cause, than her own intrinsick virtues." Had anyone ever dared to hold up Rachel to "public gaze" in this manner he would have told them "sternly but leconicly" that their action was "odious" and insulting. You should do the same, he lectured. The secret slanders against female character in this town, he continued, use their panderers at public festivals for their own political ends and have no regard for the dignity and virtue of innocent women. The very thought that the sweet name of Emily Donelson had been spewed out of their polluted mouths to insult the President of the United States affected him very deeply.[4]

The nullifiers also stirred in their reptilian nest to provoke and annoy him. Two men, not regular merchants, imported some goods to South Carolina and refused payment on their bond for the import duty required by law because they pronounced the Tariff of 1828 unconstitutional. The collector of the port went to the federal district attorney for South Carolina, a man named Frost, and handed over the bond to permit Frost to institute suit for payment. To avoid bringing suit, Frost resigned his office. When Jackson learned of these developments his first inclination "was to direct an agent to institute the suit, refuse his resignation, and impeach him for neglect of duty." But the more he thought about it the more he appreciated the need for prudence and caution. He did not wish to create a volatile situation that might explode into violence. So he accepted the resignation, appointed another district attorney, and sent instructions to him to bring the suit promptly and "prosecute it with energy." Meanwhile he dispatched a private agent to South Carolina to "look and enquire, and take the necessary testimony to expose all who are engaged in this act of intended Treason against our Government." He also kept in regular correspondence with known Unionists in Charleston, particularly Joel Poinsett. Of course he suspected Calhoun as the instigator of this unlawful action. This is what the Vice President had been advocating for the last two sessions of Congress, he argued. But Jackson reiterated his now-familiar cry: *"The union shall be preserved."*[5]

The nullifiers in South Carolina tried to force Jackson into appointing one of their number as the new district attorney, but he turned aside their demands. When they argued with him about the rights of the states he informed them flatly that under no circumstances could a state nullify congressional legislation. Said he: "I draw a wide difference between

State Rights and the advocates of them, and a nullifier. One will preserve the union of the States. The other will dissolve the union by destroying the constitution by acts unauthorized in it."[6]

The wisdom Jackson displayed in this single, minor episode demonstrated clearly his steady emergence as a statesman of the first rank. He understood the gravity of the issue but he did not rush to hasty action. He also understood his duty in enforcing the law. He showed conviction and determination in complying with his duty, which he conveyed to the public through the press, but he also avoided confrontation. In times of crisis Andrew Jackson was found to be superbly endowed to meet them.

As he sat in his study in the White House and read the newspapers conveying the dying groans of Berrien, Branch, and Ingham, and as he tried unsuccessfully to quiet his throbbing head, Jackson wistfully sighed for the pleasures of his home in Tennessee. But the dream, he knew, was impossible. "The people say 'my services are necessary to preserve the union, by restoring the constitution, by the administration of the government to its original reading, and thereby harmonize the people in every section of the U. States." To restore republicanism as he knew it would be an incalculable blessing to the American people. Besides, he could not tolerate the idea that he had been forced out of office by the schemes and conspiracies of his enemies. "I see I cannot retire now. . . . I will not be driven by my enemies." Also, he had not yet completed his reform program. Two things remained to be accomplished: "the national debt paid, and the Bank question settled." Once the public debt had been erased, a "judicious Tarriff" might be arranged which would further "harmonise" the major sections of the nation. Although he suffered another bad siege of illness in October and wondered aloud whether he could survive another year, he determined to keep to his earlier resolve to seek a second term as President—and then, he told Van Buren, "you will see me adopt a course worthy of myself, and the principles I have always advocated."[7]

His indisposition and the mounting talk of death turned Jackson's thoughts to religion. He read the Bible daily and also attended church services now fairly regularly. His correspondence to close friends and family frequently conveyed pious sentiments which he unquestionably felt very deeply. When he heard of the recovery of the wife of his good friend, John Coffee, he sent the husband a rapturous note of thanksgiving. "I rejoice to find, by the goodness of an overruling providence, that your dear wife has been restored to health. . . . how grateful should we be to our savior and our god, for her preservation, and restoration to health and for that daily preservation, and blessings which he is constantly bestowing upon us."[8]

A few bright spots appeared in the otherwise all-pervading gloom. His new cabinet seemed to take hold rather nicely. Louis McLane did not arrive from Europe until midsummer, but he too quickly adjusted to his new responsibilities. Best of all Jackson's family rejoined him on September 5. Andrew and Emily had agreed to abide by his wishes in the matter of social courtesy to his friends and guests—an agreement made easy by the imminent departure of the Eatons for Tennessee—and returned to their former positions in the White House. Jackson glowed as he welcomed back Donelson "with his little family" along with Mary Eastin and Mary McLemore, who accompanied them. The residence would come alive again. Jackson even seemed pleased to see his ward Andrew Jackson Hutchings. Young Hutchings appeared a little more mature now and told Jackson he was "determined to become a learned man." So he enrolled at the University of Virginia. Jackson gave him some shirts and $150 in cash to pay for room, board, and tuition for the semester. Unfortunately, the boy had acquired many bad habits over the years, some of which he learned at school. They teach poorly today, Jackson complained, not like they used to. "Our modern mode of teaching is all wrong. formerly the child was taught to spell & read well, then was taught arithmetic and to write well, these points gained, the gramar & geography might be commenced with advantage & not before. Writing is machancial, & unless attended to when young, never can be obtained afterwards, therefore it is, that few of our modern scholars write good hands. another advantage whilst the child is learning the art of writing well & arithmatic, his mind is expanding & preparing for the science and languages." Jackson wished teachers would make young students "spend every day at least one hour in writing." To his surprise and delight young Hutchings really applied himself this time and his professors' reports for the first quarter complimented the student on his excellent progress.[9]

More than anything else Jackson found pleasure—he was apprehensive at first—in the marriage of his only son. Andrew Jr. had met an "accomplished, amiable, & handsome" young lady by the name of Sarah Yorke. She lived in Philadelphia, the daughter of a wealthy merchant. But shortly before his death the father lost two ships at sea, "leaving two orphan daughters" with very limited means. The twenty-two-year-old Andrew met the amiable Sarah on a visit to Pennsylvania and was immediately smitten. When he proposed marriage she accepted without hesitation. Sometime around the middle of October, 1831, he told his father of his plans and showed him one of her letters. Jackson, although wary—knowing the proclivities of his son and not knowing the young lady at all—offered no objection. "Your happiness will insure mine," he wrote Andrew, "for the few years which I can expect to live. You say that Sarah possesses every quality necessary to make you happy. The amiability of her temper and her other good qualities which you represent is a sure pledge to me that she will unite with you in adding to my comfort during my life."[10]

After studying Sarah's letter and hearing his son enumerate her many qualities that would make her a fit wife, Jackson instructed Andrew to tell the young lady "that you have my full and free consent that you be united in the holy bonds of matrimony; that I shall receive her as a daughter, and cherish her as my child." He only asked that the engagement be "consummated" as soon as possible, preferably before Congress reconvened. "I shall want your aid," he explained, "and it would put it in my power to receive you and Sarah here before the bustle of congress commences."[11]

Privately, Jackson expressed some concern to his friend, John Coffee. He regretted that the Yorke family fortune had not been "carefully attended to–I know not what she is worth, as on that subject I never made inquiry–it was enough for me to know that he loved her, that she was respectable & accomplished, and not one of the modern fashionables." Still "I would have been better satisfied," Jackson admitted, "if he had married in a family I knew." But what could he do? The union would be "respectable" and "he appears to be happy."[12]

On November 20 Andrew left Washington to marry his Sarah, accompanied by Mary Eastin. The wedding took place in Philadelphia on November 24, 1831, and they honeymooned in the White House. Whatever doubts or fears Jackson entertained about the marriage quickly evaporated. Sarah became a joy and comfort to him for the rest of his days, ministering to his needs and lavishing love and affection on him which he returned in abundance. Indeed, marrying Sarah was the best thing his son ever did for him.

Jackson missed his son's wedding in order to attend to his many obligations in Washington, particularly the preparation of his annual message to Congress. The paper had been in preparation for months and, as usual, he called on his many advisers to contribute ideas and suggestions. Van Buren gave him a long list of recommendations but urged him most of all to take his "ground upon the basis of a strict construction of the Constitution." It "is the only true and saving ground," he said. Certain members of the new cabinet were "not altogether in that Sentiment," he declared, so "doctrines may be suggested and adopted, which would expose you to the charge of inconsistency" unless you exercise extreme care.[13]

Van Buren had Louis McLane in mind—and he actually named him in the letter. As a former Federalist, McLane entertained Hamiltonian ideas about some issues, especially the Bank, but otherwise could be expected to perform loyally and efficiently. Jackson acknowledged certain deficiencies within his official cabinet, despite the restoration of harmony, and wished that it were possible to bring Van Buren back home and make him his Vice President. "I miss you, and Eaton, very much," he told the Magician. "Had I you in the state Department and Eaton in the war, with the others, filled as they are, it would be one of the strongest and happiest administrations that could be formed." He respected Livingston for his writing talent and his scholarly habits of mind, but "he knows nothing of mankind" and therefore lacks judgment in assessing individuals. Also his memory was fading. Livingston loved society, had no consuming political ambition, and really wanted to go abroad, preferably as minister to France. To send Livingston to Europe and "again to have you near me," Jackson reiterated, would make a perfect situation. As for Cass, he "is an amiable talented man," and a fine writer, but he finds it hard to say no "and he thinks all men honest." This may be virtue in a private person "but unsafe in public life, for the public interest sometimes may suffer having too much confidence." Most troubling of all was Cass's unwillingness to argue with his associates. He avoids controversy at all costs and therefore tends to go along rather than stand up for what he believes and thinks.[14]

All the other members of the cabinet had talents, but nothing in Van Buren's league—or Eaton's either. Woodbury was a "trained" politician, cautious and wary. He avoided committing himself whenever possible. He always hedged his bets. But at least his opinions were his own and not those of others. When he gave an opinion—usually pried out of him—it was an honest one. A man of great industry and efficiency, Woodbury had a mastery of details. He enjoyed nothing better than arranging and rearranging complicated schedules.[15] As for Barry, the one holdover from the original cabinet, he was attached to the President and staunchly loyal, but he lacked "practical talents" and when he spoke at cabinet meetings his arguments wandered and had no point. Some thought him incredibly stupid. Almost totally without administrative ability, he nearly wrecked the post office and soon had Congress breathing down his neck. Not a few times Jackson favored him with hard stares across the room. Then there was Taney, the enigma. At first he was so busy preparing cases for the Supreme Court that he frequently excused himself from cabinet meetings. Not until the Bank War commenced did he reveal fully his tremendous talents of mind and temperament. He became Jackson's closest adviser and confidant in the official cabinet.[16]

In some ways McLane was the best of the lot. Just back from his triumph abroad he radiated confidence and decision. As former chairman of the Ways and Means Committee in Congress for a number of years, and as a friend of Nicholas Biddle and the Barings of England, McLane thought he knew a great deal about finance. His appointment as secretary of the treasury, therefore, seemed inspired. Ambitious, with aspirations for the presidency, he loved power and the exhilaration of exercising it. He was a man of consummate tact and diplomatic skill. He knew how to manage men by appealing to their patriotism, pride, vanity, fear, or whatever else it took to win them to his side. Before long he had Livingston and Cass trailing in his wake, and when Woodbury joined the group they constituted a formidable team.[17] But McLane made one serious error in his rising effort to dominate the administration. He underestimated Jackson's "strength and independence . . . and the extent of his information." He could go so far and no further. When he reached beyond his rightful limit, Jackson cut him down.[18]

Still Jackson appreciated McLane. Although they differed most notably on the Bank question, the President said it was "an honest difference of opinion." Jackson especially liked his frankness, "that open candeur with which he acts."[19] The General made it very clear that he never felt the least dissatisfaction with anyone in his cabinet who differed with him when the opposition was done "openly and fairly, and conducted with proper decorum." It was the hidden opposition, the conspiracies and whispered attacks, that he could not abide. Let his cabinet speak out honestly and forthrightly until he rendered his decision. Then he expected them to cease all opposition or resign.[19]

In the early fall of 1831 McLane began to exert his skills to bring the old man around to his way of thinking on a very serious matter. He knew of Jackson's opposition to the BUS, but he also felt the Bank necessary for the well-being of the American people. He therefore worked out a plan to resolve this difficulty for which he thought he could gain the President's approval. The central feature of his plan was the proposal to pay off the national debt before the end of Jackson's first term, that is by March 3, 1833, at the latest. This, McLane knew, would appeal irresistibly to Jackson. The debt amounted to approximately $24 million and could be retired by applying $16 million of anticipated revenue plus $8 million to be realized from the sale of the government's stock in the BUS. The liquidation of the stock—to be sold directly to the BUS itself—meant a radical alteration in the Bank's charter, something Jackson wholeheartedly approved. Once the debt was extinguished, existing revenues could be applied to improve military defense, arm the state militias, build armories, and improve the army and navy—all guaranteed to excite Jackson's interest and approval. Increased revenue also meant that the tariff could be adjusted to a more equitable level. Furthermore, McLane proposed to sell all the public lands held by the government to the states in which they lay and then distribute the proceeds from the sale to all the states. Talk about reform and reducing the operation of government! McLane's proposal staggered the old man in its scope and audacity.[20]

Only one thing the secretary asked in return: that the President refrain from mentioning the BUS in his annual message and allow McLane in his annual report to recommend recharter at the proper time and with appropriate modifications. Otherwise, he said, his report might trigger the Ways and Means Committee, chaired by Calhoun's crony George McDuffie, to prepare a bill to recharter the BUS—and such a bill he, McLane, could not oppose in good conscience.[21]

For years Jackson had urged the alteration of the operation and structure of the BUS. By 1831 it was really the centerpiece of his reform program. McLane's linking of it to the final payment of the national debt, tariff modification, national security, public land sale, and improvements seemed to embody Jackson's entire program and the principles he had always advocated. The proposal proved irresistible and Jackson immediately embraced it. The President also accepted the conditions McLane had imposed. Once he gained Jackson's approval the secretary scooted off to Philadelphia to tell Biddle personally of his success in winning the General to his plan.[22]

The Bank president sighed with relief. The snake had been scotched. Recharter, in one form or another, seemed assured. Only one thing troubled him slightly: Jackson's agreement to remain silent in his annual message about the Bank. He much preferred the President to declare that the future of the Bank was a matter for the Congress to decide.[23] Still he had to admit that McLane had solved the problem to perfection and had demonstrated the Treasury Department's independence and authority.

Meanwhile Jackson went ahead with his annual message, collecting the reports of his cabinet, listening to several advisers, and generally putting his own individual stamp on the finished product. Edward Livingston had a major hand in writing the final draft because the General liked his style of writing. But the section on the Bank came almost verbatim from McLane. By early December a completed draft was ready. Following his usual custom Jackson summoned his cabinet to a meeting to hear the message and offer final suggestions and criticisms. Since Congress would reconvene on Monday, December 5, little time remained for extensive revisions.

The meeting took place in Jackson's office. When everyone had settled down Major Donelson took out the manuscript and began to read. It was a comparatively short message. It noted the general prosperity in the country; the relations with foreign nations (which occupied more than half the text); the success of the Indian policy and the imminent extinction of all Indian titles to land within the states and the removal of all Indians who would not submit to state law; and the steady dwindling of the national debt. At the very end of the message—even after reference to conditions in the District of Columbia—Jackson mentioned the Bank. In an offhand comment he said he had brought the attention of Congress to the matter and felt content to leave it to the legislative branch to take such action as it wished.[24]

Taney's brow furrowed. Donelson concluded with the final two sentences which invoked forebearance and conciliation in the preservation of the Union. With that the members cleared their throats and shifted in their seats. No one commented. Only Taney looked distressed. He waited to see if the other members wished to say anything and when they continued to sit mute he finally raised his voice. He made his point quickly and succinctly, so much so that everyone in the room realized instantly that a keen-minded, highly articulate, and opinionated man sat in their midst.[25]

Taney asked whether the American people in reading the message would not believe that Jackson had changed his mind on the Bank. (What no one in the room knew, except McLane, was that the brief reference to the BUS resulted from the suggestion and request of Nicholas Biddle.) Would it not cause the President needless criticism and the people a certain amount of confusion if the statement on the BUS went forward as written?

McLane immediately dismissed Taney's objection. A seesaw argument ensued. Livingston and Cass sided with McLane. Barry said nothing and Woodbury interjected a comment from time to time to see if he could reconcile the differences between the two men. "I stood alone in it," commented Taney, while Jackson just watched and listened.[26] Taney kept worrying about what the people would think. Then, as Jackson had done before and would do many times later whenever a doubt arose about offending the public or individuals or a particular section of the country, he reminded his cabinet of his "abiding confidence in the virtue and intelligence of the American people." If his measures were "right," he repeatedly lectured his cabinet, the people would support him in carrying them out. Identification with the people had become fixed in his thinking.[27]

Jackson admitted that Taney's objections had not occurred to him. He said he certainly did not mean to imply that he would sign any bill for recharter, nor did he feel he should say that he would veto any bill. There was time enough to take action when an actual bill was laid before him. Meanwhile he thought the clause in question did not appear to him to be liable to the objections Taney had raised and therefore he felt disinclined to make any changes.[28]

The remark discouraged Taney. Furthermore he could see that the contest between himself and McLane worried Jackson and he wanted to end it.[29] By the time the meeting broke up Taney felt somewhat defeated. Even so, he took his defeat with good grace and went back to his duties. "But I did not know Genl. Jackson as well as I afterwards knew him," the Attorney General wrote later. The paragraph in question had been prepared by McLane and for the President to side with Taney would undercut the treasury secretary in a matter subject to his supervision. So, despite his own inclination to jab the BUS again, Jackson supported McLane at the meeting as though that were the end of it. But the next day Major Donelson called the attorney general into his office and said that a new version of the disputed paragraph had been prepared and that the President had specifically directed Donelson to show it to Taney. Donelson read slowly. "Entertaining the opinions heretofore expressed in relation to the Bank of the United States as at present organized," came the opening words of the paragraph—and then followed the passage as McLane had originally written it. Taney still thought it "studiously ambiguous" but it voided his principal objection without doing injury to McLane's overall intent.[30]

A few days later, on December 5, the Congress reconvened. Henry Clay appeared as the newly elected senator from Kentucky, smiling and shaking hands and looking rested and vigorous after his long vacation from public service. Jackson presumed of course that he and Calhoun would get together on the tariff, no doubt to cause mischief and discord.[31]

The President's message went up the following day and hardly caused a ripple of comment. Mercifully short, it said nothing to excite or frighten congressmen. But McLane's annual report! that caused a jolt. It clearly and unequivocally recommended the recharter of the Bank of the United States.[32]

"You will find Mr McLane differs with me, on the Bank," Jackson wrote to Van Buren, now safely ensconced in London, "still it is an honest difference of opinion, and in his report he acts fairly, by leaving me free and uncommitted."[33]

In approving McLane's report and allowing its publication the day following his own message, Jackson may have been enticing (as some later claimed) the Bank into believing him neutral, asking for a recharter four years before the old one expired, and then clubbing it to death with a veto when it came before him. Although not impossible, this theory is a bit farfetched. More likely, Jackson gave his consent because McLane's proposal involved "radical" modifications in the Bank charter such as selling the government's stock in the BUS and included other plans dear to his reforming heart. As he said shortly thereafter, "there were arrangements that might be favorably accommodated with the aid of a Bank provided it could be so modified or constructed as to obviate constitutional objections."[34]

Not that the radical modifications were generally noted in the commotion the report stirred among some Democrats. The ultra-Federalist tone of the proposals horrified many. "The Treasury Report," wrote Churchill C. Cambreleng of New York, "is as bad as it possibly can be—a new version of Alexander Hamilton's two reports on a National Bank and manufactures, and totally unsuited to *this age of democracy and reform.*"[35] It "is too high toned—too ultra federal for me," wrote Walter Lowrie, the secretary of the Senate.[36] John Randolph, always quick to shoot from the hip, accused the President of switching his position, which Jackson hotly denied. "Nothing more foreign to truth could have been said," the General protested. As presently chartered he still regarded the Bank as unconstitutional, as an unwarranted extension of federal power, and as "dangerous to liberty, and therefore, worthy of the denunciation which it has received from the desciples of the old republican school."[37] When Van Buren read the report he said he suffered "pain and mortification." This was the man he himself had recommended for the treasury post. "I regarded it as a state paper calculated to supersede President Jackson as the efficient head of his own administration upon a vital point by which it was destined to stand or fall."[38]

McLane did feel rather triumphant. He had supposedly "converted" the President to his own fiscal schemes and exercised considerable influence over the other members of the cabinet—with the exception of Taney. The attorney general's objections expressed in the cabinet meeting only alerted him to the presence of a nagging dissenter, one daring enough to challenge his autonomy over fiscal concerns.

The alarm of antiBank Democrats to Jackson's seeming change of heart troubled the old man. The Richmond *Enquirer* and the Albany *Argus*, two organization mouthpieces, expressed their dismay. The *Globe*, of course, could not attack McLane directly, but Blair made his position clear enough: he reprinted articles from other newspapers that did his dirty work for him.[39] Under the circumstances Jackson felt obliged to reconfirm his opposition to the Bank to various politicians and newspapermen. "Mr. McLane and myself understand each other," he wrote to one, "and have not the slightest disagreement about the principles, which will be a *sine qua non* in my assent to a bill rechartering the bank." To another he said: "Rest assured, Sir, that Mr McLane is a man of too much honor to play any game with me that may possibly make him a winner at the expense of the principles which are the rule of my administration."[40]

But McLane did in fact choose to play a game—a very dangerous game. The *Globe*'s lack of support infuriated him.[41] He felt the newspaper should have recognized the extensive revisions proposed in the report to reorganize the Bank. That was the very least Blair should have done. This failure galled him. So McLane counterattacked by organizing a conspiracy to replace Blair as editor of the newspaper. It was a stupid idea and maybe showed that McLane had less honor than Jackson supposed. Getting rid of Blair was impossible without the President's approval. Surely McLane knew that. Nevertheless he forged ahead. He risked his strong position in the cabinet by this ploy because he forced Jackson to reassert his authority and control. He jeopardized his future in a needless display of spite.

A dozen conspirators, including several members of the cabinet and such New York politicos as Churchill C. Cambreleng, Jesse Hoyt, and James Watson Webb met at McLane's house in early February, 1832.[42] They talked a great deal (McLane tried to intimate that Blair's response to his report revealed his determination to discredit Van Buren's friends in the cabinet) but they never devised a clear-cut strategy to achieve their end. For a brief moment Blair thought he could not survive such an intrigue because of Jackson's reluctance to stir another controversy within his cabinet. So he offered to resign. That was the first moment Jackson got wind of the conspiracy. When he heard it his eyes started flashing. He bridled. Then he quickly reassured the editor of his tenure. No one would replace Blair and that was final. He reaffirmed his opposition to the Bank, encouraged him in his policies, and promised him total support. "I had no temporizing policy in me," said Jackson.[43]

That ended McLane's ascendancy. He had reached the zenith of his influence and power—the climax of his career, says his biographer[44]—and then took a long slide that eventually returned him to private life. He lost the confidence of the President. He did not understand the limits of his authority. "McLane has ruined himself by taking the opposite course" from Jackson, reported Cambreleng to Van Buren. He is finished.[45] For the moment, however, McLane stayed in place. The President could ill afford another cabinet shake-up.

The National Republicans also worried over Jackson's apparent shift in policy. They expected to use his antiBank position in the coming presidential election to defeat him and restore the government to order and sanity. They called a national convention of delegates to choose their candidates, and nearly 150 party members assembled in Baltimore between December 12 and 16, 1831. Eighteen states sent representatives and they unanimously nominated Henry Clay for president and John Sergeant of Pennsylvania as his running mate. On the final day of the convention the delegates listened to an "address" which excoriated Jackson for his wretched policies and declared him "by education and character wholly unfit" for his office. If he wins reelection, the address concluded, "it may be considered certain that the bank will be abolished."[46]

Jackson informed Van Buren in London of the action taken by the National Republicans. "The other day the convention at Baltimore nominated, *as instructed,* mr Henry Clay for President. . . . I am told that several members of that body have said that it was not with any hope of his success at the next election, but for future use, and to prevent him from sinking into oblivion as a candidate for the Presidency."[47]

The meeting of National Republicans in Baltimore was not the first national nominating convention in American history. That distinction belongs to the Anti-Masonic party, the first third party, which met in Baltimore on September 26, 1831, and nominated William Wirt of Maryland and Amos Ellmaker of Pennsylvania. Ever since William Morgan's murder in 1826 the hostility against Masons had spread from New York into New England and the middle west. By the early 1830s elaborate party machinery existed in many states, complete with newspapers, local organizing committees, and such able leaders as Thurlow Weed and William H. Seward of New York and Thaddeus Stevens of Pennsylvania. Many National Republicans had hoped to entice the Anti-Masons into joining them against that "arch mason," Andrew Jackson. But Henry Clay's membership in the Masonic fraternity killed any possibility of such a union.[48]

Once Clay nailed down his own nomination he was anxious to challenge Jackson over the Bank issue. He figured that no other issue offered him as much advantage in winning the election. That meant bringing the issue forcibly before the public, and nothing could achieve that goal faster than getting a recharter bill before Congress. He therefore went to Nicholas Biddle and urged him to request recharter, arguing that

Jackson did not dare veto the bill before the election, for if he did he would surely lose the presidency. Since Biddle, in any event, must request recharter before Jackson's second term ended, Clay insisted that the bill stood a better chance for passage before the election rather than afterward. "The friends of the Bank," Clay said in a portentous tone, "expect the application to be made. The course of the President, in the event of the passage of the bill, seems to be a matter of doubt and speculation."[49]

Threatening though these words sounded, the wily Bank president did not jump at Clay's command. He understood the dangers of appearing to bait Jackson. Less than a week before he had been warned by Louis McLane against pressing the President at this time. Even William B. Lewis, another proBank ally in the White House, cautioned against bidding for recharter now since it would be seen as an open attack on some of Jackson's closest advisers and they would respond accordingly.[50] In a bit of a quandary, Biddle sent Thomas Cadwalader, a director of the BUS, to Washington to survey the situation. First, Cadwalader interviewed McLane and got a resounding command to wait. "If you apply now," the secretary said, "you assuredly will fail,—if you wait, you will as certainly succeed."[51]

But Cadwalader heard other voices. George McDuffie, chairman of the House Ways and Means Committee, counseled him to apply; Daniel Webster agreed; and Peter R. Livingston, the brother of the secretary of state, assured Cadwalader that Edward Livingston, Lewis Cass, and Louis McLane would dissuade Jackson from a veto if recharter passed the Congress.[52] When Cadwalader went back to McLane to gain his reaction if Biddle proceeded with recharter despite his admonition, he found the secretary conciliatory. McLane still opposed the move but "would not be vexed."[53]

By the first of the new year Biddle decided to go for recharter. He judged Cadwalader's report encouraging, even with McLane's warning. More than anything else, he could not resist the demands of "our friends," Clay and Webster, who may have been urging him on for their own political purposes but whose support was crucial nonetheless. He could hardly desert all his anti-Jackson allies in Congress and tag after McLane, the friend of Martin Van Buren.[54] Even at the last possible moment when Samuel Smith, another proBank senator, warned that if Biddle drove "the Chief into a Corner he will veto the Bill," the banker chose to take the risk and seek recharter anyway. The moment for action had come. The time was now.[55]

On January 6, 1832, a memorial for a renewal of the charter was formally submitted to Congress. Under ordinary circumstances Samuel Smith, chairman of the Senate Finance Committee, would have submitted the memorial, but he was not considered aggressive enough to make a vigorous case for the Bank, so Senator George M. Dallas, a Democrat from Pennsylvania, was selected to do the honors. In the House, George McDuffie guided the bill to the floor.

Quite predictably, the radical antiBank advisers in the White House howled their dismay at the sudden introduction into Congress of a bill to recharter the BUS. Blair, Kendall, and Taney, in relay, assured Jackson that Biddle had converted an economic issue into a political one for Clay's benefit, that he presumed to intrude into the electoral process to get what he wanted. Said Taney: "Now as I understand the application at the present time, it means in plain English this—the Bank says to the President, your next election is at hand—if you charter us, well—if not, beware of your power."[56]

Jackson did not need this trio to convince him of the Bank's treachery and malice. But Biddle's action was so provocative and deliberate that the President became wary. He pondered what he should do. Obviously the action challenged his leadership, disregarded his objections to the BUS, and dismissed his overtures for a compromise. With the presidential election only nine months away, and with Clay the declared candidate of the National Republicans, the move for recharter threw down the gauntlet and summoned Jackson to a life-or-death contest.

So be it. The Old Hero understood what he must do, and his fighting spirit stirred. Now the General must slay this monster, not cage it. Now he must commit himself to total warfare. For that reason he must husband his resources and plan his strategy. Intemperate explosions of anger— except when purposefully staged—would not do. He must be cautious and careful.[57]

Biddle's action wholly changed the direction of the contest between the President and the Bank. It was a formal declaration of war.

CHAPTER 21

To Kill a Minister

THE BANK OF THE UNITED STATES was indeed something of a monster, just as Jackson said. It enjoyed enormous financial and political power. To all intents and purposes it responded to the commands of only one man, Nicholas Biddle. It corrupted Congressmen with loans and regular retainer's fees.[1] It intruded into the political process to assist particular candidates for office over its possible enemies. It was the single institution that most represented the concentration of power within the nation and as such was seen by Jackson as a threat to the liberty of the American people.[2]

Despite Biddle's open declaration of war none of Jackson's letters during the first few weeks of 1832 conveyed outrage, as might have been expected. Even among his closest friends and advisers he kept his own council. He remained cool. He assured them all that he still opposed recharter (unless modified) but that he would watch and wait until the bill cleared Congress. "My friends need not fear my energy–should the Bank question come to me," he told Coffee, "unless the corrupting monster should be shraven of its ill gotten power, my veto will meet it frankly & fearlessly."[3]

This new year started very badly for Jackson. First came the application for recharter, then he suffered a severe financial reverse. A small cotton crop and the mismanagement of his overseer meant he earned nothing from his farm. Then the marriage of his son and the impending marriage of Mary Eastin, his ward, to a naval officer depleted his financial reserves. Although his salary of $25,000 a year as President (paid monthly at $2,083 per month) helped considerably, he entertained so lavishly that most of it disappeared each year with hardly a trace. Thomas Hart Benton's daughter remembered as a girl the sumptuous meals served in the White House during Jackson's tenure. She remembered the immense number of wax candles burning in all the state rooms, the "stands of camelias and laurestina" brightening each corner of every room, and the enormous supper table in the State dining room shaped like a horseshoe with a "monster salmon in waves of meat jelly" at either end. The meal itself frequently included canvasback duck, pheasant, fish, ham, mutton chops, and sweetbreads, with side dishes of oyster pie, cauliflower, macaroni, and spinach. For dessert, ice cream, cookies, cakes, custards, and fruit were served. These dinner parties were so frequent and so magnificent that Jackson practically bankrupted himself before he left the White House.[4]

On top of everything else the President contracted influenza early in 1832 that flattened him for weeks. Worse, his new set of artificial teeth did not fit properly and he was forced to remove them so his gums might heal. He felt miserable throughout most of the winter and the behavior of Congress only intensified his misery. Then his left arm started to ache again. The bullet fired by Jesse Benton in 1813 stayed in his arm for nearly twenty years and caused him periods of intense discomfort. By 1831 the bullet had worked itself downward in the inner side of his arm and stationed itself below the wound and less than an inch from the surface of the skin. It could be easily felt and moved. In April, 1831 he thought of going to Philadelphia "to get the bullet cut out of his arm" and he "would have gone but for the political motives which he knew would be imputed."[5] Nine months later the pain intensified and disturbed his work schedule. Since it was so near the skin surface his friends and family believed that it could be extracted quite easily and that its extraction would not only end the pain but have a beneficial effect on his general health. Old Hickory agreed, and so Dr. Harris of Philadelphia was summoned to perform the operation. The procedure was swift. Jackson bared his arm, gritted his jaws, grasped his walking stick, and said, "go ahead."[6] The surgeon made an incision, squeezed the arm, and out popped a "half ball" of the ordinary pistol size. The metal was "a good deal flattened by the contusion upon the bone and hackled somewhat on the edge." The wound was dressed and Jackson went right back to work. An amazing man. What awed everyone over the next three days was that the operation in no way interrupted his attention to business, notwithstanding his long bout with the flu.[7]

Another disappointment came a few weeks later when officials of the University of Virginia informed him that his ward, Hutchings, who seemingly had been doing so well, would be dismissed for absenteeism. Hutchings saved them the bother and withdrew. "How humiliating to my feelings and intelligence!" Jackson scolded the young man. "How useless has [been] my various admonitions, and your promises to me." At least his "moral conduct is without blemish," he told Coffee. Jackson sent Hutchings home to Tennessee to tend to his farm. Maybe, said the President, if he applies himself, "gets a few good books, a well selected little library, he will make a useful citizen." At least no one could say that Andrew Jackson had not tried to give him "a first rate education."[8]

But of all the disappointments Jackson suffered in the opening weeks of the new year, none compared to what happened in the Senate on January 25. The nominations of Van Buren, McLane, and Livingston finally came up for confirmation early in January. Livingston and McLane went through without incident on January 12 and 13, although Livingston complained that he was put through an "investigation in which my whole life was scrutinized and all the newspaper abuse examined . . . with all the force that party could give to them."[9] But Van Buren's nomination as minister ran into a motion to table—and lost. Not until January 24 did the Senate resume consideration, and for two days the debate over the Magician's confirmation rose to a raging duel between Clay, Webster, Poindexter, Miller, and Hayne on the one side and Forsyth, Marcy, Brown, and Smith on the other. Four main objections to the nomination were raised: Van Buren's instructions to McLane in negotiating for the West Indian trade because they repudiated the efforts and policies of previous administrations; his part in causing the breach between Jackson and Calhoun ostensibly to advance his own presidential ambitions; his part in causing the breakup of the cabinet for the same purpose; and his part in introducing the spoils system into the federal government.

Henry Clay, in full cry, said he owed it to "the honor and character of the Government" to vote against confirmation. Standing tall at his place, gesturing at all the appropriate places, looking urbane and confident, he sneeringly referred to "the pernicious system of party politics adopted by the present administration," a system introduced from New York by its onetime senator. William L. Marcy of New York, one of Van Buren's ablest lieutenants, came to his friend's defense and in the course of his remarks handed the opposition a telling quotation with which to bludgeon the administration over its reform policy. "To the victor," he said, "belong the spoils of the enemy." A snappy and cynical rejoinder, but a most unfortunate remark. Although true, it struck many senators as "semi-barbarous—and the utterance of that principle alone, lost Van Buren many, very many friends."[10]

Daniel Webster raked over the instructions to McLane, but it remained for George Poindexter of Mississippi to indulge in personal abuse. Van Buren rode the whirlwind, he orated, "to render the credulous and confiding chief, whose weakness he flattered, and whose prejudices he nourished, subservient to all his purposes, personal and political. His plans of operation were shrouded in darkness and mystery . . . for the accomplishment of his ulterior views." Insinuations about Van Buren's sex life, along with references to his behavior toward Peggy Eaton, dribbled from his "polluted mouth." Stephen D. Miller of South Carolina took obvious pleasure in repeating some of the grossest innuendoes. This prompted Alexander Buckner of Missouri to observe that "none but a liar —an infamous liar, would utter them."[11]

The Vice President gaveled Buckner to order, whereupon John Forsyth of Georgia jumped to his feet and denounced Calhoun for daring to interrupt. "What right have you, Sir, to call a Senator on this floor to order. If you remember your own decisions you must know that you are grossly out of order for this interference." Everyone in the chamber expected a "personal encounter" to follow, at least between Miller and Buckner. Tempers exploded. The "low scurrillous slanders" that flew back and forth ran to "a degree of malignity & vindictiveness never before exhibited in the Senate."[12]

Two days of debate turned the Senate chamber into an arena of ferocious politicians tearing at each other to vent their anger over past injuries and wrongs. Old wounds were picked raw. Calhoun's friends pilloried Van Buren for intriguing his way into Jackson's affections. Van Buren's supporters responded in kind, charging the Vice President with deception and hypocrisy in the Seminole and Eaton controversies. Naturally Clay, Webster, and their associates added to the mayhem with all sorts of devilish remarks and insinuations. "Clay gave a history of V.B. to shew how immoral he was."[13]

With intrigue practically a way of life in Washington, with rejection a real possibility, and with so many senators aching for revenge over one wrong or another, the idea of "rewarding" the Vice President with the distinction and honor of defeating Van Buren's nomination occurred to both Democrats and National Republicans. If there were a tie in the Senate, Calhoun would cast the deciding vote—and what a spectacle that would make. There had already been one tie the week before over a vote to table. With care and attention to vote-counting perhaps another could be "arranged." As it turned out George Bibb of Kentucky held the crucial vote. He had promised to support Van Buren's nomination but was prevailed upon to absent himself on the final vote.[14]

According to Blair, Bibb was a weak-willed, muddle-headed opportunist, "ever the tool of superiors to whom he looked for support or elevation." At the beginning of his career he clung to Clay, then deserted to Jackson, later "joined Calhoun and his nullifiers" when he reached Washington, and finally "fell out with him into Clays hands again and became the tool of the triumvirate [Clay, Calhoun, and Webster] in the conspiracy against [Van Buren]." He was an obvious dupe. He followed instructions. So it was arranged. Bibb conveniently found other things to do on January 25, the day of the final vote.

When the Senate was formally asked if it would consent to Van Buren's nomination as minister to Great Britain, twenty-three senators said yes and another twenty-three said no. Everyone in the room froze. All eyes turned to the Vice President. The senators could feel Calhoun's obvious pleasure. Calmly and deliberately he cast the deciding vote and Van Buren's nomination was defeated.[15]

As the vote was announced Thomas Hart Benton turned to Gabriel Moore of Alabama, who was sitting near him, and said in a half-mocking voice: "You have broken a minister, and elected a Vice-President."

Moore stared at him. Then intellectual dawn spread slowly over his face. "Good God!" he cried, "why didn't you tell me that before I voted, and I would have voted the other way."[16]

Minutes later Benton overheard Calhoun talking with some of his friends about the defeat. The friends were expressing their fears that by their vote they had unwittingly elevated Van Buren to a higher office. Calhoun reassured them. "It will kill him, sir," he sneered, "kill him dead. He will never kick sir, never kick."[17]

The reaction in Washington and around the country was predictable. Democrats vented their outrage and disgust. What an insult to the President, they stormed. What an affront. The friends of Calhoun, Clay, and Webster, on the other hand, gloated over their victory. The punishment they had meted out, they crowed, was richly deserved. They felt sure the people would approve this summary dismissal of a spoilsman who advanced his career by stepping on and over the prostrate bodies of former friends.[18]

What happened in the Senate had long been predicted. Still the reality of it carried a walloping impact. The Albany Regency had anticipated it and even said "that they should like to see" it happen but were "deeply mortified" when their hope materialized. Jackson, too, had been ambiguous. He told Van Buren at one point that he needed him and if the Senate dared to reject him then he would bring him home and make him Vice President. "The opposition would if they durst try to reject your nomination as minister," he wrote in December, "but they dare not, they begin to know if they did, that the people in mass would take you up and elect you vice President without a nomination."[19]

Jackson was presiding at a dinner party when the Senate vote was taken. Adjournment of the upper house came well after six o'clock. The President's guests moved into the Red Room after dinner and Old Hickory entered at their head, "talking and laughing with much animation." He took a seat near the fire. A group knotted around him. He was in rare form that evening and looked extraordinarily self-possessed. His long, narrow head, topped with thick greying hair which stood erect "as though impregnated with his defiant spirit," and his deeply furrowed brow and piercing blue eyes added to his commanding presence. He spoke with precision and point. "His whole being conveyed an impression of energy and daring." Suddenly a messenger entered the room and whispered into Jackson's ear. The President's body stiffened, his eyes flashed. He sprang from his chair.

"By the Eternal! I'll smash them!"[20]

His guests crowded to his side to learn the cause of this outburst. When they heard the devastating news they all commiserated with him. But Jackson soon calmed down and started to calculate his advantages produced by the spite of Calhoun, Clay, and company. What infuriated him, however, was the personal insult directed immediately at himself by the Senate. "The people," he told Van Buren, "will properly resent the insult offered to the Executive, and the injury intended to our foreign relations, in your rejection, by placing you in the chair of the very man whose casting vote rejected you." In his mind the negative vote was aimed at himself, to humiliate him before the electorate. Even so, he knew the people would rally to his side and show their resentment to this outrage and indignity.[21]

For Van Buren, the rejection was the best thing that ever happened to him. It forever linked him to Jackson. His career, his fortune, his reputation were now all tied to Old Hickory, and if the old man continued to enjoy unbounded public affection so, too, would he. "Your course and the Presidents are now blended," wrote Churchill C. Cambreleng, "we must strike while the iron is hot and weld it."[22]

Visitors to the White House were pleasantly surprised at Jackson's quiet demeanor over the incident. Like the introduction of the Bank recharter bill, this incident increased Jackson's outward control over himself. Still his visitors knew that he boiled inwardly. The President takes the matter "with great calmness," wrote one, "but he feels forcibly the affront cast upon him by the majority."[23] How could he not? The affront was so deliberate and premeditated. To close friends like Coffee the General revealed his true feelings. He particularly raged against Miller, Poindexter, and Moore. "They would betray their god let alone their country," he fumed. "Miller made a most disgraceful speech in the secrete session, him and Calhoun are both politically dam'd." The feeling and indignation of the people "run high," he contended, and Democrats ought to take advantage of it and hold meetings to condemn the Senate's action.[24] His suggestion needed little push. Friends of the administration held "Town county and even school district meetings to express their sympathy for their 'fallen Idol'."[25] The party organization began to stir. Thus, with Jackson's encouragement, Democrats started preparing for the coming presidential election.

More than anything else Jackson's "great calmness" and quiet demeanor reflected his growing sense of certainty about the people's approval of his overall handling of the government. He came to believe that the American electorate stood with him in his determination to preserve liberty by reducing government and excising corruption. More and more he saw himself as the sole representative of all the people.[26]

White House guests also saw it. Something in his manner, the way he spoke to them, no matter their station, seemed to tell them that he served as their representative. He not only believed he was a tribune, he acted

the part. He treated visitors with marked respect and kindness; he listened attentively to them and responded to their problems as though he
was responsible for solving them. A young woman who had spent two
years in a mental institution and had been deprived of the use of her
property came to Jackson "for support in her distresses." The old man
heard her out, "shed tears" over her tale of woe, and gave her twenty
dollars from his purse. Anyone as unfortunate as she, he told her,
"should never want while he had a shilling."[27] Everyone came to his door
with their troubles. He turned no one away. Sometimes a whole group
of people appealed to him, dozens of them at a single meeting. When they
did so he usually stood in the center of a circle and heard each one in turn.
Once he was confronted by a "throng of apprentices"—boys of all ages
with their hats on—and he treated them with great deference. According
to one observer these boys were "the vilest promiscuous medley that ever
was congregated in a decent house; many of the lowest gathering around
the doors, pouncing with avidity upon the wine and refreshments, tearing
the cake with the ravenous keenness of intense hunger; starvelings, all
fellows with dirty faces and dirty manners; all the refuse that Washington
could turn forth from its workshops and stables." Nevertheless, Jackson
was not too busy to see them, shake their hands, hear them out, and
provide them with refreshments.[28] Most visitors to the White House
invariably commented on the social and class mixture of people to be
found wandering around the President's drawing room. "Such a crowd
& such a motley crowd," said one, "from Cora Livingston [the secretary
of state's daughter] to a woman in a crimson velvet hat & gown—from
the vice President to an intoxicated canal labourer in a dirty red plaid
cloak—you have probably never seen assembled. It is a striking picture
of *democracy*, & truth to tell, it strikes me with disgust."[29]

Some visitors complained directly to the President. Inviting laborers
into the White House, along with the other riffraff, seemed to carry the
ideals of democracy a bit too far. But Jackson demurred. He said that the
White House was the "People's House" and himself "their steward." He
explained how important it was for the President to have contact with the
community—the entire community. "Our institutions," he said, "are
based upon the virtue of the community." A President draws his strength
from the community. The virtue of the American people constitutes the
bulwark of the Republic, he contended; what demoralizes the people and
diminishes their virtue corrupts their institutions. He "is a great stickler
for virtue and truth," noted one regular caller at the White House.[30]

Whether or not they enjoyed the privilege of visiting the Presidential
mansion and witnessing Jackson's democratic attitudes firsthand, the
American people generally understood or sensed his commitments and
beliefs. Much of his strength with them by 1832 was the basic moral
appeal of his thought and behavior. Despite his earlier stormy life—the
duels, the killings, and the rest—the American people came to regard

Andrew Jackson as the one man in Washington who represented the moral virtues of their revolutionary past.

Although the opening weeks of 1832 provided a series of disasters, still Jackson experienced a strengthening feeling of confidence. Certain of popular support, sure of his future direction, and exuding an aura of calm and control, he rejoiced in the knowledge that Van Buren would soon return home and help him continue his program of reform.

CHAPTER 22

Veto!

THE WHITE HOUSE GLITTERED. The great democrat was hosting a party for thirty guests and he never seemed so lighthearted and happy. As usual he paid particular court to the ladies, standing in their midst and filling their ears with pretty little compliments that had them giggling and gushing their thanks. With his family around him, now augmented by a wonderful daughter-in-law, Jackson radiated contentment. He was "in as fine a humour as I ever saw him," said one guest. As soon as anyone new entered the room the President quickly rushed to their side, seized them by the arm, and "in his usual gallant style" introduced them to all the other guests. After the party had been in progress for a while he asked one young lady to play the pianoforte for him, and when she agreed he escorted her to the instrument and stood by her side while she entertained the guests with several popular airs. At the conclusion of the recital he told her how much her playing pleased him "and then handed her back to her seat again."[1]

When the party broke up and most of the guests dispersed, one or two old friends remained behind and seated themselves with Jackson around the fireplace. Someone asked about his health, particularly in view of his recent operation. He replied that the strength of his arm had been completely restored so that he could now manage a horse with it. Indeed he had already resumed his daily rides. As he spoke his eyes suddenly grew distant as his mind slipped back twenty years. He started reminiscing and he recounted the gunfight with the Bentons and how his "arm was broken *all to pieces.*" He remembered how some of the pieces of bone came out of his arm while he campaigned against the Creek Indians and forced him to keep his arm in a sling for six months.

Some of those pieces he sent to Rachel as a souvenir. Jackson shook his head as these scenes flooded back in his mind. The things he had done in his life.[2]

The Old Hero loved to recount his adventures to an appreciative audience and he sometimes reminisced for hours, encouraged by his guests. Not that that happened very often. Only at small and select parties. At larger affairs he merely circulated among his guests and attended to their needs. For his last levee of the 1831–1832 season, given on his sixty-fifth birthday, some twelve hundred people attended "of all sorts— mostly genteel people." He was "in excellent health & spirits," reported one guest, and bore up under the fatigue of the evening until ten o'clock, when he retired. He admitted to those who inquired that "he has not been so well in 10 years." Apparently the adversity of Van Buren's rejection and the Bank bill revitalized him.[3]

The White House got even livelier in April when Jackson hosted a wedding for Mary Eastin, who had broken her engagement to the naval officer, Captain William B. Finch, to marry a hometown boy, Lucius J. Polk. Jackson had had his doubts about Finch, since he was an older man and a stranger, but he had no reservations about Polk. What he regretted was the loss of Mary from the family circle. Even more devastating to him was the loss of Andrew Jr. and the pregnant Sarah when they returned to the Hermitage on April 12, 1832. The house in Tennessee had undergone extensive alterations the previous year to suit Sarah's presence and needs. Two wings were added, the west wing becoming the dining room (it could seat a hundred persons) and pantry, and the east wing housing the library and overseer's room. Unlike the present house, both wings were gabled with cedar shingles. In addition, porticos were added at the front and back. Across the south front of the house a one-story portico was raised, except over the entrance where it rose two stories and was topped by a pediment with wreaths of laurel leaves in the frieze. Ten slender Doric columns supported the portico across the 104-foot front. The cost of this remodeling, including painting and papering the entire house, ran to $2619.50.[4]

The entire appearance of the Hermitage was dramatically altered by these changes, and what had been a large but unostentatious brick house now began to look like an imposing mansion fit for a grand seignior. At this time a new kitchen and smokehouse were also built and Jackson purchased additional pieces of furniture in Philadelphia to make the residence feel like home to his new daughter. In a relatively short time the General had grown to love this comely girl and before she left for the Hermitage he presented her—"with my affectionate regard"—the pearl necklace and earrings that had once belonged to Rachel. Upon her departure he asked her to write to him regularly. "When alone in my room your letters will be company for me," he said.

Sarah kissed him. She promised to look after things for him. "Dr

Sarah," he added, "drop a kind tear over the tomb of my Dr wife in the garden for me."[5]

Another loss from the Jackson circle of family and friends was Van Buren. The Little Magician had decided against returning home immediately lest it appear that he was in mad haste to climb to higher office. By touring Europe for a few months he could relax and enjoy himself and conveniently miss the national nominating convention to be held in Baltimore by the Democrats in May. Of course he catalogued a variety of other reasons for remaining abroad and swore he would rush home in an instant if Jackson required his services, but the General understood and offered no objection. Since the matter of Van Buren's future was already settled in Jackson's mind he played along with his friend's delicate sense of political feeling. He merely regretted not having him close at hand for consultation now that the bank question neared resolution.[6]

The rejection simplified political matters. Long ago Jackson had decided that Van Buren would run with him on the Democratic ticket, and that ticket no doubt would have been endorsed with or without the rejection. But not everyone cottoned to the prospect of Van Buren as Vice President—especially in the south, where the New Yorker's vote on the Tariff of 1828 was remembered with bitterness. He was seen as a deadweight around Jackson's neck and certain to cost the Hero votes wherever the tariff was a burning issue. "I perceive by the administration papers," wrote one southerner, "that it is highly probably this 'affair' will have the effect, to cause Mr. V. B. to be nominated by the Convention as Vice President. Would not this be carrying the vindication too far for the dictates of policy? . . . His conduct on the tariff question of '28 has been treasured up in judgement against him." The writer suggested Samuel Smith and Philip P. Barbour as far preferable in North Carolina and the rest of the south.[7]

Other states suggested other possibilities. Pennsylvania preferred William Wilkins for the second spot, Kentucky liked Richard M. Johnson, Virginia wanted William C. Rives after Barbour, Maryland offered Louis McLane, to name just a few. And of course there was always John C. Calhoun, for whom Duff Green tried heroically to dredge up support. Not that any of these men had the remotest chance of winning Jackson's acceptance, which was all that mattered. Still the efforts for Barbour and Johnson continued well past the convention date and did not fade away until weeks before the election.

There was no way to block the President's will in the matter. "Jackson is rapped up in Van Buren," reported Senator William L. Marcy to the Regency, and he will hear of no substitute for the ticket.[8] The action of the Senate had insulted the executive branch through a coalition of nullifiers and Clay men, according to the President, and only the action of the people in elevating Van Buren to the vice presidency could atone for the "disgrace done to our country and national character."[9] He expected the Democratic convention to nominate his choice by "acclamation" and to that end he directed Blair and other administration newspapers to devote their energies. Although Blair personally preferred Johnson, an old Kentucky friend, he obeyed the command.

Jackson urged the convocation of a national convention despite its novelty. His appreciation of party organization and discipline had risen considerably during his three years in office and he sensed its importance in terms of his own leadership as President and party standard-bearer. He also saw it as a means of gaining popular acceptance and participation in the selection of the President and Vice President.[10] His immediate concern, however, was in getting Van Buren nominated and in driving off other potential candidates. Thus he reckoned the convention a useful tool.[11]

State and local conventions had been operating in American politics for many years. Once "King Caucus" took a lethal blow, the extension of the convention system to national politics was natural and inevitable. Van Buren considered summoning one for the 1828 election but feared a floor fight over Calhoun's nomination.[12] Then in the spring of 1831 William B. Lewis suggested to Amos Kendall that the state legislatures "propose to the people to elect delegates to a national convention" as the best means of harmonizing the different objectives of the friends of the administration.[13] But it took Jackson's support to win acceptance of the idea. As he quickly recognized and later acknowledged, "the plan of calling Conventions of Delagates, elected by the people themselves and charged with their instructions for the purpose of selecting candidates for important trusts and of thus producing concern among the friends of the same principles" made spanking good sense because it advanced democracy in America. "This plan has had the most beneficial operation, in preventing distractions among the people . . . in selecting agents to give effect to their wishes, and in maintaining their control in the Government. It strikes me that this is the only mode by which the people, will be able long to retain in their own hands, the election of President and Vice President."[14]

Although some states continued to nominate their presidential candidates through their legislatures or local conventions—now called "democratic republican conventions"[15]—Jacksonians throughout the nation heeded a call by New Hampshire, and propagated by the *Globe,* to send delegates to Baltimore to name their ticket.[16] By means of local, city, county, and state meetings or legislative caucuses the delegates were selected. Many states sent delegations equal to their congressional representation, others decided the number in accordance with local wishes. Some 334 Democratic delegates assembled from every state but Missouri (Benton had doubts about the convention) with the eastern states, Kentucky, Tennessee, and Ohio fully represented. This first Democratic national nominating convention met on May 21, 1832, at the Athenaeum, but because of the large number in attendance moved to the Universalist Church on St. Paul Street. Isaac Hill of New Hampshire, John Overton, William Carroll, and John Eaton of Tennessee, Simon Cameron of Pennsylvania, and Silas Wright, Jr., and Azariah C. Flagg of the New York Regency were some of the delegates.[17]

Because New Hampshire had originated the call for a convention, the delegates from that state claimed the right to propose the chairman. They offered John Overton. But Eaton announced that Overton was ill and suggested instead Robert Lucan of Ohio, who was accepted. In formulating convention rules the delegates decided to require a two-thirds vote for nomination of the Vice President. Presumably this rule would encourage unity and cohesion within the party and provide the candidate with the appearance of solid support. The convention also adopted the unit rule, directing the majority of each delegation to cast the entire vote of the state. A committee was appointed, representing every state, to examine and report the credentials of all delegates.

On the evening of the first day, after the convention had adjourned, the Virginia delegation met in Congressman William S. Archer's room— possibly the first "smoke-filled room" at a convention—to decide whether they should risk Jackson's anger and push for Barbour's nomination. They realized that many southerners would vote for him regardless of their decision but finally agreed to go along with Van Buren if he captured a majority of the delegates.[18]

In the afternoon session of the second day the delegates at length reached the principal business of the convention. Without speeches or formal nominations they proceeded immediately to vote and on the first ballot awarded 208 votes to Van Buren, 49 to Barbour (representing votes from Virginia, North Carolina, South Carolina, Alabama, and Maryland) and 26 to Johnson (from Kentucky, Illinois, and Indiana). Archer then rose and announced that the Virginia delegation approved the nomination of Van Buren and would recommend him cordially to their constituents. Whereupon the delegates "unanimously" concurred "in recommending him to the people of the United States for their support."[19]

That this first Democratic convention was summoned solely for the purpose of agreeing to a vice presidential candidate became obvious when it neglected to nominate Jackson for the presidency. As Congressman William King of Alabama said, "with regard to the candidate to be supported for the Presidency, there was no diversity of sentiment among the members of the Convention—all concurring in the propriety and importance of the reelection of our present worthy and venerable Chief Magistrate, Andrew Jackson." The convention simply "concurred" in the nominations the President had already received from many states.

On the last day of the convention, May 23, the committee to prepare an address to the people reported that since the party was united on "principles and sentiments," each delegation should be left the responsibility of making "such explanations by address, report, or otherwise, to their respective constituents of the objects, proceedings and result of the meeting as they may deem expedient." The convention then established a general central committee to reside in Washington and a general corresponding committee for each state appointed by the president of the convention. A special committee headed by Robert Lucas officially notified Van Buren of his nomination. The letter eventually sent the rejected minister congratulated him that "there is in reserve for your wounded feelings a just & certain reparation as well as an ample retribution for the injury meditated against" President Jackson. The delegates then adjourned, gratified with the ease by which they had accomplished the will of their chief.[20]

Compared to the Anti-Masonic and National Republican conventions, the Democratic meeting was virtually cut-and-dried. There was no great address, no statement of principles, no exalted shout of pride over Jackson's achievements. Because of the peculiar circumstances of this convention in addressing itself solely to the question of the Vice President and the fact that they knew what was expected of them, the Democratic meeting felt no obligation to state its principles or define the issues any more than they needed to remind the American people of the virtues and talents of their presidential candidate. The delegates only worried that Jackson had made it more difficult for himself by carrying the "great intriguer" on his back as his running mate.

As for the issues, they hardly seemed relevant to the presidential campaign. Surely issues were never meant to be submitted to the people for their solution. They merely served to define a little more precisely the caliber and leadership of the candidate. And as long as Andrew Jackson sat in the White House the nation did not want for issues. At the moment two potentially lethal bills were slowly making their way through the legislative process in Congress, either of which could convulse the nation. One was the bill to renew the charter of the Bank of the United States, and the other was a bill to revise the tariff schedule in order to rid it of the "abominations" passed in 1828.

Both issues came forward simultaneously in Congress. Henry Clay, in a speech running three days, proposed a new tariff schedule. He extolled his American System and launched into a long discussion of free trade and protection. He insisted that his proposal benefitted all sections of the Union. As he spoke he hurtled one shaft after another at those who would lead us "to the prostration of our manufactures, general impoverishment, and ultimate ruin."[21] Never had he spoken so well, or so long, or to such great effect. He was "in the prime of his prime," said one contemporary.[22] His long exile from the Senate had provided him with renewed vigor. Now he was back, well rested, and in top condition. Andrew Jackson had better stand his guard.[23]

Several Senators from the middle and New England states seconded his arguments—but not his eloquence—while southern senators almost to a man groaned their fears and anxiety. "Sir," pleaded Senator Hayne from South Carolina, "I call upon gentlemen on all sides of the House to meet us in the true spirit of conciliation and concession. Remove, I earnestly beseech you, from among us, this never-failing source of contention. Dry up at its source this fountain of the waters of bitterness. Restore that harmony which has been disturbed—that mutual affection and confidence which has been impaired."[24] In the lower house the debate was even more heated as southerners insisted upon sharp reductions on woolens, cottons, and iron.

Jackson, too, proposed a tariff revision. In his annual message of 1831 he declared that the approaching retirement of the public debt necessitated a more equitable schedule of rates. He tied the reduction of the debt to the tariff but said nothing about the distribution of the surplus. He simply requested revenue to meet the basic needs of the government and opted for duties on articles necessary for national defense as counterweights to foreign trade barriers. Since Louis McLane agreed with the President's thinking on this issue he was given the task of preparing the President's proposal along with an accompanying report. McLane worked diligently on the assignment, collecting information from both manufacturers and farmers. He completed his report on April 27. What he proposed accorded precisely with Jackson's wishes, for it sought compromise between the excessive demands of Clay and the sharp reductions required by the nullifiers. Basically he recommended an overall cut in duties from approximately 45 percent in 1828 to about 27 percent. McLane preferred a gradual diminution of rates but yielded to Jackson's insistence on a speedy adjustment.[25]

As might be expected the extremists on both sides of the issue rejected McLane's rate proposal as either too much or too little. Friends of the administration in Congress applauded it, and the *Globe* assured the nation that it was based on Jacksonian principles and offered in a spirit of conciliation.[26] A few Democratic protectionists like William L. Marcy worried over the reduction on woolens but admitted that all the senators were "exceedingly anxious to conciliate the South."[27] John Quincy Adams, now a member of the House of Representatives from Massachusetts and chairman of the Committee on Manufactures, reacted favorably to the administration's proposal and set his committee to work on adjustments to make it a trifle more palatable to manufacturers, particularly woolen manufacturers. The committee also deleted a few articles, generally lowered duties on noncompetitive goods, and retained high protection on everything else.[28] With these adjustments the bill was reported to the full House on May 16.

In the spirit of conciliation Jackson accepted the revised version. It came close to his own bill, even though it still retained a number of excessive rates. Because Adams's name and reputation accompanied the bill the protectionists in the House agreed to support it. Although some of them preferred the bill reported on March 30 by the Senate Committee on Manufactures because of its higher rates, they decided to keep silent. But the Senate bill was probably scuttled on direct orders from the White House,[29] for without warning the chairman of the Committee on Manufactures, Mahlon Dickerson of New Jersey, asked the Senate to table his committee's recommendation. That done, the Senate turned to the Adams bill after it passed the House, added several amendments raising the rates, and passed it in July. "Bad as was the scheme of the Secretary of the Treasury," snorted Senator Hayne, "the bill from the House was much worse, and this is infinitely the worst of all."[30]

The conference committee of the two houses, prompted by the administration, rejected the Senate changes. Then, under pressure from Jackson, both the House and Senate passed the unamended Adams bill with impressive majorities.[31] The President used Major Lewis as his lobbyist. During the debates Lewis put in repeated appearances in the committee rooms, urging members on both sides of the question to compromise. He roamed the lobbies of the Capitol to make certain that all Democrats heard Jackson's arguments. The President, he said, wished it to be known that he believed "the just course" lay between the two conflicting opinions. Sometimes Lewis resorted to thinly veiled threats.

"You must yield something on the tariff question," he told Senator Marcy of New York, "or Mr. Van Buren will be sacrificed."

Marcy resented this crude attempt at intimidation. "I am Mr. Van Buren's friend," he snapped, "but the protective system is more important to New York than Mr. Van Buren.[32]

Suit yourself, Lewis shrugged. But Marcy got the message and his letters back home to the Regency confirmed it.[33] Lewis's threat had been idle, however. Jackson would never sacrifice Van Buren, but all the New York politicos understood nonetheless how important it was to defuse the tariff issue in an election year.

By and large the Tariff of 1832, which passed on July 9, reduced revenues approximately $5 million and lowered most rates to approximately 25 percent. But woolens, iron, and cottons retained their high protective schedules.[34] "The manner in which the Tariff was adjusted," wrote one Pennsylvania politician, "seems to meet with universal approbation."[35] Quite obviously, he was speaking about reaction in the north.

Jackson signed the tariff bill on July 14, 1832—and gladly. "The modified Tariff," he informed Coffee, "has killed the ultras, both tarifites and nullifiers, and in a few weeks that excitement that has been created by the united influence of the coalition of Calhoun Clay and Webster will cease to agitate the union." Although further mischief will be attempted, he predicted, "the virtue of the people" will dispel it.

You may expect to hear from So Carolina a great noise stired up by Calhoun Miller and Co., who has left here for that purpose, but the good sense of the people will put it down. The south being relieved, by the diminution of duties upon cotton bagging, on blanketts, on course wollings and on sugar will convince the people that the whole attempt at nullification is an effort of disappointed ambition, originating with unprincipled men who would rather rule in hell, than be subordinate in heaven, for the people must now see that all their grievances are removed, and oppression only exists in the distempered brains of disappointed ambitious men.[36]

The possible action of the nullifiers in response to the new tariff was not Jackson's only worry in the summer of 1832. Toward the close of the long debate on this issue the nation suddenly became aware of the frightful danger of the cholera plague that had swept Europe the year before and had now found its way to the United States. Henry Clay readied a resolution requesting the President to appoint a day of fast and introduced it into the Senate on June 27. Meanwhile the synod of the Reformed Church of North America recommended that the President designate a "day of fasting, humiliation and prayer." Jackson responded promptly. He had strong feelings on the subject, for it touched directly on his understanding of the function of the central government. While he concurred in the efficacy of prayer and hoped that the nation would be spared the attack of pestilence, he told the synod, he flatly refused to comply with the request because it would transcend the limits of federal authority prescribed by the Constitution and "might in some degree disturb the security which religion now enjoys in this country in its complete seperation from the political concerns of the General Government." It was the province of the states and the pulpits "to recommend the mode by which the people may best attest their reliance on the protecting arm of the almighty in times of great public distress." Not the President of the United States.[37]

Jackson also watched Clay's posturing in the Senate with undisguised annoyance and irritation. When the Kentuckian's resolution passed the Senate and went to the House the President signaled his advisers to prepare a veto message.[38] Did the Congress not see that such an action by the federal government jeopardized individual freedom and the safety of religion? Fortunately the House on July 14 tabled the resolution and Jackson put his veto aside. A number of Jacksonians mocked Clay's obvious appeal for popular approval. As a gambler, duelist, and hard drinker he seemed hardly the person to call for acts of piety. "Could he gain votes by it," said one, "he would kiss the toe of the Pope and prostrate himself before the grand lama."[39]

The other potential bombshell to work its way through Congress in the spring of 1832 was the Bank bill. Under ordinary circumstances this bill might have sailed through Congress without stirring a ripple of comment or criticism. But Jackson was now determined to kill this "hydra," and he had powerful allies in both the lower and upper houses. Still they constituted a distinct minority; and, after counting votes, they knew that a majority of Congressmen favored recharter and would probably wish to avoid a struggle over the issue if at all possible. Aware of the votes against them and the inevitable "tactics of the bank," the "course of action" for the antiBank Jackson men "became obvious, which was—to attack incessantly, assail at all points, display the evil of the institution, rouse the people—and prepare them to sustain the veto."[40] Which meant placing the final burden of defeating the monster on the President—a burden he was more than willing to bear. Congressional attack also meant forcing the Bank into a posture of defense in both houses. Once the engagement became general the President's forces would "lay it open to side-blow, as well as direct attacks."[41] They proceeded as though they were engaged in actual combat, and they mapped their strategy accordingly. To initiate their assault they asked for an investigation of the BUS by the House of Representatives. Jackson loved this approach. It appealed to his fighting instincts.

Benton got Augustine S. Clayton, a Georgian who had published a pamphlet against the Bank in his own state, to introduce a resolution in the House calling for an investigation of the BUS for misconduct and alleged violations of its charter. Since any number of congressmen received retainers from the Bank, or had obtained loans under the most favorable circumstances, or otherwise benefited monetarily from the Bank's good regard, attempts to block an investigation might well imply guilt. Once an investigation was approved, of course, "misconduct" would most certainly be found.[42] Benton gave Clayton a memorandum of seven alleged breaches of the Bank's charter and fifteen instances of imputed misconduct to look into. Several Pennsylvania representatives tried to quash Clayton's motion after he introduced it, but James K. Polk and Clayton fought them off and the motion passed. As William L. Marcy told his banker friend in Albany, Thomas W. Olcott, the proBank forces dared not object to the motion for fear of offending their "intelligent constituency" who would conclude that Congress was "little inclined to look into the alleged abuses of that mamoth moneyed aristocracy."[43]

A committee consisting of Clayton as chairman and Richard M. Johnson, Francis Thomas, Churchill C. Cambreleng, George McDuffie, John Quincy Adams, and John Watmouth proceeded immediately to Philadelphia to inspect the Bank's operation. The committee, chosen by Speaker Stevenson upon the advice of the White House, was distinctly unfriendly to the BUS, as might have been expected. The subsequent report of this committee shimmered with distortions about the Bank, although it is unlikely that it changed many votes in the House.[44] When the report was published the *Globe* and other Democratic sheets chorused their congratulations for the committee's excellent work, particularly in looking into such reprehensible behavior as discriminating against ordinary citizens in favor of "privileged persons" when granting loans or selling bills of exchange.[45] Actually the committee's greatest contribution was its success in supplying the Jackson press with innuendo and unproven allegations with which they could launch a massive propaganda attack upon the Bank. The nonpartisan newspapers, however, had a different view of the committee's report. Hezekiah Niles, who took an impartial position at the beginning of the Bank War and only later went over to Biddle's side, commented in his *Weekly Register* that the report was "the strangest mixture of *water-gruel* and *vinegar,* the most awkward and clumsy and exaggerated *ex-parte* production that we ever read: it seems to have been begotten in passion and brought forth in weakness—still born!"[46]

The strength of the antiBank organization slowly asserted itself throughout the spring of 1832. With Jackson in the White House rendering enormous aid through encouragement and lobbying tactics, with Benton in the Senate, Polk in the House, and Blair commanding the *Globe,* they constituted a powerful host, despite the Bank's many advantages of money and strong support from responsible and articulate men. With Kendall and Taney at his immediate call, Jackson had an arsenal of talent prepared to provide him any service he demanded in the fight. Even Louis McLane deserted the Bank. The arrogance of the recharter demand in a bill that offered no compromise forced him to admit that the measure must be put down. Only Edward Livingston continued to argue for recharter but Jackson simply ignored him.

The adviser who really gained in stature and importance during this opening round of the Bank War was Attorney General Roger B. Taney. Even congressmen with no quick and ready access to the President noticed his growing influence in the White House. They also heard of his strong—almost violent—resentment toward the Bank. "I verily believe," Cambreleng told Van Buren, that "Taney is the only efficient man of *sound* principles in the Cabinet."[47] As the action in Congress headed toward a final confrontation between the opposing forces, Taney kept up a constant barrage of verbal abuse of the Bank, all channeled directly at Jackson. He grasped every opportunity to see the President and catalogue for him the reasons against recharter. He graphically depicted all the dangers the Bank posed to the liberty of the American people. "It is the immense power of this gigantic machine," he hissed, "—controlling the whole circulating medium of the country—increasing or depressing the price of property at its pleasure all over the U. States . . . it is that power concentrated in the hands of a few individuals—exercised in secret & . . . constantly felt—irresponsible & above the control of the people or the government for the 20 years of its charter, that is sufficient to awaken every man in the country if the danger is brought distinctly to his view."[48]

Where Taney left off—if he ever did—Amos Kendall picked up. Kendall enjoyed a longer association with Jackson and therefore a greater intimacy. Probably Kendall and Taney always hoped to kill the monster rather than reform it. With Blair as their ally and a broadcast medium to command the attention of Democrats across the nation, they began a campaign "to awaken every man in the country" to the dangers posed by Biddle's "gigantic machine." An increasing number of Congressmen enlisted in the fight as the vote on recharter neared, and they too reached out to all levels of their constituency to convert them into enemies of the monster. "Get the Workies to be up and doing on the U.S.B. question," wrote one of them. "They are democrats in principle."[49] But the one person who made the War possible, without whose approval this assault would immediately collapse, was the President. Others might match his spite but only he commanded the forces to accomplish the Bank's destruction.

Nicholas Biddle reacted to the intensified campaign against his institution by rushing down to Washington to conduct the defense in person. He ordered petitions to be sent to Congress demanding renewal and predicting fiscal catastrophe if passage failed. He urged the Bank's retainers in Congress to deliver speeches that he could reprint and distribute around the country. To him the economic future of the nation depended on the BUS, and no wild Indian-scalping frontiersman from Tennessee was going to destroy it.

Jackson carefully observed—and Blair dutifully reported—Biddle's direct intrusion into the legislative process. The action proved all the President's fears and past warnings. Corruption, again generated by the BUS, reared its "hydra-head." Let anyone dare to challenge the power and influence of the Bank and all the horrors commanded by this monster were loosed upon the land. Jackson bemoaned Biddle's interference but he also relied on the people to help him overcome it. "I cannot refrain from shedding a tear over the immorality of our congress, and the corruption of the times," he wrote, "still there are a redeeming spirit in the virtue of the people in which I trust, to perpetuate the liberty of our country, & check the corrupting course of the ambitious demagogues. I have been lead to these expression from corrupting scenes in congress."[50]

Caught in the middle of the opening exchange of fire in the War were the proBank Jacksonians, a sorry group of congressmen who favored recharter but dared not break with the President over the issue. Realizing the futility of appealing directly to Jackson—although a few of them tried unsuccessfully—a group of them went to Biddle after his arrival in Washington and begged him to defer the fight for recharter until after the fall election. They warned of the likelihood of a veto. They even predicted failure to override the veto. The timing, they said, was all wrong. Strategic retreat was Biddle's only sensible course of action. They argued long and earnestly but Biddle refused to budge. He had already committed himself to go forward with the bill and nothing they said convinced him to change his mind.[51] So these bedeviled Democrats decided to force a retreat without Biddle's approval. They introduced delaying tactics in Congress to hold up the bill until the next session. But their tactics failed. The well-drilled Bank men beat them off. "Our life," said Thomas Cadwalader, "depends on this session, and getting the veto now, so that the nation may be roused before the autumnal elections."[52]

On June 11, 1832, despite the labored efforts of Benton and the other Jackson leaders in Congress, the bill for recharter passed the Senate by a vote of 28 to 20. Almost a month later, on July 3, it rode triumphantly through the House by a count of 107 to 85. Solid support for the BUS came from the representatives from New England and the middle Atlantic states with strong opposition from the south and almost divided reaction from the northwest and southwest. Biddle sighed with relief. "I congratulate our friends most cordially upon this most satisfactory result. Now for the President. My belief is that the President will veto the bill though this is not generally known or believed."[53]

No question that Jackson would veto. Only how? Would he leave a small opening wedge to permit approval of some sort of recharter in the future, as most of his cabinet counseled him to do, or kill the Bank outright, once and for all, as Kendall, Blair, and Taney advised? The secretary of the treasury, who should have guided the direction and language of the veto, had relatively little influence in this decision. He had long since lost the President's confidence in the matter. But Jackson was always the gentleman and a stickler for proper form. He would never deliberately offend or embarrass one of his cabinet officers by some insensitive action. As long as it was feasible to do so, he felt that the veto should be kept within his official family; therefore he called a cabinet meeting and told them of his intention. All of them—except Taney, who was away in Annapolis—urged him to place his veto on grounds that would allow him to sign a different recharter bill in the future.[54] But this Jackson positively refused to do. "He would not sign a veto placing it upon any other grounds than those upon which he acted," he informed them.[55] This meant they could offer him no help in composing his veto. This meant he must go outside for assistance. Although it pained him to disregard his cabinet, Jackson had no choice, and so he asked Kendall to begin the task of composition. At the same time he summoned Taney to the White House to assist in the preparation.

Taney spent three days with Kendall and Donelson shaping the message. They used the room that Ralph Earl had outfitted as a studio. As the message progressed, Earl painted. The President frequently interrupted the composition, listening to what had been written and "giving his own directions as to what should be inserted or omitted."[56] The first day of the preparation Amos Kendall worked practically alone except for the presence of Earl in the room. The first draft was his. The second day Levi Woodbury dropped by and in an effort to edge closer to the President's position lent a hand in some of the revisions demanded by Jackson.

By this time Taney was deep into the preparation, since he seemed to enjoy a special relationship with the General on the issue. Actually it was not so much a dissatisfaction with Kendall or his work that brought the attorney general more immediately into the drafting stage but the fact that Taney belonged to his official family and Jackson felt more comfortable having him involved. A small prejudice perhaps, but it indicated how traditional and conservative Old Hickory could be in some things. Another participant in the wording process of this most important state paper was Major Andrew J. Donelson, but his other responsibilities constantly interfered, so his contribution was relatively slight. As for Louis McLane, he denied that he was responsible for a single argument in the entire message as ultimately written.[57] Overall the presence and will of Andrew Jackson predominated. What finally emerged was precisely what he wanted to say to Congress and the American people.[58]

When completed to the satisfaction of the group who composed it, the veto was taken to the President for his consent. He read it, approved it, and summoned his cabinet for their comments and suggestions. Then he transmitted it to Congress.[59]

Martin Van Buren returned to the United States on July 4, 1832, just in time to get down to Washington to see his friend before the veto went forward. The President was anxious to see him. On the evening of Van Buren's first appearance at the White House after his return home he was startled to find Jackson on a sickbed looking like "a spectre . . . but as always a hero in spirit." The President brightened when he saw the New Yorker. He reached out his hand in welcome. The Magician gushed a greeting. Then, holding Van Buren's hand in one of his own and passing the other through his long grey-white hair, he said: "The bank, Mr. Van Buren is trying to kill me, *but I will kill it!*"[60] He said this very quietly, without passion or any tone of rage. Nor was it a boast. Just a simple statement of fact.

To destroy the Bank of the United States meant that Jackson's reform program now verged on a radical swing towards more vigorous action to terminate centralized power within the country. Henceforth Jackson's language and actions show a determination to obliterate every vestige of this liberty-threatening institution. Henceforth he sharpened his public attack. He referred to the Bank as a "hydra-headed monster" equipped with engines of terror and destruction and so dangerous that it "impaired the morals of our people," "threatened our liberty," "subverted the electoral process," and undermined "our republican institutions."[61] His reform program took a wild leap forward with the transmittal of his veto of the Bank bill, and cleared the way for further change and improvement. To succeed in his purpose would have a shattering impact on the financial and political operations of the country. Its social and intellectual consequences would be even more devastating.

Signed and transmitted to Congress on July 10, 1832, the veto hit the nation like a tornado. For it not only cited constitutional arguments against recharter—supposedly the *only* reason for resorting to a veto—but political, social, economic, and nationalistic reasons as well. The Bank of the United States, Jackson argued, enjoyed exclusive privileges conferred by the government which, for all intents and purposes, gave it a monopoly over foreign and domestic exchange. Government must never confer exclusive privileges on anyone or any institution, he asserted, for that creates inequity and leads ultimately to a deprivation of liberty. Investigation revealed, he said, that relatively few people owned stock in the BUS—"chiefly the richest class"—and yet they divided profits from investments of government funds generated from taxes on all the people. Some $8 million worth of shares belonged to foreigners, Jackson contended. By this recharter bill, therefore, "the American Republic proposes virtually to make them a present of some millions of dollars." Once the President hit this theme in his message he repeated it like the intense nationalist he was, over and over. Why should the few, particularly the foreign few, hold the special favor of this country? If the government must sell monopolies, he continued, "it is but justice and good policy . . . to confine our favors to our own fellow citizens, and let each in his turn enjoy an opportunity to profit by our bounty." Because of these foreign investments the Bank necessarily catered to their interests. "Is there no danger to our liberty and independence in a bank that in its nature has so little to bind it to our country?" Is there not "cause to tremble for the purity of our elections in peace and for the independence of our country in war?" Furthermore, control of this institution rests firmly in the hands of the wealthy. "It is easy to conceive that great evils to our country and its institutions might flow from such a concentration of power in the hands of a few men irresponsible to the people."[62]

Turning to the constitutional question, Jackson noted that the friends of the Bank had insisted that it had been settled by the Supreme Court in the case *McCulloch* v. *Maryland.* "To this conclusion," he declared, "I cannot assent." Both houses of Congress and the executive must decide for themselves what is or is not constitutional before taking any action on a bill, whether that action consists of voting for it by Congress or signing it by the President. "It is as much the duty of the House of Representatives, of the Senate, and of the President to decide upon the constitutionality of any bill or resolution which may be presented to them for passage or approval as it is of the supreme judges when it may be brought before them for judicial decision." What Jackson argued here, and argued in a way citizens in 1830 would understand, was the equality and independence of each branch of the federal government. A balance had been established by the Constitution among the three branches, and through that balance the liberty of the people was protected. To allow the Supreme Court total and final authority skews the system. Just because the court declares a bill constitutional does not mean that Congress *must* vote for such a bill when one is introduced, or that the President *must* sign it if, in their good judgment, they honestly believe the bill unconstitutional. "The authority of the Supreme Court," he averred, "must not, therefore, be permitted to control the Congress or the Executive when acting in their legislative capacities, but to have only such influence as the force of their reasoning may deserve." Since the matter of a national bank was subject to their action, Jackson simply claimed for the Congress and the executive the right to think and act as equal and independent members of the government.[63]

It is important to note that Jackson claimed legislative power for the executive in arguing this point, something Congress was certain to resent however true it might be.

The message continued examining the constitutional issue, addressing the "necessary and proper" clause and whether it applied to such institutions as banks. Jackson then turned to the accusations of the Bank's "gross abuse and violation of its charter." There was enough evidence, he said, "to excite suspicion and alarm," enough to warrant suspension of further action on this bill until a full inquiry had been completed. Since the Bank was unwilling to submit to a thorough investigation, the government should therefore "proceed with less haste and more caution in the renewal of their monopoly."[64]

Jackson not only whacked away at the Bank and its practices but he continually asserted presidential authority and privilege. "The bank is professedly established as an agent of the executive branch of the Government," he declared, "and its constitutionality is maintained on that ground." Yet neither upon the propriety nor the provisions of this act was the executive consulted. Whatever public or private interests gave birth to this act they did not include "the wishes or necessities of the executive department." The action is therefore premature and the "powers conferred . . . not only unnecessary, but dangerous to the Government and country."[65]

But the greatest devastation from this tornadolike veto came at the tail end of the message. It almost sounded like a call to class warfare. Certainly nothing like it had ever come from a President before—or ever would again.

> It is to be regretted that the rich and powerful too often bend the acts of government to their selfish purposes. Distinctions in society will always exist under every just government. Equality of talents, of education, or of wealth can not be produced by human institutions. In the full enjoyment of the gifts of Heaven and the fruits of superior industry, economy, and virtue, every man is equally entitled to protection by law; but when the laws undertake to add to these natural and just advantages artificial distinctions, to grant titles, gratuities, and exclusive privileges, to make the rich richer and the potent more powerful, the humble members of society—the farmers, mechanics, and laborers—who have neither the time nor the means of

securing like favors to themselves, have a right to complain of the injustice of their Government. There are no necessary evils in government. Its evils exist only in its abuses. If it would confine itself to equal protection, and, as Heaven does its rains, shower its favors alike on the high and the low, the rich and the poor, it would be an unqualified blessing. In the act before me there seems to be a wide and unnecessary departure from these just principles.

Nor is our Government to be maintained or our Union preserved by invasions of the rights and powers of the several States. In thus attempting to make our General Government strong we make it weak. Its true strength consists in leaving individuals and States as much as possible to themselves —in making itself felt, not in its power, but in its beneficence; not in its control, but in its protection; not in binding the States more closely to the center, but leaving each to move unobstructed in its proper orbit.[66]

Jackson then closed the message by placing his reliance on the American people. If they sustained him he would be "grateful and happy." More and more frequently Jackson spoke in his public as well as his private writings of his absolute confidence in the ability of the people to recognize the wisdom and moral worth of his actions. "In the difficulties which surround us and the dangers which threaten our institutions," he concluded, "let us firmly rely on that kind Providence which I am sure watches with peculiar care over the destinies of our Republic, and on the intelligence and wisdom of our countrymen. Through *His* abundant goodness and *their* patriotic devotion our liberty and Union will be preserved."[67]

So ended one of the strongest and most controversial presidential statements ever written. The friends of the Bank were utterly appalled by the tone and substance of the message, and some of its principles and arguments were later scored by historians and economists as "beneath contempt."[68] Nicholas Biddle likened it to "the fury of a chained panther biting the bars of his cage." It was, he said, "a manifesto of anarchy, such as Marat or Robespierre might have issued to the mobs" during the French Revolution.[69] The Democrats, naturally, hailed it as a "Second Declaration of Independence" and summoned the people to register their approval of it at the polls in the coming election. As it soon developed, the veto proved to be a realistic and hardheaded political document, exciting men to battle. As an economic statement, totally unconcerned with the Bank's financial value to the nation, it can be faulted easily. But as propaganda it is a masterpiece.

Indeed, Jackson's Bank veto is the most important veto ever issued by a President. Its novel doctrines advanced the process already in train by which the presidency was transformed and strengthened. To begin with, Jackson accomplished something quite unprecedented by writing this veto. Previous Presidents had employed the veto a total of nine times. In forty years under the Constitution only nine acts of Congress had been struck down by the chief executive, and only three of these dealt with important issues. In every instance the President claimed that the offending legislation violated the Constitution. It was therefore generally accepted that a question of a bill's constitutionality was the only reason to apply a veto. Jackson disagreed. He believed that a President could kill a bill for any reason—political, social, economic, or whatever—when he felt it injured the nation and the people. The implications of such an interpretation were enormous. In effect it claimed for the President the right to participate in the legislative process. Jackson invaded the exclusive province of Congress. According to his view, Congress must now consider the President's wishes on all bills *before* enacting them, or risk a veto. It must defer to the will of the executive if it expects to legislate successfully. Jackson's interpretation of presidential prerogatives, therefore, essentially altered the relationship between the legislative and executive branches of government. The President now had a distinct edge. He was becoming the head of the government, not simply an equal partner.

From the founding of the nation under the Constitution, the legislative branch was generally regarded as preeminent. In the minds of most, it was Congress, not the President, who embodied and secured representative government. The generation of Americans who fought the Revolution had been very suspicious of a strong chief executive. To them, executive power meant monarchical (and ultimately dictatorial) power. Thus, in dedicating themselves to the perpetuation of individual liberty they devised a system of government with a strong legislature elected by the people and in full control of the purse strings. Jackson changed that. Thenceforward the President could participate in the legislative process. Coupled with that was his total success in establishing the concept that he, as President, represented all the people. And he, as President, protected their liberty.

Critics were appalled by Jackson's claims. The editors of the Washington *National Intelligencer* later argued that the veto power "enabled the President . . . to usurp the legislative power." The question henceforth "is not what Congress will do," they jeered, "but what the President will permit."[70]

Jackson's veto message of 1832 also powerfully restated the philosophy of the minimized state. Centralized government endangered liberty, he said, and therefore it must never intrude in the normal operations of society. When it does interfere and assumes unwarranted power, such as creating a Bank, it produces "artificial" distinctions between classes and generates inequality and injustice. Americans in the Jacksonian age believed in equality in the abstract, which they felt could be realized in the concrete as equal opportunity. Therefore, no one—and no institution—should be aided (or hindered) by the government through its legislation in achieving the full fruits of his individual labor.

This ideological position concerned Jackson long after the veto was returned to Congress. In fact for the coming presidential election he felt he must "give to my opponents a full view of my opinion on the constitutional power of Congress to create corporations, as well as the impolicy & inexpediency of the measure, as well as its corrupting influence on the morals of the nation."[71]

The Democratic press amplified Jackson's arguments. By chartering the BUS, they chorused, the Congress had permitted the creation of a "moneyed aristocracy." This aristocracy, they continued, acquired "a power over our people, and an influence in their government, which threatened to change the character of our institutions, and reduce our States to a degrading dependence." Fortunately, Andrew Jackson stood guard at the helm of government. "Well it is for the people that they have him at their head . . . and well it is for the principles of republicanism and 'equal rights.' " The Bank will "receive its death-blow from the patriotic Jackson, the man of the People. He has watched its corrupting power, its unwarrantable abuses, and now . . . he will . . . put a period to its existence." The course of American freedom was secure with Old Hickory in the White House. "It is difficult to describe, in adequate language," proclaimed the *Globe*, "the sublimity of the moral spectacle now presented to the American people in the person of Andrew Jackson."[72]

The Bank War then shifted back to the Capitol. Congress had the option of accepting Jackson's decision or rejecting it by overriding his veto. No one doubted its intended course, and on July 11 Daniel Webster rose in the Senate to smite the President with the force of his eloquence and constitutional knowledge.

Again, mobs jammed the gallery to hear the "god-like Daniel," and he did not disappoint them. His words rose and fell with dramatic impact, the great head rolled to the rhythm of his cadences, and his right hand flashed through the air to punctuate his arguments. He was contemptuous of the President's constitutional arguments, outraged by its attitude toward the Supreme Court, and downright furious by its attempt to divest Congress of its full legislative authority. "According to the doctrines put forth by the President," intoned the glowering Webster, "although Congress may have passed a law, and although the Supreme Court may have pronounced it constitutional, yet it is, nevertheless, no law at all, if he, in his good pleasure, sees fit to deny it effect; in other words, to repeal or annul it." Webster's face darkened as his voice became more agitated. "Sir, no President and no public man ever before advanced such doctrines in the face of the nation. There never was a moment in which any President would have been tolerated in asserting such a claim to despotic power."

Webster hit the mark squarely. But times had changed and the people no longer feared their chief executive. Rather they identified with him. They looked to Jackson as their representative, and therefore these whiggish fears about his claim to despotic power sounded more like partisan politics than anything else. Webster further contended that Jackson's bold assertion of his prerogatives was not confined to a simple statement of presidential preeminence over the other two branches of government. He went further. Jackson "claims for the President, not the power of approval, but the primary power of originating laws."[73]

Not exactly. Although this interpretation can be inferred from the message, and the presidential practice of initiating legislation begins at this time, what Old Hickory wanted to get across to Congress was his right to be a partner in the power of originating laws, a power that he argued was properly his by virtue of his veto authority. But even this was an abrupt departure from the past. So Webster protested. "We have arrived at a new epoch," he warned. "We are entering on experiments with the government and the Constitution, hitherto untried, and of fearful and appalling aspect."[74]

Henry Clay agreed. And when he rose to speak there was even greater excitement among the visitors in the galleries, for Clay was a gut fighter, a verbal brawler whose slashing attacks on his victims (Jackson among them during the Seminole debate in 1819) delighted his audience because they were always so deliciously nasty and personal. He called Jackson's action a "perversion of the veto power." The framers of the Constitution, he said, never intended it for "ordinary cases. It was designed for instances of precipitate legislation, in unguarded moments." It was to be used rarely, if ever, something all previous Presidents had understood. "We now hear quite frequently, in the progress of measures through Congress," he cried, "the statement that the President will veto them, urged as an objection to their passage!" Imagine! Through the instrument of the veto, the President may effectively intrude into the legislative process and force his will upon Congress. This was "hardly reconcilable with the genius of representative government." It was downright revolutionary.[75]

The Democrats hooted at Clay's criticism. Thomas Hart Benton rose to reply. This big, powerful-looking man with an ego twice the size of his physique was every bit the match for Senators Clay and Webster. He invariably generated excitement when he spoke. On this occasion he referred to Webster and Clay as the "duplicate Senators," which drew a big laugh from the galleries. He scolded the pair for faulting Jackson when the BUS, the most power-mad institution in the country, corrupted everyone it touched, and was presently engaged in controlling the next election by unleashing its financial might to defeat the President. He was shocked, he said, by the disrespect toward Jackson that he had heard in the chamber during the debate. No doubt it was all part of a vicious campaign, financed by Biddle, to abuse and discredit the President before the American public.

Clay laughed at Benton. What a faker! He remembered back to 1813, he said, when Jackson and Benton were enemies and had engaged in a gunfight involving several other men including Benton's brother, Jesse. And Benton dares to talk of disrespect and abuse. At least, taunted Clay, "I never had any personal rencontre with the President; I never complained of the President beating a brother of mine after he was prostrated and lying apparently lifeless." Nor, he continued, had he ever said that if Jackson were elected President, congressmen would have to protect themselves by carrying guns and knives.

"That's an atrocious calumny," cried Benton, springing to his feet.

"What," retorted Clay, "can you look me in the face, sir, and say that you never used that language?"

"I look," bellowed Benton, "and repeat that it is an atrocious calumny, and I will pin it on him who repeats it here."

Clay flushed with rage. "Then I declare before the Senate that you said to me the very words."

"False! False! False!" screamed Benton.

Other Senators bolted to their feet, fearful the two men would attack one another on the Senate floor. Ladies in the galleries gasped in horror, while the men roared their excitment at the possibility of a fistfight on the floor—or worse.

The chair gaveled for order. After a few moments the dignity of the Senate was restored.

"I apologize to the Senate," said Benton, "for the manner in which I have spoken—but not to the Senator from Kentucky."

Clay stood his ground. The thin line that marked his mouth slowly stretched into a smile. "To the Senate," he said, "I also offer an apology —to the Senator from Missouri, none!"[76]

Thus ended the great debate over Jackson's arbitrary seizure of legislative power and his illegal "experiments with the government and the Constitution." But despite the oratorical power of Webster and Clay, the Bank men could not muster a two-thirds vote to override Jackson's veto. The 22 to 19 tally fell far short of the needed vote. On July 16, 1832, both houses adjourned. Since there would be a presidential election in the fall, the members were terribly concerned about the effects of the Bank War in political terms.[77] Jackson, in writing the veto as he did, laid the Bank issue squarely before the American people for decision. Never before had a chief executive taken a strong stand on an important matter, couched his position in provocative language, and challenged the electorate to unseat him if they did not approve. And the alternative was clear. Either Clay and the Bank—or Jackson and no Bank.

The decision rested with the American people.

CHAPTER 23

Jackson, the Union, and Democracy

THE PRESIDENTIAL ELECTION OF 1832 was the one and only time in American history that a major issue was submitted to the electorate for disposition. In that sense it is unique. The American people hate to decide issues. It frightens and confuses them. But Jackson insisted on a popular referendum. He so trusted the good judgment of the people and their devotion and affection for him, and he so despised the BUS as the worst of all corrupting agents in the country, that he believed the outcome a foregone conclusion. He reduced the contest to a simple morality struggle between good and evil, between an honest yeomanry and a decadent money power. He was less apprehensive about this election than any other he had ever engaged in; he was content that nothing further needed to be done to insure success. Proud of his veto, certain of the inevitable triumph of morality, he made no particular effort to shape and direct this election. The mechanics of victory he left to others. "The opposition you will see are reckless," he told John Coffee toward the end of the campaign, "all kinds of slander but the virtue of the people will meet the crisis and resist all the power and corruption of the bank."[1]

Small wonder the American people regarded him with such total devotion. He was more than a symbol to them.[2] He appealed to their moral sense, to their goodness and their virtue. He added to their dignity. He uplifted their pride. His appeal was never the vulgar call of the crude politician pandering for votes. Jackson's appeal went to the conscience and patriotism of the electorate.

Jackson's calm and certain attitude about the goodness of the people and their ultimate triumph seemed to give him an air of resignation and acceptance, as though he were now above mundane cares and problems.

Even the running of his plantation and the concerns at home failed to disturb his peaceful mood. "Andrew is now married," he said, "and I mean to throw the care of the farm on him, I shall never more pester myself with this worlds wealth—My only ambition is to get to the Hermitage so soon as the interest of my country and the will of the people will permit me, and there to set my house in order and go to sleep along side of my dear departed wife."[3]

Anxious to depart disease-ridden Washington, where the cholera had already begun its deadly work, Jackson waited out the adjournment of Congress before heading back to Tennessee and the quiet of the Hermitage. The details of the presidential campaign were left in the capable hands of men like Kendall, Blair, Lewis, Donelson, and a small army of politicians stationed around the country.

Amos Kendall served virtually throughout the campaign as national party chairman. A regular flow of correspondence and campaign propaganda to politicians in every state left his office each day. He urged organization; he encouraged the founding of newspapers; he prodded politicians to "proclaim" the message of Jacksonian reform. "You must try by an efficient organization and rousing the patriotic enthusiasm of the people," he told one party chieftain, "to counteract the power of money." "Have you an organization in your state?" he queried another. "Whether you have or not . . . send me a list of names of Jackson men good and true in every township of the state . . . to whom our friends may send political information. I beg you to do this *instantly.*"[4]

Francis Blair also proved to be a valuable campaigner during this election. Indeed, his newspaper kept up a steady barrage of uncommonly effective propaganda, some of it vicious but all of it effective. When the New York *Courier and Enquirer* reversed its editorial policy and came out in favor of the Bank after receiving a substantial loan, Blair nailed its editor, James Watson Webb, as "That two legged, strutting, mouthing, ranting, bullying animal . . . Webb who has just 'hopped the twig' and now sits perched on the United States Bank, chanting his cock-a-doodle-doos." Hezekiah Niles, the editor of a Baltimore sheet, was bullied for supporting recharter. The *Globe* noted that Niles had "defected to the Bank: *price unknown.*"[5] It also pummeled congressmen who supported recharter and accused them of having been "bribed." George Poindexter of Mississippi and Josiah Johnson of Louisiana were particularly singled out for "borrowing" $10,000 and $36,000 respectively. Practically all of these accusations were well founded.[6]

Blair and Kendall issued special *Extra Globes* during the campaign designed "to throw this paper into every neighborhood of the United States." They exhorted members of Congress "to assist in disseminating it among their constituents." They virtually wrapped the country in antiBank propaganda. "Extra *Globes,*" reported the Maine *Advocate,* "are sent in bundles by the Administration and its officers, into every town where a Jackson man can be found to distribute them. Letters are written and *franked* by the different officers at Washington, and sent out in all directions, soliciting 'names and money', and it is avowed to be their intention to introduce them into every house in the State, if possible. . . . At what former period have we seen the government officers, and even the President himself . . . writing electioneering letters, and circulating papers filled with political trash and the vilest falsehoods."[7]

Jackson delighted in this journalistic free-for-all. "With my sincere respects to Kendall & Blair," he wrote to Lewis from the Hermitage in August, "tell them the veto works well, & that the Globe revolves with all its usual splendor—That instead, as was predicted & expected by my enemies, & some of my friends, that the veto would destroy me, it has destroyed the Bank."[8] The language and tone of the veto inspired much of the editorial comment and mood of the campaign. Instead of attacking Clay or Wirt, the candidates of the opposing parties, Democratic editors tended to single out the BUS (or Biddle) as the principal villain of this election. The *Globe,* like Jackson, referred constantly to the Bank as a "monster," one with twenty-seven heads and a hundred hands. The "Golden vaults of the Mammoth Bank," announced Blair, were opened wide to pay electioneers two dollars a day to campaign against the President. Such "bribery" and interference into the electoral process should not go unpunished, he preached. "Let the cry be heard across the land. Down with bribery—down with corruption—down with the Bank. . . . Let committees be appointed in every township to prosecute every Bank agent who offers a bribe." What these propagandists tried to prove to the people was Jackson's contention that if the Bank, "a mere monied corporation," can direct the results of political elections, then "nothing remains of our boasted freedom except *the skin of the immolated victim.*"[9]

Of course Nicholas Biddle did not sit mute in his office on Chestnut Street in Philadelphia and allow these outrageous statements against his Bank to go unchallenged. He poured thousands of dollars into a verbal assault on Jackson to defeat him. He paid for the reprinting of speeches by Clay, Webster, and anyone else who supported recharter. He even distributed thirty thousand copies of the veto message because he considered it excellent propaganda for the Bank. "The U.S. Bank is in the field," wrote Senator Marcy, "and I cannot but fear the effect of 50 or 100 thousand dollars expended in conducting the election in such a city as New York." Isaac Hill agreed. The financial power of the Bank reached into New Hampshire to influence the election. "The Bank is scattering its thousands here to affect us," he reported. It has been estimated that the Bank probably contributed something in the neighborhood of $100,-000 to defeat Andrew Jackson, although no precise amount of money can be calculated.[10] When warned that his actions only proved Jackson's case that the Bank interferred in the free elections of the American people, Biddle dismissed the warnings with a snort.

Given Jackson's principal reason for attacking the Bank and Biddle's vigorous response, the editorial campaign against the "monster" soon widened to include broader questions of democracy and liberty. The struggle against the BUS was a struggle to preserve American liberty, the editors said. "The Jackson cause," they chorused, "is the cause of democracy and the people, against a corrupt and abandoned aristocracy."[11] Because Jackson stands with the people against tyranny and in defense of liberty he has been maligned and attacked by the citadels of money and elitism. "He is opposed because he supports the interests of the WHOLE PEOPLE," argued the Vermont *Patriot*, "—because he will not uphold corrupt monopolies—because he will not become suppliant to the Aristocracy of the land!" Liberty and democracy versus tyranny and corruption was what this election was all about, according to the Democrats.[12]

As might be expected the National Republicans took a less exalted view of Jackson's reform program. To all the propaganda about democracy and liberty, they countered with accusations of despotism and tyranny. "The spirit of Jacksonianism," insisted the Boston *Daily Advertiser and Patriot*, "is JACOBINISM. . . . Its Alpha is ANARCHY and its Omega DESPOTISM. It addresses itself to the worst passions of the least informed portion of the People." The Cincinnati *Daily Advertiser* said that Jackson had annulled "two houses of Congress, the Supreme Court and the Constitution of the United States." He had inflicted a "calamity on the prosperity" of the nation by his veto, added another journal. "Could it have any effect but to swell the power and augment the influence of the Executive, by adding money to patronage?" The "Constitution is gone!" moaned the Washington *National Intelligencer*. "It is a dead letter, and the will of a DICTATOR is the Supreme Law!"[13]

Although frequently savage, the National Republican press on the whole lacked the vigor and viciousness of the best Democratic sheets. However the National Republicans did publish a number of pamphlets which in terms of content and analysis far outdistanced the Jacksonians in documenting their case before the American people.

One such pamphlet, *A Retrospect of Andrew Jackson's Administration*, running nearly twenty-five printed pages, closely analyzed the President's career and accomplishments. In a dispassionate critique it indicted him for his failures. Jackson had come to power, said the *Retrospect*, preaching retrenchment, economy, and reform. But in four short years he had violated every one of his pledges. "He has introduced a new tenure of office, obedience to his will," claimed the *Retrospect*, and consequently dismissed 990 office holders, more than 13 times the number of those removed by his predecessors. Many new federal offices have been created, with salaries and expenses increased. Thus, instead of retrenchment, as he promised, "we find a most disastrous dereliction from the economy of those measures, on the discredit and ruin of which his advocates sought to elevate him to power." The expenses of the government currently run $10 million more than they did under President John Quincy Adams, said the *Retrospect*. It cost $22,500 alone to send John Randolph to Russia on a "pretended mission" in which he spent the "whole time, except for eleven days, in London improving his health." Another $18,000 went for Van Buren's abortive mission to Great Britain, which could have been avoided if the President had waited for the consent of the Senate as required by the Constitution. The post office spent in excess of $300,000 and needed an annual addition of $80,000 to sustain the department—and yet the postal service throughout the country has been reduced. All told, argued the *Retrospect*, the Jackson administration has cost the taxpayer more money and provided less service. If swelling the departments in terms of personnel and expenses is retrenchment and economy, "then we want no more of it."[14]

Jackson pledged reform in all the departments, continued the *Retrospect*, yet his cabinet produced nothing but dissension. And this dissension was provoked "in order to control their private families" or dictate their views about Van Buren for the vice presidency. We also believe, said the pamphlet, that the President "encouraged one of his favorites to assassinate an obnoxious member!" Some reform![15]

Jackson promised to reduce the authority and power of the central government, but had in fact increased it, according to the *Retrospect*. Instead of observing the strict letter of the Constitution, he has departed from it—repeatedly. Appointment, according to the Constitution, requires the advice and consent of the Senate. Jackson had not only appointed a minister to the Turkish dominions and other minor officials without this consent but even after the Senate had "expressly refused to give its consent." In employing the veto in such a "revolutionary" and arbitrary manner, "Jackson has shown a strong propensity to intrude upon the legislative department, and by several successive acts of power has taken from Congress almost half its powers, and from the Senate more than half." Andrew Jackson, announced the *Retrospect*, "is an Usurper and a Tyrant; and our constitution and laws, under his Chief Magistracy, are but a dead letter."[16]

Furthermore, the President has arrested internal improvements, has obscured his true position on the tariff "in ambiguity and mystery," and has drained millions from the treasury to "drench the borders of the frontiers with the blood of the wretched half-starved Indians, without taking any efficient measures to avert or diminish the calamity." He has shown nothing but contempt for the Supreme Court in refusing to interpose his authority to free men held by the state of Georgia. In sum, "General Jackson has, by his lawless usurpations, inflicted deep and dangerous wounds on the constitution, and his tyranny has gone very far to discredit the whole system of popular government. He has proved false to his promises, to his country, to his friends, to everything but his own wretched ambition."[17]

Quite a listing. Quite an indictment. The Democrats responded with categorical denials of these charges. If the truth be admitted, they said, everyone must acknowledge that Jackson had swept corruption from government and restored the virtues of the Founding Fathers. He terminated unconstitutional expenditures and saved millions of public money; he substantially reduced the national debt and was close to paying it off entirely; and he was engaged in destroying that enemy of liberty and monster of corruption, the Bank of the United States. He also restored trade with the West Indies, which had been lost through diplomatic mismanagement; concluded advantageous treaties with Denmark, Turkey, and France; and achieved a higher degree of respect from the rest of the world than had ever existed before. And he had guided the Indians to a safe haven in the west where they could preserve their culture and religion forever. A self-made man, a man of the people, he warred against monopolies, aristocrats, and stock-jobbers. He was democracy's finest image of itself.[18]

The verbal assaults on Jackson's character and achievements were nothing new to the Hero. They had accompanied his entire public life. But he never overcame his need to defend himself or strike back at those who reviled him. Even in 1832 when he seemed confident of popular support and content with the success of his administration, Jackson could not help intruding in the campaign from time to time to direct his editors in responding to some charge or complaint. When the Washington *National Intelligencer,* along with other newspapers in the country, scolded him for his rotation policy, Jackson immediately signaled the *Globe* to issue a rebuttal. "Present me to Mr. and Mrs. Blair," he wrote to William B. Lewis, "and say to him I shall expect to see a good reply to Joe Gales [Joseph Gales and William W. Seaton edited the *National Intelligencer*] attack on the administration for removals. Joe may be challenged to name one officer removed that has not been swindling the Govt. or was not a defaulter. However you know all this, and Mr. Kendall if his health and other concerns will permit can give Joe such a dressing as will quiet him, and *if possible,* put him from lying."[19]

Jackson remained in Tennessee a good part of the summer of 1832 and therefore relied totally on Kendall and Blair to counteract the "lying" propaganda of the National Republicans. He had left Washington on July 22 and did not return until October 19. On his journey home he reportedly paid all his expenses in gold. "No more paper-money, you see, fellow-citizens," he remarked with each gold payment, "if I can only put down this Nicholas Biddle and his monster bank."[20] Gold, hardly a popular medium of exchange, was held up to the people as the safe and sound currency which Jackson and his administration hoped to restore. Unlike paper money, gold represented real value and true worth. It was the coin of honest men. Rag money, on the other hand, was the instrument of banks and swindlers to corrupt and cheat an innocent and virtuous public.

The Hero spent a restful three months away from Washington and it improved both his health and temper. He told Lewis that he enjoyed "good health now—mine has very much improved—I walked the other day without halting, & without oppression, four miles; my strength is greatly improved."[21] In addition to the salubrious climate of middle Tennessee and the joy he felt over the effect his veto was producing around the country, Jackson credited the presence of his immediate family with his improved condition. His daughter-in-law was pregnant and expecting in the fall, and Jackson had no hesitation in telling his son that if Sarah presents "you with a fine daughter . . . I will claim to name it Rachel." On November 1, 1832, Sarah gave birth to a lovely daughter and she was duly christened Rachel. At age sixty-five General Jackson had become a grandfather and he doted on this child to the day he died. "I feel deeply indebted to you and my dear Sarah," he wrote his son. "Shall I be spared it will be a great pleasure to watch over and rear up the sweet little Rachel, and make her a fair emblem of her for whom she is called."[22]

During his stay in Tennessee Jackson was repeatedly asked to participate in several campaigning schemes, all of which he refused. Although he attended barbecues on his way to and from Washington, the most he would consent to do in Tennessee was meet the citizens who asked to see him. "They offered me a public dinner which I declined," he told Major Donelson, "but agreed to meet them and shake my old neighbours and friends by the hand."[23] Jackson understood the need of people to touch him and express their affection. Otherwise he contented himself with staying at home, reading the newspapers, answering his mail and writing the many politicians around the country who commanded his attention. He left his plantation to his son to manage and merely queried him periodically on the condition of the crops, livestock, and fences. He spent a good deal of time thinking about his second term as President and what he would do to further his program of "reform retrenchment and economy." The most immediate concern, he decided, was the need "to put an end to this waste of public money" by blocking expenditures for internal improvements. Until an amendment was added to the Constitution authorizing public works by the federal government he felt he must "stop this corrupt, log-rolling system of legislation."[24] Retrenchment and economy, he insisted, were still the most effective means of safeguarding the nation's liberty.

Only one issue necessitated his careful attention during the months at home in Tennessee. He knew it posed a danger even before he left the capital. The Tariff of 1832, enacted during the closing moments of Congress, seemed certain to incite ambitious men into provoking trouble in the South. Nonetheless, he felt sure that the public at large would recognize that all the grievances of the agitators had been ameliorated and that "oppression only exists in the distempered brains of disappointed ambitious men."[25]

Still he watched with a growing sense of concern as nullifiers in South Carolina announced their readiness to engage in some form of precipitate action. Reports out of that state of threatened civil strife sounded ominous. When someone said to Jackson that Calhoun "ought to be hung as a traitor to the liberties of his country" for proposing nullification, the President agreed—most emphatically. Moreover, he said, if the nullifiers carried their threats into action he planned to march ten thousand volunteers into South Carolina to "crush and hang" the traitors. "These are and must be the feelings and sentiments of all honest men who love our happy country and who wish to hand down to their posterity the liberty we enjoy."[26]

The danger of overt action by the nullifiers became acute as the summer wore on. The tension, which mounted in cities like Charleston and produced armed mobs roaming the streets at night, won regular coverage in the newspapers and captured Jackson's daily attention.[27] Angry verbal exchanges in editorials of South Carolina newspapers provoked duels, bloody fistfights, and riots in early August and September. Then, when the President heard that an attempt had been made to bring about the disaffection of the army and naval officers in command at Charleston harbor, he knew he must respond. In such situations there was never anything precipitate about his decisions. They were always carefully thought out and discussed with his aides. Instinctively he sensed when the moment had arrived to make his move, for delayed action like precipitate action can worsen a situation. This highly developed sense of timing, a product of his military career, was enhanced by Jackson's understanding of the need to keep on top of a problem and never let it run out of control. "Altho I do not believe that the Nullifiers will have the madness & folly to attempt to carry their mad schemes into execution," he told Coffee, "still you know, I must be vigilant, and not permit a surprise, and to do this effectually, I must be at my post, and scan with great care the signs of the times as they may arise." By this time Jackson's growing stature as a statesman, particularly in difficult situations, had begun to catch the attention of many Washington observers. "He is a much abler man than I thought him," commented Senator George Dallas of Pennsylvania, "one of those naturally great minds which seem ordinary, except when the fitting emergency arises."[28]

Although Jackson did not expect the events in the south to develop into a "desperate issue, yet it behooves us to be ready for any emergency," he informed Levi Woodbury, the secretary of the navy. In view of the possible efforts by nullifiers to capture the Charleston forts by subverting their command and in view of political information he had secured that the South Carolina legislature would be convened immediately after the fall election to determine the state's course of action, Jackson ordered several actions. The army and navy secretaries were told to cooperate in arranging the replacement of the officers and troops in Charleston "at any time it may be desireable." Do not withdraw the officers without the men, he instructed, because one will influence and intimidate the other. "Therefor let the officers and men be relieved by a faithful detachment, and this carried into effect as early as possible at farthest, by the 20th of October, and before their assembly meets. Let it be done without a hint of the cause until it is effected, and as the common routine of the army." If the nullifiers capture the forts they could "prevent a blockade. *This must be guarded against, and prevented.*" He then directed that General Winfield Scott take care of all preparations. He also directed that a naval squadron be readied at the Norfolk station to be deployed instantly "if we shall be required to use any." To guarantee that his orders were received and carried out he notified Major Donelson to double-check. "I do not despair of preserving the union," he said. "The influence of the Bank has not destroyed me, and I trust that a kind providence will protect our happy union, & preserve it from all the combinations of the Nullifyers & their wicked & ambitious vassels." Meanwhile he neutralized Georgia. "I have no fears of [Governor] Lumpkin," he wrote; "his letters to me give evidence of his firmness and opposition to nullification." Also, Jackson kept open his lines of communication to the unionists in South Carolina —Joel R. Poinsett, Colonel William Drayton, James L. Petigru, the Richardsons of Sumter, the Pringles, Judge David Johnson, and others—and urged them to provide him with quick and reliable information as events developed.[29]

Interestingly, even in the midst of this potentially dangerous situation in South Carolina, Jackson alluded to the Bank. It rarely left his mind during the summer. His war against the monster would reach a climax with the fall election and he wanted nothing to endanger his anticipated triumph. He delighted to hear from the many politicians who wrote him at the Hermitage about the efficaciousness of his veto, and he assured Major Donelson that had it reached Kentucky in time for the gubernatorial election it would have produced an even greater Democratic majority.[30] Virtually all the resolutions passed by Democratic state and local conventions praised the President for his stand against the Bank. They lauded his veto "as a document worthy of the purest days of our Republic. It brings us back nearer to the original principles which pervaded, and the spirit which animated the fathers of our country, than anything which emanated from the Executive since the days of Jefferson. It is the final decision of the President between the Aristocracy and the People—he stands by the People."[31]

The Democrats did not rely on the bank issue alone to win this election. As professional politicians in an age of rising professionalism, they knew the immense importance of organization. Indeed it was the extraordinary vitality of their organization that built many of the impressive majorities for the President in every section of the nation. Meetings were held at the local, county, and state levels, and a wide range of committees—corresponding and funding committees, for example—were established to generate support for the national ticket and find the necessary money to energize a presidential campaign. Most important to the organizational development of the Democratic party during the campaign of 1832 was the establishment of a long chain of "Hickory Clubs," which were intended to supplement, not replace, the work of local and state committees. The Central Hickory Club in Washington, organized by Kendall and including many Kitchen members, "gave tone and character to all other clubs throughout the country."[32] Even when the campaign ended, this Central Hickory Club retained its political potency, for it enjoyed Jackson's wholehearted encouragement and support.[33]

In Philadelphia the "Democratic Hickory Club, No. 1" set up shop to promote Jackson's reelection so that he could continue to "guard our institutions" and "our liberty" against "foreign and moneyed influences." In the west meetings were frequently spontaneous. As one man wrote, "We are up and doing. The Veto was received . . . last evening. The roaring of cannon announced that some important occasion had called forth that token of national, patriotic feeling. . . . Immediately . . . a meeting of the Democratic Republicans of this town . . . assembled at one of our public hotels, where the objections of the President on returning the bill, were read and considered. Spirited resolutions, approving of the course of the President were adopted and a feeling was imparted among the friends and supporters of the Administration seldom witnessed in this place on any public occasion."[34]

Out of the superior organization developed by the Democrats grew not only meetings but high-powered propaganda in the form of newspapers, circulars, broadsides, pamphlets, and the like, and a variety of techniques and gimmicks guaranteed to excite and entertain the voter and turn him out at the polls on election day. One of the best of these techniques was the parade. Michel Chevalier, a Frenchman traveling through the United States at this time, described one of these demonstrations in his book, *Society, Manners and Politics in the United States*. "It was nearly a mile long," he wrote. "The Democrats marched in good order, to the glare of torches; the banners were more numerous than I had ever seen them in any religious festival; all were in transparency, on account of the darkness." Then came portraits of Jackson: one showed him in the uniform of a general, another as a Tennessee farmer "with the famous hickory cane in his hand." The procession "had its halting-places; it stopped before the homes of the Jackson men to fill the air with cheers, and halted at the doors of the leaders of the Opposition, to give three, six or nine groans."[35]

Barbecues were another important technique in winning the voter's favor. Nothing beats food and drink to capture the interest of the American electorate. Even when the Democrats lost elections they seemed to think a barbecue was in order. "There seems to be no way of convincing these fellows," reported one opposition newspaper, "that they are fairly beaten. They have one sort of answering for every thing. If we show them that we have elected our Lieutenant Governor by a majority of nearly 30,000 *they reply by swallowing a pig.* If we show them that we have gained great strength in the Senate, and added to our superiority, *they reply by devouring a turkey.* If we show them that we have obtained a majority of two-thirds in the House of Representatives, *they reply by pouring off a pint of whiskey or apple-toddy.* There is no withstanding such arguments. We give it up."[36]

At these barbecues the Democrats frequently erected towering hickory poles after they had been marched around town to attract a crowd. "I remember one of these poles," wrote a foreign observer, "with its top still crowned with green foliage, which came on to the sound of fifes and drums, and was preceded by ranks of democrats, bearing no other badge than a twig of the sacred tree in their hats. It was drawn by eight horses, decorated with ribbons and mottoes." Sitting in the tree itself were a dozen Democrats, waving flags and shouting "Hurra for Jackson!" The crowd then took up the cry. "Hurra for Old Hickory," "Democracy against the Aristocracy," "Victory." Invariably these barbecues ended with the singing of "The Hickory Tree."

> "Hurra for the Hickory Tree!
> Hurra for the Hickory Tree!
> Its branches will wave o'er tyranny's grave.
> And bloom for the brave and the free."[37]

Jackson himself attended one or two of these affairs but only when they happened to occur along the route of his travels. Normally he tried to follow the accepted decorum of presidential candidates by keeping aloof from the campaign. But the people so desperately wanted to see him and "shake him by the hand" that it was difficult for him to refuse all invitations. Opposition newspapers chided him over his unseemly and indecorous behavior when he appeared at a barbecue. "This is certainly a new mode of electioneering," scolded the Washington *National Intelligencer* when the editor learned of Jackson's attendance at a barbecue in Lexington, Kentucky. "We do not recollect before to have heard of a President of the United States descending in person into the political arena." Even with all the new campaigning techniques developed during the Jacksonian age, many voters demanded personal appearances by the candidates.[38]

On September 18 the General and his party left the Hermitage to return to Washington. The timing was perfect. The weather cooperated, and his appearances along the route generated uncontrollable excitement. The crowds cheered him, waved hickory branches in his direction, and drank toasts in his honor. "General Jackson—Unconquered and Unconquerable" was a favorite toast in the west.[39] Wherever he went he experienced nothing but adulation and hysterical screaming and shouting. He was literally escorted by mobs on his entire journey through Kentucky. "Never have I seen such a gathering as met us in advance of Lexington three miles," he related to Donelson, "to say the least of the number, I may say 5000—and this too without any concert, or notification."[40] The people were so enthusiastic that he even expected to win the state over its native son, Henry Clay. "The political horizon is bright as far as we have seen or heard."[41] Because of these demonstrations Jackson averaged less than thirty miles a day on his journey, pausing only on Sunday to rest and attend church services. It was a marvelous climax to the campaign and perfectly timed to coincide with state elections in the west. For a man who was not supposed to do any campaigning, Jackson saw an awful lot of people on his trip back to Washington.

If the Democrats were expert at parades and barbecues, the National Republicans showed a remarkable flair for political cartooning, and it is very probable that the art came of age in this election. Jackson made an especially attractive target for cartoonists, and they hardly ever missed hitting the bullseye in the many pictures they drew of him. One of the most striking, entitled "Uncle Sam in Danger," showed Uncle Sam sitting in a chair, his arm lanced, with blood and specie flowing from the wound into a basin held by Amos Kendall. "Dr." Jackson stands over the victim, a scalpel in his hand. "Hold the Bason [sic] Amos," commands the President, "this is merely an Experiment but I take the Responsibility." Van Buren stands to one side, a pained expression on his face, and comments that he cannot give an opinion about the worth of the operation. A citizen in the corner laments: "Twixt the Giniril (since He's taken to Doctring), and the little Dutch Potercary, Uncle Sam stands no more chance than a stump tailed Bull in fly time."[42]

Many of the cartoons involved the Jackson–Van Buren relationship and either commented on the President's reliance on the Magician or Van Buren's cleverness in advancing his own presidential aspirations. One of these showed the President receiving a crown from Van Buren and a scepter from the devil; another portrayed Jackson, Van Buren, and others attired as burglars, aiming a large battering ram at the Bank's front door; and a third, depicting the spoils system, had a fearsome red devil flying over the country with strings attached to his feet, fingers, and tail, and tied at the other end to spoilsmen who bounce and jump as the devil jiggles the strings. Presumably Jackson was the devil and the Democrats his puppets. One popular caricature showed Jackson and Clay dressed as jockeys riding a race to the White House with Clay half a length ahead. But unquestionably the most famous cartoon drawn at approximately this time was "King Andrew the First." It depicted Jackson in full regal attire, complete with ermine robe, crown, and scepter. In his left hand he holds a rolled document labeled "veto," and he stands on a tattered copy of the Constitution and an emblem with the motto, "Virtue, Liberty and Independence." At the top of the picture are the words, "Born to Command."[43]

All of the cartoons, parades, barbecues, and other campaigning gimmicks measured the distance politicians had traveled away from serious discussions of important public issues. They also documented the concern of politicians to broaden their appeal among the masses and cater to the things they believed stimulated popular support. A striking pamphlet can influence voters, remarked one commentator, "and so does a well-conducted newspaper; but a hickory pole, a taking cry, a transparency, a burst of sky rockets and Roman candles (alas! that it should be so!) have a potency over a large third of our voters that printed eloquence can not exert." As one Ohio editor rightly observed: "There is no withstanding such arguments."[44]

No doubt politicians showed keen sensitivity to the public mood and temper as the nation continued the democratization of its institutions. With all the noise and hoopla about the virtue and wisdom of the people, perhaps good sense dictated that no one test that virtue or measure that wisdom. Better to amuse the public with skyrockets and hickory poles than frighten them with serious talk about credit, paper money, and the national banking system. It was one thing to argue about liberty and democracy and quite another to debate the merits of specie over paper or the justice of the tariff schedules. Democrats and National Republicans did not so much deliberately debase American politics as simply adjust their style and method of winning elections to conform to a changing social and economic system. The continuing development of the industrial revolution, the rapid economic growth of the 1830s, the revolution in transportation most recently advanced by the advent of railroads, the heightened mobility of the people as they raced across a continent, the apparent (at least to contemporaries) social mobility of all classes as they raised their standard of living, the preoccupation with work, money, and "getting ahead"—all these shaped a new and modern American society to which politicians quite naturally responded in ways they thought appropriate to it. An expanding economy usually produces an expanded democracy. In the United States that expansion in the 1830s possessed prodigious dimensions.

Andrew Jackson symbolized that dynamic, explosive democracy. His popularity no longer rested solely on his past military accomplishments. By 1832 he was seen less as the "Hero of New Orleans," and more as the "man of the People." Said one politician: *"Democracy and Jackson."* They are one.[45]

Because they appreciated the difficulty of unseating an enormously popular President backed by a strong national party, the National Republicans understood the absolute need of attracting Anti-Masonic votes, despite Clay's membership in the fraternity. In several states a determined effort was made to initiate cooperation between the two parties.

It was pointed out that Jackson was the real Masonic candidate, not Clay; it was shown that more non-Masons like John Quincy Adams supported the National Republican party; and it was argued that Wirt's candidacy was hopeless and would only benefit the "arch mason" himself, General Jackson. The results of these efforts of cooperation and unification were very uneven, but enough conversions took place to alarm the Democrats. "You must so manage as to break up the Anti Masons in your quarter," Gideon Welles of Connecticut was advised by Amos Kendall, "or at least to prevent their union with the Nationals."[46] The Democrats argued that Wirt, a former Mason, was actually a stalking horse for Clay. *"Be not deceived,"* warned Blair. *"All* the candidates are Masons. In this respect, they are on equal footing. The object of running Mr. Wirt, is to enable the *leaders* to transfer the votes you give to him—to Henry Clay."[47]

Although many New Yorkers cast an anti-Jackson vote for Clay, representing a coalition between the National Republicans and the Anti-Masonic parties, this union did not work in any other state.[48] Even if it had, the coalition could not approach the level of organizational strength of the Democrats or Jackson's popular appeal around the country.[49] Nevertheless, the Anti-Masonic movement scored impressive majorities in some areas as it steadily expanded from western New York and Vermont into Pennsylvania and Ohio. It put up a heroic fight against the "arch mason," but came nowhere near defeating him.

As the campaign drew to an end in midfall, Andrew Jackson arrived in Washington on the evening of October 19. He found the city still suffering from the dreaded cholera epidemic—what the newspapers called "the prevailing epidemic"—and the President had warned his nephew during the summer to desert the White House and seek refuge in the suburbs. The disease had crossed the Atlantic from Europe early in 1832 and quickly spread from one city to another. By the summer nearly three thousand persons had perished. It attacked Philadelphia, frightened Baltimore, and finally invaded Washington. It reached out to the west, besieging Cincinnati and then moving on to Chicago. New Orleans contracted it, instead of yellow fever. Washington was particularly hard hit —more than anyone imagined.

Jackson himself paid little attention to the "prevailing epidemic." Long ago he had developed a pious fatalism about such matters. "My Dr Sarah," he wrote his daughter-in-law, "knowing that we have to die we ought to live to be prepared to die well, and then, let death come when it may, we will meet it without alarm and be ready to say, 'the Lords will be done'."[50]

Actually he had a more pressing matter to think about. His mind concentrated most particularly on South Carolina. Unionists in Charleston like Joel R. Poinsett kept him informed of the situation and one of the first things he learned upon returning to the White House was the unhappy news of the defeat of the Union party at the ballot box throughout the state. "You must be prepared to hear very shortly of a State Convention and an act of Nullification," Poinsett advised him. That was a blow, a very dangerous blow. The Union party was attempting to oppose nullification, Poinsett continued, and "adhere to our allegiance to the United States. But allegiance implies protection and we rely upon the Government acting with vigor in our behalf."[51]

Vigor could be expected from Jackson, particularly to preserve the Union. Vigor best described his style of action. And when he learned that the nullifiers expected to get away with their defiance—the way Georgians defied the Supreme Court—Jackson felt personally challenged to show what vigorous measures he could provide to put down threats of treason. Poinsett could give him no advice as to the best course of action but he did try to provide an outline of what the nullifiers would do. They will proceed "by replevin," he said, and if the collector of the port refused to comply with it they will either imprison him or break open and seize the custom stores. If this action is to be resisted by the federal government, said Poinsett, then something better happen very quickly, such as providing three hundred muskets and "a number of hand granades." The customhouse and post office were "crowded with Nullifiers," reported Poinsett. "I am advised even not to put a letter in the Post office of Charleston directed to you!"[52]

A sad state of affairs when a loyal citizen could not write to the President without endangering himself. Jackson scowled as he read Poinsett's letter. But he did take comfort in Poinsett's assurance that there were many Unionists in South Carolina and that most of them were "ready to support the laws if legally called upon so to do at the hazard of their lives."[53] Words like that stirred Jackson's blood.

Almost immediately upon receiving this latest information of the defeat of the Union party in South Carolina followed by a report of the likelihood of an attack upon the federal forts in Charleston by the nullifiers, the President issued orders to the secretary of war.

Washington, October 29, 1832

Confidential

The Secretary of War will forthwith cause secrete and confidential orders to be Issued to the officers commanding the Forts in the harbour of charleston So Carolina to be vigilant to prevent a surprise in the night or by day, against any attempt to seize and occupy the Fts. by any Set of people under whatever pretext the Forts may be approached. Warn them that the attempt will be made, and the officers commanding will be responsible for the defence of the Forts and garrisons, against all intrigue or assault, and they are to defend them to the last extremity—permitting no armed force to approach either by night or day. *The attempt will be made to surprise the Forts and garrisons* by the militia, and must be guarded against with *vestal vigilence* and any attempt by force repelled with prompt and examplary punishment.[54]

In addition to directing the preparation of the forts for possible attack, Jackson also turned his attention to the customhouse and post office. He authorized George Breathitt, brother of the governor of Kentucky, to journey to South Carolina, ostensibly as a post-office inspector, to gather information about the reports of disloyalty and collusion within the revenue and postal service, "specifying the names of all officers so engaged." Breathitt had visited Jackson at the Hermitage and accompanied him back to Washington. He absorbed all the things the President wanted said and done, and he carried instructions from the secretary of the treasury to the collector of Charleston—but this Jackson did not want anyone to know. Breathitt was directed to consult with Poinsett and Colonel Drayton and other Unionists as to the best direction for the government in counteracting the schemes of the nullifiers. Jackson also wanted to know whether Sullivan's Island in the harbor could be assaulted from the rear, and the precise armament conditions at Castle Pinckney.[55]

Thus, by early November, Jackson had taken a number of important actions to maintain control of this dangerous situation. He had transferred troops to the garrisons at Fort Moultrie and Castle Pinckney as well as to the federal installations on the islands in the harbor, replacing companies whose loyalty might falter. At the same time he had committed all military preparations for this operation to the very capable hands of General Winfield Scott. In addition he stationed Breathitt in South Carolina to report directly to him on every movement taken by the nullifiers.[56]

The necessity of ordering these warlike actions against his native state was very painful for Jackson, but he had his duty. The duty of the President, he said, "is a plain one, the laws will be executed and the union preserved by all the constitutional and legal means he is invested with." He was utterly astonished that intelligent, law-abiding citizens could be deluded by the "wild theory and sophistry of a few ambitious demagogues," place themselves in an attitude of rebellion toward their government, and thus "become the destroyers of their own prosperity and liberty." These proceedings, he ventured, were "nothing but madness and folly." Surely if "grievances do exist there are constitutional means to redress them." Unfortunately, with each passing day he saw the crisis approaching and the day not far off "when the government must act and that with energy."[57] He would be ready; of that no one need doubt.

At least one bit of good news arrived during this crisis period. By mid-November it was virtually official that Jackson had been reelected to the presidency by an overwhelming popular and electoral count. Jackson received 688,242 popular votes, while Clay took 473,462 and Wirt 101,051. Old Hickory won approximately 55 percent of the popular vote as against 37 percent for Clay and 8 percent for Wirt. In the electoral college Jackson garnered 219 votes against 49 for Clay and 7 for Wirt. Clay carried Massachusetts, Rhode Island, Connecticut, Delaware, Kentucky, and a majority of the Maryland vote, while Wirt won the single state of Vermont. Jackson swept all the rest except South Carolina, which gave its 11 votes to John Floyd of Virginia. In the vice presidential contest, Van Buren gained an easy victory by taking 189 votes to Sergeant's 49 and Ellmaker's 7. South Carolina awarded its 11 votes to Henry Lee of Massachusetts, while Pennsylvania gave 30 to its favorite son, William Wilkins.[58]

In addition to Vermont, Wirt gathered respectable blocs of votes in Connecticut, Massachusetts, New York, and Pennsylvania. He also picked up a few hundred votes each from the states of Maryland, New Jersey, Ohio, and Rhode Island. Clay did relatively well in New England, the middle Atlantic states, and some parts of the west, like Ohio, where internal improvements meant a great deal to the electorate. Jackson drew his greatest support from the west and the south. He did reasonably well in the middle Atlantic states and less well in New England, although he won the states of Maine and New Hampshire, where the Democratic party had a strong organization.[59] Indeed, the cracking of the New England bloc by Jackson represented a real advance in Democratic strength. That crack widened over the next few years and terminated what some feared was a monolithic commitment to a Federalist/National Republican persuasion. Only in the south, where a two-party system had never really flourished, was there total commitment to one candidate. In Alabama, Georgia, and Mississippi, Jackson had no opposition. South Carolina, of course, acted out its anger and pique and would soon descend into "madness and folly." In Maryland, where the electoral vote was cast by district, Jackson took only 3 out of the 10 votes available. Clay received the other 7; however, two of these seven electors did not cast their ballots in the formal election that followed.

The final totals of popular votes in this election are extremely inexact. To begin with, in some states, it is impossible to distinguish between the Clay and Wirt vote because they registered their tallies as "Jackson" and "anti-Jackson." No mention of Clay or Wirt appears. In addition, Clay's Tennessee vote is suspiciously small; it is almost half the total that John Quincy Adams received in 1828. As a westerner, Clay enjoyed far greater support in Tennessee than Adams. Furthermore, the Missouri vote for Clay is never given. Some have argued that there was no opposition to Jackson in that state, but more probable is the claim that the final figure reported simply represents Jackson's majority over Clay in that state.[60]

However imprecise the popular total may be, one fact defies contradiction: Jackson won a smashing victory. Of the total votes cast he received 54.6 percent, an achievement rarely attained in presidential elections. And he did it in the face of powerful opposition: a Bank pouring thousands of dollars into the campaign to defeat him; a popular and capable opposition candidate in the person of Henry Clay; and a movement of near-religious intensity determined to expel all Masons from government.

Although the total number of votes cast in 1832 rose more than 100,-000 over the 1828 contest, the percentage of Jackson's popular majority declined by more than 1.5 percent from what he received four years earlier. Jackson is the only President in American history whose reelection to a second term registered such a decline. Perhaps too much can be made of this fact, considering the trifling extent of the decline and the inexactness of the total figure of votes cast. Still it is suggestive. The apparent decline could have been caused by the improved organizational structure of the two parties over their counterparts in the 1828 election; or by the existence of the first third party in American political contests. Also the bank issue, the tariff agitation, the question of spoils, and the Eaton affair undoubtedly cost Jackson many votes. Or it may have been his strong executive leadership that worried some Americans over the possible danger it posed to their republican system of government.

What must not be forgotten in any analysis is what this election demonstrated about Jackson's relation to the American people. Clay insisted on the Bank recharter as an issue with which to fight Old Hickory at the polls and it was as potent an issue as anyone could have desired. Still the issue and the Bank's money were not powerful enough to unseat the General —or come anywhere near it. "The devotion to him is altogether personal, without reference to his course of policy," declared *Niles Weekly Register.*[61] "Who but General Jackson would have had the courage to veto the bill rechartering the Bank of the United States," asked one man, "and who but General Jackson could have withstood the overwhelming influence of that corrupt Aristocracy?"[62]

Indeed, the only real issue in the campaign was Jackson himself, and the people by their vote reaffirmed their trust and confidence in him. They had confidence in his leadership because he stood for morality and virtue in government and because he stood as their representative. In short, then, the election was a triumph, as one Ohio politician rightly observed, for "Jackson and Democracy."[63]

If nothing else, the contest proved that one of Jackson's greatest assets was his ability to inspire the people to follow his lead, even when he frightened and worried them by raising such issues as the destruction of the Bank. But the most important objective of government is the protection and defense of the freedom of the people, and the American electorate never had any doubt of its safety in the strong and capable hands of Old Hickory. "His re-election by an expression of the public will," wrote Amos Kendall, "is deemed by us essential to the interests of our country, if not to the existence of the union."[64]

Soon newspapers talked about a third term. "My opinion," said the defeated third-party candidate, William Wirt, "is that he may be President for life if he chooses."[65] Certainly with South Carolina continuing its course into "madness and folly," many agreed that Andrew Jackson was the only man around who could preserve the Union and with it the freedom of the American people.[66]

Notes

Abbreviations and Short Titles Used in the Notes

Adams, *Memoirs*	Charles Francis Adams, ed., *Memoirs of John Quincy Adams* (Philadelphia, 1874–1877), 12 volumes.
AHR	*American Historical Review*
AJ	Andrew Jackson
ASPF	American State Papers, Finance
ASPFA	American State Papers, Foreign Affairs
ASPIA	American State Papers, Indian Affairs
Bassett, *Jackson*	John Spencer Bassett, *The Life of Andrew Jackson* (New York, 1916).
Bemis, *Adams*	Samuel Flagg Bemis, *John Quincy Adams and the Union* (New York, 1956).
Benton, *Thirty Years View*	Thomas Hart Benton, *Thirty Years View* (New York, 1865), 2 volumes.
Calhoun Papers	W. Edwin Hamphill, et al., eds., *The Papers of John C. Calhoun* (Columbia, 1963–), 12 volumes.
CHS	Chicago Historical Society
Clay Papers	James F. Hopkins et al., eds., *The Papers of Henry Clay* (Lexington, 1959–), 4 volumes.
CUL	Columbia University Library
DUL	Duke University Library
Hamilton, *Reminiscences*	James A. Hamilton, *Reminiscences of James A. Hamilton* (New York, 1869).
HL	Huntington Library
HUL	Harvard University Library

393

Jackson, *Correspondence*	John Spencer Bassett, ed., *The Correspondence of Andrew Jackson* (Washington, D.C., 1926–1933), 6 volumes.
JAH	*Journal of American History*
James, *Jackson*	Marquis James, *The Life of Andrew Jackson* (Indianapolis and New York, 1938).
JPP	Jackson Papers Project, Hermitage, Tennessee
JRDF	John R. Delafield Foundation, New York, N.Y.
JSH	*Journal of Southern History*
Kendall, *Autobiography*	William Stickney, ed., *The Autobiography of Amos Kendall* (Boston, 1872).
Latner, *Presidency of Jackson*	Richard B. Latner, *The Presidency of Andrew Jackson* (Athens, Ga., 1979).
LC	Library of Congress
LHA	Ladies Hermitage Association, Hermitage, Tennessee
MHS	Massachusetts Historical Society
ML	Pierpont Morgan Library, New York, N.Y.
Munroe, *McLane*	John A. Munroe, *Louis McLane: Federalist and Jacksonian* (New Brunswick, 1973).
MVHR	*Mississippi Valley Historical Review*
NA	National Archives
NYHS	New-York Historical Society
NYPL	New York Public Library
NYSL	New York State Library, Albany, N. Y.
Parton, *Jackson*	James Parton, *Life of Andrew Jackson* (Boston, 1866), 3 volumes.
PHS	Historical Society of Pennsylvania, Philadelphia, Pa.
PUL	Princeton University Library
Remini, *Jackson*	Robert V. Remini, *Andrew Jackson and the Course of American Empire, 1767–1821* (New York, 1977).
RG	Record Group
Richardson, *Messages and Papers*	J. D. Richardson, *Compilation of the Messages and Papers of the Presidents* (Washington, D.C., 1908), 20 volumes.
RUL	Rochester University Library
Sellers, *Polk*	Charles G. Sellers, Jr., *James K. Polk, Jacksonian, 1795–1843* (Princeton, 1957).
SHC	Southern Historical Collection, University of North Carolina, Chapel Hill, N.C.
THM	*Tennessee Historical Magazine*
THQ	*Tennessee Historical Quarterly*
THS	Tennessee Historical Society
TSL	Tennessee State Library

Van Buren, *Autobiography*	John C. Fitzpatrick, ed., *Autobiography of Martin Van Buren*, (Washington, 1920).
Webster Papers	Charles M. Wiltse, et al., eds., *The Papers of Daniel Webster* (Hanover, 1974–) 4 volumes.
Weed, *Autobiography*	Harriet H. Weed., ed., *Autobiography of Thurlow Weed* (Boston, 1883).
WUL	Washington University Library
YUL	Yale University Library

CHAPTER 1

1. For a full account of the duel see Remini, *Jackson*, pp. 136–143.

2. Jackson frequently treated himself for tuberculosis and since he obtained a measure of relief by occasionally wearing "Kelley's Consumption Jacket" he gladly provided the manufacturer of the garment with an endorsement. See Jackson Papers, LC.

3. See Remini, *Jackson*, pp. 184–186, for a full discussion of the gunfight with the Bentons.

4. AJ to Colonel James Gadsden, May 2, 1822, in Jackson, *Correspondence*, III, 161. For much of the information on Jackson's health I have relied on Frances Tomlinson Gardner, "The Gentleman from Tennessee," *Surgery, Gynecology and Obstetrics*, LXXXVIII, 408ff. See also John B. Moses and Wilbur Cross, *Presidential Courage* (New York, 1980), pp. 36–66.

5. AJ to Gadsden, May 2, 1822, in Jackson, *Correspondence*, III, 161.

6. The birth date usually given for Andrew Jackson, Jr., and included in volume I of this biography, is December 22, 1809 (p. 161). But recently the editors at the Jackson Papers Project discovered a note in the account papers for September 1822, Jackson Papers, reel 78, frame 15, LC which reads: "Andrew Jackson D. was born on the 4 of Decbr 1808." This notation appears to be in Jackson's hand, although this is not absolutely certain. The "D." presumably means "Donelson" which in itself seems strange since Jackson was hardly the man to call his son by a name other than his own. In any event the date does conform to the markings on Andrew Jr.'s tombstone. It reads: "Andrew Jackson, Adopted son of Genl Andrew Jackson, who died at the Hermitage, April 17th, 1865, in the 57th year of his age." I am grateful to Harold Moser, editor of the JPP, for bringing this matter to my attention.

7. AJ to Coffee, May 26, 1831, quoted in John H. DeWitt, "Andrew Jackson and His Ward, Andrew Jackson Hutchings: A History Hitherto Unpublished," *THM*, Series II, Volume I (January 1931), 6.

8. See volume I of this biography, pp. 193–194. Lyncoya was named by Maria Pope, the daughter of Colonel Leroy Pope, into whose care Jackson first committed the child after discovering him on the battleground at Tallushatchee.

9. Obituary notice, *United States Telegraph*, July 3, 1828.

10. Ibid.

11. AJ to Rachel, December 7, 1823, in Jackson, *Correspondence*, III, 215–216.

12. Lyncoyer to AJ, December 29, 1823, Hurja Collection, THS. I am rather suspicious of this letter. It is a copy and there is too much fake-sounding "Indian talk" in it. The copy is in poor condition and has been edited. However, I've examined it carefully and the copy appears to have been written at an early

date, possibly the 1820s or 1830s. Moreover the letter itself seems to have been written in response to Jackson's request of December 7. It is the only known Lyncoya letter in existence.

13. *Telegraph*, July 3, 1828.

14. AJ to Donelson, March 5, 1823, Donelson Papers, LC.

15. AJ to Anthony Wayne Butler, January 13, 1823, Jackson Papers, The Historic New Orleans Collection, copy JPP.

16. AJ to Donelson, December 28, 1818, Donelson Papers, LC.

17. AJ to Donelson, April 26, 1822, Donelson Papers, LC.

18. AJ to Donelson, May 20, 1822, Donelson Papers, LC.

19. Donelson to AJ, June 5, 1822, Donelson Papers, LC.

20. AJ to Donelson, June 28, July 5, 1822, Donelson Papers, LC. This particular closing is taken from the letter of April 1, 1822.

21. Rachel Jackson to John Donelson, August 25, 1821, Miscellaneous Jackson Papers, THS.

22. AJ to Hutchings, April 18, 1833, in Jackson, *Correspondence*, V, 60.

23. Henry Wise, *Seven Decades of the Union* (Philadelphia, 1881), pp. 98–99.

24. Ibid., p. 113.

25. Horace Holley to Luther Holley, August 14, 1823, Miscellaneous Papers, TSL.

26. Hamilton, *Reminiscences*, p. 70.

27. Ibid.

28. Wise, *Seven Decades*, pp. 100–101.

29. Ibid., p. 80.

30. Ibid., pp. 80, 101.

31. Ibid., pp. 102–103.

32. Nathan Sargent, *Public Men and Events* (Philadelphia, 1875), I, 36.

33. Hamilton, *Reminiscences*, pp. 76, 79.

34. Peter Cartwright, *Autobiography of Peter Cartwright* (New York, 1956), p. 134.

CHAPTER 2

1. Memorandoms, [1822], Jackson Papers, LC.

2. Ibid.

3. Richardson, *Messages and Papers*, I, 673. See Remini, *Jackson*, pp. 399–424, for the background of this quarrel.

4. Memorandoms, [1822], Jackson Papers, LC.

5. Dr. James C. Bronaugh to AJ, February 16, 1822, in Jackson, *Correspondence*, III, 151.

6. New York *Statesman*, August 6, 1822. For reports of various abuses, see *National Intelligencer*, February 22, April 24, May 8, June 7, 12, 19, 1822.

7. *National Intelligencer*, March 24, May 29, August 21, 1822.

8. Baltimore *Federal Republican*, September 4, 1822.

9. New York *Statesman*, May 12, 1822.

10. Memorandoms, [1822], Jackson Papers, LC. For a clarification of what Jackson is talking about see Remini, *Jackson*, pp. 308–320, 341–377, 399–424.

11. Ibid., pp. 341, 370, 377–379.

12. AJ to Calhoun, August 1823, in Jackson, *Correspondence*, III, 203–204; AJ to Coffee, February 14, 1823, March 28, 1824, Coffee Papers, THS.

13. For a long time I resisted Jackson's contention about the corruption of this era, believing that it was largely a figment of his overwrought imagination.

But the more I researched the period, the more the evidence convinced me that he knew what he was talking about. Besides, when politicians of the 1820s worried about corruption they did not limit their concern to stealing. As will be shown, corruption also included such things as subverting the constitutional process and showing contempt for the popular will. Some evidence to document the corruption of the era will be provided in the text and the accompanying footnotes, but a biography of Jackson is hardly the place to attempt a full examination of this phenomenon. Unfortunately, not much scholarly research on the Monroe administration has been available except for George Dangerfield, *The Era of Good Feelings* (New York, 1952) and Harry Ammon, *James Monroe: The Quest for National Identity* (New York, 1971). It must be remembered, of course, that the corruption of the 1820s cannot compare quantitatively with the spectacular corruptions of the Grant, Harding, and Nixon administrations later on. After all, it was a small country of ten million people just beginning its climb to fame and fortune. Speaking relatively, however, this period can hold its own with the worst and most corrupt eras in American history.

14. A good case in point is Daniel Webster. Here is a man who regularly took handouts from any source available and paid the expected price. As George Bancroft later said: "His meannesses in money matters & his necessities control his conduct." Bancroft to W.L. Marcy, November 5, 1841, Miscellaneous Papers, NYSL. Webster probably helped himself to public funds involved in the Webster-Ashburton Treaty, although some scholars would dispute this. Also, as secretary of state, he was accused of taking a bribe from gamblers to arrange the nomination of the consul to Rio de Janeiro. See *House Document* #945, 27th Congress, 2nd session. How Webster has managed to maintain his reputation is one of the wonders of American historiography. No one comparable to Webster today, said Senator Paul Douglas of Illinois in 1952, "would lend himself to the villainies he practiced." See Richard H. Leach, "George Ticknor Curtis and Daniel Webster's 'Villainies,'" *The New England Quarterly* (September 1954), XXVII, 391–395 and Irving H. Bartlett, *Daniel Webster* (New York, 1978), *passim.* For this information on Webster I am grateful to Harold D. Moser, present editor of the Jackson Papers project and former editor of the Webster Papers project. Perhaps it is a trifle unfair to single out Webster since he's such an easy mark. Many other congressmen in the 1820s were practically as guilty as he—from Henry Clay, who regularly falsified his travel expenses, to Thomas Hart Benton, who accepted fees from the American Fur Company to represent their interests in the U.S. Senate, to all the many congressmen who allowed their families and friends to use their franking privilege and who misappropriated government property without giving it a second thought. A number of these "petty" corruptions will be cited and documented further along in the text.

15. Fayetteville, North Carolina, a branch of the Bank of the United States.

16. J. D. Steele, Manuscript Journal, 1820–1829, HL.

17. Newspapers in Washington and New York regularly carried stories about these peculations during 1822 and 1823. See, for example, the Washington *National Intelligencer*, March 24, May 29, August 21, 1822.

18. Kenneth Wiggins Porter, *John Jacob Astor: Business Man* (New York, 1966), II, 714; Benton, *Thirty Years View*, II, 13; Herman J. Viola, *Thomas L. McKenney: Architect of America's Early Indian Policy: 1816–1830* (Chicago, 1974), p. 65. "You deserve the unqualified thanks of the Community for destroying" the factory system, wrote Astor's agent Ramsay Crooks to Benton, April 1, 1822, in Porter, *Astor*, II, 713.

19. Viola, *McKenney*, pp. 51–52.

20. *Annals of Congress*, 17th Congress, 1st Session, pp. 235–236.

21. Viola, *McKenney*, p. 68.

22. *National Intelligencer*, February 22, 1822.

23. Monroe obtained his loan during the War of 1812 and did not discharge it until nearly fifteen years later. Astor offered the loan, according to Monroe, "on hearing that I was pressed for money." Monroe to Madison, March 28, 1828, James Madison Papers, LC. In 1820 Astor took a very indulgent attitude toward the President's indebtedness. He said that he understood "that Landed proper[ty] in the US. is at present not very Saleble I presume you have not Sold any of your estates & there fore it may not bee convenient to repayme the Sume Lend to you nor am I particularly in want of it it will however bee agreable to have the Intrest paid & I have taking the Liberty to Draw on you for 2100$ favr. of my Son at 90 Days being equil to 3 years Intrest." Astor to Monroe, April 5, 1820, Monroe Papers, NYPL. According to Astor's biographer, Astor took as much advantage of his money-lending operations as possible. He constantly hounded the government "in search of favors and considerations of one kind or another . . . requesting special consideration for his agents in the Indian country." Porter, *Astor*, II, 727, n. 57. Happily for Astor, Monroe occupied the highest offices in the government during this critical period in the history of the American Fur Company, ascending from secretary of war to secretary of state to President of the United States. Astor's complaint about the order prohibiting foreigners from engaging in the fur trade can be found in Astor to Calhoun, March 14, 1818, Office of Secretary of War, Letters Received Relating to Indian Affairs, RG 75, NA, in which he said he was sending his agent, Ramsay Crooks, to Calhoun to explain his problems. The rescinding order went out to Lewis Cass, governor of the Michigan Territory on March 25, 1818, with copies to Governor Ninian Edwards of the Illinois Territory, Governor William Clark of the Missouri Territory, and General Thomas A. Smith. Cass responded on April 25 and said that the new order would be put into effect immediately. Office of Secretary of War, Letters Sent Relating to Indian Affairs and Letters Received, RG 75, NA. See also Viola, *McKenney*, p. 53. Later, Cass was also accused of accepting a $35,000 bribe from Astor.

Apparently Astor loaned money to a number of prominent politicians at the time. In 1819, for example, he loaned $20,000 to Henry Clay. That was a great deal of money, particularly in Kentucky during the panic year of 1819. When Clay later asked for an extension of time in repaying the loan, Astor was more than happy to oblige. At this time Clay also worked for the Bank of the United States and continued in that position until his appointment as secretary of state. See his many letters from 1819 to 1825 to Langdon Cheves and Nicholas Biddle. Clay, *Papers*, II, 686, III, 533, 874, for the Astor material and volumes II and III, *passim*, for the letters to the Bank presidents. See also Porter, *Astor*, II, 905 n. 1, for Clay's request for an extension of time.

24. A notorious example is Daniel Webster. But there were many others. When Senator George Poindexter of Mississippi supported a bill for the recharter of the Bank of the United States, for example, he had received a $10,000 loan from the Bank. Several months later he received an additional $8,000 while the first loan remained unpaid. This violated the Bank's own regulations. See Edwin A. Miles, "Andrew Jackson and Senator George Poindexter," *JSH* (February 1958), XXIV, 59. The history of the Bank's violations of its own regulations as well as the terms of its charter in permitting, encouraging, and authorizing improper financial operations is notorious.

25. The Indian-trade operation, army and navy appropriations, and banking operations are only a few of the instances to document this statement, evidence for which will be provided in the text in the next several pages. But again

it must be stated that a biography of Andrew Jackson is not the place for an administrative history of the presidency of James Monroe.

26. The case of Stephen Cantrell, a pension agent of Nashville, accused of paying pensioners in depreciated local bank notes instead of specie, was particularly well known to Jackson and received a measure of national attention. Details can be found in the *National Intelligencer*, March 29, 1823. Jackson said that this money went to corrupt the political process. See AJ to Coffee, May 24, 1823, Coffee Papers, THS.

27. *National Intelligencer*, March 29, 1823; AJ to Coffee, May 24, 1823, Coffee Papers, THS. See Jackson's many letters to Coffee during the 1820s on this subject in the Coffee Papers, THS.

28. Biddle Memorandum, no date, Biddle Papers, LC.

29. *House Report* #104, 17th Congress, 2nd Session, *passim*. See also Viola, *McKenney*, pp. 80, 78, 71.

30. AJ to Calhoun, June 28, 1822, in Jackson, *Correspondence*, III, 164.

31. Everette Wayne Cutler, "William H. Crawford: A Contextual Biography." Doctoral Dissertation, University of Texas at Austin, 1971, p. 158.

32. Wiltse, *Calhoun*, pp. 184–185.

33. W. Morton to John M. O'Connor, July 7, 1822, Van Buren Papers, LC.

34. Wiltse, *Calhoun*, p. 202. Johnson's speech can be found in the *Annals of Congress*, 16th Congress, 1st Session, pp. 82–84.

35. *National Intelligencer*, May 7, 1822.

36. Ibid., May 7, June 8, 12, 1822. Monroe later twice nominated Van Deventer to be the navy agent in New York City and twice the Senate rejected the nomination. Reports of these abuses and swindles, said the *National Intelligencer*, April 4, 1823, were not forgotten by the public.

37. Cutler, "William H. Crawford," p. 161. My own discussion follows the general lines developed by Cutler in his dissertation and I am grateful to him for his insights and perceptions.

38. Ibid.

39. Wayne Cutler, "The A. B. Controversy," *Mid-America* (January 1969), LI, 24.

40. Ibid.

41. Ibid., p. 32; *Annals of Congress*, 17th Congress, 2nd Session, p. 860.

42. Cutler, "A. B. Controversy," p. 35.

43. Crawford to Coles, June 14, 1823, Coles Papers, PUL.

44. Cutler, "A. B. Controversy," p. 35.

45. Chase C. Mooney, *William H. Crawford, 1772–1834* (Lexington, Kentucky, 1974), p. 244.

46. *ASPF*, V, 80–146; Mooney, *Crawford*, p. 247.

47. The petitioners for "Claims on Account of Spanish Spoliations Under the Treaty with Spain for the Cession of Florida" reads like a Who's Who of the early insurance industry. See *ASPFR*, V, 798–799. *National Intelligencer*, January 29, March 16, November 26, 1822, has some information on the Spanish claims. See also John Bassett Moore, *History and Digest of the International Arbitrations* . . . (Washington, D.C., 1898), V, 4487–4531; and Records of the Boundary and Claims Commissions, Record Group 76, NA. I am grateful to Wayne Cutler for his assistance in this research.

48. See State Department series, Applications and Recommendations for Office, RG 59, NA.

49. E. J. Hale to William R. Hale, July 3, 1824, Brock Collection, HL. The suspicions against Adams were sometimes noted by Adams himself. See, for example, Adams, *Memoirs*, VI, 302–303.

50. E. J. Hale to William R. Hale, July 3, 1824, Brock Collection, HL.

51. Baltimore *Federal Republican*, August 26, 1822.

52. Memorandoms, [1822], Jackson Papers, LC.

53. Dr. James C. Bronaugh to AJ, February 8, 1822, in Jackson, *Correspondence*, III, 148.

54. *National Intelligencer*, July 6, 1822.

55. Eaton to AJ, December 30, 1821, in Jackson, *Correspondence*, III, 141.

56. *ASPF*, III, 508.

57. AJ to Donelson, July 5, 1822, Donelson Papers, LC.

58. Cutler, "William H. Crawford," p. 204.

59. Ibid., p. 181.

60. These ideas are developed more fully in the following works: Bernard Bailyn, *The Ideological Origins of the American Revolution* (Cambridge, 1967) and *The Origins of American Politics* (New York, 1968); Gordon S. Wood, *The Creation of the American Republic, 1776–1787* (New York, 1972); Richard Buel, Jr., *Securing the Revolution: Ideology in American Politics, 1789–1815* (New York, 1972); Richard Buel, Jr., "Democracy and the American Revolution: A Frame of Reference," *William and Mary Quarterly* (1964), XXI, 165–190; Robert E. Shalhope, "Toward a Republican Synthesis: The Emergence of an Understanding of Republicanism in American Historiography," *William and Mary Quarterly* (1972), XXIX, 49–80; Lance G. Banning, "Republican Ideology and the Triumph of the Constitution, 1789 to 1793," *William and Mary Quarterly* (1974), XXXI, 167–188; and Joyce Appleby, "The Social Origins of American Revolutionary Ideology," *JAH*, (1978), LXIV, 938–940. I have borrowed freely from these several scholarly works. An excellent application of the ideas of "republicanism" to the Jacksonian era can be found in Richard B. Latner, *Presidency of Jackson* pp. 3, 11, 13, 23–25, 209–212.

61. AJ to Coffee, February 10, 1825, Coffee Papers, THS. See also AJ to Richard M. Johnson, September 1828, in Jackson, *Correspondence*, III, 431 and AJ to Major Auguste Davézac, May 4, 1828, Livingston Papers, JRDF.

62. AJ to Donelson, August 6, 1822, Donelson Papers, LC. See also AJ to Colonel Squire Grant, February 18, 1825, in Jackson, *Correspondence*, III, 276.

63. AJ to Coffee, March 28, 1824, Coffee Papers, THS. See also AJ to Coffee, May 12, 1828, Coffee Papers, THS.

64. AJ to James Buchanan, June 25, 1825, Buchanan Papers, PHS.

65. AJ to James W. Lanier, May 15 (?), 1824, in Jackson, *Correspondence*, III, 253.

66. AJ to James Hamilton, Jr., June 29, 1828, in ibid, III, 412.

67. AJ to James K. Polk, December 4, 1826, Polk Papers, LC.

68. AJ to Samuel Swartwout, December 14, 1824, in Jackson, *Correspondence*, III, 269. See also AJ to Major Davézac, May 4, 1828, Livingston Papers, JRDF.

69. AJ to Francis Preston, January 27, 1824, Jackson Papers, HL.

70. AJ to Sevier, February 27, 1797, Hurja Collection, THS. Many of these arguments are repeated in his letter to Davézac, May 4, 1828, Livingston Papers, JRDF.

71. Ibid.; AJ to Overton, January 22, 1798, in Jackson, *Correspondence*, I, 43.

72. AJ to Dr. James Bronaugh, August 27, 1822, quoted in Herbert J. Doherty, Jr., "Andrew Jackson's Cronies in Florida Territorial Politics," *Florida Historical Quarterly* (July 1955), XXXIV, 23.

73. Herbert J. Doherty, Jr., "Andrew Jackson on Manhood Suffrage: 1822," *THQ*, (1956), XV, 60.

74. AJ to L. H. Coleman, April 26, 1824, in Jackson, *Correspondence*, III,

250. Jackson is actually talking about a national debt that is encouraged by a strong central government and the rich because the rich constitute the credit class.

75. AJ to John Q. Adams, November 22, 1821, in ibid., III, 139.

76. AJ to William S. Fulton, July 4, 1824, in ibid., III, 259.

77. Memorandoms, [1822], Jackson Papers, LC.

78. AJ to Donelson, February 26, 1824, Donelson Papers, LC.

79. AJ to Francis Preston, January 27, 1824, Jackson Papers, HL.

80. AJ to James Gadsden, May 2, 1822, Jackson Papers, LC.

81. AJ to Donelson, February 12, 1824, Donelson Papers, LC. See also his letter to Coffee, February 15, 1824, Coffee Papers, THS.

82. AJ to Donelson, April 17, 1824, Donelson Papers, LC. See also AJ to Donelson, April 23, 27, 1824, Donelson Papers, LC.

83. Dr. Thomas G. Watkins to AJ, March 13, 1822, in Jackson, *Correspondence*, III, 154.

84. Calhoun to James E. Calhoun, August 26, 1827, in *Calhoun Papers*, X, has a good statement on this point.

85. This is how Jackson later remembered the arguments to induce him to run. See AJ to [John C. McLemore ?], December 25, 1830, Miscellaneous Jackson Papers, NYHS.

86. AJ to Bronaugh, July 18, 1822, Jackson Papers, LC.

87. AJ to Donelson, August 6, 1822, Donelson Papers, LC. H. M. Brackenridge in his *Letters* (Washington, 1832) claims that Jackson while serving as governor of Florida in 1821 rejected the idea that he might be a candidate for the presidency (page 8). "Do they think that I am such a d——d fool as to think myself fit for President of the United States? No, sir; I know what I am fit for. I can command a body of men in a rough way; but I am not fit to be President." Perhaps Jackson said this in 1821 but it should be noted that Brackenridge's book was published during Jackson's second campaign for the presidency in 1832. If he did say it in 1821 perhaps the letter to Donelson in 1822, quoted in the text, served to repudiate that statement.

88. AJ to Donelson, August 6, 1822, Donelson Papers, LC.

89. Grundy to AJ, June 27, 1822, in Jackson, *Correspondence*, III, 163–164.

90. AJ to Donelson, August 6, 1822, Donelson Papers, LC.

CHAPTER 3

1. For an excellent account of social changes in America from the colonial period onward, see Rowland Berthoff, *An Unsettled People: Social Order and Disorder in American History* (New York, 1971). See also Yehoshua Arieli, *Individualism and Nationalism in American Ideology* (New York, 1964), and Fred Somkin, *Unquiet Eagle: Memory and Desire in the Idea of American Freedom* (New York, 1967). A comprehensive account of the Jacksonian years is Edward Pessen, *Jacksonian America* (Homewood, Ill., 1978).

2. Useful in understanding American economic life at the beginning of the nineteenth century are: Douglass C. North, *The Economic Growth of the United States, 1790–1860* (New York, 1961) and Stuart Bruchey, *The Roots of American Economic Growth, 1607–1861* (New York, 1965).

3. The standard study of transportation for this period is George R. Taylor, *The Transportation Revolution, 1815–1860* (New York, 1951).

4. The Jacksonian era is rich in travel accounts by foreigners and I have drawn freely from the following: James S. Buckingham, *America, Historical, Statistic*

and Descriptive (New York, 1841); Michel Chevalier, *Society, Manners and Politics in the United States: Being a Series of Letters on North America* (Boston, 1839); Francis J. Grund, *Aristocracy in America* (London, 1839); Basil Hall, *Travels in North America, in the Years 1827 and 1828* (Edinburgh, 1829); Thomas Hamilton, *Men and Manners in America* (Philadelphia, 1833); Harriet Martineau, *Society in America* (London, 1838); Alexis de Tocqueville, *Democracy in America* (New York, 1966); and Frances M. Trollope, *Domestic Manners of the Americans* (London, 1832).

5. Evaluations of the degree of social and economic mobility during the Jacksonian era have undergone some revision by historians recently. The received wisdom from the profession at present seems to be that such mobility did in fact exist, but did not apply uniformly to all Americans. The classic statement on the subject is Alexis de Tocqueville, *Democracy in America.* An important criticism of the notion of widespread upward mobility is Edward Pessen, "The Egalitarian Myth and the American Social Reality: Wealth, Mobility, and Equality in the 'Era of the Common Man,' " *AHR* (1971), LXXVI, 989–1034.

6. George Dangerfield, *The Era of Good Feelings* (New York, 1952), p. 95.

7. The various attitudes toward the party system in the late eighteenth and early nineteenth centuries are fully described in Richard Hofstadter, *The Idea of a Party System: The Rise of Legitimate Opposition in the United States, 1780–1840* (Berkeley, 1969).

8. Cutler, "William H. Crawford," Doctoral Dissertation, University of Texas at Austin, 1971, p. 73.

9. Remini, *Jackson,* pp. 51ff.

10. The following discussion is based almost totally on Charles Sellers's two excellent articles, "Banking and Politics in Jackson's Tennessee, 1817–1827," *MVHR* (June 1954), XLI, 62–74, and "Jackson Men with Feet of Clay," *AHR* (April 1957), LXII, 537–551. I am extremely indebted to Sellers for his analysis and interpretation.

11. Still the best account of early Tennessee politics is Thomas P. Abernethy, *From Frontier to Plantation in Tennessee: A Study of Frontier Democracy* (Chapel Hill, 1932), pp. 115ff, although as Sellers points out he is almost completely mistaken in his evaluation of Jackson.

12. Francis P. Blair to Mrs. Gratz, April 20, 1831, in Thomas H. Clay, ed., "Two Years With Old Hickory," *Atlantic Monthly* (August 1887), LX, 193; Lewis R. Harlan, "Public Career of William Berkeley Lewis," *THQ* (March 1948), VII, 3.

13. AJ to Benton, no date, Jackson Papers, LC.

14. See Joseph H. Parks, *Felix Grundy: Champion of Democracy* (University, La., 1940), pp. 115–120.

15. Those, like Jackson, committed to "republicanism" in Tennessee began stating publicly that "banking in all its forms, under every disguise, is a rank fraud upon the laboring and industrious part of society." Campaign Circular for Henry H. Bryan, candidate for Congress, in Sellers, "Banking and Politics," p. 70.

16. Ibid., pp. 71–73.

17. AJ to Captain John Donelson, September 3, 1821, in Jackson, *Correspondence,* III, 117.

18. AJ to Lewis, July 16, 1820, Jackson Papers, NYPL.

19. AJ to Coffee, August 26, 1821, Coffee Papers, THS.

20. AJ to Benton, no date, Jackson Papers, LC.

21. AJ to Coffee, May 24, 1823, THS.

22. Jackson offered Overton "the advice of a sincere friend. he may adopt it or not as he pleases and I am done." AJ to Coffee, April 15, 1823, Coffee Papers, THS.

23. Sellers, "Banking and Politics," p. 81.

24. Ibid.

25. Ibid., p. 84.

26. Ibid.

27. A full discussion of this thesis can be found in Sellers, "Jackson Men with Feet of Clay," pp. 537–551.

28. Ibid.

29. AJ to Colonel James Gadsden, December 6, 1821, in Jackson, *Correspondence*, III, 141.

30. Overton to Clay, January 16, 1822, in Clay, *Papers*, III, 156–157.

31. *Niles Weekly Register*, August 24, 1822.

32. Sellers, *Polk*, p. 89.

33. Monroe badly mishandled the matter. He went to Eaton first and asked if Jackson would accept the appointment. This was not only appropriate but wise. Eaton told him that he frankly did not know whether Jackson would accept or not. Instead of checking further Monroe simply went ahead with the appointment. AJ to Edward Livingston, March 24, 1823, Livingston Papers, JRDF.

34. AJ to Adams, March 15, 1823, in Jackson, *Correspondence*, III, 192–193. Jackson obviously had assistance in the composition of this letter. He copied the text verbatim in letters to friends to explain his decision. See AJ to Edward Livingston, March 24, 1823, Livingston Papers, JRDF.

35. AJ to Coffee, March 10, 1823, Coffee Papers, THS. See also AJ to Coffee, February 21, 1823, Coffee Papers, THS.

36. AJ to Coffee, March 10, 1823, Coffee Papers, THS.

37. Jackson may have been privy to Overton's maneuvering. "When men standing high in society with a full knowledge of the villainy of another supports him," he told Coffee, "they participate in his crimes by supporting him, and loose their character for honesty—They by this act disgrace their county, and inflict a wound in the breast of every honest man in the county, and establish a precedent that strikes at the root of morality, religion & virtue.... The time will shortly arive when men thus acting in support of villains will meet with the indignant frowns of every honest man." AJ to Coffee, August 15, 1823, Coffee Papers, THS.

38. The details of this maneuvering can be found in William B. Lewis to Lewis Cass, no date, possibly 1844 or 1845, Jackson-Lewis Papers, NYPL.

39. Ibid.

40. Ibid.

41. AJ to Coffee, October 5, 1823, Coffee Papers, THS.

42. B. Coleman to Coffee, October 24, 1823, Coffee Papers, THS.

43. AJ to Coffee, October 5, 1823, Coffee Papers, THS.

44. The language used in Congress, Jackson said, "would disgrace the marketplace." Nothing beneficial to the public good could be done until the presidential election is over and done with, he protested. AJ to Coffee, March 1, 1823, Coffee Papers, THS.

45. AJ to Coffee, October 5, 1823, Coffee Papers, THS.

46. Lewis to Cass, no date, Jackson-Lewis Papers, NYPL.

47. AJ to Rachel, November 28, 1823, Jackson Papers, HL.

48. AJ to Rachel, December 3, 1823, Jackson Papers, HL.

49. AJ to Rachel, December 7, 1823, in Jackson, *Correspondence*, III, 215. See also AJ to Rachel, November 28, December 3, 11, 1823, Jackson Papers, HL.

CHAPTER 4

1. J. D. Steele, Manuscript Journal, 1820–1829, HL.

2. Ibid.

3. Ibid.; Benjamin F. Butler to Harriet Butler, May 7, 1823, Butler Papers, NYSL.

4. Ibid.; Cutler, "William H. Crawford," Doctoral Dissertation, University of Texas at Austin, 1971, has an excellent discussion of the secretary's background and political ideas. See also Chase Mooney, *William H. Crawford, 1772–1834* (Lexington, Ky., 1974).

5. Robert V. Remini, "The Albany Regency," *New York History* (October 1958), XXXIX, 341–355.

6. Henry S. Foote, *Casket of Reminiscences* (St. Louis, 1876), pp. 59–60; Nathan Sargent, *Public Men and Events* (Philadelphia, 1875), I, 204; "Mr. Van Buren," *The United States Magazine and Democratic Review* (1844), XV, 5.

7. Arthur M. Schlesinger, Jr., *The Age of Jackson* (Boston, 1945), pp. 82–83, catches the spirit, appearance, and public appeal of Henry Clay in a brilliant sketch.

8. See particularly Jackson's letter to Lewis, January 25, 30, 1819, Jackson-Lewis Papers, NYPL.

9. Samuel Flagg Bemis, *John Quincy Adams and the Foundations of American Foreign Policy* (New York, 1950), traces Adams's early life.

10. Wiltse, *Calhoun*, pp. 272ff; Margaret L. Coit, *John C. Calhoun, American Portrait* (Boston, 1950), pp. 123–124, 138.

11. AJ to Donelson, March 19, 1824, Donelson Papers, LC.

12. Sam Houston to Abram Maury, December 13, 1823, Miscellaneous Houston Papers, LC.

13. J. D. Steele, Manuscript Journal, 1820–1829, HL.

14. John Eaton to Rachel Jackson, December 18, 1823, in Jackson, *Correspondence*, III, 217.

15. AJ to Major George W. Martin, January 2, 1824, in ibid., III, 222.

16. Winfield Scott to AJ, December 11, 1823, AJ to Scott, December 11, 1823, Jackson Papers, HL.

17. For details of this quarrel see Remini, *Jackson*, pp. 342–343.

18. Parton, *Jackson*, III, 47–48.

19. Ibid., p. 48.

20. Clay even attended Jackson's fifty-eighth birthday party on March 15, given by Eaton and Call and attended by Nathaniel Macon, Governor Holmes of Mississippi, Edward Livingston, and others. AJ to Rachel, March 16, 1824, Jackson Papers, HL.

21. Eaton to Rachel Jackson, December 18, 1823, in Jackson, *Correspondence*, III, 217.

22. AJ to Coffee, December 31, 1823, Coffee Papers, THS.

23. AJ to Rachel, December 21, 1823, Jackson Papers, LC.

24. Call propositioned her, which she rejected with "much seeming indignation." Lewis to AJ, September 8, 1829, Jackson-Lewis Papers, NYPL; Lewis to AJ, July 2, 1829, Jackson Papers, LC.

25. AJ to Rachel, December 21, 1823, Jackson Papers, LC.

26. AJ to Donelson, January 21, 1824, in Jackson, *Correspondence*, III, 225.

27. AJ to Rachel, February 6, 1824, Jackson Papers, HL.

28. Ibid.; see also AJ to Coffee, February 15, 1824, Coffee Papers, THS.

29. Stephen Van Rensselaer to Solomon Van Rensselaer, February 15, 1824, in Mrs. Catharina V. R. Bonney, *A Legacy of Historical Gleanings* (Albany, 1875), p. 410. For Van Buren's account of this caucus see his letter to Benjamin F. Butler, February 15, 1824, Van Buren Papers, LC.

30. AJ to Coffee, February 15, 1824, Coffee Papers, THS.

31. Ibid.

32. Walter Lowrie to Van Buren, September 14, 1824, William Smith to Samuel Smith, October 17, 1824, Louis McLane to Van Buren, October 21, 1824, Albert Gallatin to Van Buren, October 2, 1824, Van Buren Papers, LC; Robert V. Remini, *Martin Van Buren and the Making of the Democratic Party* (New York, 1959), pp. 66–68.

33. For Jackson's reaction to this convention see AJ to Coffee, February 22, 1824, Coffee Papers, THS. Dallas explained his actions in a letter to Edward Livingston, March 1, 1824, Livingston Papers, JRDF.

34. AJ to Donelson, March 7, 1824, Donelson Papers, LC.

35. AJ to Lewis, February 22, 1824, Jackson-Lewis Papers, NYPL.

36. Ibid.; AJ to Donelson, March 7, 1824, Donelson Papers, LC.

37. AJ to Rachel, December 11, 1823, January 21, March 16, 1824, Jackson Papers, HL.

38. AJ to Rachel, March 16, 1824, Jackson Papers, HL.

39. AJ to Rachel, January 21, 1824, Jackson Papers, HL. Most probably Rachel had begun to show signs of heart trouble.

40. Ibid.

41. AJ to Lewis, December 7, 1823, Jackson-Lewis Papers, NYPL.

42. *Annals of Congress*, 18th Congress, 1st Session, pp. 122, 208–209, 294, 330.

43. Ibid., 137, 208, 296, 253–256, 570.

44. AJ to James W. Lanier, May 15 [?], 1824, in Jackson, *Correspondence*, III, 253. Jackson moved to amend one bill he had introduced to keep the road proposed by the measure solely within lands owned by the United States, *Annals of Congress*, 18th Congress, 1st Session, p. 209.

45. AJ to Lewis, May 7, 1824, Jackson-Lewis Papers, NYPL.

46. AJ to Coffee, June 6, 1825, Coffee Papers, THS.

47. Van Buren, *Autobiography*, p. 241.

48. *Annals of Congress*, 18th Congress, 1st Session, p. 744.

49. William Allen Butler, *Martin Van Buren* (New York, 1862), pp. 24–25.

50. AJ to L.H. Coleman, April 26, 1824, in Jackson, *Correspondence*, III, 249–250.

51. Van Buren, *Autobiography*, p. 240.

52. William Graham Sumner, *Andrew Jackson* (Boston, 1882), p. 95; Robert V. Remini, *Andrew Jackson* (New York, 1966), p. 99.

53. See, for example, *The Letters of Wyoming, to the People of the United States, on the Presidential Election, and in Favor of Andrew Jackson* (Philadelphia, 1824).

54. AJ to Donelson, April 27, 1824, Donelson Papers, LC. See also AJ to Coffee, June 18, 1824, June 18, 1824, Coffee Papers, THS; AJ to William S. Fulton, July 4, 1824, in Jackson, *Correspondence*, III, 259–261; and AJ to Lewis, May 7, 1824, Jackson-Lewis Papers, NYPL.

55. AJ to Coffee, June 6, 1825, Coffee Papers, THS

56. AJ to Lewis, February 22, 1824, Jackson-Lewis Papers, NYPL.

57. Jackson assumed, however, that an "independent court martial would have condemned them under the 2nd section of the act establishing rules and articles for the government of the army of the u.s." AJ to Monroe, January 6, 1817, in Jackson, *Correspondence*, II, 272–273.

58. This correspondence was published in the *National Intelligencer*, May 7, 9, 12, 1824, and also in *Niles Weekly Register* among other newspapers.

59. AJ to Donelson, March 6, 1824, Donelson Papers, LC.

60. VB to David Evans, June 9, 1824, Van Buren Papers, LC.

61. Van Buren, *Autobiography*, p. 125.

62. Van Buren to David Evans, June 9, 1824, Van Buren Papers, LC.

63. AJ to Donelson, March 6, 1824, Donelson Papers, LC.

64. AJ to Donelson, March 19, 1824, Donelson Papers, LC; AJ to Coffee, June 18, 1824, Coffee Papers, THS.

65. Ibid.

CHAPTER 5

1. AJ to Donelson, March 19, 1824, Donelson Papers, LC. See also Eaton to Coffee, March 2, 1824, Coffee Papers, THS.

2. AJ to Lafayette, September 10, 1824, in Jackson, *Correspondence*, III, 266.

3. Lafayette to AJ, October 18, 1824, in ibid., III, 268.

4. For a discussion of the various editions of this biography see John Reid and John Henry Eaton, *The Life of Andrew Jackson* (University, Ala., 1974), Frank Lawrence Owsley, Jr., ed., pp. v–xiv.

5. For a further analysis of this point see Robert P. Hay, "The American Revolution Twice Recalled: Lafayette's Visit and the Election of 1824," *Indiana Magazine of History* (1973), LXIX, 43–62.

6. Patchell to AJ, August 7, 1824, in Jackson, *Correspondence*, III, 262.

7. [John Henry Eaton], *The Letters of Wyoming, to the People of the United States, on the Presidential Election, and in Favour of Andrew Jackson.* (Philadelphia, 1824). For an excellent article on Eaton's role in the elections of 1824 and 1828 see Gabriel L. Lowe, "John H. Eaton, Jackson's Campaign Manager," *THQ* (1952), XI, 99–147.

8. Robert P. Hay, "The Case for Andrew Jackson in 1824: Eaton's *Wyoming Letters,*" *THQ* (1970), XXIX, 140.

9. *Letters of Wyoming*, pp. 10, 11, 14, 24, 5, 6, 93, 94. Hay, "The Case for Andrew Jackson," provides an excellent discussion of this pamphlet.

10. *Letters of Wyoming*, pp. 11, 12, 14.

11. Ibid., pp. 10, 14, 15.

12. These are Hay's conclusions in his article "The Case for Andrew Jackson," p. 149, except for the first sentence of the paragraph, which is taken from *Letters of Wyoming*, p. 28.

13. *Letters of Wyoming*, p. 36.

14. Ibid., p. 15.

15. Hay, "The Case for Andrew Jackson," cites a dozen or more of these newspapers, p. 150, footnotes 22 and 23. See also this author's article, " 'The Presidential Question': Letters to Southern Editors, 1823–1824," *THQ* (1972), XXXI, 170–186.

16. Hay, "The Case for Andrew Jackson in 1824," p. 150.

17. J. B. Mower to Weed, March 5, 1824, Weed Papers, RUL.

18. For details of this quarrel see Remini, *Jackson*, pp. 180–186.

19. Memorandum in the Jackson Papers, LC, in AJ's hand with an endorsement "Rough draft of Facts against A. Wayne, Jesse Benton etc."

20. AJ to Coffee, September 23, 1824, Coffee Papers, THS.

21. Ibid.

22. Gallatin to Walter Lowrie, May 22, 1824, Gallatin Papers, NYHS.

23. The argument that the election of 1824 involved more than personalities is ably and convincingly advanced by Paul C. Nagel, "The Election of 1824: A Reconsideration Based on Newspaper Opinion," *JSH* (1960), XXVI, 315–329.

24. A list of these historians is found in ibid., p. 315.

25. J. B. Mower to Weed, March 5, 1824, Weed Papers, RUL.

26. James F. Hopkins, "Election of 1824," in *History of American Presidential Elections,* Arthur M. Schlesinger, Jr., and Fred L. Israel, eds. (New York, 1971), I, 371.

27. The skullduggery in all its detail is described in Robert V. Remini, *Martin Van Buren and the Making of the Democratic Party* (New York, 1959), pp. 73–84.

28. Weed, *Autobiography,* p. 128.

29. On the efforts exerted to win over the Federalists, see Shaw Livermore, Jr., *The Twilight of Federalism: The Disintegration of the Federalist Party, 1815–1830* (Princeton, 1962).

30. Still the best study of Louisiana politics in the Jacksonian era is Joseph G. Tregle, "Louisiana in the Age of Jackson: A Study in Ego-Politics," doctoral dissertation, University of Pennsylvania, 1954.

31. Billie J. Hardin, "Amos Kendall and the 1824 Relief Controversy," *Register of the Kentucky Historical Society* (1966), XLIV, 196–208.

32. Donald J. Ratcliffe, "The Role of Voters and Issues in Party Formation: Ohio, 1824," *JAH* (1973), LIX, 847–870; Logan Esarey, "The Organization of the Jacksonian Party in Indiana," *Mississippi Valley Historical Association Proceedings* (1914), VII, 220–243.

33. Parton, *Jackson,* III, 52.

34. Wise, *Seven Decades of the Union,* p. 81.

35. Ibid.

36. AJ to Coffee, December 27, 1824, Coffee Papers, THS.

37. Ibid.

38. AJ to Coffee, January 23, 1825, Coffee Papers, THS. Rachel said she had the privilege of attending prayer meetings twice a week and attending church twice every Sunday. Rachel Jackson to Mary Donelson, January 27, 1825, Donelson Papers, LC.

39. McLane to Mrs. McLane, [December 9, 1824], in Munroe, *McLane,* p. 174.

40. AJ to Coffee, January 23, 1825, Coffee Papers, THS. "I have resisted all those invitations Except the 8th January," Rachel wrote to her sister. "We get two and three invitations of a day sometimes." Rachel Jackson to Mary Donelson, January 27, 1825, Donelson Papers, LC. This letter has been copied and heavily edited.

41. AJ to Lewis, December 27, 1824, Jackson Papers, ML.

42. McLane to Mrs. McLane, January 13, 1825, McLane Papers, LC.

43. Parton, *Jackson,* III, 55.

44. Clay to Francis Blair, January 8, 1825, in *Clay Papers,* IV, 9–11.

45. On this point there was an interesting exchange between Sam Houston and Representative John Sloane of Ohio, in Parton, *Jackson,* III, 57–58.

46. AJ to Lewis, January 24, 1825, Jackson-Lewis Papers, NYPL.

47. AJ to Coffee, January 10, 1825, Coffee Papers, THS.

48. AJ to Lewis, January 29, 1825, Jackson-Lewis Papers, NYPL.

49. AJ to Coffee, January 10, 1825, Coffee Papers, THS.

50. George Dangerfield, *The Era of Good Feelings* (New York, 1952), p. 338; *Niles Weekly Register,* August 18, 1827.

51. Benton, *Thirty Years View,* I, 48.

52. McLane to Mrs. McLane, January 1, 1825; McLane to J. A. Bayard, January 9, 1825 in Munroe, *McLane,* p. 170.

53. McLane to Mrs. McLane, February 6, 1825, McLane Papers, LC.

54. Adams, *Memoirs,* VI, 464–465.

55. Hayne to J. V. Grimke, January 28, 1825, Miscellaneous Hayne Papers, NYHS.

56. Van Buren, *Autobiography,* pp. 199–200.

57. Donelson to Coffee, February 19, 1825, Donelson Papers, LC.

58. *National Intelligencer,* January 31, 1825.

59. Ibid., February 4, 8, March 16, 28, 1825.

60. McLane to Mrs. McLane, February 6, 1825, McLane Papers, LC.

61. Ibid.

62. Van Buren to Mrs. McLane, February 6, 1825, Hamilton-McLane Papers, LC.

63. Parton, *Jackson,* III, 63–65.

64. Hopkins, "The Election of 1824," p. 380.

65. McLane to Mrs. McLane, February 9, 1825, McLane Papers, LC.

66. Van Buren, *Autobiography,* p. 151.

67. Adams, *Memoirs,* VI, 443, 473–475; Bemis, *Adams,* pp. 42–43.

68. *National Intelligencer,* February 10, 1825.

69. Donelson to Coffee, February 19, 1825, Donelson Papers, LC.

70. AJ to Colonel Squire Grant, February 18, 1825, in Jackson, *Correspondence,* III, 276. Jackson was actually talking about Kentucky citizens, but clearly his thought also applied to the entire nation.

71. AJ to Coffee, February 19, 1825, Coffee Papers, THS.

72. Ibid.

73. Adams, *Memoirs,* VI, 505–506.

74. AJ to Overton, February 10, 1825, Overton Papers, THS.

75. S. G. Goodrich, *Recollections of a Lifetime* (New York and Auburn, 1856), II, 403–404.

76. Bill dated February 18, 1825, in Jackson, *Correspondence,* III, 277.

77. Donelson to Coffee, February 19, 1825, Donelson Papers, LC.

78. McLane to Mrs. McLane, February 12, 1825, McLane Papers, LC.

79. Clay to Francis Brooke, February 14, 1825, in *Clay Papers,* IV, 67.

80. AJ to Lewis, February 14, 1825, Miscellaneous Jackson Papers, NYHS; also in Jackson, *Correspondence,* III, 276.

81. AJ to Lewis, February 20, 1825, Jackson-Lewis Papers, NYPL.

82. Ibid.

83. Ibid.

CHAPTER 6

1. Henry Lee to AJ, September 17, 1828, Donelson Papers, LC; George Bibb to Felix Grundy, Grundy Papers, NCSL.

2. Calhoun to AJ, June 4, 1826, in *Calhoun Papers,* X, 110.

3. Details of the movements of Radicals under Van Buren's direction can be found in Remini, *Martin Van Buren and the Making of the Democratic Party* (New York, 1959), pp. 84–146.

4. Richard H. Brown, "The Missouri Crisis, Slavery, and the Politics of Jacksonism," *South Atlantic Quarterly* (1966), LXV, 55–72, takes a somewhat different point of view. Brown's argument is more fully developed in his doctoral dissertation, " 'Southern Planters and Plain Republicans of the North': Martin Van Buren's Formula for National Politics," Yale University, 1955.

5. See, for example, Robert J. Trumbull, *The Crisis or Essays on Usurpations of the Federal Government, passim,* originally published in the Charleston *Mercury* and

later reprinted in pamphlet form in 1827, a copy in Jackson's personal library in the Hermitage, Volume XI, no. 8.

6. Henry Lee to AJ, September 17, 1828, Donelson Papers, LC. See also Calhoun to AJ, June 4, 1826, in *Calhoun Papers*, X, 110–111.

7. Rufus King to John King, February 27, 1825, King Papers, NYHS.

8. AJ to Lewis, February 22, 1824, Jackson-Lewis Papers, NYPL.

9. Adams, *Memoirs*, VI, 518.

10. Charles Wiltse, *John C. Calhoun, Nationalist* (Indianapolis, 1948), p. 309.

11. Parton, *Jackson*, III, 79.

12. AJ to Swartwout, March 6, 1825, Clermont State Historic Park, New York. For Rachel's reaction to Jackson's defeat see her letter to Katherine D. Morgan, May 18, 1825, Western Reserve Historical Society, Cleveland, Ohio.

13. *Niles Weekly Register*, July 5, 1828. This sentiment was repeated everywhere. See Henry Wise, *Seven Decades of the Union* (Philadelphia, 1881), p. 81.

14. AJ to Coffee, April 24, 1825, Coffee Papers, THS.

15. AJ to Lewis, February 20, 1825, Jackson-Lewis Papers, NYPL.

16. AJ to Swartwout, February 22, 1825, in Jackson, *Correspondence*, III, 278–279.

17. AJ to Swartwout, March 6, 1825, Clermont State Historic Park, New York.

18. "Address to the People of the Congressional District," March 26, 1825, in *Clay Papers*, IV, 161–165.

19. AJ to Coffee, April 24, 1825, Coffee Papers, THS. Jackson later contended that the bargain charge was proved when Representatives Trimble, Metcalf, and Frank Johnston of Ohio all told their constituents that they voted for Adams because they understood "that if Mr Adams was elected president, Clay would be secretary of state." AJ to Richard K. Call, March 20, 1828, CHS.

20. AJ to Swartwout, May 16, 1825, in *Some Letters of Andrew Jackson*, Henry F. DePuy, ed. (Worcester, 1922), p. 20.

21. Parton, *Jackson*, III, 95.

22. "To the Tennessee Legislature," October 12, 1825, in Jackson, *Correspondence*, III, 293–296.

23. Jackson appointed John Coffee as his agent to superintend the business of Andrew J. Hutchings while Jackson was out of the state. Statement by AJ, December 30, 1825, Jackson Papers, THS.

24. AJ to Coffee, March 16, 1827, Coffee Papers, THS; AJ to Call, May 3, 1827, Jackson Papers, NYHS; AJ to Grundy, May 30, 1826, Grundy Papers, UNCL; AJ to Lewis, March 8, 1828, Jackson Papers, ML.

25. AJ to Edward Livingston, January 30, 1826, Livingston Papers, JRDF.

26. AJ to Duval, July 25, 1826, Jackson Papers, TSL. This letter is in A.J. Donelson's handwriting, which explains the correct punctuation.

27. Parton, *Jackson*, III, 99.

28. Ibid., pp. 101–102.

29. At first the opposition newspapers called the Jacksonian party the "Combination." See the *National Intelligencer*, March, April 1826.

30. The Nashville Central Committee included Overton, Lewis, Campbell, Alfred Balch, Tom Claiborne, John Catron, Robert Whyte, John McNairy, William L. Brown, Robert C. Foster (who sometimes acted as the "chairman pro tem"), Joseph Philips, Daniel Graham, Jesse Wharton, Edward Ward, Felix Robertson, John Shelby, Josiah Nichol, and William White. The first notice of this committee in a Washington newspaper appeared in the *United States Telegraph* (a Jackson organ), April 9, 1827. For details of the process of structuring the Jackson

party on the local, state, and national levels, see Robert V. Remini, *Election of Andrew Jackson* (Philadelphia, 1965), pp. 51–120. An important study of party organization during the Jacksonian era is Richard P. McCormick, *The Second American Party System: Party Formation in the Jacksonian Era* (Chapel Hill, 1966).

31. T. Bradley to Gulian C. Verplanck, November 13, 1827, Verplanck Papers, NYHS.

32. The speech was given March 30, 1826. See *Register of Debates*, 19th Congress, 1st session, pp. 401–403. The reference to Blifill and Black George is taken from Henry Fielding's *Tom Jones*.

33. Benton, *Thirty Years View*, I, 70–77, contains details of the duel.

34. Richardson, *Messages and Papers*, II, 866–968, 872, 879, 882.

35. Edward P. Gaines to AJ, [1826], Jackson Papers, LC. See also the Jackson press for 1827 and 1828, especially the *United States Telegraph*, October 28, 1828.

36. AJ to John Branch, March 3, 1828, Branch Family Papers, SHC.

37. Macon to B. Yancey, December 8, 1825, in Edwin M. Wilson, *The Congressional Career of Nathaniel Macon* (Chapel Hill, 1900), p. 76.

38. AJ to Branch, March 3, 1826, Branch Family Papers, SHC.

39. Ibid. At the same time Jackson wrote to another: "The interest, as well as the feelings of the american people are, a friendly intercourse with the Republics of the South, commercial treaties with them on the broad basis of reciprocity, but entangling alliances with none—This is our true policy." AJ to Richard K. Call, March 9, 1826, Jackson Papers, LC.

40. Van Buren, *Autobiography*, p. 200.

41. *Register of Debates*, 19th Congress, 1st session, pp. 401–403.

42. Calhoun to AJ, June 4, 1826, in *Calhoun Papers*, X, 110–111.

43. AJ to Calhoun, [July 18, 1826], in ibid., X, 158–160.

44. Romulus Saunders to Bartlett Yancey, April 17, 1826, in "Saunders-Yancey Letters," *North Carolina Historical Review*, VIII, 456–457.

45. Richard Hofstadter, *The Idea of a Party System* (Berkeley, 1969), *passim*.

46. Van Buren to Thomas Ritchie, January 13, 1827, Van Buren Papers, LC.

47. Hamilton, *Reminiscences*, p. 68.

48. These are not the words Van Buren actually spoke to Calhoun. They are what he wrote to Ritchie a few weeks later; it is presumed that the arguments to both men were somewhat similar, for they occur in other places to other men at approximately the same time. See Van Buren to Ritchie, January 13, 1827, Van Buren Papers, LC.

49. Van Buren, *Autobiography*, pp. 513–514.

50. "We united heart and hand to promote the election of General Jackson," Van Buren recorded in his *Autobiography*, p. 514.

CHAPTER 7

1. AJ to Kendall, September 4, 1827, Jackson-Kendall Papers, LC; Kendall to Blair, February 3, 1829, Blair-Lee Papers, PUL; Ritchie to Lewis, September 16, 1828, Jackson Papers, LC; AJ to Edward Livingston, December 6, 1827, Livingston Papers, JRDF. See also Jackson's many letters to Coffee and Donelson in 1827 and 1828 in the Coffee Papers, THS and Donelson Papers, LC.

2. For Jackson's monetary views, pro and con, see Bray Hammond, *Banks and Politics in America from the Revolution to the Civil War* (Princeton, 1957); John M. McFaul, *The Politics of Jacksonian Finance* (Ithaca, N.Y., 1972); Robert V. Remini,

Andrew Jackson and the Bank War (New York, 1967); and Peter Temin, *The Jacksonian Economy* (New York, 1969).

3. AJ to Colonel John D. Terrill, July 29, 1826, in Jackson, *Correspondence*, III, 308–309.

4. AJ to T. P. Moore, July 26, 1826, in Jackson, *Correspondence*, III, 309.

5. AJ to Earl, July 10, 1828, Miscellaneous Papers, Indiana Historical Society. AJ to Committee of the Davidson County Bible Society, September 30, 1826, in Jackson, *Correspondence*, III, 315.

6. Isabel T. Kelsay, "The Presidential Campaign of 1828," *East Tennessee Historical Society Publications*, no. 5 (1933), 69–80; Culver H. Smith, "Propaganda Technique in the Jackson Campaign of 1828," in ibid., no. 6 (1934), 44–66. AJ to Call, March 20, 1828, CHS.

7. See various communications in the Jackson Papers, LC and TSL. Eaton wrote to Edward Livingston who also voted against Washington asking for an explanation of his vote and Livingston provided a long reply. See Eaton to Livingston, May 3, 1828, Livingston to Eaton, n.d., and AJ to Livingston, August 2, 1828, Livingston Papers, JRDF.

8. There are many statements about the marriage in the newspapers and private letters of the period. The one presented here is contained in the papers of John W. Taylor, January 22, 1825, NYHS.

9. *Gazette*, March 23, 1827, copy JPP.

10. Ibid., March 30, 1827.

11. Ibid., April 20, 24, 1827.

12. Ibid., April 24, 1827.

13. *United States Telegraph*, June 22, 1827. Harriet C. Owsley, "The Marriages of Rachel Donelson," *THQ*, XXXVI (1978), 479–492 presents the most "pro-Jackson" interpretation of the marriage. She argues—and this is the nub of her case—that a document dated January 28, 1791, in which Rachel is referred to as "Rachel Jackson" was registered in the April term of the Nashville court and not in the January term as stated in my *Jackson* p. 64. In any event the document itself was written on January 28, 1791.

14. January 22, 1825, Taylor Papers, NYHS.

15. Clay to Hammond, December 23, 1826, Miscellaneous Clay Papers, DUL.

16. AJ to Houston, December 15, 1826, Jackson Papers, LC.

17. *United States Telegraph*, June 22, 1827. See also sworn statements in 1826 and 1827, Jackson Papers, LC.

18. AJ to Southard, January 5, 1827, in Jackson, *Correspondence*, III, 330.

19. AJ to Houston, January 27, 1827, in ibid., III, 332–333.

20. Eaton to AJ, February 8, 1827, in ibid., III, 341–342.

21. Southard to AJ, February 9, 1827, in ibid., III, 342–343.

22. *United States Telegraph*, May 20, 1828.

23. AJ to Hugh Lawson White, February 7, 1827, in Jackson, *Correspondence*, III, 334, 341.

24. "Coffin Hand Bill," HL.

25. AJ to Colonel Allen, March 31, 1827, Jackson Papers, TSL.

26. For details of these particular "rencounters" see Remini, *Jackson*, pp. 38–39, 57ff., 102, 124, 138, 107–108, 117–124, 137–138, 140, 136–143, 184–185.

27. Lewis to Elijah Haywood, March 28, 1827, Jackson-Lewis Papers, NYPL.

28. J. D. Steele, Manuscript Journal, 1820–1829, HL.

29. AJ to Coffee, April 8, 1827, Coffee Papers, THS.

30. Andrew Erwin, *Gen. Jackson's Negro Speculations* . . . (n.p., n.d.), pp. 3, 9, 15.

31. Lewis to Haywood, March 28, 1827, Jackson-Lewis Papers, NYPL.

32. Ibid.

33. *Reflections on the Character and Public Services of Andrew Jackson with Reference to his Qualifications for the Presidency with General Remarks.* By a Native American. (New York, 1828), p. 7.

34. The *Telegraph* made its first appearance on February 6, 1826, and when the campaign heated up, Green launched the weekly *Telegraph Extra.*

35. Lewis to AJ, June 28, 1842, Jackson Papers, HL.

36. Buchanan to Ingham, August 16, 1827, Buchanan Papers, PHS; *Niles Weekly Register,* July 7, 21, August 11, 18, October 6, 1827; AJ to Lewis, September 1, 1827, Jackson Papers, ML; Buchanan to Henry F. Slaymaker, January 20, 1827, Miscellaneous Papers, HL.

37. Buchanan to AJ, August 10, 1827, Jackson Papers, LC.

38. Calhoun to Van Buren, July 7, 1826, in Van Buren, *Autobiography,* pp. 514–515. On the loans to Green, see Jackson, *Correspondence,* III, 301–302; and Eaton to Coffee, February 22, 1825, Coffee Papers, THS.

39. AJ to Green, August 13, 1827, Jackson Papers, LC.

40. AJ to Call, July 1, 1827, Jackson Papers, LC; AJ to Colonel Allen, March 31, 1827, Jackson Papers, TSL; AJ to Call, July 1, 1827, Jackson Papers, TSL; AJ to Robert Y. Hayne, July 9, 1827, Paul Hamilton Hayne Papers, DUL.

41. AJ to Call, July 1, 1827, Jackson Papers, LC; AJ to Hayne, July 9, 1827, Paul Hamilton Hayne Papers, DUL.

42. On Van Buren's tour see Van Buren to Tazewell, April 30, 1827, Miscellaneous Van Buren Papers, DUL; *National Intelligencer,* April 7, 1827; Raleigh, N.C., *Register,* March 20, 1827; Van Buren to James A. Hamilton, January 28, February 15, 1827, Miscellaneous Van Buren Papers, NYPL. Most of Van Buren's letters to Jackson are in the Van Buren Collection in the Library of Congress because Van Buren asked Jackson to return them to him to assist him in the preparation of his *Autobiography.* Foolishly, Jackson obliged without making copies. Some of these letters Van Buren may have destroyed after Jackson's death.

43. Kendall to AJ, August 22, 1827, Jackson Papers, TSL.

44. Richard Latner, *The Presidency of Jackson,* develops this thesis at length.

45. *National Journal,* February 27, March 10, 22, 31, July 24, 1827 and *National Intelligencer,* March 13, 20, 1827.

46. W.T. Barry to Alfred Balch, November 19, 1827, Jackson Papers, LC. See also Henry Lee to AJ, September 17, 1828, Donelson Papers, LC, and AJ to Edward Livingston, December 6, 1827, Livingston Papers, JRDF.

47. AJ to John Branch, June 24, 1828, Jackson Papers, LC. See also AJ's letters to Edward Livingston, Robert Y. Hayne, Richard Call, Van Buren, Caleb Atwater, Amos Kendall, John Coffee, Alfred Balch, et al. during 1827 and 1828, many of which are located in the Library of Congress or the Tennessee State Library.

48. Caleb Atwater to AJ, February 29, 1828, Jackson Papers, LC; John Nelson to Samuel Smith, January 29, 1829, Smith Papers, LC; *United States Telegraph,* January 24, 1828. See also *Kentucky Watchtower,* May 10, 1828.

49. *Niles Weekly Register,* November 10, 1827. Many of the circulars are unsigned and untitled; copies of some of them are located in JPP. Of the 265 pamphlets bound by Jackson for his library at the Hermitage, nearly 50 of them deal with the election of 1828. An inventory of these pamphlets was prepared by Stewart Lillard. The quoted passage in the text is taken from George Bibb to Felix Grundy, February 5, 1827, Grundy Papers, UNCL.

50. *Register of Debates,* 19th Congress, 1st Session, pp. 2655–2656.

51. Albany *Argus*, November 4, 1828; *Telegraph*, October 20, 1828. See also Charleston *Mercury* and Richmond *Enquirer*.

52. John Miller to Taylor, February 8, 1828, John W. Taylor Papers, NYHS.

53. Parton, *Jackson*, III, 144.

54. *National Journal*, May 24, 1828.

55. AJ to Edward Livingston, August 2, 1828, Livingston Papers, JRDF.

56. With all the talk about the six militiamen and the case of John Woods and the arrests in New Orleans, Jackson appreciated that a celebration on January 8, 1828, would serve as the best reply of all to these charges. See AJ to Livingston, December 6, 1827, Delafield Papers, JRDF. See AJ to Richard K. Call, March 20, 1828, CHS, for the many invitations from state election committees.

57. AJ to Lewis, December 25, 1827, Jackson Papers, ML.

58. Hamilton, *Reminiscences*, p. 70.

59. Parton, *Jackson*, III, 139.

60. Ibid., pp. 139–140; AJ to Livingston, February 21, 1828, Livingston Papers, JRDF; Edwin A. Miles, *Jacksonian Democracy in Mississippi* (Chapel Hill, 1960), pp. 3–4.

61. James Parton said that not until the reception given in New York City for Kossuth in the 1850s was this celebration surpassed. Parton, *Jackson*, III, 138.

62. AJ to Livingston, February 21, 1828, Livingston Papers, JRDF. The Democratic press was particularly vocal in emphasizing Jackson's role in "saving" the republic. See, for example, the *United States Telegraph* for the spring and summer, 1828.

63. AJ to Kendall, September 4, 1827, Jackson Papers, LC.

64. Robert V. Remini, *The Election of Andrew Jackson* (New York, 1963), 117–119. This work includes many more details of the 1828 election.

65. Ibid., p. 153; *National Journal*, September 4, 1828.

66. *Telegraph*, January 26, February 16, July 2, 23, 1828; *Extra Telegraph*, March 21, 1828.

67. John William Ward, *Andrew Jackson, Symbol of an Age* (New York, 1955), pp. 13–15.

68. Benjamin Perley Poore, *Reminiscences of Sixty Years in the National Metropolis* (Philadelphia, 1886), I, 90.

69. Eaton to AJ, January 21, 1828, Jackson Papers, LC.

70. AJ to Lewis, July 16, 1828, Jackson-Lewis Papers, NYPL.

71. Alexander Smyth to David Campbell, December 3, 1827, David Campbell Papers, DUL.

72. For further details see Remini, *Election of Andrew Jackson*, p. 167.

73. James K. Polk to Dr. Alfred Flournoy, December 6, 1827, Polk Papers, LC.

74. AJ to Lewis, December 19, 1827, Jackson-Lewis Papers, NYPL.

75. Worden Pope to C. A. Wickliffe, January 6, 1828, Worden Pope Miscellaneous Papers, LC.

76. Van Buren, *Autobiography*, p. 514.

77. Silas Wright, Jr. to Azariah C. Flagg, December 20, 1827, April 7, 13, 22, 1828, Flagg Papers, NYPL; *Register of Debates*, 20th Congress, 1st Session, pp. 1836–1870, 748, 2576.

78. Robert V. Remini, "Martin Van Buren and the Tariff of Abominations," *AHR*, LXIII (1958), 903–917.

79. E. Sage to Gulian C. Verplanck, March 8, 1828, Verplanck Papers, NYHS.

80. Albany *Argus*, May 20, 1828. For an opposite view see *Niles Weekly Register*, May 17, June 28, July 26, 1828.

81. Worden Pope to C. A. Wickliffe, January 6, 1828, Worden Pope Miscellaneous Papers, LC.

82. John Branch to AJ, May 23, 1828, in Jackson, *Correspondence*, III, 403.

83. AJ to Coffee, May 12, 1828, Coffee Papers, THS.

84. The best account of the origins of the antimasonic movement is Robert O. Rupp, "Social Tension and Political Mobilization in Jacksonian America: Case Study of the Antimasonic Party in New York, Pennsylvania and Vermont." Doctoral dissertation, Syracuse University, 1980. I am grateful to Rupp for his criticisms and suggestions of my account of the movement.

85. Weed, *Autobiography*, p. 297.

86. Henry B. Stanton, *Random Recollections* (New York, 1886), p. 25; Marcy to Verplanck, March 9, 1828, Verplanck Papers, NYHS.

87. Francis Baylies to Verplanck, April 6, 1828, Verplanck Papers, NYHS.

88. AJ to Hamilton, April 29, 1828, in Jackson, *Correspondence*, III, 399.

89. Van Buren to AJ, September 14, 1827, Van Buren Papers, LC. See also Van Buren to Livingston, September 4, 1828, Livingston Papers, JRDF.

90. Gulian C. Verplanck to Jesse Hoyt, January 22, 1828, in William L. Mackenzie, *Life and Times of Martin Van Buren* (Boston, 1846), p. 203.

91. AJ to Lewis, June 22, 1828, Jackson-Lewis Papers, NYPL.

92. Nicholas Trist to Donelson, October 19, 1828, Donelson Papers, LC.

93. William Rives to W. Gilmer, September 25, 1828, Rives Papers, LC; Van Buren to B.H. Norton, May 14, 1828, Charles Owen Collection.

94. Atwater to AJ, September 20, 1827, Jackson Papers, LC.

95. AJ to Lewis, September, 1828, Jackson Papers, ML.

CHAPTER 8

1. Rachel Jackson to Elizabeth Watson, July 18, 1828, Jackson Papers, YUL; AJ to Richard K. Call, December 22, 1828, in Walter R. Benjamin, *The Collector* (January 1906), p. 28.

2. *United States Telegraph*, July 3, 1828. In the first volume of this biography I mistakenly gave the date of Lyncoya's death as July 1, 1828. The reason for this error is that the undated obituary notice in the *Telegraph* of July 3, 1828 said that death occurred "on the morning of the 1st inst.," and I automatically put down July 1 without thinking. But obviously word of the tragedy could hardly have gotten from Nashville to Washington in two days.

3. Jackson Lynch to William B. Campbell, November 5, 1828, Campbell Papers, DUL; Remini, *Election of Andrew Jackson*, p. 183; *Telegraph*, October 20, 1828.

4. Virginia and Rhode Island restricted suffrage with property qualifications and Louisiana maintained tax payments as a requirement for voting. Chilton Williamson, *American Suffrage from Property to Democracy* (Princeton, 1960), pp. 182–224.

5. *Telegraph*, October 17, 22, November 5, 1828.

6. AJ to General Thomas Cadwalader, November 16, 1828, in Jackson, *Correspondence*, III, 445.

7. Green to AJ, November 12, 1828, Jackson Papers, LC.

8. Donelson to Coffee, November 16, 1828, Donelson Papers, LC.

9. Jackson to Lewis, October 19, 1828, Jackson-Lewis Papers, NYPL.

10. Kendall to AJ, November 19, 1828, CHS; AJ to Kendall, November 25, 1828, Jackson Papers, LC.

11. Clay to Webster, November 30, 1828, Webster Papers, LC.

12. Maine gave one electoral vote to Jackson.

13. Arthur M. Schlesinger, Jr., and Fred L. Israel, eds., *History of American Presidential Elections: 1789–1968* (New York, 1971), I, 492.

14. AJ to Coffee, November 24, 1828, Coffee Papers, THS. These general sentiments, namely that his victory was "a triumph of the virtue of the people over the corrupting influence" of the executive branch "to destroy the morals of the people," are repeated in numerous letters written at the time. See, for example, AJ to Thomas Butler, November 23, 1828, Louisiana State University, copy JPP, from which the above quotation is taken.

15. AJ to Coffee, December 11, 1828, Coffee Papers, THS; AJ to Edmund P. Gaines, December 4, 1828, Jackson Papers, LC.

16. Robert Wickliffe to Clay, October 7, 1828, H. Shaw to Clay, January 9, 1829, Clay Papers, LC; *Niles Weekly Register,* December 6, 1828; Edward Everett to A.H. Everett, December 2, 1828, Everett Papers, MHS.

17. See *Telegraph* and its successor as the organ of the Democratic party, the Washington *Globe,* for the period. See also Jackson's messages and other public statements in Richardson, *Messages and Papers,* II, 998ff.

18. This thesis is advanced, explained, and documented in Richard P. McCormick, "New Perspectives on Jacksonian Politics," *AHR* (1960), LXV, 288–301.

19. New York *American,* November 9, 1827.

20. John Miller to John W. Taylor, February 8, 1828, Taylor Papers, NYHS.

21. Nathan Sargent, *Public Men and Events* (Philadelphia, 1875), I, 346–347.

22. Kendall to Blair, February 3, 1829, Blair-Lee Papers, PUL.

23. E. P. Gaines to AJ, November 22, 1828, Jackson Papers, LC.

24. Parton, *Jackson,* III, 153.

25. AJ to Coffee, November 24, 1828, Coffee Papers, THS.

26. Rachel Jackson to Elizabeth Watson, July 18, 1828, Jackson Papers, YUL.

27. Eaton to Rachel Jackson, December 1, 1828, in Jackson, *Correspondence,* III, 447–448.

28. AJ to Coffee, December 11, 1828, Coffee Papers, THS.

29. Henry A. Wise, *Seven Decades of the Union* (Philadelphia, 1872), p. 113.

30. John S. Bassett states that he received this account from Mrs. Elizabeth Blair Lee (daughter of Francis P. Blair, Sr.), who remembered it from her youth and got it directly from Major Lewis. However, it is strange that Lewis did not repeat this story to James Parton, who surely would have put it into his biography as he did all the other information Lewis gave him. See Bassett, *Jackson,* p. 406 footnote 1.

31. Ibid.

32. Wise, *Seven Decades,* p. 114.

33. Francis Preston to AJ, December 5, 1828 with the endorsement in Jackson's hand: "Answered in haste 18th Dec., 1828. Whilst writing Mrs. Jackson taken violently ill." Jackson, *Correspondence,* III, 452, footnote 2. James Parton states in his biography that Jackson was in the fields some distance from the house when Rachel was taken ill. See Parton, *Jackson,* III, 154. Parton got his account from Old Hannah.

34. Parton, *Jackson,* III, 154–155. Bassett says that a local tradition insists that Rachel was seized after her arm became chilled by stirring a vat filled with pickles in strong brine. Jackson, *Correspondence,* III, 452 footnote 2.

35. James, *Jackson,* p. 478.

36. The committee in Nashville preparing the reception in Jackson's honor stated that Rachel died between the hours of 10 and 11 P.M. Parton, *Jackson*, III, 157.

Dr. Heiskell's bill for medical services rendered between October 21 and December 22 for Rachel include the following:

November 8	pills	1.50
December 17	To visit Mrs. Jackson and venesection	2.50
December 18	Attendance	
December 19	To visit Mrs. Jackson and attendance	2.00
" " "	and pulv.	2.50
December 20	To visit Mrs. Jackson and attendance	2.00
December 21	To visit Mrs. Jackson and attendance. Cast. oil 4	2.50
December 22	To visit Mrs. Jackson and attendance.	2.00

Receipt, Charles Owen Collection, Glencoe, Illinois.

37. Parton, *Jackson*, III, 156.

38. Ibid.

39. Mrs. Smith to Mrs. Kirkpatrick, January 12, 1829, in Gaillard Hunt, ed., *The First Forty Years of Washington Society* (New York, 1906), p. 259.

40. Bassett, *Jackson*, p. 407.

41. Parton, *Jackson*, III, 156.

42. Ibid., p. 157.

43. Ibid.

44. Jackson paid $60 for the casket to McCombs and Robinson on December 26, 1828. Receipt, Charles Owen Collection, Glencoe, Illinois.

45. Parton, *Jackson*, III, 158.

46. Wise, *Seven Decades*, p. 115.

47. This is inferred from remarks of Reverend William Hume, who gave the eulogy.

48. James, *Jackson*, p. 482.

49. Parton, *Jackson*, III, 158.

50. Wise, *Seven Decades*, p. 116.

51. It is not certain who composed this inscription. Certainly it had Jackson's cooperation and approval. It has been attributed to Henry Lee but John H. Eaton is the more likely author. According to Robert Chester, who married Rachel's niece, Martha Hays, the author was Eaton. "Reminiscences of Colonel Chester," *Magazine of American History*, XXVII (May 1892), p. 387.

CHAPTER 9

1. AJ to Coffee, January 17, 1829, Coffee Papers, THS.

2. AJ to Jean Plauché, December 27, 1828, Jackson Papers, TSL.

3. Ibid.

4. Hayne to AJ, December 18, 1828, in Jackson, *Correspondence*, III, 453.

5. Thomas Ritchie to Van Buren, March 27, 1829, Van Buren Papers, LC.

6. Memorandum, [December 23, 1828], in Jackson, *Correspondence*, III, 454.

7. AJ to Coffee, January 17, 1829, Coffee Papers, THS.

8. Ely to AJ, January 28, 1829, in Jackson, *Correspondence*, IV, 3; see also Lyman Beecher to Ely, January 20, 1829, in ibid, pp. 3–4.

9. Frances M. Trollope, *Domestic Manners of the Americans* (New York, 1949), I, 125.

10. *Telegraph,* January 28, 1829.

11. Thomas S. Hinde to Clay, February 3, 1829, Clay Papers, LC.

12. Trollope, *Domestic Manners,* p. 125.

13. Edwin A. Miles, "The First People's Inaugural—1829," *THQ* (Fall, 1978) XXXVII, 296.

14. See the mayor's letter to the Boards, February 3, 1829, Miscellaneous Papers, LC.

15. Remini, *Election of Andrew Jackson,* (Philadelphia, 1963), p. 195; Miles, "First People's Inaugural," p. 296.

16. Ibid.

17. Alfred Mordecai to Ellen Mordecai, February 11, 1829, in Sarah Agnes Wallace, ed., "Opening Days of Jackson's Presidency as Seen in Private Letters," *THQ* (1950), IX, 368.

18. Quoted in Miles, "First People's Inaugural," p. 297.

19. Ibid., p. 295.

20. *National Intelligencer,* February 17, 1829; Kendall, *Autobiography,* p. 288; Hamilton, *Reminiscences,* p. 98; Miles, "First People's Inaugural," p. 297.

21. AJ to Van Buren, February 14, 1829, James Hamilton, Jr., to Van Buren, February 19, 1829, Van Buren Papers, LC; Kendall to Blair, March 7, 1829, Blair-Lee Papers, PUL.

22. Silas Wright, Jr., to Van Buren, December 9, 1828, Van Buren Papers, LC.

23. AJ to Hamilton, March 4, 1829, in Jackson, *Correspondence,* IV, 13; Hamilton, *Reminiscences,* pp. 89–97.

24. Tazewell to AJ, March 30, 1829, in Jackson, *Correspondence,* IV, 15; Van Buren, *Autobiography,* p. 256; Hamilton, *Reminiscences,* p. 91. Virginians later pinned their hopes on Philip P. Barbour but Jackson passed over him. Bassett, *Jackson,* p. 413.

25. Kendall to Blair, March 7, 1829, Blair-Lee Papers, PUL; Hamilton to Van Buren, February 18, 1829, Van Buren Papers, LC.

26. Kendall to Blair, March 7, 1829, Blair-Lee Papers, PUL; James Hamilton, Jr., to Van Buren, February 19, 1829, Van Buren Papers; W. A. Ingham, *Samuel D. Ingham* (Philadelphia, 1910), pp. 6–10; Kim T. Phillips, "The Pennsylvania Origins of the Jackson Movement," *Political Science Quarterly* (1976), XCI, 489–508.

27. AJ to Rachel, February 27, 1824, Charles Norton Owen Collection.

28. VB to James A. Hamilton, February 15, 1829, in Hamilton, *Reminiscences,* p. 93.

29. Kendall to Blair, March 7, 1829, Blair-Lee Papers, PUL.

30. Louis McLane to James A. Bayard, February 19, 1829, Bayard Papers, LC.

31. Eaton to AJ, December 7, 1828, Hurja Collection, TSL.

32. Remini, *Jackson,* p. 161.

33. Eaton to AJ, December 7, 1828, Hurja Collection, TSL.

34. Eaton to White, February 23, 1829, in Nancy N. Scott, *Memoir of Hugh Lawson White* (Philadelphia, 1856), p. 266. See Jackson's account in AJ to John McLemore, December 25, 1830, Miscellaneous Jackson Papers, NYHS.

35. Kendall to Blair, March 7, 1829, Blair-Lee Papers, PUL.

36. AJ to John Overton, January 10, 1825, Claybrooke Collection, THS.

37. McLane to Van Buren, February 19, 1829, Van Buren Papers, LC.

38. Kendall to Blair, March 7, 1829, Blair-Lee Papers, PUL.

39. Hamilton, *Reminiscences*, p. 102; Bassett, *Jackson*, 414; William S. Hoffman, "John Branch and the Origins of the Whig Party in North Carolina," *North Carolina Historical Review* (1958), XXXV, 299–315.

40. C. P. Van Ness to Van Buren, March 9, 1829, Van Buren Papers, LC.

41. Kendall to Blair, March 7, 1829, Blair-Lee Papers, PUL.

42. Memorandum in Jackson's handwriting, [December 9, 1828], in Jackson, *Correspondence*, III, 451–452.

43. Thomas P. Govan, "John M. Berrien and the Administration of Andrew Jackson," *JSH* (1939), V, 448; C. P. Van Ness to Van Buren, March 9, 1829, Van Buren Papers, LC.

44. Kendall to Blair, March 7, 1829, Blair-Lee Papers, PUL; Dorothy G. Fowler, *The Cabinet Politician: The Postmasters General, 1829–1909* (New York, 1943), p. 2.

45. Kendall to Blair, March 7, 1829, Blair-Lee Papers, PUL.

46. Hamilton, *Reminiscences*, p. 99.

47. McLean resigned four days after the inaugural.

48. Kendall to Blair, March 7, 1829, Blair-Lee Papers, PUL; Hamilton, *Reminiscences*, pp. 100–101.

49. William Wirt to William Pope, March 22, 1829, John P. Kennedy, *Life of William Wirt* (Philadelphia, 1849), II, 228.

50. AJ to John C. McLemore, April 1829, Miscellaneous Jackson Papers, NYHS. A short time later Mrs. William Rives asked Jackson for his autograph. He obliged and enclosed with it a poem that says something about the sort of men he hoped to employ in his administration:

> Now to my tent, O God, repair,
> and make thy servant wise;
> I'll suffer nothing near me there,
> that shall offend thine eyes.
>
> The man that doth his neighbour wrong,
> by falsehood, or by force,
> The scornful eye, the slanderous tongue;
> I'll banish from my doors.
>
> I'll seek the faithful, and the Just,
> and will their health enjoy;
> These are the friends, that I shall trust,
> the servants, I'll employ.
>   Andrew Jackson
>   June 26, 1829

It has been stated that Jackson is the author of this poem. I frankly doubt it. The manuscript is in his hand and is carefully written and has no corrections or misspellings. He probably read the poem somewhere, liked it, and copied it. The poem and the accompanying letter to Mrs. Rives are in the Donelson Papers, LC.

51. Richard B. Latner, "The Eaton Affair Reconsidered," *THQ* (1977), XXXVI, 330–351.

52. Kendall to Blair, February 3, 1829, Blair-Lee Papers, PUL.

53. Ibid.

54. Kendall to Blair, March 7, 1829, Blair-Lee Papers, PUL.

55. Welles to Niles, February 12, 1829, Welles Papers, LC.

56. Kendall to Blair, February 3, 1829, Blair-Lee Papers, PUL.

57. Ibid.

58. Kendall to Blair, March 7, 1829, Blair-Lee Papers, PUL.

59. Kendall to Blair, January 9, 1829, Blair-Lee Papers, PUL.

60. Kendall to Blair, March 7, 1829, Blair-Lee Papers, PUL.

61. Kendall, *Autobiography*, pp. 287–288; John Niven, *Gideon Welles* (New York, 1973), pp. 60–61.

62. "Rough Draft of the First Inaugural Address," Jackson Papers, LC, and reprinted in Jackson, *Correspondence*, IV, 10–13.

63. Hamilton, *Reminiscences*, p. 104.

64. Indeed Hamilton's reliability in the *Reminiscences* is sometimes open to question. Too often his statements contradict surviving documents. There is considerable puffery in the *Reminiscences*, and Hamilton's testimony should be treated accordingly.

65. Richardson, *Messages and Papers*, II, 1000–1001. Jackson later claimed that he wanted to mention the BUS but his friends thought it belonged in his first message to Congress. See his endorsement in Polk to AJ, December 23, 1833, Polk Papers, LC.

66. Van Buren to Hamilton, February 21, 1829, in Hamilton, *Reminiscences*, p. 94.

67. Webster to Mrs. E. Webster, February 19, 1829, in Webster, *Private Correspondence* (Boston, 1857), I, 470.

68. Parton, *Jackson*, III, 169.

69. New York *Spectator*, March 13, 1829. I am very grateful to Professor Edwin A. Miles, who provided me with transcripts of dozens of newspaper reports of the inauguration which he used in preparing his article, "First People's Inaugural." The title of his article also provided the title for this chapter and is used with the author's consent.

70. New York *Evening Post*, March 10, 1829.

71. Niven, *Welles*, p. 58; *United States Gazette* (Philadelphia), March 6, 1829.

72. *Telegraph*, March 5, 1829.

73. Philadelphia *Gazette*, March 8, 1829; Gaillard Hunt, ed., *The First Forty Years of Washington Society* (New York, 1906), p. 293.

74. Ibid., p. 293.

75. Parton, *Jackson*, III, 170.

76. Albany *Argus*, March 19, 1829; Hunt, *Forty Years*, p. 291.

77. Boston *Statesman*, March 12, 1829.

78. Hunt, *Forty Years*, p. 291; Salmon P. Chase, manuscript diary, March 4, 1829, Chase Papers, LC.

79. Richardson, *Messages and Papers*, II, 999–1001.

80. Madison's first inaugural was about as short as Jackson's.

81. Hamilton to Van Buren, March 5, 1829, Van Buren Papers, LC.

82. *Telegraph*, March 5, 1829.

83. Washington *City Chronicle*, March 7, 1829; Hamilton to Van Buren, March 5, 1829, Van Buren Papers, LC; New York *Evening Post*, March 10, 1829.

84. Hunt, *Forty Years*, p. 291.

85. *Argus of Western America*, March 18, 1829. Edwin A. Miles regards Kendall's coverage of the inauguration for the *Argus* as the best of the many newspaper accounts, and I quite agree.

86. Hunt, *Forty Years*, p. 291.

87. E. P. Gaines to AJ, November 22, 1828, Jackson Papers, LC; Remini, *Election of Andrew Jackson*, p. 199.

88. Joseph Story to Mrs. Joseph Story, March 7, 1829, William W. Story, *Life and Letters of Joseph Story* (Boston, 1851), I, 563.

89. Hunt, *Forty Years*, p. 283; Hamilton to Van Buren, March 5, 1829, Van Buren Papers, LC.

90. Hunt, *Forty Years*, p. 284.

91. *Argus of Western America,* March 18, 1829.

92. Hunt, *Forty Years,* p. 295; *Telegraph,* March 5, 1829; Salmon P. Chase, manuscript diary, March 4, 1829, Chase Papers, LC.

93. Gideon Welles could not get over it. His sense of the sovereignty of the people was completely devastated by the demonstration. Niven, *Welles,* p. 65.

94. Hamilton to Van Buren, March 5, 1829, Van Buren Papers, LC.

95. Benjamin P. Poore, *Reminiscences of Sixty Years* (Philadelphia, 1886), I, 95.

96. Hunt, *Forty Years,* pp. 289, 297; Richmond *Enquirer,* March 13, 1829.

97. Hunt, *Forty Years,* pp. 288–289, 297.

98. Ibid.

99. *Argus,* March 18, 1829.

CHAPTER 10

1. *Report of the Commission on the Renovation of the Executive Mansion* (Washington, D.C., 1952), p. 30; Lewis to Edward Livingston, April 20, 1829, Livingston Papers, JRDF; William Ryan and Desmond Guiness, *The White House: An Architectural History* (New York, 1980), pp. 128–130. For a description of some of the White House rooms see Caleb Cushing's Diary, April 1829, Cushing Papers, LC.

2. Parton, *Jackson,* III, 180; Burke, *Emily Donelson of Tennessee,* I, 173. These living arrangements were altered later and will be described in volume III of this biography.

3. James, *Jackson,* p. 494; Private Memorandum Book of A. Jackson, written sometime between May 18 and June 23, 1829, Jackson Papers, LC.

4. Ibid.; see also his many letters to Coffee and Overton at this time, TSL.

5. Edward Everett to John McLean, August 1, 1828, Everett Papers, MHS.

6. Lewis to J. A. Hamilton, December 12, 1828, Van Buren Papers, LC; "Outline of principles," February 23, 1829, Jackson Papers, LC. On Jackson's administrative reforms see Albert Somit, "Andrew Jackson as Administrative Reformer," *THQ* (1954), XIII, 204–233.

7. Contrast the *National Intelligencer* with *Telegraph* for 1829 and 1830 as one example; Parton, *Jackson,* III, 206ff.

8. Ibid., p. 220.

9. Ibid., p. 692.

10. Revised thinking about Jackson and the spoils system began with Carl Russel Fish, *The Civil Service and the Patronage* (New York, 1905) and continued with Eric M. Eriksson, "The Federal Civil Service under President Jackson," *MVHR* (March 1927), XIII, 517–540. Sidney H. Aronson, *Status and Kinship in the Higher Civil Service: Standards of Selection in the Administrations of John Adams, Thomas Jefferson, and Andrew Jackson* (Cambridge, Mass., 1964), shows there was little difference between the men chosen for federal office by these three Presidents. A fine review of the various opinions among scholars about Jackson's handling of the patronage is William F. Mugleston, "Andrew Jackson and the Spoils System: An Historiographical Survey," *Mid-America* (1977), LIX, 113–125.

11. AJ to Hardy Cryer, May 26, 1829, in Jackson, *Correspondence,* IV, 33.

12. Jackson blamed much of his difficulty in the matter on "the preceding administration" whose object was to "embarrass" him. AJ to Coffee, March 19, 1829, Coffee Papers, THS.

13. Kendall had become so acceptable in the White House that there was

talk of establishing him in another Washington newspaper or making him Green's partner, but Kendall refused. Kendall to Blair, January 9, February 3, March 7, 1829, Blair-Lee Papers, PUL.

14. Kendall to Blair, February 3, 1829, Blair-Lee Papers, PUL.

15. AJ to John C. McLemore, April 1829, Miscellaneous Jackson Papers, NYHS; Benjamin Perley Poore, *Reminiscences*, I, 98.

16. Nathan Sargent, *Public Men and Events*, I, 167–168.

17. AJ to McLemore, April 1829, Miscellaneous Jackson Papers, NYHS.

18. Kendall, *Autobiography*, p. 298.

19. Ibid.; Kendall to Blair, April 25, 1831, Blair-Lee Papers, PUL; AJ to Overton, May 13, 1830, Overton Papers, THS; Albert Somit, "Andrew Jackson as Administrative Reformer," *THQ* (1954), XIII, 205, 216, 217. In this chapter when dealing with Jackson as administrator I have relied heavily on Somit's article in the *THQ* as well as his "New Papers: Some Sidelights Upon Jacksonian Administration," *MVHR* (1948), XXXV, 91–99.

20. AJ to T. L. Miller, May 13, 1829, in Jackson, *Correspondence*, IV, 31–32.

21. David Campbell to his wife, June 3, 1829, Campbell Papers, DUL.

22. AJ to McLemore, April 1829, Miscellaneous Jackson Papers, NYHS; AJ to Coffee, May 30, 1829, Coffee Papers, THS; Kendall to Blair, November 22, 1829, Blair-Lee Papers, PUL.

23. AJ to Samuel Ingham, March 28, 1829, John K. Porter Collection, LC.

24. Memorandum Book of A. Jackson commencing April 1829, Jackson Papers, LC. That Jackson understood that he needed a system approved by Congress can be seen in his letter to Van Buren, March 31, 1829, Van Buren Papers, LC.

25. Richardson, *Messages and Papers*, II, 1011–1012.

26. The people had the right, Jackson argued, "to reach through the election of the Chief Executive, every subordinate officer, and thus to remove all who shall have given dissatisfaction to the public." AJ to Joseph C. Guild, April 24, 1835, in Jackson, *Correspondence*, V, 340.

27. Eriksson, "The Federal Civil Service," pp. 517–540; John W. Forney, *Anecdotes of Public Men* (New York, 1970), I, 283.

28. Van Buren, *Autobiography*, p. 231.

29. Ibid.

30. Ibid., p. 232.

31. Lewis to Edward Livingston, March 27, 1829, Livingston Papers, JRDF. Jackson was so indisposed that he withdrew from business for a day or two. Finally he took some medicine and his health, said Lewis, "has been gradually improving ever since. . . ."

32. Benton, *Thirty Years View*, I, 737.

33. William I. Paulding, *Literary Life of James K. Paulding* (New York, 1867), pp. 287–288.

34. Benton, *Thirty Years View*, I, 738.

35. Van Buren, *Autobiography*, p. 232.

36. See Max M. Mintz, "The Political Ideas of Martin Van Buren," *New York History* (1949), XXX, 422–448.

37. Van Buren, *Autobiography*, p. 251.

38. Ibid.

39. Ibid., pp. 251–252.

40. Ibid., p. 252. See also Van Buren's "Memo of Presidential Conference," [1829], Van Buren Papers, LC.

41. Van Buren, *Autobiography*, pp. 254–255.

42. "Tazewell is a corrupt man," said Amos Kendall, an opinion appar-

ently confirmed by his defense of Miles King in the matter of King's default. Kendall to Blair, April 25, 1831, Blair-Lee Papers, PUL; Van Buren, *Autobiography,* p. 256.

43. Ibid., p. 259; Van Buren to Edward Livingston, April 19, 1829, Livingston Papers, JRDF.

44. Van Buren to Jesse Hoyt, April 13, 1829, in William L. Mackenzie, *Life and Times of Martin Van Buren* (Boston, 1846), p. 216.

45. Van Buren, *Autobiography,* pp. 246–248.

46. AJ to Van Buren, March 31, 1829, in ibid., pp. 248–249.

47. Cambreleng to Van Buren, April 15, 1829, Van Buren Papers, LC.

48. Van Buren to AJ, April 23, 1829, Van Buren Papers, LC.

49. Van Buren to Cambreleng, April 23, 1829, Van Buren Papers, LC.

50. AJ to Van Buren, April 24, 1829, in Van Buren, *Autobiography,* p. 265.

51. Van Buren to Cambreleng and William Bowne, April 1829, Van Buren Papers, LC.

52. Van Buren, *Autobiography,* p. 268.

53. AJ to Blair, January 5, 1839, Jackson Papers, LC; Van Buren, *Autobiography,* p. 269.

54. The reformers of the late nineteenth century believed that civil service would eliminate the abuses inherent in Jackson's removal policy. But they created other problems. Where will the two major parties, upon whom the country is dependent for its governmental functions, obtain the means to operate if patronage is denied them? Obviously, they will turn to the rich, both corporate and individual. And, as the scandals of the Nixon administration vividly demonstrated, that alternative is a dangerous and frightening one.

55. AJ to Van Buren, May 15, 1830, Van Buren Papers, LC. See also Jackson's many letters at this time, particularly to John Overton, June 8, 1829, Dickinson Papers, THS, and his Private Memorandum Book, and "Notes," May 1830, Jackson Papers, LC.

56. Private Memorandum Book, Jackson Papers, LC.

57. AJ to Overton, June 8, 1829, Dickinson Papers, THS.

58. For a discussion of Jackson's attitude toward the Indians and his conduct toward them as commissioner see Remini, *Jackson,* pp. 321ff., 392ff.

59. Hamilton, *Reminiscences,* p. 134; Private Memorandum Book, Jackson Papers, LC; Ronald N. Satz, *American Indian Policy in the Jacksonian Era* (Lincoln, Nebr., 1975), pp. 9–18.

60. Hamilton, *Reminiscences,* p. 134; Private Memorandum Book, Jackson Papers, LC; House document 116, *Executive Documents,* 22nd Congress, 1st session, IV, 3–9. Francis Paul Prucha argues that Jackson had four alternatives: genocide; integration between the white and red races; federal protection of the Indians within their state residences; and removal. Only removal, he argues, was feasible. See his "Andrew Jackson's Indian Policy: A Reassessment," *JAH* (1969), LVI, 527–539.

61. Private Memorandum Book, Jackson Papers, LC.

62. AJ to Van Buren, May 18, 1829, in Jackson, *Correspondence,* IV, 34.

63. John Bassett Moore, *History and Digest of the International Arbitrations to Which the United States Has Been a Party* (Washington, D.C., 1898), IV, 762–763.

64. AJ to Overton, June 8, 1829, Dickinson Papers, THS.

65. Private Memorandum Book, Jackson Papers, LC.

CHAPTER 11

1. Parton, *Jackson*, III, 287.

2. In her *Autobiography* (New York, 1932), Peggy Eaton wrote her own defense; but see also Queena Pollack, *Peggy Eaton, Democracy's Mistress* (New York, 1931), and Allen C. Clark, "Margaret Eaton (Peggy O'Neal)," *Records of the Columbia Historical Society* (1942–1943), XLV, 1–33.

3. Van Buren, *Autobiography*, p. 345.

4. AJ to Coffee, March 19, 22, 1829, Coffee Papers, THS.

5. AJ to John C. McLemore, April 1829, Miscellaneous Jackson Papers, NYHS.

6. Ibid.; Charles J. Love to AJ, April 15, 1829, in Jackson, *Correspondence*, IV, 23.

7. S. J. Hays to AJ, May 5, 1830, in ibid., IV, 23 note 1.

8. Houston to AJ, September 19, 1829, Jackson Papers, LC.

9. Ely to AJ, March 18, 1829, in Parton, *Jackson*, III, 186.

10. AJ to Stiles, March 23, 1829, in ibid., III, 188–189, 191. This letter has obviously been edited to improve punctuation if not spelling and grammar, but the tone and sense of it are pure Jackson.

11. Benton, *Thirty Years View*, I, 738.

12. Francis Hillery to Mrs. Louis McLane, October 29, 1836, in John Munroe, "Mrs. McLane's Colored Boy and Peggy O'Neal," *Delaware History* (October 1963), X, 366.

13. "Narrative by General Jackson," in Parton, *Jackson*, III, 197–199, and original in Jackson Papers, LC; see also Kendall to Blair, November 22, 1829, Blair-Lee Papers, PUL.

14. Kendall stated that the doctor's wife insisted her husband had never mentioned the matter to her. Ibid.

15. Parton, *Jackson*, III, 204.

16. Ibid., III, 205.

17. Van Buren, *Autobiography*, p. 344.

18. Emily Donelson to Mary Coffee, March 27, 1829, in Pauline Wilcox Burke, *Emily Donelson of Tennessee* (Richmond, Va., 1941), I, 178.

19. Van Buren, *Autobiography*, p. 347.

20. Ibid., p. 350.

21. Ibid., p. 352.

22. Levi Woodbury to Elizabeth Woodbury, December 24, 1829, Woodbury Papers, LC; Van Buren, *Autobiography*, pp. 353–354.

23. Before this interview took place, however, Jackson had agreed to allow Colonel Richard M. Johnson of Kentucky to interview the three men and prepare them for the coming meeting. Johnson may have asked them to invite the Eatons to their parties, which was further than Jackson wished to go.

24. Memorandum, [January 1830], Jackson Papers, LC.

25. Ibid.

26. Kendall to Blair, November 22, 1829, Blair-Lee Papers, PUL.

27. AJ to John McLemore, September 22, December 25, 1829, Miscellaneous Jackson Papers, NYHS.

28. AJ to Overton, December 31, 1829, in Jackson, *Correspondence*, IV, 108–109.

29. "Note" by William B. Lewis and endorsed by Jackson, in ibid., IV, 109, footnote 2.

30. Ibid., IV, 108.

31. Donelson to McLemore, April 30, 1830, Donelson Papers, LC.

CHAPTER 12

1. AJ to Van Buren, March 31, 1829, Van Buren Papers, LC.

2. "Outline of principles submitted to the Heads of Department," February 23, 1829, Jackson Papers, LC.

3. AJ to John C. McLemore, April 1829, Miscellaneous Jackson Papers, NYHS.

4. AJ to Coffee, May 30, 1829, Coffee Papers, THS.

5. Remini, *Jackson,* pp. 378ff; AJ to Overton, June 8, 1829, Dickinson Papers, THS; Van Buren to Joel Poinsett, August 25, 1829, Van Buren Papers, LC.

6. AJ to Van Buren, August 12, 1829, Van Buren Papers, LC.

7. Van Buren to Poinsett, August 25, 1829, "Notes on Poinsett's Instructions," in Jackson's and Donelson's handwriting, Van Buren Papers, LC.

8. Ibid.

9. Ibid.; Van Buren to Poinsett, August 25, 1829, Van Buren Papers, LC.

10. AJ to Butler, October 10, 1829, Butler to AJ, March 7, 1834, Jackson, *Correspondence,* IV, 81, V, 252.

11. Ronald N. Satz, *American Indian Policy in the Jacksonian Era* (Lincoln, Neb., 1975), p. 3; Wilson Lumpkin, *The Removal of the Cherokee Indians from Georgia* (New York, 1907), I, 43; Clarence E. Carter and John P. Bloom, comps., *The Territorial Papers of the United States* (Washington, D.C., 1944–), V, 142–146; Charles J. Kappler, ed., *Indian Affairs: Laws and Treaties* (Washington, D.C., 1893–1913), II, 24.

12. Satz, *American Indian Policy,* p. 14.

13. For an analysis of McKenney's work among church groups see ibid., pp. 14–18.

14. Instructions to Generals William Carroll and John Coffee from John H. Eaton, May 20, 1829, *Senate Documents,* 21st Congress, 1st session, document #1, serial 160.

15. AJ to Captain James Gadsden, October 12, 1829, in Jackson, *Correspondence,* IV, 81; Parton, *Jackson,* III, 279–280.

16. Eaton to Carroll and Coffee, May 20, 1829, *Senate Documents,* 21st Congress, 1st session, document #1, serial 160.

17. Satz, *American Indian Policy,* p. 13; R. S. Cotterill, *The Southern Indians: The Story of the Civilized Tribes Before Removal* (Norman, Okla., 1954), pp. 237–238; Annie H. Abel, "The History of Events Resulting in Indian Consolidation West of the Mississippi," American Historical Association, *Annual Report for the Year 1906* (Washington, D.C., 1908), I, 370–371.

18. Satz, *American Indian Policy,* p. 18; circular letter to governors of Tennessee, Mississippi, and Alabama, May 21, 1829, Records of the Office of Indian Affairs, Letters sent, Record Group 75, NA.

19. Parton, *Jackson,* III, 269.

20. Hamilton, *Reminiscences,* p. 150; Kendall's Bank draft and Kendall to AJ, November 20, 1829, Jackson Papers, LHA with copies in JPP.

21. Private Memorandum Book of A. Jackson, Jackson Papers, LC; AJ to Robert J. Chester, November 30, 1829, in Jackson, *Correspondence,* IV, 96.

22. Richardson, *Messages and Papers,* II, 1005.

23. Jackson's Draft of the First Message, Jackson Papers, LC.

24. Richardson, *Messages and Papers,* II, 1006.

25. Ibid., pp. 1010–1011.

26. Ibid., p. 1013.

27. Ibid., p. 1015.

28. Ibid., p. 1017.

29. Ibid., p. 1018.
30. Ibid., p. 1019.
31. Jackson's Draft of the First Message, Jackson Papers, LC.
32. Richardson, *Messages and Papers*, II, 1021.
33. Ibid.
34. Ibid., p. 1025.
35. Ibid.

CHAPTER 13

1. Lee had been shunted aside in the scramble for chief clerk in the State Department and had been nominated for the consular post to get rid of him. He felt badly used. For a thorough discussion of Jackson's appointments see Leonard D. White, *The Jacksonians: A Study in Administrative History, 1829–1861* (New York, 1954), and Sidney H. Aronson, *Status and Kinship in the Higher Civil Service: Standards of Selection in the Administrations of John Adams, Thomas Jefferson, and Andrew Jackson* (Cambridge, Mass., 1964).
2. White, *Jacksonians*, p. 107.
3. Parton, *Jackson*, III, 277.
4. Daniel Webster to Mr. Dutton, May 9, 1830, in *The Writings and Speeches of Daniel Webster: Private Correspondence*, Fletcher Webster, ed. (Boston, 1903), I, 501.
5. AJ to Coffee, April 10, 1830, Coffee Papers, THS.
6. Quoted in Remini, *Andrew Jackson and the Bank War* (New York, 1967) p. 65.
7. *Register of Debate*, 21st Congress, 1st session, pp. 31–35, 35–41, 43–80.
8. Ibid., p. 77.
9. Parton, *Jackson*, III, 282.
10. See editorials in the *United States Telegraph* for January and February, 1830.
11. AJ to Claiborne, November 12, 1806, in Jackson, *Correspondence*, I, 153.
12. Parton, *Jackson*, III, 282.
13. Van Buren, *Autobiography*, p. 413.
14. Ibid.
15. Parton, *Jackson*, III, 284.
16. Van Buren, *Autobiography*, p. 414.
17. Ibid.
18. *United States Telegraph*, April 15, 17, 20, 23, 1830; Kendall to Blair, April 25, 1830, Blair-Lee Papers, PUL.
19. Van Buren, *Autobiography*, p. 415.
20. Ibid.
21. Benton, *Thirty Years View*, I, 148–149.
22. *United States Telegraph*, April 15, 17, 20, 23, 1830.
23. *Register of Debates*, 21st Congress, 1st session, p. 80.
24. Latner, *Presidency of Jackson*, pp. 64–68. Latner argues that the attack on Eaton was in part an attempt to direct Jackson's program and force him to recommend radical reduction in the tariff rates.
25. Kendall to Blair, April 25, 1830, Blair-Lee Papers, PUL.
26. Parton, *Jackson*, III, 284–285.
27. Richard Pollard to William C. Rives, June 10, 1830, Rives Papers, LC.
28. Webster to Clay, April 18, 1830, Clay Papers, LC; Felix Grundy to Daniel Graham, April 5, 1830, Jacob M. Dickinson Papers, TSL.

29. Adams, Memoirs, VIII, 222. The same thought is contained in Clay to Adam Beatty, May 4, 1830, in *The Private Correspondence of Henry Clay*, Calvin Colton, ed. (Boston, 1856), p. 266.

30. Kendall to Blair, April 25, 1830, Blair-Lee Papers, PUL.

31. James B. Gardiner to Lewis, July 5, 1830, Miscellaneous Lewis Papers, LC.

32. In addition to Lewis, Kendall also agreed to a second term. Kendall to Blair, March 18, 1830, Blair-Lee Papers, PUL.

33. Adams, *Memoirs*, VIII, 209.

34. T. Childe to Thurlow Weed, March 11, 1830, Weed Papers, RUL.

35. Van Buren to James Gordon Bennett, May 2, 1830, Van Buren Papers, LC.

36. Hill to Gideon Welles, April 20, 1830, Welles Papers, LC.

37. Blair to Kendall, February 11, 1830, Blair-Lee Papers, LC.

38. Edward Everett to A. H. Everett, March 11, 1830, Everett Papers, MHS.

39. Webster to Jeremiah Mason, February 27, 1830, in Webster, *Private Correspondence*, I, 488.

40. Adams, *Memoirs*, VIII, 184–185.

41. Woodbury to Elizabeth Woodbury, March 6, 1830, Woodbury Papers, LC.

42. Mrs. Smith to Mrs. Kirkpatrick, January 26, 1830, in Smith, *First Forty Years*, p. 310.

43. Ibid., p. 311.

44. Margaret Eaton to AJ, June 9, 1830 with endorsement by Donelson, Donelson Papers, LC.

45. Adams, *Memoirs*, VIII, 185.

46. For details of this controversy see Remini, *Jackson*, pp. 367–377.

47. AJ to Hugh Lawson White, March 30, 1828, in Jackson, *Correspondence*, III, 396. Overton initially suspected Calhoun but both he and Jackson decided "that the dagger was in other hands than Mr. Calhoun." AJ to Overton, May 13, 1830, Overton Papers, THS.

48. Bassett, *Jackson*, p. 501. See also AJ to White, February 7, 1828, March 30, 1828, in Jackson, *Correspondence*, III, 334–341, 396–397, AJ's Memorandum for Major Donelson, March 8, 1831, Donelson Papers, LC, and Alfred Balch to Edward Livingston, July 24, 1832, Livingston Papers, JRDF.

49. Crawford to Van Buren, December 21, 1827, October 21, 1828, Van Buren to Crawford, November 14, 1828, Van Buren Papers, LC.

50. "Narrative by Major William B. Lewis," in Parton, *Jackson*, III, 318.

51. Ibid., p. 320.

52. Ibid., p. 323.

53. Ibid., pp. 323–324.

54. AJ to John Overton, December 31, 1829, in Jackson, *Correspondence*, IV, 109.

55. William H. Crawford to John Forsyth, April 30, 1830, in *Works of John C. Calhoun*, Richard K. Cralle, ed. (New York, 1851–1856), VI, 30. Crawford had the notion that he was still a presidential possibility and wrote Henry Clay for his support. See Crawford to Clay, March 31, 1830, Clay Papers, LC.

56. Latner, *Presidency of Jackson*, pp. 64–71.

57. Ibid., p. 64. The evidence is not conclusive but Kendall said that it was generally believed that "Mr. Calhoun's friends are the principal agitators and instigators of this business. Mr. Calhoun is a madman if he promotes it, and he is not a wise man if he does not put an end to it." Kendall to Blair, January 28,

1830, Blair-Lee Papers, PUL. This is one of the earliest letters to name Calhoun and his friends as the instigators of the plot against the Eatons. Even if Calhoun was innocent of provoking the social ostracism of the Eatons, the friends of Jackson felt he should have done something to "put an end to it."

58. Latner, *Presidency of Jackson*, p. 64.

59. AJ to Calhoun, May 13, 1830, in Jackson, *Correspondence*, IV, 136.

60. Parton, *Jackson*, III, 333.

61. Calhoun to AJ, May 25, 1830, in *United States Telegraph*, February 17, 21, 23, 26, 1831. See also Washington *Globe*, February 25, 1831 and *Niles Weekly Register*, April 2, 1831.

62. "Narrative by Major William B. Lewis," in Parton, *Jackson*, III, 326.

63. Ibid.

64. Ibid., p. 327.

65. AJ to Donelson, December 25, 1830, Miscellaneous Jackson Papers, NYHS.

66. AJ to Calhoun, May 30, 1830, in Jackson, *Correspondence*, IV, 141. Jackson apparently had help in writing this letter—the Latin quotation is correct. In his private correspondence he invariably said, "et tu Brutus." See AJ to Overton, May 13, 1830, Overton Papers, THS, for example.

67. Kendall to Blair, October 2, 1830, Blair-Lee Papers, LC.

CHAPTER 14

1. Joseph G. Cogswell to George Bancroft, February 21, 1830, Bancroft Papers, MHS.

2. AJ to Smith, May 19, 1829, in Jackson, *Correspondence*, IV, 36.

3. AJ to Andrew Jackson, Jr., July 26, 1829, in ibid., IV, 57.

4. AJ to Andrew Jackson, Jr., August 20, 1829, in ibid., IV, 63.

5. AJ to Andrew Jackson, Jr., September 21, 1829, in ibid., IV, 76.

6. AJ to Coffee, March 19, July 21, 1829, Coffee Papers, THS.

7. AJ to Coffee, April 10, 1830, Coffee Papers, THS.

8. AJ to Andrew Jackson, Jr., July 4, 1829, in Jackson, *Correspondence*, IV, 49–50.

9. AJ to Andrew Jackson, Jr., July 20, 1829, in ibid., IV, 54.

10. AJ to Andrew Jackson, Jr., August 19, 1829; AJ to Charles J. Love, December 17, 1829, in ibid., IV, 62, 105.

11. *Register of Debates*, 21st Congress, 1st Session, p. 820. The bill as introduced in Congress authorized a subscription to the stock of the Maysville, Washington, Paris, and Lexington Turnpike Road Company. The road subsidized by this stock was not actually part of the National Road system although its advocates argued otherwise. Latner, *Presidency of Jackson*, p. 101.

12. Van Buren, *Autobiography*, p. 320.

13. AJ to Van Buren, May 15, 1830, in ibid., p. 322.

14. Ibid., p. 323.

15. Ibid., p. 324.

16. Ibid.

17. Ibid., pp. 324–325.

18. "Notes—The Maysville road bill," Jackson Papers, LC; Latner, *Presidency of Jackson*, p. 102.

19. Van Buren, *Autobiography*, pp. 325–326.

20. Ibid., p. 326.

21. Ibid.

22. Richardson, *Messages and Papers*, II, 1046–1055.

23. Van Buren, *Autobiography*, p. 327. Over the next several years Jackson became more hostile to internal improvements, further narrowing the permissible area for federal involvement. He also gradually abandoned ideas about the distribution of the surplus. See Jackson's sixth message to Congress delivered on December 1, 1834, and his eighth message delivered on December 5, 1836. Richardson, *Messages and Papers*, II, 1340–1341, 1464–1465.

24. Clay to Webster, June 7, 1830, in *Private Correspondence of Daniel Webster*, I, 504.

25. AJ to Van Buren, June 26, 1830, Van Buren Papers, LC.

26. Hamilton to Van Buren, June 8, 1830, Van Buren Papers, LC. Not all Democrats were as enthusiastic. Ritchie said the message did not live up to "our Virginia Doctrines." Thomas Ritchie to Archibald Ritchie, June 8, 1830, in "Unpublished Letters of Thomas Ritchie," *The John P. Branch Historical Papers of Randolph-Macon College* (1911), III, 209.

27. AJ to Lewis, June 26, 28, 1830, Jackson-Lewis Papers, NYPL.

28. "Notes—The Maysville road bill," Jackson Papers, LC.

29. Ibid.

30. Richardson, *Messages and Papers*, II, 1165.

31. AJ to Coffee, May 31, 1830, Coffee Papers, THS.

32. AJ to Overton, May 13, 1830, Overton Papers, Murdock Collection, THS; "Notes—The Maysville road bill," Jackson Papers, LC.

CHAPTER 15

1. Governmental aspects of Indian-white relations are treated extensively in Reginald Horsman, *Expansion and American Indian Policy, 1783–1812* (East Lansing, Mich., 1967), Francis Paul Prucha, *American Indian Policy in the Formative Years* (Cambridge, Mass., 1962), and Wilcomb E. Washburn, *Red Man's Land/White Man's Law* (New York, 1971).

2. See for example, Willie Blount to AJ, December 28, 1809, Jackson Papers, LC.

3. Quoted in Francis Paul Prucha, ed., *The Indian in American History* (New York, 1971), p. 24.

4. Ronald N. Satz, *American Indian Policy in the Jacksonian Era* (Lincoln, Nebr., 1975), p. 2.

5. Ibid., pp. 9–10.

6. *Register of Debates*, 21st Congress, 1st Session, pp. 507–511; Satz, *American Indian Policy*, p. 20.

7. Latner, *Presidency of Jackson*, p. 92; *Register of Debates*, 21st Congress, 1st Session, pp. 1124–1125; Joseph H. Parks, *John Bell of Tennessee* (Baton Rouge, 1950), p. 37; L. Paul Gresham, "The Public Career of Hugh Lawson White," *THQ* (1944), III, 303.

8. *Register of Debates*, 21st Congress, 1st Session, pp. 305, 580–583; *Niles Weekly Register*, March 20, 1830.

9. *Register of Debates*, 21st Congress, 1st Session, pp. 309–320.

10. Ibid., pp. 310–311.

11. Ibid., p. 325.

12. Ibid., pp. 359–369, 345, 354, 357.

13. The pattern of anti-removal votes by National Republicans in Ohio and Missouri and pro-removal votes by Democrats from New York, New Hampshire, New Jersey, and Pennsylvania shows that nearness to the frontier had little

to do with lineup of votes. See Satz, *American Indian Policy*, p. 25. Barton, Sam Bell of New Hampshire, Burnet, Chambers, Chase, Clayton, Foot, Frelinghuysen, Holmes, Knight, Marks, Robbins, Ruggles, Sprague, and Webster voted no. *Register of Debates*, 21st Congress, 1st Session, p. 383.

14. Van Buren, *Autobiography*, pp. 288-289.

15. Ibid., p. 289.

16. *Register of Debates*, 21st Congress, 1st Session, p. 1001.

17. Ibid., p. 1002.

18. Ibid., pp. 1021-1024.

19. Ibid., p. 1030.

20. Ibid., pp. 1032-1034.

21. Ibid., pp. 1132-1133.

22. Ibid., p. 1124.

23. *Telegraph*, May 28, 1830.

24. Van Buren, *Autobiography*, p. 289.

25. Satz, *American Indian Policy*, p. 30.

26. *Register of Debates*, 21st Congress, 1st Session, pp. 1145-1146.

27. Van Buren, *Autobiography*, p. 289.

28. U.S. *Statutes*, IV, 411-412. Satz, *American Indian Policy*, Appendix, pp. 296-298 reprints the statute in full.

29. On Indian removal see Grant Foreman, *Indian Removal: The Emigration of the Five Civilized Tribes* (Norman, Okla., 1953); and Mary E. Young, *Redskins, Ruffleshirts, and Rednecks: Indian Allotments in Alabama and Mississippi, 1830-1860* (Norman, Okla., 1961).

30. The best defense of Jackson's Indian policy as policy is Francis Paul Prucha, "Andrew Jackson's Indian Policy: A Reassessment," *JAH* (1969), LVI, 527-539.

31. *Debates in Congress*, 21st Congress, 1st Session, p. 318; and see also Jackson's letters to Eaton and Lewis Cass, 1831 and 1832, Jackson Papers, LC, and Jackson to Coffee, 1831, Coffee Papers, THS. AJ to Monroe, March 4, 1817, Monroe Papers, NYPL.

32. Van Buren told Jackson that his conduct of Indian affairs would "constitute one of the most distinguished traits of your administration." Van Buren to AJ, July 16, 1831, Van Buren Papers, LC.

33. Latner, *Presidency of Jackson*, p. 97.

34. AJ to Coffee, May 31, 1830, Coffee Papers, THS; AJ to Lewis, June 21, 1830, Jackson Papers, ML; AJ to Lewis, June 26, 1830, Jackson-Lewis Papers, NYPL; Margaret Eaton to AJ, June 9, 1830 with Donelson's appended note, Donelson Papers, LC.

35. AJ to Van Buren, June 26, 1830, Van Buren Papers, LC.

36. Donelson to Coffee, June 17, 1830, Donelson Papers, LC.

37. Ibid., AJ to Lewis, June 21, 1830, Jackson Papers, ML; AJ to John Branch, June 21, 1830, Donelson Papers, LC; AJ to Coffee, June 14, 1830, Coffee Papers, THS.

38. AJ to Lewis, June 28, 1830, Jackson-Lewis Papers, NYPL. See also Felix Grundy to Woodbury, July 7, 1830, Woodbury Papers, LC. Jackson arrived at the Hermitage on July 6.

39. AJ to Van Buren, June 26, 1830, Van Buren Papers, LC; AJ to Lewis, June 21, 1830, Jackson Papers, ML. A few years later Jackson supposedly said to Van Buren, "Mr. Van Buren, *your* friends may be leaving you—but my friends *never* leave *me.*" R. H. Wilde to Gulian C. Verplanck, May 1, 1834, Verplanck Papers, NYHS.

40. Eaton to John Donnelly, August 11, 1830, Jackson Papers, LC.

41. Ibid.

42. AJ to Lewis, July 21, August 7, 1830, Jackson-Lewis Papers, NYPL.

43. AJ to Lewis, July 28, 1830, Jackson-Lewis Papers, NYPL.

44. AJ to Samuel J. Ingham, July 31, August 1, AJ to John Pitchlynn, August 5, 1830, Jackson Papers, LC; AJ to Lewis, August 10, 1830, Jackson Papers, ML.

45. Chiefs of the Choctaw Nation, east and south districts, to Eaton, August 10, 1830, Eaton to Chiefs, August 5, 1830; Jackson's address to Chickasaws, August 23, 1830, RG 46, E 326, NA; Jackson *Gazette,* September 4, 1830; *Niles Weekly Register,* September 18, 1830.

46. Ibid.

47. Ibid.; "Journal of the proceedings had with the Chickasaw and Choctaw Indians, at the late treaties," Jackson Papers, LC.

48. AJ to Lewis, August 31, 1830, Jackson Papers, ML; Arrell M. Gibson, *The Chickasaws* (Norman, Okla., 1971), pp. 176–178. The journal of Coffee's negotiations is in the Jackson Papers, LC, copy in JPP.

49. AJ to Lewis, August 25, 1830, Jackson-Lewis Papers, NYPL; Eaton to John Donelly, August 11, 1830, Jackson Papers, LC. Wirt favored removal but allowed himself to be persuaded by Daniel Webster into defending the Cherokees. William S. Hoffman, "Andrew Jackson, State Rightist: The Case of the Georgia Indians," *THQ* (1952), XI, 335–336.

50. Greenwood LeFlore to Eaton, August 10, 1830, Choctaw Chiefs to AJ, August 16, 1830, Records of the Bureau of Indian Affairs, Letters Received, Choctaw Agency, NA.

51. William Carroll to Van Buren, February 6, 1831, Van Buren Papers, LC. Angie Debo, *The Rise and Fall of the Choctaw Republic* (Norman, Okla., 1961), pp. 50–57; AJ to Choctaw Nation, August 26, 1830, RG 75, E 267, Choctaw Removal Records, NA. This "talk" is written in Jackson's own hand.

52. Arthur H. DeRosier, Jr., *The Removal of the Choctaw Indians* (New York, 1972), p. 122; Charles C. Royce, *Indian Land Cessions in the United States* (Washington, D.C., 1900), p. 726.

53. DeRosier, *Removal,* p. 128.

54. Ibid., pp. 129–147; Satz, *American Indian Policy,* p. 78.

55. "Regulations Concerning the Removal of the Indians, May 15, 1832," *Senate Document* # 512, 23rd Congress, 1st Session, pp. 124–125.

56. Satz, *American Indian Policy,* pp. 151–168; Laurence F. Schmeckebier, *The Office of Indian Affairs* (Baltimore, 1927), pp. 27–43; "Report on Regulating the Indian Department, May 20, 1834," *House Report* # 474, 23rd Congress, 1st Session, pp. 23–27.

57. Lewis Cass to Benjamin F. Curry, September 1, 1831, and Cass to James Montgomery, September 3, 1831, Return J. Meigs Papers, LC. Cass succeeded Eaton as secretary of war in 1831.

58. AJ to Coffee, November 6, 1832, Coffee Papers, THS.

59. On the Creeks and the Seminoles see John K. Mahon, *History of the Second Seminole War, 1835–1842* (Gainesville, Fla., 1967); Mary E. Young, "The Creek Frauds: A Study in Conscience and Corruption," *MVHR* (1955), XLII, 411–437. Report of the Cherokee suit against Georgia can be found in 5 *Peters* 1ff.

60. Ibid., pp. 15–20.

61. Only Worcester and Butler went to jail. Nine other apprehended missionaries accepted pardons from the governor in exchange for a promise that they would cease violating Georgia law.

62. 6 *Peters* 515. For an excellent discussion of the legal battle, particularly

its consequences, see Edwin Miles, "After John Marshall's Decision: *Worester* v. *Georgia* and the Nullification Crisis," *JSH* (1973) XXXIX, 519–544.

63. Ibid., p. 527.

64. Richard P. Longaker, "Andrew Jackson and the Judiciary," *Political Science Quarterly* (1956), LXXI, 348–350, 363–364; Charles Warren, *The Supreme Court in United States History* (Boston, 1922), II, 224; Satz, *American Indian Policy*, p. 49.

65. AJ to Coffee, April 7, 1832, Coffee Papers, THS.

66. Horace Greeley, *The American Conflict: A History of the Great Rebellion in the United States of America, 1860–'64* (Hartford, 1865), I, 106.

67. AJ to Coffee, April 7, 1832, Coffee Papers, THS.

68. Charles J. Johnson to ?, March 23, 1832, David Campbell Papers, DUL.

69. See, for example, *Niles Weekly Register*, April 28, 1832, and the New York *Daily Advertiser*, March 9, 1832. Actually the missionaries understood that Jackson could not be summoned to do anything until the court reconvened in 1833. Miles, "After John Marshall's Decision," p. 528.

70. Longaker, "Andrew Jackson and the Judiciary," p. 350.

71. Lewis Williams to William Lenoir, April 9, 1832, in Miles, "After John Marshall's Decision," p. 533, fn. 32.

72. Technically it was not a removal treaty but a clever administration scheme to get the Creeks to relinquish their land in return for a pledge that it would be alloted to the chiefs and headmen. See Mary Young, "The Creek Frauds," pp. 412–414.

73. Miles, "After John Marshall's Decision," p. 530.

74. "I trouble you with the enclosed," Van Buren wrote the President, "that my letter to Forsyth may pass through your hands. You may seal it or deliver it open to him at your election." Van Buren to AJ, December 22, 1832, Van Buren Papers, LC. See also B. F. Butler to Wilson Lumpkin, December 17, 1832, Gratz Collection, PHS.

75. Miles, "After John Marshall's Decision," p. 537 quoting Cass to Lumpkin, December 24, 1832, one an official letter, the other private.

76. Ibid., pp. 543–544. See also Marvin R. Cain, "William Wirt against Andrew Jackson: Reflection of an Era," *Mid-America* (1965), XLVII, 113–138.

77. Richardson, *Messages and Papers*, II, 1166. For the Black Hawk War see Cecil Eby, *"That Disgraceful Affair": The Black Hawk War* (New York, 1973); Ellen M. Whitney, comp. and ed., *The Black Hawk War: 1831–1832* (Springfield, Ill., 1970–1975) two volumes; and William T. Hagan, "The Black Hawk War," doctoral dissertation, University of Wisconsin, 1950. Despite Jackson's best efforts sizable numbers of Potawatomie, Winnebagos, Chippewas and Ottowas still resided in the Old Northwest at the conclusion of Jackson's term in office.

78. AJ to secretary of war, [1831], Jackson Papers, LC.

79. Satz, *American Indian Policy*, p. 152. This is the best study of Jackson's administrative reforms of the Indian bureaucracy.

80. Ibid., pp. 54–56.

CHAPTER 16

1. AJ to John Overton, September 30, 1830, in Jackson, *Correspondence*, IV, 181.

2. Jackson's address to the foreign ministers, April 6, 1829, U.S. Presidents, A. Jackson Papers, NYPL.

3. Van Buren, *Autobiography*, p. 251; Hamilton, *Reminiscences*, p. 130; Munroe, *McLane*, pp. 253–256.

4. Quoted in ibid., p. 256. If there is such a thing as a definitive biography, John Munroe's *Louis McLane* is it. The research is heroic and the analysis, organization, and writing superb.

5. Ibid., pp. 262–263. For the failures of Adams's negotiations see F. Lee Benns, *The American Struggle for the British West India Carrying-Trade, 1815–1830* (Bloomington, Ind., 1923), pp. 118–162.

6. Cambreleng to Van Buren, April 9, 1830, Van Buren Papers, LC. For the diplomacy of the Adams administration see Samuel Flagg Bemis, *John Quincy Adams and the Foundations of American Foreign Policy* (New York, 1950).

7. Relatively little scholarly work has been published on Jackson's foreign policy. For a list of books, articles, and dissertations written on this subject as of 1979 see Robert V. Remini and Edwin A. Miles, *The Era of Good Feelings and the Age of Jackson, 1816–1841* (Arlington Heights, Ill., 1979), pp. 100–101.

8. Memorandum, French Spoliation Claims, April 10, 1830, Jackson Papers, LC. This memorandum is in Jackson's handwriting and states "Private and for Mr Van Burens own eye."

9. Munroe, *McLane*, p. 275.

10. McLane to Cambreleng, March 30, 1830, Cambreleng to Van Buren, April 9, 1830, Van Buren Papers; McLane to Woodbury, August 30, 1830, Woodbury Papers, LC; Munroe, *McLane*, p. 276.

11. Richardson, *Messages and Papers*, II, 1043.

12. Van Buren to AJ, July 25, 1830, Cambreleng to Van Buren, October 11, 1830, Van Buren Papers, LC; Munroe, *McLane*, p. 277.

13. Ibid., p. 278.

14. McLane to Woodbury, August 30, 1830, Woodbury Papers, LC; see also McLane to Van Buren, August 20, 1830 in Munroe, *McLane*, p. 278, and McLane to Hamilton, August 19, 1830, in Hamilton, *Reminiscences*, pp. 172–173.

15. Cambreleng to Van Buren, October 3, 23, 1830, Van Buren Papers, LC; Richardson, *Messages and Papers*, II, 1061–1062.

16. See *Telegraph*, October 3, 1830 and *Niles Weekly Register* (not a Democratic paper), October 9, 1830.

17. AJ to Butler, October 6, 1830, in Jackson, *Correspondence*, IV, 182.

18. Nikolai N. Bolkovitinov of the Institute of World History in Moscow, USSR, has done some interesting work on United States–Russian relations; his first volume, *The Beginnings of Russian-American Relations* (Cambridge, Mass., 1975) has been translated by Elena Levin. See also Howard R. Marraro, "John Nelson's Mission to the Kingdom of the Two Sicilies [1831–1832]," *Louisiana History Quarterly* (1949), XXXII, 149–176; Richardson, *Messages and Papers*, II, 1006.

19. AJ to Overton, May 27, 1830, Overton Papers, THS; Richardson, *Messages and Papers*, II, 1068, 1044.

20. Memorandum, dated April 1829, Jackson Papers, LC.

21. Rives to Van Buren, September 8, 1830, Van Buren Papers, LC.

22. Van Buren to Rives, July 20, 1829, Diplomatic Instructions of the Department of State—France, NA.

23. Rives to Van Buren, September 18, 1830, Van Buren Papers, LC. See also Rives to Van Buren, November 7, December 17, 1829, January 16, 28, 1830, Dispatches from U.S. Ministers to France, NA.

24. Richardson, *Messages and Papers*, II, 1007.

25. Rives to Van Buren, February 16, 1830, Dispatches from U.S. Ministers to France, NA.

26. Rives to Van Buren, June 8, 1830, in ibid.

27. Rives to Van Buren, September 18, 29, 1830, Van Buren Papers, LC.

28. Richardson, *Messages and Papers*, II, 1064; Richard A. McLemore, *Franco-American Diplomatic Relations, 1816–1836* (Baton Rouge, 1941), pp. 76–77.

29. Rives to Van Buren, April 28, 1831, Dispatches from U.S. Ministers to France, NA; AJ to Livingston, September 3, 1831, Livingston Papers, JRDF; McLemore, *Franco-American Diplomatic Relations*, pp. 82–87.

30. *Globe*, October 13, 1832.

31. Richardson, *Messages and Papers*, II, pp. 1067–1068. Charles Rhind headed this commission and the treaty with Turkey was signed on May 7, 1830.

32. AJ to Butler, October 6, 1830, in Jackson, *Correspondence*, IV, 182.

33. Randolph to AJ, September 29, 1830, in Jackson, *Correspondence*, IV, 181; Richardson, *Messages and Papers*, II, 1068.

CHAPTER 17

1. AJ to Lewis, August 7, 1830, Jackson-Lewis Papers, NYPL; Donelson to AJ, November 9, 1830, Jackson Papers, LC; AJ to Mary Eastin, October 24, 1830, AJ to Emily Donelson, January 20, 1831, in Jackson, *Correspondence*, IV, 187, 226. See also the exchange of letters between Donelson and Jackson, in ibid., pp. 192–195.

2. AJ to Donelson, December 25, 1830, Miscellaneous Jackson Papers, NYHS, AJ to Emily Donelson, January 20, 1831 and Statement of Andrew Jackson Donelson, November 21, 1830 in Jackson, *Correspondence*, IV, 227, 204.

3. Donelson's statement, November 21, 1830 in Jackson, *Correspondence*, IV, 205; AJ to Coffee, December 6, 1830, Coffee Papers, THS. See also Virgil Maxcy to Woodbury, September 16, 1830, Woodbury Papers, LC.

4. Identifying Calhoun as his enemy made political good sense. It was far easier to explain to the nation the disruption of his administration in terms of personal ambition than anything else.

5. Kendall to Blair, October 2, 1830, Blair-Lee Papers, PUL.

6. AJ to Robert Oliver, October 16, 1830, Miscellaneous Jackson Papers, PHS.

7. Kendall to Blair, January 9, 1829, Blair-Lee Papers, PUL.

8. Kendall to Blair, April 25, 1830, Blair-Lee Papers, PUL.

9. Ibid.

10. Kendall to Blair, January 9, February 3, 11, 1830, Blair-Lee Papers, PUL; Parton, *Jackson*, III, 335; Latner, *Presidency of Andrew Jackson*, pp. 75–76.

11. Kendall to Blair, August 20, 1830, Blair-Lee Papers, PUL.

12. Kendall to Blair, October 2, 1830, in ibid.

13. Kendall reported that Blair hesitated about accepting and acceded only when Kendall promised to "bear an equal share in the responsibilities." Kendall, *Autobiography*, p. 372. But any hesitation was financial and Blair must have seen the advantages to a move.

14. Kendall to Blair, November 20, 1830, Blair Papers, LC.

15. Kendall to Blair, October 2, 1830, Blair-Lee Papers, PUL.

16. Kendall to Blair, November 20, 1830, Blair Papers, LC.

17. Ibid.

18. Kendall to Hill, November 26, 1830, Miscellaneous Kendall Papers, NYHS. The trouble with the *Telegraph*, said William B. Lewis, "is looking more to men than principle, and the support of the President has always been with it a secondary consideration." Lewis to Overton, January 13, 1831, Overton Papers, THS.

19. AJ to Coffee, December 6, 1830, Coffee Papers, THS.

20. Blair "comes here by invitation," John A. Dix of New York was told by a Washington Democrat. "We are his supporters. I wish you to be." C. S. Smith to Dix, December 14, 1830, Dix Papers, CUL.

21. Lewis to Overton, January 13, 1831, Overton Papers, THS.

22. Parton, *Jackson*, III, 337.

23. AJ to John C. McLemore, December 25, 1830, Miscellaneous Jackson Papers, THS; William E. Smith, "Francis P. Blair, Pen-Executive of Andrew Jackson," *MVHR* (1931), XVII, 548. See also William E. Smith, *The Francis Preston Blair Family in Politics* (New York, 1933) and Elbert B. Smith, *Francis Preston Blair* (New York, 1980).

24. Smith, "Francis P. Blair," p. 548; Parton, *Jackson*, III, 337.

25. Kendall to Blair, August 20, October 2, 1830, Blair-Lee Papers, PUL; Kendall to Blair, November 20, 1830, Blair Papers, LC; Lewis to Overton, January 13, 1831, Overton Papers, THS.

26. Smith, "Francis P. Blair," p. 548; Parton, *Jackson*, III, 337–339.

27. Smith, "Francis P. Blair," pp. 549–550.

28. AJ to Livingston, July 21, 1832, Delafield Papers, JRDF.

29. Parton, *Jackson*, III, 338.

30. Ibid., pp. 336–337. See also AJ to Overton, February 28, 1831, Overton Papers, THS.

31. Latner, *Presidency of Jackson*, p. 78; Kendall, *Autobiography*, p. 373; Kendall to Blair, November 20, 1830, Blair Papers, LC.

32. Kendall claimed to be the author of the motto. Kendall, *Autobiography*, p. 372.

33. George Crawford to Blair, March 27, 1831, Blair-Lee Papers, PUL.

34. Edward Everett to Alexander Everett, January 23, 1831, Everett Papers, MHS.

35. Van Buren to Jesse Hoyt, January 31, 1823, in William L. Mackenzie, *The Lives and Opinions of Benjamin F. Butler and Jesse Hoyt* (Boston, 1845), p. 190.

36. Jackson "likes me vastly," wrote Blair, "and . . . values my opinion in some things . . . more than he does the magician's." Blair to Mrs. Benjamin Gratz, March 2, 1831, in Thomas H. Clay, "Two Years with Old Hickory," *Atlantic Monthly* (August 1887), LX, 192.

CHAPTER 18

1. AJ to John C. McLemore, December 25, 1830, Miscellaneous Jackson Papers, NYHS.

2. Lewis to Overton, January 13, 1831, Overton Papers, THS.

3. Green to Calhoun, November 19, 1830, Green Papers, SHC; Latner, *Presidency of Jackson*, p. 77; James B. Gardiner to W. B. Lewis, July 5, 1830, Miscellaneous Lewis Papers, LC. The Lewis-Eaton connection derived from the fact that they had been brothers-in-law through Eaton's first marriage. Eaton's supposed influence over Barry resulted from endorsing a needed bank loan and housing Barry's family when they first arrived in Washington.

4. Gardiner to Lewis, July 5, 1830, Miscellaneous Lewis Papers, LC.

5. Cornelius Holland to P. J. Carter, December 26, 1830, Jackson Papers, THS.

6. Lewis to Overton, January 13, 1831, Overton Papers, THS.

7. Richardson, *Messages and Papers*, II, 1063, 1064–1071, 1074.

8. Ibid., pp. 1082, 1083.

9. Ibid., pp. 1091–1092.

10. The full argument of this decision can be found in 4 *Wheaton* 316ff.

11. See especially "Private Memorandum Book of A. Jackson," Jackson Papers, LC.

12. See manuscript, annual message, December 1830, enclosed with AJ to Van Buren, November 1, 1830, Van Buren Papers, LC.

13. Richardson, *Messages and Papers*, II, 1092. The recommendation closely resembles Kendall's draft for the bank portion of the first message, Jackson Papers, LHA.

14. Benton, *Thirty Years View*, I, 187.

15. Ibid., p. 197.

16. See editorials in the spring, 1830, especially April 6, 13, 20, 27, 1831.

17. Benton, *Thirty Years View*, I, 204.

18. Ibid.; Parton, *Jackson*, III, 343.

19. R. Smith to Biddle, December 13, 1830, Biddle to Jonathan Roberts, January 15, 1831, Biddle Papers, LC.

20. Edward Everett to Alexander Everett, January 23, 1831, Edward Everett Papers, MHS.

21. "Calhoun has no vitality but as a part of the Jackson party," wrote Edward Everett to his brother. "By breaking away he destroys himself." Ibid.

22. Van Buren, *Autobiography*, p. 377.

23. Everett to his wife, January 19, 1831, Everett Papers, MHS.

24. Van Buren, *Autobiography*, p. 379.

25. Hugh Hamilton to James Buchanan, February 20, 1831, Buchanan Papers, PHS.

26. Blair to Van Buren, December 9, 1858, Van Buren Papers, LC. Blair also says that Governor Lumpkin was a party to the consultation. Van Buren, *Autobiography*, p. 379.

27. Ibid., p. 378.

28. Ibid.

29. Ibid., p. 379.

30. See *Telegraph*, February 17, 21, 23, 26, 1831; *Globe*, February 25, 1831; *Niles Weekly Register*, April 2, 1831

31. Lewis to Overton, January 13, 1831, Overton Papers, THS.

32. Van Buren, *Autobiography*, p. 376.

33. AJ to Overton, February 8, 1831, Overton Papers, THS.

34. Blair did not recall whether he spoke to the President about the Johnson-Grundy proposal when he was first approached—"when the thing was in petto" is the way he put it—"but I am sure I did before Green made the publication." Blair also remembered speaking to Green—it was the last word he ever spoke to him in his life—in order "to tell him [a] few days before it appeared that it would produce a war between Genl Jackson & Mr Calhoun." Blair to Van Buren, December 9, 1858, Van Buren Papers, LC.

35. Edward Everett to his wife, February 11, 1831, Everett Papers, MHS. See also James A. Hamilton to Van Buren, February 3, 1831, Van Buren Papers, LC, and Granger to Weed, February 15, 1831, Granger Papers, LC.

36. "The thrusts at Van Buren will be very direct & undisguised," wrote Granger. "Matty will use the claws of others to take his own chestnuts from the fire." Granger also knew the exact date of publication. Granger to Weed, February 15, 1831, Granger Papers, LC.

37. The complete work can be found in the *Telegraph*, February 17, 21, 23, 26, 1831; the essential parts are reprinted in Remini, ed., *The Age of Jackson* (New York, 1972), pp. 33–43; Williams to Van Buren, March 22, 1831, Van Buren

Papers, LC; Henry Storrs to Abraham Van Vechten, February 22, 1831, Miscellaneous Storrs Papers, NYHS; Parton, *Jackson*, III, 345; Marcus Morton to Calhoun, March 7, 1831, Miscellaneous Papers, MHS; Edward Everett to his wife, February 17, 1831, Everett Papers, MHS; AJ to Charles J. Love, March 7, 1831, in Jackson, *Correspondence*, IV, 246.

38. Kendall to Welles, March 19, 1831, Welles Papers, LC; Blair to Van Buren, December 9, 1858, Van Buren Papers, LC.

39. Kendall, *Autobiography*, p. 373.

40. AJ to Charles J. Love, March 7, 1831, in Jackson, *Correspondence*, IV, 246.

41. William S. Archer to Van Buren, March 12, 1831, Van Buren Papers, LC.

42. Edward Everett to his wife, February 2, 1831, Everett Papers, MHS.

43. Samuel Bell to William Plumer, January 22, 1831, Samuel Bell Papers, NYHS.

44. Hamilton to AJ, February 24, 1831, in Hamilton, *Reminiscences*, p. 196; Van Buren, *Autobiography*, p. 377.

45. Henry L. Ellsworth to Van Buren, March 10, 1831, William S. Archer to Van Buren, March 12, 29, 1831, Van Buren to John Van Buren, March 27, 1831, Van Buren Papers, LC.

46. Edward Everett to his wife, February 22, 1831, Everett Papers, MHS.

47. Van Buren, *Autobiography*, p. 384; Henry Storrs to Abraham Van Vechten, February 22, 1831, Miscellaneous Storrs Papers, NYHS.

48. R. McCall to General T. Cadwalader, April 20, 1831, Cadwalader Papers, PHS.

49. Memorandum, dated February 1831, Jackson Papers, LC.

50. Jackson talked about publication but his remarks were probably intended only as trial balloons. See Lewis to Overton, January 13, 1831, Overton Papers, THS.

51. Edward Everett to his wife, February 22, 1831, Everett Papers, MHS.

52. Van Buren, *Autobiography*, p. 402.

53. Ibid., pp. 402–403.

54. Ibid., p. 403.

55. Ibid.

56. Ibid., p. 404.

57. Ibid.

58. Ibid., p. 405.

59. Ibid.

60. Ibid., pp. 405–406.

61. Ibid., p. 406.

62. Ibid.

63. Marquis James in his biography of Jackson called his chapter on the dissolution of the cabinet "Martin Van Buren's Masterpiece." James, *Jackson*, pp. 567ff.

64. Van Buren, *Autobiography*, pp. 406–407.

65. Eaton to AJ, April 7, 1831, AJ to Eaton, April 8, 1831, Van Buren to AJ, April 11, 1831, AJ to Van Buren, April 12, 1831, in Jackson, *Correspondence*, IV, 257–258, 260–263.

66. Van Buren, *Autobiography*, pp. 407–408.

CHAPTER 19

1. Benjamin F. Butler to Van Buren, April 22, 1831, Van Buren Papers, LC.

2. Van Buren to Butler, April 16, 1831, in ibid.

3. Alfred Balch to AJ, May 7, 1831, Jackson Papers, LC. Even John Quincy Adams interpreted it as an attempt to set an example for the country because of Van Buren's belief that a presidential candidate should not "with propriety be a member of the Cabinet." Adams, *Memoirs*, VIII, 358.

4. Calhoun to David F. Caldwell, May 1, 1831, Calhoun Papers, DUL.

5. Memorandum, April 18, 1831, in Jackson's handwriting, Jackson Papers, LC.

6. Ingham to AJ, April 18, 19, 1831, AJ to Ingham, April 20, 1831, in Jackson, *Correspondence*, IV, 263–265, 268; Ingham to Berrien, [April 19, 1831], April 20, 1831, in Royce C. McCrary, Jr., " 'The Long Agony Is Nearly Over': Samuel D. Ingham Reports on the Dissolution of Andrew Jackson's First Cabinet," *Pennsylvania Magazine of History and Biography* (1976), C, 235–237.

7. Branch to AJ, April 19, 1831, AJ to Branch, April 20, 1831, in Jackson, *Correspondence*, IV, 266 and Parton, *Jackson*, III, 354–356; Branch to Charles Fisher, May 5, 1831, Fisher Family Papers, SHC.

8. Berrien to AJ, AJ to Berrien, June 15, 1831, in Jackson, *Correspondence*, IV, 295 and Parton, *Jackson*, III, 356–359.

9. Ibid., p. 359; John Tyler to Littleton W. Tazewell, May 8, 1831, in Lyon G. Tyler, *The Letters and Times of the Tylers* (Richmond, 1884–1896), I, 422; Clay to Francis Brooke, May 1, 1831, in Calvin Colton, ed., *Private Correspondence of Henry Clay*, (New York, 1857), p. 299.

10. Donelson to McLemore, June 10, 1831, Miscellaneous Donelson Papers, NYHS.

11. Adams, *Memoirs*, VIII, 360.

12. Ingham to Berrien, [May 9, 1831], in McCrary, "Long Agony Is Nearly Over," p. 242.

13. Ingham to Berrien, May 7, 1831, in ibid., p. 241.

14. Hill to Amos Kendall, April 26, 1831, Jacob Bailey Moore Papers, HUL; Kendall to Welles, April 23, 1831, Welles Papers, LC.

15. Clay to Brooke, May 1, 1831, in Colton, ed., *Private Correspondence of Henry Clay*, p. 300.

16. Van Buren to McLane, April 26, 1831, Diplomatic Instructions, Great Britain, NA; Livingston to Van Buren, April 20, Van Buren to Livingston, April 23, 1831, Livingston Papers, JRDF; Van Buren to Livingston, April 9, 1831, Van Buren Papers; Hunt, *Memoirs of Louise Livingston* (New York, 1886), pp. 98, 100.

17. AJ to White, April 9, 1831, White to AJ, April 20, 1831, in Jackson, *Correspondence*, IV, 259, 267; AJ to Livingston, June 24, 1831, Livingston Papers, JRDF.

18. AJ to White, April 29, 1831, in Jackson, *Correspondence*, IV, 272.

19. White momentarily hesitated and agreed to serve and then changed his mind once more and refused to accept Jackson's offer. See AJ to White, June 1, 1831 and White to AJ, June 15, in ibid., pp. 287, 295.

20. AJ to Coffee, May 26, 1831, Coffee Papers, THS. Overton "came charged with orders to have Eaton elected, if possible, to the Senate," wrote Alfred Balch. But many Tennessee legislators realized that if they elected Eaton he would return to Washington "and the late harassing scenes" would be "renewed." Perhaps that was one reason they rejected him. Balch to Livingston, October 20, 1831, Livingston Papers, JRDF.

21. Levi Woodbury to William Plumer, January 6, 1832, Miscellaneous Papers, NYHS. Had White accepted the War Department, Drayton would probably have been offered the office of attorney general. See Donelson to McLemore, June 10, 1831, Miscellaneous Donelson Papers, NYHS. Van Buren to AJ, July 16, 1831, Van Buren Papers, LC.

22. AJ to Lewis, May 7, 1831, Jackson Papers, ML; Vincent J. Capowski, "The Making of a Jacksonian Democrat: Levi Woodbury, 1789–1831," Doctoral dissertation, Fordham University, 1966.

23. Taney had actually been considered for the post in 1829 but was passed over. See John Nelson to Samuel Smith, January 29, 1829, Smith Papers, LC. Carl B. Swisher, *Roger B. Taney* (New York, 1935), pp. 126, 139–140; Walker Lewis, *Without Fear or Favor: A Biography of Chief Justice Roger Brooke Taney* (Boston, 1965), pp. 119–123. See, also, Taney's several letters of political recommendation for 1829 and 1830 in the Jackson Papers, LC.

24. Ingham to Berrien, April 20, 1831, in McCrary, "Long Agony Is Nearly Over," p. 237.

25. AJ to Lewis, May 7, 1831, Jackson Papers, ML; George Dallas to Livingston, May 12, 1831, Livingston to Dallas, July 15, 1831, Livingston Papers, JRDF.

26. Eaton to Ingham, June 17, 1831, in Parton, *Jackson;* III, 364–365.

27. Ingham to Eaton, June 18, 1831, in ibid., III, 365. Ultimately Berrien and Branch were drawn into the public controversy and their letters were published in the *Telegraph, National Intelligencer,* and *Niles Weekly Register.* AJ to Coffee, May 26, 1831, Coffee Papers, THS.

28. AJ to Lewis et al., June 22, 1831, AJ to Ingham, June 23, 1831, in Jackson, *Correspondence,* IV, 201.

29. Parton, *Jackson,* III, 368.

30. AJ to Van Buren, June 23, 1831, Van Buren Papers, LC; AJ to Donelson, June 23, 1831, Donelson Papers, LC.

31. "Duff Green is about to open his batteries against us," wrote Jackson to Livingston, August 7, 1831, Livingston Papers, JRDF; Floyd to John Barbour, June 24, 1831, Miscellaneous Floyd Papers, LC.

32. See his letters for April, May, and June, 1831, in the Jackson and Donelson Papers, LC, many of which are reproduced in Jackson, *Correspondence,* IV, 265–312.

33. AJ to McLemore, June 27, 1831, Miscellaneous Jackson Papers, NYHS.

34. Ibid.

35. AJ to Lewis, June 26, 1831, Jackson-Lewis Papers, NYPL; AJ to Livingston, August 23, 1831, Livingston Papers, JRDF.

36. Donelson to Emily, June 16, 1831, Donelson Papers, LC.

37. Grundy to Eaton, May 25, 1831, Grundy-McGavock Letters, SHC.

38. Floyd to Barbour, June 24, 1831, Miscellaneous Floyd Papers, LC; AJ to Donelson, May 5, 1831, Donelson Papers, LC; Livingston to Auguste Davezac, July 19, 1831, Livingston Papers, JRDF. The *Globe* was accused of attacking not only congressmen but lawyers, judges, state executives, legislatures, and the United States Bank. "It is too full of . . . the Cat and Dog politics of Kentucky," complained Alfred Balch in a letter to Livingston, September 12, 1831, Livingston Papers, JRFD. See also Dallas to Livingston, July 3, 1831 in ibid. for a list of some of the *Globe's* victims.

39. Floyd to John Barbour, June 24, 1831, Miscellaneous Floyd Papers, LC.

40. Elbert B. Smith, *Francis Preston Blair* (New York, 1980), pp. 53–54; AJ to Van Buren, June 23, July 25, 1831, Van Buren Papers, LC; Dallas to Livingston, May 12, 1831, Livingston Papers, JRDF.

41. Kendall to Blair, January 28, 1830, Blair-Lee Papers, PUL.

42. Latner, *Presidency of Jackson*, argues the importance of this western connection, pp. 56–57, 197–198.

43. Donelson to McLemore, June 10, 1831, Miscellaneous Donelson Papers, NYHS; *Telegraph*, February 28, March 18, 25, 1831; AJ to Donelson, May 5, 1831, Donelson Papers, LC.

44. Richard B. Latner, "The Kitchen Cabinet and Andrew Jackson's Advisory System," *JAH* (1978), LXV, 372.

45. Blair to Mrs. Benjamin Gratz, August 29, 1833, but misdated as 1831, in Thomas H. Clay, "Two Years With Old Hickory," *Atlantic Monthly* (1887), LX, 198; Biddle to Robert M. Gibbes, December 31, 1831, Biddle Papers, LC; Latner, "Kitchen Cabinet," p. 374.

46. Edwin A. Miles, *Jacksonian Democracy in Mississippi* (Chapel Hill, 1960), pp. 46, 61–68.

47. An article signed "Veritas" (undoubtedly Poindexter) appeared in the *Telegraph* on March 13 and referred to the "Kitchen Cabinet" in defending Poindexter's vote against Van Buren's nomination. Two days later the Richmond *Enquirer* mentioned the Kitchen Cabinet. For this information, particularly Poindexter's role, I am grateful to Edwin A. Miles.

48. Benton, *Thirty Years View*, I, 678.

49. Ibid.

50. Van Buren to AJ, November 18, 1832, Van Buren Papers, LC.

51. Woodbury to William Plumer, January 6, 1832, Miscellaneous Papers, NYHS.

52. AJ to Randolph, November 11, 1831, in Jackson, *Correspondence*, IV, 372.

53. Latner, "Kitchen Cabinet," argues the concept of a White House staff but I am not entirely persuaded by it. See pp. 379–384. See also Erik M. Eriksson, "President Jackson's Propaganda Agencies," *Pacific Historical Review* (1937), VI, 209–228; Richard P. Longaker, "Was Jackson's Kitchen Cabinet a Cabinet?" *MVHR* (1957), XLIV, 94–108.

54. James C. Curtis, "Andrew Jackson and His Cabinet—Some New Evidence," *THQ* (1968), XXVII, 157–164.

55. AJ to Donelson, May 5, 1831, Donelson Papers, LC.

CHAPTER 20

1. Jackson was very much the "family man," said Blair, and needed their presence. Blair to Mrs. Banjamin Gratz, August 29, 1831, in Clay, "Two Years with Old Hickory," *Atlantic Monthly* (1887), LX, 197.

2. Blair to Mrs. Gratz, April 20, 1831, in ibid., p. 193.

3. Ibid.

4. AJ to Donelson, July 10, 11, 1831, Donelson Papers, LC.

5. AJ to Van Buren, July 23, 1831, Van Buren Papers, LC.

6. AJ to Robert Y. Hayne, February 6, 1831, Hayne to AJ, February 4, 1831, Jackson Papers, LC.

7. AJ to Coffee, November 21, 1831, Coffee Papers, THS; AJ to Van Buren, August 8, 1831, in Jackson, *Correspondence*, IV, 329.

8. AJ to Coffee, October 3, 1831, Coffee Papers, THS.

9. AJ to Coffee, September 6, 1831, November 20, 1831, but misdated 1830, Coffee Papers, THS.

10. AJ to AJ, Jr., October 27, 1831, in Jackson, *Correspondence*, IV, 365.

11. Ibid.

12. AJ to Coffee, November 20, 1831, Coffee Papers, THS.

13. Van Buren to AJ, October 11, 1831, Van Buren Papers, LC.

14. AJ to Van Buren, December 6, 17, 1831, Van Buren Papers, LC.

15. Roger B. Taney, "Roger B. Taney's 'Bank War Manuscript,' " Carl B. Swisher, ed., *Maryland Historical Magazine* (1958), LIII, 126-127; Woodbury to Van Buren, April 10, 1832, Van Buren Papers, LC.

16. Taney, "Bank War," p. 127.

17. Cambreleng to Van Buren, January 4, 1832, Van Buren Papers, LC.

18. Taney, "Bank War," p. 125.

19. AJ to Van Buren, December 6, 1831, Van Buren Papers, LC; Taney, "Bank War," p. 128.

20. *House Executive Document,* No. 3, 22nd Congress, 1st Session, pp. 5-16.

21. Munroe, *McLane,* p. 307.

22. J. R. Poinsett to Joseph Johnson, January 18, 1832, Gilpin Collection, PHS.

23. Munroe, *McLane,* pp. 305-306.

24. Taney, "Bank War," pp. 121-122.

25. Ibid.

26. Ibid., pp. 123, 125-127.

27. Ibid., p. 129.

28. Ibid., pp. 127-128.

29. Ibid., p. 127.

30. Ibid., p. 215.

31. AJ to Van Buren, December 6, 1831, Van Buren Papers, LC.

32. *House Executive Document,* No. 3, 22nd Congress, 1st Session, pp 5ff.

33. AJ to Van Buren, December 6, 1831, Van Buren Papers, LC.

34. AJ to John Randolph, December 22, 1831, in Jackson, *Correspondence,* IV, 387.

35. Cambreleng to Jesse Hoyt, December 29, 1831, in Mackenzie, *Life and Times of Martin Van Buren,* p. 230.

36. Lowrie to Van Buren, January 27, 1832, Van Buren Papers, LC.

37. Randolph to AJ, December 19, 1831 and AJ to Randolph, December 22, 1831, in Jackson, *Correspondence,* IV, 386-387.

38. Van Buren, *Autobiography,* p. 581.

39. *Globe,* December 9, 12, 17, 19, 1831.

40. AJ to Hamilton, December 12, 1831, in Hamilton, *Reminiscences,* p. 234; AJ to Randolph, December 22, 1831, in Jackson, *Correspondence,* IV, 387.

41. Munroe, *McLane,* p. 315.

42. Cambreleng to Van Buren, February 4, 1832, Van Buren Papers, LC.

43. Ibid.; AJ to Blair, January 17, 1843, in Latner, *Presidency of Jackson,* p. 116.

44. Munroe, *McLane,* p. 317.

45. Cambreleng to Van Buren, February 5, 1832, Van Buren Papers, LC.

46. *Niles Weekly Register,* December 17, 24, 1831.

47. AJ to Van Buren, December 17, 1831, Van Buren Papers, LC.

48. *Niles Weekly Register,* October 1, 1831; Harriet H. Weed, ed., *Autobiography of Thurlow Weed* (Boston, 1883), p. 389. Remini, *Andrew Jackson and the Bank War* (New York, 1967), pp. 90-91.

49. Clay to Biddle, December 15, 1831, Biddle Papers, LC.

50. Munroe, *McLane*, p. 318.

51. Cadwalader to Biddle, December 21, 22, 1831, Biddle Papers, LC.

52. Munroe, *McLane*, p. 320.

53. Cadwalader to Biddle, December 30, 1831, Biddle Papers, LC.

54. Munroe, *McLane*, p. 321.

55. Smith to Rives, January 3, 1832, in ibid., p. 321.

56. Taney to Ellicott, January 25, 1832, Taney Papers, LC.

57. Space precludes a detailed account of this opening phase of the Bank War, but I have tried to make it available in my *Andrew Jackson and the Bank War.*

CHAPTER 21

1. "I believe my retainer has not been renewed or *refreshed* as usual," Webster wrote Biddle in 1833. "If it be wished that my relation to the Bank should be continued, it may be well to send me the usual retainers." Webster to Biddle, December 21, 1833, in Biddle, *The Correspondence of Nicholas Biddle Dealing with National Affairs, 1807–1844,* Reginald C. McGrane, ed. (Boston, 1919), p. 218. See also Irving H. Bartlett, *Daniel Webster* (New York, 1978), pp. 204–209. See also AJ to Kendall, July 23, 1832, Jackson Papers, LC.

2. See, for example, AJ to Lewis, April 29, 1833, Jackson-Lewis Papers, NYPL; Kendall to AJ, March 20, 1833, Jackson Papers, LC; and Richardson, *Messages and Papers,* II, 1304, 1224–1238.

3. AJ to Coffee, February 19, 1832, Coffee Papers, THS.

4. AJ to Coffee, January 21, 1832, Coffee Papers, THS; Jessie Benton Fremont, *Souvenirs of My Time* (Boston, 1887), p. 95.

5. Blair to Mrs. Benjamin Gratz, April 20, 1831, in Clay, "Two Years with Old Hickory," *Atlantic Monthly* (1887), LX, p. 193.

6. Parton, *Jackson,* III, 415.

7. Donelson to Coffee, January 16, 1832, Donelson Papers, LC.

8. AJ to Hutchings, February 11, 1832, Jackson Papers, THS.

9. Livingston to Davezac, [January 11, 1832], Livingston Papers, JRDF.

10. *Register of Debates,* 22nd Congress, 1st Session, p. 1325; Samuel R. Foot to William H. Seward, February 28, 1832, Seward Papers, RUL.

11. *Register of Debates,* 22nd Congress, 1st Session, p. 1341.

12. S. R. Hobbie to Azariah C. Flagg, January 29, 1832, Flagg Papers, NYPL.

13. Ibid.

14. For an account of this incident from Calhoun's point of view see Wiltse, *John C. Calhoun, Nullifier* (Indianapolis, 1948), pp. 125–128; and Margaret L. Coit, *John C. Calhoun: American Portrait* (Boston, 1950), pp. 216–217.

15. Blair to Van Buren, April 25, 1859, Van Buren Papers, LC; *Register of Debates,* 22nd Congress, 1st Session, p. 1324. Samuel Prentiss of Vermont also absented himself.

16. Benton, *Thirty Years View,* I, 215.

17. Ibid., p. 219.

18. *Telegraph,* January 27, 30, February 2, 3, 4, 1832.

19. Ambrose Spencer to John Taylor, January 31, 1832, John W. Taylor Papers, NYHS; AJ to Van Buren, December 17, 1831, Van Buren Papers, LC.

20. Henry Wikoff, *Reminiscences of an Idler* (New York, 1880), pp. 29–31.

21. AJ to Van Buren, February 12, 1832, Van Buren Papers, LC.

22. Cambreleng to Van Buren, February 13, 1832, Van Buren Papers, LC. Cambreleng also predicted the outcome of the confirmation proceedings and said

it would help Van Buren even though it would also annoy him. Cambreleng to Van Buren, January 4, 1832, Van Buren Papers, LC.

23. Hobbie to Flagg, January 29, 1832, Flagg Papers, NYPL.

24. AJ to Coffee, January 27, 1832, Coffee Papers, THS.

25. T. J. Sutherland to Taylor, February 15, 1832, Taylor Papers, NYHS.

26. See especially Jackson's memoranda for 1830, 1831, and 1832, Jackson Papers, LC. Some of this sentiment is reflected in his "Protest" message to Congress, Richardson, *Messages and Papers*, II, 1295, 1301, 1298, 1304, 1305, 1309.

27. Blair to Mrs. Benjamin Gratz, May 10, 1831, Clay, "Two Years with Old Hickory," p. 194.

28. George Bancroft to S. D. Bancroft, December 25, 27, 1831, in M. A. D. Howe, *The Life and Letters of George Bancroft* (New York, 1908), I, 193, 196.

29. Alfred Mordecai to Ellen Mordecai, March 4, 1830, Mordecai Papers, LC.

30. Fremont, *Souvenirs of My Time*, p. 98; Bancroft to Bancroft, December 25, 27, 1831, in Howe, *Life and Letters of George Bancroft*, I, 193–196; see also various Jackson letters in Jackson, *Correspondence*, III, 174, 184, 204, 207, 228, 232, 242, 250, 253, 269, 276, 277–278, 287, 308, 402, 412, 431, 447, 452, 454. Jackson's democratic manner is further commented upon in Caleb Cushing's Diary, April 1829, Cushing Papers, LC.

CHAPTER 22

1. John Campbell to David Campbell, March 8, 1832, Campbell Papers, DUL.

2. Ibid.

3. Benjamin F. Butler to Harriet Butler, March 17, 1832, Butler Papers, NYSL.

4. D. Morison to AJ, December 6, 1831, Jackson Papers, LHA. See also Stanley F. Horn, *The Hermitage: Home of Old Hickory* (New York, 1950), pp. 22–23.

5. AJ to Andrew Jackson, Jr., May 27, 1832, [April 1832], in Jackson, *Correspondence*, IV, 441 fn. 1, 432; AJ to Sarah Yorke Jackson, April 25, 30, 1832, Jackson Papers, LC.

6. Van Buren to AJ, March 13, 1832, Van Buren to Marcy, March 14, 1832, Van Buren to AJ, February 20, March 6 (two letters), 9, 13, 28, April 2, 1832, Van Buren Papers, LC.

7. Spencer O'Brien to W. P. Mangum, February 26, 1832, in Henry T. Shanks, ed., *The Papers of Willie Persons Mangum* (Raleigh, 1950), I, 494.

8. Marcy to Flagg, February 6, [1832], Flagg Papers, NYPL.

9. AJ to Coffee, January 27, 1832, Coffee Papers, THS.

10. AJ to Lewis, August 18, 1832, Jackson-Lewis Papers, NYPL.

11. On the background of the convention and the reasons for its rise, see James S. Chase, *Emergence of the Presidential Nominating Convention, 1789–1832* (Urbana, Ill., 1973), pp. 69ff.

12. Remini, *Martin Van Buren and the Making of the Democratic Party* (New York, 1959), pp. 130–133.

13. Lewis to Kendall, May 25, 1832, in "Origin of the Democratic National Convention," *American Historical Magazine* (1902), VII, 270.

14. AJ to Tilghman A. Howard, August 20, 1833, in Jackson, *Correspondence*, V, 166. Jackson was talking about state conventions here but his thoughts clearly reflect his attitude about national conventions.

15. *Niles Weekly Register*, March 24, 1832.

16. Samuel R. Gammon, Jr., *The Presidential Campaign of 1832* (Baltimore, 1922), pp. 97–98; Latner, *Presidency of Jackson*, p. 129.

17. Chase, *Emergence of Nominating Convention*, p. 263.

18. Niles to Welles, May 22, 1832, Welles Papers, LC.

19. Proceedings reported in *Niles Weekly Register*, May 26, 1832.

20. Ibid.; Lucas et al. to Van Buren, May 22, 1832, Van Buren Papers, LC.

21. *Register of Debates*, 22nd Congress, 1st Session, p. 466.

22. Parton, *Jackson*, III, 451.

23. Clay's full speech is given in *Register of Debates*, 22nd Congress, 1st Session, 462–473. Much of it is reprinted in Benton, *Thirty Years View*, I, 266–275, which says something about what contemporaries thought of it.

24. Ibid., pp. 268, 274–275.

25. Latner, *Presidency of Jackson*, p. 145; Munroe, *McLane*, pp. 345–346.

26. *Globe*, April 30, 1832.

27. Marcy to Dix, May 1, 1832, Dix Papers, CUL.

28. Munroe, *McLane*, p. 347.

29. A man by the name of Moses Myers had been seen "flitting about between the House of Representatives and the Treasury Department, using his exertions to cut down the protective system," according to Henry Clay. Quoted in ibid., p. 348.

30. *Register of Debates*, 22nd Congress, 1st Session, p. 1217.

31. Munroe, *McLane*, pp. 348–349.

32. Parton, *Jackson*, III, 452.

33. Marcy to Flagg, June 28, 1832, Flagg Papers, NYPL; Marcy to Dix, May 1, 1832, Dix Papers, CUL.

34. William W. Freehling, *Prelude to Civil War: The Nullification Controversy in South Carolina, 1816–1836* (New York, 1965), p. 248.

35. George Dallas to Edward Livingston, July 23, 1832, Livingston Papers, JRDF.

36. AJ to Coffee, July 17, 1832, Coffee Papers, THS.

37. AJ to Synod, June 12, 1832, in Jackson, *Correspondence*, IV, 447.

38. See draft of this veto message by McLane in the Van Buren Papers, LC.

39. Quoted in Charles I. Rosenberg, *The Cholera Years: The United States in 1832, 1849, and 1866* (Chicago, 1962), p. 50.

40. Benton, *Thirty Years View*, I, 235.

41. Ibid., p. 236.

42. Ibid.

43. Marcy to Olcott, January 22, 1832, Olcott Papers, CUL.

44. Dallas to Biddle, March 15, 1832, Biddle Papers; Remini, *Andrew Jackson and the Bank War* (New York, 1967), pp. 78–79.

45. Benton, *Thirty Years View*, I, 238; *Globe*, March 28, 1832.

46. *Niles Weekly Register*, May 12, 1832.

47. Cambreleng to Van Buren, February 5, 1832, Van Buren Papers, LC.

48. Taney to AJ [?], February 20, 1832, Taney Papers, LC. This is a confidential memorandum.

49. Cambreleng to Jesse Hoyt, February 16, 1832, in William L. MacKenzie, *The Life and Times of Martin Van Buren* (Boston, 1846), p. 231.

50. Remini, *Bank War*, pp. 79–80; AJ to Sarah Jackson, May 6, 1832, Andre deCoppet Collection, PUL.

51. Ralph C. H. Catterall, *The Second Bank of the United States* (Chicago, 1903), p. 234.

52. Cadwalader to Biddle, May 31, 1832, Biddle Papers, LC.

53. Biddle to Cadwalader, July 3, 1832, Biddle Papers, LC.

54. Roger B. Taney, "Roger B. Taney's 'Bank War Manuscript,' " Carl B. Swisher, ed., *Maryland Historical Magazine* (1958), LIII, 226.

55. Ibid.

56. Ibid., p. 227.

57. McLane to Samuel Smith, July 23, 1832, Smith Papers, LC.

58. Taney, "Bank War," pp. 226–227.

59. Ibid.

60. Van Buren, *Autobiography*, p. 625.

61. See his many letters to Coffee, Van Buren, and Kendall in the Coffee Papers, THS, and Jackson and Van Buren Papers in LC throughout 1832 and 1833. See particularly AJ to Lewis, April 29, 1833, Jackson-Lewis Papers, NYPL; Kendall to AJ, March 20, 1833, Jackson Papers, LC; and Richardson, *Messages and Papers*, II, 1304, 1224–1238.

62. Ibid., pp. 1139–1140, 1143–1144.

63. Ibid., pp. 1144–1145. Twenty eight years later, Chief Justice Taney explained that Jackson's argument is valid when "acting as a part of the legislative power—and not of his right or duty as an executive officer." Taney to Van Buren, June 30, 1860, Van Buren Papers, LC.

64. Richardson, *Messages and Papers*, II, p. 1152.

65. Ibid., pp. 1152–1153.

66. Ibid., p. 1153.

67. Ibid., p. 1154.

68. Catterall, *Second Bank*, p. 239.

69. Biddle to Clay, August 1, 1832, Biddle Papers, LC.

70. November 22, 1834.

71. AJ to Lewis, [September, 1832], Jackson Papers, ML.

72. *Globe*, July 12, 20, 1832, and see its many editorials "The Veto and the Bank," July 23, 28, August 1, 6, 9, 17, 24, 30 and September 5, 1832 and its reprints of editorials from other newspapers, especially the Pittsburgh *Manufacturer*, July 20, 1832.

73. Daniel Webster, *Works of Daniel Webster* (Boston, 1864), III, 434, 446, 438, 447.

74. Ibid., p. 447.

75. Henry Clay, *The Works of Henry Clay*, Calvin Colton, ed. (New York, 1904), VII, 524.

76. William N. Chambers, *Old Bullion Benton: Senator from the New West* (Boston, 1956), pp. 184–186; Ben Perley Poore, *Reminiscences* (Philadelphia, 1886), I, 144.

77. Samuel Smith to AJ, June 17, 1832, Jackson Papers, LC.

CHAPTER 23

1. AJ to Coffee, October 1832, Coffee Papers, THS.

2. For the things Jackson represented best to the American people see John William Ward, *Andrew Jackson: Symbol for an Age* (New York, 1955).

3. AJ to Reverend Hardy M. Cryer, June 17, 1832, in Jackson, *Correspondence*, IV, 448.

4. Kendall to ?, July 25, 1832, Kendall Papers, NYHS; Kendall to Welles, September 12, 1831, Welles Papers, LC; Jackson memorandum, July 1832, Jackson Papers, LC; Jackson to Lewis, August 18, 1832, Jackson-Lewis Papers, NYPL.

5. *Globe,* September 8, October 16, 1832.

6. *Niles Weekly Register,* October 27, 1832; Remini, *Andrew Jackson and the Bank War* (New York, 1967), p. 97.

7. *Niles Weekly Register,* March 14, 1832; Remini, "Election of 1832," in Arthur M. Schlesinger, Jr., Fred L. Israel, and William P. Hansen, ed., *History of American Presidential Elections* (New York, 1971), I, 510.

8. AJ to Lewis, August 9, 1832, Jackson Papers, ML; AJ to Donelson, August 16, 1832, Donelson Papers, LC.

9. *Globe,* October 17, 1832.

10. Marcy to Hoyt, October 1, 1832, William L. Mackenzie, *Lives of Butler and Hoyt* (Boston, 1845), p. 113; Hill to Hoyt, October 15, 1832, William L. Mackenzie, *Life and Times of Martin Van Buren* (Boston, 1846), p. 239.

11. *Globe,* September 5, 1832; see also reprints of editorials from other Democratic newspapers, September 8, 15, 22, October 3, 6, 17, 20, 1832.

12. Quoted in *Globe,* September 5, 1832.

13. *National Intelligencer,* September 6, 1832.

14. *A Retrospect of Andrew Jackson's Administration* (n.p., 1832), pp. 3–5, 6.

15. Ibid., p. 8.

16. Ibid., pp. 9–10, 11.

17. Ibid., pp. 14, 15, 18.

18. *Globe,* October 17, 20, November 3, 1832.

19. AJ to Lewis, August 18, 1832, Jackson-Lewis Papers, NYPL. See also AJ to Kendall, July 23, 1832, Jackson Papers, LC.

20. Parton, *Jackson,* III, 420.

21. AJ to Lewis, August 9, 1832, Jackson Papers, ML; AJ to Donelson, August 9, 1832, Donelson Papers, LC.

22. AJ to Andrew Jackson, Jr., November 12, 1832, in James, *Jackson,* p. 609. Jackson's anxiety is conveyed in his letter to his son, November 8, 1832, Jackson Papers, LC.

23. AJ to Donelson, August 19, 1832, Donelson Papers, LC.

24. AJ to Kendall, July 23, 1832, Jackson Papers, LC.

25. AJ to Coffee, July 17, 1832, Coffee Papers, THS.

26. AJ to Van Buren, August 30, 1832, Van Buren Papers, LC.

27. Freehling, *Prelude to Civil War,* p. 253.

28. AJ to Coffee, August 18, 1832, Private Collection of James S. Leonardo, Des Moines, Iowa. Jackson was referring to the necessity of getting back to Washington before October 10 or 15, 1832. Dallas to Henry Gilpin, December 1, 1832, Dallas Papers, PHS.

29. AJ to Woodbury, September 11, 1832, in Jackson, *Correspondence,* IV, 474–475; AJ to Donelson, August 30, September 17, 1832, Donelson Papers, LC; Freehling, *Prelude to Civil War,* pp. 239ff; AJ to Lewis, August 23, 1832, in *New York Times,* January 11, 1875, copy JPP.

30. AJ to Donelson, August 30, 1832, Donelson Papers, LC. For the positive effect of the veto among Pennsylvania Democrats, see George Dallas to Edward Livingston, July 23, 1832, Livingston Papers, JRDF.

31. Quoted in Remini, "Election of 1832," I, 509.

32. Duff Green to Calhoun, October 23, 1832, Green Papers, SHC; Latner, *Presidency of Jackson,* p. 138.

33. See Hickory Club's invitation to Edward Livingston, January 3, 1833, Livingston Papers, JRDF.

34. Quoted in Remini, "Election of 1832," I, 509; see also *Globe,* September 22, 1832.

35. Michel Chevalier, *Society, Manners, and Politics in the United States* (Boston, 1839), pp. 306–308.

36. Quoted in Remini, "Election of 1832," I, 513; *Globe*, September 22, October 20, November 3, 1832.

37. *Globe*, November 3, 1832.

38. *National Intelligencer*, October 5, 1832.

39. *Globe*, September 22, 1832.

40. AJ to Donelson, October 5, 1832, Donelson Papers, LC. See also AJ to Andrew Jr., September 30, 1832, William K. Bixby Collection, WUL.

41. AJ to Donelson, October 10, 1832, Donelson Papers, LC. In this letter Jackson was levelheaded enough to accept the fact that his friends in Kentucky did not believe he could defeat Clay in their state.

42. The Library of Congress maintains a collection of political cartoons.

43. Parton, *Jackson*, III, 424.

44. Ibid., p. 428; Remini, "Election of 1832," I, 514.

45. Dallas to Edward Livingston, May 30, 1831, Livingston Papers, JRDF.

46. Kendall to Welles, September 30, 1831, Welles Papers, LC.

47. *Globe*, September 8, 1832.

48. Edward Everett to Lemuel Shattuck, December 24, 1832, Miscellaneous Papers, HL; Samuel J. Tilden to ?, May 25, 1832, Tilden Papers, NYPL.

49. Van Buren said the prospect for electoral success had never been brighter. Van Buren to AJ, August 29, 1832, Van Buren Papers, LC. On William Wirt's role in this election see Marvin R. Cain's "William Wirt against Andrew Jackson: Reflection on an Era," *Mid-America* (1965), XLVII, 134–135, 136–137.

50. W. S. Harvey to Donelson, Donelson Papers, LC; Blair to Livingston, August 24, 1832, Livingston Papers, JRDF; Henry R. Taylor to John W. Taylor, September 13, 1832, Taylor Papers, NYHS; AJ to Sarah Jackson, June 21, 1832, Jackson Papers, LHA.

51. Poinsett to AJ, October 16, 1832, Jackson Papers, LC; Poinsett to Edward Livingston, October 17, 1832, Livingston Papers, JRDF.

52. Ibid.

53. Ibid.

54. AJ to Cass, October 29, 1832, in Jackson, *Correspondence*, IV, 483.

55. AJ to Donelson, October 10, 1832, Donelson Papers, LC; AJ to Breathitt, November 7, 1832, in Jackson, *Correspondence*, IV, 484–485.

56. Freehling, *Prelude to Civil War*, p. 265; Lewis Cass to Winfield Scott, November 18, 1832, *American State Papers, Military Affairs*, V, 159.

57. AJ to Poinsett, November 7, 1832, in Jackson, *Correspondence*, IV, 486.

58. Svend Petersen, *A Statistical History of the American Presidential Elections* (New York, 1963), pp. 20–21.

59. Clay was accused of willfully shutting his eyes to Maine's needs and interests. The "people will remember him for it, at the ballot box." Robert Dunlap to Flagg, August 13, 1832, Flagg Papers, NYPL.

60. Petersen, *Statistical History*, p. 21.

61. *Niles Weekly Register*, April 21, 1832.

62. George Blair to Willie P. Mangum, December 8, 1832, in Mangum, *Papers*, I, 588.

63. J. H. Kirth to Flagg, October 13, 1832, Flagg Papers, NYPL. See also Cambreleng to C. W. Gooch, November 15, 1832, Miscellaneous Papers, University of Virginia Library.

64. Kendall, Autobiography, p. 302.

65. Wirt to John T. Lomax, November 15, 1832, in John P. Kennedy, *Memoirs of the Life of William Wirt, Attorney-General of the United States* (Philadelphia, 1849), II, 331.

66. It is a fact that in the presidential election of 1860, with the nation close to secession and civil war, a number of Americans voted for Andrew Jackson, even though he had been dead over fifteen years.

Index

449